LATIN AMERICA AND
THE CARIBBEAN IN
THE INTERNATIONAL SYSTEM

———————— ■ ————————

FOURTH EDITION

LATIN AMERICA AND THE CARIBBEAN IN THE INTERNATIONAL SYSTEM

■

G. Pope Atkins

Research Fellow, University of Texas at Austin;
Professor Emeritus, United States Naval Academy

Westview Press
A Member of the Perseus Books Group

Copyright © 1989, 1995, 1999 by Westview Press, A Member of the Perseus Books Group

Published in 1999 in the United States of America by Westview Press, 5500 Central Avenue, Boulder,
Colorado 80301-2877, and in the United Kingdom by Westview Press, 12 Hid's Copse Road, Cumnor
Hill, Oxford OX2 9JJ

First edition published in 1977 by The Free Press

Library of Congress Cataloging-in-Publication Data
Atkins, G. Pope, 1934–
    Latin America and the Caribbean in the international system / G.
Pope Atkins. — 4th ed.
        p.   cm.
    Includes bibliographical references and index.
    ISBN 0-8133-3382-2 (hc). — ISBN 0-8133-3383-0 (pbk.)
    1. Latin America—Foreign relations—1980–   2. Caribbean Area—
Foreign relations.   I. Title.
JZ1519.A98   1999
327'.098—dc21   98-42262
                                                                                          CIP

The paper used in this publication meets the requirements of the American National Standard for Perma-
nence of Paper for Printed Library Materials Z39.48-1984.

10   9   8   7   6   5   4   3   2   1

To Taylor, Maggie, Ginny, Jeff, and Kristy,
and Carly, Tyler, and Zachary

Contents

Illustrations

Acronyms and Abbreviations

AACC	Anglo-American Caribbean Commission
ACAT	Continental Association of American Workers
ACP	Africa, the Caribbean, and the Pacific
ACS	Association of Caribbean States
ADELA	Atlantic Community Development Group for Latin America
AFL	American Federation of Labor
AG	Andean Group
AIFLD	American Institute for Free Labor Development
ALADI	Asociación Latinoamericana de Integración
ALN	National Liberation Action
ANCOM	Andean Common Market/Andean Community
ARDE	Democratic Revolutionary Alliance
ARENA	Republican Nationalist Alliance
ATLAS	Unionized Latin American Workers' Group
ATPA	Andean Trade Preference Act
BIS	Bank for International Settlements
BOLSA	Bank of London and South America
CACM	Central American Common Market
CARIBANK	Caribbean Bank
CARICOM	Caribbean Community and Common Market
CARIFORUM	Caribbean Forum
CARIFTA	Caribbean Free Trade Association
CBI	Caribbean Basin Initiative
CCD	Committee on Disarmament
CEBs	Base Communities
CEC	Special Committee on Trade
CECLA	Special Latin American Coordinating Committee
CECON	Special Negotiating and Consulting Commission
CELADE	Latin American Demographic Center
CELAM	Conference of Latin American Bishops
CICAD	Inter-American Drug Abuse Control Commission
CICYP	Inter-American Council for Commerce and Production
CIDI	Inter-American Council for Integral Development

CIO	Congress of Industrial Organizations
CIPIC	Intergovernmental Council of Copper Exporting Countries
CIS	Commonwealth of Independent States
CIT	Inter-American Federation of Labor
CLASC	Latin American Confederation of Christian Trade Unionists
COAS	Council of the Organization of American States
CROM	Regional Confederation of Mexican Labor
CSLA	Latin American Syndicalist Confederation
CTAL	Confederation of Latin American Workers
CUTAL	Single Central Association of Latin American Workers
DEA	Drug Enforcement Agency
EAI	Enterprise of the Americas Initiative
EC	European Community
ECCB	Eastern Caribbean Central Bank
ECLA	Economic Commission for Latin America
ECLAC	Economic Commission for Latin America and the Caribbean
ECOSOC	United Nations Economic and Social Council
EIB	Export-Import Bank of Washington
ELNF	Fidelista National Liberation Army
ELN	National Liberation Army
ENDC	Eighteen Nation Disarmament Committee
EPL	Popular Liberation Army
ERP	Revolutionary Army of the People
ESAPAC	Central American Advanced School of Public Administration
EU	European Union
EXIM	Export-Import Bank of Washington
FALN	Armed Forces of National Liberation
FAP	Peronist Armed Forces
FAR	Revolutionary Armed Forces
FARC	Armed Forces of Colombia
FARN	Armed Forces of National Resistance
FDN	National Democratic Front
FDR	Democratic Revolutionary Front
FEAC	Inter-American Financial and Advisory Committee
FIR	Revolutionary Leftist Front
FLN	National Liberation Front
FMLN	Farabundo Martí National Liberation Front
FPL	Farabundo Martí Popular Forces of Liberation
FSLN	Sandinist National Liberation Front
FSO	Fund for Special Operations
FTA	Free-Trade Area

FTAA	Free Trade Area of the Americas
FTAs	Free-Trade Agreements
G-3	Group of Three
GATT	General Agreement on Tariffs and Trade
GSP	Generalized System of Preference
IAEA	International Atomic Energy Agency
IAECOSOC	Inter-American Economic and Social Council
IAS	Inter-American System
IBEC	International Basic Economy Corporation
IBRD	International Bank for Reconstruction and Development
ICAITI	Central American Institute of Industrial Research
ICFTU	International Confederation of Free Trade Unions
ICJ	International Court of Justice
ICSCC	Interdepartmental Committee on Scientific and Cultural Cooperation
IDA	International Development Association
IDB	Inter-American Development Bank
IFC	International Finance Corporation
IGOs	Intergovernmental organizations
IIAA	Institute of Inter-American Affairs
ILPES	Latin American Institute for Economic and Social Planning
IMF	International Monetary Fund
INCB	International Narcotics Control Board
INTAL	Institute for the Integration of Latin America
IOEC	Organization of Iron Ore Exporting Countries
IPEB	International Organization of Banana Exporters
IR	International Relations
IRCA	Immigration Reform and Control Act
IRELA	Instituto de Relaciones Europeo-Latinoamericanos
ITT	International Telephone and Telegraph
LAFTA	Latin American Free Trade Association
LAIA	Latin American Integration Association
LDC	Less-Developed Country
M-19	19th of April Movement
MAAG	Military Assistance Advisory Groups
MERCOSUR	Common Market of the South
MICIVIH	International Civilian Mission in Haiti
MIF	Multilateral Investment Fund
MIR	Movement of the Revolutionary Left
MISURASATA	Sandinista Unity of Miskito, Sumas, and Ramas
MNC	Multinational Corporation
MPM	Montoneros

MPSC	Popular Socialist Christian Movement
MR-13	13th of November Revolutionary Movement
MRTA	Movimiento Revolucionario Túpac Amaru
MSA	Mutual Security Act
NAFTA	North American Free Trade Agreement
NATO	North Atlantic Treaty Organization
NIEO	New International Economic Order
NJM	New Jewel Movement
NPT	Non-Proliferation Treaty
NSC	National Security Council
NSD	National Security Doctrines
OAS	Organization of American States
ODECA	Organization of Central American States
OECS	Organization of Eastern Caribbean States
OIR	Revolutionary Integration Organization
OLAS	Organization of Latin American Solidarity
ONUCA	United Nations Observer Group in Central America
OPANAL	Organization for the Prohibition of Nuclear Weapons in Latin America
OPEC	Organization of Petroleum Exporting Countries
ORIT	Inter-American Regional Organization of Workers
PAFL	Pan American Federation of Labor
PCOAS	Permanent Council of the Organization of American States
PRC	People's Republic of China
PRG	People's Revolutionary Government
PROSPEL	Programa de Seguimiento de las Políticas Exteriores Latinoamericanas
PRT	Revolutionary Workers Party
PRTC	Central American Workers' Revolutionary Party
SELA	Latin American Economic System
SEM	Single European Market
SI	Socialist International
SICA	Central American Integration System
SIECA	Permanent Secretariat of Central American Economic Integration
SL	Sendero Luminoso
SUNFED	Special United Nations Fund for Economic Development
UAR	United Arab Republic
UN	United Nations
UNCDF	United Nations Capital Development Fund
UNCED	United Nations Conference on Environment and Development
UNCLOS	United Nations Conference on the Law of the Sea

UNCTAD	United Nations Conference on Trade and Development
UNDCP	United Nations International Narcotics Control Program
UNDP	United Nations Development Program
UNEP	United Nations Environmental Program
UNMIH	United Nations Mission in Haiti
UNO	United Nicaraguan Opposition
URNG	Guatemalan United Revolutionary Front
VPR	Popular Revolutionary Vanguard
WFTU	World Federation of Trade Unions
WTO	World Trade Organization

Preface

The first edition of this book was intended to partially fill a gap in the scholarly literature. It was issued at the beginning of a heightened and sustained scholarly interest in Latin America's international relations; since then the related literature has substantially increased. Nevertheless, the original purpose of this book still seems to be appropriate—to provide a topically complete and analytically integrated survey of Latin America's international relations. As in the past, it is further intended to serve as a classroom text at the upper undergraduate or beginning graduate level and as a general reference source for anyone seeking description and analysis of the subject. A fundamental assumption also remains: Latin America and the Caribbean should be the central subject of study. This essential point of reference is reflected in a determined effort to concentrate primarily on the region—with the policies of the United States and other outsiders, which are also specifically and extensively treated, subsumed under that overall objective.

This fourth edition has been revised and reorganized thoroughly, especially in terms of the evolving characteristics of the new international era that have dramatically affected the region's international relations. Calling the current system "post–cold war" is unsatisfactory, inasmuch as it tells us only that the new era is not like the old one. The designation indicates the understanding that with the end of East-West conflict, policy reorientations are required on the part of all actors; but it does not suggest what the salient elements of the new and complex period are. "Post–cold war" is also misleading with regard to the Latin American and Caribbean region, where the end of the cold war converged with prior established trends—in particular the critical political and economic transformations in the regional states that were only partially related to superpower competition. This combination subsequently gave rise to further extant transnational phenomena (those that intimately involve nonstate as well as state actors and their relations) as basic regional characteristics.

In addition to revising and reorganizing the material in an attempt to capture the characteristics of the new international era, I have also changed the title of the book: from *Latin America in the International Political System* in the first three editions to the present *Latin America and the Caribbean in the International System*. I have added "Caribbean" because of the generally accepted recognition of the role of the "new" Caribbean states as regional actors. I have dropped "political" for the combined reasons of intensified changes in the international regional subsystem and the necessity of multidisciplinary analysis.

In order to recognize (and properly so) the emergence of certain Caribbean states and distinguish them from the long-existing Latin American states, specialists dealing with the region have adopted the term "Latin America and the Caribbean" to denominate the region. This understandable effort is an inadequate adjustment, however, since older Spanish American states had already encompassed most of the circum-Caribbean territory and population. Nevertheless, "Latin America and the Caribbean" has become a matter of general usage and, given the lack of a satisfactory alternative, is so applied in this book.

I value interdisciplinary contributions to the understanding of the subject of this study. Integrating them, however, is not without problems. Over the past four decades the array of disparate international phenomena has broadened, and inquiry increasingly has fragmented into subfields within several academic disciplines—with little coordination among them. Because the study of international relations during this period has been centered in political science—the inheritor of the unsustained effort to establish the subject as an autonomous academic field—some organization has been provided. Even within political science, however, international relations no longer constitutes a single subfield but encompasses three separate but related areas: the interstate system and its array of subspecialties, foreign policy analysis and comparative foreign policy, and international political economy. Furthermore, other disciplines—in particular history, economics, psychology, sociology, and anthropology—continue to be strongly involved from their own academic vantage points. In all disciplines the overall system has been viewed increasingly as a "global" one involving the combination of interstate and transnational phenomena.

Some organization of the disparate study of international relations has also been provided by the widespread (but far from universal) adoption of systems theory as a framework for analysis. More specifically, with regard to the subject matter of this book, a systems perspective is particularly useful for organizing an introduction to the analysis of such a complex subject. The systems paradigm views international relations as a network of structures and processes, with the focus on the actions of the units (states, interstate organizations, and nonstate transnational entities) and the consequences and outcomes of their interactions. The book remains organized around the idea of Latin America and the Caribbean as a separate international subsystem within the global system, with special consideration given to both further subsystems within the region and to the extraregional world of which it is a part. This organizing device also allows the specific regional focus to be pursued in such a way that adds to general rather than parochial knowledge. But this is not a book on methodology. Rather, theories of international and comparative politics are applied to aid in the understanding of Latin America and the Caribbean (the theories often need to be accommodated or corrected for regional realities), and the need for concepts to refer to the world of experience (my theoretical assumption and bias) is stressed.

The book is organized in terms of its purpose to construct an analytic framework for the study of the region's international relations. It integrates dimensions of the interstate system and some basic elements of foreign policy analysis, while blending the systemic and policy ingredients of international political economy. Historical and legal-institutional descriptions and interpretations are subsumed under the primary paradigm. Psychological models are referred to as elements of foreign policy analysis. Sociological and anthropological inquiries especially enlighten transnational phenomena, including the orientations of transnational actors and institutions and the interactions associated with their relations. Issues and current events are not treated separately but are melded into the overall approach. The chapter sequence is intended to be a logical progression in systemic terms, presenting material with as little repetitiveness as possible without damaging coherence or understanding. Thus, after presenting the elements of the framework in Part One, the book proceeds to an investigation of the essential characteristics of the policies of the state actors (Part Two) and the transnational actors (Part Three); to the myriad intergovernmental organizations in which the Latin American and Caribbean states have been involved at the various system levels (in Part Four); and, finally, to an analysis of the various categories of interaction in which the parties have been involved (Part Five).

Any field that studies the structures and processes of human behavior involves the problem of how analysts handle values—not only as detached observers but also as people who make interpretations and define policy preferences. Objectivity is an appropriate goal; however, "value-free" analysis on the part of the analyst is not necessarily desirable. The resolution of this problem depends on the position taken toward evidence and inference. I have attempted first to identify issues and summarize competing arguments in a detached manner and to postpone normative conclusions until after analyzing a variety of political structures and processes. At several points in the book, my interpretations appear but are intended to flow from the prior conceptualizations, descriptions, and evaluations.

I wish to extend my gratitude to colleagues in the United States, Latin America and the Caribbean, and Europe, who during the life of the first three editions and in preparation for the fourth have offered encouragement, advice, suggestions, comments, criticism, and information. Special acknowledgment is made to Allison Temple Bacon, Morris Blachman, Barabara Breeden, Jack Child, Peter Cleaves, Isaac Cohen, John Finan, Esperanza Duran, Wolf Grabendorff, René Gutiérrez, Fred Halliday, Margaret Daly Hayes, Luis Esteben Julia, John Lovell, David Myers, Stella Pérez de Villagrán, Helen Purkitt, Roberto Russell, Lars Schoultz, Max Sherman, Larry Thompson, Charles Wilson, Larman Wilson, Virginia Atkins Wilson, and Debbie Warden; and, posthumously, to the late Harold Blakemore, Harold Eugene Davis, Thomas McGann, and John Martz. I gratefully acknowledge my debt to the many undergraduate and graduate students who have come under my guidance during many years of teaching the subject. Finally, I pay special tribute to my wife, Joan Jorns Atkins, for her continuing professional and personal support. I am fully responsible for all that follows.

G. Pope Atkins
Austin, Texas

PART ONE

■

A Framework for Analysis

The first three chapters of this book establish the overall framework within which the rest of the study is cast. Chapter 1 discusses the systems concept as a way to organize analysis of international relations in general. Chapter 2 identifies Latin America and the Caribbean as a subsystem of the global system and outlines the general characteristics of the subsystem's evolution. Chapter 3 presents and critiques the major explanatory and prescriptive theories regarding the region's international relations. Using this framework for analysis, the rest of the book provides a detailed examination of the various elements of the Latin American and Caribbean subsystem's international relations.

CHAPTER ONE

■

The International System

As an overview of the international system and its constituent elements, this chapter discusses international systems theory to the extent that it provides the analytic framework used for selecting, arranging, and comparing data relating to the complex Latin American subsystem.[1] The emphasis here is on the role of theory as an organizing device rather than as explanation, prediction, prescription, or judgment (matters that are explored in Chapter 3). This does not preclude reference to such theoretical uses, however, when they clarify the reasoning behind the selection of certain organizational components.

A SYSTEMS PERSPECTIVE

The Approach to This Study

Certain developments over the past four decades in the study of IR (as analysts like to refer to the inquiry of international relations) have influenced the approach taken in this book.[2] Among the most important of these developments was systems theory, which from the late 1950s was increasingly adopted as an analytic framework and became the generally assumed paradigm (but not without criticism or dissent). Systems theory is concerned with structures and processes in the study of human behavior. Any system by definition consists fundamentally of the interaction between two or more distinct units and of the functions of that interaction. "Structure" means the system's form and configuration—the way in which its elements are organized and interrelated. The structure of a system is characterized both by differentiation (the presence and workings of separate units) and by integration (the overall organization of the system, perhaps including any subsystems). "Process" is the series of specific, continuous, and interdependent operations of the system—in effect, the activities and interactions of the units and subsystems that have consequences, results, or outcomes. Process indicates that a system is dynamic. Structure and process both imply some measure of regularity of relations and mutual dependence among the units and subsystems.

While adopting a systems approach, IR analysts distinguished between international politics and foreign policy analysis.[3] The first area addresses the overall interstate system, with an emphasis on the interactions of the nation-state units and the consequences for the system's structures and processes. This embraces a large portion of the established traditional approach to the study of IR, which includes the historical evolution of the international system, the regulatory elements such as balances of power and international organization and law, and strong attention to the "high politics" of security, diplomacy, and war. The second area, foreign policy analysis, focuses on the nation-states themselves, either singly or in comparison. It deals with the nature, attributes, and actions of states and, in particular, inquires about the way decision makers form images, expectations, and perceptions, respond to motivations and aspirations, process information, formulate interests, analyze situations, select objectives, and decide upon and execute courses of action. In foreign policy analysis, the overall system embraces the extrasocietal environments that give rise to decisions and in which subsequent policy action takes place.

Beginning in the early 1970s, analysts broadened their notions of the international system and its units in order to account for crucial transnational phenomena. They have generally acknowledged that states remained the most important actors in world affairs but insisted that the significance of transnational (nonstate) actors and relations (especially economic, social, and cultural, but also including insurgencies, drug trafficking, and common criminal activities) had increased to the extent that they should be integrated with the interstate model into a single global system. With the end of the cold war and with subsequent developments, students of IR have reemphasized these concepts.[4]

A subsystemic area of inquiry, as implied in the preceding commentary, lies between the individual actors (state and transnational) and the global system (the combination of interstate and transnational phenomena). International subsystems are defined as groupings of some of the total system's units that interact on a regular basis. Subsystemic structures and processes remain distinct, even as they form the entire system and even though the units also participate on a broader basis in the global system. Several different kinds of international subsystems may be identified—for example, the regularized interaction of two states, international organizations, ideological or common-interest groupings, and geographic regions. Most of the elements of a system apply to subsystems; their analysis likewise involves the concepts of actors, interaction, regulation, and even further subsystems. Thus regional international relations, such as those of Latin America and the Caribbean, can be viewed as subsystems.

Finally, the continuing problem of terminological ambiguity that has characterized the study of IR is relevant to this analytic framework. The very terms "international relations" and the derivative "international system" are inexact. The designation of "international" assumes too much about the homogeneity of the "nation." "Interstate" would be more accurate but would not correctly denote the scope of inquiry, which goes beyond the relations of states to encompass transnational phenomena. And the term "transnational," since it plays off the "international" concept as its counterpoint, suffers from the same inexactitude ("transstate" and "transsociety" are likewise insufficient). The notions of a "world system" or "global system" would be improved representations, but they have been co-opted by specific theoretical schools (see Chapter 3). In any event, "international relations" and "international system" remain firmly imbedded as the generic "umbrella" terms despite their deficiencies. Thus, somewhat reluctantly, I continue to use the term "international system," with the understanding that it refers to a combined interstate-transnational global system that includes regional subsystems in its structure.

Characteristics of the International System

The international system as conceived in this book is a complex political, military, economic, social, and cultural structure of both power and interdependence. It is comprised of states interacting in cooperation and conflict, informal power relationships, and formal international rules and institutions—and of transnational actors that join the mix and add to the complex array of interactions. A systems approach offers analytic advantages by providing a broad overview of international structures and processes and by facilitating the analysis of a wide range of relationships. Systemic concepts are also applicable to the specific levels of activity within the global system—from individual state and transnational actors to various groupings of them (such as in a geographic region). Within each of these interrelated levels are found discreet structures and processes involving units, subsystems, interaction, and regulation.

Nevertheless, certain assumptions of international systems thinking gives rise to some conceptual problems. Some critics argue that an international system does not exist, and, therefore, international relations are not susceptible to such analysis. This view assumes that IR should deal only with the flux of changing concrete situations that are not amenable to systemic generalization or theoretical explanation and that students in the field must be satisfied with describing particular past or current events. More specifically, it assumes that international relations are anarchic, since no centralized international decision-making authority exists, and a system, by definition, requires regularity. This view is similar to the position taken (mostly in the past) by some historians who viewed history as a series of new and unique events and who denied the existence of behavioral patterns. A similar perspective has also been expressed by some sociologists who have found individual psychological patterns of behavior but no social system as such.

One can hardly claim, in reply, that international events fall into immutable patterns, and one must acknowledge that the international system differs in fundamental ways from domestic processes. The essential problem is that of regulation: The international arena, unlike the domestic realm, lacks higher authoritative decision-making agencies able to make and enforce rules and reconcile conflicting parties. Furthermore, little feeling of legitimacy exists above the state level, which continues to be the central structural feature and decisional source in the system. Certain other actors also occupy important positions, which serves to further decentralize the system.

International relations, however, do not merely consist of anarchic competition. A degree of integration is found, although it is considerably less than within most state systems. In reality, state independence is far from absolute, whether in the domestic or the international domain. Loyalty and legitimacy remain problematical within the state itself, and state interdependence is a fact as well as a theory of international life. The distribution of power and influence among states and other actors has always had a primary structural influence; the "balance of power" has been recognized by strategists for centuries as an informal controlling device. Formal regulatory institutions are embodied in international law, organizations, and other interstate regimes; various forms of informal consensus (norms) also exist. Although any authoritative activity of such institutions is ultimately limited by the sovereign autonomy of the member states (which today seems to be to some degree an eroding concept), many formal and informal rules are voluntarily accepted and followed. In addition, the variety of sustained identifiable patterns of interstate and transnational interaction is significant. Today's international system may be characterized as primitive, rudimentary, and decentralized, but it demonstrates enough regularity to apply systemic concepts as the basis for organizing the analysis of IR and the accompanying theoretical debates.[5]

THE NATION-STATE ACTORS

The Nature of the Modern State

The most important differentiated units in international politics today, as in the past three centuries, are sovereign nation-states. At present they number about 200 and are located in all parts of the world. The nation-state has never been and is not now the only unit in the international system. Its long evolution has been an irregular one, and today it is challenged in several important ways. Nevertheless, it is and will continue for the foreseeable future to be the most prominent actor. As such, it is the central concept in world politics and the starting point for an understanding of the international system.

The state units themselves have changed over time. For example, Chinese states, Greek city-states, Egyptian and Indian civilizations, and pre-Columbian American entities such as the Aztec and Inca empires as well as European empires and feudal realms all preceded the nation-state. Some of them paralleled for a time or even survived along with the nation-state's ultimate spread around the globe.

The modern state system evolved after the collapse of feudalism and the dual empire-papacy system in Europe at the end of the Middle Ages. The new system developed throughout the fifteenth and sixteenth centuries and was legally institutionalized by the Peace of Westphalia (1648), which settled the Thirty Years War among kings, pope, and emperor (supported by feudal lords). The peace arrangement recognized the independence of secular nation-states from the Holy Roman Empire and the papacy. This system subsequently spread from Europe to all parts of the world.

The process was not essentially completed in Europe until the late nineteenth century (and then not entirely), when Italy and Germany each were finally consolidated. In the meantime, after their own emergence, the new European states began to expand their power around the globe through imperialism and trade. This movement was led first by Portugal in the early fifteenth century and Spain beginning in the 1490s, followed by France, Holland, and England in the sixteenth century. Eventually, almost all European states adopted imperialist policies, and overseas empires were established in most of the non-European world.

Independent nation-states of the European type did not appear outside of Europe until the United States of America was established in 1776 through a revolutionary process. Most of Latin America followed suit between 1804 and 1824 by forcefully breaking away from imperial Spain and Portugal; Japan did so in the late nineteenth century through a nonrevolutionary process of "opening" to the outside world. China did not effectively become a nation-state in the Western sense until after 1911, the year of Sun Yat Sen's revolution. The European empires in Asia, Africa, and the Caribbean largely broke up in the twentieth century. Most of the new states in those areas were created after World War II, including two of the most populous in the world, India and Indonesia. Thus, what originated as a European system became a cumbersome world-wide one through several kinds of change.

The modern state is endowed with two unique and abstract characteristics that it shares with no other entity—the attribute of sovereignty and the relationship of nationalism to statehood. Sovereignty and nationalism are distinct concepts, but they are related in their complex evolution over the past three and a half centuries.

Introduced in seventeenth century international law, sovereignty is traditionally defined as the state's supreme authority over its citizens—the state is the final arbiter in their lives. Whether sovereignty is, indeed, absolute and indivisible has long been a matter of debate. The idea was the product of the times that witnessed the rise of the nation-state under absolute monarchs. It replaced the medieval concept of limited sovereignty under natural (divine) law embodied in the contractual relationship of the feudal system. The concept of sovereignty stressed the superiority of the territorial state to both imperial universalism and feudal localism. It reflected the need for central government authority, embodied in the monarch ("the sovereign"), in order to create domestic order and stability within a given territory.

An analysis of the phenomenon of nationalism is complicated: first by the lack of a precise and widely accepted definition; second because the variety of nationalism is highly complex; and third because of both the fragmentation of and alternatives to nationalism. Nevertheless, the continuing importance of nationalism to the nature of the modern state and to foreign policy formulation cannot be denied.

Classic definitions characterize nationalism as a "group consciousness" in which individuals identify themselves with and give supreme loyalty to the abstraction of the nation, which reinforces the state as the ultimate source of authority and legitimacy. This definition should be modified with the caveat that particular nationalists may use nationalism in attempts to capture control of the state and its authority, claiming to speak for "the nation" in order to gain advantage over political competitors. Nationalism represents an emotional identification of the individual with the nation-state, as a psychological refuge and source of a sense of well-being that inspires devotion to the nation-state. It is also a structural and institutional phenomenon—it represents the lodging of social functions and their structural base in the nation-state.

States and nations have existed throughout recorded history, but only after the consolidation of feudal units into kingdoms in Western Europe were the two elements combined. Since then, a principal theme has been the search by multicultural states for a single nationhood and by homogeneous nations for separate statehood. These processes involve the melding of distinct entities that are not necessarily coterminous—the state (a legal-political entity defined in terms of territory, population, and effective autonomous government) and the nation (a social-cultural entity defined in terms of people who, for whatever reasons, share a sense of sameness and uniqueness). From the rise of the modern state until the late eighteenth century, European dynastic states worked to create nations of their domains, with the "sovereign" serving as the symbol of national identity among the people living within the state borders. With the American and French revolutions (1776/1789) and the subsequent development of republicanism, nationalism came to be identified with "the people." Thereafter, national groups sought to create states that conformed to national boundaries, and the idea of "national self-determination" was born. Since then, a tension has existed over the nature and relationship of nations and states.

The definitional elusiveness of nation and nationalism has been and continues to be problematical. Realities of ethnic and social identity on the part of distinct internal sectors within societies challenge their meaning. This has been true not only for the decidedly multicultural societies in the Americas but in numerous European states, where modern nationalism was born, and in other parts of the globe. Immigrants often have dual identities and loyalties: Although they are newly citizens of a state to which they give loyalty out of appreciation for the economic opportunities or political havens provided, their cultural roots are elsewhere. Other, more recent transnational considerations have compounded the problem. One of the reasons offered for the prominence of transnational actors is that people may identify their interests with nonstate entities in addition to the nation-state, so that the former compete for or share individual loyalties with the latter. At the same time, a variety of "subnational" entities—such as tribal groupings, leaders of breakaway provinces, sides in a civil war, insurrectionist forces, and governments in exile—may challenge state authority. Thus, the term "nation-state" is, to a considerable degree, a misnomer.

A major change in the concept of sovereignty also occurred with the development of republicanism in the late eighteenth century. The locus of state sovereignty shifted from the tangible person of the monarch to the abstraction of "we the people." This transition required the doctrine of popular sovereignty to emerge, in which the voice of the people *(vox populi)* replaced the voice of God *(vox Dei)* as the ultimate base of authority.

The notion of popular sovereignty, which personified the state and ascribed action to a nonhuman abstraction, raised enduring philosophical questions about the intangible nature of the nation and the state. Although, analysts have tended to attribute action to states as a convenient expression, they recognize that human beings in fact make decisions and act on behalf of states and their societies. The personification of the state is both a legal and convenient way of referring to the behavior of an identifiable collection of human beings. Questions remain, however, about the sources of "state behavior."

State Action

Foreign policy analysis focuses on how and why decision makers behave the way they do. Thus the identification of the intellectual, psychological, and institutional factors that affect the reasoning processes by which leaders arrive at decisions is the central analytic element. As in the general study of IR, most foreign policy analysts have come overtly or implicitly to employ a systems perspective as an analytic framework to guide their inquiry. Within this outlook, however, particular decision models place different emphases on the different ingredients of policy-making. (Theories of decision-making are explored in Chapter 3.)

Policy decisions put into action may be generally characterized as "orientations." They are the actual substance of policies finally decided upon. Foreign policy orientations are the result of decision makers' evaluations of the state's place in the international system and of their choice of methods for coping with the external world. Some analysts equate orientation with a state's tendencies regarding alignment. I, however, prefer to adopt a broader perspective and describe policy orientations in terms of four dimensions: ends and means, alignment, national roles, and status quo or revisionist commitments. In addition, capability analysis is crucial to foreign policy formulation at several stages of the process.

Ends-means analysis inquires into a state's calculation of purposes, interests, and goals and into the relations between the objectives and the policy instruments and techniques. It may also include reference to ethical and moral considerations. Ultimate state objectives seem usually to be articulated as those identified with the concept of "national interest," often referred to as the "vital interests" of self-preservation, security, and social and economic well-being. These interests are expressed in the most general and often symbolic or even mythical terms, which makes the idea of national interest highly ambiguous. This analytic interpretation runs the danger of ignoring or of not recognizing dissent within the decisional unit, a dissent based on differing interests, ideologies, or other values that may lead to different conclusions about what constitutes national interest.

The choice of instruments and tactics can involve varying combinations of policies: multilateral, bilateral, or unilateral, and active or passive. A multilateral orientation tends to seek joint action through international organizations, alliances, and coalitions, an approach that contrasts with bilateral (state-to-state) or unilateral ("go-it-alone") approaches. The more active a state, the more likely it is to initiate action rather than only respond to or resist the initiatives taken by others. An important aspect of activism is the degree of willingness to intervene in the affairs of other states through diplomatic, economic, or military means. Some states passively choose not to compete.

A second dimension of state orientation concerns tendencies regarding alignment. Does a state choose military alliance and economic or political coalition with other states? Or does it prefer some form of neutrality, nonalignment, or isolation? Neutrality may refer to the legal status chosen by a state during armed hostilities; such a choice entails defined rights and responsibilities that distinguish neutrals from belligerents. Another meaning of neutrality, also recognized in international law, has to do with states that are neutralized through the actions of others, usually through agreement among great powers to impose and guarantee the neutrality. Neutrality is also used somewhat loosely to mean nonalignment—a voluntary rejection of alliance, a refusal to align with the great powers or their blocs—without reference to legal status. An isolationist strategy is indicated by a low level of involvement in aspects of the international system, from attempts to seal off the country against external penetration to reducing diplomatic or commercial transactions.

The third dimension, called "national roles," refers to policy makers' views of what the nation-state should do in the world based on their perceptions of both the outside world and their own societies. Role conceptions define the kinds of actions appropriate to national values. They are associated only with states that are actively involved in global or regional affairs. For example, following the lead of K. J. Holsti,[6] we can posit some typical national roles that are suggestive of how the United States perceives its functions in the Caribbean Basin: the role of "regional defender/leader/policeman," protecting, (and intervening in the affairs of) other states in a defined area; of "mediator," assisting in and perhaps insisting on international and internal conflict resolution; and of "protector of the faith," urging, sometimes forcefully, anticommunism and democratic development during the cold war, and economic and political neoliberalism in the current era.

Finally, foreign policy orientations may be understood in terms of a state's commitment to either the status quo or to revisionism. A state may pursue a policy of the status quo if it is satisfied with its lot in the international system, or at least is willing to accept it. A state with a revisionist commitment is dissatisfied with the status quo and desires to change the distribution of the rewards of the system in a way more to its advantage. A status quo state pursues policies aimed at keeping things the way they are and thus will usually be defensive in nature, oriented toward the preservation of peace and stability. Contrarily, the revisionist state is more likely to be on the offensive and willing to take higher risks, seeing less to lose in its deprived situation and considering peaceful and stable processes as working to its disadvantage.

State Capability

Capability analysis, which is crucial to foreign policy formulation at several stages of the process, is partly an inventory of relative strengths and weaknesses as measured by a state's economic, political, military, and other resources. But analysis goes far beyond this essentially technical calculation to consider the influence of a broad range of "situational factors" that give rise to or help shape policy decisions and orientations. These factors arise in real-world settings or conditions in the international and intrasocietal environments and within the political system itself. They impinge on state actions, either limiting its freedom or offering it opportunities. Their structures and events may impose requirements on policy makers to the extent that, in some cases, they find decisions largely determined for them. The analyst should be skeptical, however, about any classification called "determinants of policy."

Among the external environmental factors that influence decisions are the capabilities and the actual or anticipated actions of other states, real and imagined threats, and considerations of coping with moves made by other states by resisting, cooperating, or accommodating them. A state's geographic setting influences such variables as world position, the presence of more or less powerful neighbors, and whether climate, terrain, and natural resources are favorable or unfavorable. The social setting of other states must also be considered, not only in terms of their strength in potential conflict but also as to their ability to cooperate in mutual enterprises. From the intrasocietal environment come such influences as nationalism, ideology, religion, the state of the economy, and the nature of social stability. Inside the political system, interest groups, political parties, and elites may interact with decision makers, and public opinion, public relations activities, the communications media, and elections also influence policy decisions. Within government, association among and within the bureaucracies and interpersonal relationships among key decision makers affect decisional outcomes. An important consideration is the influence of the nature of the governing regime itself on foreign policy decisions and actions; that is, what differences in behavior may be ascribed to the fact that a regime is democratic, authoritarian, totalitarian, or something else?

THE INTERSTATE SYSTEM

The interstate elements of the system have been integrated through the means of both power distribution and international institutions. The balance of power provides an informal mechanism for regulating international conflict. International law, organizations, and regimes represent formal attempts to control and accommodate power politics as well as to promote interstate cooperation. Competition and conflict seem to be inherent in the nation-state system, based as it is on the concept of sovereignty and characterized as it is by nationalism and a heavy emphasis on the role of power. States assume that they must use their own resources to achieve their objectives or to prevent successful challenges by other states. Consequently, the regulation of conflict—its limitation and adjustment—is a major concern for most states. At the same time, regulation also involves the search for cooperative measures designed to resolve problems relating to military force, economic interdependence, national development, and the physical environment itself.

Distribution of Power and Influence

Balance-of-power theories imply equilibrium and stability within a system composed of several largely autonomous political forces. The equilibrium concept in systems theory, as well as the more operational traditional views of the balance of power, assume that when stability or equilibrium is disturbed, either by an outside force or by internal change within certain system components, the system itself exhibits a tendency either to reestablish the original equilibrium or to adopt a new one. According to this theory, the various states in the international system, each with a different level of capability, group themselves in such a way that no single state or group of states is strong enough to dominate the system; power is balanced by opposing power. If equilibrium is maintained, then aggression is deterred, peace assured, and the independence of small states guaranteed. Conversely, war indicates disequilibrium, or a breakdown of the balance of power (a dysfunction of the balance mechanism).

The theory of power balance is not universally accepted by scholars. Some reject it outright as an artifice, whereas others note that it may be exploited by states to justify their pursuit of policies aimed not at equilibrium but at a power imbalance in their favor. Still others deny the assumption that equilibrium is the normal or natural state of a system and actually view balance as abnormal. Political leaders have often pursued balance-of-power policies, however, usually aimed at achieving a "favorable" balance; an international "pecking order" based on power considerations does seem to exist, whether power distribution is sought or accidental, balanced or random. Thus, insofar as the balance of power is defined as "distribution of power" rather than "power equilibrium," I believe that the concept correctly, if roughly, describes certain important patterns of state relationships. I further assume that an excessive shift in the balance of power tends to generate forceful reactions on the part of decision makers in those principal states adversely affected; but I reject the notion that the reaction is automatic or that the nature of the system is "organic" in this regard. Power politics are the result of human decision-making.

According to balance of power theory, the basic types of balance that have existed in the nation-state system are multiple balance and simple balance. In a multiple system, several states balance each other on a global scale with further balances found in certain regional areas. Multiple balance was the controlling pattern of international politics from the birth of the nation-state until World War II. During that time between five and seven great powers dominated the scene, with widespread dispersal of power among them. Such a pattern may contain a "balancer," or one state that remains aloof from alliance until the balance seems to be shifting, whereupon it intervenes in favor of the weaker side in order to reestablish the balance.

Simple balance involves the concentration of power around two poles of roughly equal strength. Such a bipolar system existed after World War II, with the United States and the Soviet Union leading two sides composed of large groups of states. Bipolarity began to break up and power began to become dispersed in the early 1960s with the rise of new centers of political and economic, if not military, power. Military bipolarity still existed, although the superpower-led alliances showed elements of internal fragmentation and were challenged by the large (although often internally divided) Non-aligned Movement. Politically and economically the world was increasingly multipolar.

Balance-of-power theory further acknowledges a variety of techniques for balancing power. The classic methods, aimed at either increasing the power of one pole or diminishing that of another, include shifting alliances, increasing armaments, seizing territory, creating buffer zones, intervening in the affairs of others, and setting states against each other in accordance with the principle of divide and conquer. Power balancing also involves establishing spheres of influence or control, such as the Soviet Union's influence in Eastern Europe until the late 1980s, and the U.S. influence in the circum-Caribbean throughout most of the twentieth century.

An aspect of balance-of-power theory particularly relevant to this study is the fundamental principle that proximate geographic areas are linked to a state's vital core interests. Thus, powerful states react to unfavorable events in proximate states or to actions of external states that may compete for influence in those adjacent areas. This principle accounts, for example, for U.S. opposition to other foreign influences in the Caribbean zone. Spheres of influence have been essentially nonnegotiable for great powers. They have been particularly important when the geographic interests of great powers have overlapped or when more remote powers have challenged the primacy of another great power's sphere of influence.

The "unipolar" or imperial model of power distribution is one in which dominant authority is held by a single entity. It is not a "balancing" system—indeed, a principal purpose of balance of power operations is to avoid such single-state domination. Unipolar systems were created by conquest, such as that resulting in the Roman, Ottoman, and Russian empires. Napoleon attempted to conquer Europe, and Hitler had more global ambitions. System stability depended on the dominant center's ability to control those who had been subjugated—a difficult task, evidenced by the fact that all such systems or attempts to create them engendered violent resistance.

Conditions in the post–cold war world have challenged theories of power relationships. With the sharp decline and then dissolution of the Soviet Union—leaving the United States as the only state that could claim to be, or could be perceived as, a superpower—any lingering bipolarity was definitively ended. However, multipolarity as traditionally conceived was not revived. Some analysts initially saw the new situation creating a de facto unipolar world, but most of them dismissed the possibilities for a worldwide, neo-imperial system. They understood the many limitations on the U.S. power to undertake economic or military domination and the strong U.S. public reluctance to play a global police role. Indeed, with the irrelevance of military power to many of the primary post–cold war issues and their transnational nature, one may reasonably argue for a new political-economic-social-cultural multipolarity.

Interstate Institutions

A number of institutions serve as formal regulatory instruments in the interstate system. Some regulation has been achieved by international law and intergovernmental organizations and by other specialized interstate regimes.

International law, a body of formal regulatory rules, dates from the beginning of the nation-state system and has been an integral part of its evolution. The concept of sovereignty is a central tenet of international law, but it also poses a central problem: If the state is the supreme authority within its territorial bounds, are there any international laws to which the state itself is subservient? This difficulty has forced international law to rely on consent, with states reserving to themselves legal interpretation and the nature and application of law. This decentralized legal system in the international sphere was effective when the great powers generally agreed to uphold certain rules of conduct. Such was the case for almost three centuries, until the outbreak of World War I, when European powers agreed upon and enforced the law. Since then, however, no such agreement has existed. Despite these problems, a huge amount of day-to-day international business is facilitated and guided by legal agreement.

Weaker states, old and new, have had an ambivalent attitude toward international law. On the one hand they see the need for legal restraint of the larger powers, but on the other hand they recognize that law tends to reflect the interests of those powers. They often view it as the codification of the international power structure in which violators among the weaker states are punished by the stronger ones. At the same time, their own impact on law has been significant. Their interpretation of law differs in several respects from the traditional postulates, which they view as inimical to their own interests. They stress the development of law to reflect their concerns in such areas as nationalization of foreign enterprise, territorial sea limits, and nonintervention of one state in the affairs of another.

Intergovernmental organizations (IGOs) began to develop in the nineteenth century and expanded and accelerated in the twentieth. They are created and directed by governments on the general and regional levels as well as other functional levels. The leaders of most states recognize a difficult dilemma: The nature of the system is conflictual, but mutual interdependence requires cooperation. IGOs are creations of the states themselves, developed by leaders in response to the practical necessities of international life and as attempts to make international relations function more smoothly. They are the results of state agreements to engage in regularized consultation, to follow mutually agreed upon rules of behavior, and to establish administrative machinery to implement joint decisions.

Regional organizations, as the name implies, regulate international relations within defined geographic areas. They date from the latter half of the nineteenth century, when European Public Unions and the Inter-American System were organized. Regional organizations may be classified according to their basic purposes. Some have been concerned essentially with mutual defense, such as the North Atlantic Treaty Organization and the Warsaw Pact during the cold war. Such alliances represent the formal organizational aspects of balance-of-power structures. Others have been primarily concerned with specific fields of cooperation, such as the economic and political integration schemes in Europe and Latin America and the Caribbean. Multipurpose organizations have also been created, such as the Arab League, the Organization of African Unity, and the Inter-American System.

General (global or universal) international organizations are a product of the twentieth century. Three of them have appeared: (1) The Hague System, initiated in 1899 and ending with the outbreak of World War I; (2) the League of Nations, founded in the wake of World War I and continuing until the end of World War II; and (3) the United Nations (UN), created during World War II and developing thereafter with considerable complexity. Membership in these organizations has included the vast majority of sovereign states in existence during their respective tenures. Founded fundamentally (but not exclusively) as responses to the problems of war, they have used a variety of approaches for promoting peace by attacking what their advocates assumed to be the causes of war. The Hague System dealt especially with arbitration, disarmament, the development of international law, and the creation of permanent global international agencies. These elements were continued by the League of Nations and the United Nations, although the pursuit of collective security was their primary rationale.

Those who originated the concept of collective security thought of it as the integration of power as opposed to the balance of power, with most of the powers of the world coming together in a global organization to deter aggression. Collective security has been largely a failure; attempts in the post–cold war era to resuscitate it have been partially successful but difficult and controversial. The League and the UN also sought to create a "grand debate" of the issues among their members, to promote economic and social development, to adopt common international legal standards, to bring about colonial adjustments, to facilitate pacific settlement of disputes, to control or reduce military armaments, to combat illicit drug traffic, and to improve international administration. The UN has also undertaken to deal with the law of the sea, the degradation of the physical environment, and other issues.

Another set of IGOs, of varying complexity but neither regional nor general, have performed a multiplicity of specialized functions. They include such entities as commodities agreements (the Organization of Petroleum Exporting Countries, OPEC, is probably the best-known), the Commonwealth of Nations, the Nonaligned Movement, and others.

International regimes, often but not necessarily associated with IGOs, are attempts at international governance and the regulation of international systems. One of the principal roles of IGOs is to sponsor, facilitate, or serve as regimes, but they are not the exclusive source of such governance. Regimes may be organized outside of IGOs through special conferences, bilateral or multilateral treaties, or informal agreements and understandings. Regimes focus on the congeries of forces at work in selected issue-areas and attempt to resolve tensions between order and disorder. They ideally constitute mutually accepted norms, values, expectations, rules, procedures, and perceptions of legitimacy, allowing international actors to cooperate on a regularized basis and to deal with shared problems of common concern in the absence of higher authority. Regime-building may occur on bilateral, regional, global, or other levels or on some combination of them. Many different kinds of international problems, including mutual security, terrorism, arms races, economic development, trade, financial relations, scarcity of resources, borders and waterways, and many other concerns, have given rise to regimes.

Some random examples illustrate the phenomenon. The combined UN financial institutions—the International Monetary Fund, the World Bank, the General Agreement on Tariffs and Trade, and its successor the World Trade Organization—form a global economic regime. The Third World challenged that regime and offered its alternative New International Economic Order. The corpus of arms control agreements and the law of the sea are important treaty-based functional regimes. The Antarctic Treaty creates a specific geographic regional mode of governance in the uninhabited continent. The Organization of American States includes (among other things) extensive provisions and organizations seeking to protect and promote human rights among the states of the Western Hemisphere. The Panama Canal Treaties between Panama and the United States illustrate an important bilateral regime.

Interstate Interactions

Once a state has decided upon a course of action, it mobilizes its resources or its "instruments of policy." The kinds of policy instruments and techniques available to decision makers to pursue their objectives cover a wide gamut of options. Positive action is not necessarily a consequence of the decisional process, for a state may decide to do nothing. Beyond nonaction, instruments may be classified in such categories as diplomatic, political, psychological, cultural, economic, or military resources. Thus, interactions in the system are largely identical with policy instruments. For example, war and economic assistance are policy instruments as well as forms of interaction. When the instruments of state action, once selected through the policy process, are implemented, they then constitute part of international political processes and result in patterns of interaction that give further structure to the system.

Capability analysis, a concept introduced earlier, is also essential to understanding international interactions. In fact, the most meaningful view of foreign policy capability theorizes a range of power relationships. Capability is relative with respect to other states; it cannot exist without having one party to assert claims and another to respond. Brazil is considerably more powerful than, say, Romania, but the lack of significant interaction between them renders such an observation meaningless. A state may be weak in general terms relative to one state and powerful relative to another. This principle would apply to the relations of Mexico to the United States and to Guatemala, respectively. A state may have power over another in one area of activity, but the roles may be reversed in another area. For example, in military terms, the United States is infinitely more powerful than Venezuela; but Venezuela, due to its huge petroleum resources, sometimes has great leverage with regard to the energy needs of the United States. Capability also depends on the problem or situation in which it is being exercised. In 1965 the United States was capable of invading the Dominican Republic, quelling domestic chaos there, and restoring public order, but afterward it was incapable of establishing the U.S. system of democracy for Dominicans.

We often classify the large number of diverse state instruments and interactions in political, economic, military, and other categories. It is also useful to cut across these categories and think of them as either cooperative or conflictual in character.

"Cooperation" (or "collaboration," which is synonymous) means willingly working with others for a common purpose in harmonious relationships. It involves the conscious behavior of all of the actors and is designed to produce results of value to all of them. Cooperative measures include diplomatic representation, cultural activities, technical assistance, capital investment, economic aid, trade, military grants and aid, arms transfers, personnel exchanges, armed service missions, and other transactions. Thus, cooperation is perceived by the various actors as enhancing their own ability to achieve goals while also being compatible with the interests of others. Interests need not be mutual in the sense of sameness, but cooperation requires that they be complementary and noncontradictory, even if different. Cooperation implies a symmetry of relations acceptable to all parties, even if full satisfaction is lacking or some resentment is present.

Conflict is the opposite of cooperation. It refers to instruments of policy and patterns of politics involving coercion, contention, hostility, tension, struggle, divisiveness, and discord of action—in general, a variance of principles and interests and asymmetry of relations. Conflict is present in war, intervention, blockade, clandestine actions, subversion, hostile propaganda, covert intelligence activities, terrorism, guerrilla warfare, diplomatic nonrecognition of new governments, rupture of relations, economic pressures such as embargoes, boycotts, frozen assets, blacklists, denial of aid, and the nationalization and expropriation of foreign enterprise. International conflicts arise out of incompatible objectives between states, which often resort to threats and sometimes ultimately to the use of force. The regulation of conflict and search for cooperation through direct negotiation, third-party activities (by states or IGOs), or the creation of international regimes are among the most constant, persistent, and even poignant themes of international politics.

The cooperation-conflict dichotomy is not exact, nor is either category fixed or static. Even in the most cooperative relationships some level of conflict may arise; cooperative relations may become conflictual, and conflict may be transformed into cooperation. As a policy matter, cooperative and coercive instruments are rarely applied singly or in isolation; usually they come in some sort of tactical "mix" of tools. This being so, interstate processes are probably best understood in terms of diplomacy and violence.

The concept of diplomacy has more than one meaning. In a narrow sense, "diplomacy" refers to the conduct of negotiations and other relations between states, the practices and procedures whereby they exchange official representatives and communicate with each other. In its broader meaning, "diplomacy" is synonymous with "bargaining," which is the general process, either formal or informal, whereby parties reach agreements. These agreements may relate to obligations undertaken in cooperative transactions or to the resolution of conflict. Bargaining entails the politics of influence, the process by which states and other actors seek to achieve their ends by influencing others to behave in a desired fashion through the mobilization of appropriate resources. Bargaining may include promises and rewards ("carrots") as well as threats and punishments ("sticks"). It may go on between friends, neutrals, opponents, and enemies.

The relationship between diplomacy (bargaining) and violence (the threat or use of force) is a subject of debate. Some would define bargaining as the attempt to induce or persuade without resorting to physical coercion. In this view, diplomacy may require "the stick," but it falls short of the actual use of armed force or other forms of violence; that is, states resort to force only when diplomacy fails. Another school extends the meaning of diplomacy to include the selective use of force, or the "diplomacy of violence." They consider war as an instrument of policy in the tradition of Karl von Clausewitz's famous dictum that "war is the continuation of policy by other means," a deliberate and rational part of bargaining.

A fine line separates the use of diplomacy and of force as bargaining vehicles, but it is a critical distinction because cost and risk tend to rise sharply once armed action has been undertaken. Furthermore, the use of armed force goes far beyond the purposes of a bargaining tool. In the twentieth century, two world wars on an unprecedented scale—in the technology of killing and destruction and the massive slaughter of both combatants and civilians—were utterly irrelevant to notions of a Clausewitzian "policy by other means." Something of the same could be said of many past wars as well. Numerous analysts understand Clausewitz's position as a prescription for what war and strategy should be—an instrument of policy—but are skeptical that it accurately describes what war actually is.

Thus war, in theory or practice, has ranged from being a limited political instrument to a broad assertion of raw power; it may aim to influence, to compel, or to seize. It may be a rational bargaining exercise, or it may be irrational or accidental. Even if initially conducted rationally, war may get out of control, and its termination, under many circumstances, rational or otherwise, may be difficult. Increasingly since World War II and clearly in the post–cold war international system, the actuality of warfare is characterized by internal wars (as opposed to interstate wars).

TRANSNATIONAL ACTORS AND RELATIONS

Transnational interactions describe movements across state boundaries when at least one significant actor is not an agent of a government or international governmental organization. Governments may or may not be involved in specific transnational processes; if they entail only governments they are categorized as interstate relations. Pluralists have argued compellingly for the essentiality of transnational phenomena for understanding the evolving new era. These scholars emphasize the importance of a diverse assortment of transnational actors—such as multinational corporations, nongovernmental organizations, churches, international political parties and labor associations, immigrants and refugees, and guerrilla groups. They have directed attention to the critical interactions—among them commercial activities, religious networks, migration of people, cultural dissemination, insurgency, and drug trafficking—in which these and others actors are involved, often alongside states. It is clear that students of IR must account for transnational phenomena and combine them with the analyses of the interstate system and state policies into a single overall international system.[7]

The idea of the transnationalization of the international system is understood in combination with that of globalization. The terms, however, tend to be loosely used and are marked by conceptual disparity. As employed in this book, globalization alludes not to a literally globalized order but to a continuing dynamic globalizing process, involving the uneven expansion of relations at all system levels. Although globalization refers prominently to the international economic system, it is far from restricted to it, as some commentators assert or imply. Just as meaningful is an array of political and social-cultural phenomena and issues. Thus transnationalization inherently accompanies globalization. It elevates the prominence of a broad array of non-nation-state actors and intensifies phenomena that evolve in a largely autonomous manner parallel with interstate relations. Consequently, states and IGOs are joined by transnational actors to engage in a wide variety of activities and transactions having multiple effects and immense consequences.

When the defenders of the established state-centric analytic tradition were challenged by the advocates of increased recognition of transnational relations, their primary defense was that transnational phenomena did not significantly affect the overarching functions of the international system—the "high politics" of security, diplomacy, war, and peace. For that reason, the "low politics" of transnational phenomena were understood as part of the interstate system's environment within which states operated. The dissenters counterargued that although interstate relations were clearly of crucial importance, transnational phenomena often challenged and eroded state authority and sometimes superseded it. Of more importance than "who won" these state-transnational debates, however, was the reality of both widespread bargaining between states and IGOs with transnational entities over a broad range of issues and the formation of agreements, coalitions, and associations. Furthermore, the distinctions between high and low politics were becoming increasingly difficult to discern and perhaps meaningless, so that transnational relations could not simply be dismissed or marginalized as subordinate low politics.

Considerable evidence supports the assertion that the old notion of high politics has been superseded by a complex mix of critical interstate and transnational phenomena. As early as the latter part of World War II, the substance of international economics was deemed a matter of national and international security; states had in fact long behaved as if this were the case. In the early 1980s numerous states, led by the United States, officially declared the illicit drug traffic a matter of security concern. In the post–cold war era the list was expanded to include other high-priority transnational phenomena, including matters of representative democracy and respect for human rights, immigrants and refugees, and the protection of the environment. In addition, certain issues involving military threats, both interstate and internal wars, continue as major security concerns. Many issues are closely identified with domestic society and are not appropriate for the use of state force, nor particularly amenable to diplomacy. The decline of state power should not be exaggerated, however. Not only do diplomacy and war remain as convincing undertakings, but states can play major roles in transnational relations.

The question arises of how we account for the violation of sovereignty in the face of state power differentials.[8] This problem of reconciling absolute sovereignty and relative power, inherent to the modern (Westphalian) interstate system since the introduction of the idea of absolute state sovereignty in the mid-seventeenth century, became more and more problematical with increasing state interdependence and the rise of ideologies that fractured consensus over the meaning of the state and of international norms. From the beginning states were willing to accept the myth of consent to disguise power intrusions and preserve the principle of absolute sovereignty. Transnational developments have further complicated this enduring puzzle.

The problem of sovereignty has been openly revived in the post–cold war era with the emergence of new international norms. A number of states around the globe (and notably those of the Americas) have engaged in a process of redefining national and international security. The preponderance of the intertwined concerns indicated above are extensions of essentially domestic considerations and imply an admission that states cannot alone effectively surmount them. If their resolution requires they be approached in a multilateral and transnational context, then a redefinition of sovereignty is also required; that is, if fundamental state problems do not stop at physical borders, then neither does sovereignty. A definitive solution to this difficulty has not been agreed upon.

SYSTEM CHANGE

An important area of inquiry has to do with systemic change or transformation. How does a system shift from one historical dividing line to another? That is, how does it move in time? How do we detect the transformation of a system from one with certain characteristics to a new era with changed or different features?

Many analysts have measured systemic change in terms of revised state capabilities and their power relationships. They have pointed to such factors as major military victories or defeats, collapsed or reshuffled alliances, and alterations in state capability levels and the instrumentalities they use. For example, in the global system, the Thirty Years War, the Napoleonic wars, and the two world wars ended prior system configurations, introduced new ones, and precipitated continuing fundamental changes in their aftermath. More specifically, World War II elevated the United States and the Soviet Union to a new superpower level, thus altering the nature and stratification of the state units. The introduction of nuclear weapons permanently changed the nature of warfare and power, and nuclear proliferation further transformed the way the system was integrated. Then, with the recovery of traditional power centers, and with energy resources and industrialization thrusting previously weak states into important international roles, the bipolar configuration was seriously eroded.

Other analysts have focused on significant shifts in both the distribution of political-military power and the patterns of economic-social interdependence. Certain elements with regard to the transnational impact on system change have always been present to some degree. In a general sense, the beginnings of today's globalization and transnationalization can be traced back five centuries to the Age of Discovery (on the part of Europeans) and the subsequent expansion of imperialism and trade and the flow of people, capital, technology, and ideas. They became particularly important during the nineteenth century with the industrial and scientific revolutions, the concomitant developments in communications and other technologies, and the dramatic increase in commerce and capital investment and in human migration. Until World War I, however, much of the world did not participate in transnational occurrences, and globalization as we know it today was relatively slow. The processes were then disrupted by world depression, followed by World War II. Since then, the expansion of transnational phenomena in a globalizing context has increasingly characterized the international system. Disguised for four decades by the imperatives of the cold war, the cessation of East-West conflict gave them great impetus. The end of the cold war revolutionized the international system, not only by ending superpower confrontation and its broad implications but also by allowing transnational-global phenomena to take center stage and further profoundly alter the system.

INTERNATIONAL SUBSYSTEMS

Component subsystems of the international system operate at a level between states and transnational actors and the worldwide system. Most of the elements of a system apply equally to subsystems, which are also marked by differentiation and integration. The analysis of subsystems involves the concepts of individual unit-actors, foreign policy, interstate and transnational interactions, regulation, further subsystems, and change. Although some modifications must be made in these conceptual categories to accommodate the study of regional international relations, the same analytic questions and criteria already posed in the context of foreign policy analysis and the international system are directly relevant.

Subsystems may be identified by examining the differentiation and integration of various actors—states, interstate organizations and associations, transnational actors, and mixes of all kinds. The regularized interaction of two states could be considered a subsystem, such as that between Mexico and the United States or between Argentina and Brazil. International organizations of all kinds, irrespective of geography, may also be considered subsystems. Ideological or common-interest groupings that form international subsystems have included the industrialized states, the Communist world, and the Third World. Of particular importance, and of primary interest to this study, is the concept of the geographic regional subsystem, such as Latin America and the Caribbean, the Middle East, Europe, Asia, and so on.

International subsystems are not considered independent systems. Today, one worldwide system encompasses virtually all actors, subsystems, and their interactions. (The "boundary" of a system is defined as that limit within which all system components are contained and outside of which no system interaction takes place.) Regional groupings and other associations are considered to be subsystems even though they are marked by all of the elements of a system for several reasons: (1) their units interact significantly with other units and subsystems beyond their boundaries; (2) outside actors are subsystem relevant; (3) regional actors may also form parts of other subsystems; and (4) subsystem groupings remain functionally inseparable from the global system.

Although regions are relatively new foci for systems theory as such, the concept of the region has long been evident in both the study and practice of international relations. The concept of regional politics is nothing new, especially if one considers older concerns with regionalism, political and economic integration, and the voluminous literature on European international relations. International political processes have been interpreted to include regional spheres of influence in the balance of power, regional organization, regional integration (economic and political), regional security, and regional policies of the great powers, as well as the notion of regional subsystems. An academic concern with regional topics appeared even before World War I, but such concerns were not widespread until after the failure of collective security under the League of Nations to prevent World War II and the sanction of "regional arrangements" by the United Nations Charter. Latin American studies were an exception, as inter-American organizations, beginning in 1889, were the object of historical and institutional-legal scholarship. If we consider inter-American relations in general, a literature had begun to develop even before 1889. By and large, however, strong scholarly interest in regional topics is a post–World War II enterprise.

The early postwar writings were caught up in the debate between regionalists and universalists about the best arrangements for creating world order. Regionalists were primarily concerned with peace and security arrangements for dealing with aggression and controlling conflict in delineated geographic areas and with describing existing organizations in legal terms. The regionalism versus globalism debate centered on the regional commissions and activities of the United Nations and the activities of specialized regional organizations. In the mid-1950s, regionalist scholarly interest began to focus on economic and political integration; scholars searched for ways in which national political actors within defined geographic zones could shift at least part of their loyalties and decision-making to supranational regional institutions for their mutual benefit. Officials and analysts dealing with the Inter-American System and with economic integration within Latin America were especially prominent in these debates. Finally, with the impact of systems theory on the study of politics in general and international relations in particular, regional concerns became part of systems theory. The idea of region has been revived in the post–cold war era even as the system has increasingly globalized.

All of these approaches to the study of regions are linked by the common idea that geographic proximity defines one of the limits of inquiry. Consequently, the problem of defining what constitutes a region is common to all. The fundamental difference is that the peacekeeping, functional, and integration approaches include prescriptive doctrines and normative statements of preference (although scientific studies have attempted to determine their effectiveness), whereas systems theory is designed to order the objective study of reality (it is flexible enough to allow prescriptions and judgments to be considered, but not accepted as norms). Furthermore, the view of a given region as a subsystem is topically more inclusive than in the other regional approaches because it deals with the totality of regional policies and relations among actors. It includes and integrates consideration of structures, processes, and issues in other approaches and goes beyond them with an array of systemic elements. Latin America and the Caribbean composes a particularly pertinent "living laboratory" for analysis. It is to that regional subsystem that we now turn our attention.

NOTES

1. An "organizing device" is designed to assist in the understanding of social science data, such as those related to the study of international relations, by ordering seemingly disparate facts and events into some meaningful pattern that can be analyzed. An organizing device may be called an *approach*, a *paradigm*, a *quasi-theory*, a *conceptual framework*, or an *analytic framework*. All of these terms are roughly synonymous (though I prefer the term *analytic framework*). Regardless of which one is used, such terms have three specific purposes: (1) to provide a method of systematically determining which facts are pertinent and which may be ignored; (2) to enable one to present methodically the selected data in a coherent and logical manner; and (3) to facilitate the orderly comparison of related sets of phenomena. If one is not satisfied with data-gathering in a non-selective fashion and wishes to make complex problems analytically manageable and to bring them into some sort of focus, then such a strategy is essential. For a clear statement of the nature and use of analytic frameworks, see Karl W. Deutsch, *The Analysis of International Relations*, 3d ed. (Englewood Cliffs, N.J.: Prentice-Hall, 1988).

2. An insightful and thorough intellectual history of the IR field is William C. Olson and A.J.R. Groom, *International Relations Then and Now: Origins and Trends in Interpretation* (London: HarperCollins Academic, 1991).

3. A landmark collection of essays among the early sources that draw this analytic distinction are the two editions—in effect, two volumes—edited by James N. Rosenau, *International Politics and Foreign Policy* (New York: Free Press, 1961, 1969).

4. An early influential evocation was Robert O. Keohane and Joseph S. Nye Jr., eds., *Transnational Relations and World Politics* (Cambridge: Harvard University Press, 1972), followed by Keohane and Nye, *Power and Interdependence: World Politics in Transition* (Boston: Little, Brown and Co., 1977).

5. A number of textbooks analyze the international system, addressing interstate relations, foreign policy processes, international political economy, and (to varying degrees) other transnational phenomena. Collectively they expand the synoptic treatments of the specific topics in this chapter. The highly selective list includes: Seyom Brown, *International Relations*

in a Changing Global System: Toward a Theory of World Polity, 2d ed. (Boulder, Colo.: Westview Press, 1995); David N. Farnsworth, *International Relations: An Introduction,* 2d ed. (Chicago: Nelson-Hall Publishers, 1996); K. J. Holsti, *International Politics,* 6th ed. (Englewood Cliffs, N.J.: Prentice-Hall, 1992); Barry B. Hughes, *Continuity and Change in World Politics: The Clash of Perspectives* (Englewood Cliffs, N.J.: Prentice-Hall, 1991); Lloyd Jensen and Lynn Miller, *Global Challenge: Change and Continuity in World Politics* (Harcourt Brace, 1993); Charles W. Kegley Jr. and Eugene R. Wittkopf, *World Politics: Trends and Transformation,* 5th ed. (St. Martin's Press, 1997); Daniel S. Papp, *Contemporary International Relations: Frameworks for Understanding,* 4th ed. (New York: Macmillan, 1997); Frederic S. Pearson and J. Martin Rochester, *International Relations: The Global Condition in the Late Twentieth Century,* 3d ed. (New York: McGraw-Hill, 1992); James N. Rosenau and Ernst-Otto Czempiel, eds., *Governance Without Government: Order and Change in World Politics* (New York: Cambridge University Press, 1992); John T. Rourke, *International Politics on the World Stage,* 4th ed. (Guilford, Conn.: Dushkin, 1993); Bruce Russett and Harvey Starr, *World Politics: The Menu for Choice,* 4th ed. (New York: W. H. Freeman, 1992); and Gordon C. Schloming, *Power and Principle in International Affairs* (New York: Harcourt Brace Jovanich, 1991).

6. K. J. Holsti, "National Role Conceptions in the Study of Foreign Policy," *International Studies Quarterly* 14 (March 1970): 232–309.

7. Keohane and Nye, in their two books cited above, argued for a combined interstate, transnational, and transgovernmental "world politics paradigm." More recently, IR scholars have sought to integrate the elements of the present changing system for analytic purposes; for example, Robert C. North, *War, Peace, Survival: Global Politics and Conceptual Synthesis* (Boulder, Colo.: Westview Press, 1990) attempts to construct a conceptual framework of "a set of generic, even *universal,* processes that . . . function across societies and through time to encompass social, psychological, technological, economic, political, military, and other phenomena and somehow capture their interplay."

8. This discussion is taken from G. Pope Atkins, "Redefining Security in Inter-American Relations: Implications for Democracy and Civil-Military Relations," in *To Sheathe the Sword: Civil-Military Relations in the Quest for Democracy,* ed. John P. Lovell and David E. Albright (Westport, Conn.: Greenwood Press, 1997).

CHAPTER TWO

———————— ■ ————————

The Latin American and Caribbean Regional Subsystem

Identifying the structures and processes of the Latin American and Caribbean subsystem and tracing its evolution links the real-world region with the concepts explored in the previous chapter. The first part of this chapter delineates the subsystem in light of criteria applicable to any international regional subsystem. It posits a structure comprising the overall regional subsystem and its subsystems and the region's position in extraregional patterns in the Western Hemisphere and the rest of the world. With these factors in mind, the chapter then traces the subsystem's changing contours from its beginning to the present, which not only reinforces a sense of the regional international structure but also gives a sense of the subsystem's dynamism.

IDENTIFYING REGIONAL SUBSYSTEMS

Criteria

Scholars have proposed differing definitions of regional subsystems, and their work on related issues is marked by conceptual disparity. An early survey of the literature on regional subsystems by William Thompson remains especially helpful in establishing the criteria that should be applied in determining the validity of geographic regions as international subsystems.[1] Thompson concluded that three criteria were necessary and sufficient: (1) that the regional actors be in geographic proximity; (2) that there be both internal and external recognition of the region as a distinctive area; and (3) that the interaction among the actors and their patterns of relations exhibit a degree of regularity and intensity. A regional subsystem, then, consists of a set of geographically proximate and regularly interacting states that share to some degree a sense of regional identity and are so perceived by external actors. These same criteria also identify further subsystems within the region.

In studying a particular regional subsystem, one must first identify the boundary that delimits the region and sets it apart from other components of the larger international system. This condition is implied by the term "region," and it includes the identification of the differentiated units. In an autonomous system, the boundary is defined as that limit containing all of the components and outside of which none of their interaction takes place. The term "subsystem" is applied to regional elements since, clearly, actors outside of a regional subsystem are significant because transboundary interaction takes place. Nevertheless, the boundary must set off the components of one subsystem from those of others, even if these distinctions may be less clearly defined than in an independent system.

The establishment of a typology of subsystem-relevant actors further helps us to identify regional boundaries. The units include the regional states within the boundary, the external states that have regularized interaction with the regional actors, and several kinds of intraregional and external transnational entities.

Geographic proximity within a physical boundary is a necessary characteristic of a regional subsystem, but it alone does not define the subsystem. Students of regional studies must guard against geographic determinism and beware of unwarranted assumptions about the character of relations within a given territory. The result may be a contrived region based merely on geographic convenience; if the proposed subsystem units have nothing more than their proximity in common, then the proposition is invalid. Therefore, after establishing the geographic limits of a region, the analyst must search for additional indications of subsystem qualities.

The second aspect of analysis is the extent of regional self-perception and the views of the external actors about the region. Shared attributes among subsystem actors may help to delineate the region if they contribute to a regional self-consciousness. In systemic terms, however, common sociocultural, economic, and political traits, even if revealing indicators, are not definitional requirements. Proximate and interacting states may be rich or poor, culturally complex or simple, or politically and socially advanced or not (however defined) without violating the subsystem concept. The key consideration in international subsystem analysis is the degree of mutual identity, for whatever reason, among the actors.

In this regard, several questions might be asked: Do subsystem actors exhibit cultural, social, political, or economic homogeneity or cohesion and, if so, has it furthered their mutual identification in international relations? Do they share common problems or interests in their foreign policies that have led to some sort of unity? What degree of interdependence, as well as mutual dependence on external actors, exists in the political, economic, military, social, and cultural arenas? Does the power, influence, or actions of external actors contribute to regional consciousness? Do intraregional perceptions distinguish the region from other parts of the world and in what ways? Do intraregional organizational linkages (such as security arrangements, intergovernmental organizations, and economic integration), regularized interactions (such as diplomatic activities, commercial trade, military support, and human migration), or identifiable power stratifications among the regional actors play roles in promoting regional self-consciousness?

The region, finally, is also defined by the regularity of relationships among the units, including the patterns and intensity of the various forms of interaction engaged in by the regional and external state and nonstate actors as well as the subsystem-related regulatory institutions and processes. This condition is implied by the concept of "subsystem" and is closely related to the notion of systemic integration. What are the patterns and effects of such international contacts as diplomatic exchanges, trade and investment, economic aid, various kinds of military relations, communications, and cultural relations? Does an identifiable power configuration emerge among the regional actors or in regard to the region as part of the global structure? What is the degree of their economic and social-cultural interdependence? What is the role of conflict, both within the region and with outside actors, in structuring the subsystem? What formal associations give further structure to regional relations?

The Problem of Latin America and the Caribbean

How valid is the view of Latin America and the Caribbean as a regional subsystem? Do the thirty-three independent states in the region—defined as inclusive of that territory in the Western Hemisphere south of the United States—form a coherent entity for study? This question is the system theorist's version of the Latin Americanist's age-old query: To what extent can the area be regarded as a significant unit in the conduct of international affairs? In other words, do the independent states in the region form a coherent entity for study, or is Latin America only a convenient geographic description? These questions raise the problem of the appropriate "levels of analysis" in the general study of IR as applied to the Latin American-Caribbean context.

Many specialists on Latin America are skeptical of region-wide conceptualizations, saying that the great differences and heterogeneity among the states within the region and their tremendous diversity in numerous aspects are so profound that generalizations are virtually impossible. Some even argue that Latin America no longer exists as a region susceptible to precise analysis.[2] Many of them prefer to concentrate on the individual countries and subregions within Latin America. Others emphasize a larger regional level, an inter-American system of informal interaction and formal organization among all of the states in the Western Hemisphere. In particular, they see regularized inter-American cooperation as required for the resolution of the salient international issues and problems. Others, for different reasons, see the region, or parts of it, as an element in special extraregional associations, such as Third World, Pan-Hispanic or Pan-Iberian, and Pacific Rim communities, among other possibilities. They make no claims for exclusivity, however.

The globalist-regionalist debate, referred to at the end of the previous chapter, continues. Globalists say that the most important interstate and transnational structures and the most critical issues are worldwide in scope; consequently, analytic efforts should concentrate on this highest level, with a view to resolving current issues within global regimes. Considerable evidence suggests the simultaneous regionalization and globalization of the international relations of Latin America and the Caribbean. The international system is not a coherent whole, nor is globalization a seamless web. Even as the international system has become more interdependent globally, it is concurrently defined more sharply by regions and subregions. In fact, the Latin American and Caribbean region and subregions have in recent years actually increased their cohesion.

In my view, an accurate picture of the international relations of Latin America and the Caribbean requires that we recognize and link individual state, subregional, regional, hemispheric, global, and other extrahemispheric levels of interaction. This demanding analytic task is required if we do not accept the idea that one or even a few levels of analysis offer the key to understanding, at the exclusion or slighting of the others. In addition, the nature of the issues compel action on the part of interested parties in all arenas. In any event, the regional subsystem is the principal focus, as it is both divided into its own subsystems and placed in the context of the global system. These possibilities may complicate the structure of the Latin American and Caribbean subsystem (as well as the global system), but they do not refute the central regional concept as a point of departure. Latin America and the Caribbean may be set apart as both a conceptually defensible and an analytically important region.

THE LATIN AMERICAN AND CARIBBEAN REGION

Although much truth is evident in the argument that the Latin American and Caribbean region is so internally different and the world so interdependent that it cannot be treated as a whole, it is exaggerated and misleading. This level of analysis and interaction does have considerable limitations, but in terms of the systemic criteria delineated above, the Latin American region for many years has constituted a significant unit as such in the international system.[3] Even as the international system has become more interdependent, it has been defined more sharply by its regions. Latin America and the Caribbean is a prime example; in some respects its coherence has actually increased in the post–cold war world.

Geographic Demarcation and the Regional States

Identification of the regional line of demarcation begins with the notion of a geographic boundary delimiting the region and enclosing a set of physically proximate states. In spatial terms, the region of Latin America and the Caribbean measures some 7,000 miles from northern Mexico to Cape Horn at the far southern reaches of Chile and Argentina. It comprises an area roughly two and a half times larger than the United States and is populated by about 491 million people (as of mid-1998). The region is mostly occupied by thirty-three sovereign states, with the small remainder consisting of British, Dutch, French, and U.S. dependencies. The northern part of the region—Mexico and the Caribbean area—is mostly south of the United States. Almost all of South America, however, lies east as well as south of North

MAP 2.1   *Latin America and the Caribbean*

America; the Natal region (the "Brazilian Bulge") is only 1,900 miles from the closest point on the African continent. The South American continent itself measures 4,600 miles in length and about 3,000 miles at its widest point, and it contains about 85 percent of all of Latin America's territory.

The regional states located within the subsystem boundary form the central focus of the subsystem's international relations. These states may be subdivided into groupings that reflect their colonial beginnings: *Ibero-America* refers to the nineteen nation-states of Spanish and Portuguese origin, all of them the "old" or "traditional" states in the context of Latin American studies. Eighteen of them form *Spanish*

America, with widely varying stages of development and international capabilities. They are, in alphabetical order, Argentina, Bolivia, Chile, Colombia, Costa Rica, Cuba, Dominican Republic, Ecuador, El Salvador, Guatemala, Honduras, Mexico, Nicaragua, Panama, Paraguay, Peru, Uruguay, and Venezuela. They occupy some 57 percent of the total Latin American land area. Most of them achieved their independence from Spain between 1810 and 1824; the Dominican Republic became independent of Spain in 1822 but was soon occupied by Haiti and did not regain its independence until 1844. Cuba overthrew Spanish authority as a result of the U.S. military defeat of Spain but was not technically sovereign until the end of U.S. military occupation in 1902. Panama, a province of Colombia, seceded in 1903 with U.S. assistance to become formally independent. *Portuguese America*, or *Luso America*, refers to Brazil, which was under the colonial rule of Portugal until becoming independent in 1822. This giant of Latin America, the largest regional state in both population and territory (larger than the continental United States), covers about 40 percent of the Latin American terrain. Tiny *Haiti* is the oldest regional state and is also a "traditional" one for Latin Americanists. Haiti broke away from France in 1804, the first Latin American state to gain independence, in a successful black slaves' revolt. It has maintained its West African culture to a remarkable degree to the present day. These twenty "old" Latin American states—eighteen Spanish American ones plus Brazil and Haiti—together account for some 97 percent of Latin America's territory and population.

The remainder of the regional actors are thirteen small "new" states, twelve of which are former British colonies that gained their independence between 1962 and 1984 and are part of the collectivity called the *Commonwealth Caribbean Countries* (which also includes certain remaining British dependencies, noted below). The independent states are Antigua and Barbuda, Bahamas, Barbados, Belize, Dominica, Grenada, Guyana, Jamaica, St. Kitts-Nevis, St. Lucia, St. Vincent, and Trinidad and Tobago. *Suriname*, a former colony of the Netherlands, became independent in 1975.

The external sector is made up of those states, intergovernmental organizations (IGOs), and transnational actors outside the boundary that have significant relations with the regional actors. They are identified in terms of regularized interaction with the region or parts of it, such as influencing the regional distribution of power; engaging in significant commercial relationships; participating in regional organizations, alliances, or alignments; being part of intrasocietal movements (such as immigrants and refugees); and engaging in internal war (insurgents) or criminal activities (drug traffickers). These elements (they are a few among many) are merely noted here and are further discussed below.

Political dependencies located within the regional boundary, numbering eleven administrative entities, represent the continuing territorial presence of controlling external states—the United Kingdom, France, the Netherlands, and the United States. Each of the eleven entities were originally acquired as part of the earlier imperial actions of one of these nations. Today the non-sovereign members of the Commonwealth Caribbean Countries have a constitutional status of "States in Association with

Great Britain," which are self-governing but dependent on the United Kingdom for external affairs. They are Anguilla, Bermuda, British Virgin Islands, Cayman Islands, Montserrat, and the Turks and Caicos Islands. The Falkland Islands, located in the far South Atlantic Ocean, constitute a British crown colony. France has converted its colonies to overseas departments; they are French Guiana, Guadeloupe, and Martinique. The Netherlands' former colonies, with coequal commonwealth status, are the Netherlands Antilles and Aruba. United States dependencies are Puerto Rico, a commonwealth, and the U.S. Virgin Islands, a federal territory.

Perceptions

The evidence supporting the existence of a regional awareness is varied. Fundamental differences, and even uniqueness, among the regional states are obvious in Latin America and the Caribbean. Diversity and exceptionality should not be overemphasized, however. Although few generalizations would apply to all of the Latin American states, a degree of commonality exists among them; and certain generally, if not universally, applicable patterns and shared experiences and traits emerge out of the diversity. (Chapter 4 discusses this complexity, noting elements of both commonality and multiformity.) More important are the significant ways in which mutual identification, regularized informal interactions, and formal organization are prevalent.

Regional self-consciousness is difficult to measure, but evidence suggests a "push-pull" force working in Latin American relations, an ambivalent situation of mutual repulsion and attraction. The most obvious expressions of ambivalence are found in the relations between Brazil and Spanish America. Great diversity exists among the eighteen Spanish American states, but they also exhibit a certain cultural similarity and mutual identity. At certain times within Spanish America, ambivalence has been reflected in the competition for leadership between Mexico and Argentina and sometimes between Colombia, Chile, Peru, and Venezuela. Mutual identity is further revealed by the sensitivity of political groups in one state to developments in others. During extended periods of time, military establishments have communicated with their regional counterparts, as have certain political parties; to a lesser extent labor unions and student groups have done so. In the intellectual sphere, it seems significant that regional debates have sometimes centered on competing Latin American solutions to the problems of development and change, with minimal reference to nonregional prescriptions.

External states have tended to increase subsystem cohesion in Latin America by their very presence. From the earliest days of statehood, Latin Americans have tended to band together when outsiders intervened or exerted other pressures. No Latin American state has been a great power in global politics, although a few have come close to breaking this mold at certain times. All have operated from a position of weakness relative to the world powers, with some special circumstantial exceptions.

Most of the Latin American states have tended to band together against threats, real and imagined, from the outside world. For example, from the time of the wars for independence from Spain until the mid-1860s, Spanish American unity, insofar as it existed, was based largely on fear of foreigners and a desire to ally against them. Plans for economic integration since World War II have been motivated not only by hopes for mutual economic benefit but also by the possibility of escaping from economic dependence on external industrialized states. Furthermore, Latin Americans have tended to side with each other when outsiders have exerted pressure in the region, even when individual state interests have not been involved. For example, U.S. intervention in the Caribbean during the first third of the twentieth century evoked strong protests even from the remote Rio de la Plata region, which was largely unaffected by U.S. actions. By the mid-1970s, the Panama Canal issue was no longer simply a confrontation between Panama and the United States but had become a matter of concern for virtually all of Latin America, which supported Panamanian interests against the United States. In the 1980s conflict in Central America led to organization of the Contadora Group by Mexico, Colombia, Venezuela, and Panama, which was subsequently endorsed by a Support Group of South American states not directly affected by the Central American crisis. Another example of regional unity was the majority decision among Latin American states to express support for Argentina in its 1982 war with the United Kingdom over the Falkland/Malvinas Islands, despite their own unhappiness with Argentine aggression. The U.S. invasions of Grenada in 1983 and Panama in 1990 provoked a similar, if less intense, mutual condemnation. We must acknowledge that Latin Americans have often had difficulty in presenting a sustained unified front with enough consistency to be effective, but this does not change the fact of mutual identification.

A number of external actors have viewed the Latin American region as a distinct area. Thus external perceptions of the region as an international unity have been reflected in the "Latin American policies" of various states and in their foreign policy-making apparatus (Latin American bureaus of one kind or another), including, consistently, the United States, at times the former Soviet Union, and more recently the European states, Canada, and others. This external perception has been true of intergovernmental organizations and transnational actors as well. For example, the Holy See, the United Nations, the European Union, international political parties and labor groups, and some multinational corporations and nongovernmental organizations have formulated regional Latin American policies and administrative structures.

Regularity of Interaction

Latin Americans have formally organized among themselves, which indicates forms of regularized interaction and further strengthens the notion of regional self-awareness. A few examples since World War II illustrate the point. The eleven-member Latin American Free Trade Association (LAFTA), established in 1961 and reorganized in 1980 as the Latin American Integration Association, includes all of the large regional economies, so that it represents an important cross-regional if not a total regional association. In 1975 the Latin American Economic System was created and has near-universal regional membership. In order to caucus on a regional basis before confronting the outside world, Latin American groups have been organized within or with reference to other international organizations, such as the United Nations, Third World associations, and the European Union. The Latin American Parliament, created in 1965, has been resuscitated in the 1990s. In 1964 most Latin American states joined the Special Latin American Coordinating Committee as an informal regional caucusing group, which in 1972 was replaced by the formally constituted Latin American Economic System. Organized in 1986, the eight-member Rio Group expanded to include almost all of the Latin American and Caribbean states and became the preeminent Latin American organizational voice on the new agenda of issues. These organizations have taken on new significance in the post–cold war era and have given renewed impetus to interregional cooperation as well as to some coordinated involvement with the outside world.

THE REGIONAL SUBSYSTEMS

Viewing Latin America in terms of a single unit is appropriate but incomplete. We also need to highlight those subsystems with different conditions. Several subsystems are possible, involving both subregions and the bilateral relations of individual Latin American states. The most relevant ones are Mexico, the circum-Caribbean, South America, and Brazil (also a key South American actor). Also significant are further subordinate levels, such as Central America and the Caribbean Commonwealth within the circum-Caribbean, and, in South America, the overlapping Southern Cone, Platine, Andean, and Amazonic areas.

Mexico

Mexico stands apart in Latin America because it is a large and important state that borders a superpower.[4] It has a special structure of intense bilateral relations with the United States, as well as inter-American and other international connections. Mexico is part of a North American continental subsystem shared with Canada and the United States—a great area, most of which is outside of Latin America. Consequently, much of the Mexican international subsystem has been and is largely divorced from the broader inter-American arena, although the latter has also been important. Mexico has at times been of significant interest to one or another of the world's great powers, sometimes intensely in the nineteenth century and mostly episodically in the twentieth. But the United States has long been the principal foreign presence in Mexico (the foreign menace, in the eyes of many Mexicans). Because of territorial proximity, periods of protracted violence and other forms of strife and conflict, increasingly integrated economic and social structures, and close association with the domestic concerns in each country, many of the issues have been bilateral, Mexican-U.S. ones.

Yet the evolution of the Mexican subsystem, beginning in the late nineteenth century but sharply accelerated during World War II and continuing thereafter, has resulted in a basic reality: The special and complicated Mexican-United States bilateral association is one of strong mutual dependency. Although the United States has clearly been the stronger partner, Mexico has had considerable say. This view of the relationship has been sharply challenged by those who have emphasized Mexico's relative weakness in most respects and have said that the United States could dictate the relationship. But developments in the 1980s and 1990s have confirmed that the connection is symbiotic and unavoidably linked and that the United States cannot coerce Mexico without damaging itself. The trilateral North American Free Trade Agreement (in effect in 1994) is a dramatic indication of Mexican-U.S. interdependence; with Canada a party, it also furthers the coherence of a nascent North American subsystem.

The Circum-Caribbean

The circum-Caribbean is a complex geographic, political, social, and cultural region.[5] Its boundary as an international subsystem has been perceived by both local and external states to include the islands of the Caribbean Sea and those nearby in the Atlantic Ocean, the entire Central American isthmus and Yucatan peninsula, and the north coast of South America extending into the Atlantic Ocean. Thus, Colombia, Venezuela, Guyana, and Suriname are considered Caribbean states. U.S. policy makers have preferred the idea of a "Caribbean Basin" that conforms to the above definition. That notion is often viewed by Europeans as a self-serving U.S. invention, although in the nineteenth century Britain seemed to have held the same idea, as do Venezuela and Mexico today. Within the boundary, in addition to the regional states, are all but one of the remaining American dependencies of the United Kingdom (the exception is the Falkland Islands in the South Atlantic) and all of those of France, the Netherlands, and the United States.

Caribbean states have been relatively small and weak, with the exceptions of Colombia and (more recently) Venezuela. Consequently, the region has continuously been the object of rivalry, pressure, intervention, and domination by greater powers. Nothing is new about great-power conflict in the area. International relations have not changed for centuries; only the actors have shifted. In the nineteenth century, Britain was preeminent, although challenged by France and the United States. Their interest in a transisthmian canal was a major issue.

The U.S. presence in the circum-Caribbean has been one of the clearest cases of hegemony in the international system. The United States has been the international policeman in the area, more assertive and consequential there than in South America beyond the Caribbean. In Latin America the United States has engaged in unilateral military intervention only in Mexico and the circum-Caribbean; the last intervention in Mexico was in 1914, but it intruded with arms as late as 1989–1990 in Panama; and in 1994 it led a United Nations-sanctioned force in the military occupation of Haiti. Most of the Caribbean area is part of a U.S. bilateral trading system.

U.S. hegemony, however, has not been total, constant, or simple and has been subject to numerous challenges. The territorial holdings of Britain, France, and the

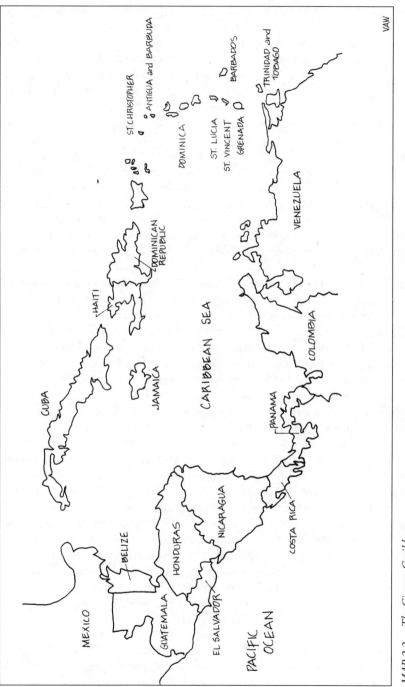

MAP 2.2   The Circum-Caribbean

Netherlands have constituted a constant, although generally non-threatening, diversion from U.S. primacy. The principal external challenge arose when Cuba became the Soviet Union's first high-priority Latin American interest with their alignment after 1959; later, after 1979, the Soviets supported the Sandinistas in Nicaragua and by extension the insurgents in El Salvador. In the 1980s a number of local Latin American and nonhemispheric states and organizations disagreed with U.S. unilateral and military policies in the Central America conflict and pressed for changes. Furthermore, U.S. actions in the Caribbean over the years have often engendered strong domestic opposition in the United States. On balance, however, U.S. power and influence have been and continue to be the primary factors in Caribbean international relations.

The circum-Caribbean may be further subdivided. Central America, the isthmian area between Mexico and South America, has displayed systemic characteristics. From their independence to the present, the traditional five Central American states (Costa Rica, El Salvador, Guatemala, Honduras, and Nicaragua) have intermittently banded together among themselves in political and economic unions. Central American conflict has provided a parallel subsystemic structural element. The Central American crisis of civil war and international conflict in the 1980s is the most recent dramatic example. The resolution of the conflict in terms of a peace plan initiated by the Central American's themselves strengthened the cooperative structures.

Until recently, the five traditional Central American states did not consider Panama or Belize as "Central American." They continued to view Panama, a former province of Colombia that gained independence in 1903, as the beginning of South America and as not sharing their local interests. They saw Belize as absorbed with Commonwealth Caribbean affairs after it became independent in 1981. In the 1980s, Panama and Belize were increasingly involved in Central American affairs, and in the mid-1990s the other states accepted them as formal members of subregional organization.

The Commonwealth Caribbean Countries also make up a further subsystem. Ten of them are island states in the eastern Caribbean; one of them (Guyana) is nearby on the South American continent, and another (Belize) is on the Central American isthmus. Guyana, by virtue of its location, is also a part of the loosely structured South American subsystem (see below); and, as indicated, Belize has also become identified with the Central American subsystem. Several of the Commonwealth Caribbean states failed to unite in a proposed single independent state in 1962. But shortly thereafter they began their continuing economic integration as they individually emerged as independent states, with the effort culminating in the formal Commonwealth Caribbean Community integration organization. Certain of them also felt they had special interests and created another level of subsystem within that Community—the Organization of the Eastern Caribbean States.

South America

The entire South American continent below Central America arguably forms an international subsystem.[6] South America beyond the Caribbean, however, is a more coherent entity. This majority part of the continent is largely (but not entirely) synonymous with what is called the Southern Cone of South America. The states in Southern Cone international relations are Argentina, Bolivia, Brazil, Chile, Paraguay, Peru, and Uruguay. Excluded are the northern tier states of Colombia, Venezuela, Guyana, and Suriname (as well as Ecuador, a non-Caribbean state). Their concerns overlap those of the South American subsystem, especially territorial and border questions, but the thrust of their attention is more often oriented toward the circum-Caribbean.

The Southern Cone thus defined forms a regional subsystem distinguished by a number of characteristics that make it dramatically different from the northern sector of Latin America. A principal characteristic has been the region's relative isolation from the mainstream of international politics, largely a function of its strikingly unique geographic situation. In addition, the leading Southern Cone states are relatively institutionalized. Their remote global location a long distance from Europe and the United States, combined with the relative strength of the key local states, has helped them resist outside pressures and domination. The region has not been part of a global balance-of-power system in which a great power has played the role of an international policeman enforcing the peace and thus has enjoyed relative foreign policy autonomy.

Southern Cone states have a broad array of external relationships that add to their ability to balance outside influences. The subregion is a multilateralized trading area. Unlike Mexico and the Spanish Caribbean, the Southern Cone states have longstanding economic (as well as cultural) ties with Europe. Japan is also an important economic partner. Brazil, especially, has diversified its economy and developed a broad set of bilateral relationships. The United States, by and large, has been one of several competitors in South America, never approaching a position of dominance as in the circum-Caribbean or of primary importance as in Mexico. Thus, as a general matter, the United States in its Latin American relationships has had the least interest and influence in the Southern Cone, with the exception of Brazil, and its influence with Brazil declined dramatically after the mid-1960s.

Relative isolation from global power politics has allowed the major Southern Cone states to establish independent patterns of interaction involving their own subregional issues. The issues have involved local rivalry for leadership as well as state searches for security, power, well-being, prestige, and resources, depending on the relative capabilities of the states involved. They have had intense patterns of interactions among themselves, largely shaped by regional factors with minimal reference to outside states or intergovernmental organizations.

The subregion has been an area of local conflict, with roots in the colonial period. The legacy includes a long list of territorial and boundary disputes, national power struggles that have led to warfare and threats of war, and competition for prestige, regional leadership, and resources. Subregional international relations have brought strategic-geopolitical components to the foreign policies of the major Southern Cone states, which further distinguishes the subregion from the more northerly sector where this phenomenon is not found. The Southern Cone states have developed such calculations primarily in regard to their own subregion, extended to include the South Atlantic and the Antarctic. Since the late 1970s, the subregion's traditional international rivalries have been muted, generally paralleling domestic democratic trends.

This development is reflected in the intra-Southern Cone state integration organization, the Common Market of the South (MERCOSUR), which began forming in 1990. In 1998 MERCOSUR consisted of Argentina, Brazil, Paraguay, and Uruguay, with Bolivia and Chile as associate members; other South American countries beyond the Southern Cone will probably join. The Platine countries of Brazil, Argentina, Uruguay, Paraguay, and Bolivia have a mutual self-identification, reflected, among other ways, in their organization of the Cuenca del Plata accord in 1969 for regional infrastructure development. The Amazonic countries—Brazil, Suriname, Guyana, Venezuela, Colombia, Ecuador, Peru, and Bolivia—have considered themselves an international unit, in as much as in 1978 they signed the Amazon Pact for the controlled development of the Amazon Basin. The Andean countries—Venezuela, Colombia, Ecuador, Peru, Bolivia, and Chile—formed the Andean Group within the Latin American Free Trade Association in 1966 to foster their own integration; it has continued to the present.

Brazil

Brazil is the largest and strongest state in the region of Latin America and the Caribbean. In several respects its bilateral relationships, like those of Mexico but for different reasons, should be viewed as a discrete subsystem. Brazil has long stood apart from the rest of Latin America because of its Portuguese cultural heritage, large size (territory, population, and economy), and (sometime) ambition and potential to be an influential state in global politics. Brazil was long the "sleeping giant" of Latin America, first under British tutelage and then as the junior partner in a cooperative alignment with the United States. But in the 1960s Brazil began to increase its self-confidence toward the United States and its overall ability to pursue an independent foreign policy without an assumption of mutual interests. More than any of the other regional states, Brazil diversified its economy and developed a multilateral network of international trade and strong ties with its immediate neighbors, with Europe, the Middle East and Africa, and with Japan, in addition to those with the United States.

THE EXTRAREGIONAL WORLD

The Inter-American System

The term "inter-American system" is used in two ways. On the more general level it means all structures and processes of inter-American relations within the boundaries of the Western Hemisphere, identifying all of the Americas as another regional subsystem—in which Latin America and the Caribbean are joined by Canada and the

United States—within the global system. Included within this broad configuration is a group of formal western hemispheric inter-governmental organizations also bearing the collective name "Inter-American System" (indicated by the use of capital letters). Latin American states, along with the newer Caribbean states since the early 1960s, have been majority participants in the informal and formal elements of the inter-American system. The United States has been the key hemispheric actor as well as, in the twentieth century, a global great power or superpower. Canada, long a marginal presence in hemispheric affairs, began in the 1960s to take a strong interest in Latin America and significantly increased its activities from the mid-1980s. The informal inter-American relationships have been alluded to above and will be further detailed below; the matter of the formal system requires some further clarification.

The Inter-American System originated in 1889 and has evolved to the present day; it refers to multipurpose, hemisphere-wide organizations among the American states. The designation denotes not a centralized institution overseeing subordinate organizations but an "umbrella" concept covering an uneven yet uninterrupted history and current network of institutional principles, policies, procedures, and organizations. Today the system largely consists of the separate but coordinated Organization of American States (OAS) and the Inter-American Development Bank (IDB). Other post–World War II elements have included a scattered system for the peaceful settlement of disputes and the Inter-American Treaty of Reciprocal Assistance (Rio Treaty) regime, both of which are presently moribund. In 1991 the OAS achieved universal membership of all thirty-five sovereign states in the Americas—the thirty-three Latin American and Caribbean states, the United States, and Canada. (Cuba has been a "non-participating" member since 1962.) The OAS has also conferred observer status on forty extrahemispheric states and the United Nations. The IDB, founded in 1960, has evolved a membership of forty-nine states, including twenty-one from outside the hemisphere. The Inter-American System's activities have evolved to promote purposes along a broad front: economic, social, and cultural cooperation; conflict resolution; nonintervention and sovereign equality; codification of international law; mutual security; representative democracy and human rights; and measures against drug traffic and environmental degradation.

Global and Extrahemispheric Levels

The Latin American and Caribbean regional actors have been part of the global system beyond the inter-American system, both as objects of the actions of outsiders and as active participants in their own right. They have also been involved with certain extrahemispheric subsystems.

Historically the European states were among the most important actors of the external sector, with Britain the single most important actor in the nineteenth century. The European states engaged variously in cooperative and conflictual relations with the Latin American states. A number of them reasserted their Latin American interests, especially from the early 1970s; today, operating in concert through the European Union as well as individually, European states have taken on a new significance. The Soviet Union expanded its sometimes subversive, sometimes diplomatic activities after 1959, beginning with its alignment with Cuba. Since the dissolution of the Soviet Union, Russia and the other successor states have been minor or nonexistent presences. Japan became a continuing economic force, also dating from the 1960s. An array of other external states have special bilateral or other particular relationships.

Latin American states have sought to join the international system as juridically equal participants. Only Brazil participated in the First Peace Conference at The Hague in 1899, but in 1907 twenty of the twenty-two Latin American states sent delegates to the Second Peace Conference and thus joined The Hague System. During the life of the League of Nations (1920–1945), all Latin American states participated at some time or another, although all of them were never members at the same time. Latin Americans were instrumental in shaping the United Nations, beginning in the late-World-War-II planning stages; they remained active participants in the UN, and the UN was active in the region, as it is today. All Latin American and Caribbean states are members of the United Nations.

Over the years other extraregional international subsystems have involved different combinations of Latin American and Caribbean states. A few non-inclusive examples may begin with their identification with the Third World. Beginning in 1961, sixteen states from the region eventually joined the Nonaligned Movement. They took leadership roles in the New International Economic Order, a formal Third World association that almost all of the regional states joined. Formally organized in 1974, after some thirteen years of evolution, it was pursued especially in the serial United Nations Conference on Trade and Development and in the General Assembly. Latin American and Caribbean interest declined in these Third World associations with the end of the cold war.

As former British colonies, the twelve English-speaking states in the circum-Caribbean are members of the Commonwealth, where they make up almost a quarter of the membership of fifty-three states. Spain has taken the lead during the twentieth century in fostering Pan-Hispanic connections and sometimes Pan-Iberian ones to include Portugal and Brazil; their purposes have varied under the different sponsoring Spanish governments. Some analysts and governments posit numerous Latin American states as part of an emerging Pacific Basin or Pacific Rim subsystem; a huge and somewhat amorphous undertaking, it is perceived predominately as economic in nature. For two South American states, territorial interests also extend to the Pacific Ocean; Chile has sovereignty over the Easter Islands and Ecuador over the Galapagos Islands.

TRANSNATIONAL PHENOMENA

Non-nation-state actors and unofficial activities, mixed with, paralleling, or competing with interstate relationships, have always been part of what evolved into the Latin American and Caribbean subsystem. The consequences of transnational phenomena expanded greatly after World War II, with another wave of enlargement after the end of the cold war. But not until the 1970s did the idea of transnationalization appear as an analytic concept, and since the end of the cold war it has been increasingly advanced, in concert with the notion of globalization, as fundamental for understanding Latin American and Caribbean international relations. In the regional context globalization may be seen as an uneven process of the outward expansion of transnational phenomena at all systemic layers of interaction (individual society, regional, subregional, and extraregional); that is, each of these varied levels responds to global economic, political, social, and cultural change. In this conceptualization, the simultaneous globalization and regionalization of transnational relations is part of the same irregular process that moves unevenly from one level to another.

With regard to the region and transnational phenomena, a few examples may be cited for illustrative purposes. The oldest continuing transnational actor is the Holy See (itself a sovereign state) and the Roman Catholic Church global organizational structure. Migration was critical to the peopling of the Americas, beginning in the modern era with European conquest and colonization (following the prehistorical migrations); today's movement of people as immigrants and refugees dates especially from the latter nineteenth century. Pirates, privateers, and buccaneers were significant in the colonial era, as were autonomous European trading companies. International business enterprise entered the scene with Latin American independence, and multinational corporations have played increasingly important roles, especially since World War II. Guerrilla insurgents date from the movements of independence and were found from time to time thereafter; since the late 1950s they have been a regular phenomenon of varying intensity. The illicit drug traffic, beginning in the late nineteenth century, has also had an irregular history; it became a problem of intense policy interest in the early 1980s. International labor movements and political party organizations have been active throughout much of the twentieth century and are prominent today; they have varied in their impact. The number of international nongovernmental organizations has grown rapidly in recent decades; they diverge tremendously in the activities pursued, the resources at their disposal, and in their levels of influence.

SUBSYSTEM CHANGE

After Latin American independence and through the mid-twentieth century, subsystem transformation depended not so much on intraregional events as on external influences in the region and on individual regional actors. The primary factors in subsystem alterations were primarily related to interstate power relationships, although elements of interdependence were also in play. After World War II, the transnational phenomena, always present as part of the Latin American international scene, increasingly became integral subsystemic characteristics and joined the interstate elements as important measures of subsystem change. Furthermore, after the mid-1960s, internal state and societal considerations became increasingly important. We may identify different eras in the development of Latin America's international relations by referring to some combination of the distribution of state power and influence, levels of economic and social interdependence, and internal domestic developments.

The Latin American subsystem and its subregional components have gone through distinct stages, with transitional periods signaling the end of one era and the initiation of another. The various subregions did not develop in exact parallel, however, so that most dates assigned in the following discussion should be considered approximate.

From Colonies to States

The Latin American subsystem evolved out of the colonial period, from the late fifteenth to the early nineteenth centuries, when colonialism bound the entire region to European powers. The vast portion of the region was part of the Spanish and Portuguese crowns, although France, Britain, and the Netherlands challenged their regional primacy. Up to the end of the three-century colonial period the Spanish and Portuguese empires were largely intact, with the relatively minor exceptions of the British, French, Dutch, and Danish West Indies.

Latin American independence, like that of the United States earlier, began largely as a sidelight of European international politics. The Napoleonic Wars, with France occupying Spain and Portugal, facilitated the Spanish American and Brazilian revolutions (French armies had invaded the Iberian peninsula in 1807–1808). By the time Spanish King Ferdinand VII returned to the throne in Madrid in 1814, most of Spanish America was in revolt against him. By 1824 the once vast Spanish American Empire was reduced to Cuba and Puerto Rico. In 1822, a year after the Portuguese royal Bragança family returned from Brazil to Lisbon, Brazilians declared their independence. In contrast to the long and bitter struggle between Spain and its colonies, Portugal relinquished control with little opposition. Brazilians called upon the willing Portuguese prince (the heir to the throne), who had remained in Brazil as regent, to make the declaration of independence and rule as monarch of the new state.

European Dominance

The nineteenth century after the mid-1820s roughly marks the first era of the independent Latin American subsystem. The severance of the colonial ties that had bound the region to overseas powers for more than three centuries, and that had almost entirely isolated it from the rest of the world outside Spain and Portugal, submitted the new Latin American states to the power vagaries of the international system. In addition, the independence of the vast Latin American territory affected the international system by changing the distribution of power among European states and by stimulating rivalry among them to gain regional influence or control. Throughout the nineteenth century, the Latin American states played passive roles in global politics, where they were subordinate to the outside world.

The major external actors were European and had a preponderance of economic, military, and technological capabilities as well as long experience in statecraft. The United States played an important role in areas contiguous to it, but it was otherwise weak in relation to the European states. The United Kingdom was the dominant external actor and held the primary position in most of the region into the first years of the twentieth century. Britain's naval and merchant fleets dominated the Atlantic and discouraged other power excursions into the area until the turn of the century. It is true that Mexico lost half its territory to the United States between 1836 and 1848, that Mexico and the Dominican Republic were occupied by France and Spain, respectively, in the 1860s, and that other armed interventions were initiated in the area by France, Spain, the United States, Britain itself, and, later, Germany and Italy. Nevertheless, Britain shielded the Western Hemisphere from many other European designs, especially those of France and Spain, by largely controlling ocean communications between Europe and America. In 1881 a private French company began construction of the Panama Canal but abandoned the bankrupt project eight years later. Germany and Italy entered the scene with their respective national-state unifications in the 1870s. Germany became highly competitive, especially in commercial and military affairs.

European imperialism during the nineteenth century took on special characteristics in Latin America. The Latin American states had a low capability level in relation to the outside world, making them subject to pressures from the more dynamic European powers. From the Latin American point of view, the external powers were not effectively restrained by the global balance-of-power system. Nevertheless, certain aspects of that system helped protect the Latin American states. Europeans were not uninhibited and conceivably might have been even more unheeding of Latin American sovereignty. The era of "new imperialism" in the latter half of the nineteenth century and up to World War I—which involved highly competitive European great-power activities in the Middle East, Africa, and Asia—also marked the height of European interest in Latin America. The region figured in no significant way in the worldwide imperialism-colonialism thrust, however, and the Latin American states managed to maintain a measure of independence in comparison with much of the rest of the non-North Atlantic world. This situation was a curious one on the surface, considering that imperialism was then viewed as a normal product of international competition, that it was characterized by the development of the alliance system in Europe and by the division of colonial spoils, and that its causation is generally ascribed to economic motives.

At the beginning of the nineteenth century, the United States was a relatively weak external actor. It steadily rose in power during that century, expanding its territory almost three times over from 1802 to 1852 and, after the end of its Civil War in 1865, developing its industrial and military capabilities and increasing its population at rapid rates. The United States finally emerged as a great power at the turn of the century. In general, it was not a major factor in the nineteenth century balance of power beyond North America, although some European leaders, particularly in Britain, recognized its power potential.

Despite the warning to Europe by President James Monroe in 1823 to keep "hands off" the Americas, the United States did not dominate affairs in the Western Hemisphere. This statement of the U.S. position was issued in the shadow of the British navy, for at that time the United States lacked the military power necessary to keep continental European forces out of the Americas, although it knew that Britain could and would do so. Monroe's statement remained virtually forgotten in the United States for many years; only later was it elevated to the status of "doctrine." Thus, Britain realized Monroe's purposes in the sense that it assured to some degree Latin American independence from the imperial designs of continental Europeans.

Until the mid-1890s, the United States displayed little interest in Latin American affairs beyond its own continental expansion, the possibility of an interoceanic canal in Central America, and the unrealized proposals to annex Cuba, the Dominican Republic, and the Danish West Indies. The major exceptions to U.S. weakness in Latin America were its relations with its immediate neighbor, Mexico, and with Britain in Central America. The United States acquired about half of Mexico's national territory as the result of the annexation of Texas and the later war settlement in 1848. Britain was the chief U.S. rival in Central America, where the construction of a transisthmian canal was of continuing concern to both states and brought them into serious conflict. The two states signed the Clayton-Bulwer Treaty in 1850, which softened their intense rivalry by providing that neither would construct or exclusively control a canal or "exercise domain" over any part of Central America.

Distinctive subregional structures and self-consciousness in Latin America were not as clear in the post-independence period as they would later become. Nevertheless, the various subregional subsystems had begun to emerge, with some of their elements shaped during the colonial period. For example, Spanish control of the Caribbean, in contrast to its firm hold on other parts of the Spanish American Empire, had been eroded by other European challengers who acquired territories there, and Brazil's separate identity was evident throughout most of the colonial period. Intra-Latin American distinctions became clearer as the century progressed. Important South American conflicts—between Argentina and Brazil on the Atlantic side and, on the Pacific coast, between Chile and the alliance of Peru and Bolivia—that developed in the early independence period became continuing elements of the Southern Cone subsystem.

The Mexican identity was shaped by the aggressive policies of outsiders. Severe blows came with territorial losses to the United States as a result of Texas independence in 1836 and the disastrous war of 1845–1848. Later, from 1862–1865, France occupied Mexico and incorporated it into the French empire; Mexican patriots, led by Benito Juárez, managed to expel the foreign presence. The dictatorship of Porfirio Díaz (1876–1910) allowed the United States and certain European states (especially Britain and Belgium) to dominate its economy. After the Mexican Revolution of 1910 overthrew Díaz, Mexico adopted highly protectionist economic policies and an essentially isolationist political orientation toward the outside world, although the protracted violence and other forms of strife that had characterized

Mexican-U.S. relations for much of the nineteenth century extended into the first two decades of the twentieth.

The circum-Caribbean subsystem did not undergo major systemic change until the turn of the century, which saw the retirement of Britain and the emergence of the United States as the dominant power in the area. In contrast, during the 1860s the Southern Cone subsystem went through a transition period that solidified its identity and further set it off from northern Latin America. Southern Cone states developed more viable political systems. They strongly desired to modernize their nations in all respects and looked to foreigners for aid in doing so. Now secure from most threats of European intervention, they concentrated on internal problems and national development involving cooperative rather than conflictual relations with Europeans and the United States. The remoteness of these states played an important role in their development, as the external great powers concentrated on a new era of energetic imperialism in other parts of the world.

The Southern Cone balance-of-power system began with intense rivalry among Argentina, Brazil, and Chile (the "ABC" states), with Peru drawn in and "buffer" status for Uruguay, Paraguay, and Bolivia.[7] The system resembled but was not an imitation of contemporary European regional power politics and stood apart from global balances. Major developments in Southern Cone international relations during the nineteenth century included: Chile's Policy of the Pacific, aimed at domination of the west coast; Argentina's determination to be preeminent in the Rio de la Plata area and to restore the old viceregal boundaries (which had included Uruguay, Paraguay, and part of Bolivia) under its control; and Brazil's preoccupation with expanding and securing its own borders. Thus, Argentina contended with Chile for influence in Bolivia and Peru, and with Brazil over Paraguay and Uruguay. In intraregional politics, the century witnessed a series of major South American wars or threats of war as well as other forms of power struggle.

The subregional power structure in the latter nineteenth century was especially coherent, after it began to change in the 1860s. Argentina developed rapidly after its unification as a state in 1861. Brazil extended its territory greatly, actually beginning in 1851 and continuing into the 1900s, by gaining territory from all eight of its neighboring states except for Peru. Brazil, however, was unable to match Argentina's spectacular economic growth. The Argentine-Brazilian competition was inconclusive for the remainder of the century.

A period of "condominium hegemony" extended from 1883 until 1924. Chile began to act in broader terms; it sought to preserve its power position by currying favor with Ecuador and Colombia against Peru and with Brazil and Paraguay against Argentina—out of fear that Argentina might cooperate with Bolivia and Peru to challenge its Policy of the Pacific. Chile and Argentina, after narrowly averting war in the 1890s, reached an accord in the Pactos de Mayo (1902). They explicitly recognized each other's sphere of influence, agreed to naval parity, and formalized the balance of power system between them. This agreement temporarily left Chile secure in the west, but the Atlantic rivalry between Argentina and Brazil continued. Largely confined to the Rio de la Plata region in the nineteenth century, the rivalry expanded in the twentieth century when both parties adopted policies asserting leadership of South America. The ABC concept effectively ended in the mid-1920s. Chile clearly was left behind, in terms of power, by both Argentina and Brazil, although Chile continued to maintain its power position as best it could. The Argentine-Brazilian competition remained indecisive for about four more decades.

The Rise of the United States and the Decline of Europe

The second era of subsystem development dates roughly from the 1890s until the middle of World War II. Latin American international relations had entered a four decade period characterized by rising U.S. power and declining European influence. The United States and the United Kingdom were the most significant external actors, but the former expanded its power whereas the latter declined in influence. The United States emerged as a great power, signaled by its military victory over Spain in 1898. Yet the Latin American states became active for the first time in global affairs, with their participation in the Second Peace Conference at The Hague, and then in the League of Nations. They also joined the formal Inter-American System, which had been established at U.S. initiative with the First International Conference of American States (1889–1890). The system became regularized and increasingly complex, with Latin Americans at first participating reluctantly but compliantly under U.S. direction. By the late 1920s, however, they were assertively defiant of U.S. paternalism and interventionism. Inter-American relations became significantly more harmonious when the United States reduced and then disavowed forceful intervention and adhered to multilateral consultation for issue resolution (the bases for its Good Neighbor Policy). With the U.S. focus on gaining Latin American support in the war effort, the cooperative thrust was as a general matter carried over into World War II. Good neighborly collaboration did not change the realities of the state power asymmetry in the United States' favor. During 1943, when the United States realized that war developments had turned to the Allies' advantage, its interest in and attention to Latin America began to wane.

The United States pursued imperialism in the circum-Caribbean, and U.S. interests and power dominated most of the area. Britain retired from its preeminent position in the Caribbean, leaving the United States free to assert its hegemonic ambitions. The United States assumed the role of international police power in the Caribbean, converted most of it into a bilateral trade area, and engaged in various forms of coercive unilateral intervention. Interventions were primarily designed to preempt European meddling, to enforce stability in the environs of the Panama Canal, and to secure the Caribbean approaches to the isthmus that the United States considered vital to its strategic interests. The other outside states generally recognized and conceded the U.S. sphere. The exceptions to total U.S. hegemony were the holdings of Britain, France, the Netherlands, and (until 1917) Denmark.

By the mid-1920s imperial policies had fallen into disrepute in the United States and that orientation and its instruments were incrementally abandoned. The process was completed by the mid-1930s. Elements of a sphere of influence structure persisted, however, not with direct military intervention but in terms of power differentials and economic dependency.

In the South American subsystem, the United States was only one of several competitors to the powerful British position. France and Germany were also important contenders. U.S. influence outside of the Caribbean area did not begin to rival that of Europe until World War I. After the war, Britain, which had been the major source of capital for South America, continued to play a major role but yielded first place to the United States.

The stronger Southern Cone states became relatively more autonomous at the beginning of the twentieth century, even though their new roles coincided with the rise of U.S. power. With the opening of the Panama Canal under U.S. control, with the U.S. domination of the Caribbean region, and with the beginning of the Mexican Revolution in 1910, the Southern Cone subsystem was further set apart. Furthermore, far-reaching changes occurred in Southern Cone social, economic, and political systems, as well as in power relationships among the states of the area and with outside powers, during the first three decades of the twentieth century. Brazil emerged from under British tutelage and sought more autonomy in an "unwritten alliance" with the United States. In intraregional relations, many of the same conflicts continued.

U.S. Hemispheric Hegemony

The third phase of change in the Latin American regional subsystem began during World War II and continued throughout the postwar period until the mid-1960s.[8] It was given impetus with the advent of the cold war but shifted direction after 1959, following the Castro revolution in Cuba and its subsequent alignment with the Soviet Union.

Soon after World War II the international system was characterized by a loose bipolarity. U.S. officials tended to integrate the Latin American region as a unit in their global conceptualizations of East-West conflict, initially emphasizing its relative remoteness behind the front lines of the cold war.

The United States had replaced all foreign powers throughout the hemisphere, except for their small and problematic colonies. The United States was the region's largest trading partner and capital investor, and it monopolized military relations. Between 1945 and 1948 the Inter-American System was formalized by the Inter-American Treaty of Reciprocal Assistance (Rio Treaty), which joined the Latin American states with the United States in a formal inter-American security alliance, and by the Charter of the Organization of American States (OAS), which formally organized the region into a bloc under U.S. leadership. Thereafter the United States was able to convert the Inter-American System into an anticommunist alliance. These developments were accompanied by the largely successful U.S. effort to mold a mostly reliable Latin American voting bloc in the United Nations. Most Caribbean states were U.S. clients. The Southern Cone was less strictly under U.S. domination but also less autonomous than before.

Outside powers offered little challenge to U.S. dominance because Latin America was not related to their primary concerns. West European states retreated from strong competition. They were first absorbed with their own recovery and reconstruction and then preoccupied with intra-European affairs, with relations with the superpowers, with their own security arrangements, and with the dissolution of their empires in Asia and Africa. The Soviet Union indicated slight interest as well. It was fundamentally concerned with its own contiguous regions and the cold war with the United States and Western Europe. At the same time it regarded Latin America as inevitably a U.S. sphere of influence that precluded Communist advances. The United States dealt with the infrequent occurrences it perceived as threats on an individual basis, such as its provision of covert support for the overthrow of a leftist government in Guatemala in 1954. The United States calculated that international communism posed little threat to Latin America, a view that, when coupled with the dominant U.S. power position, meant that the United States devoted minimal policy attention to the region.

After Cuba aligned with the Soviet bloc following the Castro Revolution of 1959, U.S. regional policy perceptions were dominated by fears of Soviet expansionism. At the same time, Latin Americans increasingly resisted the U.S.-led transformation of the Inter-American System into an anticommunist alliance. The global structure came to be widely perceived (not entirely accurately) as consisting of three "worlds": the First (industrialized and noncommunist) World, the Second (Communist) World, and the Third (developing and nonaligned) World. U.S. officials tended to view Latin America as part of the Third World, grouping the region with Asia and Africa especially in the developmental sense and ambiguously in terms of nonalignment.

The Soviet Union accepted the opportunity to erode the U.S. power position in the Caribbean. This development posed the first significant challenge to U.S. predominance in Latin America since World War II. The United States consequently assigned a prominent position to Latin America in its global policies and temporarily devoted more resources to the region. Its policies included cooperative instruments through aid programs and coercive means through various forms of intervention. The policy emphasis had special implications for the circum-Caribbean.

U.S. and Latin American interests converged in what came to be called the Alliance for Progress. From 1959 to the mid-1960s, the United States temporarily defined the concept of security to include national development, which coincided with the Latin Americans' primary economic interests. The Inter-American Development Bank was created in 1959, with the United States the prime donor of lending funds. The United States also pursued coercive strategies, which included the sponsoring of an exile invasion of Cuba in 1961 and the multilateral agreements in the OAS to impose sanctions on Cuba in 1962 and 1964. Once Cuba left the fold, the United

States said it would not allow a similar occurrence again. It forcibly returned the Dominican Republic to its sphere of influence through military intervention in 1965 in order to prevent "another Cuba." That intervention effectively ended the Alliance for Progress and the convergence of interests.

In the meantime, a major series of cold war events occurred with the U.S.-Soviet confrontation in the Cuban missile crisis of October 1962. The clash over the presence of Soviet missiles in Cuba was a major episode in the cold war, the significance of which went far beyond the Caribbean area and the rest of Latin America. It was a great world crisis in which the both antagonists seemed to perceive a potential shift in the global power balance. A debate over whether Soviet missiles in Cuba in fact could have altered the strategic military balance ensued at the time and continued thereafter. At any rate, Fidel Castro was largely ignored in what was essentially a superpower showdown. An important outcome was the Soviet agreement to remove its newly placed weapons in return for a U.S. pledge not to invade Cuba.

Regional Pluralism

The Latin American subsystem entered its fourth era beginning in about the mid-1960s. It became even more independent from outside actors and more shaped by the regional actors themselves than had previously been the case. The period lasted roughly until the end of the cold war. Developing international relationships involved changes in U.S. policy in response to shifting calculations of "the Communist threat," the revival of activities by European and Asian states, and rising Latin American foreign policy assertiveness. The argument was heard that, with the intense application of U.S. power in the circum-Caribbean after 1981 and the severe economic crisis and heavy debt burden throughout Latin America and the Caribbean in the 1980s, the subsystem had entered a new era of dependency relationships. The evidence suggests, however, that the hemispheric position of the United States was increasingly challenged, resulting in a relative decline in U.S. influence, increased pluralism in the distribution of power, and elevated levels of economic and social interdependence.[9]

For more than a decade beginning in the latter 1960s, the United States chose policies that again placed a low priority on Latin America, even in the circum-Caribbean. The Southern Cone recaptured its contours as a semi-autonomous subsystem, perhaps eroded but still intact after the brief postwar period of U.S. predominance in the hemisphere. The Soviet-Cuban threat seemed to recede in the wake of the missile crisis. The United States abandoned developmentalist policies, so that levels of funding for economic and military assistance programs declined sharply, and direct arms sales were severely limited. Certain bilateral relationships were important, such as U.S.-Panamanian bargaining over new canal treaties and the array of concerns with Mexico.

The erosion of global bipolarity was evidenced by Latin American positions and actions toward the United States, as many of them resisted U.S. power—with some success. They stated their lack of support for a united American front, which they viewed as a device to maintain their subordinate status under U.S. influence. This attitude was a culmination of trends gathering force after the mid-1960s, which included expropriating foreign enterprises and assuming control of national resources, broadening contacts with other world power centers, challenging the United States in the Inter-American System, and devoting more attention to organizing among themselves and excluding the United States. Most Latin American states were prompted to cooperate and unite in order to bargain with the United States, but their cooperative efforts were limited and their bargaining power undermined by their own continuing rivalries and disputes. Latin Americans also increasingly joined with the Third World. The west coast states in the mid-1970s came to acknowledge a "Pacific Rim" identity and interest, an informal and ambiguous grouping of about fifty states with an emphasis on mutual trade and investment. Within the Inter-American System, Latin Americans were increasingly dissatisfied with an anticommunist alliance, especially after the U.S. military intervention in the Dominican Republic in 1965 and its insistence on converting the situation into an inter-American problem. The United States, emphasizing mutual security, was unhappy with the Latin American's lack of cooperation and preoccupation with economic matters. The Inter-American System became ineffective in mutual security; it continued economic development activities but was not an important arena for addressing the external debt difficulties.

The other external states took only partial advantage of the waning U.S. regional influence. Japan became an economic force in the region; European governments and nonstate actors expanded their activities; and the Soviet Union increased its diplomatic, economic, and military presence. But none of them, with the exception of the Soviet Union, calculated Latin American operations in strategic terms.

Economic debilities bearing on the Latin American states in the 1980s, including a large external debt owed to U.S. banks, clearly reduced their foreign policy capabilities. The regional states' ability to pursue independent foreign policies was eroded, but U.S. leverage as a creditor was far from absolute. The debt situations involved risks for all parties. This is not to argue that they placed equal constraints on creditors and debtors alike; indeed, Latin American governments were forced to adopt stabilization measures that caused domestic hardships and political tensions. Yet all of the major Latin American states, and even some of the smaller ones, maintained international orientations and policies in opposition to those of the United States. It is difficult to measure how U.S. financial influence was translated into political leverage on issues other than the rescheduling of debt repayments.

The regional subsystem era saw U.S. dominance in abeyance, but limitations on U.S. capabilities should not be overstated. Furthermore, subsystemic distinctions in the various parts of Latin America revealed different power relationships.

Mexico was absorbed with its bilateral U.S. relations and with such issues as trade, investment, capital flows, energy supplies, migration (both legal and illegal), boundary settlements, sharing of water resources, border communities, tourism, and fishing

rights. Of particular importance, the United States was Mexico's largest trading partner, and Mexico occupied third place in total U.S. trade. With regard to the dominant
inter-American issues—Central American conflicts, intervention, Cuba, trade and investment, external debt, human rights, arms transfers, and the drug traffic—Mexico
tended to differ with and oppose the United States on all of them. The United States
was not in a position to bring about any fundamental reorientation of Mexican foreign
policy, in spite Mexico's severe debt problems, which began in 1982 and were later exacerbated by internal Mexican political and social problems. The United States continued as the much stronger nation, but Mexico was far from being merely its client.

Although the United States was increasingly isolated in the circum-Caribbean
during the 1980s, its power and influence continued to be the primary considerations in the subregion's international relations. U.S. relations with Cuba further deteriorated after 1975 because of its expanded African adventures in concert with the
Soviet Union, and President Jimmy Carter accused the Soviet Union and Cuba of
increased activities in Central America. The Reagan administration, inaugurated in
1981, was determined to increase the U.S. presence in the Caribbean and to recapture U.S. influence, beginning in Central America. These determined efforts included the U.S. military invasion of Grenada in 1983. From the U.S. point of view,
the principal challenge to Caribbean security arose from the Soviet relationships
with Cuba and Nicaragua. Although the Soviet Union and its partners showed caution in their Caribbean activities, they did not retire in the face of strongly assertive
U.S. actions. U.S. activities also engendered strong opposition in the United States
itself. And challenges came from other sources as well, including the NATO allies.

One of the most striking new conditions in the circum-Caribbean was the new assertiveness of Latin American states. Four of them—Mexico, Venezuela, Colombia,
and Panama—organized the Contadora Group in 1983 to offer a formula for the
negotiated settlement of Central American conflict. Four geographically-removed
South American states—Argentina, Brazil, Peru, and Uruguay—later joined this effort and formed the Contadora Support Group in direct challenge to U.S. policies.
Even more striking was the multilateral peace plan agreed to by the five Central
American governments in August 1987; the United States initially opposed the plan,
which in time enjoyed considerable success. Latin American dissatisfaction was also
reflected in resistance to U.S. leadership in the Inter-American System, which was
no longer available to legitimize U.S. actions. Thus the United States was challenged
by the regional states themselves, including the weakest among them and those considered to be U.S. clients. Nevertheless, although the United States was not able to
get its own way in Central America, it retained sufficient influence to hinder Latin
American initiatives.

Numerous European actors presented something of a challenge to U.S. domination of the Caribbean zone. They did not view Latin America in general in terms of
security interests because of geographic, cultural, and political distance and higher
priority concerns elsewhere; and they tended to defer to the United States on
Caribbean strategic matters. NATO members had only the contingency security

concern that the Gulf of Mexico and Caribbean Sea be open for movements of military forces and supplies in the event of European war. After the Nicaraguan Revolution of 1979, Europeans took a political interest in the evolving Central American crisis and by and large dissented from the U.S. approach. Their concern had to do not so much with geopolitics, strategy, or balances of power as with the nature of commitments by the West to social change in the Third World. Europeans tended to agree that Soviet influence should be minimized and to be concerned about Nicaragua's authoritarian trends. But they opposed unilateral coercion by the United States and argued against military solutions. They applauded the Contadora initiative and the Central American peace plan.

But European opposition did not develop to the extent anticipated during the period immediately following the Nicaraguan Revolution when the situation was in flux. They exercised little influence on Central American events or on restraining U.S. actions. Most of all, the 1983 U.S. military intervention in Grenada signaled a new and more serious phase. Without primary interests in the region, European governments drew back so as to avoid another alliance problem with the United States. At the same time, however, they warned the United States that more coercive actions in Central America would engender more problems with its European allies.

Certain continental and global trends converged to alter the nature of the Southern Cone's international relationships. The U.S. presence, especially economic, remained highly important. Nevertheless, a more open international environment and diffused external influences allowed local actors greater latitude in the conduct of their foreign relations and permitted extraregional states to engage in substantial involvement—some building on traditional relationships, others evolving into new ones. By the mid-1980s almost all of the subregional states had moved away from military regimes to constitutional democracies. Intra-Southern Cone relationships underwent dramatic evolution, particularly with more cooperative Argentine-Brazilian and Argentine-Chilean relationships. A Brazilian-Argentine rapprochement began in 1979, survived the Anglo-Argentine war of 1982 and the dramatic changes of government in both states, and was extended thereafter. Argentina and Chile settled their Beagle Channel dispute. The Anglo-Argentine dispute over the Falklands/Malvinas continued, although the British and Argentines negotiated directly and eventually restored relations. The Southern Cone maintained its long-standing ties to Europe and established closer economic relations with Japan. Argentina after 1979 engaged the Soviet Union as its primary trading partner.

U.S. influence with Brazil declined dramatically after the mid-1960s. Brazil developed a multilateral network of international trade, became not only self-sufficient in military affairs but one of the world's major arms exporters, and reduced its dependence on imported oil. It developed strong ties in Europe, the Middle East and Africa, and Japan, in addition to those with the United States. Brazil's freedom of action was limited by its heavy external debt burden, yet it still maintained a high degree of independence. Although Brazil suffered serious debilities as the world's largest portfolio-debtor nation, it also had a well-diversified market economy, which was ranked the world's eighth largest. Under military governments in the 1960s and 1970s, Brazil sought great-power status. Although those ambitions receded, cooperative relations with Brazil for all external states stemmed from a convergence of interests rather than from an assertion of superior power.

Post–Cold War Era

During the latter part of the 1980s into the 1990s, the global international system entered the post–cold war era.[10] In the case of Latin America and the Caribbean, the end of East-West conflict combined with other already existing elements to produce a new international period, which in turn spurred the development of other trends.

The principal "end of the cold war" consequence was the understanding on the part of all actors that, with East-West conflict no longer relevant, the old analytic and policy frameworks were no longer valid. The United States abandoned its long-standing preoccupation with minimizing what it saw as hostile foreign intrusions in the Western Hemisphere. Latin Americans were no longer required to calculate how to respond to U.S. anticommunist policies, with which most of them had disagreed. This new understanding was a critical consideration but by itself did not capture the complexity of regional international relations.

The regional context had been changing well before the end of the cold war, in certain ways not directly related to superpower competition. Principal among them were Latin America's political and economic transformations away from authoritarian governance and state-dominated economies, trends that had been in motion since the early 1980s. By 1990 the transition away from military regimes to constitutional democracies had generally been completed, although democracy was under stress, and "partial democracies" more often than not characterized government development. By then the new governments had generally adopted "neoliberal" economic reform, although the process had been a difficult one and domestic opposition to the changes persisted. As these governments revitalized cooperation among themselves on both regional and subregional levels, they were also determined to be active participants in the evolving global system. They sought cooperative relations with the United States and with other outside states, IGOs, and transnational actors.

The inter-American level was of particular significance. Relations were facilitated by Latin Americans adopting a more positive nationalism and by the United States returning to a more multilateral orientation. The formal Inter-American System was revived as an organizational setting within which to address hemispheric problems. In the late 1980s into the 1990s, the OAS, via its performance as part of the Central American peace process, reversed its two-decade decline. Member states again perceived the system as an appropriate problem-solving forum. An important development was Canada's decision to become an important actor in inter-American security affairs. From 1987 Canada was closely involved in the Central American peace process, an involvement that included command of the UN peacekeeping force in the subregion; and in 1990 it joined the OAS as a full member.

As a consequence of the end of the cold war and of the regional political and economic changes, the American states elevated a set of urgent issues to the top of the inter-American agenda. Among them were problems of democracy, human rights, state governance, and civil-military relations; of international trade, investment, external debt, and economic integration; of the degradation of the physical environment and sustainable development; of immigration and refugee problems; and of illicit drug trafficking and other criminal activities. Although problems of insurgencies and interstate conflicts were greatly reduced from past situations, they continued to receive attention. A general consensus emerged that democratic development and economic reform constituted the overarching norms in hemispheric relations and should provide the subtext for the salient issues; that is, the resolution of problems depended directly on favorable political and economic conditions. The OAS and the IDB took measures to support these principles and objectives.

These top priority issues were essentially an extension of the domestic concerns of the state parties—"intermestic" issues with a strong mix of international and domestic components that required resolution in a context different from that of the cold war. Although the end of the cold war did not alter the reality of asymmetrical inter-American power relations within the Inter-American System, the high domestic content of the issues seemed to mute the consequences of asymmetry inasmuch as they required multilateral resolution. Thus, transnationalization and globalization—which had been increasingly critical elements of regional international relations since the end of World War II but partially disguised by cold war imperatives—were essential characteristics of the new era.

Inter-American trade and investment were of particular importance. President Bush presented his Enterprise for the Americas Initiative in June 1990, which proposed a western hemispheric free-trade area. The United States eventually signed "framework agreements" with almost all of the regional states as the foundation for the future negotiation of free trade. The regional states themselves had already begun to reform and expand their own subregional integration, a process further stimulated by the Bush initiative and reflected in the Inter-American System's declared goal of creating a hemispheric free-trade area by the year 2005. However, its realization has been pursued in a halting and complex manner.

Latin American and Caribbean leaders were fully aware that hemispheric free trade, if realized, would link their integration organizations more closely to the U.S. economy. Concerned over the possibility of becoming a U.S. dominated economic preserve, they acted to expand extrahemispheric connections, and outsiders responded. The European Community (in 1992 redesignated the European Union—EU) began to hold annual foreign ministers meetings with the Rio Group; it revived annual meetings with the Central American states; and it commenced formal discussions with Southern Cone states and Mexico about the progressive liberalization of trade. Certain Latin American states pursued their economic interests in terms of an evolving Pacific Rim trading system. At the same time, Latin American and Caribbean interest in the Nonaligned Movement and the New International Economic Order declined; alignment was no longer an issue in the former instance, and the demise of the Soviet Union reduced the leverage of the latter.

Mexico and the United States fundamentally reoriented their policies toward one another. As inter-American tensions eased in the latter 1980s, Mexico abandoned its protectionist trade and investment policies and pressed the United States for a free-trade agreement. The United States responded positively, and Canada, in order to protect itself from trade diversion, joined in. The historic trilateral North American Free Trade Agreement (NAFTA) went into effect on January 1, 1994. Mexico also broadened its external relationships, as reflected in its free-trade talks with the EU.

Changes were extensive in the circum-Caribbean, where East-West conflict had been most dramatic. The Soviet Union actually became a part of the Central American peace process, ceasing its weapons transfers to Cuba and Nicaragua and pressuring them to end arms deliveries to insurgents in El Salvador. With the decline of Soviet power and then the breakup of the Soviet Union itself, commitments to Cuba were reduced and then virtually canceled. Cuba itself was internationally isolated and absorbed with its internal problems. The Central American peace process suffered delays and other problems after 1987 but also enjoyed considerable success; the United Nations and the Organization of American States provided critical assistance, and the United States eventually supported it. The U.S. unilateral military intervention in Panama in 1990, and its guiding role in the UN-sponsored peacekeeping operation in Haiti beginning in 1994, indicated that the United States was still willing to use armed compulsion in the area even in the post–cold war era.

The UN roles in the Central American peace process and in Haiti represented a historic juncture, in that the UN had formerly deferred to the Inter-American System on such matters.

NOTES

1. William R. Thompson, "The Regional Subsystem," *International Studies Quarterly* 17 (March 1973): 89–117. Thompson inventoried and evaluated twenty-one attributes that had been proposed by eighteen analysts to define a regional subsystem.

2. This notion also implies that a Latin American policy of the United States (or of any other entity) is an outdated concept—if one cannot treat the region as a whole, then pursuing a regional foreign policy is futile.

3. A large number of broad-gauged studies from history, political science, and economics have detailed Latin American international relations from a region-wide perspective, while acknowledging subregional and country realities. An early, complete, and still-useful history is J. Fred Rippy, *Latin America in World Politics,* 3d ed. (New York: F. S. Crofts, 1938); see also J. Fred Rippy, *Globe and Hemisphere* (Chicago: Henry Regnery, 1958). More recent histories are Harold Eugene Davis, John J. Finan, and F. Taylor Peck, *Latin American Diplomatic History: An Introduction* (Baton Rouge: Louisiana State University Press, 1977); Demetrio Boersner, *Relaciones Internacionales de América Latina: Breve Historia,* 4th ed. (Caracas: Nueva Sociedád, 1990); and Lester D. Langley, *America and the Americas: The United States in the Western Hemisphere* (Athens: University of Georgia Press, 1989). A broad range of phenomena in

terms of the international system and Latin America's place in it are addressed by Peter Calvert, *The International Politics of Latin America* (Manchester: Manchester University Press; New York: St. Martin's Press, 1994) Hélio Jaguaribe, *El nuevo escenario internacional* (México: Fondo de Cultura Económica, 1985, 1994); and Luciano Tomassini, Carlos J. Moneta y Augusto Varas, *El sistema internacional y América Latina* (Buenos Aires: Grupo Editor Latinamericano, 1991). Latin American international political economy is dealt with by Jonathan Hartlyn and Samuel A. Morley, eds., *Latin American Political Economy: Financial Crisis and Political Change* (Boulder, Colo.: Westview Press, 1986). David W. Dent, ed., *Handbook of Political Science Research on Latin America: Trends from the 1960s to the 1990s* (Westport, Conn.: Greenwood Press, 1990); part 2 provides bibliographic essays.

4. For insights regarding the historical theme of integrated-yet-separate Mexican-U.S. relationships, see Lester D. Langley, *Mexico and the United States: The Fragile Relationship* (Boston: G. K. Hall, 1991).

5. The notion of a circum-Caribbean subsystem is explicated by G. Pope Atkins, "The United States and the Caribbean Basin," in David J. Myers, ed., *Regional Hegemons: Threat Perception and Strategic Response* (Boulder, Colo.: Westview Press, 1991); it is further supported by the analyses in Lester D. Langley, *Struggle for the American Mediterranean: United States-European Rivalry in the Gulf-Caribbean, 1776–1904* (Athens: University of Georgia Press, 1976); Lester D. Langley, *The United States and the Caribbean in the Twentieth Century*, 4th ed. (Athens: University of Georgia Press, 1989); Anthony P. Maingot, *The United States and the Caribbean: Challenges of an Asymmetrical Relationship* (Boulder, Colo.: Westview Press, 1994); and P. Sutton, ed., *Europe and the Caribbean* (London: Macmillan, 1991).

6. On South America, to include Brazil, see G. Pope Atkins, ed., *South America into the 1990s: Evolving International Relationships in a New Era* (Boulder Colo.: Westview Press, 1990); Samuel L. Baily, *The United States and the Development of South America, 1945–1975* (New York: New Viewpoints, 1976); Glen St. John Barclay, *Struggle for a Continent: The Diplomatic History of South America, 1917–1945* (London: Whitefriars, 1971); and Jack Child, *Geopolitics and Conflict in South America: Quarrels Among Neighbors* (New York: Praeger, 1985).

7. Robert N. Burr, *By Reason or Force: Chile and the Balancing of Power in Latin America, 1830–1905* (Berkeley: University of California Press, 1967) is the authoritative treatment; the topic is also analyzed by Norman A. Bailey, *Latin America in World Politics* (New York: Walker, 1967), chapter 3.

8. See especially F. Parkinson, *Latin America, the Cold War, and the World Powers, 1945–1973* (Beverly Hills, Calif.: Sage, 1974). Of special-topic interest are Jan F. Triska, *Dominant Powers and Subordinate States: The United States in Latin America and the Soviet Union in Eastern Europe* (Durham, N.C.: Duke University Press, 1986); and Edy Kaufman, *The Superpowers and Their Spheres of Influence: The United States and the Soviet Union in Eastern Europe and Latin America* (London: Croom Helm Kaufman, 1976).

9. On the limits of U.S. influence, see Robert Wesson, ed., *U.S. Influence in Latin America in the 1980s* (New York: Praeger, 1982); and Kevin Middlebrook and Carlos Rico, eds., *The United States and Latin America in the 1980s: Contending Perspectives on a Decade of Crisis* (Pittsburgh: University of Pittsburgh Press, 1986).

10. The evolving post–cold war era is dealt with by G. Pope Atkins, ed., *The United States and Latin America: Redefining U.S. Purposes in the Post-Cold War Era* (Austin: Lyndon B. Johnson School of Public Affairs, University of Texas at Austin, 1992), Abraham F. Lowenthal and Gregory F. Treverton, eds., *Latin America and the United States in a New World* (Boulder, Colo.: Westview Press, 1994), and Lars Schoultz, William C. Smith, and Augusto Varas, eds.,

Security, Democracy, and Development in U.S.-Latin American Relations (Miami: N-S Center Press; New Brunswick, N.J.: Transaction Publishers, 1994), Luciano Tomassini, con colaboración de Carlos J. Moneta y Augusto Varas, *El Sistema Internacional y América Latina: La Política Internacional en un mundo Postmoderno* (Buenos Aires: Grupo Editor Latinoamericano, 1991).

CHAPTER THREE

■

Explanations and Prescriptions

A number of theories have appeared in the study of international relations that purport to explain Latin America in the international system, and some have been formulated with particular reference to the region. In several instances they also offer policy prescriptions for the various actors. The theories address matters that have long been the subject of intense debates about the consequences of policies and interactions in the region, and they raise issues and questions over which serious analysts disagree. This chapter completes the book's framework for analysis with a presentation and critique of these theories, which are especially relevant to Latin America.

THE THEORETICAL ENTERPRISE

The principal groups of IR theories, in the order presented and analyzed below, are realism and idealism; Marxism-Leninism; liberal developmentalism; structural and neo-Marxist dependency; world-system; modernism, monetarism, and neoliberalism; and pluralism. As a general matter, these theories are concerned both with explaining state behavior and the international system and with influencing state policies and the decisions of other actors, either as prescriptions for or in opposition to them. Prior to engaging in specific theoretical critiques, therefore, a brief review of the nature of theory (itself a matter of dispute) and its relationship to policy advocacy is in order.

Most IR scholars agree on the importance of theoretical inquiry. A theory is a set of propositions designed to explain a class of phenomena, such as those analyzed in this book. Furthermore, IR specialists tend to be practical as well as scientific and philosophical; they are interested in policy prescriptions along with objective analysis and subjective understanding. Indeed, the latter two concerns have often led to interest in policy problems.

"Theory" is often used colloquially or pejoratively to connote an untested idea or opinion in political discourse. For the purposes of this book, this meaning and practice are emphatically rejected. A mere subjective preference is not the equivalent of theoretical judgment in any critical sense. A cardinal rule for serious political analysts (including those who wish to influence policies) is to be self-conscious about their intellectual processes—to understand the nature of one's thoughts and those of others in the theorizing process.

The various intellectual operations that people may engage in are represented by the different kinds of statements they make. In the case of IR, we should distinguish five categories of assertions: descriptive, explanatory, predictive, normative, and prescriptive. Explanatory statements give meaning to descriptive (factual) statements, typically answering some form of the question "why?" Predictive statements are usually derived by extrapolating trends and applying explanations to presume future conditions. Normative (value-laden) statements express a preference in terms of right and wrong, desirable and undesirable, and other value-based objectives. Prescriptive statements go beyond assessment or contemplation to offer advice with the purpose of affecting events. Prescriptive statements usually have normative and predictive elements. They are normative in the sense that purposes proceed from some image or view of a desirable state of affairs. They are predictive when stating what course of action will accomplish a given purpose.

These statements are reflected in three generic kinds of theory: (1) the combined category of behavioral (empirical) theory and formal (mathematical) theory, which analyzes politics by scientific methods; (2) normative theory, which studies politics in philosophical, ethical (often tied to legal), or ideological terms; and (3) policy theory, which offers advice for courses of action. These theories are separate but not mutually exclusive; in fact, each of the theories examined in this chapter includes empirical, normative, and policy elements.

No matter what specific purposes one may bring to the study of IR, the beginning point is to strive to understand objectively the world in which we live. Thinking may then shift to normative evaluations. Both objective and subjective understanding may be applied to policy prescription. Normative conclusions may go beyond clarifying values about proper behavior by recommending what should be done in matters of action. Empirical theory (and, less overtly, formal theory) may tell policy makers the best way to achieve a desired goal—what is possible or not—after what is desirable has already been determined. Thus, knowledge of politics may be applied to solving actual problems.

The expectation of theorists to "use" political knowledge in the policy arena raises questions about both scholarship and motive. Should theorists go beyond objective and ethical analysis about political behavior to prescribe policy? Those who answer in the affirmative (and I am among them) argue that, since all policy is ultimately based on values, a detached approach may not necessarily be desirable. As Charles Lerche succinctly put it, "If the serious scholars suspend normative judgment on events, the function of assigning value to policy choices falls to political leaders, journalists, and other manipulators of the mass psyche."

Nevertheless, a caveat about policy prescription must be noted. Political knowledge cannot tell us whose problem definition or policy prescription is right, because it cannot tell us what political ends we ought to seek or to what particular goals our factual knowledge ought to be applied. Furthermore, since prescriptive statements almost always have normative overtones, political knowledge may be used for purposes that one may thoroughly disapprove of.[1]

REALISM AND IDEALISM

The Realist-Idealist Dichotomy

The realist and idealist theoretical schools represent the oldest concepts in IR theory and practice. Although the idealist alternative to realist thinking has been mostly overshadowed by the latter as an operational guide, it has been persistent and at times has achieved prominence to the extent that analysts have referred to a "realist-idealist dichotomy."[2] The two schools offer competing theories of human nature, the international system, and the bases for formulating and evaluating foreign policy.

Realism is fundamentally pragmatic. In general terms, it is a view of the world as it is, as distinguished from abstract or speculative preferences. Realism focuses on the centrality of the state as a unitary, rational "power unit" and posits a state-centric model of the international system. Realists perceive that system as anarchic, meaning for them the absence of any central authority over states. Consequently, the system is a "self help" one on the part of states under conditions of both cooperation and conflict. Realists emphasize "the national interest" as the fundamental guide to policy-making in the sense of the state's most vital needs of self-preservation, independence, territorial integrity, military security, and economic well-being. Thus a state pursues a realist policy when it is based on strategic national interest and power politics. The realist school starts with the assumption that power is the key factor in all international relationships, and that the wise and efficient use of power by a state in pursuit of its national interest is the main ingredient of a successful foreign policy.

Neorealism departs from the classic realist school by de-emphasizing the causality of human nature and stressing the structure of the system as both a determinant of policy formulation and a constraint on policy action (hence neorealists are also known as "structural realists"); that is, the central concepts are the "high politics" of security, diplomacy, and war, which give structure to the system and are most fundamentally expressed in balances of power.

Idealism is the pursuit of high principles, purposes, or goals in international relations, such as justice and peace. It is a representation of things as they might or should be rather than as they are. The idealist approach to international relations is based on standards involving international norms, legal codes, and moral-ethical values. Idealists, like realists, have thought within the framework of interstate relations and state interests, but they have sought to reform the system and the way policy makers think about and use power. They believe that foreign policies based on moral-legal principles are more effective than power politics because they are more durable and better promote unity and cooperation among states. Idealism involves not force and coercion but winning over the minds and allegiances of people to accept rules that ought to govern state conduct. This view assumes that foreign policies should strive to create a better world order and emphasizes international law, organization, and other regimes that reduce conflict and facilitate cooperation. Idealists regard the potency of ideas, as opposed to the power politics of realists (or the materialism of Marxists), as capable of overcoming resistance to asserting human values in foreign policy and international relations.

Since the late nineteenth century, and especially in the wake of the two twentieth century world wars, idealists have sought to develop structures that would facilitate international peace and mitigate war. They ascribed international violence to reliance on power politics and the failure of balances of power; they generally assumed that more adequate institutional arrangements could prevent war. The idealist school has included a variety of approaches by advocates who by and large shared assumptions but often disagreed strongly over the measures to be taken. Within the bounds of idealism have been found pacifists, legal reformers, world federalists, and classic political and economic laissez-faire liberals and social democrats. They argued for a number of measures and emphases, all of which were implemented to some degree: institutional cooperation within general international organizations for collective security and other purposes; the rule of international law; disarmament and arms control; and the enlightened internal political, social, and economic reform of the states themselves.

Realists are closely identified with the "rational actor" or "rational choice" model of foreign policy decision-making. The model assumes foreign policy makers to be rational individuals who follow (or should follow) a detached architectonic plan of state purposes and goals and logical strategic and tactical procedures. Accordingly, strategic decisions—an overall design to achieve certain goals and objectives—are made with reference to state interests and power in the context of an external structure of power relationships. Thus decisions are predictable in those terms, and what goes on inside the state in the way of individuals or organizations is of little analytic importance.

The rational choice model is not restricted to the realist school. Others with different values underlying their preferences for state purposes and policies, including those with idealist inclinations, use the rationalist language of strategic setting and external challenges, state interest and capability, and the need for effective purposeful action. International political economists also adopt rationalist concepts in their concern with policies based on macroeconomic models and goals that stress the interrelationship of economic policies and the international political and economic systems. Numerous international historians, most military strategists, and many journalists base their analyses and commentary on rational model tenets. Unqualified adherence is rare, however.

Power Politics and Latin America

Practices associated with realism—balance-of-power, strategic and geopolitical calculations, and conflict—have been important aspects of the Latin American subsystem (only recently to include the new Caribbean states) from its beginnings to the present. The policy implications of conflict in Latin American international relations have been especially profound for the United States, as the most powerful external actor and the most willing and able to use coercive diplomacy. It was not the first of the states to engage in power politics in Latin America, nor in recent years has it been the only one. According to European leaders themselves, European imperialism in Latin America during the nineteenth century was largely based on the region's position in European-centered balance-of-power calculations (although other factors were also in play for individual states). Power politics have also characterized a significant portion of the relations between and among the Latin American states themselves.

In the case of the United States and power politics, especially throughout the twentieth century, the realist-idealist dichotomy relates particularly to the debates over the preferred approach to foreign policy-making. A strategic calculation seems to have dominated U.S. policy action in the region when policy makers perceived a threat to U.S. interests from outside powers operating in Latin America; but a strong strain of American (Wilsonian) idealism has also been interjected, especially in the persistent debates over the degree to which Latin American democratization should be a part of U.S. policy calculations. Realists think that popular attitudes and moral self-righteousness have misled the United States into adopting idealistic guidelines in the making of foreign policy decisions. The result, according to the realists, is the inability of the United States to compete effectively with other states that base their policies on the hard realities of national self-interest. Idealists tend to reject the power-centered realist approach as a Machiavellianism that produces only short-term gains. For the idealist, the most successful policies have been based on values that have won both domestic and overseas support. The realist-idealist dichotomy in today's world should not be overstated, however. Realism and idealism may converge, and policy debates and decisions often attempt to reconcile the two. In practice, policies often have combined some mixture of realism and idealism, with realism specifying the means for achieving goals and idealism justifying the policies adopted.

Latin American leaders have also formulated policies in terms of national interests and security. They have been concerned about military threats to their territorial integrity and physical safety posed by foreign incursions, whether of the European great powers, the United States, or other Latin American states. From the earliest days of statehood, Latin Americans tended to band together when outsiders intervened or exerted other pressures. Since World War II, however, in most Latin American countries for most of the time, national security has been synonymous with national development, with an emphasis on internal unity and economic well-being. External threat perceptions have tended to be limited to border and territorial disputes and, in the circum-Caribbean, to great-power intervention.

The most coherent expression of Latin American *realpolitik* has been found in the Southern Cone, most notably in Brazil, Argentina, and Chile. Dating from the nineteenth century, military men and their civilian associates in particular adopted geopolitical strategic perspectives. These theories were based on the organic theory of the state, an extreme version of power politics that views conflict as natural, inevitable, and necessary if a nation is to survive and achieve its "destiny." This kind of thinking also justified domestic repression, especially by military regimes from the 1960s into the 1980s. Geopolitical bases for policy declined dramatically in the 1980s with the return to constitutional civilian governments.

MARXISM-LENINISM

From the mid-nineteenth century through World War I, Marxism and then its Leninist interpretation appeared as theoretical dissents from realism and imperialism and prescriptions for action against the associated evils of capitalism. Marxist-Leninist ideas also offered alternatives to what their proponents considered ineffective idealism and liberalism.

As developed by Karl Marx and Friedrich Engels in the middle to late nineteenth century, Marxism was a set of economic and political doctrines emphasizing the theories of dialectical materialism and class struggle. Marx adopted the Hegelian dialectic of history—the assertion that entities and events were understood in terms of the clash of contradictory ideas expressed in a central thesis and an opposing logical antithesis; they were eventually reconciled in a synthesis of higher truth. Marxism replaced the Hegelian battle over ideas with the inevitability of class conflict based on materialism—that is, class struggle created by contradictions in the means of production to which the classes were related. Class struggle between dominant and exploited strata was a Marxist dialectical constant. In feudalism, the aristocracy owned the land and exploited the labor of the peasants, a contradiction that led to the rise of a new dominant class. In capitalism, the state was a device for the exploitation of the masses by a dominant class: The bourgeoisie owned capital and exploited the labor of the proletariat. Marx predicted that contradictions inherent to capitalism would precipitate a proletarian revolution (which he also advocated, under favorable conditions). The revolution would crush the bourgeoisie and overthrow the capitalist system, create a "dictatorship of the proletariat," and proceed through a period of socialism to the end of a stateless and classless communist society.

Marxism argued that the functioning of the international system was rooted in social and economic factors. Although Marx said little about Latin America beyond a brief tract on Mexico, some of today's theories about the region's international relations recall the earlier Marxist arguments. This has been especially true of neo-Marxist dependency theory and world-system theory (see below). Of more immediate importance, however, were Lenin's interpretations, which have also provided the basis for subsequent theorizing.

Lenin made the most influential extensions of Marx's concepts. His theory of imperialism was set forth most cogently in his 1912 essay, *Imperialism—the Highest Stage of Capitalism*. Lenin addressed the matter of Marx's faulty predictions and argued that the advanced capitalist states had avoided revolution by co-opting their own workers and shifting their exploitation to other lands through an imperialist in-

ternational capitalist system. History nevertheless remained on the side of communist revolution inasmuch as imperialism represented the highest and last stage of
capitalism. To Lenin, the capitalist economic system was the driving force behind
both colonization and war. Economic factors dominated the capitalist states' policies, which were inevitably imperialist. Lenin's influence was even greater after his
seizure of power in Russia in 1917 and the creation of the Soviet Union.

Initial Soviet assessments of Latin American society were heavily dependent on
Marxist ideas of class struggle, with the conclusion that both "objective" and "subjective" conditions necessary for a proletarian revolution were lacking. The region was
too advanced industrially to fit the Marxist precapitalist idea, but it was not describ-
able as a mature capitalist industrial economy either. Thus, Latin America was
unique in Marxian terms; it stood midway between precapitalist and mature capitalist stages. In addition, the middle and upper classes were too strong for a successful
revolution by the small working class, which itself seemed too interested in achieving
middle-class status.

Following World War II, Soviet writers tentatively explored the notion that the region shared some common characteristics with the newly independent, precapitalist,
noncommunist, underdeveloped Third World in Asia and Africa. In particular, U.S.
economic domination offered the possibility of an anti-imperialist revolution, even
though Latin America continued to have unique social and economic characteristics.
Beginning in the mid-1960s Soviet writers emphasized the decline of U.S. influence
in the region.[3] At the same time, traditional Marxism-Leninism in Latin America
was challenged by Latin American guerrilla groups who advocated Trotskyism, Maoism, and especially, Fidelismo. With the end of the cold war, the disappearance of
the Soviet Union, and the general eclipse of communism and its associated intellectuals, Marxist-Leninist theory declined precipitously.

LIBERAL DEVELOPMENTALISM

From the mid-1950s into the 1980s, certain theorists—especially in comparative
politics, history, and development economics—purported to place Latin America
in a larger than regional mold. They did so in terms of development theory and the
concept of modernization. Although the study of IR has since entered a "postmod-
ernist" period, many Latin Americanists (including myself) long before concluded
that development theory failed to explain convincingly Latin American development or to use satisfactorily Latin American data to support general assertions.[4]
Nevertheless, the theory was the basis for important state policies and was prominent in debates over them, so that a consideration of it in the Latin American context is in order.

With the emergence of formerly colonial peoples as new sovereign states over
much of the globe after World War II, certain scholars detected the seeming irrelevance of the West European and North American experiences to the analysis of the
new "developing world." In this sense, development theory provided a necessary cor-

rective to traditional modes of comparative analysis, which tended to be misleading when applied outside the North Atlantic area.

Development theory loosely grouped Latin America with the "emerging nations" of Asia and Africa under the rubrics of "underdeveloped" or "developing," as distinguished from the "developed" nations of Western Europe and North America. The idea of "developed" was equated with the notions of "modern," "industrial," and "Western"; conversely, the "underdeveloped world" was characterized as "traditional," "preindustrial," and "non-Western," with its members often referred to as "new nations." Development theory suggested further that underdeveloped states go through a "transitional" process, moving from traditional to modern societies. Some development theorists suggested that certain imperatives of change moved societies inexorably through a transitional process toward modernity.

Although development theory properly alerted us to the fact that Latin America was fundamentally different from Western Europe and North America, this awareness did not justify an assumption that the region was to be equated with Asia and Africa. Much of the Latin American region shared with other regions the challenges of change: It went through social, economic, and political transformations, experienced frustration associated with economic dependence on the major industrial states, and desired to refrain from involvement in great-power rivalries. But crucial and fundamental differences existed between Latin America and the rest of the developing world, as well as between the region and developed states and between states within Latin America itself.[5] (Asianists and Africanists made similar claims.)

The various classifications associated with developing states—new, non-Western, and industrializing—were highly questionable in the Latin American context. In the first place, Latin America was not composed of "new nations." Most of the states gained their sovereign independence between 1804 and 1824, well over a century before most Asian and African nations "emerged" into statehood. Developmental theorists eventually accommodated this obvious reality, but they still tended not to understand the importance of the established traditions of Latin American statehood. The earlier and different colonial heritage and the longer history of independence, as opposed to the rest of the developing world, combined with a unique sociocultural base to produce a distinct Latin American developmental tradition.

The region was difficult to classify with certainty as either Western or non-Western. The Roman Catholic heritage, European languages, and some other cultural aspects were Western. But non-Western Native American Indian and imported African cultures were interwoven in important patterns. Inasmuch as Spain and Portugal imposed a large degree of their Iberian culture and politics on Latin America, then it could be described as Western. Yet Spain and Portugal were long on the periphery of what was usually posited as Western civilization but could not be described as non-Western in terms of development theory. Furthermore, the Latin American colonial heritage was different from most of the rest of the developing world.

The level of industrialization varied widely in Latin America. Some states, such as Haiti, Ecuador, Bolivia, and others, might have been considered preindustrial. Others, such as Mexico and Argentina, had reached relatively high levels of industrialization, and, most notably, Brazil had constructed a well-diversified and heavily industrialized economy. Furthermore, it did not necessarily follow that every nation with a low industrial level was correspondingly low in social or political modernity, or that industrialized nations were modern in other respects. Uruguay and Costa Rica, for example, reached modern levels of social organization within representative democratic frameworks while their traditional, agriculture-pastoral, nonindustrial economies persisted. Argentina, high in most "indicators of modernity," had been governed by military regimes that may be characterized as primitive. Brazil, the most industrialized regional economy, had continually suffered from a rigid social system and exceptionally high levels of poverty.

Some broader methodological problems were associated with development theory. Latin America (and other regions as well) fit erratically into any theory of unilinear, inexorable movement from traditionalism to modernism. The assumption that there was such a steady progression from the old to the new may be criticized as a form of historicism, the idea of inevitable deterministic "forces of history." It also implied ethnocentrism, the view that developing nations ought to become like the model, equating modernism with old, Western, industrialized states. With regard to Latin America, the region's history revealed no inevitable progression along a traditional-modern continuum. Latin American economic, social, and political traditions proved remarkably resistant to change.

This view does not deny that societal change is susceptible to theoretical explanation, nor does it argue against inter-area comparisons of the process. Rather, it suggests that development theory as offered was only partially useful. Today other theories in comparative politics and political economy have superseded the development theory discussed here; they are taken up below. The point to be made now is that Latin America and the Caribbean should be included in the broader perspective of the international system, but its special place in that system must be recognized. As a theoretical as well as a policy matter, the region also deserves attention on its own terms.

Development theory provided the basis for a significant portion of the Latin American policies of the United States and of Europe. U.S. policy makers after World War II assumed that economic growth led to stable democratic societies. Many held the view that democracy must be based on a free-enterprise economic system. During the Alliance for Progress period, actually beginning in 1959 and effectively ended in 1965, economic planning combined with social reform was stressed. A further assumption, reflected in aid programs, was that Latin American political violence was linked to poverty and that economic development would deter such political "instability." Development came to be subordinated to "anticommunism." In 1968 the adoption of the Nixon "low profile" policy overtly abandoned developmentalism. It was rediscovered and amended by the Reagan administration and provided the initial rationale behind the Caribbean Basin Initiative and some other policies in Central America. Developmentalism also continued to be the favored alternative to coercion in the U.S. debate over Latin American policy at the time, as well as in the advice coming from Europe and Latin America.

A debate over the relationship between foreign economic assistance and political and social change in recipient states was carried on in the context of development theory. These problems had (and may still have) important implications for U.S. policies, as well as for those of other actors, such as the European Union and the international lending institutions. Critics of developmentalism charged that economic aid, either purposely or unwittingly, supported the Latin American status quo rather than stimulated reform. Other analysts suggested that economic aid would lead to violence by breaking down existing social structures. Either connection between economic development and political change seems tenuous. The United States attempted with little success to influence political forms with economic aid; the failure of such experimentation under the Alliance for Progress is primary evidence. Although a connection doubtless exists between economics and politics, and although Latin American economic needs are susceptible to influence from external states, the lesson seems to be that economic development cannot substitute for political development. Whereas technology and investment capital can be exported to facilitate economic development, the institutions and traditions of representative and social democracy cannot. Evidence suggests that political forms must evolve according to national configurations rather than by copying foreign models.

DEPENDENCY THEORIES

Structuralist Dependency

In the immediate aftermath of World War II, the Economic Commission for Latin America (ECLA) published a comprehensive analysis of economic development in the region. That analysis, inspired by the emerging theories of the Argentine economist Raúl Prebisch, marked the formal introduction of structuralist economic theory, which challenged orthodox approaches. The structuralists were the intellectual offspring of Latin American economists, led by Prebisch and including the Mexican Víctor Urquidi and the Brazilian Celso Furtado.[6] Their theories gained increasing favor as the basis for Latin American economic policies until they, too, were challenged and fell out of favor. The theory of structural economic dependency was often at the center of ongoing debates about the economic aspects of Latin American development and related policies.

Prebisch's structuralist theory visualized the world economy in terms of a "center-periphery" structure, with industrialized states forming the center and underdeveloped ones the periphery. Underdevelopment, the theory said, was perpetuated by this structure primarily because the center sold increasingly expensive manufactured goods to the periphery in return for raw materials at increasingly unfavorable terms for underdeveloped markets. The unfair terms of trade, Prebisch said, were a form of colonialism, a dependence escapable only through the industrialization and sustained growth of the peripheral economies. Prebisch advocated prescriptions for economic development on a regional and global scale, involving convergent domestic and international reforms and measures. Prebisch advocated that the Latin American states reduce their external dependency through the integration of their economies and that they broaden the size of their markets for local industry and join with other producers of primary exports in commodity agreements, limiting supply and increasing the prices received. He appealed to the center for help in the way of public economic assistance, private investment, and trade preferences; but he emphasized that poor nations must depend primarily on themselves and not rely on external aid. He said that external cooperation was important as a means of supplementing and stimulating internal action but should not be considered a substitute for it.

Structuralists argued that the causes of Latin American inflation were to be found in economic structural (institutional) rigidities and inelasticities. They concluded that monetary policy alone could not reduce inflation over the long run or stimulate economic growth. They advocated the structural reform of traditional institutions that proved incapable of adjusting to change. Although Latin American industrialization, population growth, and urbanization increased the demand for food, the archaic land tenure system (*latifundia*) had not been able to increase the food supply significantly, with inflationary results. Industrial institutions and foreign trade patterns were also structured so as to increase inflation and retard growth. When imports grew faster than the export of primary mineral and agricultural products, balance-of-payments problems were created.

Structuralists had little faith in monetary policies, saying that austerity retarded growth, and they looked to government to bring about basic reforms. They advocated agrarian reform and government credits for the modernizing of agricultural methods; government policies to encourage export diversification, including industrial products; heavy taxes on imported luxury goods and inefficiently utilized land holdings; and more public investment in the capital goods industry. They recognized the need to import capital in money and kind but argued that Latin America should pursue import substitution industrialization so as to become less dependent on imports. They were among the strongest advocates of Latin American economic integration.

In the 1980s Latin Americans began to abandon structuralism and the attendant policies. As redemocratization in the 1980s came to be widely accompanied by economic neoliberalism (see below), policies relying on state intervention into the economy were discredited and eventually replaced with laissez-faire policies of reduced government controls, privatization of state-owned enterprises, free trade, and openness to external investment. Economic integration was revived but reformed and sought to seek parallel free-trade arrangements with the United States and Europe.[7]

Neo-Marxist Dependency

A major school of dependency theory employed a generally Marxist frame of reference. In an important sense it was the "radical school" that offered an array of theories and prescriptions for economic development over the years.[8] The theory went far beyond the essentially economic parameters of structuralism, however, to construct further a general sociopolitical theory of international relations. These dependency theorists also saw an international structure of the core and periphery. They tended to agree with structuralists that archaic institutions were at the root of underdevelopment, emphasizing that the existing "modern" social sectors exploit national productivity rather than generate it for development. They rejected the structuralists' "reform the system" approach, however, and advocated a socialist revolution. Radicals would have eliminated the existing private agricultural system, instituted state ownership of large industries, and either excluded foreign investment or allowed it to operate only under the strictest controls. In the 1980s they called for renunciation of the foreign debt or for greatly reduced service payments.

These solutions were attempted to differing degrees by certain different Latin American regimes, including the revolutionary Castro rule in Cuba, the elected government of Salvador Allende in Chile, and the military socialist juntas in Peru and Bolivia. The Sandinista government in Nicaragua and the APRA government in Peru also advocated and in some ways were able to pursue such policies. Some liberation theologians subscribed to this dependency theory.

A basic premise of the theory was that Latin American economic development was determined by the interests and activities of external capitalist states and multinational corporations (MNCs) operating in the world capitalist market. Latin American economies were dependent because they were conditioned by external capitalist forces over which they had little control. Economic dependence was seen as an inevitable result of international capitalist politics, with foreign investment—a corollary to the expansionist tendencies of capitalist economies, especially in the United States—invariably detrimental to the recipient. The dependency relationship ultimately was conflictual; in something of a restatement of the Leninist theory of imperialism, conflict was said to be the result of the search by industrial capitalist societies for raw materials, insufficiently supplied at home, and for outlets for manufactured products and capital, which were in an overabundance at home.

Economic dependence was said to have had a profound effect on internal Latin American economies—stagnation, unemployment, income inequality, and disequilibrium were seen as directly related to the underdeveloped state's subordinate position under the dominant capitalist states and MNCs. These economic effects in turn helped shape social and political structures. International inequalities retarded domestic economic development, consequently weakening power bases for the establishment of egalitarian social policies. Some dependency theorists spoke of "internal colonialism" within Latin American nations, whereby resources were continuously transferred away from majority underdeveloped social sectors to the minority advanced sector. The latter was linked to foreign capitalists and the international capitalist economy, thus intensifying unequal internal distribution of income and social rewards. Dependistas further argued that external military relationships were responsible for Latin American militarism—the widening gap between classes caused national disintegration that led to the installation of military regimes for the support of oligarchic or bourgeois interests.

Many other Marxist theorists implicitly rejected the idea of dependency. For example, studies by Marxist scholars at the Institute of Latin American Studies at the Academy of Sciences of the USSR (Moscow) emphasized the growing independence of many Latin American states from U.S. domination.[9] This position was ideologically consistent with Leninism, as anti-imperialism had to assume that independence was possible. It was also consonant with cautious Soviet policies when they emphasized diplomacy with Latin American states rather than subversion or revolution.

Critics challenged the assumptions of dependency theory. Many of them acknowledged that the theory contained elements of truth, but they argued that it had major logical and empirical fallacies. They contested the assertions that economic dependence was a necessary consequence of capitalist economies and that private foreign investment in Latin America invariably was exploitive, pointing out that powerful states, whether capitalist or noncapitalist, had always imposed economic dependence on weaker ones. They further noted that dependency theorists ignored the possibility of Cuba's economic dependency on the Soviet Union and confined their observations to relationships dominated by capitalist powers.[10] Attention may also be called to cleavages within Latin America, where relatively weaker states complained of domination by the stronger ones. For example, such claims were common among the majority of members of the Latin American Free Trade Association against their colleagues: Mexico, Brazil, and Argentina. This position was also taken by small states in the Southern Cone subsystem, which had little to do with the world capitalist economy. The basis for dependency was not capitalism but a disparity of several power dimensions in which weak actors were vulnerable to exploitation in whatever kind of markets they operated.

WORLD-SYSTEM THEORY

The original theorists of the world-system school of analysis defined that system as the global capitalist order that developed after about 1500 and eventually embraced the entire world. For them the European discovery and subsequent domination of the Americas was the defining element in the worldwide spread of capitalism. Immanuel Wallerstein is the most prominent world-system theorist.[11] He developed a comprehensive framework of world history that grew out of neo-Marxist dependency theory, but in time it superseded the declining dependency school and stood on its own terms.

World-system theory denies the validity of state-centric models for analysis, since, it says, the state is merely an artifice as an instrument of the key source of power—the elite capitalist classes. Wallerstein also chides state-centrism for its short-term historical perspective, which embraces too little of human experience. World-system theory opposes modernization (developmental) theory for its misguided focus on internal societal ("national") dynamics and their comparative analysis, since they are in fact the outcome of global historical developments. Thus it contradicts development policy—political, economic, and social reform—as an impossibility. Finally, Wallerstein and his followers contest the conjectures of other world historians who also have been dissatisfied with state-centrism but have applied civilization approaches. Their most notable target in IR scholarship is Arnold Toynbee, who argued that humankind had expanded geographically over the centuries from an initial core to a number of comparable civilizations and whose rise and fall had followed essentially parallel paths.[12] World-system theory posits transcivilizational patterns in world history but stresses the primacy of historical materialism as the essential concept.

Wallerstein argued that the appearance of capitalism and the rise of European imperialism were not characteristics of a new period in the evolution of interstate power relations revolving around autonomous state actors; instead, they had created a new and increasingly integrated global system. That system was shaped by the "historically imposed logic" of evolving capital markets. Wallerstein asserted the creation of the first "world economy" in history, which was distinct from the prior politically imposed "world empires." States and societies were defined in terms of their positions within the world system, itself a hierarchical, political-economic-social structure. The core-periphery concept, introduced by structural dependency and shared by neo-Marxist dependency, was further adopted and adjusted by world-system theory: The core at the center of the system comprised the most powerful industrialized states led by dominant capitalist classes; the periphery constituted the weakest and most exploited societies; and the intervening level, the semi-periphery, included those entities with a degree of internal authority but incapable of competing on a par with the core units.

According to Wallerstein, three developments had been essential to the establishment of the capitalist world economy: the expansion of the geographical scope of the capitalist world, the development of different methods of labor control, and the creation of strong state machineries in what would become the core states. In William McNeil's assessment, this perspective carried Marx's historical materialism to the global level: The world system, the consequence of historical materialism, was a single and complex "division of labor" in which social classes and their interests were both national and international; thus dynamics within individual societies were understood in terms of the evolution of unequal distribution of economic benefits on the world-system level.[13]

The New World, with Latin America closely linked as a separate region, loomed large in the theoretical design.[14] The world system and the Americas were simultaneously born in the sixteenth century as "geosocial constructs." The European discovery and colonization of the Americas were the "constitutive act" of the modern world system. They were the prime testing ground for labor control methods and the model for the entire world system as it evolved over the centuries. For the first three centuries of the modern world system all of the Americas were subordinated in all respects as formal colonies to a few European states. The United States progressively moved from the periphery to the semi-periphery to the core to post–World War II world-system hegemony. But Latin America remained on the periphery of the capitalist world economy throughout the nineteenth and twentieth centuries; independence, rather than undoing "coloniality," had "merely transformed its outer form."

Revisionist world-system theorists have disagreed on how far back in history their basic constructs apply. Their position also raises questions about the neo-Marxist basis of the world system (even though most—but not all—revisionists are in the Marxist position). Andre Gunder Frank, a founder of the neo-Marxist dependency school, had joined Wallerstein as a capitalist world-system advocate but then became the leading revisionist.[15] Frank and others have traced economic cycles backward in time and discovered earlier beginnings of the world system, of which they consider the capitalist world system to be a continuation. They claim to see the world through the same basic analytic framework as Wallerstein; but they argue that all of the elements associated with the current 500-year-old world system had their counterparts as long as 5,000 years ago (some revisionists claim as much as 8,000 years). Historical materialism with a capital-accumulating core, they say, has existed in different locations throughout history, independently of particular modes of production. The modern capitalist system is only the most recent form and is perhaps a passing occurrence. Prior to 1492, the "New World" was home to some world-systems elements of its own, long before its incorporation into the modern world system. Wallerstein retorts that the Americas were not merely assimilated into a pre-existing, capital-accumulating economy, that there would not have been such an economy without the Americas, and that the system requires the particular capitalist mode of production.

William McNeil attempts to resolve some problems in the revisionist position, in particular the inexactness of the term "world system" and the role of Marxist concepts.[16] He acknowledges that a global market arose only after 1500, so that the name "world system" for ancient and medieval relationships is an obvious misnomer. But, he says, if the modern process took centuries to complete, then the earlier lack of globalism does not really matter inasmuch as the interrelatedness expressed in world-system thought actually shaped the past and future. With regard to the Marxist requirement of the uniqueness of modern capitalism, the world-system framework "seems fully capable of absorbing and profiting from a Marxist (or ex-Marxist) stream."

MODERNISM, MONETARISM, AND NEOLIBERALISM

The political-economic alternatives to dependency and world-system theories are less abstract in their analysis and prescriptions, although they have also been associated with forms of Latin American developmental nationalism. The traditional or "classical" view of what came to be known as "economic development" dated from the middle to the late nineteenth century in most Latin American states. That was the period when Latin American elites began to lead a conscious thrust for economic modernization, usually in alliance with foreign entrepreneurs. This position was part of the category of nationalism that has been labeled "modernism."[17] Economic development was seen as requiring the attraction of foreign capital by means of cooperation. Modernization, in concert with foreign assistance, was actively encouraged by certain elites who sought increased wealth for themselves as well as a cultural milieu comparable to that of the world's most prestigious nations. Modernism continued in recent years in modified form as a school of economic thought sometimes labeled the "neoclassical" model.

An important economic policy debate developed after World War II when monetarists challenged the emerging structuralist dependency school.[18] This debate was especially intense in the late 1950s and early 1960s, until structuralism carried the day. Monetarist thinking was later identified with the orthodox economics championed by the International Monetary Fund (IMF), and with MNCs and the governments of industrialized states. The monetarist theory essentially argued that price stability is the main prerequisite for economic growth. Therefore, the major task in Latin American economic development was to control the inflation that retards long-term investment, undermines wages, leads to labor strikes, and in general inspires social and political instability as well as economic chaos. The principal causes of inflation were expansive monetary and fiscal policies and the increased role of government as the promoter of development through public spending and deficit financing. The monetarist solution was to return to a free-market system by increasing the economic role of the private sector and reducing government intervention. Disciplined monetary policies reducing aggregate demands—such as rejecting large wage demands, restricting credit, raising taxes, and reducing government spending and employment—sufficed to reduce inflation. Such austerity programs were said to decrease the demand for consumer goods imports, which increased exports and relieved balance-of-payment pressures. Control of inflation attracts foreign investment, a crucial source of investment capital.

Neoliberalism, which caught hold in the 1980s and into the 1990s, is something of the inheritor of modernism and monetarism. It became dominant among the new generation of democratic leaders, and in turn is a rejection of structuralism. The thinking is rooted in the economic liberalism of the nineteenth century, which was closely linked to the political liberalism of the times (with its own origins in the seventeenth and eighteenth centuries). In the political sphere the emphasis was on democracy, individual dignity and freedom (liberty), constitutionalism and republicanism, civil liberties, and limited government. In the economic arena the stress was on individual initiative, free enterprise, free trade, and opposition to state intervention in the economy (laissez-faire). Both political and economic liberty were to be achieved through a minimalist, and therefore liberal, state. In Latin America, this dominant ideology of the capitalist, industrializing world was challenged by mercantilism, a theory carried over from the colonial era that emphasized state-centered and directed economies and high levels of international trade protectionism. Inasmuch as those structures continued after World War II, they were sometimes referred to as neomercantilist.

As the cold war faded and then ended, and trade and investment assumed primacy in the international system, most Latin American leaders embraced the new liberalism in their international economic relations. It is reflected in such actions as the privatization of state enterprises, assistance to private sectorial development, the lowering of barriers to trade, and the embracing of intraregional free trade as well as of trade with the outside world (most notably the United States). These policies further reflect a number of Latin American attitudinal changes: They are generally less defensive toward and more willing to cooperate with the outside world, are eager to reintegrate with and be an integral part of whatever new global system finally emerges, are disillusioned with the old defensive nationalism and economic models (which involved import substitution industrialization and protectionism and which are seen as failed), and are willing to apply alternative models for economic reactivation.[19] All of this has been facilitated by the return to democracy and civilian rule and by its increasing, if tenuous, popular legitimacy.

Neoliberalism has its strong critics. Some fear that free trade with the United States will lead to another kind of economic dependency. Others stress the domestic consequences—that even if neoliberalism has macroeconomic benefits and certain sectors may prosper from it (usually those who already hold most of the wealth), too many other people remain poor and have only marginal opportunities for betterment.[20]

PLURALISM

At the beginning of the 1970s a growing "pluralist" (or "multicentric") perspective of the international system and its actors emerged as another important theoretical challenge to the dominant realist, state-centric model. The end of the cold war and subsequent developments stimulated a resurgence of analysis from pluralist perspectives.[21] Pluralism, an old philosophical concept, reflects suspicion of any single system that claims to explain the world and advocates instead multiple perspectives as the way to truth. Pluralism is heterogeneous in its theoretical inclusiveness. In the case of the study of IR, pluralists are defined in terms of their mutual discontent with state-centrism for its neglect of transnational actors and relations, and in terms of their insistence that the interstate perspective of the international system be combined with transnational phenomena to produce one of a global system of "complex interdependence" (see Chapter 1). Latin Americanists had long understood or at least sensed the importance of transnational phenomena, which had always been part of what evolved into the Latin American and Caribbean subsystem, but without solid theoretical underpinnings. Today students of IR and of the region generally assume the significance of transnational phenomena, although they sharply debate the theoretical significance.

Pluralism, rather than a single parsimonious theory, is a relatively inclusive category of approaches within a framework of generally shared assumptions but with differences over important particulars. It embraces a wide range of nonstate phenomena, so that at the heart of research efforts and conceptual debates are the relationships between states and societies. Consequently, the pluralist effort in method is broadly interdisciplinary, even fragmented, as contributors from economics, comparative and international politics, sociology, anthropology, history, and psychology, as well as the humanities and theology, examine the relevance of various phenomena to the international system. Nevertheless, a number of theoretical implications flow from the pluralist outlook.

Transnationalism

On the system level the key pluralist concept is transnationalism. James Rosenau defines transnationalism as "the process whereby international relations as conducted by governments have been supplemented by relations among private individuals, groups, and societies that can and do have important consequences for the course of events."[22] Transnational relations involve at least one significant actor that is not an agent of a government or international governmental organization; the latter may or may not be participants. Thus states and intergovernmental organizations are joined by transnational actors to engage in a wide variety of activities and transactions having multiple effects and immense consequences.

The assortment of transnational actors is highly diverse. It has included international business enterprises and multinational corporations, international nongovernmental organizations of all kinds (educational foundations, humanitarian and voluntary organizations, and professional associations, to name but a few categories), international political party associations and labor movements, the Holy See and the transnational Roman Catholic Church network, other churches, immigrants and refugees, travelers and tourists, communications media, entertainment and sports enterprises, educational institutions, the accompanying business people, journalists, artists, entertainers, athletes, educators, students, scientists, and a wide range of other individuals—as well as pirates, privateers, buccaneers, revolutionaries, terrorists, guerrilla groups, mercenaries, drug traffickers, and organized criminal elements.

Pluralists sometimes consider international governmental organizations, dating from the nineteenth century, to be transnational actors. Realists have long acknowledged IGOs as parts of the interstate system inasmuch as they were created by and served as instruments of the states. Certain pluralists also include transgovernmental actors, in which linkages or coalitions are forged among official government representatives that may bypass central government control. Many theorists consider this phenomena difficult to demonstrate and probably exceptional.

With the variety among transnational actors and the resources available to them, their level of influence and the outcomes of relations vary considerably. Certain actors are in fact relatively autonomous units in the system itself. As a general matter, transnational actors have engaged in a wide variety of activities and transactions having multiple effects and immense consequences. Goods, money, people, organizations, information, ideas, images, beliefs, doctrines, and popular culture flow across and transcend state boundaries, creating their own political, economic, ethnic, social, and cultural patterns that are by and large not subject to state control. Most phenomena are closely identified with domestic society. Most issues are not appropriate for the use of state force or necessarily responsive to diplomacy.

Globalism and Modernism

Transnationalization is further comprehended in association with the concept of globalization. As used in this book, globalization does not mean a literally globalized order. It rather alludes to the continuing, dynamic, irregular, uneven, multilineal, often contradictory growth of transnational phenomena at all system levels. Although globalization tends to link individual societies, they are experiencing and responding to the changes associated with globalization in different ways. In sum, globalization is not a single process affecting the world as a whole; it is instead creating an overlapping patchwork of linkages and relationships.

Globalization is understood as a consequence of modernization, in the sense of the development of the modern world. A pluralist definition of modernization is "the social, political, and economic prerequisites for, and consequences of, industrialization and technological development."[23] The various systemic levels have had a common exposure to modernism; what has varied is the nature of that exposure and the consequences of it.

Analysts debate the beginnings of modernization, but all agree that it was in full swing by the nineteenth century and continued unabated in the twentieth century, increasing rapidly after World War II and accelerating in the early 1980s. Modernization has included such factors as the earlier industrial and scientific revolutions and the more recent electronic discoveries and applications. Industrialization gave rise to mass consumption, foreign investment, movement of people, and modern ideologies. The growth of scientific technology made improvements in transportation, communications, and information flows, which were spectacularly advanced by the electronics age. These developments have helped tie the world together by surmounting geography and political boundaries. They have furthered the rapid flow of culture, ideas, financial resources, commerce, energy sources, migrants, and tourists. They have facilitated the development of a global economy, the spread of representative democracy and respect for human rights, and the formation of religious networks—as well as environmental degradation, the drug traffic, insurgency, and international crime. These are all signs of complex interdependence in the senses of both interconnectedness and vulnerability. In terms of the international system, modernization has so transformed societies and linked them that the distinction between domestic and foreign policy has become blurred. This has increasingly created more opportunities for subnational entities to form transnational contacts (for good, ill, or neutral purposes).

Foreign Policy Analysis

The pluralist category embraces those foreign policy analysts who see the rational model associated with state-centrism as fundamentally flawed in assuming decisions to be the result of consistent monolithic state processes overseen by logically reasoning decision makers. Theorists in this category have constructed alternative theories emphasizing the centrality of fallible human beings, and have argued that the human element in decision-making not only intrudes on but departs from rational processes. No satisfactory overarching alternative pluralist theory of foreign policy has emerged to explain the behavior of decision makers, and in important ways the designers of competing approaches consider them mutually exclusive. Nevertheless, the theoretical effort has produced models that, when taken together, alert us to other factors that may influence decisional processes.

Cognitive theories rooted in psychological and anthropological concepts address what and how people perceive, think, and know. Particularly important for these theories when they are applied to foreign policy analysis is the response of decision makers to perceptions and images that they hold of the world, their own societies, and themselves, and the way they form foreign policy motivations, aspirations, and expectations in response to stimuli from both intrasocietal and extrasocietal environments. Cognitive analysts distinguish between the decision maker's objective environment (reality) and psychological environment (the perception or image of reality), and they address the difficulty of reconciling the two. Another group of theorists, advocating a *bureaucratic and organizational process model* of decision-making, focuses on the psychology of group behavior. They contend that foreign policies most often are the result of group dynamics and institutional biases within competing bureaucracies and other organizations central to the policy process. They focus on the roles of governmental subunits or nongovernmental subnational actors with distinct foreign policy interests and perceptions and their own preferred strategies and tactics. Critics of this approach say it aspires to explain too much from a narrow conceptual base, but they acknowledge that it does offer insights about the limitations of groups that make it a useful corollary to more comprehensive models. The *political process model* assumes that foreign policy decisions are made within the broad context of the overall political system, thus taking into account a wide range of factors (and thus denying the notion of a unitary state-actor model). The model essentially operationalizes the systems perspective on the state level: A variety of influences that arise in the intrasocietal and extrasocietal environments are filtered through the political system and brought to bear on decision makers. These influences are converted through a decision process (which may include some combination of rational, perceptual, bureaucratic-organizational, or other considerations) into policy and action. A political process approach gives due consideration to transnational elements that influence official foreign policy-making. It also accounts for transsocietal actors who, via external linkages, have policy preferences that bypass official political leadership.

NOTES

1. This point is made by John C. Wahlke and Alex N. Dragnich, eds., *Government and Politics* (New York: Random House, 1966), 16–17. They cite, for illustrative purposes, Book V of Aristotle's *Politics*, which proposes knowledge about the causes of revolution. That knowledge may

serve very different purposes, such as those of a tyrant protecting his power against rebellious subjects, of a democratic leader working for stability in an open society, of an ego-gratifying agitator manipulating the revolution, or of a leader using revolution as a means to human progress.

2. Jack C. Plano and Roy Olton, *The International Relations Dictionary*, 4th ed. (New York: Holt, Rinehart, Winston, 1988), 18ff, from whom the dichotomy designation is borrowed, offer useful synoptic definitions and discussions. For a clearly presented extended discussion of realism, see Paul R. Viotti and Mark V. Kauppi, *International Relations Theory: Realism, Pluralism, Globalism*, 2d ed. (New York: Macmillan, 1993), chapter 2.

3. For a Marxist analysis of Latin America's international relations by a well-known Soviet analyst, see Anatoly Glinkin, *Inter-American Relations from Bolivar to the Present* (Moscow: Progress Publishers, 1990).

4. See essays by Douglas A. Chalmers and Philippe Schmitter in Douglas A. Chalmers, ed., *Changing Latin America: New Interpretations of Its Politics and Society* (Philadelphia: *Proceedings of the Academy of Political Science* 30, 1972); John D. Martz, "The Place of Latin America in the Study of Comparative Politics," *Journal of Politics* 28 (February 1966): 57–80; and Alfred Stepan, "Political Development Theory: The Latin American Experience." *Journal of International Affairs* 20, no. 2 (1966): 63–74.

5. Howard J. Wiarda, ed., *Politics and Social Change in Latin America: Still a Distinct Tradition?*, 3d ed. (Boulder, Colo.: Westview Press, 1992) makes a strong case for a distinct Latin American developmental tradition.

6. Some works by Raúl Prebisch are: *Capitalismo periférico: crisis y transformación* (México, D. F.: Fondo de Cultura Económica, 1981); *Change and Development: Latin America's Great Task* (Washington, D.C.: Inter-American Development Bank; New York: Praeger, 1970); *The Economic Development of Latin America and Its Principal Problems* (New York: United Nations, 1950); "Five Stages in My Thinking on Development," in *Pioneers in Development*, ed. Gerald M. Meier and Dudley Seers (New York: Oxford University Press); *Nueva política comercial para el desarrollo* (México: Fondo de Cultura Económica, 1964); *Towards a Dynamic Development Policy for Latin America* (New York: United Nations, 1963). Some studies by Víctor L. Urquidi are: *The Challenge of Development in Latin America* (New York: Praeger, 1964); and *Free Trade and Economic Integration in Latin America* (Berkeley: University of California Press, 1962).

7. Osvaldo Sunkel, ed., *Development from Within: Toward a Neostructuralist Approach for Latin America* (Boulder, Colo.: Lynne Rienner Publishers, 1993) offers an updated alternative to neoliberalism.

8. Three works by the militant pioneer dependency theorist, Andre Gunder Frank, are: *Capitalism and Underdevelopment in Latin America: Historical Studies of Chile and Brazil* (New York: Monthly Review Press, 1967); *Latin America: Underdevelopment or Revolution; Essays on the Development of Underdevelopment and the Immediate Enemy* (New York: Monthly Review Press, 1969); and *Lumpenbourgeoise-Lumpendevelopment: Dependence, Class, and Politics in Latin America* (New York: Monthly Review Press, 1972). He was followed by Susanne Bodenheimer, *The Ideology of Developmentalism: The American Paradigm-Surrogate for Latin American Studies* (Beverly Hills, Calif.: Sage, 1971); Fernando Henrique Cardoso and Enzo Faletto, *Dependency and Development in Latin America* (Berkeley: University of California Press, 1979); James Petras, ed., *Latin America: From Dependence to Revolution* (New York: John Wiley, 1973); Theotonio dos Santos, *Dependencia económica y cambio revolucionario en América Latina* (Caracas: Ed. Nueva Izquierda, 1970); A. Syzmanski, *The Logic of Imperialism* (New York: Praeger, 1981); and C. Thomas, *The Rise of the Authoritarian State in Peripheral Societies* (New York: Monthly Review Press, 1984).

9. See note 3 above; Glinkin was associated with the Institute of Latin American Studies at the Academy of Sciences.

10. General works analyzing and criticizing dependency theory are Frank Bonilla and Robert Girling, eds., *Structures of Dependency* (Stanford: Stanford University Press, 1973); Ronald Chilcote and Joel Edelstein, eds., *Latin America: The Struggle with Dependency and Beyond* (New York: Halsted, 1974; and José Ocampo et al., *Dependency Theory* (Riverside, Calif.: Latin American Perspectives, 1976). Cogent critiques are David Ray, "The Dependency Model of Latin American Underdevelopment: Three Basic Fallacies." *Journal of Inter-American Studies* 15 (February 1973): 4–20; and Tony Smith, "The Underdevelopment of Development Literature: The Case of Dependency Theory." *World Politics* 31 (January 1979): 247–288. Robert A. Packenham, *The Dependency Movement: Scholarship and Politics in Development Studies* (Cambridge: Harvard University Press, 1992) says (and laments) that dependency theory is alive in its long-term politicizing of the social sciences.

11. A sociologist and Africanist, Wallerstein's pioneer work is *The Modern World System,* 3 vols. (New York: Academic Press, 1976, 1980; San Diego: University of California at San Diego, 1989).

12. William A. McNeil, "Introduction," in *The World System: Five Hundred or Five Thousand Years?* ed. Andre Gunder Frank and Barry Gills (London: Routledge, 1993).

13. McNeil, "Introduction."

14. Aníbal Quijano and Immanuel Wallerstein, "Americanity as a Concept, or the Americas in the Modern World System," *International Social Science Journal* 134, (November 1992): 549–557—a concise overview of the authors' view of the critical position of the Americas in the world-system theoretical construct.

15. An important source is Frank and Gills, *The World System: Five Hundred or Five Thousand Years?* In addition to those of the editors, contributions are made by nine other revisionist world-system analysts, with a rebuttal and restatement by Wallerstein. See also Terence Hopkins, Immanuel Wallerstein et al., *The Age of Transition: The Trajectory of the World System, 1945–2045* (Atlantic Highlands, N.J.: Zed Books, 1996) and Thomas Richard Shannon, *An Introduction to the World System Perpsectives* (Boulder, Colo.: Westview Press, 1989).

16. McNeil, "Introduction."

17. Arthur P. Whitaker and David C. Jordan, *Nationalism in Contemporary Latin America* (New York: Free Press, 1966).

18. Monetarism and traditionalism are represented by Roberto de Oliveira Campos, *Reflections on Latin American Development* (Austin: University of Texas Press, 1967); and Adalbert Krieger Vasena and Javier Pazos, *Latin America* (London: E. Benn, 1973).

19. See Isaac Cohen, "Economic Questions," in *The United States and Latin America: Redefining U.S. Purposes in the Post-Cold War Era*, ed. G. Pope Atkins (Austin: Lyndon B. Johnson School of Public Affairs, 1992).

20. William C. Smith, Carlos H. Acuña, and Eduardo A. Gamarra, eds., *Latin American Political Economy in the Age of Neoliberal Reform: Theoretical and Comparative Perspectives for the 1990s* (New Brunswick, N.J.: Transaction Press, 1994) is a sharp criticism of neoliberalism that advocates rethinking Latin American political economy.

21. A highly influential early work was Robert O. Keohane and Joseph S. Nye Jr., eds., *Transnational Relations and World Politics* (Cambridge: Harvard University Press, 1972), followed by Robert O. Keohane and Joseph S. Nye Jr., *Power and Interdependence: World Politics in Transition* (Boston: Little, Brown, and Co., 1977). Also among the earlier important works were Richard W. Mansbach, Yale H. Ferguson, and Donald E. Lampert, *The Web of World Pol-*

itics: Non-State Actors in the Global System (Englewood Cliffs, N.J.: Prentice-Hall, 1976), which includes a chapter on the Latin American region; Edward L. Morse, *Modernization and the Transformation of International Relations* (New York: Free Press, 1976); James N. Rosenau, *Linkage Politics* (New York: Free Press, 1969); and James N. Rosenau, *The Study of Global Interdependence: Essays on the Transnationalization of World Affairs* (New York: Nichols, 1980). Some more recent works broadly analyzing transnationalization and globalization from various perspectives are Michael Banks and Martin Shaw, eds., *State and Society in International Relations* (New York: St. Martin's Press, 1991); Hans-Henrik Holm and George Sorensen, *Whose World Order? Uneven Globalization and the End of the Cold War* (Boulder, Colo.: Westview Press, 1995); Thomas Risse-Kappen, ed., *Bringing Transnational Relations Back in: Non-State Actors, Domestic Structures and International Institutions* (Cambridge, U.K.: Cambridge University Press, 1995); James N. Rosenau, *Along the Domestic-Foreign Frontier: Exploring Governance in a Turbulent World* (Cambridge: Cambridge University Press, 1997); James N. Rosenau, *Turbulence in World Politics: A Theory of Change and Continuity* (Princeton: Princeton University Press, 1990); and Robert K. Schaeffer, *Understanding Globalization: The Social Consequences of Political, Economic, and Environmental Change* (Lanham, Md.: Rowman and Littlefield, 1977).

22. Rosenau, *The Study of Global Interdependence*, 1.

23. See the helpful discussion in Viotti and Kauppi, *International Relations Theory: Realism, Pluralism, Globalism*, 7–8, chap. 3.

PART TWO

■

The Nation-State Actors

The next three chapters analyze the foreign policies of the Latin American and Caribbean states and the external states most important to the regional subsystem. The treatments focus on classifying the policy orientations and related policy doctrines adopted and on identifying the essential influences on the decision makers who adopted them. They take into consideration, as appropriate to the state or group of states involved, the decisional environment for the choices made in terms of the most important external, intrasocietal, and political system factors. Limited reference is made with respect to political system structures for foreign policy-making. More detailed discussions of specific policy decisions and the execution of policy through various instruments on the part of all actors are presented in other parts of the book.

CHAPTER FOUR

■

The Latin American
and Caribbean States

Comparative foreign policy analysis of the Latin American and Caribbean states encounters the problem of dealing with the thirty-three entities composing the regional sector. In a sense their foreign policies are as diverse as the countries themselves. Nevertheless, the regional states share certain basic elements, so that we may make some generalizations that help us understand their foreign policy behavior. Certain aspects of three broad areas are considered from the perspectives of the regional states themselves that shed light on foreign policy choices: (1) the external environment within which foreign policies are formulated and executed and that impinge on policy formulation; (2) intrasocietal and political system elements that also shape the options for decision makers; and (3) specific policy orientations adopted toward the outside world as a result of the above influences brought to bear on the decisional process. Such an analysis reveals a number of common traits as well as important distinctions. The elements investigated in this chapter also serve to present a significant part of the milieu within which outsiders operate when Latin America is the object of their policies. The purpose of the chapter, however, is to analyze foreign policy from the point of view of the Latin American and Caribbean states themselves, in terms of how they pursue their own interests and attempt to satisfy their own needs.[1]

THE EXTRASOCIETAL ENVIRONMENT

Decision makers' perceptions of the world and their state's position in it exerts a substantial influence on what they determine is possible for them to do. From a global perspective, all of the Latin American and Caribbean states have been lesser ranking in terms of power in the international system, so that on extraregional levels a number of frequently similar policy ends and means may be postulated. Within the region, however, considerable diversity with regard to capability is evident. At one extreme is Brazil, unquestionably the most powerful Latin American country with at times the desire and potential to move into world power ranks, followed closely by middle powers such as Mexico and Argentina. At the other extreme are small countries severely lacking in relative capability. Between these limits are a broad range of middle-power states. Thus, in intraregional relations relative capability levels vary so greatly that no such policy commonality is evident. Nevertheless, yet those relations have a regularity that distinguishes Latin America and the Caribbean from the rest of the world.

For the regional decision makers, the linkages between the international and intrasocietal environments are crucial to foreign policy choices. In this context, decision-making is understood as the mutual impact of the political system and extrasocietal structures and processes. Much of this book delineates what in effect is the external environment within which Latin American and Caribbean states must operate, and the details need not be repeated here. A historical reality has been the regional states' relative weakness in relations with world powers. European states and the United States, in different times and places, have been primary factors in the decisional processes of the regional states. Yet evidence suggests that the great powers of past eras (including the United States), and even the United States as a post–World War II superpower, have not been omnipotent in pursuing their goals in Latin America, despite their relative preponderance of power.

Individual regional states have by and large been neither entirely dependent on nor independent from the outside world. The norm is some (highly variable) degree of interdependence in complex interstate and transnational relationships. Although the international system has and does shape to a great extent the regional actors' foreign policies, it is mistaken to see external forces behind every foreign policy decision (only the most reductionist dependency theorist or tough-minded realist reaches this extreme). At times foreigners dominated or overwhelmed decisional processes. Such would seem to be the case, for example, in the Caribbean area during the period of intense U.S. imperialism in the first third of this century and, to a lesser but important extent, in the 1980s. The same was said for Cuba, which was characterized as a Soviet "puppet" until the end of the cold war. Even for the weakest and most externally dominated states, however, this generalization is not entirely accurate, even when extreme foreign pressures are being applied. For example, in the 1980s, El Salvador and Cuba, in their relations with the United States and the Soviet Union, respectively, exhibited a certain independence in their decision-making capacities and were adept at manipulating their respective patron's strong commitment to their survival.

Too much emphasis on the extraregional influences obscures power configurations within the region. This view of foreign dominance ignores the political complexity and relative foreign policy autonomy of some of the major regional states, as well as the isolated international environment of certain ones. Thus a basic distinction should be made between regional states' policy orientations formulated for intraregional relations and those formulated for relations with external actors. Many regional situations and issues require decisions largely divorced from external pressures. In the politics of the inter-American arena several states have made decisions, played roles, and employed tactics in largely autonomous ways.

The geographic settings within the region should be highlighted in the analysis of Latin American and Caribbean foreign policy. The physical locations of different parts of Latin America combined with other subregional factors have shaped states' perceptions and orientations toward the outside world as well as toward each other. The categories follow the subsystem contours identified in Chapter 2.

The northern part of the region—Mexico and the circum-Caribbean—has always been subjected to intense foreign pressures. The intense interest of outside states in their affairs has been a primary policy-making factor for all states in this portion of Latin America. Mexico's position on the U.S. border has fundamentally affected Mexican foreign policy decisions, which are intimately related to domestic policy. For many years Mexico experienced the threat or actuality of military intervention as well as economic dominance. That proximity has also facilitated, perhaps compelled, Mexico to engage in a broad range of interactions with the United States. The historic North American Free Trade Agreement (NAFTA), which went into effect on January 1, 1994, is a dramatic case in point; Mexico took the initiative that led to the trilateral agreement among Mexico, the United States, and Canada.

The Caribbean area was the scene of initial colonial European rivalry and of U.S.-British contention in the nineteenth century; in the twentieth century it was drawn into a sphere of pervasive U.S. influence until that was challenged by the Soviet Union in Cuba and later Nicaragua. By 1990 the United States was again the dominant external influence. The United States intervened militarily and otherwise with varying intensity throughout this period. The latest unilateral military invasion occurred in Panama in 1989–1990; under the imprimatur of the United Nations Security Council, the United States led a force into Haiti in 1994. The United States has also been the dominant external economic factor. Thus, the intense interest of outsiders in their affairs has been a primary policy-making factor for all states in northern Latin America.

Geography and power disparities have influenced intraregional relations as well, as certain local states have exerted their own intraregional leverage. Venezuela's expansion of international influence in the 1970s, based on large financial resources garnered from the sale of petroleum, extended into the rest of the Caribbean area. Even with the decline of those resources in the 1980s, Venezuela joined Colombia, Mexico, and Panama in the Contadora Group in a sustained effort to resolve the Central American conflict, which they perceived as posing a serious threat to themselves. The proximity of five small Central American states to relatively huge Mexico has influenced their foreign policies. The Central American states briefly joined the Mexican empire in the 1820s; the isthmian crisis and its resolution in the 1980s was of primary concern to Mexico. Mexico has been especially concerned with events in its immediate neighbor, Guatemala, involving competing territorial claims, immigrants and refugees, and guerrilla incursions. Mexico and Guatemala long had competing claims to Belize, which delayed for many years its gaining of independence from Great Britain.

The five "traditional" Central American states have been intimately concerned with each other in a love-hate, push-pull process since their independence, ranging from the creation and dissolution of a Central American federation after independence to the post–World War II establishment, decline, and revival of integration organizations. Recent events are particularly illustrative. Considerable intra-Central American violent conflict ensued after 1979, yet in 1987 the Central American states themselves devised a complex long-term plan for peace and recovery in the region, which they continued to pursue with slow but steady success into the 1990s.

The states in the Southern Cone of South America have a strikingly unique geographic situation. Their location places them at great distances from both Europe and the United States, outside the mainstream of great-power global politics and beyond the immediate sphere of U.S. influence. Although they have been subject to external coercion and rely on the outside world to provide their principal export markets, most of the time distance has given those states a measure of freedom in the international system and the opportunity to pursue policies toward each other relatively free of outside considerations. Subregional international politics have resulted in strategic components to several local states' foreign policies, a phenomenon not found so coherently in other parts of Latin America (see below).

A number of physical features have also affected the intraregional policies of several states. Mountains form the dominant characteristic of much of Latin America. They are found in many of the Caribbean islands and begin almost at the Mexican border with the United States, continuing south through Central America, along South America's Caribbean coast and western continental reaches, and into Brazil. The Andes mountain chain (*cordillera*) extends from the Patagonian region of southern Chile and Argentina along the west coast of the continent near the Pacific shores to the Caribbean coast, traversing Colombia and Venezuela. In width the mountains vary from less than 100 miles in the south to a 400-mile plateau in Peru and Bolivia. They have provided a security barrier between Chile and Argentina, Chile and Bolivia, and Bolivia and Peru. The large Atacama desert between Chile and Peru has served the same function. Mountainous terrain in all parts of the region has provided haven for insurgent groups. The vast Amazon jungle basin—the heartland of South America, which even today has large undeveloped zones—has traditionally formed a barrier between Brazil and most of its neighbors.

South America contains several great river systems linking the states. The Amazon River is the world's largest. It carries, by conservative estimate, 20 percent of the world's fresh water, and 40 percent of the South American surface waters, found in the territories of eight states, drain into it. Ocean ships are able to navigate some 900 miles upriver to Manaus, and smaller vessels can proceed 1,400 miles farther to Iquitos in Peru. Other important South American river systems are the Magdalena-Cauca in Colombia and the Orinoco in Venezuela, both of which rise in the interior and flow into the Caribbean Sea; both are navigable for considerable distances. The river complex of the Uruguay-Paraguay-Paraná-Pilcomayo, which empties into the Rio de la Plata estuary, is of great commercial and, in the minds of some local leaders, military significance. Navigable for 2,000 miles by oceangoing vessels, the system connects southern Brazil, Uruguay, Paraguay, and Argentina. Bordering states have established formal agreements to cooperate based on the two great South American river systems: the Amazon Cooperation Treaty and the Rio de la Plata Basin Accord. Elsewhere in South America, and overlapping with the Southern Cone, certain groups of states have acted in informal and formal concert to deal with perceived mutual interests—especially those in the Andean, Amazonic, and Rio de la Plata regions.

INTRASOCIETAL ELEMENTS

Nationalism

Nationalism is a fundamental influence in Latin American and Caribbean foreign policy-making.[2] An analysis of this phenomenon is complicated, however, because the Latin American variety of nationalism is highly complex. It involves several forms and different orientations. It assumes multiple ideologies and loyalties even within individual countries. The nationalism, variously, stems from both internal and external sources, is based on indigenous social values, reflects political and economic interests, imitates the values of outsiders, or stands in opposition to external values or interference. The effects of nationalism have varied, ranging in style from militant, intolerant, xenophobic, aggressive, and divisive at the one extreme, to pacific, benign, internationally cooperative, and domestically unifying at the other extreme. The diversity of nationalism has led to domestic political tensions and resulted in a variety of foreign policies.

The following discussion will identify only those variants of nationalism that have foreign policy relevance, ignoring most of those addressing specific themes or countries and those of essentially domestic consequence. The newer Caribbean states are treated separately because their nationalism has emerged in the context of historical experience and political-social cultures distinct from the older Latin American societies.

Early Nationalist Sentiments. The roots of Latin American nationalism are found in the colonial era, when some native elites developed a sense of separate identity from Spain and Portugal. Between 1810 and 1824, when most of Spanish America ended its colonial status and achieved national independence, the fighting intensified the anti-Spanish feeling that had been building for some time. This Spanish American aversion has been called "creole nationalism," a term that grew out of the bitterness of *criollos* (Spaniards born in the New World and their offspring, representatives of whom made up most of the ruling classes after independence) toward the privileged Spanish authorities in America (called *peninsulares*). This form of nationalism survived throughout the nineteenth century, prodded on by Spanish hostility toward the lost colonies and by xenophobia among some Spanish Americans to whom anything Spanish was anathema.

The nationalist outcome in Brazil was very different. In 1820 the royal Portuguese Bragança family, who had fled from Portugal to Brazil during the Napoleonic inva-

TABLE 4.1   Country Profiles (estimates for the end of 1997)

State (capital city)	Area (square miles)	Total Population (thousands)	Growth Rate (% annual)	Literacy (%)	Regular Armed Forces (number of personnel)			
					Army	Navy	Air Force	Total
Antigua-Barbuda (St. Johns)	171	66	0.7	89	(defense force)			150
Argentina (Buenos Aires)	1,072,068	35,047	1.1	95	41,000	20,000	12,000	73,000
Bahamas (Nassau)	5,389	263	1.1	90	(defense force)			860
Barbados (Bridgetown)	166	2.57	0.2	99	500	110		610
Belize (Belmopan)	8,867	224	2.4	91	1,000	50		1,050
Bolivia (La Paz)	424,163	8,259	2.3	80	25,000	4,500	4,000	33,500
Brazil (Brasilia)	3,286,473	164,595	1.2	80	200,000	64,700	50,000	314,700
Chile (Santiago)	286,400	14,586	1.5	94	51,000	29,800	13,500	94,300
Colombia (Bogotá)	439,513	37,431	1.7	88	121,000	18,000	7,300	146,300
Costa Rica (San José)	19,653	3,569	2.2	93	(civil guard/border security)			7,000
Cuba (Havana)	44,218	11,091	0.7	98	38,000	5,000	10,000	53,000
Dominica (Roseau)	305	83	0.4	94				
Dominican Republic (Santo Domingo)	18,703	7,691	1.2	83	15,000	4,000	5,500	24,500
Ecuador (Quito)	104,506	11,327	2.0	87	50,000	4,100	3,000	57,100
El Salvador (San Salvador)	8,083	6,105	2.0	73	25,700	1,100	1,600	28,400
Grenada (St. Georges)	133	95	0.5	98				

Country (City)							
Guatemala (Guatemala)	42,040	11,549	2.5	55	33,500	1,500	700	35,700
Guyana (Georgetown)	82,978	712	-0.8	96	(defense force)			1,600
Haiti (Port-au-Prince)	10,714	6,736	1.5	53	(public security force)			4,000
Honduras (Tegucigalpa)	43,277	5,755	2.7	73	16,000	1,000	1,800	18,800
Jamaica (Kingston)	4,470	2,615	0.8	82	(defense force)			3,320
Mexico (Mexico, D.F.)	759,530	97,557	1.9	88	130,000	37,000	8,000	175,000
Nicaragua (Managua)	53,668	4,425	2.6	57	15,000	800	1,200	17,000
Panama (Panama)	29,208	2,783	1.9	89	(national police force)			11,800
Paraguay (Asunción)	157,047	5,647	2.7	90	14,900	3,600	1,700	20,200
Peru (Lima)	494,293	24,954	1.8	82	85,000	25,000	15,000	125,000
St. Kitts-Nevis (Basseterie)	150	42	0.9	97				
St. Lucia (Casteries)	238	160	1.2	67				
St. Vincent Grenadines (Kingston)	150	119	0.7	96				
Suriname (Paramaibo)	55,000	444	1.6	95	1,800			1,800
Trinidad-Tobago (Port of Spain)	1,864	1,274	0.1	97	2,100			2,100
Uruguay (Montevideo)	72,172	3,268	0.7	96	17,600	5,000	3,000	25,600
Venezuela (Caracas)	347,029	21,929	2.1	90	34,000	15,000	7,000	79,000
Total	7,872,639	490,592						1,355,390

Sources: Central Intelligence Agency, *The World Factbook, 1995*; and International Institute of Strategic Studies, *The Military Balance, 1997–1998*. Projections and estimates by the author.

sion of the Iberian peninsula in 1807 and 1808, returned to Lisbon, leaving Prince Pedro to rule Brazil as regent. He came under the influence of Brazilian nationalists and, with a tolerant father, actually represented the successful independence movement in 1822 with little bloodshed. Anti-Portuguese feeling was found among native Brazilians, but it was modified by the wide acceptance of two members of the old royal family (who would have succeeded to the Portuguese throne) as sovereigns of Brazil until 1889.

A strong sense of "Americanism" and Spanish American solidarity existed among some leaders of the new states. Sometimes called "continental nationalists," such prominent patriots as Simón Bolívar and José de San Martín hoped for political unity in Spanish America and visualized some sort of league of states to be organized along the lines of the viceregal boundaries. These plans were frustrated, however, as the Spanish American empire broke up into sixteen separate states. A number of boundary conflicts among them, inter-American wars, and foreign interventions helped to develop individual nationalist sentiments and to erode continental nationalism. Loyalties were often local rather than national in scope, although international conflict promoted some national unity in the face of foreign threats.

A great deal of nineteenth-century Latin American nationalism, largely restricted to the small, elite power groups, was often a superficial imitation of European and North American strains. Independence was won just as modern nationalism was taking shape in these other areas of the globe, stimulated by the American and French Revolutions (1776/1789). These elites, however, were divided among themselves.

In Spanish America, competing groups were organized into primitive political parties, actually cliques, labeled Conservative and Liberal (a European borrowing), each with a different nationalist perspective. Conservatives generally wished to perpetuate the colonial system, but with themselves rather than the Spaniards as leaders; they looked to the past for national identity and unity—a past that included authoritarian central governments, Roman Catholicism, rigid social stratification, and other elements of the Hispanic colonial tradition. Liberals rejected the colonial past. They were anti-Spanish to varying degrees and to some extent opposed the political, social, and educational roles of the Church, adopted anticlerical positions, and sought to replace the authoritarian political system with progressive forms and principles copied, especially, from France, Britain, and the United States.

Modernization and Nationalism.   Later forms of Latin American nationalism were rooted in the values and tensions associated with the processes of political, social, and economic modernization. They dated essentially from the late nineteenth century, when modernization, largely fostered by native elites in league with foreign interests, helped to create new, politically aware socioeconomic groups. The rise of new social classes stimulated nationalist sentiments among the mobilized groups, as they attempted to establish a broad consensus that would better serve their interests and as they challenged traditional elite power structures. The continuing process of economic development and social conflict was further shaped by the impact of two world wars, the repercussions of the interbellum worldwide depression, the cold war, and foreign military intervention, as well as investment and economic assistance.[3]

Modernism refers to the pursuit of national unification and development by progressive elites, usually with foreign help. The drive to develop, beginning in the nineteenth century, was itself a nation-building process looking to Europe and the United States for inspiration and identifying with political and economic liberalism and cultural cosmopolitanism. Modernist advocates asserted that the best way to strengthen the nation was to draw as fully as possible on foreign sources, including capital investments, managerial skills, and mass immigration. Modernism was especially vigorous in Brazil, Argentina, Chile, Uruguay, and Mexico, where foreign enterprise and European immigration (of less significance in Mexico than the other states) assumed great importance in national development.

Nativism was a Spanish-American nationalist reaction to modernism. Opposing the influx of foreign immigrants and other influences, it was based on both *criollo* national values and opposition to the values of others. Nativists such as the Argentines José Hernández, writing in the late nineteenth century, and Ricardo Rojas, in the early twentieth, urged that tradition be protected and their nation ridded of European cultural hegemony. Nativists often viewed their national pasts nostalgically and romantically and saw the nation's history as a struggle between native-born Spanish-Americans and immigrants.

Antiyankeeism was related to nativism during the first third of the twentieth century. Traces of anti-Americanism were found throughout the nineteenth century, but they were not sustained until many Latin Americans were outraged by U.S. intervention, military and otherwise, in the Caribbean area. The expansion of U.S. interests stimulated nationalism not only in politics and economics but in cultural matters as well. A number of literary expressions of *antiyanquismo* during that time declared disillusionment with the course the U.S. democratic experiment had taken and warned of the threat of North American materialism to Hispanic spiritualism. Such sentiments existed in Brazil, but they were less pronounced there than in Spanish America, since Brazilian leaders encouraged friendship with the United States. Brazilians, to the present day, do not hold the same suspicions and hostility toward foreigners as Spanish Americans.

The United States was severely criticized for its interventions. Antiyankeeism increased gradually during the three decades after World War II and sharply in the 1980s, not only because of such events as the military invasion of the Dominican Republic in 1965, the subversion in Chile in the 1970s, the U.S. support of the United Kingdom in the 1982 Anglo-Argentine war, coercive policies in the circum-Caribbean in the 1980s, the 1989 U.S. military intervention in Panama, and other occurrences, but also because of resentment over U.S. economic and trade policies and its hard-line stance during the debt crisis in the 1980s. At the same time, Latin American governments themselves were under pressures stemming from economic dislocations and social change, and the United States presented a tangible object for resentment. Some political candidates appealed to this kind of nationalism, calculating that anti-U.S.

rhetoric could enhance their popularity. Although considerable xenophobia was undoubtedly behind antiyankeeism, the Latin American majority also seemed to be insisting, not unreasonably, on having a greater say in the rules of the international game.

Economic nationalism was first embraced by the new upper middle class, primarily the industrial and entrepreneurial sectors, that emerged from the modernization process. It was later adopted by representatives of the other middle sectors, organized labor, and the student movement. (The appearance of the student movement paralleled modernization in the early twentieth century.) In contrast to the foreign orientation of the earlier modernists, economic nationalists stood for a modified statism. Although economic nationalism may allow an important role for private enterprise, its basic tenets held that the nation owns the subsoil and natural resources and that the national good prevails over private property rights.

Economic nationalism intensified after World War II and again in the late 1960s and then the 1980s. In these periods the major stimulus was provided by U.S. economic policies. A prominent rallying point was a program of economic nationalism formulated by the United Nations Economic Commission for Latin America under the leadership of, first, the Argentine Raúl Prebisch and then the Mexican Víctor Urquidi. They argued that Latin America should develop its own industry by establishing protective tariffs and creating common markets. They also advocated commodity agreements and better terms of trade with other states in the United Nations Conference on Trade and Development. They did not reject the use of foreign capital but argued that foreign interests should not interfere with Latin American industrialization. More radical schools of economic nationalism advocated the expropriation and nationalization of existing foreign enterprises and the exclusion of further foreign investment. Prebisch and Urquidi would allow such investment but only under closely supervised conditions.

Revolutionary nationalism presented a different set of considerations. Many Latin Americans have viewed the United States as an oppressive power whose interests conflicted widely with their own. This nationalism has been associated with movements that seek to destroy their own systems, which they view as allied with the United States, and replace it with something else. The radical Left attempted to use popular nationalism to further their cause. In the 1930s and 1940s Soviet-oriented Marxist movements tried to capture nationalism for the proletariat, often working with popular fronts composed of other leftist and sometimes centrist parties. Although Communists supported populism, they never controlled it. Their greatest successes occurred in Chile, where a Popular Front of Communists, Socialists, and Radicals governed under a Radical Party president from 1938 to 1952 (the Communists separated in 1947). A coalition of leftist parties was again in power under President Salvador Allende from 1970 to 1973.

Revolutionary nationalism was vividly expressed by the Cuban Revolution of 1959. Fidel Castro's combination of Cuban nationalism (in the tradition of José Martí) and Marxism-Leninism during the 1960s forced Latin America as well as the United States to recognize the slowness of economic and social development in the region. The Castro revolution provided ideological inspiration for other groups that began to use violence aimed at overthrowing the existing order and to express hatred for the United States. The new radical left was hostile to the orthodox Communist parties and scornful of their tactic of peaceful coexistence. They abandoned traditional modernist social values, including constitutional processes, claiming to have lost faith in the ability of "bourgeois democracy" *(democracia burguesa)* to achieve social justice. Revolutionary nationalism was not successful in gaining power outside of Cuba until the Sandinista movement eventually gained control of the government in Nicaragua after the revolution of 1979.

Commonwealth Caribbean Countries. The nationalist orientations of the former British dependencies in the circum-Caribbean that gained their independence beginning in 1962 are marked by special considerations. The former British colonies, never "Latin" and no longer linked to the United Kingdom, have searched for an American identity. Ten of them formed the West Indies Federation between 1958 and 1962, anticipating the emergence of a single independent state. It dissolved, however, and separate entities were created with their own national identities, with others remaining dependent on the United Kingdom.

A British cultural facade had been superimposed, variously, on African, East Indian, Asian, and other ethnicities. Barbados is the most "English" among these new nations, duplicating old-world ways to a remarkable degree. Trinidad and Tobago perceives itself as "American" more than the others but has not rejected the British tradition. All but Guyana have governors-general representing the British crown (but with no political power). Although they criticize British policies, especially regarding aid and trade, anti-British nationalism is minimal.

Post–Cold War Nationalism. A salient characteristic of the post–cold war era is the emergence in Latin America of a new, more positive nationalism that contrasts with the prior prevailing defensive postures.[4] The change actually began to occur in the 1980s before the end of the cold war and was consonant with the region's transformation away from military regimes and statist economies toward democracy and open economies. The result is that Latin Americans are generally less defensive toward each other and the outside world than at any time since the mid-1960s. They are more willing to engage in international cooperation (including, prominently, with the United States) and are eager to be an integral part of the emerging global system. The new nationalism sought to reinsert the regional states into the global system (after the isolation and isolationism of the military regimes) and to cooperate closely among themselves and with outsiders. This new mood facilitated the reactivation and reform of Latin American regional international organizations and the resurgence of the Inter-American System.

This is not to deny the continued existence of xenophobia, antiyankeeism, economic nationalism, and revolutionary nationalism, which have declined but not disappeared. A distinct minority still argued that Latin Americans must organize among themselves as a way to assert their independence against imperialism. Some voiced apprehension about U.S. offers of hemispheric free trade, saying they were aimed at resurrecting and institutionalizing U.S. regional imperialism. However, much of the Latin American Left, which is marked by considerable diversity, has deserted, at least temporarily, these and related arguments. They say that anti-imperialism is not a viable basis for a united Latin American front toward the outside world. Likewise, much of the nationalism of the politically heterogeneous Right, a substantial portion of which had an inherent suspicion of the outside world, has been marginalized or undergone changes in its perceptions and prescriptions.

The new nationalism is a good measure of changes in Latin American foreign policies. Statements from a majority of Latin American and Caribbean governments and their multilateral organizations, backed by policy actions, demonstrate that they seek to (1) strengthen their democracy through economic and social development and regional cooperation and integration; (2) create a free international trading system; (3) deal jointly with problems of clandestine arms trade, terrorism, drug trafficking, and environmental degradation; and (4) promote discussions with other states and IGOs in a climate of goodwill. This means that the regional states, despite continuing suspicions and apprehensions, tend to share issue-paradigms with each other, the United States, Europe, and other international actors.

The ascension of the new nationalism is a consequence of the confluence of a number of factors: First, Latin Americans had dismal experiences with military regimes, especially their repression and economic failure, which led to disenchantment not only with the Right and the Left but with the dominant defensive foreign policy models generally adopted after World War II. Second, in the midst the most severe depression in half a century, Latin Americans, having decreased the polarization of their domestic politics, searched for alternative developmental models for economic reactivation. Third, the return to democratic forms and civilian rule combined with the adoption of economic neoliberalism to bring an unprecedented degree of homogeneity to prevailing Latin American political systems and a consensus about foreign policies. Fourth, the end of East-West conflict elevated other issues of more importance to the regional states—especially economic development and democratic strengthening—to the top of a mutually agreed upon inter-American agenda. Finally, despite certain apprehensions, Latin Americans perceived that the United States, free of its cold war obsessions, was less inclined to intervene or place itself on the side of the status quo and was more willing to cooperate on a partnership basis. The positive nature of this nationalism is not necessarily permanent, however. It could revert to xenophobia if improvements in living standards and other areas of social equity are not forthcoming.

Political Systems

The Primacy of Domestic Politics.   Foreign policy decision-making by its nature differs somewhat from the domestic process. Nevertheless, Latin American foreign policy analysis emphasizes the interplay of domestic politics and foreign policy, recognizing that the latter tends to be a projection of the former. International relations are regarded as one means of furthering domestic goals, or, perhaps more correctly, of attaining objectives that are categorized as neither foreign nor domestic but simply as national objectives. For example, foreign policy has often been viewed in terms of its possible contribution to internal economic development. Foreign policy can also be an important mode for achieving or maintaining political power, especially in the hands of opportunistic politicians who lack popular support or wish to divert attention from domestic political crises by focusing on nationalist foreign policy causes. Political advantage has been sought, and often gained, by both government and opposition leaders by raising such issues as territorial disputes with neighboring states, intervention by external powers, exploitation by foreign entrepreneurs, and nationalization of foreign enterprises.

Some exceptions have existed to the rule of domestic political dominance, especially the Southern Cone military-state security doctrines and actions based on geopolitical theories and strategies (see below). In the new conditions of the post–cold war international era, however, with the major issues related to transnational, intersocietal phenomena, the Latin American and Caribbean states make little distinction between domestic and foreign policy.

Political Stability and Instability.   Some internal or domestic factors affect policy-making capability. Another source of strength or weakness on the part of Latin American states, in addition to their individual size or location, is their own political system. Of particular importance is the matter of political stability and instability, the former adding to national strength and the latter both a source and an expression of weakness—and an invitation to foreign meddling. The politically unstable states in Latin America are less united on international issues and less able to deal with their own national development. Preoccupied with domestic problems or crises, they tend to consider foreign policy as relatively less important. In contrast, the Latin American states with the most effective foreign policies are also the most politically stable. They are more able to devote resources to international questions, and they have gained a certain amount of respect from other states.

The international effectiveness of the major states has depended largely on their internal stability. During the early national period, few Latin American states were able to maintain internally stable political systems. Instability and lack of economic development initially led to European and later U.S. military intervention and domination in other respects. Conflict and factionalism, including civil war and rebellion, as well as corrupt administrative practices, were common. This weakness frequently invited foreign intervention. Brazil experienced little turmoil in the nineteenth century and was the major exception in this regard. The heir to the Portuguese crown gave up his claim and, as constitutional monarch, was the "moderating power" from 1822–1831; his son similarly reigned until 1889. Chile was the first Spanish American state to work its way out of chaos when, in the early 1830s, it entered a period of consolidating "oligarchical democracy." In the latter part of the century, Argentina began to move toward relatively stable systems, although a great deal of violence accompanied the process.

Mexico's political turmoil, beginning in 1910, for all practical purposes retired it from international politics for two decades. Mexico regained stability after the 1930s, however, and became an important actor in inter-American and, at times, world affairs, despite its geographic disadvantage in proximity to the United States. Brazil's stability since the mid-1960s, as in an earlier era, was fundamental to its uneven drive for world power. As Brazil's authoritarian government became fragmented in the late 1970s, its foreign policy followed suit. Brazil's main rival, Argentina, although loath to admit it, effectively dropped out of the Latin American leadership race, primarily because of problems directly related to political instability beginning in the late 1920s and accelerating after 1955. Argentina's return to popular civilian rule in 1983, replacing a military regime that had terrorized its own populace, instituted a policy of "reinsertion" into the international system.

Chile's domestic political crisis beginning in 1970 caused severe foreign policy problems as well as weakness in dealing with them. A decade of civil war in Colombia beginning in 1948 and subsequent guerrilla insurgency and violence associated with narcotraffic have kept Colombia from developing the international influence that should be possible, given its size and physical and human resources; later the consequences of the illicit drug industry had the same effect, and in the mid-1990s Colombia was a state in turmoil. In contrast, Venezuela's capability has been enhanced by a democratically legitimized political system and its vastly increased oil riches—especially in the 1970s—despite its small population and serious domestic social inequities. But as Venezuela's national income dropped with the decline in oil revenues in the 1980s, its domestic political consensus was reduced, which led to several manifestations of political crisis.

Political stability is also of importance to the foreign policies of small states. Uruguay, for example, influenced inter-American relations for many years because of its prestige stemming from stable democratic governance. It suffered a great loss in prestige, however, when political stability deteriorated along with its economic life in the decade after 1966, resulting in the armed forces taking over government. Costa Rica is another example of a small state respected for its democratic stability, developed after World War II; this reality enhanced, for example, its remarkable leadership in the Central American peace process from the late 1980s to the mid-1990s. Conversely, small states can be particularly weakened by domestic political problems. For example, political instability in the Dominican Republic after 1961 led directly to the U.S. military intervention in 1965. Civil war and insurgency in Central America in the 1980s led, variously, to U.S., Cuban, Soviet, and other external involvement in local politics. Internecine strife in Grenada, Panama, and Haiti were principal reasons for the U.S. military interventions in 1983, 1989, and 1994, respectively.

Economic, military, and social factors are also of considerable importance and are approached in specific contexts in this book. In general, economic problems trouble states, although examples of real economic strengths are also evident. Latin American military capability generally has not been significant in world politics, but it has had substantial impact in inter-American relations. Population pressures, combined with other factors of nationalism, economic hardship, and repression, have led to considerable transnational migration and sometimes to war. Social tensions and lack of homogeneity have had different impacts on the capabilities of the various states.

The Commonwealth Caribbean states exhibit dissimilarities in territorial and population size, economies, and ethnicity. But all of them have high literacy rates, and most pride themselves on their functioning parliamentary systems ("Westminster democracies"), although events in several states have at least somewhat blemished their reputations for democracy and political stability. Nevertheless, but for highly exceptional cases, they have not had problems of intervention into politics on the part of their small armed forces.

FOREIGN POLICY ORIENTATIONS

Foreign policy decisions are expressed in action terms as a set of "orientations"—the result of calculations about purposes, goals, objectives, strategies, and tactics a state can reasonably pursue, as well as the establishment of the means that can be plausibly employed to realize or sustain them. Considerations of state power and capability variations, discussed above, bear strongly on the choice of policy orientations. In the global arena, the fact that Latin American and Caribbean states have operated from a position of relative weakness has significantly affected their selection of policy purposes, instruments, and strategies. Intraregional politics are more complex, in that the region is a microcosm of the global system with a wide range of relative power positions and, consequently, of orientations adopted by the regional states toward each other.

Ends and Means

Objectives and Tactics. When dealing with the outside world, the diverse Latin America and Caribbean states demonstrate a similarity in the objectives sought and even the means used.[5] The Latin American and Caribbean states pursue national interests that are common to virtually all states as they attempt to ensure their survival, security, and well-being. In the regional context, these ultimate objectives translate into long-range goals that reflect capability levels, national consciousness, and domestic politics. Their primary purposes with regard to the outside world have been to maintain sovereignty and to lessen dependence on and demonstrate independence from other states—global, regional, or local. They further seek especially to strengthen their economies and promote economic development. In a more abstract but real manner, they champion national prestige. The states also promote particular interests and pursue objectives limited to a single state or only a few of them. We should also recognize that government officials do not always openly state their objectives; they may have "hidden agendas" or may not have clear conceptions of their objectives (a phenomenon not restricted to Latin America).

In general, the range of techniques available to the regional states in global politics has been limited because they must rely on other than physical power, either military or economic. In this context, the most important criticisms of both realist theory and neo-Marxist dependency theory is that they underestimate the extent of policy recourse available to relatively weak states. They long ago developed tactics reflective of their limited capabilities toward the outside world, and they pursue them to the present day. They exert influence as best they can with such tactics as: (1) playing active roles in international organizations and attempting to align among themselves in relations with the outside world; (2) promoting international law and supporting such principles and procedures as nonintervention and peaceful settlement of disputes; (3) appealing to humanitarian sentiments and moral principles; (4) exploiting the rivalries of greater powers while remaining as noncommittal as possible themselves; (5) bargaining with the outsiders that provide markets for their natural resources and other goods; and (6) expanding their international contacts so as to "diversify dependency" to a degree that no single outsider has overwhelming influence.

In intraregional politics, the local great powers have played the game of power politics within the subregions—most notably, but not exclusively, in the Southern Cone—including the pursuit of imperialist goals and the use of military force as well as other techniques. The other states are thus reduced to using small-state tactics in their relations with the larger Latin American states. They attempt to restrain the larger ones through international organization and law and by capitalizing on regional rivalries—a combination of persuasion and manipulation.

Latin American and Caribbean governments have also cooperated among themselves, both within international organizations and through informal means of association. From the national beginnings to the present day, they have participated in organizations on all levels—among themselves within their own region, in the Inter-American System of multilateral cooperation with the United States and Canada, and in global, Third World, and specialized extrahemispheric institutions. In the extraregional institutions, Latin Americans tend to associate among themselves as a regional bloc. They have generally worked together in order to realize mutual goals and to facilitate their common bargaining power with the outside world. In the latter instance, their reasoning is that cooperation among themselves and presentation of a united front to the outside world partially compensates for their individual weaknesses in international relations. Despite many failures, frustrations, and disappointments over the years, Latin Americans have persisted in the organizational-associational tactic.

Beginning in the 1980s and continuing into the post–cold war era, Latin Americans have engaged in a form of association called *concertación*—meaning intra-Latin American foreign policy collaboration and cooperation.[6] It has been pursued in the revival of intergovernmental organizations dealing with virtually all of the multilateral issues. It was further reflected in the moving away from old diplomatic formality and protocol to intraregional consultation involving frequent personal contacts at all levels of authority. For skeptical observers, the revived enthusiasm for concerted action represented nothing new and so was not especially significant—it was, they said, no more than a new version of the old rhetoric about Latin American unity. For others, however, *concertación* was not the mere extension of the long-established inclination to mutual association toward the outside world but an important qualitative change involving shared Latin American policy orientations and increased assertiveness toward the United States and other outsiders. These analysts explain collaboration as the combination of a decline of U.S. hegemonic capabilities and Latin American democratic governments seeking collective self-protection. Some of the latter analysts say that the convergence of Latin American foreign policies has been profound but not total—that each government retains its own foreign policy framework and interests that reflect its traditions, objectives, conditions, and capabilities. The factors inspiring the "new nationalism" in Latin America, discussed above, were also behind the thrust for *concertación*.

Independence and Autonomy.   The desire for an independent or autonomous role in international relations, not defined in an absolute sense but as "more freedom of action," is a reflection of Latin American national consciousness. The realization of independence in foreign policy, however, has been frustrated by capability deficiencies, and in important ways the regional states have been subordinate to or at times even subjugated by external states. Thus a corollary objective has been to reduce their political, military, and especially economic reliance on outside actors. Freedom of action is difficult for all relatively small states. Nevertheless, although many regional actors stand in a dependent relationship to external actors, others have achieved a modicum of autonomy, and independence is a serious aspiration with almost all of them. The pursuit of autonomy in foreign policy is not only difficult for many states but often paradoxical. Latin American states want to achieve or maintain independence in their international actions, but to do so they must be strong in relation to the outside world; to become strong they must obtain some sort of assistance from the outside world toward which they wish to be independent, thus increasing the chances for a dependent relationship. Much of Latin America's continuing dilemma, then, is this: How are states to improve their capability and modernize their societies while preventing inordinate influence in their economies and political systems?

The greatest dependence on others has been economic and financial, areas in which the Latin American states as a whole are the most vulnerable to external influences. Their reliance on public and private investment and loans has circumscribed their independence to varying degrees. Because export markets are crucial to their well-being, most Latin American states strive to maintain friendly relations with their best customers. They have long sought foreign investment capital and assumed it was necessary for economic growth. Increasingly, however, expropriation of foreign enterprise was demanded by certain nationalist groups and effected by some governments. Beginning in the 1930s and increasingly throughout the 1960s and 1970s, governments were forced to calculate the relative economic and political benefits, costs, and risks between maintaining their appeal to foreign investors and pursuing expropriation. The thrust for expropriation declined in the 1980s and then was replaced with a new effort to engage in free trade with outside states and to attract private foreign investment. Although the process reflects a sense of urgency and determination, it is politically difficult, entailing as it does dislocations and abrupt changes.

Latin Americans have often attempted to remain independent from external actors by playing them against each other. The exploitation of great-power rivalries has long been a favored technique. For example, Colombia played on the rivalries among Great Britain, the United States, and France throughout the nineteenth century and thereby maintained control of the isthmus of Panama; but when the rivalry faded after 1901, and the United States was left unchallenged, Colombia lost control of its province. In addition, Latin American states seek to diversify their dependence by accepting economic, military, and other aid from a variety of external states, hoping that no single one will have an overpowering position of influence. On the inter-American scene, the small states have attempted to exploit local great-power rivalries. For example, both Uruguay and Paraguay, with varying success, have tried to balance Argentina and Brazil. During the cold war, Latin Americans were well aware of U.S. concern about the growth of communism in Latin America and were sometimes able to exploit it to their benefit by persuading the United States to commit relatively large amounts of aid and make trade concessions. The lack of such leverage since the end of the cold war has been evident.

A certain foreign policy autonomy of the Latin American states was evident before the end of the cold war. After the mid-1960s most Latin American governments increasingly sought more freedom of action, with varying success. They generally had no more than a nominal commitment to U.S.-defined strategic concepts and emphasized their own economic development. U.S. relations with Mexico were increasingly characterized by mutual dependence. Brazil and other key South American states did not simply follow the lead of the United States (or of anyone else) in international relations, despite such debilities as their huge external debt. Even in Central America the United States did not get its way easily. Two peace initiatives, the Contadora process and the Esquipulus II accord, meant that U.S. primacy was challenged by the Latin American states themselves, including all of the most important ones and several weak ones who were supposed to be U.S. clients. In the post–cold war period, the thrust for independence in foreign policy has become more pronounced. Latin Americans themselves have taken greater initiative in international relations, a fact revealed in their determined regional and subregional organizational activities and regular interstate consultations and in the informal understandings from which the United States and other outsiders are excluded.[7]

Economic Policy.   International economic policy represents the clearest nexus between Latin American domestic and foreign policy. In virtually every Latin American state since independence, and more recently since the independence of the

newer Caribbean states, foreign policy has to some degree been an extension of domestic economic interests and concerns.[8] The foreign trade of every regional state is
crucial to its well-being. Exports are required to generate the foreign currency necessary to pay for essential imports and to help repay foreign debt. Export taxes and import duties provide a significant source of government revenue for various operations, including development programs. Latin American diplomats spend a great
deal of their time aiding exporters. They play the traditional diplomatic game of pro-
jecting a favorable national image, at least partly to promote the confidence of outsiders in their economic worthiness. Economic policies tend to be highly pragmatic;
many external relations revolve around economic needs, which in turn temper ideological positions or compromise other objectives. For example, even the most anticommunist governments (including military regimes) adopted pragmatic stances toward the Soviet Union and Eastern Europe when advantageous trade relations were
offered, and much of the increase in Latin American relations with Communist
states from the late 1960s was explained in terms of economic necessity.

National Security Calculations.   Closely related to ends-means choices, especially
regarding "vital" state interests, are judgments about and doctrines of national security.[9] Latin Americans have long formulated policies in terms of traditional national
security concerns about threats to territorial integrity and physical safety posed by
foreign incursions from the great powers and disputes with neighbors. After World
War II, "national security" in the Latin American policy lexicon was increasingly focused on national development. The emphasis was on internal unity and economic
well-being, with external threat perceptions tending to be limited to contiguous border and territorial disputes and, in the circum-Caribbean, great-power intervention.
For most governments other than most dictatorships and military regimes, when the
subject of security entered the policy debate, the imperative to promote national socioeconomic well-being tended to supplant military defensive preparations.

Individual Latin American and Caribbean states as well as subregional groupings
have had special security considerations. Mexico is an important example of one with
particular interests. It took a unique position after the 1910 Revolution, refusing even
to use the term "security" in foreign policy statements until the mid-1980s. From the
1960s Mexicans regarded "security" as a synonym for military rule and repression, saying disdainfully that they did not want to "South Americanize" their political system.
"Security" finally entered their foreign policy vocabulary, but it referred to economic
integrity or the specific concern with insurgency threats to the southern oil fields.[10]

The clearest exceptions to the trend leading to the primacy of domestic politics
were found in the geopolitical security orientations in the Southern Cone states,
most notably in Brazil, Argentina, and Chile.[11] They are the only states in Latin
America to have developed significant strategic schools of thought. Their geographic
location beyond any outsiders' sphere of influence allowed these states to develop local great-power approaches; and in the process they acted on the basis of a geopolitical view of international politics applied to the combined Southern Cone-South

Atlantic-Antarctic regions in response to their individual national interests. The other states have done so to a lesser extent or not at all.

Southern Cone geopolitical perspectives included general theories of IR, explanations of Southern Cone international politics, and prescriptions for specific state action. Dating from the nineteenth century, geopolitical doctrines were adopted as the bases for security thinking primarily among armed forces officers and their civilian allies. The dominant strains of Southern Cone geopolitics were initially borrowed from European geopolitical thinking. They drew heavily on the German traditions of extreme versions of power politics, viewing international relations as a Darwinian process in which the strongest and most ruthless states survive and dominate the weaker ones. States were viewed as living organisms that competed and struggled in a world where might makes right, and that sought to expand to their full capacity through the extension of "living frontiers." Consequently, international conflict was deemed natural, inevitable, and necessary if a state was to survive and achieve its destiny. In disrepute in Europe and the United States after its absorption by fascist theorists in the 1930s, these ideas survived in Southern Cone writings and later formed one of the principal bases for military government practices. In my view, this version of geopolitics does not espouse serious theories of international relations, but its conjectures must be taken seriously in order to understand an important source of military behavior in the Southern Cone.

Brazil produced the most significant geopolitical schools, whereas Argentine thinking largely rested on perceptions of Brazilian expansionism and encroachment into Argentina's natural sphere of influence. Argentine schools adopted a more maritime orientation than the Brazilian ones. Chilean geopolitics, the least developed of the three, was also largely maritime in content. One major theme in Southern Cone geopolitics is the "ABC" rivalry for influence, extended to include security and ambitions in the South Atlantic and Antarctica. Brazil's security concerns further extend to West Africa and Chile's to the South Pacific; Brazil also relates geopolitics to its thrust to be a world power as its "destiny" *(grandeza)*.

From the early 1960s through the 1980s, Southern Cone military regimes, led by those in Argentina, Brazil, and Chile, devised and were guided by National Security Doctrines (NSD).[12] Essentially an extension of the Darwinian school of geopolitics described above, the NSD rationalized creation of "authoritarian national security states" in their different forms. They furnished a doctrinal base and rationale for both foreign and domestic security policies. In the former instance, the NSD inspired aggressiveness toward long-standing interstate conflict issues, heightened concern about external military threats to state territorial integrity posed by nearby states, and gave impetus to arms races in the Southern Cone subsystem (nuclear considerations were particularly ominous in Argentine and Brazilian calculations).

The military regimes also used NSD to justify domestic repression. They violently overwhelmed all opposition ("the enemy within") by propelling "security forces" into "internal wars" (the "dirty war" in Argentina). The wars started as counter-insurgency operations but quickly went far beyond to the widespread killing of thousands of civilians and the gross distortion of civil-military relations. The international tensions were frequently cited in the geopolitical literature as justification for augmented military establishments.

Darwinian geopolitical bases for policy were abandoned with the return to democratic civilian governments. A simultaneous fundamental shift in geopolitical thinking began in about 1982, arising among reformist geopoliticians associated with the Peruvian army and spreading from there. It advocated an end to chauvinism, argued that democracy was weakened by geopolitically-based conflicts and competition with neighbors, and called for integrated interstate approaches to common problems. It was also critical of the United States and its domination of the Inter-American System to the detriment of Latin American interests, although this element has faded with the end of the cold war. This school's concern in the latter 1990s is with regional economic cooperation and integration, interstate cooperation replacing power competition, and democracy and harmony over militarism and conflict—a far cry from the organic state *realpolitik* model discussed above.[13]

The Redefinition of Security.   The end of the cold war and the political and economic transformations in Latin America (especially redemocratization) complicated even further the meaning of security, as policy makers fundamentally revised their established ways of thinking about such matters.[14] Latin Americans continued to define security in such a way that it had a close relationship to domestic politics; it was now formulated in terms of the post–cold war transnationalization of the issues, and was compatible with a similar orientation that the United States had adopted for significant elements of its foreign policies. Latin Americans expanded the notion of international security so as to apply it to all of the major issues, including not only the established categories of interstate conflicts, insurgency, and economic well-being but also expanded aspects of international trade, debt and investment, democracy and human rights, socioeconomic elements in national development, the narcotics traffic, immigration and refugee policy, and environmental issues. These were matters of national debate, with different outcomes in different countries; nevertheless, Latin Americans were aware of the problem of applying security thinking to a primarily transnational world.

Widespread agreement was achieved about the democratic and economic subtext of almost all the problems but not about the degree to which all of them should be expressed in terms of security. For example, some people worried about revived or expanded national security roles for the armed forces, since in the recent past "security" was often an excuse for overthrowing constitutional governments and instituting brutal repression. Others counterargued that a broadened definition of national security would strengthen the hand of civilian authorities in their relations with military personnel. Nevertheless, Latin Americans were faced with defining the role of the armed forces, both in civil-military relations and outside their boundaries—and especially with regard to the new possibilities of participating in multilateral peacemaking or peacekeeping operations. The armed forces themselves were often reluctant to undertake these expanded roles.

Alignment

Isolationism and Neutralism.   Latin American states have generally come to accept their small-power roles in global politics. Concomitantly, they have assumed non-committal positions in great-power conflicts as much as possible.

Upon becoming independent, most Spanish American states and Brazil were the first "new states" to understand and oppose imperialism by attempting isolation and considering neutrality. Yet Latin Americans sought the support of European states in order to assist their national development, and they reconciled finally to the United States as chief guarantor of their sovereignty and security. During World War I, Latin America failed to respond to U.S. urging for hemispheric solidarity. The leading states of Argentina, Chile, Colombia, and Mexico were neutral. During World War II, however, only Argentina and Chile remained neutral until the latter months of the hostilities.

After World War II, Latin American states sought to remain aloof in the cold war, with varying degrees of success. Isolationist positions toward global rivalries were pursued in a political and military sense, but Latin Americans remained active in world economic relations. "Aloofness" and "isolationist" did not mean "neutrality" or "nonalignment," however, except in a few instances, and only a small minority of Latin American states adopted neutral positions in international politics. Then, in the late 1960s, a number of Latin American states began to adopt some form of the nonaligned orientation.

One of the earliest and most important neutralist postures was *justicialismo* in Argentina, a "third position" claiming to reconcile capitalism and communism and adopted under President Juan Perón (1946–1955). Perón's strategy did not represent a link between Latin America and the incipient Afro-Asian bloc, which developed into the Nonaligned Movement during the cold war, although his strategy was watched closely in Latin America and gained global attention. His concept was more akin to the "third way" advocated by President Charles de Gaulle of France and was reflected in the slogan: *Ni Yanquis ni Marxistas: Peronistas* (Neither Yankees nor Marxists: Peronists). It was a Peronist version of the Argentine traditions of neutralism, nonintervention, and policy independence, which were reflected in the rejection of alliances in the nineteenth century and later neutrality in the two world wars.

Neutralist orientations were articulated by the administration of Jacobo Arbenz Guzmán in Guatemala (1950–1954) and by the brief presidency of Janio Quadros in Brazil (January–August 1961). Their neutralism paralleled the Nonaligned Movement's concept of "noncommitment," but neither of them became members (although Brazil sent observers to the Belgrade meeting in 1961). Costa Rica in 1948 implied a form of unarmed neutrality when it abolished its armed forces; in 1983 the government made official its particular form of neutrality.

Strong Latin American political forces worked against neutralism following World War II. The armed forces generally desired close relations with the United States,

and the internationalist upper and middle classes recognized the importance of traditional trading relationships and the perils of radical change to their social and economic positions. In fact all Latin American states joined in formal military alliance
with the United States in the Rio Treaty of 1947. Beginning in the early 1960s, however, and accelerating thereafter, a large number of Latin American states joined the
Nonaligned Movement.

Nonalignment.   Latin American nonalignment has been a multifaceted objective
variously interpreted by Latin American governments. Interest in the Nonaligned
Movement revealed mixed motives, with domestic imperatives helping to explain
the degree of commitment or level of activity. Although all of the Latin American
states except Cuba were among the original signatories in 1947 and remained formally allied with the United States through the Inter-American Treaty of Reciprocal
Assistance (Rio Treaty), eight of them joined the Nonaligned Movement because
they saw their interests as more congruent with those of Asia and Africa. Cuba withdrew from the treaty and aligned with the Soviet Union—as well as joined the Nonaligned Movement. Nicaragua also sought political-military unity with the Soviet
Union but did not abrogate the Rio Treaty. Only one of the new states (Trinidad and
Tobago) adhered to the treaty after becoming independent, and still it joined the
Nonaligned Movement, along with six other new states. As a general matter, since
1982 the Rio Treaty has been moribund.

Nonalignment was also part of the overall Latin American strategy aimed at reducing dependence on the United States by developing diversified, external, bilateral, and organizational relationships as alternatives to the status quo balance of
power. The Nonaligned Movement had the practical advantage of placing participants in a position to bargain for assistance from both sides in the East-West competition. Other Latin American states did not participate in the movement—some because their U.S. alignment was more beneficial to them, and others because they
found little value in a neutral posture.[15]

Eventually sixteen Latin American and Caribbean states became full members of
the Nonaligned Movement: Argentina, Belize, Bolivia, Chile, Colombia, Cuba,
Ecuador, Grenada, Guyana, Jamaica, Nicaragua, Panama, Peru, St. Lucia, Suriname,
and Trinidad and Tobago. Eight more had attended as observers: Barbados, Brazil,
Costa Rica, Dominica, El Salvador, Mexico, Uruguay, and Venezuela. The nine Latin
American states not participating in the Nonaligned Movement were Antigua-
Barbuda, Bahamas, Dominican Republic, Guatemala, Haiti, Honduras, Paraguay, St.
Kitts-Nevis, and St. Vincent. In addition, three Latin American regional organiza-
tions—the United Nations Economic Commission for Latin America and the
Caribbean, the Latin American Economic System, and the Latin American Energy
Organization—sent observers to nonaligned meetings over the years. With the end of
the cold war, Latin American and Caribbean interest in the Nonaligned Movement
declined considerably to the point that it is rarely mentioned in policy statements.

NOTES

1. The first comprehensive work to apply foreign policy analysis to the processes of almost all of the regional states was Harold E. Davis, Larman C. Wilson, and others, *Latin American Foreign Policies* (Baltimore: Johns Hopkins University Press, 1975); it was followed by several comparative foreign policy analyses within conceptual frameworks: Gerhard Drekonja K. and Juan G. Tokatlian, eds., *Teoría y práctica de la política exterior latinoamericana* (Bogotá: Universidad de los Andes, 1983); Elizabeth G. Ferris and Jennie K. Lincoln, eds., *Latin American Foreign Policies: Global and Regional Dimensions* (Boulder, Colo.: Westview Press, 1981); Jennie K. Lincoln and Elizabeth G. Ferris, eds., *The Dynamics of Latin American Foreign Policies* (Boulder, Colo.: Westview Press, 1984); Heraldo Muñoz and Joseph S. Tulchin, eds., *Latin American Nations in World Politics,* 2d ed. (Boulder, Colo.: Westview Press, 1996); Juan Carlos Puig, ed., *América Latina: políticas exteriores comparadas* (Buenos Aires: Grupo Editor Latinoamerinano, 1984); and Luciano Tomassini, ed., *Relaciones internacionales de la América Latina* (México: Fondo de Cultura Economica, 1981). Good histories of the subject are provided by Demetrio Boersner, *Relaciones internacionales de América Latina: breve historia,* 4th ed. (Caracas: Nueva Sociedád, 1990); and Harold Eugene Davis, John J. Finan, and F. Taylor Peck, *Latin American Diplomatic History: An Introduction* (Baton Rouge: Louisiana State University Press, 1977). Highly useful are the thematic compilations by the Programa de Seguimiento de las Políticas Exteriores Latinoamericanas (PROSPEL), *Anuario de políticas exteriores latinoamericanas* (individual titles vary), comp. Heraldo Muñoz (Buenos Aires: Grupo Editor Latinoamericano, 1985–1988; Caracas: Editorial Nueva Sociedad, 1989–1990). See also Roland H. Ebel, Raymond Taras, and James D. Cochrane, *Political Culture and Foreign Policy in Latin America: Case Studies from the Circum-Caribbean* (Albany: State University of New York Press, 1991). On the foreign policies of the English-speaking states, see Jacqueline Anne Braveboy-Wagner, *The Caribbean in World Affairs: The Foreign Policies of the English-Speaking States* (Boulder, Colo.: Westview Press, 1986); Anthony T. Bryan and Andrés Serbín, eds., *Distant Cousins: The Caribbean-Latin American Relationship* (New Brunswick, N.J.: Transaction, 1994); Michael Erisman, *Pursuing Post-Dependency Politics: South-South Relations in the Caribbean* (Boulder: Lynne Rienner Publishers, 1992); Ivelaw Lloyd Griffith, *The Quest for Security in the Caribbean: Problems and Promises in Subordinate States* (Armonk, N.Y.: M. E. Sharpe, 1993); and Jorge Heine and Leslie F. Manigat, eds., *The Caribbean and World Politics: Cross-Currents and Cleavages* (New York: Holmes and Meier, 1988). See also Hilbourne A. Watson, ed., *The Caribbean in the Global Political Economy* (Boulder: Lynne Rienner Publishers, 1994).

2. The most thorough general work on Latin American nationalism is by Arthur P. Whitaker and David C. Jordan, *Nationalism in Contemporary Latin America* (New York: Free Press, 1966), which should be read with Whitaker's later article, "The New Nationalism in Latin America," *Review of Politics* 35 (January 1973): 77–90. Also important are books by Victor Alba, *Nationalists Without Nations* (New York: Praeger, 1968); Gerhard Masur, *Nationalism in Latin America* (New York: Macmillan, 1966); and readings collected and analyzed by Samuel L. Baily, ed., *Nationalism in Latin America* (New York: Knopf, 1971).

3. The following discussion identifies the main forms of nationalism stimulated by modernization, following certain of the categories posited by Whitaker and Jordan, *Nationalism in Contemporary Latin America.*

4. See Isaac Cohen, "Economic Questions," in *The United States and Latin America: Redefining U.S. Purposes in the Post-Cold War Era,* ed. G. Pope Atkins (Austin: Lyndon B. Johnson School of Public Affairs, University of Texas, 1992); and Isaac Cohen, "A New Latin

American and Caribbean Nationalism," *Annals of the American Academy of Political and Social Science* 526 (March 1993).

5. Harold Davis and Larman Wilson conclude that "on the whole, the most striking fact emerging from this survey [of Latin American foreign policies] is that they share many political objectives and that on many major questions their policies have been virtually identical." Harold E. Davis, Larman C. Wilson et al., *Latin American Foreign Policies* (Baltimore: Johns Hopkins University Press, 1975), 445.

6. On the concept of *concertación* and related aspects of Latin American foreign policies, see Alicia Frohman, *Puentes sobre la turbulencia: La concertación política latinoamericana en los ochenta* (Santiago: Facultad Latinoamericana de Ciencias Sociales, 1990); and Luciano Tomassini, comp., *El sistema internacional y América Latina: Nuevas formas de concertación regional en América Latina* (Buenos Aires: Grupo Editorial Latinoamericano, 1990).

7. John D. Martz, "Democracy and Human Rights," in Atkins, *The United States and Latin America: Redefining U.S. Purposes in the Post-Cold War Era*, 49.

8. Albert O. Hirschman, *Journeys Toward Progress: Studies of Economic Policy Making in Latin America* (New York: Twentieth Century Fund, 1963) is a classic treatment of the subject.

9. This discussion is taken from G. Pope Atkins, "Redefining Security in Inter-American Relations: Implications for Democracy and Civil-Military Relations," in *To Sheathe the Sword: Civil-Military Relations in the Quest for Democracy*, ed. John P. Lovell and David E. Albright (Westport, Conn.: Greenwood Press, 1997).

10. David Ronfeldt, ed., *The Modern Mexican Military* (San Diego: University of California, 1984).

11. This subject relies on three studies by Jack Child: *Geopolitics and Conflict in South America: Quarrels Among Neighbors* (New York: Praeger, 1985); *Antarctica and South American Geopolitics: Frozen Lebensraum* (New York: Praeger, 1988); and "Geopolitical Thinking," in *The Military and Democracy: The Future of Civil-Military Relations in Latin America*, ed. Louis W. Goodman, Johanna S. R. Mendelson, and Juan Rial (Lexington, Mass.: Lexington Books, 1990). See also Philip Kelly and Jack Child, eds., *Geopolitics of the Southern Cone and Antarctica* (Boulder, Colo.: Lynne Rienner Publishers, 1988).

12. David Pion-Berlin, "Latin American National Security Doctrines: Hard- and Softline Themes," *Armed Forces and Society* 15, no. 3 (Spring 1989): 411–429.

13. See Child, "Geopolitical Thinking"; and Philip Kelly, *Checkerboards and Shatterbelts: The Geopolitics of South America* (Austin: University of Texas Press, 1997).

14. Atkins, "Redefining Security in Inter-American Relations."

15. H.C.F. Mansilla, "Latin America Within the Third World: The Search for a New Identity, the Acceptance of Old Contents," *Ibero-Amerikanisches Archiv* 11, no. 2 (1985): 171–191.

CHAPTER FIVE

■

Nonhemispheric States
and Canada

The Latin American and Caribbean policies of selected states outside the Western Hemisphere and of Canada are examined in this chapter. Much of the study of Latin America's international relations was traditionally preoccupied with the role of the United States. As the following discussion should indicate, however, other external states have been closely involved in the region, a matter well recognized by analysts. European involvement reached its greatest height prior to World War I. It was revived in the 1970s and has been carried forward to the present day. The presence of the Soviet Union was notable after 1917 but not prominent until the connection with Cuba after 1959. Since the Soviet Union's dissolution in 1991, Russia and the other successor states have had little interest in the region. Japan, a relative newcomer to the scene, after World War II developed overwhelmingly economic interests in the region but has recently added a more political content. The position of Canada is analyzed in some detail, in recognition of its increasingly significant regional activity. A broad array of other nonhemispheric states developed Latin American policies, two of which are treated in this chapter: the People's Republic of China, a highly significant global actor with vacillating Latin American policies; and Israel, which has an essentially political approach toward Latin America and was, for a time, an important military supplier.[1]

EUROPE

Origins of Policies

During the colonial period most of the Latin American region was ruled by Spain and Portugal, with the small Caribbean remainder belonging to other European masters.[2] The region was of immense importance to the two primary imperial powers. For the challengers to the Iberian position in the Americas, actions in the region were a part of, and often a sidelight to, their competition with other European states on a sometimes global scale. Nevertheless, the foundations for Spanish, Portuguese, and other European views of Latin America as a weak and even inferior set of entities were established during the colonial era. Furthermore, certain Spanish, British, French, Dutch, and Danish colonies that were obtained during the active colonial presence, some as late as the first third of the nineteenth century, remained territorial intrusions in the Latin American subsystem. In the meantime, after the successful movements for independence, the emergence of new Latin American states between 1804 and 1824 and their subsequent search for nationhood stimulated rivalry among the external powers to gain regional influence or control.

The United Kingdom's interests in Latin America date from the colonial period, when it gained territorial and commercial positions in the region.[3] During an early stage of the Latin American movements for independence, while Spain was ruled by Napoleon, the British apparently intended to annex large portions of Spanish territory. However, after an unsuccessful military effort in the Plata River region in 1807 and 1808 and an aborted one in Mexico in 1808, Britain changed its approach. From 1808 to 1824 Britain covertly assisted the Spanish American patriots in order to prevent France from taking advantage of the situation, correctly assuming that Britain would be able to dominate the new states sufficiently to achieve its purposes without colonizing them. In 1825 Britain recognized the independent Latin American republics, even though it preferred they choose some kind of monarchy. Thereafter, Great Britain was the dominant external power in Latin America until the end of the century, with the important exception of Mexico.

British goals were first and foremost commercial in nature. Holding a primary position in most of the region, Britain was primarily interested in extending its new industrial strength by consolidating and expanding its economic position in Latin America. Its merchant fleets and superior naval power dominated the Atlantic and served to support British commercial objectives while denying expansion by other external states. Great Britain became especially well-entrenched in southern South America, holding preeminent commercial positions in Argentina, Brazil, and Uruguay. British interests were not entirely economic, however, at least not in the Caribbean area, where it had ambitions to build and control a Central American canal and to protect existing colonies. Great Britain felt obliged to prevent or impede French intrusion and U.S. expansion into the area. It initially attempted to act in concert with the United States to deter other European expansion. In 1823, Britain proposed a bilateral declaration asserting that neither party had territorial designs on the Spanish Empire and opposing any attempt by the Holy Alliance and Spain to recapture the latter's colonies. U.S. President James Monroe refused to join in such a declaration and issued his own unilateral statement. Britain encountered strong U.S. opposition over the canal issue. In order to soften the intense rivalry, Britain agreed with the United States, in the Clayton-Bulwer Treaty of 1850, that neither would unilaterally pursue a transisthmian canal project.

Acquisition of further territory was not an important aspect of British policy by this time. The only land annexed during the Latin American national period was the remote Falkland Islands in the South Atlantic Ocean, acquired by force from Argentina in 1833 but based on an earlier claim. Between 1844 and 1860, Britain exercised a protectorate over the Central American Mosquito coast, roughly the Caribbean coast of Nicaragua today. Already existing colonies gave rise to a number of boundary disputes with Latin American states, some of which lasted into the 1980s and 1990s. They included conflict with Argentina over the Falkland Islands (called the Islas Malvinas in Argentina), with Venezuela over British Guiana (now Guyana), and with Mexico and Guatemala over parts of British Honduras (now Belize).

Spain, the preeminent colonial power in Latin America, was reduced to marginal importance after Spanish American independence.[4] Spain sought to recover its former colonies from time to time, but it was then a minor European power and did not figure prominently in regional affairs. After unsuccessfully opposing the independence of its American colonies, Spain was obsessed with the desire to regain the empire. When Ferdinand VII returned to the Spanish throne in 1815, he attempted to gain support for Spanish reconquest of the region. But British opposition restrained France and other European states sympathetic to Spain, and by 1824, reconquest was an unrealistic prospect. Nevertheless, long after most of Spanish America was independent, Spain refused to recognize its ex-colonies and intermittently plotted to recover them.

For most of the nineteenth century, beginning in 1820, Spain was deeply divided by revolution and civil war. Policies toward the Americas reflected the cleavages in Spanish politics. The Liberal government, which came to power after Ferdinand's death in 1833, temporarily abandoned plans for reconquest and pursued a conciliatory policy toward Spanish America. Despite violent opposition from traditionalists, Spain began to recognize the sovereign independence of Latin American states, beginning with Mexico in 1836. It also began to negotiate for indemnification for damages sustained by Spanish nationals during the preceding years of violence and over the question of nationality status for Spaniards who had chosen to remain in America or who were then beginning to emigrate there. Questions of recognition, debt, and citizenship dominated relations until they had been substantially settled, with some exceptions, by the mid-1860s.[5]

In contrast to the bitterness that prevailed between Spain and Spanish America during the movements for independence and the early national period, Portugal relinquished control of Brazil in a relatively peaceful manner.[6] Portugal had not exercised as strict control over Brazil as Spain had in its American empire, except during the Portuguese royal family residence in Brazil from 1808 to 1821, while the French occupied Portugal. When the Brazilians decided to declare their independence in 1822, they were led by the heir to the Portuguese throne, who was then regent in Brazil. He and his son ruled as emperors of Brazil until 1889. Portugal almost immediately reconciled itself to the loss of its American colony, recognizing the independent Brazilian state in 1825. This Portuguese policy was heavily influenced by Great Britain, which had maintained an alliance with Portugal since the early eighteenth century and continued to exercise influence throughout the nineteenth century and beyond. In 1810, Great Britain and Portugal, whose government was then in Brazil, had signed trade agreements giving the British a preeminent position in Brazilian markets. The British had been responsible two years earlier for the royal family's escape to Brazil aboard a British ship during the Napoleonic invasions. Subsequently, Britain had acted as the diplomatic intermediary between Portugal and Brazil during their negotiations for recognition. An independent Brazil was favorable to British interests, and Britain used its influence over the subservient Portuguese government. Portugal was also the weaker partner in the Portuguese-Brazilian relationship.

By the time of Latin American independence, France had lost much of its American empire, but it persisted more than any other external state in its designs on Latin American territory during the nineteenth century. The French imperialist thrust eventually ended in total frustration. The vast Louisiana Territory, which France had acquired from Spain by treaty in 1800, was sold to the United States in 1803. France's prize possession, the western part of the island of Hispaniola (today's Haiti), ceded by Spain in 1697, gained its independence in 1804 after a long and particularly bloody slave revolt. France refused to recognize Haitian independence until 1837. France attempted to use the Holy Alliance, a continental European anti-republican league formed after Napoleon's final defeat in 1815, to assist Spain in regaining its American empire, after which France expected to have dominant influence. Britain, by then in control of the seas, made its opposition clear, and France abandoned the scheme in 1823. France sent naval forces to blockade Vera Cruz and Buenos Aires in the 1830s to assert the claims of its citizens, but to no avail. France joined Britain in another blockade of Buenos Aires from 1845 to 1849 in support of Argentines and Uruguayans opposing Argentine dictator Juan Manuel de Rosas (who was conducting his own siege of Montevideo), but the intervention gained little.

The Latter Nineteenth Century to World War I

European involvement with the new Latin American states reached its height during the latter half of the nineteenth century and in the twentieth century up to World War I. Britain's commercial interests and France's frustrated imperial ambitions continued as before. Germany and Italy entered the Latin American scene in the 1870s as their respective national unifications were taking place. Germany became highly competitive, and by the end of the century occupied third place in Latin American trade, behind Great Britain and the United States and well ahead of France. Italy sent large numbers of immigrants, especially to southern South America, and to Argentina in particular. Britain, France, the Netherlands, Spain (until 1898) and Denmark (until 1917) continued to maintain relatively small colonies, all in the Caribbean area except for the British Falkland Islands colony. European armed intervention occurred from time to time, sometimes in concert. Increasingly, however, with the development of major South American states and the rise of U.S. power in the circum-Caribbean, Europeans turned to more cooperative relationships. Their last military intervention was a combined British-German-Italian blockade of Venezuela in 1902–1903.

European objectives were mixed. Latin America was not an arena of European power politics and imperialism to the same extent as in other parts of the world. It was, however, the object of rivalry for economic, political, cultural, and military influence. The rapid industrialization of European states led to an increase in their need for food and raw materials and to a more intense search for markets for their manufactured goods, investment capital, technical and managerial skills, and surplus population. In addition, the international rules of the game dictated that if one great power aided in economic development, cultural exchange, or military modernization, the other great powers were obliged to follow suit. Various goals were interrelated: The exportation of military expertise and technology or of cultural benefits might bring increased exportation of economic goods and assist political expansion into a peripheral and neglected area at relatively low cost. For some political and military leaders in Germany and France, Latin America assumed some importance in their strategic calculations for then present and future contingencies. From 1885 until the outbreak of World War I, the European military missions in the Southern Cone, and the provisions for training Latin American officers in Europe, were aimed at strengthening military and political relations that might become important in the event of European war. They also served economic and prestige purposes. Of particular note were the military advising and training activities of Germany in Chile, Argentina, and Bolivia, and of France in Peru, Brazil, Uruguay, and Paraguay—whereby they extended to the Americas their world-wide competition to establish useful military relations.

British domination of the seas, aided by the possession of naval bases in Latin America, and after the advent of steam shipping, was directed toward economic ends. Britain intervened at times to protect its citizens and investments and to collect debts, on occasion in concert with other European powers, but all in all it resorted to little military interference in Latin American affairs. Britain continued to be the major investor and trader. It was especially well entrenched in Argentina and had important investments in and trade with Brazil, Uruguay, Mexico, Venezuela, and Colombia. British emigration to Latin America was also important, but it did not approach the numbers of some other European countries. British settlers were largely, but not exclusively, connected with British capital enterprises.

Britain began to retire from the Caribbean at the turn of the century and to give the United States a largely free hand in the area. The Hay-Pauncefote Treaty of 1901 replaced the Clayton-Bulwer Treaty of 1850, allowing the United States to build and exclusively control an interoceanic canal. Britain maintained its Caribbean colonies and economic interests, but it became a secondary external influence in the area. It retained major interests in South America, however, especially in commercial and financial affairs, although to its chagrin its preeminence eroded after the turn of the century through the efforts of the United States and Germany. Nevertheless, Britain's investments and trade levels in Latin America reached a peak on the eve of World War I. The investments constituted about one-fourth of Britain's overseas total, with special concentrations in Argentina and Brazil.

Throughout the remainder of the nineteenth century, Spanish foreign policy was fundamentally European oriented, and Spanish America was of slight and mostly emotional concern. Spain again took up efforts to recover at least part of the old empire after the end of the Carlist civil wars. In 1861, taking advantage of political chaos in Santo Domingo, Spain persuaded its former colony to petition for reannexation. Dominicans again rebelled in 1865 and regained independence. Also in 1861, Spain joined Britain and France in a military intervention against Mexico for payment of debts, but Spain and England retired when French desires to occupy Mexico became clear. In this case Spain did not intend to extend control over Mexico. In 1864 Spain sent a small naval squadron to attack Peru and Bolivia, and then bombarded Chile for coming to the aid of its neighbors. The adventure gained nothing for Spain.

Despite these events, Spanish American conservatives had a great deal of sympathy for Spain. Liberals, on the other hand, tended toward hispanophobia and yankeephilia. Spain ruined the remaining potential for Spanish American goodwill, however, by its harsh treatment of its remaining colony in Cuba (which included Puerto Rico). Spanish American public opinion widely supported the Cuban patriot cause. After Spain relinquished its last American territory as a result of a brief war with the United States in 1898, however, sympathy with Spain was revived as hostility toward the United States increased.

In reaction to the war with the United States over Cuba, a number of well-known Spanish intellectuals promoted the idea of a common civilization or cultural community between Spain and Spanish America. The Spanish government expressed sympathy for what was called *hispanismo* but devoted minimal resources beyond financing some cultural exchange. The Spanish government saw cultural solidarity as a way to make Spain more competitive economically and to promote Spanish influence and prestige in Latin America, but Spain's economy was unable to compete in Latin American markets with the rest of Europe and the United States.

French interest in Latin America by the time of World War I had became essentially economic, in contrast to the earlier nineteenth-century imperialist thrust. In addition, the height of French cultural influence and the beginnings of its military cooperation in South America occurred at the turn of the century and up to World War I. These changes in emphasis came, however, after France had engaged in two more disastrous colonial adventures—its occupation of Mexico in the 1860s and its support for a private French company's Panama Canal enterprise.

Mexican civil war beginning in 1857 led to the repudiation of foreign debts and to a joint French-Spanish-British military intervention in 1861–1862 to force a debt agreement. After Great Britain and Spain withdrew, French troops took Mexico City. Prince Maximilian of Austria became emperor of Mexico in April 1864, supported by the French army. However, continued resistance of Mexican patriots under Benito Juárez—and, with the end of the U.S. Civil War, U.S. opposition to the French occupation—ended French imperial ambitions in Latin America with a humiliating departure from Mexico and the execution of Maximilian.

France soon took up a new American scheme—the linking of the Atlantic and Pacific oceans with a transisthmian canal. With British and U.S. power neutralized in Central America by their 1850 treaty, a private French company began construction of the Panama Canal. Mismanagement, unsound engineering, yellow fever, and corruption led to bankruptcy and abandonment of the project in 1888, with less than a quarter of the canal completed. The canal equity was eventually sold to the United States in 1902.

France had important economic interests in Latin America in the latter part of the century. During the 1890s and until the eve of World War I, it occupied fourth place in commercial trade with the region, behind Britain, the United States, and Germany. France was not really competitive with the three leading states, however, lagging far behind Germany. Moreover, France was already burdened at the time with heavy investments in Russia, Spain, North Africa, and the Middle East.

A German interest in Latin America can be traced to the colonial period when Spain allowed individual German families to make economic investments in Venezuela. After Latin American independence, Germans were prominent in the great European migrations to America, and the city-states of Hamburg and Bremen established important trading relations in Latin America. Following German unification and the establishment of the empire in 1871, Germany wove political, military, cultural, and economic relations into a complex series of policies toward Latin America. In particular, trading relations and migrations of people and capital increased.

Germans settled in large numbers in Argentina and Brazil, and to a significant but lesser degree in Chile, Peru, Bolivia, Mexico, Guatemala, and Venezuela. Germany's economic performance was especially impressive from about the turn of the century to the eve of World War I. By 1913 Germany was third in both exports to and imports from Latin America. Argentina was Germany's most important trading partner, with Brazil, Chile, and Bolivia also of significance. The extent of German trade and investment in Latin America is all the more remarkable in view of the fact that Germany suffered from an inadequate supply of foreign investment capital during that period, and in view of the fact that the focus of its investment and trade was in Central Europe, even while it recorded impressive gains in the United States, Great Britain, and the Middle East. The spread of German enterprise around the world created an urge to establish colonies and naval strength to promote and protect German overseas markets. Germany did not seek Latin American colonies, however, presumably deterred by the possibility of British and U.S. economic retaliation.

The Interbellum Period

European interest in Latin America sharply declined as a result of World War I but was rekindled throughout the 1920s and 1930s. European policies, however, remained relatively constant in concept if not in intensity during the interbellum period. All European states now pursued primarily commercial interests, with Britain retaining the largest share but strongly challenged by the United States, Germany, and France. Germany and France again played leading roles in the development of South American armies, with essentially the same partners as during the pre-World War I period. Because of a strong German presence in Latin America in the 1930s, supported by some local political groups sympathetic to Nazi Germany and fascist Italy, Europe temporarily and peripherally included the region in its strategic concerns.

British influence in Latin America, which had begun to wane at the turn of the century, declined considerably after World War I. A mild boom occurred in the 1920s, when the Prince of Wales, later King Edward VIII, traveled in 1925 to Chile, Argentina, and Brazil attempting to bolster British trade with them. Argentina continued to be the most important state in British economic calculations. In almost every year until 1946, at least 10 percent of total British capital invested abroad, and 30 percent of that in Latin America, was in Argentina. In 1947 the Perón government purchased the British-owned railway and tram lines, eliminating Britain's largest capital enterprise in Argentina.

Spain had little interest in Latin America between the wars. Its policy was restricted largely to an emotionalized form of cultural activity, although a modicum of economic, political, and even military cooperation took place. Before (but not during) World War II, Spain received small numbers of Latin American officers at its training centers.

The Spanish Civil War from 1936 to 1939 sharply divided Latin American public opinion. After its conclusion in 1939, General Francisco Franco adopted a new form of Pan-Hispanism called *hispanidad* and made it the basis for Spanish policy toward Latin America. *Hispanidad* was an amalgam of some of the cultural tenets of *hispanismo* with *falangismo*, the Spanish variant of fascism. The overblown rhetoric of *hispanidad* notwithstanding, the reestablishment of the American empire was an unrealistic goal. Franco probably aimed for the development of a Spanish American bloc supportive of Spain in international politics. He was successful in only the most reactionary sectors.

World War I had seriously interrupted German relations with Latin America. During the post-war Weimar period, Germany recovered its trading position somewhat, although it reached its prewar levels only in Argentina. German investments remained low. Germany was deeply affected by the world depression, and its economic relations suffered drastically. Military relations were revived in the 1920s along prewar lines with Chile, Argentina, and Bolivia and continued to World War II.

German National Socialist (Nazi) policy in Latin America beginning in 1933 succeeded in increasing trade, and by 1938 Germany had regained its prewar commercial position in the region. Germany's principal economic efforts were consistent with past interests, but the policies took on new strategic overtones consistent with Germany's desire to stockpile war-related raw materials as well as to encourage German export of manufactured goods for the sake of balance of payments. Hitler reorganized the German Chamber of Commerce to assist in collecting information regarding military and political conditions abroad as well as financial and commercial intelligence information. He also exerted pressure on German overseas firms to dismiss Jewish employees and to withhold advertising from newspapers unfriendly to the Third Reich.[7]

The Hitler regime introduced a new ideological factor in German foreign policy as it sought to mobilize German communities in Latin America in support of the Nazi Party in order to project a positive image of the New Germany and to further its economic goals there. Although the number of German communities existing in Latin America was small, the homeland considered them significant. Some cultural organizations had been established in years past, and Germany had always prevailed on German migrants to support the "mother culture." Hitler demanded political as well as cultural loyalty. The Nazi Party had attempted to organize and control counterparts in Latin America as early as 1930, more than two years before coming to power in Germany, and it continued its efforts after 1933. The infusion of German overseas schools with Nazi ideology received special attention, along with other forms of propaganda and often clumsy fifth-column efforts. All of these attempts caused friction within the German communities and between Germany and virtually every Latin American state where they were attempted, including Argentina and Brazil, where otherwise sympathetic regimes were in power. World War II as much as severed Germany's contacts with Latin America.

Post–World War II and Cold War

Following World War II, war-exhausted Europeans retreated from competition in Latin America. Initial postwar European policies in Latin America were subordinate to their preoccupations with essentially European affairs. They were absorbed with recovering from the war and then maintaining the new prosperity, managing relations with the superpowers, organizing the North Atlantic Treaty Organization (NATO), and developing formal European integration associations that culminated with the establishment of the European Community (EC). Several of them were also faced with making new arrangements with their old colonial empires. Latin America had only a peripheral place in these concerns.

Eventually, European states revived their interests in Latin America and again assumed important roles there. Especially after the mid-1960s, they expanded existing relations and initiated new ones. They undertook diplomatic contacts, cultural exchanges, economic assistance, private investment, and, especially, trade relations, including arms sales. Trade and investment were of paramount importance, supported by increased diplomatic contacts and some economic assistance. Even with the expanded relationships, Latin America generally was not as important to the European states as other world regions.

None of the European states viewed Latin America in security terms in the post–World War II period because of geographic and political distance and higher priority concerns elsewhere. They tended to defer to the United States on security issues. Their policies were not devoid of such content, however. NATO members had a contingency concern that the Gulf of Mexico and Caribbean Sea be open for movements of military forces and supplies in the event of European war. This concern was latent, however, and not an essential factor in policy calculations.

In the 1980s Europeans emphasized three areas of concern regarding Latin America, largely in reaction to U.S. policies: (1) the question of debt, as a political as well as financial issue; (2) the problems of Latin American democracy as the region moved away from military regimes; and (3) the phenomenon of Third World revolution, as manifested in Central America. European transnational parties—especially Social Democratic parties and the Socialist International, and Christian Democratic parties and the Christian Democratic World Union—began to pay more attention to their Latin American colleagues and emphasized these issues.

A number of political interests and activities in specific countries were particularly notable, sometimes including ideological elements. Spain, under General Franco, courted Latin America through the medium of a less aggressive version of *hispanidad* in an attempt to win votes for Spanish entry into the United Nations. The first UN General Assembly refused membership to Spain because of its nondemocratic, fascist government, but finally, in 1956, Spain joined the world body, with the support of sixteen of nineteen Latin American votes. Thereafter, Spain attempted, with some success, to gain Latin American support in the UN for its otherwise quixotic quest to force Britain to return Gibraltar to Spain. But Spain turned more attention to Europe, as it had come to equate security and the economic future with European involvement, and otherwise paid scant attention to Latin America. The main issues for Spain in Latin America involved continuing Mexican hostility toward Franco and the question of Cuban indemnification for Spanish property seized by the Castro government in 1959. After Franco's death in 1974, Spanish officials suggested a new era of Latin American relationships. After joining NATO and the EC, Spain made overtures to serve as a cultural and political bridge between the two regions.

The postwar peace settlement restructured Germany, dividing it into east and west sectors, the latter constituting the Federal Republic of Germany (West Germany). This development ushered in a new foreign policy era for Germany. Some ideological concerns motivated aspects of German policy. It wanted to break with its National Socialist past, but publicity concerning Nazi personalities who had migrated to Latin America occasionally caused embarrassment. Of more importance were German attempts to prevent Latin American recognition of East Germany and to promote German reunification. The Hallstein Doctrine of 1955 stated that Germany considered the recognition of East Germany an unfriendly act. In general, Latin American governments supported Germany regarding Eastern Europe. *Ostpolitik*, led by Willy Brandt beginning in 1969 and culminating with a treaty between the two German entities in 1972, defused the anticommunist element of German policy. In 1979, Chancellor Helmut Schmidt visited Latin America to signal increased trade and investment, but this eventuality was deterred by the region's severe debt crisis beginning in 1982.

The United Kingdom, France, and the Netherlands had Caribbean dependencies to accommodate. British policies also involved long-standing conflicts: (1) with

Mexico and Guatemala over parts of Belize, which was finally settled in 1981; (2) with Venezuela over Guyana, which is presently moribund but not legally resolved; and (3) with Argentina over the Falkland or Malvinas Islands (the Anglo-Argentine war of 1982 and its aftermath was the most dramatic of the disputes), the sovereignty over which continues in dispute. Other states also looked for Latin American support on individual matters in the United Nations. For example, Portugal sought and usually received Brazil's supporting vote in the UN, even on colonial issues. Some countries based certain policies on the fact that they had large national populations resident in Latin American countries, such as Italy's policies toward Argentina and Portugal's toward Brazil.

The European Community was a new post–World War II actor in the Latin American and Caribbean subsystem.[8] It played an expanding role as European states increasingly chose to pursue their interests mutually through the EC as well as bilaterally. In the early 1970s, the EC began to look beyond its own integration and to formulate policies toward the developing world. The EC established permanent consultation mechanisms with Latin America on the ambassadorial level in Brussels. Beginning in 1971, a regular series of multilateral diplomatic meetings were held semi-annually to discuss interregional relations. The EC worked directly with the several Latin American economic organizations and, in time, with the Latin American Economic System (SELA). In October 1984, through the initiative of the Commission of the EC, the Institute for European-Latin American Relations (Instituto de Relaciones Europeo-Latinoamericanos—IRELA) was created; it was located in Madrid and directed by the German Latin Americanist Wolf Grabendorff. Among its several functions, IRELA organizes conferences and colloquia, collects and analyzes information on a range of specific subjects, and issues a large number of publications.[9]

In 1971 the EC established a Generalized System of Preference (GSP) giving concessional terms of trade for certain Third World exports, including those in Latin America. In 1974 the EC signed the Lomé convention; the third revision (Lomé IV) went into effect in 1990 and extended the treaty for a ten year period. The agreement gives further special trade concessions and development aid to former European colonies, which in Latin America include the twelve Commonwealth Caribbean Countries, Suriname, and, as special cases, the Dominican Republic and Haiti. But the majority of Latin Americans complained that their most important export items were not on the GSP list and that further disadvantages caused by the Lomé convention worsened their terms of trade in relation to other developing economies.

EC concerns went beyond economics with their role in Latin American subsystem conflict. Specifically, the EC took positions in the Anglo-Argentine war of 1982—a move that created discord among member states. After Argentina invaded the United Kingdom's Falkland Islands colony on April 2, 1982, the EC responded to a British appeal for its support by deciding on April 16 to condemn Argentina for its aggression and to impose sanctions; it banned European arms sales to and embargoed imports from Argentina. Members made it clear, however, that the measures were designed to convince Argentina to abandon force and did not imply an endorsement of

British counterforce. Support eroded especially after May 2, when a British subma-rine torpedoed and sank an Argentine cruiser, an act widely perceived to have violated Britain's own rules of engagement. The British engaged in intense diplomacy with their reluctant EC partners, and the majority decided to extend the sanctions indefi-nitely, although Ireland and Italy refused to vote in favor. The EC lifted its sanctions on June 20, 1982, after British armed forces had prevailed in the South Atlantic.

Post–Cold War Trends

New developments paralleled the ending of the cold war and influenced European policies toward Latin America. Primary among them was the notion of "Europe 1992"—the plan laid out in the intra-EC Maastricht treaty to create a Single Euro-pean Market (SEM) by December 31, 1992, and to transform the EC into the Euro-pean Union (EU). But the ratification process revealed sufficient public skepticism or hostility and forced compromises in the depth and speed of increased integration. Movement toward the SEM continued but fell short of that originally planned. In addition, the dissolution of the Soviet bloc in Eastern Europe led the states there to seek EU membership or other association.

A great deal of Latin American speculation on the future of their relations with Europe was distinctly pessimistic. Some writers emphasized the disequilibrium cre-ated by strong political bonds and weak economic ties and were skeptical about both Europe's willingness and Latin America's capability to implement new economic strategies.[10] They stressed Latin America's frustrated expectations about relations en-gendered by EC protectionism and passivity toward the external debt; and they called attention to Europe's lack of the political will to establish complementary rela-tions with Latin America and halt further "distancing" of the two regions.

Europeans applauded Latin America's recovering and opening economies and re-democratized polities (though some expressed doubts about their sustainability), but European economic relations with Latin America had increasingly declined. From the mid-1960s to early 1990s, the Latin American portion of the EC's total trade had fallen by about half. Latin American exports to the EC, consisting mostly of agricultural and mineral commodities, were especially vulnerable if stricter EC regu-lations and preferences for Eastern European products became realities. The prospect of a more intensely integrated EC, and its expansion to include the essentially "de-veloping" economies of the former Eastern European states, threatened indirect trade diversion from Latin America.[11] For the Caribbean signatories of the Lomé convention, the preferential arrangements set out would continue unchanged.

The possibility of an inter-American free-trade system, and then the slowness of its realization, captured European attention and exposed Europe's own vulnerabili-ties and opportunities with regard to Latin American trade and investment. Presi-dent Bush presented in June 1990 his Enterprise for the Americas Initiative, which proposed a western hemispheric free-trade area that was to be negotiated once the North American Free Trade Agreement (NAFTA) had been agreed upon. Europeans initially saw both opportunities and dangers in NAFTA (which began to operate in January 1994) and its possible extension to the rest of the Americas, depending on what rules of origin were adopted. The EU then made strong efforts to increase its interaction and influence with all parts of Latin America and to expand the agenda of issues beyond commercial ones. The Latin American states, concerned about the EU's commitments in Europe and seeking a counterpoise to the United States weight in any inter-American free-trade agreements, responded positively.

A number of significant actions and agreements ensued; they posed a significant challenge to the slowly developing western hemispheric free trade. In 1991 the EU and the Rio Group, the most important Latin American and Caribbean regional association, organized and held the first gathering of the Institutionalized Meeting of Rio Group-European Union Foreign Ministers. This formal association held annual meetings thereafter, alternating between European and Latin American country locales. The central questions related to regional and subregional integration, interregional trade and investment, and the strengthening of economic and commercial relations. The ministers agreed on significant measures, such as developing a new and expanded strategy for commercial exchange and adopting new regulations for the GSP in agricultural products. They also expanded the array of issues discussed. Both sides were concerned about the drug traffic, since much of the illicit narcotics entering Europe originated in Latin America. They also issued statements on democracy, human rights, poverty, the environment, and sustainable development.

Beginning in 1995, EU initiatives on free trade with Latin American subregional organizations and certain individual states moved rapidly. In December 1995 the EU and the Common Market of the South (MERCOSUR) signed an Inter-Regional Framework Agreement as a first step toward progressive liberalization of trade and increased commercial ties and political dialogue over the subsequent decade. The EU signed similar framework agreements with Chile in 1996 and with Mexico in 1997. Further negotiations ensued in all instances. In addition, the EU held meetings with the Central American states, seeking to revitalize their relationship; in 1996 they agreed to renew their San José Dialogue, which had been established at a meeting in 1984 in the midst of the Central American conflict and continued for some years thereafter. In June 1996 the EU and the Andean Community signed a declaration on political dialogue, which was followed in May 1998 by their formation of the Euro-Andean forum.[12]

The EU also took initiatives with respect to the specific controversial issue of its relations with Cuba. Steps were taken in June 1995 to commence an expanded European-Cuban relationship, but on May 7, 1996, the European Commission announced that "the necessary conditions did not yet prevail" to formalize the cooperation agreement. Nevertheless, informal talks continued, with the EU emphasizing that any agreement required movement on the part of the Cuban regime to establish a democratic transition in Cuba. The EU also criticized the hostile U.S. policy toward Cuba—in particular the Helms-Burton legislation, which threatened judicial proceedings against business enterprises in other countries that acquired U.S. properties that had been expropriated by the Cuban government after the 1959 revolution—as contrary to international law.[13]

In the EC/EU Spain sought to play the intermediary role as the regional "bridge" between Latin America and Europe. Spain, as a reflection of its own political transformation and new openness to the outside world, also endeavored to promote democratization and conflict resolution in Latin America through multilateral means. In 1991 Spain initiated the organization of the Iberoamerican Community of Nations, to be composed of Spain, Portugal, the Spanish American states, and Brazil. The First Iberoamerican Summit of heads of state or governments was held in Guadalajara, Mexico, in July 1991 and was followed by annual summits held in different member states.[14] Spain also supported the opening of Cuba and became the largest private capital investor there, in defiance of U.S. wishes and laws. With the reunification of Germany after the collapse of the Soviet Union and its domination of Eastern Europe, Germany experienced deep economic and social problems as it reintegrated the former German Democratic Republic. Nevertheless, among the European states, Germany continued to have the largest volume of Latin American trade and investment.

THE SOVIET UNION AND AFTER

Latin America in Soviet Policy

Prior to the establishment of the Soviet Union in 1917, tsarist Russia had paid little attention to geographically remote Latin America. Russia had only sporadic contacts with the region during its colonial period and throughout the nineteenth century. The first formal relations with a Latin American state came only in 1885, when diplomatic and commercial ties were established with Argentina, which were soon followed by similar arrangements with Mexico in 1887 and Uruguay in 1890.

The Soviet Union, from 1917 until its dissolution in 1991, went through several distinct periods in its Latin American policies.[15] The Soviet Union initially showed little interest in Latin America. Its policy was preoccupied with Europe, Asia, and the Middle East. The Soviet view of Latin America and commitment of minimal resources there conformed with the earlier Imperial Russian lack of interest. Following the Russian Revolution of 1917, Soviet foreign policy espoused world revolution. Soviet leaders did not ignore Latin America—the Bolshevik government attempted to create and control Latin American Communist parties and sporadically established diplomatic relations with Latin American governments—but the region did not occupy a prominent place in their calculations. They openly stated that other areas were more urgent for Soviet policy. The Soviet Union attached more importance to the Latin American area after World War II, but its interest was still limited. The rigidity of Stalinist policy and the intransigence of local Communist parties at the height of the cold war all but made it impossible for the Soviets to collaborate with the Latin American states. Only after Stalin's death in 1953 did the Soviet Union establish diplomatic, commercial, and cultural ties.

The Soviet presence in Latin America became especially significant after the Soviet attachment to the Castro revolution in Cuba. Even then, the acceptance of Marxism-Leninism by the Cuban revolutionary leadership apparently took Soviet leaders by surprise, offering them unsought and unexpected opportunities in the Caribbean. Nevertheless, a close relationship with Cuba provided the Soviet Union with its first high-priority interest in the region. Soviet activities increased around the rest of Latin America after 1964, especially in the form of expanded trade and diplomatic relations. The new attention was reflected in the establishment in 1961 of the Institute of Latin American Studies in the Academy of Sciences of the USSR at Moscow. Even with this heightened awareness of Latin American, the area remained of relatively low priority in Soviet calculations compared to that of other world regions.

Policy Calculations

After the Revolution of 1917, a difficult analytic question was posed: To what degree was Soviet policy rooted in Marxist-Leninist ideology and to what extent did it simply reflect the pursuit of national interest by a state in the international political system? The ultimate Soviet objective may have been to achieve political power in Latin America and to communize the area. The evidence suggests, however, that even in the long run this world revolutionary purpose was not a primary motivation for policy toward Latin America. Rather, Soviet goals seemed continuously to have been aimed at weakening U.S. influence in the region and at increasing the Soviet Union's as much as possible. Soviet policy makers generally perceived limited opportunities in Latin America, and their actions were cautious, the major exception being the reckless attempt to install missiles in Cuba in 1962. Their tactics, by and large, were prudent and opportunistic, taking advantage of existing conditions rather than attempting to create more favorable situations. The Soviet Union seemed to concentrate modestly on building its own influence and detracting from that of the United States, whether or not situations seemed to offer immediate prospects for Communist revolution. In sum, the Soviets assigned Latin America a low priority, sought limited objectives there, and applied generally cautious policies.

It may be argued that Soviet policies on Latin America resulted from the confluence of ideology and pragmatism. Pragmatic considerations restrained Soviet policy and discouraged imprudent "revolutionary" activities, and ideological justifications fitted power calculations of cost and risk.

For a half-century prior to the Cuban Revolution, Soviet policy makers took into account several practical considerations, which were summed up in their concept of "geographic fatalism." They viewed Latin America as an area in which the Soviet Union was placed at a great disadvantage because of geography, which meant that few opportunities to influence regional affairs would arise. The area was physically remote from the Soviet Union and far from its primary concerns; vigorous Soviet activity would require resources it did not have or could not profitably invest. The concept of geographic fatalism would seem to differ little from traditional balance-of-power calculations about geographic settings and strategic conditions. In these terms, Latin America was also seen to be dominated by the United States, which would tolerate no revolutionary government there nor allow Soviet influence to gain a strong foothold. The main constraint, however, was that the Soviet Union was deeply absorbed in its own domestic problems and involved in international affairs of higher priority than those with Latin America.

Events seemed to confirm to Soviet leaders the persistence of geographic fate. After the Bolshevik revolution and through World War II, the Soviet Union worked primarily with Latin American Communist parties through the Latin American section of the Comintern. Direct diplomatic relations with other states were few and slow in coming, so that little opportunity was presented for interstate relations. From 1917 until 1933, most Latin American states followed the U.S. lead in refusing to recognize the Soviet Union. The Good Neighbor Policy after 1933 softened Latin American's criticism of U.S. policies even as they recognized the Soviet Union. During the cold war years after World War II, Soviet probes into Latin America brought strong U.S. responses. For example, the United States successfully supported an intervention in 1954 against a leftist regime in Guatemala that had been mildly aided by the Soviet Union. The Soviets were not particularly active in the region during the first fifteen postwar years, as the United States seemed to have a controlling influence in the area.

Related to the notion of geographic fatalism was the Soviet willingness to compromise its Latin American activities when good U.S. relations were desired. Prior to 1933 Soviet objectives in the region were shaped by its desire to attain formal U.S. recognition. After recognition was granted in that year, its objective was to maintain good relations with the United States. Partly for these reasons, Soviet activities in Latin America in competition with the United States were subdued. Later, the Soviet policy of peaceful coexistence with the United States during the 1960s and détente in the 1970s had the same effect.

The Cuban Revolution of 1959 and the unexpected survival of the Castro regime changed this Soviet view of geographic fatalism, at least temporarily. The Soviet Union initially watched the course of the Cuban Revolution with skepticism and surprise, assuming first that it was not a radical revolution and then, when it proved to be one, that the United States would not allow it to survive. Under these circumstances, there seemed to be no advantage in supporting Castro's struggle in the 1950s. The Soviets made the first tentative contacts in 1960, when the new regime had been in power for more than a year. Within Cuba the Communist Party did not ally with Castro until his victory had been virtually assured. Only then did the Soviet Union seem to believe that Castro represented a genuine Latin American social revolution that could resist the United States. The Soviets first gave verbal support, then provided economic and finally military assistance. After 1961 it seemed for a time that the United States might no longer be able to dominate affairs in the Caribbean, that Castro was a precursor of regional change toward leftist regimes, and, consequently, that the Soviet Union could influence at least part of Latin America. But Soviet policy received a major blow when the United States forced it to remove its offensive missiles so boldly placed in Cuba in 1962.

Soviet intentions and power calculations leading to superpower confrontation in the missile crisis of 1962 are difficult to assess because of the secretiveness of the Soviet decision-making process. Nevertheless, strong opinions on the subject were put forward. Most of the participating U.S. decision makers at the time, and later a number of scholarly analysts, accepted as plausible the Soviet strategic objective to enhance its first-strike nuclear missile capabilities. Graham Allison, for example, saw as "the most satisfactory explanation" of Soviet action its attempt to close the "missile gap" with the United States, since the missiles in Cuba "amounted to a doubling of Soviet first strike capabilities."[16]

Revised Policy Calculations

When the United States intervened in the Dominican Republic in 1965 to prevent a "second Cuba," it signaled the Soviet Union that it remained determined to dominate the Caribbean region. Nevertheless, the Castro revolution proved durable, and other governments hostile to the United States emerged in several parts of the hemisphere. Most important, Marxist Salvador Allende was elected president of Chile (he was leader of the Socialist Party and not a Communist). Although these occurrences seemed to refute the notion of U.S. regional invincibility, other events were in the mold of past Soviet expectations. Cuban revolutionary hero Ernesto "Che" Guevara died in 1967 while leading a guerrilla band against Bolivian military forces, and a reactionary military coup deposed President Allende in 1973. The United States was linked to both actions. The Soviet Union again tested the United States in 1970 by planning the construction of a submarine base in Cuba, but vigorous U.S. protests led it to abort the plan rather than risk another military crisis with the United States.

Other calculations seemed further to restrain Soviet policies in Latin America. Ironically, because of its "success" in Cuba, the Soviet Union became more aware of the financial and political costs and risks of policy and of its military limitations. The Cuban experience suggested three basic lessons for the Soviet Union. First, the financial costs of a Soviet commitment to an economically underdeveloped ally were high and tended to escalate. It was widely assumed that during the 1960s Cuba cost the Soviet Union the equivalent of between $350 and $400 million per year and that this cost rose to about $500 million annually in the 1970s and at least doubled to $1 billion in the 1980s. To support a comparable revolution in a larger Latin American nation presumably would cost proportionally more and would involve potentially staggering financial commitments.

Second, a close relationship with a Latin American state did not guarantee that the Soviet Union would have its way politically, or that political gains would be worth the economic costs. Cuba at times asserted its independence from Soviet leadership and publicly attacked Soviet policies toward the rest of Latin America. The

Soviet Union, by its very presence, stirred nationalist resistance to its overtures. As in other parts of the world, communism proved to be compatible with nationalism rather than monolithic and was subject neither to overriding intellectual orthodoxy nor necessarily to Soviet direction. Soviet military strength was not present in Cuba to enforce compliance as it was in Eastern Europe. Political, economic, and military support to a movement like that in Cuba could not easily be reduced or terminated. The collapse of a regime closely allied with the Soviet Union because of insufficient assistance would mean a great loss of prestige.[17]

Central American Conflict

Soviet motivations for its Central American involvement after the late 1970s were sharply debated. The Reagan administration, reinforced by the Kissinger Commission report of January 1984, offered one explanation of Soviet policies. It contended that the principal thrust was Soviet expansionism, in particular Soviet-backed and Cuban-managed support for violent revolution in Central America, aimed at establishing Cuban-style Marxist-Leninist dictatorships allied with the Soviet Union. The U.S. government also advanced the "domino-theory"—that the Soviet Union, enjoying a permanent presence in the Caribbean through its Cuban surrogate, was acting to reinforce and expand this penetration into Nicaragua. Cuban assistance, the argument continued, sought to transform additional countries into Marxist states, beginning with El Salvador. From there communism would spread to the other small Central American countries and then threaten the major bordering states of Mexico to the north and Colombia and Venezuela to the south; Mexico was the "big domino."

Certain implications evolved from this calculation of Soviet motives. In particular, Communist expansion, leading to a more extensive permanent presence, would offer the Soviet Union significant military advantages with the establishment of military bases in the region. Such bases, in addition to threatening the Panama Canal and lines of communication in the Caribbean, would allow the placement of hostile forces and weapons (conventional and nuclear) capable of striking deep within the United States and Latin American states. They would allow extended Soviet naval operations without the necessity of returning to the Soviet Union. Such a situation would force significant alterations in the U.S. forward-deployment strategy, as a previously secure area would either require resources to be diverted from other areas or the creation of new ones.

U.S. assumptions about the expansionist purposes of the Soviet Union and its aligned partners may be challenged by plausible alternative explanations. The Reagan administration-Kissinger Commission analysis about the sources of Soviet behavior, with its exclusionary emphasis on ideology and expansionism, was incomplete. Those who held this view made assertions about Soviet motivations but did not ask the same questions about the Soviets that, we may assume, they asked of themselves. What goals were realistically attainable? What costs and risks were acceptable? If Soviet policy exhibited a certain ideological consistency, it also behaved as a state in the international system. Soviet perceptions of historical inevitability and their impact on Soviet behavior could not be ignored, but, in the meantime, the Soviet Union was required to make more proximate strategic and tactical decisions. It seemed likely that maximum Soviet objectives in Central America conformed to its traditional Latin American purposes—to weaken U.S. influence and increase its own as much as possible—but within the limits of modest political and financial cost and risk. That is, the Soviet Union probably saw Central America as a target of opportunity, not of deep strategic value, and as a vulnerable investment. Furthermore, viewing Cuba and Nicaragua simply as Soviet surrogates, proxies, or puppets erroneously assumed that Cuba and Nicaragua would simply follow the Soviet lead under any circumstances. Evidence suggested diverging as well as complementary interests among them.

Yet the Soviet Union did not respond to strong U.S. anticommunist, anti-expansionist actions in Central America. This persistence defied the U.S. assumption that the Soviet Union would retreat in the face of strong counterpressures to its expansionist probing. The decline of U.S.-Soviet relations after 1979 under both President Carter and President Reagan helped explain the lack of Soviet response to forceful U.S. actions. From the Soviet view, meddling in Central America was appropriate as long as "détente" and "peaceful coexistence" were already eroded. Conversely, better general relations with the United States, particularly regarding arms control, might lead the Soviets to reduce their Central American activities.

The motivations behind Soviet behavior, however, were more complex than the above might imply. The world, including Central America, presented a highly complex picture; dialectically, it was dynamic and in constant flux. Soviet historicist ideology demanded the promotion of Communist influence, but only under favorable circumstances. The Nicaraguan Revolution of 1979 gave heightened possibilities for Soviet influence in Central America and shifted its thinking about opportunities in the U.S. sphere of influence. But the latter part of the ideological equation ("under favorable circumstances") led the Soviet Union to more pragmatic modes of ends-means and capability calculations. Although Soviet actions might respond to a "new détente," more important factors were at work—external problems involving Afghanistan, Poland, China, and the Middle East; internal economic and leadership concerns; and recognition of the high cost concomitant to the survival of a revolutionary regime.

Post–Cold War

Remarkable Soviet foreign policy reorientations after 1985, and the subsequent end of the cold war and dissolution of the Soviet Union, had profound consequences for the Soviet and then the Russian presence in Latin America. These eventualities were precipitated by the rise of Mikhail Gorbachev to premier of the Soviet Union in 1985 and his adoption of *glasnost, perestroika,* and "New Thinking" in foreign policy. In the late 1980s, Gorbachev replaced the officials controlling the Soviet Communist Party with his reform-minded supporters. The Soviet leadership concluded that under socialism the Soviet economy was actually falling farther behind the major industrial states. Furthermore, Soviet officials no longer viewed the United States as a military threat or competitor, in view of U.S.-Soviet convergence on many issues. These realities called for pragmatism in foreign policy. In Latin America, New Thinking led to a retreat from involvement in Central America and reduced priorities in Cuban relations.

The Soviet Union dramatically changed its Central American actions. It stopped delivery of heavy weapons to Cuba and Nicaragua, and in October 1989, Soviet Foreign Minister Eduard Sheverdnadze visited those two countries and applied pressure to end shipments to the Farabundo Martí National Liberation Front (FMLN) in El Salvador. The Soviet Union worked with the United States in the UN Security Council, which, in November 1989, unanimously passed a resolution creating a UN peacekeeping force in Central America. All of these moves supported the Central American peace process set in motion by the Esquipulus II initiative (see Chapter 11). The remarkable elections in Nicaragua in February 1990 ended Sandinista rule as well as the Soviet role there. According to Cole Blasier,[18] Soviet advice to undertake free elections and abide by the results may have influenced the Sandinista's decision to do so. (Castro strongly disagreed with the advice because of the disturbing implications for Cuba.) Blasier also notes the muted Soviet reaction in December 1989 to the U.S. invasion of Panama.

The long-standing relationship with Cuba was profoundly altered after 1985. With the decline of the Soviet economy and political-military power, commitments and assistance to Cuba were drastically reduced, as Soviet officials saw various generous subsidies and aid to Cuba as a significant area in which to economize. They also concluded that the new Soviet political-strategic priorities were not enhanced by Cuban cooperation. In April 1989, Gorbachev visited Castro in Havana to alert him about reduced Soviet economic support. Castro, with a huge stake in the status quo, vehemently resisted the changing relationship. Nevertheless, in 1990 the Soviets discontinued subsidizing petroleum deliveries to Cuba and Cuban sugar exports to the Soviet Union, which were especially heavy blows to the Cuban economy. In fact, the Soviets put all trade on a commercial basis at world market prices. In 1990–1991 they sharply cut Cuban grant and technical aid programs, including the number of technicians and advisers in Cuba.

Soviet decision-making regarding Cuba was a controversial matter within the changing Soviet political system. To again rely on Blasier's analysis,[19] after Gorbachev's visit to Cuba in 1989, "the USSR stood balanced between the old and new"—feeling a continued responsibility toward Cuba while fundamentally restructuring the relationship. The official policy was to remain helpful to Castro and to protect the long-term Soviet policy investment in Cuba to the extent that it could be protected, even though it had become so costly for the Soviet economy and not politically important enough to justify support at the previous generous levels. This compromise approach was strongly opposed by two contending groups. On one side, "conservative" military and intelligence officers and Communist Party traditionalists, placing value on Castro's ideological orthodoxy and his survival as a Soviet ally, favored continued abundant economic support. On the other side, "reformists" urged reducing assistance to Cuba even more, not only because of the economic drain but also because of the political cost of supporting the personalist and repressive Castro regime. The failed August 1991 coup against Gorbachev largely decided the issue in favor of the reformists, since the leaders of the pro-Castro conservative group had been among the elements of the unsuccessful coup makers.

The reformists had been increasingly impatient with Gorbachev before the coup and were by and large allied with Boris Yeltsin when he succeeded Gorbachev as premier. When the Soviet Union dissolved and was replaced by Russia and the other members of the Commonwealth of Independent States (CIS), Moscow undertook the relations with Latin America. On June 15, 1993, the Soviet combat brigade departed from Cuba as planned, ending the Russian military presence, except for some 500–1000 Russian soldiers and technicians who remained at the electronic intelligence gathering facility in Lourdes, Cuba. In July 1993, Russia granted Cuba a $380 million credit for trade cooperation and for the completion of projects earlier initiated by the Soviet Union. It was only a fraction of the assistance issuing from Moscow in previous years.[20] Since then, Soviet trade with the rest of Latin America, already at a low level, has decreased even more. Russia has been inwardly absorbed with its own continuing and severe political, economic, and social problems, and with its foreign policy toward its Eurasian neighbors and the United States. Consequently, its concern with Cuba and the rest of Latin America is of very low priority, although relatively friendly formal diplomatic relations were maintained.

JAPAN

Japan historically had a modest interest in Latin America until after World War II. Its new and expanded role was impressive, restricted as it was to economic affairs and concern for overseas Japanese communities. After 1960 Japan greatly increased its activities to become a leading investor and trader, but with virtually no political dimension to its diplomacy. This approach was consciously and carefully pursued by Japanese decision makers. With the end of the cold war and Latin America's adoption of economic neoliberalism and democratization, Japan accelerated it regional activities and added certain political dimensions to its calculations. Nevertheless, its policy remains primarily oriented toward economic objectives. Japan is much less interested in trade and investment relations with Latin America than with the United States, Europe, and neighboring Asian states. But its global economic power makes its relations with Latin America among the latter's high foreign policy priorities.

Japan's self-imposed isolation from the early seventeenth until the middle of the nineteenth century precluded ties with Latin America.[21] Toward the end of the nineteenth century and thereafter, Japan gradually increased relations through trade treaties and emigration. Even then, policies were fundamentally apolitical. Following World War II, Japan began to expand its regional involvement, with policies again revolving around economic relations and migration. Although Latin America did not rank high compared to most of Japan's other regional economic involvements, the development of relations with Latin America over the succeeding decades was particularly striking in view of Japan's past isolationism.

Japan undertook its postwar policies on Latin America in the context of its general foreign policy positions. Largely imposed after the war by the victorious United States, and reflected in Japan's new constitution, these positions also comported with the Japanese public's preferences. They focused energies almost exclusively on economic matters, allocating few resources toward defense, and placing Japan under the protection of the U.S. security umbrella. In the mid-1970s Japan began to reappraise its defense doctrines, but this reappraisal had little impact on its Latin American outlook. Japan's alliance with the United States remained too important to be eroded by taking contrary positions on relatively peripheral political or security matters like the Central American crisis. Other benefits also derived from this apolitical diplomatic posture. Not only was it considered appropriate to Japan's purposes of economic expansion and protection of overseas Japanese, it allowed Japan to avoid involvement in local Latin American conflicts and to carry on its burgeoning trade with all regime types, from right to left.

Latin America became Japan's principal postwar emigration outlet, with Brazil the most prominent recipient. About a million Japanese migrated to South America from the end of World War II to the early 1980s. About half the total number settled in Brazil, with some 80,000 in Peru, 30,000 in Argentina, and 10,000 in Bolivia. Trade relations, virtually nonexistent in the 1950s, increased from only $600,000 in 1960 to $15 billion in the early 1980s; they were supported by substantial investment and financial and technical assistance. Japanese communities in South America facilitated the trading relationships.

Japanese economic expansion in Latin America rested on a striking economic complementarity, involving trade, investment, and technical and financial assistance. Japan was required to import raw materials and food, whereas certain Latin American economies needed to export them; Japan had to export large quantities of its manufactured goods, and Latin America provided markets. Japan aimed its investment, as well as financial and technical assistance, at developing Latin American raw materials and agricultural products for export to Japan; the exchange earned was then devoted to purchasing Japanese goods. In this closed process, Latin Americans received capital and technology.

After the mid-1980s, global and regional developments further influenced Japan's Latin American policies. Japan's interest in Latin America increased with the opening of the region's economies to increased external trade and investment. Nevertheless, Japanese officials were cautious and wary of Latin America's ability to sustain economic reform, maintain political stability, and avoid xenophobia; yet they were attracted to the region's natural resources and potentially large market. In 1991

Japan's exports to Latin America surpassed the level of 1981, the year prior to the onset of the debt crisis.[22] At the behest of the United States and as part of the Enterprise for the America's initiative, Japan agreed to contribute $500 million over five years to a multilateral investment fund administered by the Inter-American Development Bank (IDB). Japan demonstrated support for Latin American democratization and respect for human rights with its involvement in Organization of American States (OAS) observer missions, with support of the Central American peace process, and with response in concert with the OAS to antidemocratic events in Peru (with which Japan had long had a special economic-social relationship).

Given Japan's almost purely economic orientation in its Latin American policies in the past, it seems that the new thrust for democracy and human rights, like its overseas development assistance and contributions to the IDB, are primarily adjuncts to economic objectives—to support the further development of Latin American market economies with which Japan trades and invests. Nevertheless, Japan also has indicated ancillary purposes in its aid policies to promote cooperation regarding environmental and narcotics issues. Japan also differentiates among the regional states. It has increased its investments especially in Mexico, Brazil, and Argentina (in that order).

CANADA

Canada's serious interest in Latin America began only recently, essentially in the late 1960s.[23] Until then, Canada's activity in Latin America was muted by wariness toward the predominant U.S. regional role and the enormous importance of its bilateral relationship with the United States. It was further restricted by Canada's orientation toward Europe and its membership in the Commonwealth and, after World War II, in NATO.

In 1867 the United Kingdom formed the Dominion of Canada as a self-governing entity, but Canada conducted its international relations through the British diplomatic system. In 1931 Canada gained sovereign independence within the British Commonwealth and commenced to prosecute its own foreign policy. Yet, as Thomas Bruneau points out, Canada did not send its first diplomatic missions to Latin America until 1941, and only in 1960 did it organize the Latin American Division in the Department of External Affairs.[24] In the private sector, as Bruneau further notes, Canadian economic involvement dated at least from the late nineteenth century with the activities of Canadian banks, mining firms, and commercial enterprises. But Canada declined to join the Inter-American System when it was founded in 1889 and when it was organized around the Organization of American States (OAS) in 1948.

Canadian commercial banks undertook an important post–World War II role in the English-speaking Caribbean, becoming active in the British colonies and then continuing to dominate their banking systems after they gained independence beginning in the early 1960s. Canadian banks expanded into other states in the

Caribbean as well. Canada took independent action in Latin America in 1962, when Prime Minister John G. Diefenbaker's Conservative government decided to continue diplomatic and trade relations with Fidel Castro's Cuba after they had been ruptured by both the United States and almost all of the Latin American states.[25]

Beginning in 1968, the Liberal government of Prime Minister Pierre Trudeau reoriented Canadian policies in Latin America. Canada's increased attention was reflected in its augmented diplomatic representation in the region. In 1972 Canada became a member of the Inter-American Development Bank (the first nonmember of the OAS to do so) and a permanent observer to the OAS. Its primary regional interest continued to be commercial and economic, and its policies had little political-security content. In about 1976 Canadian officials adopted a "hemispheric middle power" concept that emphasized bilateral relations, especially trade, with certain Latin American states.[26] The priority partners were Brazil, Mexico, Chile, Colombia, and Venezuela, with whom Canada's trade expanded significantly. Canada not only counted on their expanding economies but also perceived them as becoming relatively independent of the United States and as sharing common positions, not in congruence with those of the United States, on the law of the sea negotiations, on conflict in Central America, and on the issue of Cuba. Development assistance was extended almost entirely to the Commonwealth Caribbean Countries, where Canada felt it had special interests and responsibilities.

The Latin American debt crisis of the 1980s, beginning in 1982, caused Canada to alter both its positive view of the region's potential and its own role in the region. The idea of hemispheric middle power partnerships was abandoned and replaced by a Third World perception. Canada paid more attention to Central America, sharing European views that conflict there was the result of internal social, political, and economic factors, and not, as the United States said, a function of East-West conflict. It shifted economic relations to Asia and the Pacific Rim, although its presence in the Commonwealth Caribbean continued. The result was the neglect of the larger Latin American countries with whom Canada had recently established strong relationships.

Canada's inter-American policies entered a new phase in 1989, facilitated by Latin America's return to democratic governance, the adoption of market-economies, and the end of the cold war. In that year the Conservative government of Brian Mulroney adopted a new "Latin American Strategy" calling for higher priority in Latin American relations. Canadian officials responsible for the region found worrisome the existing unbalanced and neglectful approach, especially in view of the end of the cold war and the rapid evolution of global and inter-American developments. Canada revived its partnership with the major South American states. The hemispheric agenda included a number of problems of interest to Canada that it saw as amenable to multilateral cooperation, such as those related to political violence, democracy and human rights, immigrant and refugee flows, trade, investment, debt, development, drug trafficking, and environmental degradation. Even as the Latin American Strategy was being formulated, Canada began to play a role in the Central American peace process (see Chapter 13), especially in the creation and operation of the UN Observer Group in Central America; in May 1991 a Canadian general was appointed its commander.[27] In the meantime, in January 1990, Canada finally became a full member of the OAS. In 1991 Canada joined the United States and Mexico in trilateral negotiations that resulted in the historic North American Free Trade Agreement (NAFTA), which went into effect on January 1, 1994.

Thus Canada had undertaken a significant role in inter-American relations. Its regional policy-making was consequently more complex, in consonance with the dynamism of the region itself and the multifarious agenda of the Inter-American System. Although Canada's newly adopted regional activism and partnership in NAFTA are in addition to its traditional globalism, they are consonant with other policy principles in place since World War II: a self-perception as a "middle power"; a commitment to multilateralism as the way to deal with pressing international problems in which it was particularly concerned, including active participation in global peacekeeping and (more recently) peacemaking; a diplomatic role as a third-party "honest broker"; a search for global and regional security based on international law; and a pursuit of Third World development through social and economic equity. The new orientation was not problem-free, however. Strong domestic forces opposed NAFTA—from trade unions to certain business enterprises to general public opinion. Canada continued to disagree strongly with the United States over the latter's persistent isolation of Cuba. Peacekeeping and other multilateral actions were a costly burden to Canada's government resources and a generally worrisome undertaking for many Canadians. Nevertheless, Canada had chosen to play a high-profile role in the hemisphere and had made long-term institutional commitments to do so.

PEOPLE'S REPUBLIC OF CHINA

From the establishment of the People's Republic of China (PRC) in 1949, following Mao Tse Tung's revolution, until the Cuban Revolution of 1959, the PRC evidenced slight interest in Latin America.[28] This lack of interest was based on a combination of factors, including China's preoccupation with consolidating its own revolution, its concerns with strengthening its relations with the Soviet Union and the United States, Latin America's geographic remoteness, and the Chinese assumption that it was in the U.S. sphere of influence. Chinese policy, to the extent that it existed, rhetorically opposed U.S. imperialism and advocated armed guerrilla struggle to overthrow Latin American regimes. Latin America generally followed the U.S. lead in isolating the PRC in world politics, including opposition to its admission to the United Nations.

The PRC attempted to establish a close relationship with Cuba after the Castro revolution. It stressed the parallel nature of their revolutions and the compatibility of Maoist and Fidelista theories of rural guerrilla warfare. By then China and the Soviet Union had fallen out over a number of fundamental issues. Thus, in Latin America only Cuba had diplomatic ties with the PRC, and only Cuba supported China's admission to the UN. The two states also commenced a modest barter trade of sugar for rice. The relationship turned conflictual, however. Castro accused the PRC of subversive activities and complained of Chinese deceit in their trading relationship. The Soviet Union simultaneously outmaneuvered the PRC with economic and military assistance to Cuba, and Cuba refused to align with the PRC against the Soviet Union.

The PRC developed only a few cooperative relationships in Latin America. It began to trade with Mexico in 1963, then with Argentina and Brazil. The divisive Cultural Revolution (1966–1969) isolated the PRC in world politics and drastically reduced what contacts existed with Latin America.

After 1970 the PRC leadership shifted away from dogmatic revolutionary ideology. The PRC's friendlier relations with the United States in 1971 enhanced its acceptance among Latin Americans. Although the PRC did not become an important actor in Latin America, its regional relations increased and changed in style. A turning point for China's relationship with the rest of the world was its entry into the United Nations in October 1971. A majority of Latin American governments voted in China's favor, and China reciprocated by supporting Latin American positions in the complex law of the sea negotiations. PRC propaganda continued its anti-imperialist rhetoric against both the United States and the Soviet Union and in support of armed struggle. In practice, however, the PRC expressed a desire for diplomatic and trade relations with Latin American governments, both civilian and military. Propaganda statements were softened in the 1980s. In the meantime, diplomatic exchanges were established after 1971, and two decades later China had relations with most of the Latin American and Caribbean states. International trade was slow to develop, but in the late 1980s it began to increase significantly, and in the early 1990s it reached an all-time high in volume and value.

ISRAEL

Israel has approached Latin America in essentially political terms. Those political interests initially centered on gaining support for the creation of an independent Israeli state and later on combating competing Arab influences, and always on protecting local Jewish communities. Policies also focused on protecting Israel's domestic arms industry (for a time Israel earned foreign exchange through large arms sales to Latin American states) and on supporting U.S. security interests in certain direct ways. Overall, Israel's objectives in Latin America may be described as active but of low priority.[29]

Prior to the establishment of the state of Israel in 1948, and even before World War II, the Zionist movement sought and gained Latin American support for the legitimation of an Israeli state. As Latin American membership in the UN initially constituted more than a third of the total, Latin American voting power was crucial to Israel for decisions made following the withdrawal of the British Mandate from Palestine. The Latin American bloc overwhelmingly supported the Israeli cause. Israeli policies toward Latin America developed slowly thereafter, as Israel devoted its scarce resources to establishing a presence in Europe and the United States. Israeli aims in Latin America always sought to protect the well-being of Jewish communities, found in all parts of the region, and to keep their support.

Israel began to place more importance on Latin America in the early 1960s. Some issues were temporary, such as the diplomatic crisis with Argentina over the kidnapping of the former Nazi Adolph Eichmann. More lasting were those issues related to the Israeli perception, during the chronic Middle East conflict, that Latin American support for its independence was eroding. As Arab states and, later, the PLO increased their activities in Latin America, Israel redoubled its diplomatic efforts. By 1968 Israel had diplomatic relations with seventeen Latin American states, excluding only some small countries. Cuba severed ties in 1973 as part of Castro's drive for leadership of the Nonaligned Movement. Israel was shocked by the support of a number of Latin American delegations for the anti-Zionist resolution passed by the General Assembly in 1975. By that time, with the decline of Latin America's relative voting power and of Israel's position in the UN, Israel had shifted its instrumental emphasis in Latin America to bilateral diplomatic efforts.

Israel attempted to garner what economic gains it could in Latin America, but economic aims were of low priority and commercial transactions modest. Argentina, Chile, Brazil, Mexico, and Venezuela were its major regional trading partners. Part of the activity was in banking, which was tied to local Jewish communities, particularly in Brazil. Oil imports from Mexico were a security matter for Israel, representing part of its effort to diversify its sources. Israel became particularly active in the transference of armaments and related technical assistance as well as other forms of technology.

Israel saw arms transfers to Latin America as of commercial value as well as helpful to keeping Israeli arms factories in production during periods of relative peace. Military transfers were a post-1967 phenomenon; they began after the Six-Day War, when Israel decided to build its own heavy arms industry. When the domestic demand was low, exports kept the arms industry at a high level of readiness. In addition, with weaponry quickly becoming obsolete, the export sale of "older generation" products helped cover the high costs of defense. Arms export policies generally had broad party support in the Israeli Knesset, but some cleavages surfaced from time to time. Criticism was voiced by prominent political leaders, yet both major parties when in power made extensive arms sales to Latin America. Sales to Argentina when it was under a military government from 1977–1983 was a particularly sensitive issue, because of both the brutal nature of the regime and the large number of Jews who were victims of repression there.

Israel saw Latin America as an arena where it could both further its own national interests and demonstrate its usefulness to its all-important ally, the United States. Consequently, Israeli diplomacy involved itself in Central American conflict after 1979—with Guatemala and El Salvador and with the *contra* movement in Nicaragua—in order to supplement U.S. efforts in the region. Israel publicly expressed sympathy with the U.S. invasion of Grenada in 1983. Thus, part of Israel's Latin American policies stemmed from its perception of the region as a U.S. sphere of influence in which Israel might benefit its bilateral relations with the United

States. With the end of the cold war, the military dimension of Israel's Latin American relations declined, to the relief of many Israelis who found the Central American military connection and the activities of certain Israeli agents highly embarrassing.

NOTES

1. Herbert Goldhamer, *The Foreign Powers in Latin America* (Princeton: Princeton University Press, 1972) is a comparative analysis of the nonhemispheric states' policies toward Latin America, organized in terms of interaction processes rather than by states; William Perry and Peter Wehner, eds., *The Latin American Policies of U.S. Allies: Balancing Global Interests and Regional Concerns* (New York: Praeger, 1985) has chapters on seven nonhemispheric states and Canada (cited individually below).

2. On European policies in general, see Esperanza Duran, *European Interests in Latin America* (London: Routledge and Kegan Paul, 1985); and Wolf Grabendorff and Riordan Roett, eds., *Latin America, Western Europe, and the U.S.: Reevaluating the Atlantic Triangle* (New York: Praeger, 1985).

3. The sovereign state actor was England until 1707; Great Britain (which comprised England, Scotland, and Wales) from 1701 to 1801; the United Kingdom of Great Britain and Ireland from 1801 to 1922; and the United Kingdom of Great Britain and Northern Ireland since 1922. In accord with British custom, the term "Britain" is used here informally to mean the United Kingdom. On British regional policies and relations, see Victor Bulmer-Thomas, ed., *Britain and Latin America: A Changing Relationship* (Cambridge: Cambridge University Press, 1989); William W. Kaufmann, *British Policy and the Independence of Latin America, 1804–1828* (New Haven, Conn.: Yale University Press, 1951); Rory Miller, *Britain and Latin America in the Nineteenth and Twentieth Centuries* (London: Longman, 1993); George Philip, "British Involvement in Latin America," in Perry and Wehner, *The Latin American Policies of U.S. Allies;* and D.C.M. Platt, *Latin America and British Trade, 1806–1914* (New York: Barnes and Noble, 1973).

4. On Spanish policies and relations, see Howard J. Wiarda, ed., *Iberian-Latin American Connection: Implications for U.S. Foreign Policy* (Boulder, Colo.: Westview Press, 1989). A provocative treatment is provided by Victor Alba, "Spanish Diplomacy in Latin America and a Note on Portuguese Diplomacy," in *Latin American Foreign Policies,* ed. Harold E. Davis, Larman C. Wilson, et al. (Baltimore: Johns Hopkins University Press, 1975). The most important work on *hispanismo* and *hispanidad* is Frederick B. Pike, *Hispanismo, 1898–1936: Spanish Conservatives and Liberals and Their Relations with Spanish America* (Notre Dame: University of Notre Dame Press, 1971). Silvia Enrich, *Historia diplomatica entre Espana e iberoamérica en el contexto de las relaciones internacionales, 1955–1985* (Madrid: Ediciones de Cultura Hispánica, 1989) deals with themes during the Franco era and with subsequent "new Spain." See also Antonio Sánchez-Gijon, "Spanish Involvement in Latin America," in Perry and Wehner, *The Latin American Policies of U.S. Allies*; and Celestino del Arenal, *La política exterior de España hacia Iberoamérica* (Madrid: Editorial complutense, 1994).

5. Alba, "Spanish Diplomacy in Latin America and a Note on Portuguese Diplomacy."

6. Alba, "Spanish Diplomacy in Latin America and a Note on Portuguese Diplomacy," includes an analysis of Portugal's overall policies toward Latin America with particular reference to Brazil. For synopses of some other European states' policies, see Manfred Mols, "West German Involvement in Latin America," Georges Fauriol and Eva Loser, "French Involvement in

Latin America," and Paul Seidenman and Joseph J. Spanovich, "Dutch Involvement in Latin America," in Perry and Wehner, *The Latin American Policies of U.S. Allies.*

7. See Alton Frye, *Nazi Germany and the American Hemisphere, 1933–1941* (New Haven, Conn.: Yale University Press, 1967).

8. See Alfred Glenn Mower Jr., *The European Community and Latin America: A Case Study in Global Role Expansion* (Westport, Conn.: Greenwood Press, 1982); and Peter H. Smith, ed., *The Challenge of Integration: Europe and the Americas* (New Brunswick, N.J.: Transaction, 1993).

9. Grabendorff noted in the latter 1980s that although the EC had made notable efforts to improve relations with Latin America, limited resolution of the basic problems had occurred and institutional relations were slight: "European Community Relations with Latin America," *Journal of Interamerican Studies and World Affairs* 29, no. 4 (Winter 1987/1988): 69–87.

10. See, for example, Luciano Berrocal, "Perspectivca 1992: El Mercado Unico Europeo. ¿Nuevo desafío en las relaciones Europa-América Latina?" *Pensamiento Iberoamericano* 15 (enero/junio 1989): 205–225; and Christian L. Freres C., Alberto van Klaveren, and Guadalupe Ruiz-Giménez, "Europa y América Latina: La busqueda de nuevas formas de co-operación," *Síntesis* 18 (septiembre/diciembre 1992): 91–178.

11. Wolf Grabendorff, "European Integration: Implications for Latin America," in *Strategic Options for Latin America in the 1990s,* ed. Colin I. Bradford Jr. (Washington, D.C.: Inter-American Development Bank, 1992).

12. Institute for European-Latin American Relations, *Bulletin* (October 1996, November 1997, and June 1998); Institute for European-Latin American Relations, *Annual Report* (1996).

13. Institute for European-Latin American Relations, *Annual Report* (1996).

14. Howard J. Wiarda, *Iberia and Latin America: New Democracies, New Policies, New Models* (Lanham, Md.: Rowman and Littlefield, 1996) discusses the nature and possibilities of the Iberian-Latin American relationships with an emphasis on mutual democratic transitions and democracy as the basis for a model of development. See also Eric Baklanoff, "Spain's Economic Strategy Toward the 'Nations of Its Historical Community': The 'Reconquest' of Latin America?" *Journal of Interamerican Studies and World Affairs* 38, no. 1 (Spring 1996): 105–127; and Robin L. Rosenberg, *Spain and Central America: Democracy and Foreign Policy* (New York: Greenwood Press, 1992).

15. Among the works on Soviet policies are Cole Blasier, *The Giant's Rival: The USSR and Latin America,* rev. ed. (Pittsburgh: University of Pittsburgh Press, 1988); W. Raymond Duncan, *The Soviet Union and Cuba: Interests and Influence* (New York: Praeger, 1985); Robert G. Carlton, ed., *Soviet Image of Contemporary Latin America: A Documentary History, 1960–1968* (Austin: University of Texas Press, 1970); Stephen Clissold, ed., *Soviet Relations with Latin America, 1918–68: A Documentary Survey* (London: Oxford University Press, 1970); Leon Gouré and Morris Rothenberg, *Soviet Penetration of Latin America* (Miami: University of Miami Press, 1975); D. Bruce Jackson, *Castro, the Kremlin, and Communism in Latin America* (Baltimore: Johns Hopkins Press, 1969); Nicola Miller, *Soviet Relations with Latin America, 1959–1987* (New York: Cambridge University Press, 1989); Eusebio Mujal-Leon, ed., *The USSR and Latin America: A Developing Relationship* (Boston: Unwin Hyman, 1988); J. Gregory Oswald, comp. and trans., *Soviet Image of Contemporary Latin America* (Austin: University of Texas Press, 1970); J. Gregory Oswald and Anthony J. Strover, eds., *The Soviet Union and Latin America* (New York: Praeger, 1970); Ilya Prizel, *Latin America Through Soviet Eyes: The Evolution of Soviet Perceptions During the Brezhnev Era 1964–1982* (New York: Cambridge University Press, 1990); and Augusto Varas, ed., *Soviet-Latin American Relations in the 1980s* (Boulder, Colo.: Westview Press, 1987).

16. Official Soviet versions of the Cuban missile crisis are found in Andrei Gromyko, "Some Implications of the Cuban Missile Crisis," in *The Foreign Policy of the Soviet Union*, 3d ed., ed. Alvin Z. Rubinstein (New York: Random House, 1972); Nikita S. Khrushchev, *Khrushchev Remembers*, trans. and ed. Strobe Talbott; introduction, commentary, and notes by Edward Crankshaw (Boston: Little, Brown, and Co., 1971).

17. The above line of analysis, further reflected in the following section, generally concurs with that of Duncan, *The Soviet Union and Cuba*, and Blasier, *The Giant's Rival*.

18. Cole Blasier, "Latin America Without the USSR," *North-South Issues* 2, no. 4 (1993). See also Jan Adams, *A Foreign Policy in Transition: Moscow's Retreat from Central America and the Caribbean, 1985–1992* (Durham: Duke University Press, 1993); Cole Blasier, "Moscow's Retreat from Cuba," *Problems of Communism* 40 (November-December 1991); W. Raymond Duncan, "Russian-American Cooperation in Latin America Since Gorbachev," in *The End of Superpower Conflict in the Third World*, ed. Melvin A. Goodman (Boulder, Colo.: Westview Press, 1992); Blanca Torres Ramírez, *Las relaciones cubano-sovieticas, 1959–1968* (México: El Colegio de México, 1971); and Wayne S. Smith, ed., *The Russians Aren't Coming: New Soviet Policy in Latin America* (Boulder, Colo.: Lynne Rienner Publishers, 1992). Of interest is Sergio A. Mikoyan, "Soviet Foreign Policy and Latin America," *Washington Quarterly* (Summer 1990): 179–191, by a prominent Soviet Latin Americanist and supporter of *perestroika*.

19. Blasier, "Latin America Without the USSR," and Blasier, "Moscow's Retreat from Cuba."

20. Blasier, "Moscow's Retreat from Cuba."

21. The following commentary is based on Peter Wehner and Eric Fredell, "Japanese Interests in Latin America," in Perry and Wehner, *The Latin American Policies of U.S. Allies*; Susan Kaufman Purcell and Robert M. Immerman, eds., *Japan and Latin America in the New Global Order* (Boulder, Colo.: Lynne Rienner Publishers, 1992); and Barbara Stallings and Gabriel Székely, *Japan, the United States, and Latin America: Toward a Trilateral Relationship in the Western Hemisphere* (Baltimore: Johns Hopkins University Press, 1993).

22. Purcell and Immerman, *Japan and Latin America in the New Global Order*.

23. On the evolution of Canada's relations with Latin America, see J.C.M. Ogelsby, *Gringos from the Far North: Essays in the History of Canadian-Latin American Relations, 1866–1968* (Toronto: Macmillan, 1976). Of special interest is Jonathan Lemco, *Canada and the Crisis in Central America* (New York: Praeger, 1991). Canadian policy reorientations since 1989 are treated by Thomas C. Bruneau, "Canadian Involvement in Latin America," in Perry and Wehner, *The Latin American Policies of U.S. Allies*; Jerry Haar and Edgar Dosman, eds., *A Dynamic Partnership: Canada's Changing Role in the Americas* (New Brunswick, N.J.: Transaction Press, 1994); Hal P. Klepak, *Canada and Latin American Security* (Quebec: Méridien, 1994); and James Rochlin, *Canada as a Hemisphere Actor* (Toronto: McGraw Hill-Ryerson, 1992). For the official statement, see Canada, Department of External Affairs, *Foreign Policy for Canadians: Latin America* (Ottawa: Queen's Printer, 1970).

24. Bruneau, "Canadian Involvement in Latin America."

25. John D. Hebron, "Turning over a New Leaf in the Americas," *Hemisfile* 4, no. 1 (January/February 1992): 8–9.

26. Edgar J. Dosman, "Canada and Latin America: The New Look," *International Journal* 47, no. 3 (Summer 1992): 529–544.

27. See Jonathan Lemco, *Canada and the Crisis in Central America* (New York: Praeger, 1991).

28. See Marisela Connelly and Romer Cornejo Bustamante, *China-América Latina: Génesis y Desarrollo de Sus Relaciones* (México, D. F.: El Colegio de México, 1992); Cecil Johnson,

Communist China and Latin America, 1959–1967 (New York: Columbia University Press, 1970); and He Li, *Sino-Latin American Economic Relations* (New York: Praeger, 1991).

29. See Edy Kaufman, Yoram Shapira, and Joel Barromi, *Israeli-Latin American Relations* (New Brunswick: Transaction Books, 1979), to be read with Edy Kaufman, "Israeli Involvement in Latin America," in Perry and Wehner, *The Latin American Policies of U.S. Allies.* Damián Fernández, *Central America and the Middle East* (Gainesville: University Presses of Florida, 1990) deals with Israel and its neighbors.

CHAPTER SIX

■

The United States

The United States is the most important external actor in the Latin American and Caribbean subsystem. The purpose of this chapter is to present a broad overview of the policy of the United States toward that region. The discussion begins with an analysis of various factors affecting the position of Latin America, and more recently of the newer Caribbean states, in U.S. foreign policy decisions. The evolution of policies and accompanying doctrines are then traced in some detail, in terms of the factors previously identified.

THE LATIN AMERICAN POSITION IN U.S. POLICY

Policy Ends and Means

U.S. relations with Latin America seem to be characterized by abrupt changes in U.S. policy, especially in the twentieth century after the rise of the United States to great-power and then superpower status. The intensity of U.S. interest and the extent of its activities have varied over time and according to the subregions involved. However, from the beginning of U.S.-Latin American relations in the early nineteenth century to the end of the cold war, U.S. policy was consistent and continuous at a fundamental level. Although purposes were often couched in moral rhetoric, they were almost always calculated in terms of national security. Thus the U.S. approach to decision-making seemed to be in consonance with the realist school's assumptions that policy was and should be based on national interests and calculations about state capability and interstate balances of power. Inasmuch as the United States made an essentially strategic calculation, that is true; but other elements—especially ideology, perceptions, and the nature of the U.S. political system—erode this notion. Furthermore, in recent years as transnational phenomena have increased in importance, a realist-rational choice process has been difficult to maintain.[1]

For 180 years, from the beginning of U.S.-Latin American relations until the end of the cold war, the U.S. goal of keeping hostile foreign influences out of the Western Hemisphere was the key to understanding U.S. policy behavior in Latin America. Lars Schoultz has labeled this special way of thinking about the region as "strategic denial."[2] U.S. policy makers were preoccupied with threats that great powers outside the hemisphere might pose to U.S. security through their operations in Latin America. They attempted to prevent, exclude, or minimize foreign (nonhemispheric) influence and control in Latin America. Such intrusions were viewed as inimical to U.S. military, political, and economic interests (as specifically defined at different times and places). The United States feared some part of the region might serve as a military base of operations against it, and it competed vigorously against the economic influence of other external industrial states. This mentality was relatively constant from as early as 1811 until the late 1980s, whether the extrahemispheric rival was Great Britain in 1811, France and Spain in the 1820s, Great Britain again in the 1850s, Germany at the turn of the century and again in the 1930s, or the Soviet Union after 1947.[3]

A related ideological element was present: The United States feared that threats might penetrate the region in such forms as monarchism in the nineteenth century, fascism in the 1930s, and communism during the cold war. Some realists say that these ideological considerations undercut the realism and rationality of U.S. decisions. According to them, a concern with ideology tends to disguise the prime importance of power as the key to understanding foreign policy goals and strategies, and to introduce a distracting emotional element to decision-making.

Geographic distinctions and capability estimates were factored into the security calculations. Policy makers adopted differentiated views of the subregions within Latin America, and distinct capability considerations were applied to these separate policy arenas. Thus, the degree of U.S. concern with Latin America and the level of its activities there fluctuated with perceptions of foreign threats. Shifting U.S. policy approaches, whether interventionist, noninterventionist, developmentalist, or benign neglect, sprang initially from the objective of excluding foreign threats if they were perceived to exist.

Other objectives were sought, but more often than not they were linked to the long-range purpose of strategic denial. Once the preliminary concern with Latin American security with respect to nonhemispheric actors was minimally satisfied, the United States felt free to pursue closer objectives, which were usually (but not always) justified by linking them to the long-term concerns with "foreigners." The goal of promoting, encouraging, or developing political and economic stability in Latin America derived from the assumption by U.S. leaders that the overall interests of the United States, as a major, industrial, metropolitan, status quo state, were best served in a secure, peaceful, and stable world. This general goal, when applied to Latin America, was often a corollary to that of excluding foreign influence, in that the maintenance of Latin American stability was presumed to be a prerequisite for reducing nonhemispheric threats in the region. Likewise, the consistent pursuit of commercial advantage and vacillating attempts to "democratize" Latin America were often seen as "springboards" to realize the superior objectives. Economic and democratic development were seen as paths to stability and as ways to preempt certain foreign overtures by offering economic and political alternatives. Military interventions, occasioned by the fear of intervention by other outsiders and designed to preempt them, also sought to bring stability to what were considered chaotic situations.

This interpretation runs counter to arguments that the "strategic denial" framework is really a cover for commercial interests and economic domination, or, after World War II and especially in the 1980s, a pretense for simplistic anticommunism. The historical evidence suggests, however, that security concerns transcended other considerations. That is, U.S. policy goals and orientations toward the other Americas derived on the basis of external threat perceptions or the lack of a sense of threat. The intensity of U.S. interest and activities paralleled the degree of external threat perception. As a general matter, over time the United States was most active in Latin America when nonhemispheric states seemed most threatening; and, conversely, during periods when such threats seemed to be low or nonexistent, policy became less connected with security problems. At those times, the United States was inclined to slight the region. This allowed private interests a free hand in their commercial activities, perhaps supported by U.S. policy. In a stance more often than not justified in terms of the quest for security through political stability, the United States at times pressed Latin America for procedural democracy, a concern that in recent decades was linked to demands for human rights. A lack of foreign threats muted even the concern with stability, with the United States sometimes choosing to do little if anything.

This interpretation is also disputed by dependency schools of IR. From 1898 until the late 1920s, the United States clearly practiced classic imperialism in the circum-Caribbean, but this policy was then dismantled and disappeared. But anti-imperialist critics of U.S. policy, especially after World War II, referred to neocolonialism as the operating concept in U.S. policies. In my view, the Latin American policy of the United States was better explained in terms of an often exaggerated fear of Soviet expansionism, a benign neglect when that fear abated, and vacillating attempts to "democratize" Latin America, all within the context of inherent power disparities. Elements of a sphere-of-influence structure persisted, however, in terms of power politics and economic dependency. They were reasserted from time to time, most clearly in U.S. coercive interventions. But U.S. actions were not so much a concerted or systematic imperial policy as an ad hoc application of instruments to deal with problems related to perceptions of extrahemispheric threats in the circum-Caribbean as they arose.[4]

Strategic denial sometimes led to positive actions, such as inter-American cooperation in the 1930s and World War II and the Alliance for Progress in the 1960s. Some threats were truly provocative, as during the Cuban missile crisis in 1962 when the Soviet Union placed nuclear weapons in Cuba. But more often than not, in my view, strategic denial resulted in misguided policies based on exaggerated threat perceptions, and in dysfunctional consequences—as, for example, the consequences that followed from Caribbean imperialism during the first third of the twentieth century and from Central American policies in the 1980s.[5]

Perceptions

Since the strategic denial paradigm concentrated on what great-power rivals might do in Latin America that would affect U.S. security, U.S. policy makers tended to view Latin Americans themselves as unimportant players on the international stage. Although the approach meant attempting to assure the independence and self-determination of Latin America with regard to the other external states, a strain of paternalism also ran throughout U.S. policy. U.S. officials have often taken a paternal attitude toward Latin Americans and have been reluctant to relinquish predominance in the region (especially in the Caribbean area), assuming that Latin Americans were incapable of handling their own affairs and needed U.S. supervision.

These paternalist attitudes were reinforced with a negative appraisal of Latin American culture. Analysts who have investigated the perceptions that U.S. decision makers have had of Latin Americans tend to be struck by the persistence of negative stereotypes and paternalistic attitudes. A disdain for the peoples and institutions of the region was evident in the earliest days of inter-American relations and was carried forward thereafter. John Johnson, in a study of the Spanish American struggle for independence (at the time that strategic denial was first articulated), analyzes the pronounced shift in U.S. views, from a pro-insurgent perspective prior to Latin American independence to one of limited interest and disdain by 1830. He concludes that in the complexity and confusion of U.S. policy in the 1980s, the early policy reveals "more than mere glimmerings of why a cloud of misunderstanding, apprehension, and distrust has overhung hemispheric relations for more than two centuries." Frederick Pike argues that U.S. stereotypes of Latin Americans date from the first colonial-period contacts and have continued to impinge on relations to the present day. The stereotypes derive, Pike says, from the U.S. view of Latin America's civilization as "primitive." Lars Schoultz also finds U.S. belittlement of Latin America a historical constant. Schoultz asserts that "a belief in Latin American inferiority is the essential core of United States policy toward Latin America because it determines the precise steps the United States takes to protect its interests in the region." He goes on to say that "other beliefs would not have changed U.S. interests, but they would have led to different policies for protecting those interests." Howard Wiarda, with reference to U.S. outlooks and practices in the 1980s, says that "U.S. policies are shrouded in myths, stereotypes, and inaccuracies, growing from our condescending and patronizing attitudes."[6] Realists would also argue in this instance that such stereotyping, like ideology, erodes the realist-rational decisional processes.

Policy Arenas

The United States further formulated its Latin American policies on the subregional levels. Geographic and other extrasocietal conditions affected U.S. strategic calculations, perceptions, and capabilities. Consequently, the United States had overlapping but distinct policies toward the overall Latin American region, Mexico, the circum-

Caribbean and its subdivisions, and South America beyond the Caribbean (the Southern Cone), with a special view of Brazil. It simultaneously pursued the entire range of bilateral relations. In other words, distinct U.S. policy arenas followed along the lines of the various Latin American subregions identified in Chapter 2.

The United States has always had a special and intense interest in Mexico.[7] As discussed earlier, U.S. policy toward Mexico was determined primarily by territorial proximity. Many of the considerations in this relationship were largely divorced from those at work in the larger inter-American arena. Issues tended to be "North American" in content and closely associated with U.S. domestic concerns. In the nineteenth century the United States gained immense territory from Mexico as a result of Texas independence and the war of 1845–1848. European interventions also occurred, most notably Mexico's incorporation into the French empire from 1862–1865, while the United States was occupied with its civil war. But during the dictatorship of Porfirio Díaz (1876–1910), U.S. entrepreneurs dominated aspects of the Mexican economy. After the Mexican Revolution of 1910, Mexico adopted highly protectionist economic policies and an essentially isolationist political orientation toward the outside world. After War II the United States clearly was still the stronger partner. Yet it confronted the reality of increasing mutual dependency, shaped especially by expanding economic and social linkages. Mexico fit awkwardly into U.S. cold war constructs. In the post-cold war era the issues are overwhelmingly the extension of the critical domestic concerns of both parties, not easily fitted into an overall foreign policy strategy for either side.

U.S. officials always considered the circum-Caribbean—which they preferred to call the Caribbean Basin—to be especially important to U.S. security and well-being.[8] In fact, the concept of strategic denial was developed with primary reference to the circum-Caribbean and was most actively pursued there. That element was less sustained toward the Southern Cone and was reserved for special circumstances. During periods of intense interest based on perceived external threats, the United States attempted to dominate the Caribbean, whereas it was usually satisfied with a more restricted role in the South American zone. The United States intervened militarily only in Mexico and the Caribbean; it never landed its troops in the Southern Cone.

Brazil also occupied a special role in U.S. policy.[9] The United States long cultivated amicable relations with the "sleeping giant" of Latin America, accelerating its efforts in the mid-1970s as Brazil seemed to be on the verge of realizing its world-power ambitions. Once Brazil became the junior partner in a cooperative alignment with the United States, U.S. policies implied a regard for Brazil's increasing regional and even world importance; but that regard declined with Brazil's increasing economic and political problems in the 1980s. Those overtures were revived in the post-cold war period, but Brazil emphasized its relationships with neighboring states.

As a general matter, the United States generally assigned the Southern Cone, except for Brazil, the lowest priority in its Latin American policies. It did exert leverage there (especially economic) and sometimes applied coercive measures. But the United States only intermittently felt threatened by the activities of extrahemispheric interests there, as during the two world wars and episodically during the cold war. U.S. officials, except perhaps for a brief time after World War II, did not consider the Southern Cone to be part of its sphere of influence.

Democracy and Human Rights

Historically, one of the most perplexing and chronically troublesome aspects of U.S. policy on Latin American was the proper official attitude to be taken toward Latin American governmental forms and behavior and the extension of U.S. values to other states.[10] The fundamental issue was whether to pursue republican forms of government (representative democracy) and the protection of human rights as goals of policy. The U.S. government and its articulate populace generally sympathized with democratic elements in Latin America, and formal commitments to democratic processes were made through several inter-American conventions. The actual promotion of democracy, however, received shifting emphasis over the years.

U.S. attempts to extend the practices of representative democracy and the protection of human rights were ambiguous and vacillating. The concepts were rooted in American idealism and were not shared, until recently, by European states, who saw such efforts as misguided and not in keeping with their own widely shared realist tenets. Yet when the United States committed resources to the goal of democratic development, it was usually viewed as an instrumental objective aimed at achieving stability and thus contributing to security against outside threats. (For a discussion of the policy analytic problem, see Chapter 14.)

The Search for a New Paradigm

As the international system entered the post–cold war era in the late 1980s, the United States faced the problem of redefining its purposes in Latin America and reorienting its policies there.[11] Because the Soviet Union and Communist expansionism had been the focus of strategic denial for more than four decades, the declaration of an end to the cold war had a major impact on U.S. policy calculations toward Latin America. With the end of East-West conflict and the eventual collapse of the Soviet Union, and with no other security threats (as traditionally conceived) on the horizon, the notion of strategic denial was rendered irrelevant as a foundation for Latin American policy and had to be discarded. The critical issues had nothing to do with extrahemispheric threats. Consequently, U.S. decision makers abandoned the 180-year old idea of strategic denial and searched for a new general framework for processing the issues. In time they adopted a framework that focused on the essentiality of Latin American democracy and the respect for human rights coupled with economic well-being; other high-priority problems were subsumed within the new paradigm on the grounds that their resolution depended on Latin American democratic and economic success. The U.S. military operations commenced in Panama in 1989 and in Haiti in 1994 indicated a continuing willingness to act as policeman of the Caribbean. Some commentators feared that with the elimination of the anti-Soviet geopolitical underpinning for policies, the United States would adopt substitute rationales for strategic denial.[12] In fact, the drug traffic seemed to replace Central American conflict as the intractable problem that compromised multilateralism and rationalized policy ends justifying covert means.

The Policy-Making System

The nature of the U.S. policy-making system itself influences the content of U.S. policy toward Latin America and the Caribbean. U.S. officials make decisions in a political system that encourages conflict over policy and its fragmentation and makes difficult its accommodation and coordination.[13] This reality puts limits on U.S. capabilities, but it also reflects internal disagreements over the selection of policy ends and means.

Policy conflict involves variance of principles and interests held by the key players and disharmony and divisiveness in the policy process. Conflict, inherent to the constitutional system of checks and balances, is most notable in the relations of the executive and legislative branches and in the public opinion and constituent pressures to which they are sensitive; it is found in the bureaucratic politics within those branches as well. In addition, the federal system allows the individual states a role in the process; although the national government is preeminent in foreign policy, the growth of transnational phenomena has facilitated independent international activities on the part of the states. The entire process is intensified by the competing perceptions and policy preferences of the influential nongovernmental actors (such as business, labor, church, human rights, and other groups and the media). Policy fragmentation results in a government that speaks with many voices—a lack of central policy coordination that contradicts the realist school's image of a unitary state. Fragmentation and conflict have been found throughout U.S. history, with infrequent exceptions (such as in World War II and at certain times during the cold war). These elements were intensified in the latter 1960s, initially as a result of the Vietnam War, and have characterized Latin American policy-making up to the present, with only a brief respite.

Bipartisanship, strictly speaking, is the cooperation between the two major political parties, manifested especially in the willingness of the Congress and President to collaborate. The expression is also used in the broader sense of general cooperation within the political system. Cooperation may be based on consensus but seems to rely more often on agreement. Consensus involves a common purpose and a harmony of interests and outlooks among the key policy players, whereas agreement, rather than commonly held values, involves a willingness to compromise and accommodate differences in order to produce mutually acceptable results or something of value to all parties.[14]

Globalization and transnationalization have made U.S. policy-making even more fragmented and complicated by increasing the numbers of actors on the foreign policy stage, and have thus further eroded any notion of an authoritative "foreign policy community." Nonstate actors have extended their external linkages and increased their determination to influence foreign policy-making. The states, traditionally on the periphery of foreign policy, now participate in a major way, such as sending foreign trade missions and lobbying on immigration policy.

EVOLUTION OF POLICY

The Nineteenth Century

Isolationism and the Western Hemisphere Idea.   The U.S. foreign policy orientation, beginning with independence in the late eighteenth century and continuing throughout most of the nineteenth century, was characterized by isolationism.[15] However, policy was never founded on a literally isolationist basis of absolute nonintercourse with the rest of the world. Isolationism was relevant primarily to Europe, and then in the special sense of political "nonentanglement."

The principle of noninvolvement did not extend to relations with Latin America in the same sense that it was applied to European affairs. The initial U.S. orientation toward Latin America was contained in the Western Hemisphere Idea, also known as the Doctrine of the Two Spheres.[16] This concept posited a special relationship among all the American states, based on the geographic separation of the Americas from Europe and on the notions of political, economic, and social separation of the morally superior New World from the evil, autocratic Old World. The essence of the idea was that the Western (American) Hemisphere was separate and distinct from Europe and had its own set of interests. In general, this notion served as the basis both for the isolation of the Americas from Europe and for ties among the Americas themselves.

The Western Hemisphere Idea did not contradict the negative U.S. perception of Latin America indicated above. As a result of its own successful independence movement and creation of a constitutional representative political system, the United States expressed strong criticism of Europe's corrupt, royal, and hierarchical political systems and rigid class order of privilege based on birth and wealth. But the United States also developed a superiority complex about its institutions and values in the New World. Historians have called this a nationalist conviction of "exceptionalism": the belief that the United States held an exceptional historical position because of its special characteristics—a republican political system, economic opportunity for all, and triumph over an open continent. This notion of exceptionalism also included an understanding of the nation as white, Anglo-Saxon, and Protestant; it adversely affected relations with multiracial, Iberian, and Roman Catholic Latin America (and was complicated by the divisive slavery issue in the United States).

Fear of Foreign Influences and the Monroe Doctrine.   Initial contacts with Latin America were slow in developing. The United States began the recognition process there in 1822, partly out of sympathy with Latin Americans' desire for independence but more in the unfulfilled hope that they thereby would not be dependent on Britain or recolonized by France or Spain. The United States did not desire closer political relations, turning down Latin American overtures to form an inter-American defense alliance against Europe. The United States was eager for expanded commercial contacts but was preempted by British economic power.

Strategic denial was established at the beginning of inter-American relations in the first quarter of the nineteenth century, in consonance with the isolationist orientation and the Western Hemisphere Idea. The emergence of new Latin American states stimulated international rivalry to gain regional influence or control. The United States was weak in relation to the European powers, but it nevertheless enunciated principles that laid the foundations for the strategic denial approach. The first such statement was the U.S. Congress's No-Transfer Resolution of 1811.[17] At the time, Great Britain was on the verge of war with the United States and threatened to seize Spanish Florida and use it as a military base. In response, the U.S. Congress adopted the resolution that asserted, among other things, that the United States "cannot without serious inquietude see any part of the said territory pass into the hands of any foreign Power." The United States was also worried that the British might take Cuba as well. The No-Transfer Resolution accorded with the Western Hemisphere Idea, in that although the United States had no objection to Spain's retention of its American possessions, it would view unfavorably the transfer of lands bordering the United States to a third party (meaning Britain).

U.S. fear of nonhemispheric influences, as well as the idea of hemispheric separateness, were further revealed in 1823, when President James Monroe issued a warning to Europe to keep "hands off" the Western Hemisphere. This broader expression of strategic denial was later called the Monroe Doctrine and considered the "cornerstone" of overall U.S. foreign policy.[18] The policy had its genesis in President Monroe's "declaration" or "principles"; the term "doctrine" was not used until much later. Monroe's statement defined the contemporary U.S. attitude toward Europe's relationship with the Americas, and that of the United States toward Latin America. It reflected more than anything else the U.S. desire to limit foreign influence in the Americas. Elements had already been stated in the 1811 congressional No-Transfer Resolution.

Monroe's statement, included in his annual message to Congress on December 2, 1823, was inspired by the perception of two separate threats.[19] The first was the fear of Russian colonization of the North American Pacific coast, which led to the general declaration "that the American continents, by the free and independent condition which they have assumed and maintain, are henceforth not to be considered as subjects for future colonization by any European power." The second part addressed the challenge represented by Spain's desire to retrieve its New World empire with the help of the French-led Holy Alliance. After noting that "the political system of the allied powers is essentially different . . . from that of America," Monroe said:

> We owe it therefore to candor, and to the amicable relations existing between the United
> States and those powers, to declare that we should consider any attempt on their part to

extend their system to any portions of this Hemisphere, as dangerous to our peace and safety. With the existing Colonies or dependencies of any European power, we have not interfered, and shall not interfere. But with the governments who have declared their independence, and have maintained it, and whose independence we have, on great consideration, and on just principles, acknowledged, we could not view any interposition for the purpose of oppressing them, or controlling them in any other manner, their destiny, by any European power, in any other light, than as the manifestation of an unfriendly disposition towards the United States.

Monroe also arrogantly assured Europe of U.S. reciprocity: "Our policy in regard to Europe, which was adopted at an early state of the wars which have so long agitated that quarter of the globe, nevertheless remains the same, which is, not to interfere in the internal concerns of any of its powers."

Monroe's declaration was unilateral, fairly narrow in scope, and intended to be temporary. Its unilateral nature was made clear when the United States turned down a prior British proposal that the two states issue a joint declaration. Furthermore, immediately after the pronouncement, the United States rebuffed Latin American suggestions for treaties of alliance. Monroe restricted his warning to future colonization and was tolerant toward existing colonies; he mentioned nothing of prohibiting other forms of European intervention or influence as later interpretations were to do. That the policy was intended to be temporary was indicated by the fact that, for most of the half-century following Monroe's pronouncement, it was largely ignored as a policy guide. Once the immediate danger had passed, and during the long period of U.S. military weakness and domestic preoccupations, Monroe's words were virtually forgotten. President James K. Polk did "restate" Monroe's principles in 1845, with the possibility of Europeans gaining concessions or colonies in areas of North America. But a number of European military interventions and even colonizations occurred in Latin America and brought little response by the United States; it was willing to let Britain take the responsibility for the region from the designs of other European powers.

Continental Expansion and Manifest Destiny.   During the first half of the nineteenth century, the United States was preoccupied with continental expansion. This was expressed in the ideology of "manifest destiny," the widespread idea that the United States was entitled to expand its control across the virgin continent from one ocean to the other.[20] The process of continental expansion inevitably brought the United States into conflict with Mexico and eventually led to Caribbean imperialism.

In only fifty years, between 1803 and 1853, continental U.S. territory expanded from the area occupied by the original thirteen colonies to essentially its present boundaries, with most of the added territory taken from what was originally Spanish America. The first and largest single acquisition was the purchase in 1803 of the Louisiana Territory from France, to whom Spain had ceded the area in 1800. Its addition more than doubled the U.S. territorial size. For fifteen years after the Louisiana Purchase, the United States negotiated with Spain for the "Floridas," actually seizing some territory in 1810 and 1813. In 1819, the two states signed the Adams-Onís Treaty (it went into effect in 1821), in which Spain ceded to the United States all of its Gulf Coast lands east of the Mississippi River.

Years of conflict with Mexico culminated in war between the two states, which resulted in huge territorial gains for the victorious United States. The United States and Mexico had clashed for decades over the Texas question. Texans had won their independence from Mexico in 1836 after a violent struggle, and finally, in 1845, Texas had become a state in the union. Mexican objections to the annexation and to continuing U.S. expansionist tendencies led to war (1846–1848). Under the Treaty of Guadalupe Hidalgo, signed in 1848, Mexico ceded half its national territory to the United States, including what today constitutes much of the U.S. West and Southwest. In 1853, exactly fifty years after the Louisiana Purchase, the continental dimensions of the United States were completed with the Gadsden Purchase from Mexico, except for some later minor adjustments.

In addition, the United States felt that the future of the Caribbean region directly affected its security. U.S. leaders from time to time considered pursuing territorial gains in the Caribbean region, but their efforts were frustrated by a recalcitrant Congress that refused to approve them. Cuba was of special importance, as was the interest in building a Central American isthmian canal. The U.S. public sympathized with Cuban insurgents revolting against Spanish authority between 1868 and 1878, but the United States remained neutral even though the Cubans requested its intervention in their favor. Schemes to purchase the Danish West Indies and to annex Santo Domingo as well as Cuba were advanced but came to nothing. No further Latin American territory was taken by the United States until after its war with Spain in 1898.

Democratic Policy and Pan Americanism. A U.S. policy tradition on the question of relations with nondemocratic regimes was established at the very start of inter-American relations. Throughout the nineteenth century and into the twentieth, Spanish American political processes were characterized by personalist dictatorships (Brazil was successfully governed under a constitutional monarchy). The United States enunciated broad policy outlines in the spirit of its recognition of the revolutionary French government in 1793. On that occasion, Secretary of State Thomas Jefferson said: "We surely cannot deny to any nation that right whereon our own government is founded that everyone may govern itself under whatever form it pleases." Later, as president, Jefferson applied this principle specifically to Latin America. With few exceptions, such as Secretary of State William H. Seward's opposition to monarchy in Mexico in 1865 (in fact, an opposition to French occupation), the Jeffersonian tradition guided policy until the presidency of Woodrow Wilson after 1913.

The United States inaugurated the Pan-American movement in the 1880s, primarily for the purposes of promoting hemispheric trade and developing procedures for the peaceful settlement of disputes. It was not interested in security questions, the primary Latin American concern, and consistently strove to keep them off conference agendas. The First International Conference of American States, held in Washington in 1889–1890, initiated the Pan-American policy of the United States. It reflected the interests of U.S. businesspeople who had recently discovered trade and investment opportunities in Latin America. Policy was also motivated by the potential for promoting international stability through peaceful settlement procedures and for gathering Latin America together in a single organization under U.S. leadership, thus preempting other foreign influences.

The Latin American policy of the United States from the last decade of the nineteenth century through the first third of the twentieth was characterized by tension between the Monroe Doctrine and Pan Americanism; the latter began in earnest in 1889, but the former dominated until the 1930s. Both of these policy approaches flowed from the Western Hemisphere Idea and posited a special relationship among the Americas. But they were also contradictory, in that the Monroe Doctrine was a unilateral policy that came to justify U.S. Caribbean intervention, whereas Pan Americanism was based on the idea of international equality and cooperation. Even though the inter-American conferences beginning in 1889 posited a policy of U.S. cooperation with Latin America, multilateral diplomacy on a partnership basis was not a commitment of U.S. policy until the 1930s. Until then, unilateral imperialism superseded multilateral cooperation.

The Twentieth Century to World War II

The Imperialist Era.   During the last few years of the nineteenth century, the United States changed its policy orientation from traditional isolationism to a rudimentary internationalism. The nation passed through a period of policy transition that resulted in active participation in world affairs and elevation to the status of a great power. The new orientation revived U.S. interest in Latin America and ended its policy inaction, but it resulted in the beginnings of imperialism and coercive policies in the Caribbean area (as well as the far reaches of the Pacific Ocean).[21] The United States demonstrated a new assertiveness in 1895, when it was willing to defy even Great Britain in the latter's dispute with Venezuela over the boundary with British Guiana. Richard Olney, secretary of state under President Grover Cleveland, asserted the Monroe Doctrine against Great Britain during the dispute. His note to the British foreign minister, which claimed U.S. hegemony in the Americas, was dubbed the Olney Corollary to the Monroe Doctrine.

A new wave of nationalism that swept the United States in the 1890s led to war with Spain and resulted in territorial acquisitions in the Caribbean area. A new interpretation of manifest destiny reaching beyond continental limits was typified by the "Expansionists of 1898" who helped mold U.S. public opinion; the Caribbean region loomed large in their thinking. The most important of them was Captain (later Admiral) Alfred Thayer Mahan, who shaped official strategic thinking about the Caribbean for many years to come. Among his converts were Senator Henry Cabot Lodge and President Theodore Roosevelt.

Mahan was the founder of strategic-geopolitical thought in the United States. Like other geopolitical analysts, Mahan was a realist who looked to strategic positions that were rooted in the relationship of geographic and power-political realities in order to determine policy choices. Mahan's sea power thesis, dating from the 1890s and developed from his study of naval history, revolved around his concern with the relationship of mercantilist imperialism and sea power to national security and progress ("destiny").[22] Mahan's influence was reflected to some degree in the thinking of U.S. policy makers until the end of the cold war. Yet it may be argued that almost as soon as Mahan's theories became accepted as the foundation for U.S. policy in Latin America, their relevance began to be eroded by military technological developments—first by the submarine and aircraft and later by nuclear weapons. Nevertheless, until mid-century they were accepted by U.S. strategists as an article of faith, evidenced by the sacrosanctity of the Panama Canal in statements by military officials and diplomats until well into the nuclear age.

According to Mahan, national greatness depended on the three related factors of maritime strength, sea power, and imperialism; therefore, no great nation could be isolationist. U.S. action in the circum-Caribbean was a critical matter; Mahan strongly advocated the construction of an isthmian canal because it would draw the Pacific, Atlantic, and Gulf Coasts of the North American continent closer together. But he warned of the "many latent and as yet unforeseen dangers to the peace of the Western Hemisphere, attendant upon the opening of the canal," because the then comparatively deserted Caribbean Sea would become, like the Red Sea, a great thoroughfare of shipping that would attract "the interest and ambition of maritime nations." Such increased rivalry from Europe in the Caribbean would be a disaster to the United States "in the present state of her military and naval preparation." Thus if the United States were to build a canal it must also look to its own continental defenses, build a strong navy for offensive power, control the entire Caribbean area through the acquisition of bases, and fortify and exclusively control any canal. For Mahan, Mexico was of less strategic importance than most of the Caribbean, largely because the Gulf of Mexico lacked a satisfactory harbor for warships. Thus he emphasized the acquisition of bases in the Caribbean islands, circling the eastern approaches to the Central American isthmus.

The war with Spain in 1898 lasted only ten weeks, after which a peace treaty was concluded under terms dictated by the United States.[23] As a result, the United States annexed Puerto Rico, established a protectorate over Cuba, and occupied some smaller Caribbean islands. U.S. leaders became unequivocally determined to build and exclusively control a transisthmian canal, and concrete arrangements were so made. In 1917 the United States purchased the Danish West Indies (the U.S. Virgin Islands). Spain was now completely ejected from the hemisphere; Great Britain was willing to retire from the Caribbean area; and U.S. public opinion supported the new U.S. strategic position.

In 1904 President Theodore Roosevelt enunciated the broadest extension of Monroe's principles by far. Known as the Roosevelt Corollary, the principle asserted that U.S. interventions in the Caribbean were justified. Two years before, Germany, Great Britain, and Italy had blockaded Venezuela to enforce their financial claims, but at the behest of the United States they agreed to submit the dispute to The Hague Court of Arbitration. The court's ruling, which upheld the argument of the European powers that they should receive preferential treatment in the payment of their claims, legitimated the use of force in the collection of public debts in international law. In 1904 European creditor nations threatened force against the Dominican Republic to collect defaulted debts as they had in Venezuela. In response to the Dominican situation, Roosevelt included a statement in his annual message to Congress in 1904, which became his Corollary to the Monroe Doctrine:

> Chronic wrongdoing, or an impotence which results in a general loosening of the ties of civilized society, may in America, as elsewhere, ultimately require intervention by some civilized nation, and in the Western Hemisphere the adherence of the United States to the Monroe Doctrine may force the United States, however reluctantly, in flagrant cases of such wrongdoing or impotence, to the exercise of an international police power. . . . We would interfere . . . only in the last resort, and then only if it became evident that their inability or unwillingness to do justice at home and abroad had violated the rights of the United States or had invited foreign aggression to the detriment of the entire body of American nations.[24]

Although Roosevelt's words were intended primarily as a strategic statement, the references to "a general loosening of the ties of civilized society" and to "intervention by some civilized nation" reflected continuing cultural arrogance.

The United States invoked the Roosevelt Corollary for the next quarter-century to justify its many interventions in a number of Caribbean states (an eventuality not mentioned in Monroe's original statement). Interventionist policies begun under President Roosevelt continued under Presidents William Howard Taft, Woodrow Wilson, and Calvin Coolidge. Several coercive instruments were employed, including the use or threat of armed invasion and military occupation, the imposition of treaties giving the United States the right to intervene, the establishment of customs receiverships and financial control, the recognition and nonrecognition of new governments, and the supervision of elections.

The exclusion of other foreign influence and the promotion of regional stability were the general objectives of the Caribbean interventions. More specifically, they were used to secure and later protect the Panama Canal, to maintain order and protect the lives and property of citizens, to support U.S. investments and loans, and, later, to promote representative democracy. U.S. imperialism was aimed primarily at preventing other outside influences from dominating the area and at preempting European intervention. But after the U.S. position against outside threats was secured and stability enforced, it vigorously pressed for further advantages.

Not all of these proximate goals were sought at once by all U.S. administrations, but all of them were considered to be concomitant with national security interests. For example, "dollar diplomacy," encouraged by the Taft administration, involved the manipulation of loans and investments by U.S. consortia in the Caribbean region (especially Nicaragua and Honduras). This practice was followed by military landings ("pecuniary intervention") to protect private U.S. commercial interests. Dollar diplomacy appeared simply to further the interests of investors, but historians have since concluded that, from the point of view of the U.S. government if not that of the investors themselves, dollar diplomacy was also aimed at serving broader goals. It was hoped that U.S. investments would keep out other foreign interests, as well as support stability in small Caribbean states. Military intervention would protect U.S. investors at the same time that it would enforce a degree of political stability. U.S. investors benefited from coercive U.S. diplomacy, but they did so as a part of U.S. security policy.[25]

When President Woodrow Wilson came to office in 1913, he altered the traditional Jeffersonian view of Latin American regimes and revised U.S. democratic policies. The Wilson credo reconciled the president's liberal political principles with his policy of frequent intervention in the Caribbean (and, presumably, in Mexico) by considering the following: Political instability in Caribbean countries was a threat to U.S. interests; instability was caused by political immaturity; maturity was measurable by the extent of progress toward constitutional democracy. As a policy matter, Wilson assumed that democracy could be imposed by external pressure or force and that the United States, as the most politically mature (that is, democratic) and powerful nation in the Americas, was responsible for taking an active role in the political development of at least certain parts of Latin America.

U.S. imperialism in the Caribbean was only briefly popular with the public, and negative public opinion was an element in ending bipartisan support and forcing the dissolution of imperialist policies. Some early sharp dissent was expressed toward the imperialist thrust by the Anti-Imperialist League, established in 1898. Its members argued that the national domain should be confined to North America, that foreign populations could not properly be assimilated into U.S. society as states of the union, and that the control of overseas colonies would violate basic tenets of U.S. democracy as well as the dictates of American conscience. The Democratic Party also condemned the Republican imperialist program, although both political parties favored the U.S. construction, ownership, and control of an isthmian canal. The imperial course was chosen and sustained, however, until more effective public misgivings (and other factors) developed later.

The Good Neighbor Policy.   U.S. policies from 1929 to 1945 contrasted sharply with those of 1895 to 1928. Basic U.S. goals, however, remained constant. The United States under the Good Neighbor Policy, adopted in 1933, largely abandoned direct interventionary techniques. But the goals of foreign exclusion and Latin American stability remained, to be sought through cooperation rather than coercion. Intervention had aroused opposition in the United States. This occurred simultaneously with official calculations of a changing strategic situation. After World War I European threats to hemispheric security were virtually nonexistent, and Latin

American instability posed little direct threat to the United States. In addition, Latin American governments had made it clear that inter-American cooperation depended on the U.S. abandonment of interventionist practices. Consequently, coercion was greatly reduced.

Some features of what became known as the Good Neighbor Policy were tentatively established during the administration of Herbert Hoover (1929–1933).[26] President Hoover repudiated the Roosevelt Corollary to the Monroe Doctrine and significantly reduced Caribbean intervention. A memorandum written by Under Secretary of State J. Reuben Clark in 1928 and circulated to the Latin American governments in 1930 dissociated the Roosevelt Corollary from the doctrine, although it did not renounce the use of intervention as a policy instrument. Some U.S. troops were removed from the Caribbean area, and certain U.S. investors were told that they must seek local remedies for their problems.

President Franklin D. Roosevelt explicitly enunciated a larger design and called it the Good Neighbor Policy.[27] In his inaugural address on March 4, 1933, President Roosevelt vowed that "in the field of foreign policy I would dedicate this nation to the policy of the good neighbor." The following month, he specifically applied the Good Neighbor Policy to Latin America in a Pan American Day speech, with these words: "The essential qualities of a true Pan Americanism must be the same as those which constitute a good neighbor, namely, mutual understanding, a sympathetic appreciation of the other's point of view. It is only in this manner that we can hope to build up a system of which confidence, friendship, and good will are the cornerstones."[28] In this spirit the United States gave up intervention as a policy instrument (in law and practice) and reinvigorated Pan-American cooperation.

A salient aspect of the Good Neighbor Policy, as directed by Secretary of State Cordell Hull and by Sumner Welles in his various official positions, was the Pan-Americanization of the Monroe Doctrine; that is, direct intervention was renounced by the United States, and regional organization was embraced as a major (but far from exclusive) policy instrument. In 1933 the United States accepted, with reservations, an inter-American treaty stipulating nonintervention by one American state in the affairs of another. Three years later it accepted another treaty without reservation agreeing to the principle of absolute nonintervention. The United States abandoned its five Caribbean protectorates—in Cuba, Haiti, the Dominican Republic, Nicaragua, and Panama—and abrogated or revised the treaties on which they were based. Situations that before would have occasioned intervention were dealt with through direct bilateral diplomatic negotiations, notably Mexico's expropriation of U.S. oil company properties.

Policies of nonintervention required a return to tradition with regard to U.S. efforts at democratization. Abandoning the nonrecognition of unconstitutional governments and adopting a policy of noninterference in the internal affairs of others meant dealing with dictatorships often on a partnership basis. As a result, nonintervention came under attack because it permitted the continued existence of dictators and allowed others to seize power. U.S. officials rejected the criticism, restated the commitment to nonintervention, and complained that those who deplored the effect of nonintervention were the very ones who had opposed prior intervention.

With the rise of the fascist dictators in Europe and their increased activities in Latin America, and especially with the threat of European war in the late 1930s, the United States was again concerned with foreign influences and Latin American stability. With intervention discredited, a cooperative hemispheric security system was constructed in the late 1930s and extended during World War II. Although some important Latin American states remained neutral until near the end of the war, sufficient political, economic, and military cooperation occurred, and enough domestic stability was maintained, from the U.S. point of view.

Post–World War II Changes

The United States emerged from World War II as the most powerful state in the world with involvements on a global scale. Beginning in 1947, cold war criteria were fundamental to U.S. policy formulation. The connected themes of worldwide interests and cold war concerns shaped U.S. policy on Latin America. As a result, the degree to which Latin America received attention in U.S. policy priorities depended essentially on the extent of the perception of a Communist threat in the other Americas and the degree of U.S. involvement in other parts of the world. As an arena of cold war conflict, Latin America was a minor theater until the advent of Castro's Cuba in 1959. The United States resumed direct interventionist techniques on a reduced scale in the Caribbean area.

Nineteenth-century doctrines were seriously challenged after World War II. The Western Hemisphere Idea of a "special relationship" among the Americas lost most of its meaning. With its acceptance of broad international roles and its pursuit of intimate relations with Europe, the United States all but abandoned the idea of two separate and distinct world spheres. The idea lingered on, at least in U.S. rhetoric concerning its Latin American policy, but in reality no special inter-American relations existed in the sense of either exclusivity or high priority.

Doubt was cast on the extent to which the United States considered the Monroe Doctrine to have been multilateralized and intervention made illegal. Even though the principle of reciprocity was dead with U.S. involvement in Europe and around the globe, and even though the United States enjoyed the right of self-defense to protect its own security aside from doctrinal expressions, U.S. governments overtly or implicitly used the Monroe Doctrine to justify certain unilateral interventions (see below). It did not do so in the 1980s, however, and in the post–cold war era the lack of external threats made the doctrine irrelevant.[29]

The United States showed declining interest in Latin America during the latter part of World War II, as Secretary Hull's ideas about globalism had become dominant. "Good Neighbor" rhetoric was continued after the war, but U.S. interest in Latin America was superseded by problems related to the devastation of Europe, the "containment" of the Soviet Union, and, later, communism in Asia. The apparent lack of a serious foreign (that is, Communist) threat in Latin America did not allow the region to be easily fitted into global cold war policies. Soviet expansion in Latin America seemed as remote as the prospect of internal Communist subversion.

The Truman and Eisenhower Administrations

President Harry S Truman and his secretaries of state, George C. Marshall and Dean Acheson, made clear to Latin America that U.S. leaders felt that world problems were more crucial elsewhere. They candidly stressed the remoteness of Latin America from cold war problems.

Truman's policies toward the different types of Latin American regimes and democratization vacillated. Toward the end of World War II, the Truman presidency had briefly returned to the idea of intervention on behalf of democracy and in opposition to dictatorship. Electoral intervention was pursued in Argentina in 1945 and 1946. U.S. officials openly opposed the presidential candidacy of Colonel Juan Perón, whom they considered to be fascist-inclined. He subsequently won the presidency with ease; shortly thereafter, the United States ceased intervening in the name of democracy.

After the war, foreign aid programs, especially military, became caught up in debates concerning Latin American dictators and democrats. Both the Truman and Eisenhower administrations signed mutual defense assistance pacts with several Latin American governments, including dictatorial and military regimes. Officials insisted that in each case the granting of aid was determined by its value in promoting mutual security rather than by the political form of its recipient.

After President Dwight D. Eisenhower was inaugurated in 1953, he and Secretary of State John Foster Dulles indicated that bold Latin American policy departures were imminent.[30] During the 1952 presidential campaign, the Republican Party had sharply criticized the Truman administration for its "neglect" of Latin America. President Eisenhower appointed his brother, Dr. Milton Eisenhower, a scholar with Latin American interests, to visit and report on the region with a view to U.S. policy reform. Dr. Eisenhower's subsequent report, submitted on November 18, 1953, stressed the need for additional U.S. economic assistance to the area and for a general upgrading of Latin America in U.S. policy priorities.[31] As it turned out, the Eisenhower policy contained little that was new for Latin America. The policy emphasis, until late in the administration, still focused on East-West conflict outside the hemisphere.

The only significant cold war occurrence in Latin America prior to the Castro revolution in Cuba had to do with Communists in Guatemala gaining important positions in the leftist government of Jacobo Arbenz Guzmán (1951–1954). The United States considered that government to be Communist-infiltrated; it obtained the adoption of a formal declaration against communism in the Americas at the Tenth Inter-American Conference at Caracas in 1954. The United States then covertly sponsored a military coup that overthrew Arbenz. Secretary of State John Foster

Dulles declared the "intrusion of Soviet despotism" to be "a direct challenge to our Monroe Doctrine, the first and most fundamental of our foreign policies." (In 1960, in response to assertions by Soviet Premier Nikita Khrushchev that the Monroe Doctrine was dead, the Department of State proclaimed that its principles were "as valid today as they were in 1823.")

Otherwise the United States did not perceive a Communist threat in Latin America. Secretary Dulles, never complacent about communism, said at a press conference on November 5, 1957, that "we see no likelihood at the present time of communism getting into control of the political institutions of any of the American republics." Nevertheless, in its Latin American policies, the United States aimed to convert the Inter-American System into an anticommunist alliance in consonance with its global policies.

U.S. policy changed during the last two years of the Eisenhower presidency, in orientation if not in purpose. The first catalyst for change was the treatment of Vice President Richard M. Nixon while he was conducting a "goodwill" tour in 1958. Violent riots in Peru and Venezuela, at times threatening Nixon's physical safety, dramatized Latin American dissatisfaction with U.S. policy. The second and more enduring impetus for change was the Castro revolution in Cuba, coming to power on January 1, 1959. Castro's highly nationalist movement was strongly anti-United States in its ideological content; *antiyanquismo* eventually led to the embrace of Marxism-Leninism and alignment with the Soviet Union and its East European bloc. This foreign intrusion in the Caribbean shook the United States from its assumption of Latin American immunity from the cold war. The president proposed his "Eisenhower Plan" in 1960 for increased economic aid to Latin America, and corresponding funds were appropriated by Congress. Further plans were laid for forceful intervention against Castro. Both approaches of aid and intervention were carried out by the Kennedy presidency.

The Kennedy Administration

During the abbreviated presidency of John F. Kennedy, Latin America assumed a major position in U.S. policy under the Alliance for Progress. In his inaugural address on January 20, 1961, Kennedy offered a "special pledge" to Latin America, promising to convert U.S. "good words into good deeds, in a new alliance for progress, to assist free men and free governments in casting off the chains of poverty." At a White House reception for Latin American diplomats on March 13, 1961, the president proposed a ten-year Alliance for Progress plan of inter-American cooperation for Latin American economic, social, and political development. In August, the Alliance for Progress was formally multilateralized at an inter-American conference, which enacted the Charter of Punta del Este detailing the goals and means of the effort.[32]

President Kennedy, who had been highly critical of the Eisenhower administration's policies toward Latin American dictators and military regimes, stressed that eco-

nomic development and social reform should take place within an emerging democratic framework with political freedom. The multilateral charter stated twelve goals
for the Alliance, the first of which was "to improve and strengthen democratic institutions through application of the principle of self-determination by the people."

Thus President Kennedy adopted a high-priority policy on Latin America. That
policy, however, was also formulated in a cold war context and in pursuit of established long-range goals. The administration feared that Communists would capture
the revolutionary aspirations of a changing Latin America—that Fidelismo would
spread from Cuba to other parts of the region. Policy was directed at preventing foreign influence and maintaining political stability against communism through "developmentalism." It was hoped that social reform and economic growth would create political stability and deter Communist success. The purpose of economic
assistance always had been to create the necessary economic conditions conducive to
political stability. Now social conditions were also included in the stability formula.
The efforts toward democratic development were also based on the premise that a
counter-ideology to communism was needed. The purpose of military assistance was
clearly stated to be a support for political stability, aimed especially at counterinsurgency and the maintenance of internal order considered necessary for economic and
political development; only modest attention was paid to defense against offshore incursions. The United States attempted further to consolidate the Inter-American
System into an anticommunist alliance; in 1962 it succeeded in gaining multilateral
agreements to exclude Cuba from participation in the OAS, and in 1964 to impose
diplomatic and economic sanctions on the Castro regime.

The United States also practiced military intervention. In April 1961, a U.S.-
organized and financed band of Cuban exiles invaded Cuba at the Bay of Pigs hoping to stimulate a popular uprising that would overthrow Castro. The intervention,
planned under Eisenhower and carried out by Kennedy, was a total failure; the invaders were easily subdued by Cuban forces. In the wake of the defeat of the U.S.-
sponsored Cuban exile invasion, President Kennedy said, in an address widely referred to as the "Kennedy Corollary to the Monroe Doctrine," that if the principle
of nonintervention merely concealed or excused a policy of nonaction, then the
United States would not hesitate to act to protect its national security.

The Alliance for Progress immediately faced serious problems. From 1961 to
1963 military coups overthrew constitutionally elected governments in seven Latin
American countries—and challenged the democratic commitment and assumptions
of the Alliance. The United States refused to recognize the new governments, suspended diplomatic relations, and terminated economic and military assistance. In
1963 the U.S. position regarding military aid and democracy shifted and remained
unchanged until the mid-1970s. The Kennedy policies went further than pragmatic
accommodation to military regimes; they asserted that Latin American armed forces
played valuable and necessary roles in nation building.

In the meantime, the Soviet Union had stationed its ballistic missiles in Cuba. The
dramatic "missile crisis" of October 1962 was a confrontation between the United

States and the Soviet Union over the weapons in Cuba.[33] Intense U.S. decision-making and action ensued following the discovery of the missiles on October 14, 1962. President Kennedy temporarily organized his advisers as the Executive Committee of the National Security Council. His sought to compel the Soviet Union to remove its nuclear weapons from Cuba while avoiding nuclear war. The committee and congressional and military leaders together assessed the costs and risks of several options. The president finally decided to impose a blockade of Cuba, which was euphemistically referred to as a "quarantine." He came to favor pressing for removal of the weapons rather than destroying them through military action. The argument favoring air strikes or invasion contended that since the missiles had already arrived in Cuba, a blockade would be futile. When President Kennedy announced the quarantine, he warned that any missile launched from Cuba on the United States would invite a U.S. retaliatory blow not on Cuba but on the Soviet Union.

The Cuban missile crisis came to an end in November 1962. The Soviet Union agreed to stop building bases in Cuba and to withdraw its nuclear weapons, bomber aircraft, and ground combat troops. In return, the United States lifted the blockade and pledged nonintervention in Cuba, subject to verification that Soviet weapons had been withdrawn. Thus, the United States was successful on the issue of ballistic missiles in Cuba; the Soviet Union did not, however, withdraw its combat unit as promised.

The Johnson Administration

President Lyndon B. Johnson carried on the Alliance for Progress after his inauguration in November 1963, following the assassination of President Kennedy. In April 1965, Johnson initiated a massive U.S. intervention in the Dominican Republic civil war. After U.S. troops landed, the president, in a speech some called the "Johnson Corollary" to the Monroe Doctrine, expressed determination not to accept a "second Cuba."

As the United States became more involved in the Vietnam conflict, however, its concern with Latin America receded. Furthermore, the Cuban case eventually proved to be atypical of Latin American politics. Cuba failed to export its revolution, and after 1967 it abandoned serious attempts to do so for more than a decade. The lack of a Communist threat to the hemisphere coincided with U.S. congressional disillusionment with foreign aid as a policy technique in the world at large and a with general decline in available U.S. economic and military assistance funds. Latin Americans again complained that the United States was neglectful of their problems, despite U.S. protestations to the contrary.

The Johnson administration's approach to military governments continued to reflect a disagreement with the former policy and a belief in the need for "realism," as well as an optimistic attitude toward the military role in economic development and social reform. The administration also argued that it must work with existing military establishments even if they were corrupt or unprofessional in order to transform them through training over a period of time. It did not raise the issue of democracy in its relations with military governments coming to power from 1963 to 1968 in the Dominican Republic, Brazil, Peru, and Panama.

The Nixon and Ford Administrations

During the Nixon and Ford administrations (1969–1977), Latin America continued to be viewed as a low-priority area. In his first major address on Latin American relations before the OAS on April 14, 1969, President Richard M. Nixon indicated the abandonment of "developmentalism." He referred to the Alliance for Progress as a "great concept" but expressed disillusionment with the results of its programs. He then sent Governor Nelson Rockefeller of New York on a series of "study missions" to twenty Latin American states in May and June, 1969. The governor's visits to three states were canceled because of rioting, and fourteen others experienced serious disorders upon his arrival. The Rockefeller Report was submitted on September 3, 1969, but few of its recommendations were implemented as policy.[34]

President Nixon further outlined his policy in an address on October 31, 1969, adopting what came to be known as a "low-profile" approach. He called for a "new partnership" in inter-American affairs in which the United States "lectures less and listens more." He again rejected the social and economic developmental content of the Alliance for Progress, but he promised certain trade concessions and increases in economic aid. President Nixon showed no inclination to alter the pragmatic policies toward military governments already established.

The Nixon administration said that its Latin American policy was based on the principles of respect for diversity, mutual cooperation, and peaceful resolution of differences. Latin Americans were expected to take a larger leadership role in hemisphere affairs. In practice, the U.S. government largely ignored the region, although certain concerns were highlighted: Castro in Cuba, the Marxist (but not Communist) government of Salvador Allende, the specific issues of border questions with Mexico, the nationalization of U.S. properties in Peru, and the revision of the Panama Canal treaty. The U.S. Congress was unwilling to approve increased economic aid for Latin America, and the executive vacillated on trade concessions.

In October 1973, soon after becoming secretary of state, Henry Kissinger announced that Latin American policy was in the process of reformulation aimed at starting a New Dialogue with the other American states. The gist of Kissinger's policy statements, reinforced by remarks made by President Nixon and other U.S. officials, was to urge a new spirit of inter-American collaboration within the context of an interdependent world. The United States, the secretary said, recognized Latin American complaints that Washington had put aside its special commitments to the hemisphere, but he asserted that it sought not dominance but community and a sharing of responsibilities with Latin America. He promised that the United States would not impose its political preferences on Latin American states and would seek a close and free association with them. The United States was prepared to consult with those nations and to adjust its positions on trade and monetary matters, on rules regarding private investment and the roles of multinational corporations in underdeveloped nations, on the law of the sea, food and population programs, the transfer of technology, energy problems, development assistance, and on the restructuring of the OAS. Kissinger pointed out that the United States and Mexico had solved their long-standing Colorado River salinity dispute, that the United States and Panama had made significant progress toward a new canal treaty, and that the United States and Peru had settled their dispute concerning compensation for nationalized property.

Prospects for the New Dialogue declined beginning in mid-1974. President Nixon's attention was primarily directed toward defending himself against possible impeachment by the U.S. Congress, and Secretary Kissinger's energies were concentrated on problems in the Middle East. After Nixon's resignation in August 1974 and the succession of Gerald Ford to the presidency, U.S.-Latin American relations further deteriorated. President Ford contradicted the principles of the New Dialogue at a press conference in September 1974 by defending CIA activities in Chile preceding the fall of Allende, which he claimed were in the best interests of the Chilean people. The 1974 Trade Act excluded Venezuela and Ecuador from a generalized system of trade preferences because of their OPEC membership, even though they had not participated in the earlier OPEC-sponsored oil embargo. Consequently, Latin Americans insisted on postponing the meeting of foreign ministers that had been scheduled for March 1975 in Buenos Aires as the next step in the New Dialogue.

The United States attempted to reconcile its difficulties with Latin America. President Ford asked Congress in April 1975 to grant him the authority to waive restrictions in the 1974 Trade Act, which he said had an unintended impact on Latin American relations. Secretary Kissinger offered, in a speech on March 1, 1975, "to continue the dialogue in a spirit of friendship and conciliation" despite some "temporary interruptions." The United States ceased opposing the Latin American majority that wished to end the isolation of Cuba, and in August 1975 the OAS in effect dropped some of the sanctions that had been imposed in 1964. But the State Department also chastised Latin Americans for succumbing to "the temptation to blame disappointment on the intrigues and excesses of foreigners." It complained that "Latin America is perennially tempted to define its independence and unity through opposition to the United States."[35]

Balance-of-power thinking during the Nixon-Ford administrations, with foreign policy directed throughout by Kissinger, helps to account for Latin America's continuing low priority in U.S. policy calculations. Détente between the superpowers indicated that the United States and the Soviet Union shared a mutual interest in maintaining the existing distribution of rewards and power in the international system. In this arrangement the United States assumed key responsibility for system maintenance in Latin America, sometimes as "policeman" and at least as power broker. Thus, with no strategic threat to the United States posed by either the regional states themselves or by an external state operating in the region, the United States was free to concentrate its efforts in other areas of the world.

The Carter Administration

President Jimmy Carter (1977–1981) stated at Notre Dame University in May 1977 that "we are now free of that inordinate fear of communism which once led us to embrace any dictator who joined us in that fear." After discounting the Soviet threat, Carter rested his global policies on three commitments: (1) to consider human rights as a fundamental tenet of U.S. foreign policy; (2) to reduce the danger of nuclear proliferation and the spread of conventional weapons; and (3) to rely on all forms of military cooperation as exceptional rather than normal instruments of policy. President Carter's policies on Latin America, based on these commitments, further isolated the United States from much of Latin America. U.S. relations with numerous states were strained over human rights, nonproliferation, and other issues. Furthermore, the Carter administration did not respond to Latin America's primary interests—namely, its economic demands, especially better access to U.S. capital and technology and more concessions for their commodity exports.

U.S. relations with Southern Cone states were reduced to low levels of activity. The United States banned Argentina, Chile, Paraguay, and Uruguay from receiving further arms transfers and certain forms of economic aid. Brazil, offended by the State Department's 1977 report on its human rights situation, refused to accept any more U.S. military assistance. President Carter further annoyed Brazil by opposing its acquisition of a nuclear reactor from West Germany, citing his commitment to nuclear nonproliferation. Brazil insisted that it was related to development of energy sources and had nothing to do with weapons.

In 1977 President Carter discussed placing a new emphasis on the long-neglected Caribbean region. High-level official visits were made around the area. At the same time, the president proposed restoration of U.S.-Cuban relations and tolerance for various ideologies in the region. However, his Caribbean policies met with several difficulties. U.S.-Cuban relations deteriorated after the Soviet Union and Cuba expanded their military activities in Africa. U.S. sanctions related to human rights abuses were applied to El Salvador, Guatemala, and Nicaragua. New canal treaties were signed with Panama and ratifications exchanged, but debate in the U.S. Senate and throughout the nation was vociferous, even though the treaties had been negotiated by four presidents from both political parties. Their conclusion reflected an official U.S. view, held since the mid-1960s, that the strategic and economic importance of the canal and the Caribbean had greatly decreased.

U.S.-Mexican relations were awkward despite the Carter administration's intent to improve them. The two governments strongly disagreed over several issues, especially those of Mexican migration to the United States and the price of Mexican natural gas exports.

The Carter administration's Latin American policy underwent important adjustments after 1979. At the end of 1979, the president stated that the Soviet Union was more threatening and less accommodating than he had anticipated. In the meantime, he revised his policies toward certain parts of the Caribbean because of increased Soviet-Cuban activity; his policies toward the rest of Latin America, however, remained essentially unchanged. After the overthrow of Anastasio Somoza in Nicaragua, U.S. policy in time was antagonistic toward the Sandinista-dominated government on the grounds that it was providing Soviet arms to guerrillas in El Salvador. Fearing that events in El Salvador would parallel those in Nicaragua, Carter in January 1981 (only five days before the end of his term of office) lifted its ban on military assistance and resumed shipments to the military government despite the absence of any reforms. In the meantime, the United States also responded with hostility to a 1979 coup in Grenada led by the leftist New Jewel Movement, to which the Soviet Union and its East European bloc had extended aid (as had numerous noncommunist countries).

The Reagan Administration

When Ronald Reagan became president in 1981 he resolved to regain a dominant hemispheric role for the United States. He had sharply criticized President Carter's Latin American policies and set out to reverse them. President Reagan's worldview was based on the proposition that international disorder and terrorism resulted from the activities of the Soviet Union and its surrogates, of which Cuba was the most important. Opposition to Communist expansionism formed the basis for his global and regional policies. This approach necessitated reducing human rights concerns to a secondary position—not abandoning them but greatly reducing their emphasis. His anticommunist policies also included a resuscitation of arms transfers and other military programs, which had been considerably diminished in prior years. Although the administration viewed all of Latin America in terms of East-West conflict, its most intense concern was with the circum-Caribbean, particularly Central America. Consequently, with the exception of Mexico, U.S. efforts concentrated on small countries and paid relatively little attention to the major states in South America until events forced an extended range of concern.

Central America immediately became a front line in the new global cold war. The Reagan administration evolved a geopolitical strategic view of the Caribbean Basin with an emphasis on Central America in terms of a global "Reagan Doctrine." The Reagan administration was determined to recapture U.S. control of Central American events. The Reagan Doctrine, articulated soon after the president's inauguration in 1981, emphasized the need to reverse what was perceived as the continuing expansion of Soviet influence in strategically important Third World regions, notably Central America.[36] The creation of Soviet clients in Third World countries (referred to as surrogates and proxies) provided bases for subversive Communist operations against neighboring states, created the beginnings of an infrastructure for a global terrorist network, and made military bases available for Soviet use. Soviet activities in these surrogate nations enhanced the chances for Marxist revolutions while minimizing the risk of direct confrontation with the United States. The Vietnam experience had paralyzed U.S. resistance to Soviet expansionism. But the Soviets also had vul-

nerabilities, especially the failure of Marxist revolutions to meet popular expectations, which the United States should exploit. The key assumptions of the Reagan
Doctrine were that a "democratic revolution" was under way in the Third World and
that direct U.S. support for anti-Marxist forces would stop Soviet expansionism and
further democracy. The administration, however, did not define an explicit tactical
doctrine, arguing for a case-by-case approach.

In July 1983 President Reagan appointed the National Bipartisan Commission on
Central America, headed by former Secretary of State Henry Kissinger, to recommend policies. The Kissinger Commission report, issued in January 1984, served as
the basis for the U.S. strategic rationale for its actions in Central America.[37] The
principal assumption was that the global balance of power could be shifted by the
advance of Soviet power in that area. The security of the Caribbean Basin was vital
to the United States, whose interests were threatened by activities aimed at establishing Cuban-style, Marxist-Leninist dictatorships allied with the Soviet Union. The
"domino theory" was advanced. The Soviet Union, already enjoying a permanent
presence in the Caribbean through its Cuban surrogate, was seen as acting to reinforce and expand this penetration into Nicaragua. At the same time, Cuban assistance to El Salvador threatened to convert that state to Marxism. From there, the argument continued, communism would spread to the other Central American
countries and then threaten the major bordering states—Colombia and Venezuela to
the south and, most ominously, Mexico to the north.

This calculation of U.S. interests and Soviet-Cuban motives led to a number of
further assumptions: (1) vital Caribbean sea lanes and unimpeded passage through
the Panama Canal, already threatened by Cuba's geographic position, would be more
vulnerable with additional Soviet surrogates; (2) a more extensive permanent Soviet
presence would offer the Soviet Union other significant military advantages by allowing the placement of hostile forces and weapons (conventional and nuclear) capable of striking deep within the United States and in Latin American states, as well
as extended Soviet naval operations; (3) these factors would force significant alterations in the U.S. forward-deployment strategy, since a previously secure area would
either require new resources to be created or existing ones to be diverted from other
areas; (4) Communist takeovers would inevitably cause a vast increase in illegal immigration to the United States; and (5) U.S. worldwide credibility was at stake—in
the words of the Kissinger report, "The triumph of hostile forces in what the Soviet
Union calls the 'strategic rear' of the United States would be read as a sign of U.S.
impotence." The conclusion was that the United States must act to prevent the
transformation of its southern border into a hostile region.

In July 1983 President Reagan appointed members to the National Bipartisan
Commission on Central America, headed by former Secretary of State Henry
Kissinger, to formulate and recommend U.S. strategy and tactics. The Kissinger
Commission report, issued in January 1984, reinforced the administration's assumptions and policies but with qualifications and extensions.[38] The report served as the
basis for subsequent administration proposals to Congress and provided authority for
its strategic rationale. It may be noted that the Monroe Doctrine was not invoked and

rarely referred to during the 1980s. It was not asserted in the Reagan Doctrine toward Central America or used to justify the U.S. invasion of Grenada in 1983.

The United States instituted a program of assistance to the anti-Sandinista Nicaraguan guerrillas (the *Contras*), to the armed forces in El Salvador engaged in counterinsurgency efforts, and to Honduras for related services. U.S. actions were also directly interventionist; the most notable of these were the military invasion of Grenada in October 1983 and the mining of Nicaraguan harbors in March 1984. They were also developmental. The administration proposed the Caribbean Basin Initiative (CBI), which, at least in its initial form, insisted on the necessity for continued aggressive opposition to Soviet expansionism, but also recognized poverty as a source of instability and outlined a program for trade preferences and economic aid to friendly Caribbean governments. The administration placed increasingly strong pressure on the Salvadoran government to follow a centrist course, effectively institute an agrarian reform program, hold free and fair elections, and curtail right-wing death squads. A similar course was urged on other Central American states.

Policy conflict and fragmentation were especially notable regarding the Reagan administration's Central American policies. U.S. actions received less than enthusiastic public support, and the issues were difficult to manage with Congress. Many people, including certain key military leaders, feared "another Vietnam" in which the United States would become mired in an unwinnable Central American war unsupported by the American people. Although much of the conflict was along partisan lines, the president had difficulty getting the support of his own party in Congress for aid to the Contras, and Republicans joined Democrats in denouncing the U.S. mining of Nicaraguan harbors and the subsequent awkward and losing U.S. position in the World Court. Disagreements also occurred within the administration itself, as agencies and individuals competed for influence, and bitter differences arose among high level officials. The Kissinger Commission not only failed to inspire congressional and public unity but was itself divided over basic issues.

A controversy arose over what was known as "the Iran-Contra affair" in the United States. The National Security Council staff, located in the Executive Office of the President, directed and "privatized" covert operations in Central America in concert with private individuals and organizations. Congressional hearings in 1987 and subsequent legal proceedings against some of the participants revealed that these operations were designed to circumvent congressional prohibitions on CIA covert operations to and direct U.S. armed forces—as well as to bypass U.S. Defense Department, State Department, and CIA cognizance. The Iran-Contra affair was particularly debilitating. The affair increased the distrust between the president and Congress, intensified intra-executive competition, and decreased the president's personal authority in the policy process.[39]

In the meantime, other subregional and transregional problems intruded. Because U.S. policies in the Southern Cone had revolved around questions of human rights and military assistance during the Carter administration, President Reagan had to observe legislative controls and the prior prohibition of arms transfers because of human rights violations in Argentina, Chile, Paraguay, and Uruguay (Peru had followed constitutional procedures since 1978). With the return of democracy to Argentina and Uruguay, the prohibitions on arms transfers were lifted; they remained in effect for Chile and Paraguay.

Transnational regional problems became increasingly important during the Reagan administration. The debt question was a particularly difficult issue in U.S. policy toward all of the Latin American and Caribbean states. In April 1986, President Reagan issued a National Security Decision Directive declaring drug trafficking a threat to U.S. national security. The United States made extensive efforts to control the international narcotics traffic, but bilateral programs designed to cut off the drug flow at its sources enjoyed little success.

Post–Cold War

The presidencies of George Bush (1989–1993) and Bill Clinton (inaugurated in 1993) coincided with the end of the cold war and the search for a new Latin American policy paradigm to replace strategic denial. (The retirement of the Soviet Union from western hemispheric affairs and then its dissolution, along with the lack of other external threats, ensured the irrelevance of the Monroe doctrine.) In concert with Latin Americans, they settled on democratic and economic reform and development as the overarching norms. The region's level of priority in U.S. policy, however, was ambiguous.[40]

With the inauguration of President Bush, U.S. policy toward Latin America, and Central America in particular, moved toward the political center and was made more multilateral in orientation. President Bush and Secretary of State James Baker negotiated bipartisan cooperation with Congress on Central American policy—and in the process confirmed the end of strategic denial. The agreement they reached with congressional leaders on March 24, 1989, repudiated, in effect, the basic tenets of the Reagan policies, of which Bush as vice president had been an active part. The plan agreed to support the Central American-led peace plan, to exclude the idea of overthrowing the Sandinistas, and to deny military support to the Contras (aid for humanitarian purposes was continued).

The Bush administration joined most Latin American states in adopting a primarily economic foundation for inter-American relationships, with agreement on the essentiality of continued democratic development. President Bush's surprise proposal in a speech on June 27, 1990, for a hemispheric free-trade area—the Enterprise of the Americas Initiative—was a historic undertaking. It extended what had begun as a "primacy of Mexico" approach—reflected in a North American Free Trade Agreement (which turned out to include Canada)—to a "primacy of economics" policy extended to all the Americas. Other high priority items, all closely linked to U.S. domestic concerns, were considered to depend on Latin American economic and democratic success.

Another consideration was the possibility of seeking military or other coercive solutions. The U.S. invasion of Panama in December 1989 indicated that such action was a continuing reality in the post–cold war world. It was the first U.S. military intervention in the Caribbean area that had not been designed to preempt an external threat, and the first since World War II that had not been explained in terms of a Communist menace. The Bush administration insisted that Panama was a unique case and did not set precedents for dealing with the drug traffic or dictatorship (the primary aspects of the rationale for invading Panama, along with protecting American lives and the canal).[41]

President Clinton's secretary of state, Warren Christopher, said in May 1993 that the United States would make promotion of democracy, human rights, and the rule of law, and the expansion of prosperity through economic development and trade, the main elements of policy toward Latin America. Other officials subsequently emphasized that the bases for U.S. security policies were America's core values of representative democracy and market economies. In sum, the Clinton administration essentially continued President Bush's approach by emphasizing economics and democracy (President Clinton's approach made them coequal components) and by seeing the resolution of other high-priority problems as dependent on Latin American democratic and economic success.

The U.S. military occupation of Haiti in September 1994, undertaken under UN Security Council resolutions, was justified in terms of supporting Haitian democracy (it was intended to restore President Jean-Bertrand Aristide, who had been overthrown by a military coup in September 1991) and of helping develop democracy, the economy, and stability thereafter. It also indicated continuing U.S. willingness to apply coercive military diplomacy to Caribbean affairs.

President Clinton exerted a strong and successful effort to gain congressional approval of NAFTA after a bitter political battle; strong opposition came from the president's Democratic Party and left lingering intra-party bitterness. The administration then stated the intent to extend U.S. free trade around the hemisphere, but, reluctant to raise an issue that continued to divide Democrats during the 1996 campaign, the president waited until November 1997 to ask Congress to renew his "fast-track" free-trade negotiating authority. Prior to that he made two trips to Latin America in 1997, seeking to build congressional support by drawing attention to Latin America's democratic governments and free-market economies. His efforts did not succeed, however, as Congress refused to extend fast-track authority. Many congressional Democrats—supported by organized labor, who argued that free-trade agreements would cost U.S. jobs, and by environmental groups seeing threats to the environment—were opposed to further free-trade agreements. Republicans, who in the past were in favor of free trade as a general principle, refused again to rescue the president from the opposition in his own party. This occurrence severely undercut the bases for U.S. policies toward the other Americas.

NOTES

1. For discussions of the literature on the applicability of various decision models (identified in Chapter 3) to U.S. Latin American policy-making, see David W. Dent, ed., *U.S.-Latin*

American Policymaking: A Reference Handbook (Westport, Conn.: Greenwood Press, 1995), especially chapter 1, David W. Dent, "Introduction: U.S.-Latin American Policymaking"; chapter 2, G. Pope Atkins, "The External Environment"; and chapter 10, Harold Molineu, "Making Policy for Latin America: Process and Explanation."

2. Lars Schoultz, *National Security and United States Policy Toward Latin America* (Princeton: Princeton University Press, 1987). "If one wants to understand the core of the United States policy toward Latin America," Schoultz says, "one studies security."

3. G. Pope Atkins, "Reorienting U.S. Policies in the New Era," in *The United States and Latin America: Redefining U.S. Purposes in the Post-Cold War Era,* ed. G. Pope Atkins (Austin: Lyndon B. Johnson School of Public Affairs, University of Texas at Austin, 1992), 2–3.

4. This is the conclusion reached in G. Pope Atkins and Larman C. Wilson, *The Dominican Republic and the United States* (Athens: University of Georgia Press, 1998), 228.

5. Atkins, "Reorienting U.S. Policies in the New Era," 3.

6. See John J. Johnson, *A Hemisphere Apart: The Foundations of United States Policy Toward Latin America* (Baltimore: Johns Hopkins University Press, 1990); Frederick B. Pike, *The United States and Latin America: Myths and Stereotypes of Civilization and Nature* (Austin: University of Texas Press, 1992); Lars Schoultz, *Beneath the United States: A History of U.S. Policy Toward Latin America* (Cambridge: Harvard University Press, 1998); and Howard J. Wiarda, *In Search of Policy: The United States and Latin America* (Washington D.C.: AEI Press, 1984); see also J. Valerie Fifer, *United States Perceptions of Latin America, 1850–1930: A New West South of Capricorn* (New York: St. Martin's Press, 1991).

7. Some general historical surveys of U.S.-Mexican relations are Howard F. Cline, *The United States and Mexico,* rev. ed. (Cambridge: Harvard University Press, 1963); George W. Grayson, *The United States and Mexico: Patterns of Influence* (New York: Praeger, 1984); Lester D. Langley, *Mexico and the United States: The Fragile Relationship* (Boston: G. K. Hall, 1991); W. Dirk Raat, *Mexico and the United States: Ambivalent Vistas* (Athens: University of Georgia Press, 1992); Karl M. Schmitt, *Mexico and the United States, 1821–1973: Conflict and Coexistence* (New York: Wiley, 1974); and Josefina Zoraida Vázquez and Lorenzo Meyer, *The United States and Mexico* (Chicago: University of Chicago Press, 1985).

8. G. Pope Atkins, "The United States and the Caribbean Basin," in *Regional Hegemons: Threat Perception and Strategic Response,* ed. David J. Myers (Boulder, Colo.: Westview Press, 1991). Caribbean policies are analyzed by Lester Langley, *Struggle for the American Mediterranean: United States-European Rivalry in the Gulf-Caribbean, 1776–1904* (Athens: University of Georgia Press, 1976); Lester D. Langley, *The United States and the Caribbean in the Twentieth Century,* 4th ed. (Athens: University of Georgia Press, 1989). On Central America, see John E. Findling, *Close Neighbors, Distant Friends: United States-Central American Relations* (New York: Greenwood Press, 1987); and Thomas M. Leonard, *Central America and the United States: The Search for Stability* (Athens: University of Georgia Press, 1991).

9. See Robert G. Wesson, *The United States and Brazil: The Limits of Influence* (New York: Praeger, 1981).

10. See Lars Schoultz, *Human Rights and United States Policy Toward Latin America* (Princeton: Princeton University Press, 1981); Abraham F. Lowenthal, ed., *Exporting Democracy: The United States and Latin America* (Baltimore: Johns Hopkins University Press, 1991); and Howard J. Wiarda, *Democracy and Its Discontents: Development, Interdependence, and U.S. Policy in Latin America* (Lanham, Md.: Rowman and Littlefield, 1995).

11. The following discussion is based on Atkins, "Reorienting U.S. Policies in the New Era," and G. Pope Atkins, "Redefining Security in Inter-American Relations: Implications for

Democracy and Civil-Military Relations," in *To Sheathe the Sword: Civil-Military Relations in the Quest for Democracy*, ed. John P. Lovell and David E. Albright (Westport, Conn.: Greenwood Press, 1997).

12. For example, the fear that the drug traffic or immigration deterrence would fill the void was expressed by the distinguished Mexican scholar, Jorge Castañeda, "Latin America and the End of the Cold War," *World Policy Journal* 7, no. 3 (Summer 1990): 469–492.

13. For treatments of U.S. policy toward Latin America from political-system perspectives, see Michael J. Kryzanek, *U.S.-Latin American Relations*, 3d ed. (Westport, Conn.: Praeger, 1996); John D. Martz, ed., *United States Policy in Latin America: A Quarter Century of Crisis and Challenge, 1961–1986* (Lincoln: University of Nebraska Press, 1995); and John D. Martz, ed., *United States Policy in Latin America: A Decade of Crisis and Challenge* (Lincoln: University of Nebraska Press, 1995). On U.S. purposes in Latin America within recent time frames, see Cole Blasier, *The Hovering Giant: U.S. Responses to Revolutionary Change in Latin America*, rev. ed. (Pittsburgh: University of Pittsburgh Press, 1985); Tom J. Farer, *The Grand Strategy of the United States in Latin America* (New Brunswick, N.J.: Transaction Books, 1988); Margaret Daly Hayes, *Latin America and the U.S. National Interest: A Basis for U.S. Foreign Policy* (Boulder, Colo.: Westview Press, 1984); Abraham F. Lowenthal, *Partners in Conflict: The United States and Latin America*, rev. ed. (Baltimore: Johns Hopkins University Press, 1990); John D. Martz and Lars Schoultz, eds., *Latin America, the United States, and the Inter-American System* (Boulder, Colo.: Westview Press, 1980). Guy Poitras, *The Ordeal of Hegemony: The United States and Latin America* (Boulder, Colo.: Westview Press, 1990) is a theory-based analysis of the decline of U.S. hegemony in Latin America.

14. I have concluded elsewhere ("Reorienting U.S. Policies in the New Era," 9–10) the following: "Accommodation, bipartisanship, and coordination among the key actors in the U.S. policy-making process are necessary but insufficient prerequisites for effective foreign policy action. That is, domestic political cooperation and bipartisanship do not necessarily ensure successful policies in the sense either of achieving stated goals (an empirical observation) or of wisdom (a value judgment on the part of the observer). Given the nature of the U.S. political system, however, the lack of these elements virtually ensures policy failure (in the same two senses). Some adjustment is required in the inherently normative selection of purposes, goals, tactics, and instruments."

15. Thorough histories of U.S. policies toward Latin America include the classic work by Samuel Flagg Bemis, *The Latin American Policy of the United States* (New York: Harcourt Brace, 1943); Gordon Connell-Smith, *The United States and Latin America* (New York: Halsted, 1974); J. Lloyd Mecham, *A Survey of United States-Latin American Relations* (Boston: Houghton Mifflin, 1965); and Graham H. Stuart and James L. Tigner, *Latin America and the United States,* 6th ed. (Englewood Cliffs: Prentice-Hall, 1975). More interdisciplinary and analytic than earlier works are Lester D. Langley, *America and the Americas: The United States in the Western Hemisphere* (Athens: University of Georgia Press, 1989); and Harold Molineu, *U.S. Policy Toward Latin America: From Regionalism to Globalism,* 2d ed. (Boulder, Colo.: Westview Press, 1990); Schoultz, *Beneath the United States*; and Peter H. Smith, *The Talons of the Eagle: Dynamics of U.S.-Latin American Relations* (New York: Oxford University Press, 1996).

16. The major work is Arthur P. Whitaker, *The Western Hemisphere Idea: Its Rise and Decline* (Ithaca: Cornell University Press, 1954). See also Wilfred Hardy Callcott, *The Western Hemisphere: Its Influence on United States Policies to the End of World War II* (Austin: University of Texas Press, 1968).

17. John A. Logan, *No Transfer: An American Security Principle* (New Haven: Yale University Press, 1961).

18. Dexter Perkins, *A History of the Monroe Doctrine* (Boston: Little, Brown, and Co., 1963) is a summary of Perkins' voluminous work on the subject. See also Donald M. Dozer, ed., *The Monroe Doctrine: Its Modern Significance* (New York: Alfred A. Knopf, 1965); Ernest R. May, *The Making of the Monroe Doctrine* (Cambridge: Harvard University Press, 1975); and Gaddis Smith, *The Last Years of the Monroe Doctrine, 1945–1993* (New York: Hill and Wang, 1994).

19. For the text of Monroe's message, see James D. Richardson, ed., *A Compilation of the Messages and Papers of the Presidents* (New York: Bureau of National Literature and Art, 1907), 2:209, 218-219.

20. The standard work is Albert K. Weinberg, *Manifest Destiny* (Baltimore: Johns Hopkins University Press, 1935).

21. On U.S. imperialism in the circum-Caribbean, see Robert Freeman Smith, ed., *The Era of Caribbean Intervention, 1898–1930* (Malabar: Krieger Publishing, 1981); Dana G. Munro, *Intervention and Dollar Diplomacy in the Caribbean, 1900–1921* (Princeton: Princeton University Press, 1964); Dana G. Munro, *The United States and the Caribbean Republics, 1921–1933* (Princeton: Princeton University Press, 1974); and Whitney T. Perkins, *Constraint of Empire: The United States and Caribbean Interventions* (Westport, Conn.: Greenwood Press, 1981).

22. Alfred Thayer Mahan, *The Interest of America in Sea Power, Present and Future* (Boston: Little, Brown, and Co., 1918).

23. See Ivan Musicant, *Empire by Default: The Spanish American War and the Dawn of the American Century* (New York: Henry Holt, 1998); John L. Offner, *An Unwanted War: The Diplomacy of the United States and Spain Over Cuba, 1895–1898* (Chapel Hill: University of North Carolina Press, 1992); and, for a radical view, Philip S. Foner, *The Spanish-Cuban-American War and the Birth of American Imperialism* (New York: Monthly Review, 1972).

24. For Roosevelt's statement, see A. H. Lewis, *Messages and Speeches of Theodore Roosevelt* (Washington D.C.: 1906), 2:857.

25. The standard reference is Herbert Feis, *The Diplomacy of the Dollar: First Era, 1919–1932* (Baltimore: Johns Hopkins University Press, 1950).

26. See Alexander DeConde, *Herbert Hoover's Latin American Policy* (Palo Alto, Calif.: Stanford University Press, 1951).

27. See Donald Marquand Dozer, *Are We Good Neighbors? Three Decades of Inter-American Relations, 1930–1960* (Gainesville: University of Florida Press, 1971); Irwin F. Gellman, *Good Neighbor Policy: United States Policies in Latin America, 1933–1945* (Baltimore: Johns Hopkins University Press, 1979); Frederick B. Pike, *FDR's Good Neighbor Policy: Sixty Years of Generally Gentle Chaos* (Austin: University of Texas Press, 1995); Bryce Wood, *The Making of the Good Neighbor Policy* (New York: Columbia University Press, 1961); and Bryce Wood, *The Dismantling of the Good Neighbor Policy* (Austin: University of Texas Press, 1985).

28. *The Public Papers and Addresses of Franklin D. Roosevelt* (New York: 1938), 2:130-131.

29. G. Pope Atkins, "Monroe Doctrine," in *The Oxford Companion to Politics of the World*, ed. Joel Krieger (New York: Oxford University Press, 1993), 602–603.

30. See Steven G. Rabe, *Eisenhower and Latin America: The Foreign Policy of Anticommunism* (Chapel Hill: University of North Carolina Press, 1988).

31. Milton S. Eisenhower, *The Wine is Bitter: The United States and Latin America* (Garden City, N.Y.: Doubleday, 1963).

32. From the extensive literature on the Alliance for Progress, see Jerome Levinson and Juan de Onís, *The Alliance That Lost Its Way: A Critical Report on the Alliance for Progress* (Chicago: Quadrangle Books, 1970); Herbert K. May, *Problems and Prospects of the Alliance for Progress* (New York: Praeger, 1968); and L. Ronald Scheman, ed., *The Alliance for Progress: A Retrospective* (New York: Praeger, 1988). A good treatment of overall policies is Edward Mc-Cammon Martin, *Kennedy and Latin America* (Lanham, Md.: University Press of America, 1994).

33. Some analyses of U.S. actions during the Cuban missile crisis, from the voluminous body of writing, are Graham T. Allison, *Essence of Decision: Explaining the Cuban Missile Crisis* (Boston: Little, Brown, and Co., 1971); Abram Chayes, *The Cuban Missile Crisis: International Crises and the Role of Law* (New York: Oxford University Press, 1974); Herbert S. Dinerstein, *The Making of a Missile Crisis: October 1962* (Baltimore: Johns Hopkins University Press, 1976); and Robert A. Divine, ed., *The Cuban Missile Crisis,* 2d ed. (New York: Marcus Wiener Publishing, 1988). Treatments by U.S. officials include Robert F. Kennedy, *Thirteen Days: A Memoir of the Cuban Missile Crisis* (New York: Norton, 1969); Arthur M. Schlesinger Jr., *A Thousand Days: John F. Kennedy in the White House* (Boston: Houghton Mifflin, 1965); and Theodore C. Sorenson, *Kennedy* (New York: Bantam, 1965).

34. Nelson A. Rockefeller, *Rockefeller Report on the Americas* (Chicago: Quadrangle, 1969).

35. U.S. Department of State, *United States Foreign Policy: An Overview* (May 1975), 19–20.

36. For official explanations, see William R. Bode, "The Reagan Doctrine," *Strategic Review* (Winter 1986): 21–29; and Nestor D. Sanchez, "The Communist Threat," *Foreign Policy* 52 (Fall, 1983): 43–50. See also James M. Scott, *Deciding to Intervene: The Reagan Doctrine and American Foreign Policy* (Durham: Duke University Press, 1996).

37. *The Report of the President's Bipartisan Commission on Latin America* (New York: Macmillan Publishing Company, 1983).

38. *The Report of the President's National Bipartisan Commission on Central America.*

39. Theodore Draper, *A Very Thin Line: The Iran-Contra Affairs* (New York: Hill and Wang, 1991) is an exceptionally thorough critical analysis of Iran-Contra. Gerald Felix Warburg, *Conflict and Consensus: The Struggle Between Congress and the President over Foreign Policymaking* (New York: Harper and Row, 1989) includes Central America among the issues of the 1980s. For an excellent, more extended policy study, see Cynthia Arnson, *Crossroads: Congress, the Reagan Administration, and Central America* (New York: Pantheon Books, 1989). Of theoretical interest is Jeremy M. Brown, *Explaining the Reagan Years in Central America: A World System Perspective* (Lanham, Md.: University Press of America, 1995).

40. On the end of the cold war and its meaning and challenges for U.S. policies, see the essays in Atkins, *The United States and Latin America*; Michael C. Desch, *When the Third World Matters: Latin America and the United States Grand Strategy* (Baltimore: Johns Hopkins University Press, 1993); Jonathan Hartlyn, Lars Schoultz, and Augusto Varas, eds., *The United States and Latin America in the 1990s: Beyond the Cold War* (Chapel Hill: University of North Carolina Press, 1992); Abraham F. Lowenthal and Gregory F. Treverton, eds., *Latin America and the United States in a New World* (Boulder, Colo.: Westview Press, 1994); and Robert A. Pastor, *Whirlpool: U.S. Foreign Policy Toward Latin America and the Caribbean* (Princeton: Princeton University Press, 1992). Concerning the democratic context, see Lars Schoultz, William C. Smith, and Augusto C. Varas, eds., *Security, Democracy, and Development in U.S.-Latin American Relations* (New Brusnwick, N.J.: Transaction Press, 1994); Howard J. Wiarda, *The Democratic Revolution in Latin America: History, Politics, and U.S. Policy* (New York:

Holmes and Meier, 1990); and Howard J. Wiarda, *Democracy and its Discontents: Development, Interdependence, and U.S. Policy in Latin America* (Lanham, Md.: Rowman and Littlefield, 1995).

41. Martha L. Cottam, *Images and Intervention: U.S. Policies in Latin America* (Pittsburgh: University of Pittsburgh Press, 1994), argues that Caribbean interventions will not cease even in the post–cold war era if the U.S. decisions continue to be shaped by paternalistic views of Latin American cultures and people.

PART THREE

■

Interstate Institutions

A large number of international governmental organizations (IGOs) are relevant to Latin American international relations. IGOs sometimes behave as subsystem actors, and IGOs themselves often constitute international subsystems where regularized interaction takes place. They also serve as policy instruments of states and provide regulatory elements at various levels of international relations. Latin American states, since their sovereign beginnings, have used IGOs as favored policy instruments. Thus, a large number of IGOs need to be analyzed as a category unto themselves.

This part of the book proceeds through a hierarchy of IGOs. Chapter 7 addresses intra-American organizations. It deals with Latin American and Caribbean integration and multipurpose organizations, the Latin American nuclear-free-zone regime, and certain arrangements in the Western Hemisphere in which Latin American states have participated. Chapter 8 addresses the Inter-American System of organization and law, which reflects the western hemispheric regional search for peace, security, and national well-being. Chapter 9 is concerned with global organizations, some specific extrahemispheric regimes, and Third World structures in which Latin America and Caribbean states have participated.

CHAPTER SEVEN

■

Intra-American Integration
and Other Associations

Latin American and Caribbean state participation in international organizations at the Latin American regional and subregional levels is the subject of this chapter. Initiatives toward integration or other association in some combination of Latin American states date from the movements for independence to the present day. The nineteenth-century Spanish American congresses (called primarily to establish security communities) are discussed, followed by the complex post–World War II Latin American and Caribbean projects aimed at economic integration and/or political union. The discussion then proceeds to organizations designed to promote foreign policy coordination among the Latin American and Caribbean states and to increase their bargaining power with the rest of the world. The chapter also includes a treatment of the Latin American nuclear-free zone, a specialized regional international regime. Finally, it considers some other western hemispheric regimes: U.S.-Panamanian arrangements for the Panama Canal, governance of the U.S.-Mexican border, and the North American Free Trade Agreement and its possible extension to the other Americas.

THE MOVEMENT FOR SPANISH AMERICAN UNION

Americanismo

Subregional integration was first attempted in Latin America during the nineteenth-century movements for independence, when some Spanish American states sought to form larger political entities.[1] The efforts revealed an ambivalent intra-Spanish American "love-hate" relationship that has survived to the present day. The underlying ideology was called *americanismo* or, sometimes, "continental nationalism." Americanismo was the idea of a kindred Spanish American spirit growing out of a common colonial heritage, revolutionary experience, and culture, with a shared perception of Spanish American community that might form the basis of political union. Simón

Bolívar, the prestigious leader of independence in northern South America, was the chief advocate of Americanismo, along with other important leaders, and the most active exponent of Spanish American solidarity. Americanists variously wanted to form from one to four sovereign states out of the Spanish Empire in America. But geographic realities, localism and regionalism, and interstate disputes led instead to the establishment of separate states that were often in conflict with one another.

The four viceroyalties of the Spanish American Empire soon divided into sixteen (later eighteen) separate states. Mexico and the former colonial Spanish captaincy-general of Guatemala (i.e., Central America) joined in a single empire in 1821. Two years later Central America broke away and formed its own federation, but in 1838 the provinces split into five separate states (Guatemala, El Salvador, Honduras, Nicaragua, and Costa Rica). In 1830 Gran Colombia divided into three states (Colombia, Venezuela, and Ecuador). After Peru gained independence in 1824, its province of Upper Peru separated to form the state of Bolivia. The leaders of Buenos Aires attempted to mold a single independent state out of the Viceroyalty of La Plata, which they misnamed the United Provinces of La Plata, but it disintegrated into modern day Argentina, Uruguay, Paraguay, and part of Bolivia.

As the separate states were attempting to develop a self-conscious sense of their national identities and traditions, they also endeavored to form a security confederation among themselves. Americanismo referred to unity against outside threats as well as to kinship; in practice the former turned out to be the more powerful motivation. Four international congresses were held between 1826 and 1865, with a minority of the Spanish American states attending at any time. They signed agreements occasioned by fear of external threats, but once those threats subsided the proposals for union or alliance disintegrated into nationalism and particularism. Only one of the treaties, signed in 1848, actually went into effect.

Spanish American Congresses and Conferences

In December 1824 the Gran Colombian government, led by Bolívar, sent invitations to several states to attend a congress in Panama (a Colombian province). Bolívar's objective was to establish a Spanish American union; his immediate concern was the possibility that Spain, with help from the Holy Alliance led by France, would reclaim its American empire by force. Four states were represented—Gran Colombia, the Central American Federation, the United Mexican States, and Peru. The United Kingdom and the Netherlands, both enemies of Spain, sent unofficial observers at the invitation of conference organizers. Argentina declined to attend, unwilling to accept Gran Colombia's regional leadership. Brazil and the United States received invitations (Bolívar had at first been opposed to this) but neither participated. Bolivia and Chile accepted invitations, but their delegates did not reach Panama in time to participate.

The Congress of Panama met from June 22 to July 15, 1826. The major theme was Spanish America's unity and the defense of its new sovereignty and territorial integrity. Four agreements were signed. The most important of them, the Treaty of Perpetual Union, League, and Confederation, called for mutual defense "against all foreign domination." During the conference the threat from Spain and the Holy Alliance subsided. Only Gran Colombia ratified the agreements.

The second meeting was not held until almost two decades later. A conference in Lima, called the American Congress, met from December 11, 1847, to March 1, 1848. Five South American states were represented—Bolivia, Chile, Ecuador, Colombia, and Peru. Mexico, preoccupied with its war with the United States, did not attend; Venezuela, Argentina, and Brazil declined their invitations. The United States refused an unauthorized invitation, although even it was retracted inasmuch as the United States was at war with Mexico. The primary concern, however, was Spain's attempt to reconquer the west coast of South America.

The third conference, a one-day meeting, took place in Santiago, Chile on September 15, 1856. Only three states—Chile, Ecuador, and Peru—attended what was called the Continental Congress. Cooperation was again inspired largely by fear of foreign aggression, this time the filibustering expeditions of William Walker and other U.S. adventurers in Central America and Mexico, which heightened anxiety over U.S. territorial ambitions. The conference adopted yet another convention for alliance and confederation called the Continental Treaty. It provided for a permanent league of Latin American states with mutual aid. The other Spanish American states and Brazil were invited to join the union; the United States was not approached. None of the parties ratified the Continental Treaty.

The Second Lima Conference, the fourth and final Spanish American conference, was held from November 14, 1864, to March 13, 1865. It was attended by Bolivia, Chile, Colombia, Ecuador, El Salvador, Guatemala, Peru, and Venezuela. Argentina and Brazil still refused to participate, and the United States was not invited. Major European interventions were in progress—the French occupation of Mexico, the Spanish reoccupation of Santo Domingo, and the Spanish war with Peru and Chile. The Treaty of Union and Defensive Alliance was among the four conventions approved, which agreed to confederation and pledged mutual defense against aggression. None of the treaties were ratified.

After the congress in 1865 the disillusioned Spanish American states abandoned initiatives directed toward union. They did cooperate in efforts to codify private international law into inter-American law by organizing two gatherings: The Congress of Jurists at Lima (December 13, 1877–March 27, 1879), and the First South American Congress on Private International Law at Montevideo (August 25, 1888–February 18, 1889). The latter congress agreed to eight treaties and one protocol, which were ratified and remain in force today among the seven signatories.

In Central America, endemic interstate conflict led in 1907 to a U.S.-sponsored peace conference in Washington, D.C. The five Central American states created the Central American Court of Justice, intended to be a supranational instrument for the peaceful settlement of their international disputes. The five-member court heard ten cases during its life and successfully averted some armed conflicts, but certain justices exhibited considerable national partisanship. In 1917 the court ruled that the Bryan-Chamorro canal treaty between Nicaragua and the United States injured Costa Rica and El Salvador. Nicaragua then withdrew from the court, and it ceased to exist in 1918.

INTEGRATION MOVEMENTS

Initial Concepts

Initial Latin American integration efforts after World War II included both economic and political considerations.[2] From a purely economic standpoint, free-trade theory was embraced and applied to regional integration theory.[3] Free trade was assumed to mean more trade, redounding to everyone's benefit. Proponents further assumed that successful integration required complementary economies among the member states, meaning that the national economies must produce different goods. With complementarity, "economies of scale" would develop, a modern version of the classic economic concept of "comparative advantage." With complementarity, economic specialization exists in each national economy, with each member state exporting those products that it produces most efficiently and importing those that others produce most efficiently. Thus, the theory goes, various products originate at their most efficient and therefore least expensive source, which leads to lower prices. With costs and prices lowered to everyone's benefit, markets expand, giving incentive to increased investment and, consequently, to the expansion of existing industries and the creation of new ones. In sum, the theory of economies of scale within a regional integration context predicted that increased, sustained, and mutually beneficial economic growth would occur among member states.

The dangers of regional economic integration were also recognized. If economies of scale did not exist—that is, if "substitute" rather than complementary economies were the rule—the result of integration would be trade stagnation or trade diversion. Stagnation would occur because similar economies had little to trade. Trade diversion was the opposite of trade creation: Instead of creating low-cost sources, trade is diverted from foreign sources to higher-cost regional sources, a scenario in which integration could worsen rather than better the economic situation. For example, before integration, a South American state imported automobiles from Europe, where particular models were produced most efficiently. Integration revised the common tariff structure, making the European source more expensive, and the state then imported similar automobiles from a regional state. However, the automobiles were produced less efficiently and more expensively than at the prior pre-integration European source, resulting in higher costs and, perhaps, lower quality.

Early Planning Efforts

Latin American economic integration grew out of immediate post–World War II proposals by the United Nations Economic Commission for Latin America (ECLA).

ECLA proposed at its first meeting in 1948 that the Latin American states consider arranging themselves into a series of subregional customs unions. The rationale for subregional groupings was that their markets would be more cohesive and viable than a single larger regional one and that, after subregional markets became operational, they could be melded into a larger entity. ECLA later urged that the subregional approach be abandoned in favor of integrating the entire Latin American region. The shift in emphasis, occurring in about 1958, was based as much on political as on economic concerns. ECLA theorists argued that the integration of all Latin American states would increase the region's collective leverage to serve as a counterpoise to U.S. regional hegemony.[4]

The actual practice of Latin American integration favored the subregional approaches. Planning for the integration of five Central American states was well under way by the time ECLA shifted its position away from subregional integration, and those states were unwilling to give up the Central American Common Market (CACM), which was established in 1959. The Latin American Free Trade Association (LAFTA), composed of eleven members, was founded in 1960; in 1980 LAFTA was superseded by the Latin American Integration Association (LAIA). LAFTA, and later LAIA, did not form a Latin American regional enterprise, although it included all of the large economies and most of the region's population and resources. Efforts continued to create an all-inclusive market, but without success. In fact, further subregional integration took place that signaled movement away from institutional convergence, and that indicated the problems besetting LAFTA that led to new ways of thinking about economic integration. The Andean Group was organized in 1966 within LAFTA, at about the same time that the Caribbean Free Trade Association (later the Caribbean Community) was being organized.

The Inter-American System encouraged economic integration, favoring region-wide integration over subregional markets. The Organization of American States adopted economic integration as one of the purposes of the Alliance for Progress in the 1960s. The meeting of American presidents at Punta del Este in 1967 agreed to establish an organization linking the CACM and LAFTA and making it fully operative by 1985. The Inter-American Development Bank (IDB) actively supported the efforts, lending funds to the CACM for integration projects and underwriting multinational programs in South America aimed at physical infrastructure development. The IDB founded the Institute for the Integration of Latin America (INTAL) in Buenos Aires in 1966. INTAL served as a research institute, training center, and technical assistance source; it issued policy studies and trained (as well as attempted to persuade) Latin American governments, businesses, and labor officials.

Problems of Integration

The 1960s were years of great expectations for economic integration, but the subsequent efforts tended to be slow and formalistic. At the same time, economic and social problems continued to grow, and the Latin American desire for more freedom from external pressures remained unabated. Economic integration proceeded unevenly and by the end of the 1960s had already slowed considerably. Among the problems were deeply ambivalent attitudes toward integration in both Latin America and the United States.[5] The integration concept had at first conflicted with U.S. policy traditions of bilateral relations and support of private economic enterprise and free trade. Under the Alliance for Progress, the United States generally endorsed and subsidized integration efforts because they promised to aid in Latin American economic development and political stability. At the meeting of American presidents in 1967, President Johnson formally endorsed integration as a means of promoting Latin American economic growth. Shortly thereafter, however, U.S. assistance and commitment were reduced. Preoccupation with the Vietnam War and with domestic problems led to reduced foreign aid expenditures and commitments to Latin America in general, including support of economic integration.

Economic integration had appeal in Latin America as a means to development and as an "independence movement" against external (especially U.S.) economic domination. However, important political and economic groups whose cooperation was necessary for successful integration did not accept or were ambivalent toward integration policies. Business establishments were divided over integration issues. Certain industrialists and exporters formed interest groups that urged continuation of trade barriers. In addition, a more general Latin American view developed that integrated markets would be especially vulnerable to U.S. economic penetration. The change in U.S. policy after 1967 further fueled these misgivings.

A number of endogenous problems reduced the effectiveness of the integration organizations and worked against their expansion. The chief problems were the wide disparities in size, diversity, level of development, and rate of growth of the different economies; they were exacerbated by national rivalries and competing ideologies. Central American conflict was particularly disruptive of the CACM. Certain successes also were evident, however, so that efforts toward economic integration continued among most Latin American states outside of Central America.

Changing Concepts

Some conceptual changes regarding economic integration were advanced as ways to alleviate certain existing problems. The Andean Group was organized in consonance with positions worked out by theorists who challenged the free-trade model of regional integration. They said that free-market forces worked to benefit the economically more advanced members much more than the less-developed members. They accepted the view that the integration of developing states based on free-markets actually increased the chances for foreign penetration, especially by multinational corporations, rather than strengthened the member states relative to the rest of the world and allowed them increased independence in their collective policy-making.[6] These theorists and other critics of free trade recommended controlled markets to some degree, in order to include various forms of preferences or compensation for weaker states and strict rules for external capital investment.

By the 1980s, with the decline of the integration efforts, serious doubts arose that Latin American integration could succeed in stimulating economic development and independence. Two important developments then occurred to revive the movement: (1) Latin American political democratization accompanied by the adoption of economic neoliberalism; and (2) the end of East-West conflict and the rise of free trade and investment to primacy in the international system.

Latin American governments and IGOs—the renamed Economic Commission for Latin America and the Caribbean (ECLAC) prominent among them—reevaluated how they should respond to the rapidly changing international economic system and reoriented their integration strategies. According to Issac Cohen,[7] they concluded that the prior purposes of economic integration—to enhance import-substitution behind high import barriers as much as to expand free trade—was no longer appropriate. The U.S. Enterprise of the Americas Initiative (EAI) that was announced in June 1990 held out the possibility of hemispheric free trade, which further stimulated Latin American integration reform. Although Latin American governments anticipated increased access to the U.S. market, they realized the eventuality of hemispheric free trade meant a heavy U.S. presence in the process.

Important institutional developments ensued. Of particular importance, in 1991 Argentina, Brazil, Paraguay, and Uruguay formed, within Asociación Latinoamericana de Integración (ALADI), the Common Market of the South (MERCOSUR); Chile and Bolivia later joined as associate members. In 1994 the charter of the Association of Caribbean States was agreed to, with twenty-six member states and a number of associate members. Although the reform movement encountered difficulties, it reflected a sense of necessity and determination.

INTEGRATION IN THE CIRCUM-CARIBBEAN

The Organization of Central American States

Founded in 1951, the Organization of Central American States (ODECA) was designed to promote Central American political and economic unity.[8] ODECA, with headquarters in San Salvador, was composed of the five original Central American states. The ODECA Charter was signed on October 14, 1951, but did not go into effect until 1955. A revised charter was signed on December 12, 1962, and became effective in 1965. Panama accepted the invitation to join as a signatory of the new treaty. Article 1 of both treaties stated that the member states "are an economic-political community, which aspires to the integration of Central America." The agreement created a structure of eight organs: Meeting of Heads of State, Conference of Ministers of Foreign Affairs, Permanent Executive Council, Legislative Council, Court of Justice, Economic Council, Cultural and Educational Council, and Defense Council. Their combined purposes were to promote uniform legislation; decide legal conflicts; plan and coordinate economic integration; promote educational, scientific, and cultural interchange; achieve uniformity in the educational systems; and advise on regional defense and security. Later, a general secretariat, the Central American Bureau, was created.

ODECA was not effective in realizing its purposes. It was of some importance in assisting economic unity but its companion organization, the Central American Common Market, took the lead after being founded. ODECA was confronted with a variety of disputes and had little success in settling them. For example, in December 1967 the foreign ministers sought without success to settle the violent Honduras-El Salvador border dispute; Honduras withdrew from ODECA in 1970. The intraregional Central American conflicts after 1979 rendered ODECA moribund.

The Central American Common Market

The idea for Central American economic integration developed during the June 1951 ECLA meetings. Finally, between 1958 and 1960, the Central American states signed a series of preliminary agreements anticipating creation of the Central American Common Market (CACM). The process culminated in 1960 with two instruments: the General Treaty of Central American Economic Integration and the Convention Chartering the Central American Bank for Economic Integration. Together they consolidated, extended, and superseded the prior agreements. The General Treaty provided for the gradual realization of a Central American customs union, envisioning the eventual elimination of all trade barriers among its members and the establishment of a common external tariff for the rest of the world. It also projected a common customs administration, a unified fiscal policy, a regional industrial policy, and coordinated policies in public health, labor, education, transportation, and agriculture. The General Treaty became effective for Guatemala, El Salvador, and Nicaragua on June 4, 1961; for Honduras on May 6, 1962; and for Costa Rica on September 9, 1963.

The CACM institutional structure consisted of the Economic Council, the Executive Council, and the Permanent Secretariat (located in Guatemala City). The Central American Bank for Economic Integration (located in Tegucigalpa) and the Central American Clearing House, both established in 1961, were recognized by the General Treaty. Two training schools created years before came under CACM sponsorship: the Central American Advanced School of Public Administration (ESAPAC), instituted in 1954 in San José, Costa Rica, and the Central American Institute of Industrial Research (ICAITI), organized in 1956 in Guatemala City. Mexico joined the clearing house, providing funds to the banks and lending technical advisers to various bodies.

CACM enjoyed some success in its early years. Elimination of most tariff barriers between member countries during the years 1961–1970 brought about a 700 percent increase in intraregional trade and a 10 percent increase in trade with outside markets. CACM was almost wholly responsible for augmented foreign investment and was an important factor in increasing the gross national products of member states. Economic benefit went mostly to the industrial sector, whereas agriculture, the greatest contributor to the GNPs of individual countries, involved few economies of scale and thus was not emphasized in CACM policy.

The CACM faced economic and political disagreements that created serious conflict among its members. Economic gains were not shared equally by member states. Honduras and Nicaragua, the two least developed members, gained only slightly, whereas Guatemala and El Salvador, the most developed members, improved their trade considerably. Costa Rica held a middle position. Nicaragua and Honduras had large trade imbalances with their colleagues. They also suffered from trade substitution, importing products from other CACM members that were more expensive and of lesser quality than similar products formerly imported from the United States and Europe. The market agreements had envisioned the planned distribution of industries among member states through an integrated industries scheme that assigned plants and production rights, but CACM was unsuccessful in getting industries to locate in the less developed countries.

Trade disputes were difficult to resolve and led to various forms of penalties and retaliation that seriously disrupted the flow of trade. The El Salvador-Honduras war of 1969 further complicated the economic tensions. The economic difficulties were superseded by political and military conflicts after 1979 that as much as ended the functioning of the common market.

The Central American Integration System

In the latter 1980s, the five Central American leaders undertook initiatives as part of a regional peace process (see Chapter 13) to revive economic and political integration. In 1991 they signed the General Treaty for Central American integration, which created the Central American Integration System (SICA).[9] Designed to serve as a multipurpose "umbrella" organization comprising extant and future Central American institutions, SICA came into being with the signing of the "Succession Act" on May 31, 1994. In essence, the institutions and purposes of ODECA and CACM were combined and reconstituted in the new regime that superseded them. The secretariat was renamed the Permanent Secretariat of Central American Economic Integration (SIECA). SICA absorbed the Central American Parliament, which the five Central American presidents had created in 1987 (all parties except Costa Rica had ratified the enabling treaty); it integrated the presidential summit meetings that had been instituted in the mid-1980s (they are held every six months). The new Central American Commission on the Environment and Development was created. Panama had joined ODECA in 1965 but not CACM; Belize had become an independent state in 1981. Neither state was invited to join SICA, but the presidential meetings were opened to them—they attend irregularly. Panama is a member of some of the lower-level SICA functional agencies.

The Central American presidents continued to hold the summit meetings they had initiated in 1987 as part of the peace process. Of particular significance was the

Seventeenth Central American Presidential Summit (December 13–15, 1995), when the seven heads of government signed several agreements seeking to reinforce Central American integration. One treaty extended the terms of the Central American Alliance for Sustainable Development, a plan the presidents had adopted two months previously at a special meeting. Another pact, the Democratic Security Treaty of Central America, included provisions addressing legal systems, corruption, organization and internationalization of common crime, drug trafficking, terrorism, and arms smuggling, as well as stipulations concerning the balance of military forces for both national needs and intraregional relations.

Caribbean Dependencies

Early Developments.   The United States and the United Kingdom cooperated in 1942 to establish the Anglo-American Caribbean Commission (AACC)[10] The bipartite commission was designed to deal with certain wartime emergencies in the U.S. and British Caribbean dependencies. It developed measures to relieve the lack of ocean shipping and the disruption of world markets and devised plans to defend them from attack. In 1940 the United States had leased British West Indian areas for use as military and naval bases, giving it a direct interest in those areas governed by Britain (at the time threatened by German invasion) as well as its own Puerto Rico and Virgin Islands. The AACC largely succeeded in dealing with immediate economic and military emergencies and in beginning long-term economic projects.

In 1946 the AACC was reconstituted as the Caribbean Commission. It was broadened to include the participation of France and the Netherlands, acting on behalf of their Caribbean dependencies, as well as the participation of delegates from the nonsovereign Caribbean entities themselves. More formal than the AACC, the four-power Caribbean Commission held the regularly scheduled West Indian Conference. Its Caribbean Research Council and the General Secretariat were located in Trinidad and headed by a secretary-general. During its fifteen-year life, the Caribbean Commission undertook projects in agriculture, trade, fisheries, education, health, and other functional areas.

The four metropolitan powers agreed in 1959 to end the Caribbean Commission; it was succeeded by the Caribbean Council in 1961. The members of the new council included the Caribbean entities themselves, except France participated as a member "on behalf of" its American overseas departments. The Caribbean Council survived for three years. Among the problems leading to its dissolution (on June 30, 1965) were the breakup of the West Indies Federation in 1962, one of its largest members; the awkward position of France; and the impatience of Puerto Rico over what it perceived as the council's ineffectiveness in dealing with Caribbean problems.

The West Indies Federation.   After World War II, the United Kingdom was concerned with arrangements for the future of its American colonies.[11] After the political eclipse of Winston Churchill, both major British political parties agreed that the colonial territories around the world should be guided toward independence within the Commonwealth through economic, social, and political development. They admitted that some were deficient in population or resources to the point that self-government should not go beyond internal affairs. By 1955 the British-American territories were grouped together in ten crown colonies. The British Caribbean Territories, also known as the British West Indies, included nine crown colonies; the Falkland Islands, in the far-removed South Atlantic Ocean, were a separate crown colony within a grouping called the Atlantic Ocean Dependencies (along with the crown colonies of St. Helena and Ascension). The idea of an independent federal state composed of some of the British Caribbean Territories had been discussed for years; the British Colonial Office had begun a plan to this end in 1945 in cooperation with the local governments involved. They finally realized the goal of federation in 1958.

The West Indies Federation was composed of ten entities—Antigua, Dominica, Montserrat, St. Christopher and Nevis-Anguilla, St. Lucia, St. Vincent, Barbados, Grenada, Jamaica, and Trinidad and Tobago. It was to be internally self-governing for a four-year transition period, with Britain responsible for foreign affairs and defense. Then the federation was to be given complete independence as a sovereign federal state. In 1962 the most important entities, Jamaica and Trinidad and Tobago, decided in favor of separate independence; the federation was dissolved.

After the collapse of the federation, Britain and the dependencies agreed in 1966 to end the latter's colonial status by making them States in Association with Great Britain (meaning they were internally self-governing but depended on Britain for defense and foreign affairs). Most of them subsequently opted for sovereign independence. In the meantime, the Commonwealth Caribbean Countries looked to integrate their economies.

The Caribbean Free Trade Association

The agreement establishing the Caribbean Free Trade Association (CARIFTA) was signed in Antigua and Barbuda on December 15, 1965, by Antigua, Barbados, and British Guiana. Two years later, when additional entities agreed to join the association, the agreement was revised.[12] CARIFTA finally came into being on May 1, 1968, and eventually its membership included four independent states (Barbados, Guyana, Jamaica, and Trinidad and Tobago), seven States in Association with Great Britain, and one British colony. They all were located in the circum-Caribbean and were members of the Commonwealth.

CARIFTA members chose the free-trade area so as to eliminate tariffs and quota systems on each other's products. They allowed for exceptions based on varying levels of economic development and whether a member was a sovereign state or a nonsovereign entity. CARIFTA's governing body was the Council of Ministers, made up of representatives from each member state and responsible for broad policies. Administration was lodged with the Commonwealth Caribbean Regional Secretariat, located in Georgetown, Guyana. In 1969 CARIFTA established the Caribbean Bank (CARIBANK), with headquarters in Bridgetown, Barbados. The members, and Canada and Britain, contributed to the general fund. CARIBANK also established special funds for agricultural development and soft-currency loans, to which the United States contributed funds.

The Caribbean Community

CARIFTA's founders had envisioned the association as a first step in Caribbean Commonwealth economic integration. In April 1972 the member states adopted a treaty establishing the Caribbean Common Market (CARICOM) to replace CARIFTA; it went into effect in May 1974 and eventually had thirteen members. Twelve members were sovereign states: Antigua and Barbuda, the Bahamas, Barbados, Belize, Dominica, Grenada, Guyana, Jamaica, St. Christopher and Nevis, St. Lucia, St. Vincent, and Trinidad and Tobago. The nonsovereign member was Montserrat, still an Associated State. Four neighboring non-Commonwealth Caribbean states were made permanent observers—the Dominican Republic, Haiti, Suriname, and Venezuela; three of them later became full members—the Dominican Republic and Suriname in 1995 and Haiti in 1996.

CARICOM's objective was to create a common market of the member states, thus establishing a common external tariff in addition to removing tariffs among the members. A Common Protective Policy was adopted to "operate by way of imposing quantitative restrictions for promoting industrial and agricultural development." The less-developed countries, apprehensive about the distribution of benefits, were again given preferred status. The Commonwealth Caribbean Countries had enjoyed trade preferences with the European Community/European Union under the Lomé convention (see Chapters 5 and 12). In 1991 the two organizations formed CARI-FORUM ("Caribbean Forum") to facilitate their discussions.

CARICOM's governing board was the Conference of Heads of Government. It was assisted by the Common Market Council, composed of a minister from each participating member state. In 1973 the Commonwealth Caribbean Secretariat was renamed the Caribbean Community Secretariat. Seven additional institutions were created. They were four standing committees of ministers in the fields of agriculture, finance, labor, and mines, and three "associate institutions"—CARIBANK, the Caribbean Investment Corporation (created in 1973 to support investment programs in the less-developed countries), and the Regional Shipping Council. CARIBANK resources were expanded. In addition to its eligibility to borrow from the World Bank, the bank received contributions from Britain, Canada, the United States, and other states.

The Standing Committee of Ministers of Foreign Affairs was created for the members to "aim at the fullest possible coordination of their foreign policies within their respective competencies and seek to adopt as far as possible common positions in major international issues." This committee made advisory recommendations to CARICOM. Other noneconomic functions were carried out by the Conference of Ministers of Health and by other institutions for education and meteorology.

CARICOM, like other regional integration organizations in the 1990s, undertook organizational reform. In July 1991 the annual meeting of heads of government agreed to move toward a single market and economy. In the same month, CARICOM and the United States signed a framework agreement establishing the intent to negotiate free trade. The CARICOM summit meeting in June 1992 adopted plans to establish a CARICOM investment fund and to implement a Common External Tariff, a key element in creating a single market. Progress was slow, however, and tensions arose over specific aspects of increased integration. During this time, CARICOM added environmental problems and sustainable development as part of its continuing agenda.

The Organization of Eastern Caribbean States

In July 1981, seven small Commonwealth Caribbean island-states formed the Organization of Eastern Caribbean States (OECS) within CARICOM. The members are Antigua and Barbuda, Dominica, Grenada, Montserrat, St. Christopher and Nevis, St. Lucia, and St. Vincent and the Grenadines. They primarily sought to pool economic resources and promote their own economic integration. Secondary goals were to coordinate foreign affairs, defense, and security arrangements and to promote political stability in their locale. The OECS was the culmination of prior efforts undertaken by the member entities. In 1968, after becoming British "associated states," they had established the Eastern Caribbean Common Market, which the OECS superseded after the members became independent. The British Virgin Islands became an associate member in 1984. In 1983, the OECS members established a companion financial and economic development organization—the Eastern Caribbean Central Bank (ECCB). Anguilla joined the bank in 1987 but did not adhere to the OECS.[13]

The U.S. invasion of Grenada in October 1983 deeply divided the OECS (as well as CARICOM). Ignoring collective security provisions of the Rio Treaty and the OAS Charter, the United States, as legal justification for the intervention, persuaded the OECS majority to request U.S. military assistance under a minor provision of its charter. The minority bitterly opposed the invasion. In time the divisiveness faded within both the OECS and CARICOM.

Some New Arrangements

Additional multilateral and bilateral free-trade agreements were negotiated in response to the reformation of the extant integration organizations and the EAI proposal. They were based on the assumption that wider and deeper Latin American and Caribbean integration would make the regions' markets more interesting for traders in the United States, Europe, and Japan. Of the twenty-five agreements, the creation of the Group of Three (G-3) was particularly significant. In September 1990, the presidents of Colombia, Mexico, and Venezuela issued a declaration forming the Group of Three to coordinate their energy policies (all are oil-exporting countries); in 1994 they agreed to remove trade barriers among themselves and to seek trade cooperation with the rest of the Caribbean. Mexico and Bolivia agreed to joint ventures and to Mexican financing of Bolivian exports to Mexico through the Andean Development Corporation, of which Mexico is a member. Chile made bilateral agreements with Mexico, Venezuela, Colombia, and Ecuador, respectively, to abolish tariffs on their trade. Other accords focusing on the circum-Caribbean formed part of a process leading to a potentially significant trans-Caribbean organization.

The Association of Caribbean States

A series of intraregional, multilateral and bilateral free-trade-oriented discussions and agreements culminated in 1994 with formation of the Association of Caribbean States.[14] In addition to the G-3, several other arrangements were precursors of the association. In January 1991 the presidents of Mexico and the five member states of the CACM agreed to set up a free-trade area. Also in 1991, Venezuela agreed to give immediate duty-free access to the products of Central America and the Caribbean, with the expectation of reciprocity. In January 1992 CACM and CARICOM held a joint conference to consider melding the two organizations and extending the membership. Delegations were present from twenty-three circum-Caribbean states and dependencies; Haiti and Cuba were not invited because of the autocratic nature of their governments. In October of that year, CARICOM formally decided to take the lead in creating the Association of Caribbean States.

On July 24, 1994, twenty-six heads of state signed the charter of the Association of Caribbean States (ACS). All signatories ratified the charter within a year. The twenty-six members were divided into subgroups: CARICOM (fourteen members), Central America (six states, including Panama but not Belize, a member of CARICOM), the Group of Three, and the Greater Antilles (an informal grouping of Cuba, the Dominican Republic, and Haiti). They made provision for nonsovereign entities to join as associate members. Anguilla, the Turks and Caicos, and Guadalupe so joined; also eligible were Bermuda, the Caymans, Martinique, U.S. Virgin Islands, British Virgin Islands, French Guiana, and Puerto Rico. The membership of Cuba was significant, inasmuch as it was shunned by other regional associations because of the requirement by each that only democratic governments could join. The charter-stated purpose of ACS was to form a free-trade area. Unstated were the concerns of smaller states to increase their bargaining leverage in the hemispheric free-trade process.

TRANSREGIONAL AND SOUTH AMERICAN INTEGRATION

The Latin American Free Trade Association

In February 1960 seven Latin American states signed the Treaty of Montevideo establishing the Latin American Free Trade Association (LAFTA).[15] The seven charter members when the treaty went into effect in 1961 were Argentina, Brazil, Chile, Peru, Paraguay, Mexico, and Uruguay. Joining later were Colombia and Ecuador

(1961), Venezuela (1966), and Bolivia (1967), bringing the total number of members to eleven. Thus, the market area included most of South America plus Mexico.

LAFTA, with headquarters in Montevideo, was administered by an annual conference where members negotiated trade liberalization and established programs. The Permanent Executive Committee of ambassadorial representatives, assisted by a secretariat, implemented the conference decisions. In 1965 LAFTA created a series of ministerial councils (foreign ministers, heads of central banks, transportation and communications ministers, and agriculture ministers) with a view to later integration beyond the level of free-trade area.

LAFTA sought to establish only a free-trade area in which the members eliminated tariffs and other restrictions on "substantially all" of their trade with one another. The elimination of internal trade barriers was to be achieved incrementally over a twelve-year period and completed by 1973. However, some members resisted certain tariff reductions. Difficulties stemmed from the diversity in the levels of economic development among the member states. The less-developed ones were unwilling to drop their import trade barriers irrevocably without parallel allocation of industrial growth from which they would benefit. They felt that the "Big Three"—Mexico, Brazil, and Argentina—were benefiting disproportionately from intra-market trade and should make concessions to the weaker states. The Treaty of Montevideo had recognized Ecuador and Paraguay as "least developed" members that required certain special treatment. But the other members (Chile, Colombia, Peru, and Uruguay) insisted that they, relative to the Big Three, were also disadvantaged. Consequently, in 1963, reliance on free-market forces to determine economic growth was essentially discarded; the middle-economies were classified as "insufficient markets" and granted some preferential treatment.

The 1963 compromises were unable to realize a mutuality of interest, and LAFTA's subsequent progress was unimpressive.[16] Trade barriers were not lowered on schedule, and industry was not stimulated to the extent hoped for. By 1968 LAFTA had virtually ceased to function, deadlocked over the free-trade versus regional planning issue. Few complementation agreements were signed. The failure to agree upon a program of joint development was the principal factor slowing the tariff-cutting process among LAFTA members. This situation led to its moribund state and then to the creation of the Andean Group.

The Andean Group

The Andean Common Market (ANCOM), usually referred to as the Andean Group (AG), was formed within the LAFTA structure by members who were dissatisfied with the course of integration but unwilling to leave LAFTA.[17] The governments of Chile, Colombia, Venezuela, Ecuador, and Peru joined in the Declaration of Bogotá in August 1966, announcing their intention to form a common market aimed at accommodating the differing levels of development of their economies. They sought a common market through planned industrialization rather than reliance on free-market forces. Two treaties were subsequently drafted, one creating the Andean Development Corporation to help finance development projects and the other establishing the Andean subregional common market itself, with its headquarters in Lima. The charter of the Andean Development Corporation was signed in February 1968, and the Andean Pact (the Agreement of Cartagena) was signed in May 1969. The charter members of the AG were Bolivia (which had joined the negotiations in 1967), Chile, Colombia, Ecuador, and Peru. Venezuela delayed joining because of domestic counter-pressures but became a member in 1973.

The objectives of the AG were to (1) eventually create a common market with virtually no trade barriers among its members and a common policy toward the outside world; (2) establish an internal market for industrial production, with new industries assigned exclusively to different members; (3) limit the power of multinational corporations in their dealings with the AG; and (4) accommodate the less-developed members (Bolivia and Ecuador) with special concessions. The organizational machinery included the following bodies: (1) the Mixed Commission of ambassadorial representatives as supreme organ; (2) a council charged with presenting technical proposals to the commission; (3) an advisory consulting committee of integration experts; and (4) an economic and social council representing the interests of business and labor groups. A separate convention later established the Andean Development Corporation to serve as a regional development bank.

The AG first aspired to a free-trade area by eliminating tariffs among members in steps over a ten-year period, which was accomplished on schedule in 1982. A common external tariff was instituted by 1976 to encourage the manufacture of certain goods within the market. Industrial development was to be stimulated by an investment program and complementation agreements.

The AG gave special attention to the role of private foreign investment within the integrated market. Members claimed that MNCs had inordinately benefited from integrated economy arrangements by using their mobility and huge resources to establish industries within the region and to produce for protected and expanded markets. Those members also acknowledged the need for foreign capital and decided to control rather than exclude it.

The Andean Pact Statute on Foreign Capital ("Decision 24"), adopted in January 1971 and later modified, was the only Latin American multilateral attempt to control foreign investment. A comprehensive code, it provided for step-by-step reductions of foreign-controlled investment, regulation of the international transfer of technology, planned distribution of industries throughout the Andean zone, conversion of foreign manufacturing firms to at least 51 percent local ownership, and restrictions on existing foreign banks. Major problems emerged with regard to Decision 24. Waivers and exceptions were granted extensively. After the 1973 coup in Chile, the military regime adopted free-market economic policies directly opposed to the AG strategy, and in 1976 Chile withdrew from the agreement. A more general problem was the fact that most members had insufficient markets to support the development of industries that would be large and efficient enough to compete effectively with external industries in terms of cost and price.

After 1976 AG members substantially modified the Cartagena agreement with a series of protocols and formal decisions. Decision 24 was so altered that it was virtually abrogated, and in 1987 it was annulled. Deadlines for internal free trade and common external tariffs were extended. Industrial programs were delayed, and state roles in them were reduced. The organizational structure was also extended, with the creation in 1979 of the Andean Tribunal of Justice, the Andean Parliament, and the Council of Ministers of Foreign Affairs. With the formation of the foreign ministers council, the AG became actively political. For example, a resolution was passed by the Andean foreign ministers in June 1979, recognizing the popular Sandinista forces in Nicaragua as a belligerent in their fight with the Somoza dictatorship, thus legitimating them with legal personality and opposing the U.S. view of the matter.

The AG went through another crisis in 1980 and 1981, owing to a coup in Bolivia and border fighting between Ecuador and Peru. The members formally declared a "relaunching" of the integration movement in September 1981. Afterwards progress was slow, and the original "directed development" was all but forgotten. In 1989 the AG further broadened its purposes to include nuclear non-proliferation and a modicum of political integration.

The AG joined in the revival of Latin American interest in subregional integration. Chile rejoined the organization in 1990, following the replacement of the military regime by an elected civilian government; Chile provided the most stable and open Andean economy. In December 1991 an AG presidential summit agreed to establish the common market with common external tariffs within five years. AG overcame much of its divisiveness and in 1995 converted itself to the Andean Community (ANCOM). In December 1995 the European Union proposed the possibility of a free-trade area with ANCOM; in June 1996 the two regional organizations signed a declaration on political dialogue.

The Latin American Integration Association

In the late 1970s the LAFTA membership decided to reform extensively their integration arrangement. A new Treaty of Montevideo was signed in August 1980 by all LAFTA members to institute the Latin American Integration Association (LAIA).[18] The treaty entered into effect with full ratification in March 1981, superseding the 1960 treaty and replacing the LAFTA structure. Further development took place during a transition period in which further negotiations took place.

In certain ways LAIA is a continuation of LAFTA, with specific aspects of the old scheme incorporated into the new one. The 1980 treaty also introduced fundamental changes in both the concept and operation of economic integration. First, LAIA provided for multiple levels of negotiation and cooperation. Argentina and Brazil had been the prime movers behind LAIA so that they could make bilateral agreements between themselves and with Mexico. LAIA also allowed multilateral agreements not involving the full membership—LAFTA had sanctioned only multilateral agreements of a full market scope. Second, LAIA expanded LAFTA's activities by specifying three additional functions: the promotion and regulation of reciprocal trade, the creation of economic complementation, and the development of enlarged markets. Third, although LAFTA had recognized a special status for the relatively less-developed economies, the new scheme incorporated more extensive provisions in their favor. It also has a category of intermediate economic development, so as to add certain states that receive special treatment. Finally, LAIA provided for limited participation by certain nonmember states and private entities. In sum, LAIA was designed to have greater negotiation and operational flexibility than LAFTA, to recognize the different levels of economic development among member countries, and to provide for a wider range of agreements. LAIA added a parliamentary assembly to the institutional structure. Over time LAIA gave observer status to seven circum-Caribbean states: Costa Rica, Cuba, the Dominican Republic, El Salvador, Guatemala, Honduras, and Nicaragua.

The Common Market of the South

The Common Market of the South (MERCOSUR) was created in 1991 within LAIA but operating independently (as does ANCOM).[19] MERCOSUR is rooted in the Brazil-Argentina Program for Integration and Cooperation agreement signed in July 1986, which called for economic cooperation as well as cooperation in diplomatic and even nuclear realms and was linked to the reestablishment of democracy in both states. The agreement was then offered to neighboring states, and in March 1991, Argentina, Brazil, Paraguay and Uruguay signed the Asunción Treaty, agreeing to set up MERCOSUR.

After going into operation, MERCOSUR sought to expand its membership to other South American states. (In 1996 the members formally agreed to suspend integration privileges to any state that violated democratic principles.) In 1996 Bolivia and Chile became associate members as a prelude for both to join as full members (which would raise the MERCOSUR population to about 210 million). Brazil and Argentina, Latin America's first and third largest economies, respectively, are the core of MERCOSUR and account for its potential as an integration organization.

MERCOSUR opened to the outside world. In 1991, shortly after being organized, MERCOSUR signed a framework agreement with the United States with a view to negotiating free trade as part of a future hemispheric free-trade arrangement. In December 1995 MERCOSUR and the European Union signed an Interregional Framework Agreement looking toward the reciprocal free trade; further negotiations continued thereafter. MERCOSUR negotiated for reciprocal trade preferences with a wide range of other countries. Among them was a group of sixty developing countries, as well as Japan and Russia.

South American River Basin Development Agreements

The Cuenca del Plata Accord.   On April 23, 1969, five South American states (Argentina, Bolivia, Brazil, Paraguay, and Uruguay), all part of the complex Río de la

Plata system, signed a treaty for the development of the river basin *(cuenca)*. An example of integration of physical infrastructure resources, the Cuenca del Plata accord called for the multilateral development of international communications and water resources, especially hydroelectric power potential. It provided for a standing intergovernmental committee and annual meetings on the ministerial level. A consortium of international financial institutions, led by the Inter-American Development Bank, agreed to cooperate; a development fund was established in June 1974.

The Cuenca del Plata group achieved successes but revealed serious debilities as well. Some highway and hydroelectric projects were completed, but no development funds were expended. The most serious problem was essentially political, involving rivalry between Argentina and Brazil over regional strategic concerns and over competition for influence with the buffer states in the Southern Cone. Mutual suspicions resulted in several uncoordinated bilateral river project agreements.

The Cuenca del Plata's fortunes improved in the 1980s. The solidification of an Argentine-Brazilian rapprochement after 1979 facilitated cooperation in basin projects. Construction of the Itaipú dam on the Paraná river—a project that created the world's largest source of hydroelectric power—was completed after years of delay due to Argentine-Brazilian bickering.

The Amazon Pact.   Representatives of eight Amazon region states—Bolivia, Brazil, Colombia, Ecuador, Guyana, Peru, Venezuela, and Suriname—signed the Amazon Cooperation Treaty in July 1978.[20] The treaty called for the coordinated development of the Amazon Basin's communications and transport systems and natural resources and for the protection of the region's fragile ecology. It also gave Latin American enterprises first opportunity to develop the region. In sum, the treaty called for Amazonic regional cooperation that would enable member nations to benefit from the basin's resources, and it spelled out the projects to be accomplished. The organizational structure was simple: meetings of ministers were to convene annually (later, biannually) in different member countries. In 1992 the presidents of the Amazon Accord member states met to study proposals for the United Nations Conference on Environment and Development, held in Rio de Janeiro later in the year; they subsequently increased their emphasis on the concept of sustainable development.

MULTIPURPOSE ASSOCIATIONS

Beginning in the mid-1960s, primarily political multipurpose associations were organized among different sets of Latin American states. Their creation was largely based on the assumption that Latin American states would be more influential in the international system if they adopted common positions and regional unity toward the rest of the world. They became more important after the mid-1970s and took on new significance in the post–cold war era. The six organizations discussed below are the most notable of those that have materialized.

The Special Latin American Coordinating Committee

In 1964 Latin American states joined informally in the Special Latin American Co-ordinating Committee (CECLA).[21] CECLA was created by the Inter-American Economic and Social Council, an agency of the Organization of American States, as an autonomous Latin American forum on tariff and trade matters. No formal agreement was signed or organizational apparatus established; CECLA was an informal caucusing group that could be called by any member state willing to host it. CECLA was intended to increase regional unity for economic bargaining power with external states and international organizations.

The foreign ministers from all Latin American states except Cuba attended CE-CLA's first meeting in February 1964, to establish regional policy positions for the first meeting of the United Nations Conference on Trade and Development (UNC-TAD I). CECLA continued as a conference, reconvened as its participants desired. The ministers held a series of meetings after 1964 to plan regional bloc positions for UNCTAD II (1967) and III (1971) and worked together within other international fora such as the General Agreement on Tariffs and Trade, the International Monetary Fund, and the World Bank. CECLA provided a medium for negotiations with the United States and the European Community.

CECLA enjoyed some success but also confronted difficulties in achieving Latin American unity. One of its most significant statements was the Consensus of Viña del Mar, formulated at a meeting in June 1969 at the Chilean resort town of the same name. This set of common Latin American positions on trade and economic development issues was sent directly to President Nixon. The following year CECLA used the same tactics toward Europe. In July 1970, Latin American foreign ministers issued a statement calling for more favorable terms of trade with and increased economic assistance from the EC. CECLA reacted again in 1971 in response to the Nixon administration's general 10 percent trade surcharge. It issued the Manifesto of Latin America, pointing out that Latin America, with net deficit trade with the United States, was not responsible for the unfavorable U.S. trade balance. The manifesto asked the United States to exempt the region from the surcharge and to grant general trade preferences.

CECLA achievements were limited. Latin Americans generally were disappointed with the outcomes of the UNCTAD meetings. President Nixon responded favorably to the Consensus of Viña del Mar and exempted Latin America from the 1971 trade surcharge, but the U.S. Congress was unwilling to give in to the other demands. In 1970 the EC agreed to explore ways to improve its trade relationships with Latin America but on a non-preferential basis. CECLA meetings resulted in a high degree of Latin American unity and coordinated positions on a number of economic issues, but intraregional disagreements similar to those within the economic integration organizations also arose. The large economies, especially Mexico, Brazil, and Argentina, tended to differ with the rest over economic policy positions. Rivalry among the larger states for leadership of CECLA also reduced its unity.

The Latin American Economic System

The establishment of the Latin American Economic System (SELA) was almost entirely the result of initiatives taken by Mexican President Luís Echevarría. At a meeting in Caracas in November 1974, Echevarría persuaded President Carlos Andrés Pérez of Venezuela to establish a joint permanent consultation arrangement in order to arrive at common economic and social policies, especially those regarding Latin American natural resources. The bilateral agreement was opened to adherence by other Latin American states, without exception. In October 1975, twenty-three Latin American states signed a formal act, virtually identical to the Mexican-Venezuelan declaration, establishing SELA. By 1998 twenty-seven regional states, including Cuba, had signed the charter.

The SELA charter says the organization is "for consultation, coordination, and joint economic and social promotion." The agreement proposed to pool the resources of member states in order to form agencies for the production and sale of Latin American raw materials (a purpose unrealized). SELA also serves as an international bargaining forum with the rest of the world, and in this sense it is a political arrangement. SELA proposed to formulate common regional positions prior to attending other international meetings and thus replaced CECLA as the regional caucus. SELA is not an economic integration scheme itself, but it has the purpose of supporting regional integration.

SELA's principal organ is the Latin American Council, composed of ministers meeting at least once yearly. Council decisions, usually adopted by a two-thirds majority, are nonbinding; members are committed only to multilateral consultation. It appoints ad hoc Action Committees to supervise specific projects. A Permanent Secretariat, located in Caracas, provides operational support; a secretary-general serves a four-year term.

The Rio Group

The Central American crisis of the 1980s combined with the earlier decline of the Inter-American System to inspire Latin American organizational initiatives to resolve them.[22] Out of these efforts grew the Rio Group, the informal name of a new and important multipurpose, transregional association.

In January 1983, four states—Mexico, Venezuela, Colombia, and Panama—organized the Contadora Group and offered a plan for the negotiated settlement of Central American conflict. In July 1985, Argentina, Brazil, Peru, and Uruguay organized the Contadora Support Group, and joint meetings of the eight foreign ministers were held over the next year and a half. In December 1986 the foreign ministers adopted a declaration creating the Permanent Mechanism of Consultation and Political Coordination, known as the Rio Group. (It was widely referred to at the time as the Group of Eight, but as membership expanded the numerical designation gave way to "Rio Group.") The declaration said that, based on their experience of joint action in the Contadora process, the signatories would expand the agenda beyond Central America to include other salient issues. In practice, in addition to the Central American peace process, the Rio Group addressed a number of expanding, salient issues: the strengthening of Latin American democracy through sustained economic and social development and regional cooperation and integration; the matter of agreements with external creditors; the need to create a free and fair international trading system; the creation of a Latin American common market; and the problems of disarmament, the clandestine arms trade, terrorism, drug trafficking, and environmental degradation; as well as scientific, technical, cultural, and educational interchange. They also expanded discussions with other states and IGOs and advocated strengthening the Organization of American States.

The founding declaration provided for regular meetings of foreign ministers. In addition, annual summit meetings of heads of state were begun in November 1987, and regular conferences of finance ministers were instituted beginning in December 1988. In June 1988, representatives from SELA, LAIA, ECLAC, and IDB were invited to participate in foreign ministers meetings.

In 1991 the Rio Group and the European Union (EU) established the Institutionalized Meeting of Rio Group-EU Foreign Ministers and began to hold regular annual meetings. They initially focused on strengthening interregional economic relations; other matters were increasingly taken up, including democracy and human rights, the international drug traffic, women's rights, and sustainable development.

The Latin American Parliament

The Latin American Parliament was created in 1964 and permanently located in Caracas.[23] In 1987, a "treaty of institutionalization" gave it a stronger legal position as an IGO. Nineteen states are members. Their delegations must proportionately represent the political parties represented in the state legislatures. The parliament's decisions are not binding on governments or political parties. It was intended to promote region-wide economic integration and development and to advocate political coordination among state congresses for community cooperation, but these purposes remain vague and are stated in highly general terms. It nevertheless serves as a focal point for the discussion of economic integration and even political confederation.

THE LATIN AMERICAN NUCLEAR-FREE ZONE

In the early 1960s Brazil proposed that Latin America be made a nuclear-free zone.[24] It noted that no nuclear weapons were present in Latin America and that any regional nuclear weapons acquisitions would stimulate an expensive and dangerous arms race. In 1961 Brazil formally proposed to the UN General Assembly that the Latin American region be made a nuclear-free zone, but the assembly did not vote on the resolution.

The Cuban missile crisis of 1962 gave great impetus to the idea of a Latin American nuclear-free zone. Following the initiative of President João Goulart of Brazil, the presidents of Bolivia, Brazil, Chile, Ecuador, and Mexico signed the Five Presidents Declaration, expressing readiness to sign an enabling treaty. The UN General Assembly formally supported the declaration on November 27, 1963. Mexico then assumed the initiative, led by Ambassador Alfonso García Robles, Mexican deputy foreign minister (and later recipient of the Nobel Peace Prize for his efforts). A Latin American conference in 1965 created a commission that prepared a draft treaty. The Treaty for the Prohibition of Nuclear Weapons in Latin America was signed by fourteen states on February 14, 1967, in Tlatelolco, the section of Mexico City where the Foreign Ministry is located, and is therefore known as the Treaty of Tlatelolco. The UN General Assembly endorsed the treaty on December 5, 1967; it entered into force April 22, 1968. By 1994, all of the regional states but Cuba had ratified the treaty.

The Tlatelolco treaty is the first seeking to establish a nuclear-free zone in a populated world region. In fact, the fundamental concept of the treaty is to prevent the introduction of nuclear weapons into a geographic region already free of them. Article 1 unambiguously states the obligations of the Latin American signatories: They "undertake to use exclusively for peaceful purposes the nuclear material and facilities which are under their jurisdiction," and they agree to prohibit "the testing, use, manufacture, production, or acquisition" of any nuclear weapons, as well as their "receipt, storage, installation, deployment, and any form of possession of any nuclear weapons, directly or indirectly." Article 13 places all peaceful nuclear activities in Latin America under the safeguards system of the International Atomic Energy Agency (IAEA), a UN-sponsored organization with headquarters in Vienna. In 1969 the Organization for the Prohibition of Nuclear Weapons in Latin America (OPANAL) was established as a further control mechanism.

An overwhelming majority of Latin American states accepted the idea of a nuclear-free zone. Cuba justified its non-adherence with reference to the strained U.S.-Cuban relations and the U.S. presence at Guantánamo. Argentina, Brazil, and Chile signed the treaty and protocols, but when Argentina did not ratify the treaty, the other two attached reservations to their ratifications, saying that the treaty did not go into force for them until Argentina had adhered. Finally, in 1994, after elected civilian governments had replaced military regimes in all three states, Argentina ratified the treaty, and Chile and Brazil rescinded their reservations.

The basic treaty, restricted to the Latin American states themselves, was supplemented by two protocols designed to further ensure the region's nuclear-free condition. Protocol I commits external states with dependent territories inside the zone to place those territories under the same restrictions. Among the states responsible for territories within the geographical treaty limits, the Netherlands, the United Kingdom, and the United States have signed and ratified the protocol. The United States, whose territories include Puerto Rico and the Virgin Islands (and, for treaty purposes, the naval base at Guantánamo), delayed ratification until 1981. France signed but did not ratify the protocol; thus French Guiana, Martinique, and Guadeloupe are not militarily denuclearized. France says that since those Caribbean entities are integrated with the metropole it has the prerogative to make nuclear policies as it wishes.

Under Protocol II, nonregional nuclear weapons states agree to respect the non-nuclear status of Latin America, and not to contribute to violations of the treaty by states in the zone or to use or threaten to use nuclear weapons against them. Five nuclear powers—the United States, the United Kingdom, France, the People's Republic of China, and the Soviet Union—ratified Protocol II.

OTHER INTRA-AMERICAN ARRANGEMENTS

The Panama Canal

The idea of a canal across the Central America isthmus dates from the Spanish conquest in America.[25] Columbus had made his voyages in search of a shorter sea route from Europe to Asia, and Hernán Cortés proposed that a canal be constructed along one of the five routes that even today are considered to be the most practicable. Although Spanish kings were interested in such a project, they never began construction.[26] After Latin American independence and through the remainder of the nineteenth century, the idea was taken up by Britain, the United States, and France.

The United States took the first important step to secure control of a Central American route. On December 12, 1846, the United States and New Grenada signed a treaty that guaranteed the right of passage across the Colombian province of Panama to the United States. In the meantime, Britain had established sovereignty over British Honduras and the Bay Islands and, in 1844, proclaimed a protectorate over the "Mosquito Kingdom," which consisted roughly of today's Caribbean coast of Nicaragua. In 1849 the United States signed treaties with Nicaragua to obtain a concession for a canal, contravening British claims in the area, and a treaty with Honduras granting U.S. control of Tigre Island in the Gulf of Fonseca. Britain promptly sent a naval force that took possession of the island. A compromise was achieved in the Clayton-Bulwer Treaty of 1850, in which both the United States and Britain, in essence, promised not to claim exclusive control over any canal in Central America and to guard the safety and neutrality of any canal that should be built.

With U.S. and British canal interests mutually neutralized, the French position became dominant. A private company organized by Ferdinand de Lesseps, the Suez Canal engineer, purchased a Colombian concession in 1879 to construct a canal across Panama. Construction began in February 1881, but eight years later the enterprise ended in bankruptcy and scandal with only about one-third of the canal completed.

When the United States emerged as a great power after its war with Spain in 1898, it determined to build and control a canal. By then Britain was more amenable to compromise. The Hay-Pauncefote Treaty of 1901, negotiated by U.S. Secretary of State John Hay and the British ambassador to Washington, Lord Pauncefote, abrogated the Clayton-Bulwer Treaty, giving the United States the freedom to build and exclusively control a canal. It provided that the canal should be equally open to commercial and war vessels of all states with no discriminatory charges. Since the treaty contained no prohibition to the contrary, the United States assumed the right to fortify and defend the canal. With U.S.-British issues settled, the United States shifted its attention to choosing a canal site.

In 1899 the U.S. Congress had charged its Walker Commission to study all possible routes. In its voluminous report of November 1, 1901, the commission had narrowed the choice to two of five possible routes, one through Panama and the other through Nicaragua. When the French project failed in 1889, a new Panama Canal Company had taken over the property and attempted to sell its interest to the U.S. Congress. The Walker Commission calculated the total value of the Panama Canal Company's rights and property to be $40 million, as opposed to the company's demand for some $109 million. The commission favored the Panama route from an engineering standpoint but recommended the Nicaragua site because of the high Panama price. The U.S. House of Representatives, in accordance with the Walker Commission's recommendations, passed the Hepburn Bill in January 1902, authorizing the construction of a canal across Nicaragua. The French company responded in panic by offering to sell its interest to the United States for $40 million. Consequently, the Spooner Amendment to the Hepburn Bill authorized the Panama route as an alternative to the one across Nicaragua.

The United States negotiated an agreement with Colombia concerning its province of Panama. The Hay-Herrán Treaty of 1903 granted the United States exclusive rights to construct and operate the Panama Canal and authorized the French Panama Canal Company to transfer its concession. The U.S. Senate promptly consented to ratification, but the Colombian Senate decided to press for more advantages and unanimously rejected the treaty. French creditors were dismayed by the jeopardy to their interests, as the United States could exercise the Nicaraguan option. Agents of the French company organized a rebellion in Panama, taking advantage of long-standing Panamanian resentment against the central government for its neglect and of the current threat to their potential benefits from a Panama canal.

The Panamanian revolt began on November 2, 1902. A U.S. warship prevented Colombian troops from interfering by blockading their only route over water to Panama. Four days later, the United States recognized Panama's sovereign independence. A Panamanian employee of the French canal company became the first president of the Republic of Panama, and the former chief engineer, Philippe Bunau-Varilla, who also had engineered the revolution, was appointed Panama's minister to the United States. He negotiated a canal treaty that was signed on November 18, 1903, only two weeks after the revolt had begun.

The Hay-Bunau-Varilla Treaty provided for U.S. use, occupation, and control, "in perpetuity," of a ten-mile strip of territory extending across Panama (the Canal Zone). The United States gained the use and occupation of other lands and waters outside the zone necessary to the canal's construction, operation, or protection. Panama agreed to U.S. treaty rights to intervene in Panamanian domestic affairs if necessary to maintain order and ensure Panamanian independence so as to protect the future canal. (The Panamanian Constitution of 1904 included Article VII of the

1903 treaty, which permitted U.S. military intervention "in case the Republic of Panama should not be, in the judgment of the United States, able to maintain ... order.") In return, the United States agreed to pay Panama $10 million plus an annual subsidy of $250,000 beginning nine years after ratification of the treaty.

With the Panamanian route secured, the United States purchased the French company's assets. Construction began in 1906, and the Panama Canal, generally acknowledged to be an engineering marvel for the times, opened to traffic in 1914.

The U.S. Good Neighbor Policy coincided with the rise of Panamanian nationalism, which centered on protests about the canal. The agitation culminated in the Hull-Alfaro Treaty in 1936, which amended the original 1903 treaty. The United States renounced its right to intervene in Panamanian affairs. In case of aggression endangering Panama or the canal, the two governments were to consult about mutual defense. The annual U.S. rental subsidy was raised to $430,000, and the United States accepted stricter limitations on the conduct of business and rights of residence in the Canal Zone. During World War II, Panama gave the United States temporary permission to use certain existing military facilities and to construct new ones in Panama outside of the Canal Zone. In 1947 the two states signed a treaty providing for U.S. retention of fourteen military bases, but the Panamanian National Assembly refused to ratify the treaty in the face of a strong negative public reaction. The United States evacuated the bases. Panamanian dissatisfaction led to negotiations and resulted in further treaty amendments. The Eisenhower-Remón Treaty, signed in 1955, increased the U.S. annuity to $1.93 million and transferred certain U.S. rights and properties to Panama.

Many Panamanians, considering the U.S. concessions in the 1936 and 1955 amendments inadequate, continued to agitate against the arrangement. Riots and clashes between Zonians and Panamanians occurred on several occasions. Especially serious was a confrontation in 1964 in which four U.S. citizens and twenty-two Panamanians were killed. As a result, treaty revision talks were resumed.

Panama asserted a number of specific grievances. It complained that during the 1903 negotiations its dependence on the United States for national survival forced it to accede to U.S. demands, and that Bunau-Varilla, the principal negotiator for Panama, had primarily represented the interests of the French canal company rather than those of Panamanians. Panama charged that it had never been adequately compensated for its concessions and expressed resentment over the affluence of people who lived in the Canal Zone. Most objectionable were treaty provisions giving a foreign power virtual sovereignty over a portion of Panama that physically divided the state.

Following discussions of the canal issue in the Organization of American States and the United Nations, Panama and the United States agreed in 1964 to pursue bilateral negotiations for a new treaty. Agreements were reached in 1967 on three draft treaties that provided for canal operation by a joint U.S.-Panamanian authority and for U.S. defense responsibilities, but a nationalist military government came to power in 1968 in Panama and formally rejected them. Negotiations, resumed in 1971, were intense but inconclusive. Panama, to the chagrin of the United States, brought up the issue before the UN Security Council, meeting in Panama City in March 1973. Panama introduced a resolution calling for a treaty that would give Panama "effective sovereignty" over the Canal Zone. The United States blocked the resolution by casting a veto, but it agreed to adjust its differences with Panama. The two governments signed a Statement of Principles on February 7, 1974, designed to serve as guidelines for further treaty negotiations.

The final negotiation was left to President Jimmy Carter. On September 7, 1977, President Carter and the President of Panama, General Omar Torrijos, signed two Panama Canal treaties. At the same time, a protocol to the neutrality treaty was signed by most other Latin American nations, thereby showing their strong approval. The bilateral treaties were sent to the U.S. Senate for advice and consent, where a particularly bitter and acrimonious process took place. The mobilization of the opposition was impressive. Its basic argument was that the Canal Zone was U.S. territory, legally agreed to by Panama, and that in the new treaties the United States unnecessarily gave away an important possession. Supporters of the treaty, who finally but narrowly prevailed, argued that the treaties would remove a major source of friction not only in U.S.-Panamanian relations but in inter-American affairs in general and would signal a new era of hemispheric cooperation. They pointed out that both the economic and military security importance of the canal, although still significant, had declined considerably. They said that under the new relationship the United States would have operational and defense rights for a time sufficient to work out future contingencies. They also warned of sabotage if agreement was not reached, noting that the canal was particularly vulnerable.[27]

The new treaties, memorandum, and supporting documents were finally ratified by both states and entered into force on October 1, 1979. The treaties establish the new Panama Canal regime. The basic Panama Canal Treaty arranges for the canal's operation, maintenance, and defense through December 31, 1999. Its salient articles provided for: (1) assigning to Panama the normal local government functions in the former Canal Zone; (2) joint United States-Panamanian management and defense of the canal until the end of the century; (3) increasing Panamanian participation at all levels of operations leading to its sole management; (4) continuing control by the United States of all land and water areas necessary for the operation and defense of the canal; and (5) increasing the annuity paid to Panama with money derived from tolls and other canal revenues. The United States will operate the canal, with Panamanian participation, until the year 2000, when Panama will assume control. Until then, a nine-person board of directors will operate the canal, with five members from the United States and four from Panama. The canal is expected to be self-supporting.

The Treaty Concerning the Permanent Neutrality and Operation of the Panama Canal, with no termination date, provides for the canal after the year 1999. It guarantees that the canal will be kept permanently neutral in times of both peace and war and that nondiscriminatory access and tolls will be provided for the vessels of all countries. The United States is permitted to act militarily to defend the canal's neutrality and to keep it open.

The Statement of Understanding clarifies U.S. rights under the neutrality treaty. It confirms the permanent U.S. right to protect and defend the canal against any armed attack or threat to its security or to the free passage of ships of all nations. U.S. warships have the permanent right to transit the canal expeditiously and without conditions and, in case of need or emergency, to go to the head of the line of vessels (when the United States deems it necessary). The same obligations apply with regard to any other canal constructed in Panama. Although the former U.S. Canal Zone ceased to exist when the treaties went into force, the United States retains the right to use areas and facilities necessary to the operation and defense of the canal. The United States may take military action to ensure an open and safe canal, but it does not have the right to intervene against Panamanian territorial integrity or political independence.

Three parallel transition processes were provided for, all dating from October 1, 1979. The first was a transition that ended March 31, 1982, when Panama assumed total responsibility for local government and the U.S. community became subject to Panamanian authority. The transfer of full canal control to Panama entailed two transitional phases. One ended as scheduled on December 31, 1989, when the U.S. administrator of the Panama Canal Commission was replaced by a Panamanian. The final phase will close at midnight on December 31, 1999, when Panama will assume full responsibility.

Mexican-U.S. Riverine Agreements

A U.S.-Mexican treaty in 1884 created the mixed International Boundary Commission to decide frontier questions.[28] Some problems were settled by the commission, but not the important Chamizal dispute. The Rio Grande had continuously shifted its course southward, especially rapidly in the 1860s, transferring about 630 acres known as the Chamizal to the Texas side of the river. The Boundary Commission was unable to resolve conflicting claims and referred the problem to an international arbitral commission, which in 1911 gave the Chamizal to Mexico. The United States refused to accept the award, and the dispute dragged on for another half-century. Finally, in 1962, the United States agreed to abide by the 1911 decision. In the Chamizal convention of 1963 the United States acknowledged Mexican sovereignty over the region, and Mexico ceded the northern half of Córdova Island, lying in the Rio Grande, to the United States. The agreement also provided for the construction of a channel to divert the river, so as to place the Chamizal on the Mexican side, and for the building of three highways and two railway bridges across the river. Costs of these projects were to be shared equally by the two states.

The dispute concerning the Colorado River, flowing from Nevada into Mexico south of California, arose from the fact that, in an apparent treaty violation, the United States was not delivering water of adequate quantity or quality to Mexico. In 1944 the United States agreed to deliver a minimum amount of water to Mexico from the Colorado River, water received from the Morelos International Dam on the

Mexico-Arizona border. In 1961 the U.S. Wellton-Mohawk Reclamation District began rinsing soil with methods that involved pumping highly saline waters into the Gila River near its confluence with the Colorado. Contaminated water began to kill the cotton crops in the Mexicali Valley of Mexico. After a decade of dispute, an agreement was put into effect in 1973. Under it the United States agreed to cleanse the water to a certain degree before sending it to Mexico.

Hemispheric Free Trade

Enterprise for the Americas Initiative.   In a speech on June 27, 1990, President George Bush announced the Enterprise for the Americas Initiative (EAI), which contemplated a western hemispheric free-trade area (FTA).[29] The EAI visualized hemispheric free trade linked to the promotion of investment, debt relief, and environmental protection. The United States made clear that the first priority was the successful completion of the Uruguay Round of the General Agreement on Tariffs and Trade (GATT), followed by the establishment of a North American Free Trade Area, and then by the extension of free trade to the rest of the hemisphere.

North American Free Trade Agreement.   The North American Free Trade Agreement (NAFTA) grew out of separate U.S. bilateral relations with Canada and Mexico. The Canada-United States Free Trade Agreement had gone into effect on January 2, 1988, after two years of difficult negotiations. In the meantime, in 1987, Mexico and the United States had signed a framework agreement as the basis for further bargaining. Canada, seeking to protect its agreement with the United States, indicated its interest in taking part, and trilateral talks commenced in June 1991. The U.S. Congress required that they include parallel bilateral U.S.-Mexican discussions on labor and environmental issues. The United States consequently negotiated "side agreements" with Mexico on these matters. Congress also made progress on the NAFTA talks a prerequisite to extending accords elsewhere in the hemisphere. After rigorous bargaining, NAFTA was signed and ratified by the three states and went into effect on January 1, 1994.

NAFTA unites the three North American states in the world's largest free-trade zone, a market of more than 360 million people. The United States and Canada are each the other's largest trading partner and compose the world's largest bilateral trade. The United States is by far Mexico's largest trading partner, and Mexico is the United States' third largest. Consistent with GATT rules, NAFTA will phase out barriers to trade in goods and services in North America, eliminating some immediately and others over different periods of up to 15 years. NAFTA eliminates barriers to investment, and strengthens the protection of intellectual property rights—such as high technology, publishing, and entertainment—that rely for protection on patents and copyrights. NAFTA includes specific safeguards and escape clauses. It allows suspension of trade on some items in order to protect domestic industry, a dispute mechanism to solve trade conflicts, and any of the parties to withdraw from

NAFTA by giving six-months' notice. With NAFTA's implementation on January 1, 1994, the Border Ecological Cooperation Commission and the North American Development Bank were authorized to begin operations.

Free Trade Area of the Americas.   The EAI proposal said that the "United States stands ready to enter into free-trade agreements with other markets in Latin America and the Caribbean, particularly with groups of countries that have associated for purposes of trade liberalization." The United States negotiated a series of separate framework agreements, which were preliminary guidelines for future talks that might lead to free-trade agreements (FTAs). By mid-January 1992, the United States had concluded FTAs with two multilateral organizations—the Common Market of the South (MERCOSUR) and the Caribbean Common Market (CARICOM)—and 14 individual states. It had excluded Cuba, because of opposition to the Castro regime, and Haiti, because of the overthrow of its elected government in September 1991; after the restoration of the deposed president, Haiti joined CARICOM and thus was included in the agreement with the United States. As a general matter, these developments reflected the fact that all of the parties had decided on an export-led strategy for economic recovery and development. The developments were facilitated by the Latin American perception that the United States, no longer burdened with cold war security calculations, was less paternalistic toward the region, and by the Latin American trend away from economic nationalism and toward more openness to the outside world.[30]

Elements of the Organization of American States showed strong interest in hemispheric free trade, and the Inter-American Development Bank in 1992 established a supporting Multilateral Investment Fund. The Economic Commission for Latin America and the Caribbean strongly supported the effort. The OAS-sponsored Summit of the Americas in December 1994 promoted hemispheric free trade. The gathering adopted a Declaration and Plan of Action that resolved "to begin immediately to construct the 'Free Trade Area of the Americas' (FTAA), in which barriers to trade and investment will be progressively eliminated." Negotiations were to be completed no later than 2005, with the OAS playing "a particularly important" supporting role. The hemispheric free-trade process was stalled indefinitely, however, when the U.S. Congress refused to grant President Clinton "fast-track" negotiating authority (see Chapter 6). Nevertheless, a second Summit of the Americas convened in April 1998 and again emphasized the goal of constructing the FTAA.

NOTES

1. On the nineteenth-century Spanish American attempts at union, see Francisco M. Cuevas Cancino, *Del Congreso de Panamá a la Conferencia de Caracas, 1826–1954: El genio de Bolívar a través de la historia de las relaciones interamericanas,* 2 vols. (Caracas: Ragon, 1955); Samuel Guy Inman, *Inter-American Conferences, 1826–1954: History and Problems,* ed. Harold Eugene Davis (Washington, D.C.: University Press of America, 1965), chapters 1 and 2; J. Lloyd Mecham, *The United States and Inter-American Security, 1889–1960* (Austin: University of Texas Press, 1961), chapter 2.

2. The general subject of post–World War II integration efforts is analyzed in Sidney Dell, *A Latin American Common Market?* (London: Oxford University Press, 1966); Altaf Gauhar, ed., *Regional Integration: The Latin American Challenge* (Boulder, Colo.: Westview Press, 1985); Joseph Grunwald, Miguel S. Wionczek, and Martin Carnoy, *Latin American Economic Integration and U.S. Policy* (Washington: Brookings Institution, 1972); Felipe Herrera, *Desarrollo e Integración* (Santiago de Chile: Editorial Emision, 1986); Ronald Hilton, ed., *The Movement Toward Latin American Unity* (New York: Praeger, 1969); Gordon Mace and Jean-Philippe Thérien, eds., *Foreign Policy and Regionalism in the Americas* (Boulder, Colo.: Lynne Rienner Publishers, 1996). José Nuñez del Arco, Eduardo Margaín, and Rachells Cherol, eds., *The Economic Integration Process of Latin America in the 1980s* (Washington, D.C.: Inter-American Development Bank, 1984); Peter H. Smith, ed., *The Challenge of Integration: Europe and the Americas* (Miami: University of Miami, North-South Center; New Brunswick, N.J.: Transaction Publishers, 1993); and Víctor L. Urquidi, *Free Trade and Economic Integration in Latin America* (Berkeley: University of California Press, 1962). A useful documentary collection is Inter-American Institute for International Legal Studies, *Instruments Relating to the Economic Integration of Latin America* (Dobbs Ferry, N.Y.: Oceana Publications, 1968).

3. In strictly definitional terms, economic integration among sovereign states may occur at several levels of intensity: A *free-trade association* provides for common trade among the member states free of tariffs and other trade barriers, but with each state determining its own economic relations with the rest of the world; a *customs union* involves common trade among the members, as in a free-trade association, and, in addition, common policies toward trade with the rest of the world; a *common market* provides for common trade both among the members and with the rest of the world, and also allows free movement within the market of factors of production such as labor; an *economic union* is full economic integration that includes all of the features of a common market plus common fiscal and monetary policies and a common currency.

4. Economic Commission for Latin America, *The Latin American Common Market* (New York: United Nations, 1959).

5. Grunwald, Wionzcek, and Carnoy, *Latin American Economic Integration and U.S. Policy.*

6. A leading proponent of this view was Philippe Schmitter, *Autonomy or Dependence as Regional Integration Outcomes: Central America* (Berkeley: University of California Press, 1972).

7. Isaac Cohen, "Economic Questions," in *The United States and Latin America: Redefining U.S. Purposes in the Post-Cold War Era*, ed. G. Pope Atkins (Austin: Lyndon B. Johnson School of Public Affairs, University of Texas, 1992) analyzes changing Latin American outlooks from the late 1980s.

8. For information on ODECA and on CACM (discussed below), see James D. Cochrane, *The Politics of Regional Integration: The Central American Case* (New Orleans: Tulane University Press, 1969); Isaac Cohen Orantes, *Regional Integration in Central America* (Lexington, Mass.: Lexington Books, 1972); Félix G. Fernández-Shaw y Baldasano, *La integración Centroamérica* (Madrid: Ediciones Cultura Hispánica, 1971); George Irvin and Stuart Holland, eds., *Central America: The Future of Economic Integration* (Boulder, Colo.: Westview Press, 1989); Thomas L. Karnes, *The Failure of Union: Central America, 1824–1960* (Chapel Hill: University of North Carolina Press, 1961); Royce Q. Shaw, *Central America: Regional Integration and National Political Development* (Boulder, Colo.: Westview Press, 1979).

9. Comisión económica para América Latina y el Caribe; Banco interamericano de desarrollo, *La integración centroamericana y la institucionalidad regional* (México, D.F.: Comisión económica para América Latina y el Caribe, 1998).

10. This section relies on Herbert Corkran, *Patterns of International Cooperation in the Caribbean, 1942–1969* (Dallas: Southern Methodist University Press, 1972); see also Bernard L. Poole, *The Caribbean Commission* (Columbia: University of South Carolina Press, 1951).

11. See David Lowenthal, *The West Indies Federation* (New York: Columbia University Press, 1961); John Mordecai, *Federation of the West Indies* (Evanston: Northwestern University Press, 1968); and Hugh W. Springer, *Reflections on the Failure of the First West Indian Federation* (Cambridge, Mass.: Harvard University Press, 1962).

12. On the integration of the Commonwealth Caribbean, see W. Andrew Axline, *Caribbean Integration: The Politics of Regionalism* (London: Francis Pinter, 1979); Chandra Hardy, *The Caribbean Development Bank* (Boulder, Colo.: Lynne Rienner Publishers, 1995); and H. Michael Erisman, *Pursuing Post-Dependency Politics: South-South Relations in the Caribbean* (Boulder: Lynne Rienner Publishers, 1992).

13. Larman C. Wilson and David W. Dent, *Historical Dictionary of Inter-American Organizations* (Lanham, Md.: Scarecrow Press, 1998, 78–79).

14. Atkins, *Encyclopedia of the Inter-American System*, 310–311; Wilson and Dent, *Historical Dictionary of Inter-American Organizations*, 34–35.

15. LAFTA is studied by Edward G. Cale, *Latin American Free Trade Association* (Washington, D.C.: Department of State, 1969); F. J. Mathis, *Economic Integration in Latin America* (Austin: University of Texas Press, 1969); and Edward S. Milenky, *The Politics of Regional Organization in Latin America: The Latin American Free Trade Association* (New York: Praeger, 1973).

16. Grunwald, Wionczek, and Carnoy, *Latin American Economic Integration and U.S. Policy*, 51.

17. See Robert N. Seidel, *Toward an Andean Common Market for Science and Technology* (Ithaca: Cornell University Press, 1974).

18. Asociación Latinoamericana de Integración (ALADI), *La Asociación Latinoamericana de Integración: Un análisis Comparativo* (Buenos Aires: Secretaría General de ALADI, 1980).

19. Institute for European-Latin American Relations, *A New Attempt at Regional Integration: The Southern Cone Common Market,* dossier no. 30 (Madrid: 1992); and Luigi Manzetti, "Economic Integration in the Southern Cone," in *North-South Focus* (University of Miami: North-South Center, December 1992).

20. Franco Filho, Georgenor de Sousa, *O Pacto Amazónico: ideis e conceitos* (Belém: Falangola, 1979).

21. United Nations, Secretariat, *Recopilación de documentos básicos de la Comisión Especial de Coordinación Latinoamericana* (New York: 1972) is a collection of CECLA documents.

22. Institute for European-Latin American Relations, *The Group of Eight: A New Regional Actor for Latin America?* dossier no. 17 (Madrid: March 1989); Boris Yopo H., "The Rio Group: Decline or Consolidation of the Latin American Concertación Policy?" *Journal of Interamerican Studies and World Affairs* 3 no. 4 (Winter 1991): 27–44.

23. Institute for European-Latin American Relations, *The Latin American Parliament and its Relations with the European Union* (Madrid: 1995).

24. For discussions of the Tlatelolco Treaty from the perspective of the prime mover in having it adopted, see Alfonso García Robles, *The Denuclearization of Latin America* (New York: Carnegie Endowment for International Peace, 1967); Alfonso García Robles, *The Latin American Nuclear-Weapon-Free Zone* (Muscatine, Iowa: Stanley Foundation, 1979).

25. General studies regarding the Panama Canal are provided by Lawrence O. Ealy, *Yanqui Politics and the Isthmian Canal* (University Park: Pennsylvania State University Press, 1971); Sheldon Liss, *The Canal: Aspects of United States-Panamanian Relations* (Notre Dame: Univer-

sity of Notre Dame Press, 1969); David McCullough, *The Path Between the Seas: The Creation of the Panama Canal* (New York: Simon and Schuster, 1977); and John Major, *Prize Possession: The United States and the Panama Canal: 1903–1979* (Cambridge: Cambridge University Press, 1993).

26. Graham H. Stuart and James L. Tigner, *Latin America and the United States,* 6th ed. (Englewood Cliffs: Prentice Hall, 1975), 184.

27. U.S. Library of Congress, Congressional Research Service, *Background Documents Relating to the Panama Canal. Prepared for the United States Senate Committee on Foreign Relations* (Washington, D.C.: 1977) is a lengthy compendium of documents. George D. Moffett III, *The Limits of Victory: Ratification of the Panama Canal Treaties* (Ithaca: Cornell University Press, 1985) analyzes the uninspiring U.S. ratification process.

28. On Mexican-U.S. riverine questions, see Norris Hundley, *Dividing the Waters: A Century of Controversy between the United States and Mexico* (Berkeley: University of California Press, 1966); Alan C. Lamborn and Stephen P. Mumme, *Statecraft, Domestic Politics, and Foreign Policy Making: The El Chamizal Dispute* (Boulder, Colo.: Westview Press, 1988); and Sheldon Liss, *A Century of Disagreement: The Chamizal Conflict, 1864–1964* (Washington, D.C.: University Press, 1965).

29. The United States expressed the ideal of hemispheric free trade at the First International Conference of American States (1889–1890), but Latin Americans showed little interest. This and the following two sections are based largely on G. Pope Atkins, "Institutional Arrangements for Hemispheric Free Trade," *Annals of the American Academy of Political and Social Science* 526 (March 1993): 183–194. See Ricardo Grinspun and Maxwell A. Cameron, *The Political Economy of North American Free Trade* (New York: St. Martin's Press, 1993); Ambler H. Moss Jr., ed., *Assessments of the North American Free Trade Agreement* (New Brunswick, N.J.: Transaction, 1993); William A. Orme Jr., *Understanding NAFTA: Mexico, Free Trade, and the New North America,* 2d ed. (Austin: University of Texas Press, 1996); Paul Rich and Guillermo De Los Reyes, eds., *NAFTA: Expectations and Realities,* special issue of *Annals of the American Academy of Political and Social Science* 550 (March 1997); Sylvia Saborio et al., eds., *The Premise and Promise: Free Trade in the Americas* (New Brunswick, N.J.: Transaction, 1992); Sidney Weintraub, ed., *Free Trade in the Western Hemisphere,* entire issue of *Annals of the American Academy of Political and Social Science* 526 (March 1993); and Sidney Weintraub, ed., *Integrating the Americas: Shaping Future Trade Policy* (New Brunswick, N.J.: Transaction, 1994).

30. See Cohen, "Economic Questions." Also see Gary Clyde Hufbauer and Jeffrey J. Schott, *Western Hemisphere Economic Integration* (Washington, D.C.: Institute for International Economics, 1994).

CHAPTER EIGHT

———————— ■ ————————

The Inter-American System

Western Hemisphere organizations for law, peace, security, and national well-being collectively form the Inter-American System of institutionalized, multilateral cooperation among the American states. The name "Inter-American System," which came into general use in the late 1920s and persists to the present day, is an "umbrella" concept covering the historical evolution and present setup of interrelated organizations and their purposes and actions. The Inter-American System traces its genesis to 1889 through a direct lineage of multilateral conferences and other institutional paraphernalia. Over the past few decades it has largely consisted of the Organization of American States, the Inter-American Development Bank, and the Inter-American Treaty of Reciprocal Assistance regime.[1]

REGIONAL AMERICAN ORGANIZATION

The Pan-American Idea

The term "Pan-American" came into use in the 1880s in connection with proposals that resulted in the First International Conference of American States (1889–1890).[2] It then for many years provided the underlying doctrine and mystique for the Inter-American System. The Pan-American concept was an outgrowth of the earlier Western Hemisphere Idea (see Chapter 6).

In the nineteenth century the United States and Latin America adopted isolationist postures toward Europe; they decided their interests were compatible enough to be promoted by a degree of formal multilateral cooperation. Tensions between unilateralism and multilateralism persisted, however, especially during U.S. imperialism in the Caribbean from 1898 to about 1930. The relative isolation of the Americas in the international system during the 1930s, followed by inter-American cooperation during World War II, helped to temporarily revive Pan Americanism.

The Pan-American idea dwindled after World War II and virtually disappeared after the mid-1960s, although occasional policy statements would allude to it. The elevation of the United States to superpower status with global interests (even if reluctantly accepted) eroded the basis for perceptions of special relationships in the Americas. In fact, the United States attempted, with awkward results, to meld its Latin American policies into a global structure divided into First, Second, and Third Worlds. It first fit Latin America into the East-West divide and then further associated the region with the developing Third World. Latin Americans for their part increasingly sought more foreign policy autonomy in their relations with the United States. Nevertheless, after World War II the Inter-American System was placed on a permanent juridical basis and actively helped settle inter-American disputes; in the first half of the 1960s it vigorously administered the Alliance for Progress. It then suffered a general decline for some two decades after the mid-1960s, but since then it has undergone a revival. Thus the level of effectiveness of the Inter-American System has fluctuated over time. One might ask if without the Pan-American mystique the regional organization would nevertheless have been sustained, and if changing state interests account for the system's changing fortunes.

Regional Organization as a Policy Instrument

The institutions of the Inter-American System have partly regulated hemispheric relations by offering opportunities to and imposing limitations on the member states. The historical evidence suggests that the Inter-American System has worked best, in the sense of maximum cooperation for complementary objectives and minimal conflict among the member states, when mutuality of interests has been present. Convergence of interests has been difficult to achieve, however, since the regional states and the United States have usually sought diverging foreign policy goals.

For its part, the United States, until the end of the cold war, sought primarily to exclude other foreign influences in Latin America and, as a corollary, to support political stability in the region. To these ends the United States attempted to unify Latin America in a formal organization characterized by friendly relations but under primary U.S. leadership.[3] In fact, the United States pursued many of its region-wide Latin American policies through the multilateral institutions of the Inter-American System. With the end of the cold war, and with no external state posing a threat to the hemisphere, the United States reevaluated its purposes in Latin America and the Caribbean and indicated its willingness to deal with the major inter-American issues within the Inter-American System, to a large extent.

Although Latin American and Caribbean interests and attitudes toward regional organization vary from state to state, as a general matter they have sought as much foreign policy autonomy as possible, but their capability deficiencies have made them dependent to varying degrees on outsiders for protection and assistance. Consequently, they have attempted to limit the coercive actions of external states, while gaining help from them through international organization. They have also worked for international economic cooperation, development funds, and trade preferences and rules more compatible with their interests. The system also provides machinery for the peaceful settlement of disputes and mutual security—concepts compatible with the interests of militarily weak states. In addition, the rule of law, under which might does not necessarily make right, may be sought through international organization. Inter-American law, developed largely by Latin American jurists, stresses the corollary of nonintervention in the affairs of others. The regional states have viewed the system as serving their interests to some degree, even as they have disagreed among themselves on specific elements.

INSTITUTIONAL DEVELOPMENT

From 1889 Through World War II

The institutional history of the Inter-American System began with the First International Conference of American States in Washington, D.C., in 1889–1890.[4] The system developed thereafter in an ad hoc manner over the next fifty-five years. Seven more International Conferences of American States, the central institution, were held between 1901 and 1938 in different Latin American capitals. The Second International Conference in 1901–1902 inaugurated a system of supplementary gatherings to consider technical matters or specific subjects. By 1940 at least 159 such meetings had been held, including unofficial ones; they included single meetings as well as serial conferences, which established a number of special agencies.

Two "special" conferences (as they were later called) were convened with specific but significant agendas: the International Conference of American States on Conciliation and Arbitration (1928–1929), and the Inter-American Conference for the Maintenance of Peace (1936). Out of the latter assembly came the high-level Meeting of Consultation of Ministers of Foreign Affairs to deal with urgent matters of peace and security. The foreign ministers convened on three occasions during the wartime period (1939, 1940, and 1942). In addition, during this period the American states adopted eleven formal instruments that formed a regime for the pacific settlement of disputes. Over time the system developed a multiplicity of purposes and policies.

The international conferences adopted changing nomenclature for what came to be known as the Inter-American System, and created a supporting agency that underwent its own development. The first conference, in 1889–1890, established a rudimentary regional structure by naming the system the International Union of American States and creating an administrative instrument called the Commercial Bureau of the American Republics. The bureau, under the supervision of the U.S. State Department in Washington, D.C., had the narrow function of "the prompt collection and distribution of commercial information." The second conference, in 1902, expanded the agency's duties and renamed it the International Bureau of the American Republics. The fourth conference, in 1910, simplified the name of the overall system to the Union of American Republics; and it transformed the bureau into the Pan American Union, with broader functions and increased responsibilities. It was administered by a director general, with control vested in a Governing Board chaired by the U.S. secretary of state. Thereafter the Pan American Union expanded its activities and

TABLE 8.1   Prinicipal Inter-American Conferences, 1889–1998

International Conferences of American States

First (Washington, 1889–1890)
Second (Mexico, 1901–1902)
Third (Rio de Janeiro, 1906)
Fourth (Buenos Aires, 1910)
Fifth (Santiago, 1923)
Sixth (Havana, 1928)

Seventh (Montevideo, 1933)
Eighth (Lima, 1938)
Ninth (Bogotá, 1948)
Tenth (Caracas, 1954)—name
   changed to Inter-American
   Conference

Special Conferences

International Conference of American States on Conciliation and Arbitration (Washington,
   1928–1929)
Inter-American Conference for the Maintenance of Peace (Buenos Aires, 1936)
Inter-American Conference on Problems of War and Peace (Mexico, 1945)
Inter-American Conference for Maintenance of Continental Peace and Security (Rio de Janeiro, 1947)
First Meeting of American Presidents (Panama, 1956)
First Special Inter-American Conference (Washington, 1964)
Second Special Inter-American Conference (Rio de Janeiro, 1965)
Third Special Inter-American Conference (Buenos Aires, 1967)
Second Meeting of American Presidents (Punta del Este, 1967)

Meetings of Consultation of Ministers of Foreign Affairs

First (Panama, 1939)
Second (Havana, 1940)
Third (Rio de Janeiro, 1942)
Fourth (Washington, 1951)
Fifth (Santiago, 1959)
Sixth (San José, 1960)
Seventh (San José, 1960)
Eighth (Punta del Este, 1962)
Ninth (Washington, 1964)
Tenth (Washington, 1965–1966)
Eleventh (Washington, Buenos Aires,
   Punta del Este, 1967)

Twelfth (Washington, 1967)
Thirteenth (Washington, 1969)
Fourteenth (Washington, 1971)
Fifteenth (Quito, 1974)
Sixteenth (San José, 1975)
Seventeenth (Washington, 1978)
Eighteenth (Washington, 1979)
Nineteenth (Washington, 1981)
Twentieth (Washington, 1982)
Twenty-First (Washington, 1989-1990)

Regular General Assembly Sessions

First (San José, 1971)
Second (Washington, 1972)
Third (Washington, 1973)
Fourth (Atlanta, 1974)
Fifth (Washington, 1975)
Sixth (Santiago, 1976)
Seventh (St. Georges, 1977)
Eighth (Washington, 1978)
Ninth (La Paz, 1979)
Tenth (Washington, 1980)
Eleventh (Castries, 1981)
Twelfth (Washington, 1982)
Thirteenth (Washington, 1983)
Fourteenth (Brasilia, 1984)

Fifteenth (Cartagena, 1985)
Sixteenth (Guatemala, 1986)
Seventeenth (Washington, 1987)
Eighteenth (San Salvador, 1988)
Nineteenth (Washington, 1989)
Twentieth (Asunción, 1990)
Twenty-First (Santiago, 1991)
Twenty-Second (Nassau, 1992)
Twenty-Third (Managua, 1993)
Twenty-Fourth (Belém, 1994)
Twenty-Fifth (Montrouis, 1995)
Twenty-Sixth (Panama, 1996)
Twenty-Seventh (Lima, 1997)
Twenty-Eighth (Caracas, 1998)

developed a more complex administrative structure. The fifth international conference, in 1923, redesignated the overall setup the Union of the Republics of the American Continent; in 1928 the sixth conference changed the name again, to the Union of the American States, which was retained until 1948. The 1923 and 1928 meetings agreed on certain reforms of the Pan American Union, as the Latin American states sought more influence, but U.S. dominance prevailed. The 1928 conference signed the Convention on the Pan American Union that would have placed the Inter-American System on a permanent coordinated juridical basis; that instrument required unanimous ratification, however, which was not achieved.

Post–World War II Developments

Three conferences were held between 1945 and 1985 that produced documents forming permanent treaty bases for the Inter-American System. The first of these meetings, the special Inter-American Conference on Problems of War and Peace, met in 1945 at the end of World War II. It envisioned the consolidation, reform, and codification of the American regional arrangements that had developed over the previous five and a half decades. Latin Americans, fearful that the Inter-American System was in danger of being downgraded or even dissolved because of U.S. enthusiasm for the United Nations (then being organized), sought to regularize the regional arrangements. To this end, the conference authorized the drafting of three basic integrated documents: (1) a treaty of reciprocal assistance; (2) a constitution for regional organization; and (3) a treaty to coordinate agreements on the pacific settlements of disputes. The triad of inter-American documents was soon forthcoming.

In 1947 the special Inter-American Conference for Maintenance of Continental Peace and Security adopted the Inter-American Treaty of Reciprocal Assistance, referred to as the Rio Treaty or Rio Pact. It went into effect on December 3, 1948, after ratification by the required two-thirds of the member states, and created a mutual security regime.

The Ninth International Conference of American States in 1948 approved the Charter of the Organization of American States (Charter of Bogotá) to serve as the basic constitution for American regional organization. The charter, which superseded the unratified 1928 document, went into effect in 1951; in practice, its provisions were immediately adhered to, as authorized by the 1948 meeting.

The ninth conference also adopted the Inter-American Treaty on Pacific Settlement (Pact of Bogotá), intended to order the disparate extant procedures for the peaceful resolution of inter-American disputes. Unlike the Rio Treaty and the charter, the Pact of Bogotá entered into force only with respect to the states that ratified it, which eventually were fourteen in number. The earlier instruments remained operative for the other states that had ratified them.

When the OAS Charter was adopted, the Union of the American States became the Organization of American States. The OAS was intended to be the Inter-American System, integrating all of the American regional interstate institutions. The term

Inter-American System was still used, however, to refer to the historical experience dating from 1889. The framers of the charter decided that incorporating all of the Rio Treaty and the Pact of Bogotá would be impracticable and that their coordination with the charter would suffice. The overarching position of the OAS did not last, however, as other institutions acquired autonomous identities. In 1959 the Inter-American Development Bank (IDB) was created as a new agency outside the OAS structure in order to preserve its independence of action, and by the late 1960s the Rio Treaty had acquired its own identity. Thus the OAS, the IDB, and the Rio Treaty, operating under their own conventions and evolving to include overlapping but different state participants, became the principal separate parts of the Inter-American System.

THE OAS STRUCTURE

Charter of Bogotá

The 1948 charter provided for six principal organs to govern the OAS and carry out its purposes (see Figure 8.1).[5] The Inter-American Conference (the new name for the International Conference of American States) was established as the supreme OAS decisional body. It was to meet at least every five years, but the last time it assembled was in 1954. The next conference, scheduled for 1959, was indefinitely postponed because of certain inter-American conflicts. The meeting was never held, and major OAS business came to be conducted by other agencies.

The Meeting of Ministers of Foreign Affairs was also made one of the principal organs. The foreign ministers of all member states were to meet and consult on matters dealing with threats to hemispheric peace, with the settling of inter-American disputes, and with resistance to external attacks on the Americas. The Advisory Defense Committee of high-ranking military officers from the member states was authorized but has never been activated. With the demise of the Inter-American Conference after 1954, the foreign ministers meeting became the central authority on political-security matters.

The Council of the Organization of American States (COAS), the third major organ, was composed of a permanent ambassadorial representative from each member state. The COAS handled matters referred to it by the meeting of foreign ministers and the Inter-American Conference. It supervised the Pan American Union and coordinated the activities of the Specialized Conferences. The Rio Treaty authorized the COAS to act provisionally as the Organ of Consultation when hemispheric security or peace was threatened, until it called a meeting of consultation. Three organs were created subordinate to the COAS. The most important, as it turned out, was the Inter-American Economic and Social Council (IAECOSOC), which in 1962 established subordinate entities with special responsibilities in the administration of Alliance for Progress programs. It also filled the gap of the moribund Inter-American Council in social-economic areas. Another COAS subsidiary, the Inter-American

214

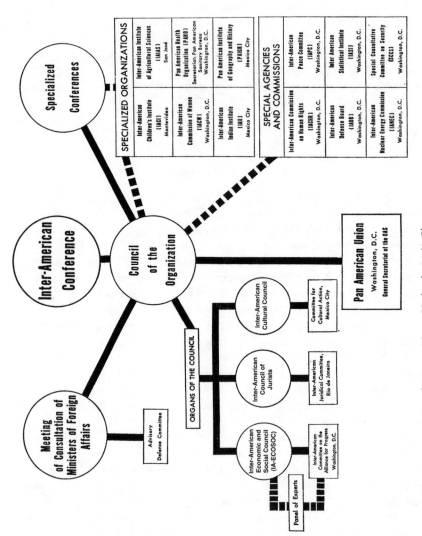

FIGURE 8.1   Organization of American States Under the 1948 Charter

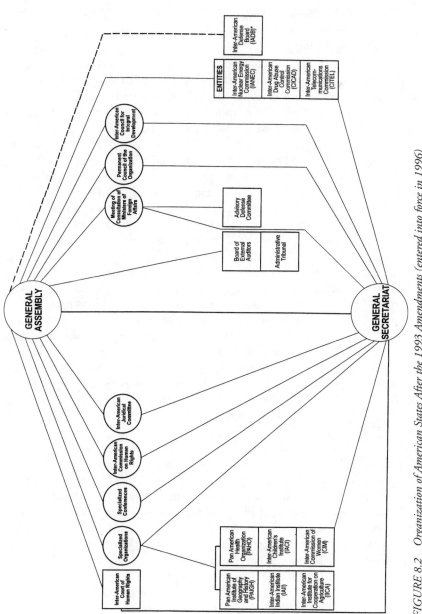

FIGURE 8.2   Organization of American States After the 1993 Amendments (entered into force in 1996)

Council of Jurists, was served by its subordinate Inter-American Juridical Committee. The Juridical Council had originated in 1939 as the Inter-American Neutrality Committee, which became the Inter-American Juridical Committee in 1942. The third COAS subunit was the Inter-American Cultural Council, with a subagency, the Committee for Cultural Action.

The Pan American Union was transformed into the general secretariat of the OAS. (The old Governing Board of the Pan American Union was converted into the Council of the OAS.) From 1948 through 1957 the secretariat was formally designated "Pan American Union" and from 1958 through 1970 as "Pan American Union, General Secretariat of the Organization of American States." It occupied a key position in the organization as a principal organ, serving in some manner all other entities and the member governments. The secretary-general directed the secretariat, along with the assistant secretary-general. Both officials were elected by the COAS for ten-year terms; their successors might not be of the same nationality.

The last two organs were actually categories of entities. The Specialized Conferences (not to be confused with the "special conferences" mentioned elsewhere) were to meet and "deal with special technical matters or to develop specific aspects of inter-American cooperation." The Specialized Organizations were intergovernmental organizations established by multilateral agreements and having specific functions with respect to technical matters of common interest to the American states. The charter did not name the specific elements composing the Specialized Organizations; that task was left to the OAS Council, which in 1950 decided on the following: Inter-American Children's Institute (founded in 1927 as the American Institute for the Protection of Childhood), Inter-American Commission of Women (established in 1928), Inter-American Indian Institute (founded in 1940), Inter-American Institute of Agricultural Sciences (founded in 1944); Pan American Health Organization (founded in 1902 as the Pan American Sanitary Bureau), and Pan American Institute of Geography and History (founded in 1929).

Other bodies not addressed by the charter were organized. The OAS created four of them after the charter had gone into effect and resurrected two others, both founded in 1940 but ignored in the charter. Grouped together in the category of Special Agencies and Commissions, they were relatively autonomous within the OAS framework. They were: Inter-American Commission on Human Rights (created in 1959); Inter-American Peace Committee (established in 1940 but not holding its first meeting until 1948); Inter-American Defense Board (also created in 1940), which in 1962 established its Inter-American Defense College; Inter-American Statistical Institute (established in 1941); Inter-American Nuclear Energy Commission (created in 1959); and Special Consultative Committee on Security (created in 1962).

Protocol of Buenos Aires

The Third Special Inter-American Conference, held in Buenos Aires in 1967, approved a Protocol of Amendment to the charter of the OAS. Called the Protocol of

Buenos Aires, it entered into force in February 1970. The amendments were intended to strengthen economic and social functions relative to political ones, reflecting a shift in organizational emphasis away from the political-security interests of the United States toward the economic-social ones of the Latin American members. The amendments also aimed to improve the organization's administrative efficiency.

The protocol increased the number of principal organs to ten. It abolished the non-functioning Inter-American Conference and created the General Assembly as the new supreme organ. The assembly was to meet at least annually to decide on general policy guidelines, discuss any matter of interest to the members, and coordinate the work of other organs. It assumed some functions of the former COAS, such as approving the OAS program budget, electing the secretary-general and assistant secretary-general, approving the admission of new members, and establishing working standards for the General Secretariat.

The General Assembly had two subordinate bodies. The Inter-American Juridical Committee, a merging of the former Inter-American Council of Jurists and its subordinate Inter-American Juridical Committee, was composed of eleven jurists from different states, who were elected by the General Assembly for four-year terms. The committee was to advise the OAS on juridical matters and promote the development and codification of international law. The second body, the Inter-American Commission on Human Rights, was elevated from being a Specialized Conference to an organ supervised by the General Assembly. It was charged with promoting the observance and protection of human rights in the Americas and investigating complaints of their violation.

The amendments did not touch the Meeting of Consultation of Ministers of Foreign Affairs, but its relative importance was reduced with the elevation of the authority of three councils. The Inter-American Economic and Social Council was raised to full council level and charged with increased responsibilities: to coordinate economic and social development programs, evaluate the progress of states receiving development assistance, and promote Latin American economic integration. The Inter-American Council for Education, Science, and Culture was an expanded and updated form of the old Inter-American Cultural Council. Its primary purpose was to promote educational, scientific, and cultural cooperation and exchange among the American states.

The Permanent Council (PCOAS) succeeded the COAS but did not hold the central position occupied by the latter. The PCOAS's basic role was as peacekeeping mediator, handling matters referred to it by the General Assembly or the Meeting of Consultation of Ministers of Foreign Affairs. It also served as the preparatory committee for the General Assembly, to prepare draft agendas, review the various matters to be considered by the latter, and recommend measures to the General Assembly regarding the General Secretariat. Like its predecessor, it was authorized to act as the Provisional Organ of Consultation until a meeting of foreign ministers might be convened. The Inter-American Committee on Peaceful Settlement was established as a subsidiary body to assist the PCOAS with its peacekeeping responsibilities; it replaced the Inter-American Peace Committee (which had been one of the Specialized Agencies and Commissions). The Inter-American Commission on Human Rights was elevated from its former position as a Specialized Organization to be an organ of the OAS.

The protocol dropped "Pan American Union" from the title of the secretariat and redesignated it "General Secretariat of the Organization of American States." The protocol increased the secretariat's duties and established a more flexible relationship between it and the other OAS organs. It changed the tenure of the secretary-general and the assistant secretary-general from ten- to five-year terms, with a provision for one reelection.

Charter provisions were unchanged regarding Specialized Conferences and Specialized Organizations. The Inter-American Institute of Agricultural Sciences was later renamed the Inter-American Institute for Cooperation on Agriculture. The 1967 protocol remained silent about Special Agencies and Commissions. The name of the category was changed on organization charts to Other Entities, which—with the new status of the Human Rights Commission, the disappearance of the Inter-American Peace Committee, and, in 1975, the abolishment of the Special Consultative Committee on Security—included the Inter-American Defense Board, Inter-American Statistical Institute, and Inter-American Nuclear Energy Commission.

The Inter-American Commission on Human Rights underwent later institutional development, which spawned a companion agency. The Inter-American Specialized Conference on Human Rights in 1969 produced the American Convention on Human Rights (Pact of San José), which finally went into effect in 1978. It incorporated and extended the 1948 American Declaration on the Rights and Duties of Man (which at the time had not been put into treaty form as some members desired). The 1969 instrument "recreated" the Inter-American Commission on Human Rights and further defined its procedures. It also created the Inter-American Court of Human Rights, located in Costa Rica and with jurisdiction limited to cases voluntarily brought by signatory states.

Protocol of Cartagena de Indias

In 1985 a special conference approved the Protocol of Cartagena de Indias, which became operative in November 1988. The action signaled the beginning of the organization's revival after institutional decline and almost two decades of conflicting purposes among the members. Economic and social purposes received special attention, with measures adopted regarding economic development, trade, and finance. The amendments sought to make interagency relations less cumbersome, to strengthen the role of the secretary-general, and to enhance the role of the Permanent Council in the peaceful settlement of disputes.

The charter still ignored the Other Entities category and did not mention the Inter-American Court of Human Rights. On the organization charts the court appeared alone on the same level as most of the organs. The charts changed the designation of Other Entities to simply Entities, which was composed of three bodies: the extant Inter-American Nuclear Energy Commission; the Inter-American Telecommunications Commission (created in 1963 as a special committee of the Inter-American Economic and Social Council); and the new Inter-American Drug Abuse Control Commission (created in 1986). The Inter-American Defense Board was taken off the Entities list and placed alone on the charts.

Additional Protocols

In 1993 the General Assembly approved the Protocol of Managua further amending the OAS Charter. It went into force in January 1996. With institutional support for regional democratic and economic development in mind, the protocol eliminated the Inter-American Economic and Social Council and the Inter-American Council on Education, Science, and Culture and created the Inter-American Council for Integral Development (CIDI) to assume their combined functions.

In December 1992 the General Assembly approved the Protocol of Washington, which went into effect in September 1997. The relatively brief document amended the charter not with regard to OAS agencies but with regard to multilateral responses to internal threats against constitutionally elected member governments. Its significance was seen as requiring formal treaty consent.

The Secretaries-General

The post of OAS secretary-general has in practice been reserved for a Latin American.[6] The first was Alberto Lleras Camargo, a former president of Colombia who in 1947 had been appointed director general of the Pan American Union for a ten-year term. In 1948, when the Pan American Union was designated the General Secretariat of the OAS, the Council of the OAS appointed him secretary-general. He served until 1954, when he resigned in frustration. Lleras returned to his native Colombia to help end civil strife there and to serve as president of the country, and then to become publisher of the news magazine, *Visión*. The second secretary-general was Carlos Dávila, a former president of Chile, journalist, and diplomat. Dávila served for a brief period from 1954 until his death in 1955. He was succeeded in 1956 by former Uruguayan Foreign Minister José A. Mora as interim secretary-general; Mora served the two years remaining on Davila's term and then a full ten-year term (1958–1968). Mora was succeeded by Galo Plaza Lasso, former president of Ecuador and United Nations official, who served for seven years (1968–1975). He was succeeded by Alejandro Orfila, who had been serving as the Argentine ambassador to the United States. Orfila resigned the post in 1984, a year before his second five-year term ended. He was succeeded by João Clemente Baena Soares, a professional Brazilian diplomat who had spent most of his career in international organization posts; he served two five-year terms (1984–1994). In 1994, César Gaviria Trujillo, president of Colombia from 1984 until that year, was inaugurated as seventh secretary-general for a five-year term.

INTER-AMERICAN DEVELOPMENT BANK

The IDB was the world's first regional multilateral bank, a lending agency designed to promote the economic and social development of its Latin American members.[7] The first president was Chilean economist Felipe Herrera, who served two five-year terms (1960–1970). He was succeeded by Antonio Ortiz Mena, a former Mexican finance minister, who was IDB president for seventeen years; he resigned in February 1988 during his fourth term. Enrique Iglesias, Uruguayan economist and diplomat, assumed the presidency in 1988. He had been executive secretary of the UN Economic Commission on Latin America (ECLA) for thirteen years (1972–1985) and then foreign minister of Uruguay.

IDB operations have been financed largely by member contributions and by special funds donated by individual states. When the bank was first organized an ordinary capital account was established for orthodox "hard loans," and the Social Progress Trust Fund was created to finance social development projects with longer terms and lower interest rates. By 1965 the trust fund had been almost entirely disbursed; its remaining resources were transferred to the new and further capitalized Fund for Special Operations (FSO) to continue "soft loans." Total IDB capital resources, which are replenished every four years, rose from $1.4 billion in 1960 to almost $100 billion in 1996.

The United States has been the largest subscriber to the IDB from the beginning. Its reduced support in the early 1970s led the bank to search for additional capital resources. Canada, new Caribbean states, and then nonhemispheric state members pledged additional capital shares. Expanded membership broadened the IDB's financial base, with Latin Americans hoping that it would erode U.S. domination.

The issue of U.S. predominance in IDB lending decisions—voting power is weighted according to the relative size of a member's contribution in proportion to the total—has been debated throughout the life of the bank. The Board of Directors approves loans from the ordinary capital account by simple majority. FSO loans, however, require a two-thirds majority. Until 1976 the United States had about 40 percent of the FSO weighted voting; with new member contributions after that date, the U.S. voting proportion dropped, standing at 34.5 percent in 1988. Latin American members then collectively controlled 54 percent, and the remaining nineteen members, 11.5 percent.

From its inception, both advocates and critics of the bank's operations have viewed the institution as a "borrowers' bank," as voting power was as much in the hands of loan recipients as in those of the principal contributors. The United States argued that it should have an even greater share of the weighted voting. The U.S. Treasury, the primary voice in U.S. international financial matters, from the late 1960s resisted the vision of development elaborated by Felipe Herrera. For example, the IDB pioneered in agrarian reform lending, a practice the United States considered outside the realm of sound development standards. The United States also expressed displeasure from time to time (especially during the Reagan administration) at the lack of a free-enterprise approach in Latin America and at the notion of the state as the primary force for development.

The IDB took on a role in the investment element of the slowly evolving hemispheric free-trade system, as envisioned in U.S. Enterprise for the Americas Initiative (EAI) in 1990. The EAI called for a special Multilateral Investment Fund (MIF), to be administered by the IDB and aimed at the promotion of regional private investment. The fund was established in February 1992 with an initial capital of about $1.3 billion, with pledges from the United States, Japan, Canada, France, Portugal, Spain, and some Latin American states. The fund was designed to provide financial support and technical help to privatization moves in Latin America and the Caribbean.

MEMBERSHIP IN THE INTER-AMERICAN SYSTEM

A near-universal majority of the American states have belonged to the Inter-American System from its beginning.[8] At the First International Conference (1889–1890), seventeen of the eighteen existing Latin American states (all except the Dominican Republic) plus the United States participated. Canada was not present. The Dominican Republic joined subsequent conferences, as did Cuba and Panama after they became independent in 1902.

As indicated above, the three principal components of the post–World War II Inter-American System—the OAS, the IDB, and the Rio Treaty regime—developed different lists of state participants. This is a fundamental way in which they are distinguished from each other.

The charter members of the OAS in 1948 were the same twenty-one states that had made up the system since 1902. Cuba under the Castro government technically remained a member, although OAS sanctions applied in 1962 suspended its participation. In 1967 the first of the newly independent Commonwealth Caribbean states began to join the OAS, and the others followed. Belize and Guyana were not allowed to enter because of unsettled boundary disputes with member states Guatemala and Venezuela, respectively, as provided for in the OAS Charter. The 1985 charter amendments, in effect in 1988, dropped the membership-denial provision, and Belize and Guyana both became full members in 1991. Thus all twelve of the independent Commonwealth Caribbean Countries became members of the OAS. Suriname, a former colony of the Netherlands, joined in 1975, the year it became independent. Canada took full membership in 1990—bringing OAS membership to all thirty-five sovereign American states, the only component of the Inter-American System to achieve universality.

In 1972 the OAS began to invite representatives from nonhemispheric states and other entities to attend its meetings as permanent observers. In 1998 there were forty-one of them: Algeria, Angola, Austria, Belgium, Bosnia and Herzegovina, Croatia, Cyprus, Czech Republic, Egypt, Equatorial Guinea, European Union, Finland, France, Germany, Greece, Holy See, Hungary, India, Israel, Italy, Japan, Kazakhstan, Latvia, Lebanon, Morocco, Netherlands, Pakistan, Poland, Portugal, Republic of Korea, Romania, Russian Federation, Saudi Arabia, Spain, Sri Lanka, Sweden, Switzerland, Tunisia, Ukraine, United Kingdom, and United Nations.

The Rio Treaty was signed in 1947 by the same twenty-one states that were to be charter OAS members. Cuba unilaterally abrogated the treaty in 1962. When the new Commonwealth Caribbean Countries sought membership in the OAS, they were allowed to join without being required to adhere to the Rio Treaty. Trinidad and Tobago is the only new signatory.

The charter members of the IDB were nineteen of the twenty Latin American states (Cuba refused to join) and the United States. In mid-1998 the IDB had forty-nine members. They included twenty-six of the thirty-five sovereign states in Latin America and the Caribbean, the United States, Canada, and twenty-one extraregional states. Six Eastern Caribbean island states did not join the bank: Antigua and Barbuda, Dominica, Grenada, St. Christopher and Nevis, St. Lucia, and St. Vincent. Their small economies did not allow them to contribute to the bank's capital funds; the IDB, in turn, was willing to help finance their development projects with contributions to the Eastern Caribbean Development Bank. Canada and Guyana were members of the bank before joining the OAS. Since 1976, when the IDB began seeking capital resources from extraregional states, twenty-two of them have joined: Austria, Belgium, Croatia, Denmark, Germany, Israel, Japan, Spain, Switzerland, United Kingdom, Austria, Finland, France, Italy, Netherlands, Norway, Portugal, Slovenia, Sweden, Switzerland, and the Holy See, all of which are presently members; Yugoslavia was a member until it fragmented into several entities.

A seemingly common misunderstanding about the OAS sanctions imposed on Cuba in 1962 should be clarified. Cuban membership in the Inter-American System was not revoked. The OAS Charter and other instruments at the time made no provision for expulsion of a member. Rather, the Castro government was denied participation in the OAS and other agencies and conferences of the Inter-American System, a provision that remained in effect even after other sanctions were effectively dropped in 1975. As noted, Cuba unilaterally abrogated the Rio Treaty and refused to join the IDB.

COMPETING PURPOSES

The various constitutional bases for the Inter-American System created the machinery described above in order to implement organizational principles. Those developed since 1889 may be grouped under seven main categories: (1) codification of international and inter-American law; (2) nonintervention and sovereign equality; (3) peace and security; (4) representative democracy and human rights; (5) economic cooperation and development; (6) opposition to the drug traffic; and (7) environmental protection. None of the policies appeared full-blown; they were introduced at different times and then evolved. The members have assigned them varying levels of commitment, revealing the competing interests and purposes at work in the system.

The Inter-American System has gone through several historical phases of development, with shifting levels of tension or cooperation among the members (usually, but not always, focused on Latin American-United States relations).[9] The first phase spanned the years from 1889 and the First International Conference to 1928, when the Sixth Conference revealed such bitter Latin American hostility toward the United States that the survival of the system was in jeopardy. During that time the United States was primarily interested in expanding hemispheric commercial relations; it secondarily sought to establish procedures for the peaceful settlement of Latin American disputes, which would promote regional political stability, facilitate international trade, and preempt nonhemispheric influences. The United States rebuffed Latin American desires for a regional mutual security arrangement, insisting on a unilateral security policy. The Latin American states shared U.S. interests in trade expansion and pacific settlement but viewed the Inter-American System primarily as a possible way to achieve security against outside intervention, first from Europe and then from the United States itself. With the extensive U.S. intervention in the circum-Caribbean, Latin American dismay with the system increased. Restrained hostility toward the United States in the early 1900s developed into bitter public denunciations by the late 1920s.

The second era, beginning in about 1928 and continuing into World War II, was marked by a general convergence of interests. The principal developments involved the progressive acceptance of nonintervention by the United States as part of the evolution of its Good Neighbor Policy, followed by the building of regional security arrangements. Most members saw mutual advantages and concurring interests in regional organization, and the period represented a particularly harmonious one.

The third phase, from the middle of World War II to the late 1950s, was again marked by diverging goals and conflicting relations. The United States and Latin America completely reversed their respective priorities in inter-American organization from those previously held. The United States wanted primarily mutual security action in the context of the global cold war, whereas Latin America generally sought to promote economic cooperation. A brief period of converging interests, during what came to be known as the Alliance for Progress, extended roughly from 1959 to 1965. The United States broadened its notion of security to include economic and social concerns, so that a temporary complementarity of interests was evident.

The fourth phase spanned the years from about 1965 to 1979. The United States did not perceive a serious threat in Latin America, so its interest in the region's economic development declined. Latin American states shared the view that U.S. trade and aid restrictions were a major source of their economic problems, and they sought through the Inter-American System to gain more favorable arrangements. After 1979, when Central American conflict renewed U.S. perceptions of security threats in the circum-Caribbean, the importance of the system declined for most parties. Latin American and Caribbean states refused to respond to U.S. attempts to reinvigorate collective security procedures, and the United States pursued its security policies outside the Inter-American System; it was unwilling to commit significant resources to developmental programs.

The current phase, beginning in the late 1980s, parallels the emergence of a global post–cold war era. Interest was revived in resuscitating formal inter-American cooperation. Security threats from outside the Americas were nonexistent, although a number of intraregional situations remained problematical. Consequently, other issues rose to the top of a common inter-American agenda, including international trade and investment, democracy and human rights, immigration and refugees, drug trafficking, and the physical environment. The foundation for inter-American relationships was a combination of free trade and democratic development. The revival of the Inter-American System was enhanced by diminished U.S. paternalism and the rise of Latin American democratic and economic reforms.

INTER-AMERICAN POLICIES

Codification of International Law

The Inter-American System first addressed the codification of international law at the Second International Conference (1901–1902).[10] The delegates signed a convention for that purpose, but only three states ratified it. The United States opposed the codification of an inter-American law at the time and for many years thereafter, reiterating its preference for global international law. The Third International Conference (1906) established the International Commission of Jurists to draft codes of international law, but the project moved slowly. Alejandro Alvarez, an eminent Chilean jurist, was the leading advocate of juridical Pan Americanism. He developed the idea of separating inter-American from general international law, considering the former the legal extension of Pan Americanism. Beginning in 1905 Alvarez advanced the idea that "because of geographical, ethnological, historical, social, political, economic, moral, and spiritual reasons the states of the New World were developing an American international law which supplemented existing international law and would eventually lead the way in molding the future of nations."[11]

As head of the International Commission of Jurists, Alvarez supervised a project drafting a separate code of inter-American law, submitting a report on it in 1923 to the Fifth International Conference. Alvarez led the International Commission after it was reestablished in 1923; it submitted twelve draft conventions on public international law to the Sixth International Conference (1928), which adopted seven of them.

Between 1928 and 1938, the process of creating and reorganizing the large number of codification agencies and revising their highly complicated procedures eclipsed codification itself. With the outbreak of European war in 1939, the meetings of the existing agencies were indefinitely postponed. The Inter-American Neutrality Committee was created to formulate recommendations for legal actions by individual governments related to neutrality; in the process it also dealt with some elements of codification. In 1942 the committee was reconstituted as the Inter-American Juridical Committee and charged with "the formulation of specific recommendations relative to the international organization in the juridical and political fields, and in the field of international security." It was an active body during World War II.

In 1948 the Juridical Committee submitted draft conventions to the Ninth International Conference. The conference used them as the bases for the American Treaty on Pacific Settlement, the Declaration of the Rights and Duties of Man, and the Inter-American Charter of Social Guarantees.

The 1948 OAS Charter reformed the unwieldy codification process. It created the Inter-American Council of Jurists as one of three organs under the Council of the OAS, with the purpose of promoting codification of public and private international law, and it made the Juridical Committee a subordinate agency of the Council of Jurists. The council and the committee were active in preparing studies relating to legal considerations of the Alliance for Progress. The 1967 Protocol of Buenos Aires reconstituted the Inter-American Juridical Committee as one of the principal organs "to serve the Organization as an advisory body on juridical matters." Since then it has drafted a broad array of instruments of private and public international law, many of which the OAS has adopted. Secretary General Gaviria submitted proposals to the Permanent Council in early 1996 to strengthen the OAS in the field of international law. He argued for the necessity of a redefined juridical agenda and new legal instruments to enable the Inter-American System to face the post-cold war challenges stemming from greater interdependence, closer relations of all kinds, common threats and problems, and increased collective action.

Nonintervention

The principle of nonintervention flows from the corollaries of state sovereignty and juridical equality.[12] The Latin American desire for nonintervention as an inter-American legal doctrine, which long predated the First International Conference in 1889, was a primary goal. Latin Americans finally succeeded in the 1930s; from their point of view, nonintervention was the paramount principle of inter-American relations.

The Argentine jurist Carlos Calvo, in his book published in 1868, enunciated a doctrine that became the rallying point for early Latin American efforts to establish nonintervention as a rule of international conduct. The Calvo Doctrine challenged the European legal position that foreign residents had special rights to "just" treatment by their host states, especially with regard to pecuniary claims. Calvo asserted that intervention by foreign governments to enforce the claims of their own citizens residing abroad was illegal, no matter what sort of treatment had been given them, because it violated the host state's sovereign independence. He stressed the absolute equality of states and the inviolability of sovereignty, and that intervention to enforce pecuniary claims under any circumstances was invalid.

A resolution incorporating the essence of the Calvo Doctrine was proposed at the First International Conference in 1889. It declared that states were under no obligation to favor foreigners with more protection than was afforded to native citizens;

the former had only the same legal rights as the latter. The United States voted against the resolution, the only state to do so.

The Calvo Doctrine was modified in 1902, when three European states threatened Venezuela with intervention in order to collect public debts. Argentine Foreign Minister Luís M. Drago proclaimed the illegality of armed intervention to force payment of foreign governmental debts, but with reference to public rather than private debt. The Drago Doctrine, which also stressed absolute sovereignty and territorial inviolability as superior to pecuniary claims, became the new point of departure for Latin American demands in the Inter-American System. With U.S. interventions in the Caribbean, Latin Americans definitively shifted their complaints from Europe to the United States.

At the four international conferences convened between 1906 and 1928, the United States attempted to keep the conference agendas devoid of the intervention issue. The Latin American states, however, succeeded in using the meetings to attack U.S. intervention as unjust and illegal interference in their domestic affairs and as a violation of their sovereignty and to demand nonintervention as an inter-American legal principle. The ensuing debate revealed sharply conflicting views as to what constituted intervention. The Latin American definition was a broad one, including diplomatic, economic, and military incursions. The United States saw intervention as military activities justified in terms of international security.

By the time of the fifth conference in 1928, an impasse had been reached over the intervention issue. Latin Americans made it clear that future cooperation was contingent on the United States dropping its opposition to nonintervention. Because of the urgency of the problem and the lack of European threats to the hemisphere, the United States abandoned the Roosevelt Corollary and then accepted nonintervention in treaty form. The United States commenced action in 1928 (see Chapter 5) and by 1933 was proceeding along multilateral lines.

The Seventh International Conference in 1933 adopted the Convention on the Rights and Duties of States. The key clause flatly stated that "no state has the right to intervene in the internal or external affairs of another." The United States signed and ratified the convention but with the ambiguous reservation of its rights "by the law of nations as generally recognized," which cast doubt on its commitment. Three years later, however, the United States accepted nonintervention as an unqualified legal principle. All of the American states adhered to a convention signed at the special Inter-American Conference for the Maintenance of Peace in 1936, entitled Additional Protocol Relative to Non-Intervention. It confirmed the 1933 principles, if anything in even stronger language.

After 1936 nonintervention was reaffirmed at various conferences and incorporated into the OAS Charter and other treaties. The charter provides that "No State or group of States has the right to intervene, directly or indirectly, for any reason whatsoever in the internal or external affairs of any other State." This principle prohibits not only armed force but "any other form of interference or attempted threat against the personality of the State or against its political, economic, and cultural elements." In addition, "No State may use or encourage the use of coercive measures of an economic or political character in order to force the sovereign will of another State and obtain from it advantages of any kind." The charter also establishes the inviolability of state territory, which may not be the object of even temporary military occupation "or of other measures of force taken by another State, directly or indirectly, on any grounds whatever." The signatories of the charter pledged "not to have recourse to the use of force, except in the case of self-defense in accordance with existing treaties." Finally, with reference to possible multilateral sanctions against a member state, the charter said that "Measures adopted for the maintenance of peace and security in accordance with existing treaties" did not violate the above principles.

The inter-American law of nonintervention has not entirely deterred the United States from intervening in Latin America and the Caribbean—nor Latin Americans from interfering in each other's affairs—although it could be argued that without the provision, interventions would have been more numerous. The United States has departed from the nonintervention principle on eight occasions that qualify as interventionist according to a minimal definition: in Argentina in 1945–1946, Guatemala in 1954, Cuba in 1961, the Dominican Republic in 1965, Chile in 1970–1973, Grenada in 1983, Nicaragua in 1984, and Panama in 1989. Latin Americans also have been guilty of intervention, especially in a series of acts in the Caribbean region beginning in the late 1940s and continuing, off and on, into the 1980s.

In the post–cold war era, the Inter-American System has adopted a new set of high-priority issues led by concerns of democratic development and economic well-being. Their designation as matters of international security raises questions about the principle of nonintervention, inasmuch as the redefinition of security implies the erosion of sovereignty. If the high-priority transnational issues are matters of security requiring multilateral resolution, then sovereignty no longer stops at state borders.[13] Arguments have been presented that sovereignty must give way to collective action (which would not be intervention) in the face of threats to democracy, human rights, economic well-being, and other situations (discussed below in specific contexts). Although Latin Americans have indicated a degree of acquiescence to this view (they have, for instance, permitted outside electoral monitors and observers), they remain sensitive to anything that might facilitate or legitimate U.S. military intervention.

Peace and Security

Standards of peaceful settlement of disputes and collective security combined to form an inter-American regime of peace and security.[14] This was not always the case or intent, however, as the two domains were originally considered distinct endeavors based on different concepts. They were introduced into the system at different times and followed separate evolutionary paths. Concern with peaceful settlement of disputes dates from the beginning of the Inter-American System in 1899–1890; collective security was introduced in 1936. Peaceful settlement was the juridical-legal-diplomatic resolution of inter-American conflict; collective security was a political-military approach to deal with aggression from abroad. In World War II the two domains began to merge, and afterwards they were intertwined to the point of forming a single system of peace and security.

Peaceful Settlement Developed.   A conflict resolution regime in terms of the peaceful settlement of inter-American disputes was formed between 1902 and 1938. A proposal for compulsory arbitration had been debated at the First International Conference (1889–1890), but Chile, unwilling to jeopardize its recent territorial gains in the War of the Pacific, forced a compromise that negated the compulsory nature of the proposed treaty. It was not adopted. Despite the initial impasse, eleven conventions, treaties, and protocols were subsequently signed and went into force. Taken together, they composed an inter-American pacific settlement regime. It was an uncoordinated system, however, with different states subscribing to one or another of the treaties and their varied procedures.

The Second International Conference in 1902 adopted the Treaty on Compulsory Arbitration. So many reservations were entered, however, that the original compulsory intent was virtually negated. The Fifth International Conference in 1923 established further peacekeeping procedures with the adoption of the Treaty to Avoid or Prevent Conflicts Between the American States, the most comprehensive of the eleven instruments adopted. Sponsored by Manuel Gondra, the foreign minister of Paraguay, it was known as the Gondra Treaty. It provided that all disputes threatening armed conflict and not amenable to direct diplomacy be submitted to a commission of inquiry. The signatories agreed to a "cooling off" period in which they made no preparations for a specified period after the commission had convened.

The special International Conference of American States on Conciliation and Arbitration (1928–1929) added three instruments. The General Convention of Inter-American Conciliation, intended as a supplement to the Gondra Treaty, added conciliatory functions to the duties of the commissions of inquiry and provided for states to resort to the commissions on a voluntary basis. The General Treaty of Inter-American Arbitration bound the contracting parties to submit to arbitration any dispute arising from a claim that could be decided by the application of law. The Protocol of Progressive Arbitration to the general treaty of arbitration, signed separately, established a procedure where exceptions or reservations to the general treaty might be abandoned from time to time, thus "progressively" expanding the limits of arbitration. Four years later, in 1933, the Seventh International Conference adopted the Additional Protocol to the General Convention of Inter-American Conciliation of 1929. Whereas the General Convention (and the Gondra Treaty) relied on ad hoc conciliation agencies, the protocol instituted permanent commissions to be available when disputes arose.

Further at the Seventh International Conference, certain states agreed to the Anti-War Treaty of Non-Aggression and Conciliation, sponsored by Argentine Foreign Minister Carlos Saavedra Lamas (for which he received the Nobel Peace Prize). At the Inter-American Conference for the Maintenance of Peace in 1936, the final four instruments were signed: the Convention for the Maintenance, Preservation and Reestablishment of Peace; the Treaty on the Prevention of Controversies; the Inter-American Treaty on Good Offices and Mediation; and the Convention to Coordinate, Extend and Assure the Fulfillment of the Existing Treaties between the American States. Together they sought to consolidate the provisions of the earlier agreements.

Collective Security Introduced.   Based on the idea of "one for all and all for one" in combating aggression, collective security was incorporated into the American regional system in 1938 and refined during World War II. The prohibition of unilateral intervention, solidified in 1936, required the fashioning of multilateral security arrangements.

From time to time a Latin American state had suggested that the unilateral Monroe Doctrine be multilaterally defined and enforced. One of the most important of those proposals was made in April 1920 by President Baltasar Brum of Uruguay. The Brum Doctrine called for the Monroe Doctrine to be multilateralized and an American League of Nations established. This proposal was submitted to the Fifth International Conference in 1923, but neither the other Latin American states nor the United States offered encouragement—the Latin American states were intent on attacking the United States for its intervention in the name of the Monroe Doctrine, and the United States insisted on unilateral security policies.

The first tentative step toward the multilateral defense of the hemisphere was taken in 1936 at the Inter-American Conference for Peace. The United States urged some sort of hemispheric defense plan, revealing a willingness to change its unilateral security policies. The conference adopted only a rudimentary form of the idea of collective security in the Convention for the Maintenance, Preservation, and Reestablishment of Peace. It provided that in the event of threats to the peace, members of the Inter-American System should "consult together for the purpose of finding and adopting methods of peaceful cooperation."

Further measures were adopted in 1938 at the Eighth International Conference. The conferees agreed on the Declaration of Lima, stating, in part, that all American states "affirmed the intention of the American Republics to help one another in case of a foreign attack, either direct or indirect, on any one of them." The declaration later formed the basis for wartime inter-American security collaboration.

Three Meetings of Consultation of Ministers of Foreign Affairs were held during the World War II period (in 1939, 1940, and 1942). Soon after the German invasion of Poland in September 1939, the first foreign minister's meeting convened and agreed on the General Declaration of Neutrality. It affirmed and defined inter-American neutrality in the European war and established a neutrality zone around the Americas. The second meeting in July 1940, shortly after the fall of France, adopted, among other things, the Declaration of Reciprocal Assistance and Cooperation for the Defense of the Americas. It stated that an attack by a non-American state would be considered an attack on all the Americas and that cooperative defense measures would be taken after consultation.

After the Japanese attack on Pearl Harbor (December 7, 1941), the third foreign minister's meeting was held in January 1942 in pursuance of the 1940 declaration. The United States sought a resolution requiring the severance of diplomatic relations by all the American states with Japan, Germany, and Italy, and most Latin American states were willing to accept the measure. Opposition from Argentina and Chile, who remained neutral, resulted in a resolution only recommending the rupture of relations. Another resolution created the Inter-American Defense Board, which was composed of military and naval advisers from all member states and charged with studying the problems of hemispheric defense and recommending solutions. The foreign ministers agreed to establish the Emergency Advisory Committee for Political Defense to investigate and coordinate measures to counter Axis subversive activities.

Prior to the third meeting, twelve Latin American states had severed relations with the Axis, and nine of those had declared war. After the meeting, all other regional states except Argentina and Chile broke relations, and four more declared war. Chile and Argentina eventually ruptured relations and declared war, in 1944 and 1945, respectively. Most of Latin America's armed forces did not have a major position in hemispheric defense and generally were assigned supporting roles, although Brazil's navy assisted the U.S. Navy in antisubmarine patrols off the Atlantic coast of South America. (Brazil sent an expeditionary force into combat in Italy and Mexico and an aircraft squadron to the Philippine Islands.) Most Latin American states helped counter Axis espionage and granted U.S. requests for base rights.

Peace and Security Merged.   The Inter-American Conference on Problems of War and Peace in 1945 addressed the peaceful settlement of disputes and collective security. These broad endeavors were codified in 1947 in the Rio Treaty and, in 1948, in the charter of the OAS and the Inter-American Treaty of Pacific Settlement. All three documents explicitly linked both areas of activity. Action agencies subsequently mixed pacific settlement and collective security methods when dealing with problems considered to threaten inter-American peace and security.

The OAS Charter listed among the organization's "essential purposes" those of peace and security. In separate brief chapters on "Pacific Settlement of Disputes" and "Collective Security," and in other articles, the charter restated the members' obligation to present all of their international conflicts to pacific processes and to commit themselves to collective security against aggression.

The Inter-American Treaty of Pacific Settlement called for obligatory settlement by the signatories. It also sought to link its principles to those of mutual security in the OAS Charter and Rio Treaty. It sought to fill the need for a single treaty to coordinate the various measures providing for the peaceful settlement of disputes, but the framers sharply debated the perennial issue of obligatory or voluntary settlement. The treaty entered into effect only for the fourteen states ratifying it and superseded all prior agreements to which they were party. For other states, the earlier instruments remained in force for those who had ratified them. Even states adhering to the

Pact of Bogotá rarely resorted to its provisions, and conflict resolution has relied on the OAS Charter and Rio Treaty.

The Rio Treaty, in its own words, was concluded "in order to assure peace, through adequate means, to provide for effective reciprocal assistance to meet armed attacks against any American state, and in order to deal with threats of aggression against any of them." As a consequence, the contracting parties "undertake to submit every controversy which may arise between them to methods of peaceful settlement." The key collective security provision stated that "an armed attack by any State against an American State shall be considered as an attack against all the American States" and required a collective response "to assist in meeting the attack." Thus the Rio Treaty envisioned conflicts requiring defense against aggression from within or outside the hemisphere, as well as those amenable to peaceful settlement. It reaffirmed and elaborated the various wartime measures against aggression on a continuing basis. It distinguished between armed attack and other forms of aggression and between aggression occurring within and outside of a precisely designated western-hemispheric geographic zone. The Organ of Consultation would "meet without delay" to examine the facts and agree on the collective measures to be taken (the options were specified in the treaty); it was authorized to identify aggression not covered by the treaty's categories (later classified as "acts of political aggression" and "aggression of a non-military character") and to decide how to respond.

Between 1948 and 1990, Rio Treaty or OAS Charter procedures were implemented in thirty-four situations and conflicts deemed to be threats to hemispheric peace and security. On most occasions the Council of the OAS or the successor Permanent Council met provisionally as the Organ of Consultation, and in eighteen cases they convoked a Meeting of Consultation of Ministers of Foreign Affairs. Eight of the foreign ministers meetings proceeded under the Rio Treaty and ten in accordance with the OAS Charter. The Inter-American Peace Committee and the Inter-American Commission on Human Rights also played roles, the former because of the close relationship between mutual security and conflict resolution, and the latter on the grounds that human rights abuses within the member states threatened the peace and security of the Americas. Most of the cases involved inter-American disputes—which inevitably blended matters of collective security and conflict resolution—and a large majority had to do with the Caribbean area. Sanctions were applied against the Dominican Republic in 1960 and against Cuba in 1962 and 1964. The Inter-American System was generally able to halt hostilities but not to resolve the underlying causes of the conflict.

As indicated above, from the mid-1960s until the latter 1980s, inter-American peace and security activities declined. Latin Americans resented the U.S.-forced creation of an inter-American peacekeeping force as a post hoc legitimation of its unilateral military intervention in the Dominican Republic (1965–1966). Thereafter, the United States did not perceive similar security threats; and Latin Americans expressed dissatisfaction with the U.S. insistence on an anticommunist alliance. In the Central American crisis after 1979 the United States pursued its policies on unilateral and bilateral bases with only peripheral reference to the Inter-American System, and Latin Americans went outside of the system to initiate their most important multilateral peace proposals. Inter-American meetings devoted to the Anglo-Argentine war in 1982 turned out to be a bitter debate on U.S. policy. The Inter-American System was not a factor in the settlement of the Beagle Channel dispute between Argentina and Chile, decided in 1984 with the Holy See serving as mediator; the United States invaded Grenada in October 1983, entirely ignoring the system.

Concepts Expanded. Beginning in 1987 the OAS, at the behest of Central American leaders, played a significant role in the Central American peace process by undertaking operations in conjunction with the United Nations (see Chapter 13). In that effort, operational concepts long associated with diplomatic-juridical peaceful settlement of disputes (now referred to as peacemaking) were extended to include peacekeeping, peace building, peace verification, and peace observing, as well as treaty verification, election monitoring, and the use of sanctions to protect democracy and human rights.[15] Overall, conflict resolution and security processes were melded to the point of being indistinguishable.

The end of the cold war following the political and economic transformations in Latin America further complicated the meaning of inter-American peace and security, in that the pressing common problems were increasingly viewed in security terms. Most policy makers around the hemisphere agreed to expand notions of security beyond extrahemispheric threats (which were nonexistent) and intraregional conflicts (some of them still problematical) to include all of the pressing problems on the inter-American agenda. They agreed upon democratic consolidation and economic well-being as the fundamental bases for international security, and they saw that the resolution of problems of armed insurgencies, drug trafficking, immigration and refugees, and environmental degradation depended on favorable political and economic contexts. However, ambiguity remained about how these concepts should be operationalized.[16]

Democracy and Human Rights

The member states have committed the Inter-American System to the promotion of representative democracy and the protection of human rights.[17] The Inter-American System paid some attention after 1901 to aspects of human rights, and made representative democracy in the latter 1930s and World War II the basis for hemispheric "political defense," but a comprehensive approach was not developed until after the war. The Rio Treaty in 1947 and the OAS Charter in 1948 strongly reaffirmed principles of democracy and human rights. In addition, the American Declaration of the Rights and Duties of Man, adopted in 1948 by the Ninth International Conference, included articles on political and legal rights as well as social, economic, and moral rights, and professed representative democracy as the necessary foundation for them. Nevertheless, actions were hesitant and qualified. For most Latin American members, nonintervention transcended democratic development. Consequently, the system has been faced with this question: How can representative democracy be promoted and human rights enforced (particularly in the face of nondemocratic regimes) without violating the principle of nonintervention? Most Latin American states have adopted a preferential position toward nonintervention. From time to time, and increasingly from the 1980s to the present, others have been willing to allow some sort of collective action.

Soon after the Rio Treaty and OAS Charter were adopted, inter-American judicial procedures began to be applied to Caribbean conflicts (see Chapter 12). These procedures largely resulted from ideological differences between closely proximate dictatorial and (more or less) democratic states. The problem for the OAS was that two fundamental principles—the doctrines of nonintervention and democratic development—had been pitted against one another. The principle of nonintervention received higher priority, as the OAS Council made clear in April 1950 when it resolved the following:

> [Considering] that both the principle of representative democracy and that of nonintervention are established in many inter-American pronouncements, and that both are basic principles of harmonious relations among the countries of America; and that there exists some confusion of ideas as to the means of harmonizing the effective execution and application of the basic principle of nonintervention and that of the exercise of democracy; [be it resolved] to reaffirm the principles of representative democracy [but] to declare that the aforementioned principles do not in any way and under any concept authorize any governments to violate inter-American commitments relative to the principles of nonintervention.

The OAS appeared in one case to serve as an "antidictatorial alliance," but it in fact demonstrated a commitment to the nonintervention principle.[18] The Sixth Meeting of Consultation in August 1960 condemned the Trujillo dictatorship in the Dominican Republic for its assassination attempt against Romulo Betancourt, the democratically elected president of Venezuela. The foreign ministers voted to impose sanctions on the Trujillo regime, including the breaking of diplomatic relations and the imposing an arms embargo. The debate did not revolve around a preoccupation with nonintervention, and the Trujillo dictatorship was almost universally detested. However, the Dominican government itself had violated the nonintervention principle and was guilty of aggression as well as of the gross violation of human rights. The reason for the sanctions was not primarily to promote democracy and human rights but rather to punish Trujillo for intervening in Venezuelan affairs.

Eighteen years later, another "antidictatorial alliance" occurred with regard to the Nicaraguan civil war. The Seventeenth Meeting of Consultation convened in September 1978 to consider the worsening civil war in Nicaragua (governed by dictator Anastasio Somoza), which also involved conflicts with neighboring countries. The foreign ministers censured Nicaragua for its international actions. The ministers reconvened in June 1979 and issued a final resolution, referring to the Somoza regime's inhumane conduct and calling for its immediate replacement by a pluralist representative government. It also demanded the guarantee of respect for human rights for all Nicaraguans and the holding of free elections as soon as possible. Although the ministers resolved that OAS member states scrupulously respect the principle of nonintervention, their action was unprecedented: For the first time, the Inter-American System had overtly sought replacement of a head of state.

The Inter-American System pursued cases of human rights violations. Included in the provisions of the American Convention on Human Rights are the right to life, liberty, personal security, habeas corpus, due process, equality before the law, fair trials, freedom from arbitrary arrest, and freedom of speech, assembly, association, political participation, and religion. The Inter-American Commission on Human Rights, when established in 1960 as an OAS advisory group, was limited to the use of moral suasion and was required to work in concert with an accused government. Cuba refused to allow the commission to investigate its situation in the early 1960s, and later Guatemala was unwilling to receive it in an investigatory role. The commission then played an active role in the Dominican crisis of 1965–1966, under an expanded mandate from the Second Special Inter-American Conference in 1965. It followed with investigations in Honduras, El Salvador, and Haiti; its factual findings were accepted, but no further actions were taken. In 1970 the Commission was empowered to "keep vigilance over the observance of human rights."

The reluctance of OAS members in the 1970s and 1980s to apply multilateral sanctions in cases of human rights violations was reflected in a series of cases. In 1970, in response to complaints filed against Brazil, the Human Rights Commission was refused permission from the Brazilian government to conduct an on-the-scene investigation. It continued to investigate from outside the country for four years, however, and presented a detailed report with considerable evidence of grave human rights violations to the OAS General Assembly in 1974. The General Assembly took note of and tabled the report.

The Human Rights Commission, in response to complaints against the military regime in Chile, made a two-week visit to that country in July and August 1974. Its lengthy report made charges of "extremely serious violations" of human rights. Two years later, in March 1976, three of the seven commission members—jurists from Uruguay, Argentina, and the United States—announced that they would not seek reelection, and in April the executive secretary from Bolivia, who had served for sixteen years, resigned the post. All of them cited the lack of OAS action on their report on Chile as a major reason for their resignation and questioned whether OAS members sincerely desired to further the cause of human rights.

The Human Rights Commission's annual report to the OAS General Assembly in June 1976 found flagrant human rights violations by sixteen member states, including the United States, and documented large numbers of abuses. The chief target was Chile, the subject of a special report charging that most human rights abuses continued. The General Assembly voted to "take note" of the commission's findings and to continue monitoring human rights in the hemisphere with special attention to Chile.

At the General Assembly meeting in 1977, U.S. Secretary of State Cyrus Vance introduced a resolution stating, in part, that "there are no circumstances which justify torture, summary executions or prolonged detention without trial contrary to law." The resolution passed by a vote of 14–0, with 8 abstentions and 3 absences. At the General Assembly meeting in 1981, however, Secretary of State Alexander Haig emphasized the Communist threat in Central America and dismissed human rights issues. The Human Rights Commission had submitted reports on violations in Argentina, Bolivia, El Salvador, Guatemala, and Nicaragua. The assembly simply acknowledged their receipt.

In the late 1980s and continuing into the 1990s, when almost all Latin American states had constitutional governments, an inter-American consensus emerged that democratic governance (in concert with economic reform) constituted the overarching hemispheric norm. The OAS strengthened the proposition that it should take direct action to defend representative democracy and human rights against internal infringements. At its regular annual meeting in June 1991, the OAS General Assembly issued a declaration called the Santiago Commitment to Democracy and the Renewal of the International System. It declared the members' "firm political commitment to the promotion and protection of human rights and representative democracy as indispensable conditions for the stability, peace, and development of the region," and mandated "adoption of efficacious, timely, and expeditious procedures to ensure the promotion and defense of democracy." An accompanying resolution specified required actions following any "sudden or irregular interruption" of democratic government in any of the member states. OAS members acted in terms of the Santiago Declaration when constitutional rule was abrogated in Haiti in 1991, Peru in 1992, Guatemala in 1993, and Suriname in 1994, with certain multilateral responses in all cases without the approval of the respective governments.

The 1992 Protocol of Washington, which went into effect in September 1997, amended the OAS Charter to provide for the temporary suspension of member states in which the democratic process had been illegally interrupted. The measure stated that a member of the OAS whose "democratically constituted government has been overthrown by force, may be suspended from the exercise of its right to participate in the meetings of the General Assembly" and in the meetings of several other OAS bodies. The new articles recommended negotiations prior to the eventual suspension, a decision requiring a two-thirds majority. In June 1993, the General Assembly issued the Declaration of Managua for the Promotion of Democracy and Development, a sweeping call for the strengthening of democratic institutions in the Americas and for inter-American cooperation and OAS programs to help the process.

Since 1990 about half the Latin American and Caribbean states have allowed OAS electoral observation missions to monitor and sometimes to assist in their elections (several of them more than once). Ranging from relatively small teams for brief periods to larger parties for the entire electoral process, missions have gone to Bolivia (1997), Colombia (1997), Costa Rica (1990), Ecuador (1998), El Salvador (1991), Dominican Republic (1990, 1996, 1998), Guatemala (1990, 1996), Guyana

(1997), Haiti (1990–1991, 1995), Honduras (1990, 1993), Mexico (1994), Nicaragua (1989–90, 1996, 1998), Panama (1990), Paraguay (twice in 1991, 1993, 1998), Peru (1993), Suriname (1991, 1993), and Venezuela (1993).

Economic and Social Cooperation

During the initial stages of the Inter-American System in the late nineteenth century, the United States was primarily interested in expanding its commercial relations, whereas Latin Americans were attracted for political and legal reasons (physical security and the nonintervention principle). The U.S. proposal at the First International Conference in 1889–1890 for an American customs union received almost no Latin American support. During the period of U.S. interventions from 1898 to 1933, Latin Americans were suspicious of U.S. economic overtures and more interested in security matters.

Important developments in inter-American economic cooperation occurred during the period surrounding World War II. The First Meeting of Consultation of Ministers in 1939 created the Inter-American Financial and Advisory Committee (FEAC), consisting of an economic expert from each member state, to anticipate economic problems consequent to war. The Second Meeting of Consultation in 1940 expanded FEAC's functions and endorsed a number of its projects. FEAC pursued programs for the marketing of surplus products, the concluding of commodity agreements, and the aiding of Latin American economic diversification. The Third Meeting of Consultation in 1942 gave FEAC the additional tasks of developing programs for the production of strategic materials, obtaining capital investments, improving transportation facilities, and breaking economic relations with Axis states.[19]

In the initial post-World War II years, the United States was primarily interested in persuading the Inter-American System to organize itself against communism in the Americas, whereas the Latin Americans emphasized multilateral technical assistance and economic development programs. Concomitant to the establishment of U.S. technical assistance programs on a worldwide scale after 1949, the OAS conducted relatively small but effective programs. The United States clearly was unwilling to establish large multilateral economic development programs.

With mounting Latin American pressure in the late 1950s, U.S. positions began to change. In September 1958 President Juscelino Kubitschek of Brazil proposed an "Operation Pan America" to an informal meeting of American foreign ministers in Washington. This economic development program was designed primarily to raise Latin American social and economic living standards. The foreign ministers recommended two important measures: (1) establishment of an inter-American financial institution for economic development; and (2) creation of a committee to recommend additional measures for economic cooperation.

The Inter-American Development Bank was established on December 31, 1959. In 1960 the United States formally offered the Eisenhower Plan, an economic development program to be administered by the IDB; it received inter-American support in the Act of Bogotá of 1960. The Alliance for Progress, proposed by President

Kennedy, was multilateralized by the Charter of Punta del Este in August 1961, which set out a series of ambitious economic goals to be accomplished during the decade of the 1960s (see Chapter 13).

After 1969 the United States reduced its economic assistance and rejected the social and economic developmental content of the Alliance for Progress. The importance of trade over aid and of foreign investment capital for economic development was reemphasized. The negative Latin American reaction was expressed in the idea of "collective economic security for development"—that is, the idea that economic-social problems be taken as seriously as the political-military conception of security. In the 1980s economic policy attention focused on the severe Latin American and Caribbean external debt problem, but the Inter-American System was not an important arena for resolving the situation. By the end of the decade the debt problem was considered to be worrisome but no longer in crisis and was subsumed under the new thrust for increased inter-American trade and investment, which did involve the Inter-American System.

The IDB and OAS actively responded in support of the U.S. Enterprise for the Americas initiative of June 1991 and its prospects for hemispheric free trade. In February 1992 the IDB established the Multilateral Investment Fund (MIF). Within the OAS, the General Assembly formally endorsed the EAI within days after it was proposed in June 1991. Secretary-General João Baena Soares attended meetings of the subregional integration organizations to speak strongly in favor of the EAI. The Special Negotiating and Consulting Commission (CECON), a subordinate and inactive body of the Inter-American Economic and Social Council, was activated as the primary forum for consideration of the role of the Inter-American System in a hemispheric free-trade system. In 1994 the General Assembly elevated and converted CECON into the Special Committee on Trade (CEC). The Economic Commission for Latin America and the Caribbean (ECLAC) strongly favored the EAI and coordinated its efforts with the IDB and CECON/CEC. The question remained of how specifically the OAS and IDB would participate in the future administration of a hemispheric free-trade system.

The Summit of the Americas meeting in December 1994 vigorously promoted the development of hemispheric free trade. In concert with the protection of democracy, the matter of free trade led the agenda of issues. The summit adopted a declaration "to begin immediately to construct the 'Free Trade Area of the Americas' (FTAA), in which barriers to trade and investment will be progressively eliminated" no later than the year 2005. The OAS was to play "a particularly important role" with respect to inter-American free trade, with the support of the IDB. A second Summit of the Americas met in 1998 and reaffirmed the creation of the FTAA. By then, however, enthusiasm had waned with political opposition in several countries, most notably the United States, whose participation was absolutely essential (see Chapters 6 and 7).

The Drug Traffic

Action on the part of the Inter-American System with regard to the illegal international drug traffic was highly limited until the 1980s.[20] The trafficking became an international issue in the 1890s; International Conferences of American States adopted occasional resolutions urging member states to exercise control of the drug traffic and to ratify certain international instruments. During World War II, which halted global efforts against the drug trade, the Inter-American System did not emphasize drug control in the Americas and deferred to bilateral measures trying to deal with the enormous illegal drug traffic. Its expansion after the late 1970s made it both a huge business enterprise with devastating social consequences and an acrimonious issue in U.S.-Latin American relations. Eventually cooperation increased and OAS action was undertaken in the mid-1980s.

In 1984 the General Assembly recognized illicit drug trafficking as a crime affecting all humanity and convoked the Specialized Inter-American Conference on Drug Trafficking, held in April 1986 in Rio de Janeiro. The conference drafted a regional initiative (the Program of Action of Rio de Janeiro). The General Assembly adopted the Program of Rio and created the Inter-American Drug Abuse Control Commission (CICAD).

The Program of Rio defined specific individual state and inter-American regional measures required for a sustained attack on the supply of and demand for illegal drugs, and called for unified planning and action by national and international drug control agencies. CICAD was given the responsibility "to develop, coordinate, evaluate and monitor those measures." In 1990 the Meeting of Ministers Alliance of the Americas Against Drug Trafficking convened in Ixtapa, Mexico, and assessed progress under the Program of Rio. The ministers reaffirmed the program and set the priorities for CICAD's efforts in the 1990s. They specified measures for cooperation on reducing demand, interdicting shipments, disrupting supply, and coordinating efforts by judicial and law enforcement agencies. The conferees emphasized the need for OAS cooperation with national, subregional, and UN programs. They noted that recent UN plans of action were similar to the Rio and Ixtapa programs and urged member states to ratify without delay the 1988 UN Convention against Illicit Traffic. Later in the year the General Assembly adopted the Ixtapa recommendations, and CICAD crafted policies and programs to implement them.

The Summit of the Americas in December 1994 addressed the problem of illicit drugs, drug trafficking, and related crimes, said to be among the most serious threats to democracy in the hemisphere. The Miami Declaration proposed that (1) policies be established to identify drug trafficking and money laundering networks in the region, and to bring criminals to justice and seize the proceeds of illicit activities; (2) programs be adopted to prevent and reduce the demand for consumption of illicit drugs; (3) international cooperation systems be instituted for follow-up and control of chemical precursors, weapons, and explosives; and (4) international coordination actions be taken to interdict the flows of narcotics in the hemisphere. The declaration recognized CICAD as the key agency for implementing the recommendations.

Environmental Protection

Until the 1970s, problems associated with the degradation of the natural environment were absent from the inter-American agenda except for isolated instances. Inter-

American attention expanded as a result of the 1972 United Nations World Environment Conference in Stockholm. The conference made the environment-development connection and compellingly publicized the notion of environmental protection as a crucial international objective. The Inter-American System still resisted action. Not until 1989 did the Inter-American Development Bank adopt policies (concurrently with the World Bank) interjecting an environmental element into its lending practices. In 1991 the OAS finally made the problem a high priority and strengthened its capacity to deal with environmental issues. The Permanent Council adopted the Inter-American Program of Action for Environmental Protection, which declared the intent "to use the OAS as a forum for a rational, constructive, hemisphere-wide debate, free of recrimination, aimed at developing a specific regional approach in order to contribute to implementation of the proposals of global scope that environmental protection requires." The council established a permanent standing committee on environmental policy, chaired by Heraldo Muñoz—a professor of Latin American international relations and then Permanent Representative of Chile to the OAS—and charged with proposing both environmental policies and measures for coordinating and evaluating them. The committee initiated numerous activities prescribed in the Program of Action, ranging from coordination with other entities of the OAS to conducting seminars and training workshops and issuing publications.[21] It represented the OAS at the 1992 Rio Summit, which extended global commitments to the Americas and served the basis for further inter-American efforts. The committee held seminars in 1992 and 1993 on the environment and sustainable development.[22] The Inter-American Conference on the Environment took place in 1996 in Bolivia to seek a balanced inter-American framework of common interests. The Secretary-General's Office set up a Unit for the Environment to provide support for organizational decisions and assistance to the member states in carrying them out.

NOTES

1. G. Pope Atkins, *Encyclopedia of the Inter-American System*, (Westport, Conn.: Greenwood Press, 1997) is a comprehensive single volume reference work that gives full information on the subjects presented in this synoptic chapter. A thorough recent work on the OAS is O. Carlos Stoetzer, *The Organization of American States*, 2d ed. (Westport, Conn.: Praeger, 1993). General institutional-legal histories of the Inter-American System and OAS tend to be dated but a number of them are still useful: Rodrigo Díaz Albonico, ed., *Antecedentes, balance y perspectivas del Sistema Interamericano* (Santiago: Editorial Universitaria, 1977); Charles G. Fenwick, *The Organization of American States: The Inter-American Regional System* (Washington, D.C.: Kaufman, 1963; University Press, 1965); Inter-American Institute of International Legal Studies, *The Inter-American System: Its Development and Strengthening* (Dobbs Ferry, N.Y.: Oceana Publications, 1966); César Sepúlveda, *El Sistema Interamericano: genesis, integración, decadencia*, 2d ed. (México, D. F.: Editorial Porrua, 1974); and Ann Van Wynen Thomas and A. J. Thomas Jr., *The Organization of American States* (Dallas: Southern Methodist University Press, 1963); Political-historical works are by M. Margaret Ball, *The OAS in Transition* (Durham, N.C.: Duke University Press, 1969); Gordon Connell-Smith, *The Inter-American System* (London: Oxford University Press, 1966); J. Lloyd Mecham, *The*

United States and Inter-American Security, 1889–1960 (Austin: University of Texas Press, 1961); and Jerome Slater, *The OAS and United States Foreign Policy* (Columbus: Ohio State University Press, 1967). Works with political frames of reference and more current assessments are Tom J. Farer, ed., *The Future of the Inter-American System* (New York: Praeger, 1988); and L. Ronald Scheman, *The Inter-American Dilemma: The Search for Inter-American Cooperation at the Centennial of the Inter-American System* (New York: Praeger, 1988).

2. Joseph Byrne Lockey, *Pan Americanism: Its Beginnings* (New York: Macmillan, 1920).

3. See Larman C. Wilson, "Multilateral Policy and the Organization of American States: Latin American-U.S. Convergence and Divergence," in *Latin American Foreign Policies: An Analysis*, ed. Harold E. Davis, Larman C. Wilson, et al. (Baltimore: Johns Hopkins University Press, 1975).

4. Thorough documentary collections for the period 1889–1954 are Carnegie Endowment for International Peace, *The International Conferences of American States, 1889–1928*, ed. James Brown Scott (New York: Oxford University Press, 1931); Carnegie Endowment for International Peace, *The International Conferences of American States: First Supplement, 1933–1940* (Washington, D.C.: Carnegie Endowment for International Peace, 1940); and Pan American Union, Department of Legal Affairs, *The International Conferences of American States: Second Supplement, 1942–1954* (Washington, D.C.: Pan American Union, General Secretariat, Organization of American States, 1958).

5. See Atkins, *Encyclopedia of the Inter-American System*, 370–373; General Secretariat, Organization of American States, *Organization of American States: A Handbook* (Washington, D.C.: 1972).

6. For more biographical data, see Atkins, *Encyclopedia of the Inter-American System*, 32–33, 117, 187–188, 319–320, 343, 365–366, 411–413.

7. Inter-American Development Bank, *Basic Facts, Inter-American Development Bank, 1993* (Washington, D.C.: The Bank, 1994); and Diana Tussie, *The Inter-American Development Bank.* (Boulder, Colo.: Lynne Rienner Publishers, 1994).

8. Atkins, *Encyclopedia of the Inter-American System*, 337–340, 373–376.

9. See John Edwin Fagg, *Pan Americanism* (Malabar, FL: R. E. Krieger, 1982); Heraldo Muñoz, "A New OAS for the New Times," *Latin America in a New World*, ed. Abraham Lowenthal and Gregory Treverton, (Boulder, Colo.: Westview Press, 1994); Scheman, *The Inter-American Dilemma*; Sepúlveda, *El Sistema Interamericano*.

10. See José Joaquín Caicedo Castilla, *El derecho internacional en el Sistema Interamericano* (Madrid: Ed. Cultura Hispanica, 1970); and Nigel S. Rodley and C. Neale Ronning, eds., *International Law in the Western Hemisphere* (The Hague: Martinus Nijhoff, 1974).

11. Samuel Flagg Bemis, *The Latin American Policy of the United States* (New York: Harcourt Brace, 1943) 238–239. See Alejandro Alvarez, *International Law and Related Subjects from the Point of View of the American Continent* (Washington: Carnegie Endowment for International Peace, 1922).

12. William E. Kane, *Civil Strife in Latin America: A Legal History of U.S. Involvement* (Baltimore: Johns Hopkins University Press, 1972); C. Neale Ronning, ed., *Intervention in Latin America* (New York: Knopf, 1970); and Ann Van Wynen Thomas and A. J. Thomas Jr. *Non-Intervention: The Law and Its Import in the Americas* (Dallas: Southern Methodist University Press, 1956).

13. G. Pope Atkins, "Redefining Security in Inter-American Relations: Implications for Democracy and Civil-Military Relations," in *To Sheathe the Sword: Civil-Military Relations in the Quest for Democracy*, ed. John P. Lovell and David E. Albright (Westport, Conn: Greenwood Press, 1997).

14. Atkins, *Encyclopedia of the Inter-American System*, 93–100, 343–351; see Richard J. Bloomfield and Gregory F. Treverton, eds., *Alternative to Intervention: A New U.S.-Latin American Security Relationship* (Boulder, Colo.: Lynne Rienner Publishers, 1990); General Secretariat of the Organization of American States, *Inter-American Treaty of Reciprocal Assistance: Applications,* 3d ed., 3 vols. (Washington, D.C.: General Secretariat of the Organization of American States, 1973–1982); J. Lloyd Mecham, *The United States and Inter-American Security, 1889–1960* (Austin: University of Texas Press, 1961); Jerome Slater, *A Reevaluation of Collective Security: The OAS in Action* (Columbus: Ohio State University Press, 1965); and Robert D. Tomasek, "The Organization of American States and Dispute Settlement from 1948 to 1981—An Assessment," *Revista Interamericana de Bibliografía/Inter-American Review of Bibliography* 39, no. 4 (1989): 461–476.

15. Jack Child, *The Central American Peace Process, 1983–1991: Sheathing Swords, Building Confidence* (Boulder, Colo.: Lynne Rienner Publishers, 1992), see especially chapter 1.

16. I have written elsewhere that a minority of analysts (myself among them) acknowledged that officials would be foolish not to think in security terms regarding real external threats; these analysts saw the advantages in forging a consensus on the meaning and implementation of hemispheric security in order to mobilize concerted action, but they questioned whether all the issues should be defined either primarily or at all in security terms. They were skeptical that redefinitional rhetoric would change security policies that are inherently based on threat perceptions, which implied the constant potential of determining them in terms of irreducible military threats (Atkins, "Redefining Security in Inter-American Relations").

17. See Thomas Buergenthal, Robert Norris, and Dinah Shelton, *Protecting Human Rights in the Americas: Selected Problems,* 3d. ed. (Kehl, Germany: N. P. Engel, 1990); Inter-American Commission on Human Rights, Inter-American Court of Human Rights, *Basic Documents Pertaining to Human Rights in the Inter-American System,* updated to 1 March 1988 (Washington, D.C.: General Secretariat, Organization of American States, 1988); Cecilia Medina Quiroga, *The Battle of Human Rights: Gross, Systematic Violations and the Inter-American System* (Dordrecht; Boston: M. Nijhoff, 1988); Alfred Glenn Mower Jr., *Regional Human Rights: A Comparative Study of the West European and Inter-American Systems* (New York: Greenwood Press, 1991); Lars Schoultz, *Human Rights and United States Policy Toward Latin America* (Princeton: Princeton University Press, 1981).

18. Jerome Slater, *The OAS and United States Foreign Policy* (Columbus: Ohio State University Press, 1967), chapter 6.

19. J. Lloyd Mecham, *A Survey of United States-Latin American Relations* (Boston: Houghton Mifflin, 1965), 133–135, 142–145, 150.

20. See Peter H. Smith, ed., *Drug Policy in the Americas* (Boulder, Colo.: Westview Press, 1992), see especially part 3; Irving Tragen, "World-Wide and Regional Anti-Drug Programs," in *Drugs and Foreign Policy: A Critical Review,* ed. Raphael F. Perl (Boulder, Colo.: Westview Press, 1994); and William O. Walker, *Drug Control in the Americas,* rev. ed. (Albuquerque: University of New Mexico Press, 1989).

21. See Heraldo Muñoz, ed., *Environment and Diplomacy in the Americas* (Boulder: Lynne Rienner Publishers, 1992); and Heraldo Muñoz and Robin L. Rosenberg, eds., *Difficult Liaison: Trade and Environment in the Americas* (Coral Gables: North-South Center, University of Miami; Washington, D.C.: Organization of American States, 1993).

22. Muñoz, *Environment and Diplomacy in the Americas*; and Joseph S. Tulchin, ed., with Andrew Rudman, *Economic Development and Environmental Protection in Latin America* (Boulder, Colo.: Lynne Rienner Publishers, 1991).

CHAPTER NINE

■

Global and
Extraregional Arrangements

This chapter deals with the many international institutions outside of the Western Hemisphere that are important to the international relations of Latin America and the Caribbean. With slight exception these institutions are twentieth-century creations. They include The Hague Peace Conferences, the League of Nations, and the United Nations System; arms control agreements, the Antarctic Treaty, and the law of the sea; the Nonaligned Movement, the New International Economic Order, and certain commodities agreements.

EARLY GLOBAL ORGANIZATIONS

The Hague System

Two great currents of international politics—arbitration and disarmament—played conspicuous roles in the international system at the beginning of the twentieth century. The first attempts to devise multilateral approaches to the problems of war and peace took place at two peace conferences at The Hague in 1899 and 1907.[1] The Permanent Court of Arbitration (The Hague Court) was established in 1899 and revised in 1907, and its declarations placed some prohibition on certain instruments of war. Plans for holding a third conference were dropped because of the increasing interstate conflicts immediately preceding World War I.

Planners of the First Peace Conference at The Hague (1899) largely ignored the Latin American states. Only Brazil and Mexico were invited, and only the latter attended. However, all twenty Latin American states were invited to the Second Peace Conference (1907) at the behest of the United States. Eighteen of them participated, with only Costa Rica and Honduras passing up the forty-four-state gathering. Prestigious Latin American representatives played active roles at the conference, especially Ruy Barbosa of Brazil, Luis M. Drago of Argentina, and Santiago Pérez Triana of Colombia. U.S. Professor Leo S. Rowe, later director general of the Pan American

242

Union, said at the 1907 meeting of the American Political Science Association that Latin American participation "was but the formal recognition of an accomplished fact—the establishment of a group of sovereign and independent states in the southern hemisphere, whose political importance can no longer be ignored." Their participation brought the Latin American region into international prominence for the first time.

Once offered the Second Peace Conference as a forum, the Latin American states mounted a concerted effort to have nonintervention accepted as a principle of international law. This effort paralleled their attempts to do the same in inter-American law. A resolution had been approved at the International Conference of American States at Rio de Janeiro in 1906 recommending that the forthcoming Hague Conference discuss the Drago Doctrine regarding the legal prohibition of force for the collection of public pecuniary claims. The Latin American delegates succeeded in having a version of the Drago Doctrine considered as a principle of general international law, but they were greatly disappointed over the extent to which it was modified. The conference adopted the Porter Doctrine (submitted by U.S. delegate General Horace Porter), which prohibited the use of force in the collection of public debts unless the debtor state refused to submit the claim to arbitration or, having gone to arbitration, failed to comply with the decision. The Drago Doctrine itself tolerated no intervention whatsoever.[2]

Because of the relative military insignificance of Latin American armed forces at the time, they received little consideration in disarmament questions. Yet one South American arrangement was of some importance. During discussions on the limitation of armed forces, the arms control agreements between Argentina and Chile (the "Pacts of May" of 1902) were given serious consideration by the European representatives, who viewed the agreements—which provided for the arbitration of all differences between the two states and for the limitation of their naval forces—as among the most modern of arms control arrangements.

The League of Nations

The Latin American states that had declared war on or severed relations with Germany during World War I participated in the subsequent Versailles Peace Conference.[3] They strongly supported President Woodrow Wilson's project for a League of Nations. Ten of them signed the Versailles Treaty, which included the Covenant of the League of Nations, and thereby became charter members of the organization. Fifteen Latin American states were members when the first League Assembly met in 1920. Eventually, all twenty of them joined the League for at least a limited time, but never were all of them members at the same time.

A regional consciousness was reflected both in Latin American behavior in the League and in the attitudes of the other members toward Latin America. An informal Latin American bloc was formed, primarily in order to assure the election of Latin American representatives to the Assembly and the Council and to obtain positions for their nationals in the Secretariat. Anxious to keep them as members in pursuit of the ideal of universality, the League established a special Latin American Liaison Bureau.[4]

Latin American delegates in Geneva used every opportunity to lecture about their contributions to world peace. They also expressed basic principles that anticipated their later actions under the UN System. For example, in 1927 Chile proposed a system of regional Latin American agreements designed to prevent any competitive armaments. Security requirements in the region, the delegates said, were unique, and European standards therefore should not apply; security should be achieved by means of arbitration and conciliation. Most Latin American states opposed arms control through global arrangements, emphasizing that the region was appreciably different from the rest of the world. In 1928 Argentina declared arbitration to be "an essentially American principle" and a sufficient guarantee of security.

The Latin American states were attracted to the League for several reasons, including the prestige that membership might bring, the League's adherence to such principles as arbitration and judicial settlement, and its potential as a counterpoise to U.S. intervention. The League offered little opportunity for Latin America to press for economic advantages in the way of aid or trade preferences, as such activities were of peripheral importance to the organization. The Latin American states succeeded in accumulating a certain amount of prestige from their League activities and participation: They gained nonpermanent seats on the League Council and representation on the World Court and elected presidents of the Assembly. On the other hand, the League paid little attention to Latin American disputes and played almost no role in limiting U.S. power in Latin America.

The first major disappointment for Latin Americans occurred at the Versailles Conference itself, when the League Covenant was adopted. Article X of the Covenant seemed to fulfill the Latin American desire for an international law of nonintervention. It read: "The Members of the League undertake to respect and preserve as against external aggression the territorial integrity and existing political independence of all Members of the League." However, Article XXI, included despite Latin American protests that it contradicted Article X, stated: "Nothing in this Covenant shall be deemed to affect the validity of international engagements, such as treaties of arbitration or regional understandings like the Monroe Doctrine, for securing the maintenance of peace." Article XXI was designed to make the Covenant more acceptable to the U.S. Senate. The Covenant made no other mention of regional arrangements.

Later events further eroded the League's utility as a counterweight to U.S. power in Latin America. The United States refused to join the League, freeing it from the limitations that might have been imposed by membership. Furthermore, the League largely refrained from dealing with inter-American problems. It ignored the Tacna-Arica dispute involving Chile against Peru and Bolivia, as well as a dispute between Panama and Costa Rica, largely because of U.S. protests in both instances. The League attempted to settle two inter-American disputes—the Chaco War between

Bolivia and Paraguay, and the Leticia conflict between Peru and Colombia—but both times it deferred to U.S. actions, even though it was not a member of the League (see Chapter 12).

THE UNITED NATIONS SYSTEM

Latin American Participation

Regional participation in the United Nations has been universal and continuous, in contrast to the intermittent nature of Latin American membership in the League of Nations.[5] Consequently, the Latin American states have always formed a significant proportion of the UN membership, although their relative voting strength declined as UN membership increased. The number of Latin American members remained constant at twenty from 1945, when the first General Assembly convened, until 1962. At that time, new Caribbean states began to join the UN, and with their addition regional membership grew in number to thirty-three. Total UN membership increased from fifty-one original members in 1945 to 185 as of 1998; the Latin American proportion in 1945 had been about 39 percent, and that of Latin America and the Caribbean in 1998 was about 18 percent.

Prior to 1960 the regional states generally supported the United States on cold war issues, but their twenty votes were never automatically assured. On "anticolonial" (dependent area) questions, they tended to favor increased colonial self-government and independence, including UN supervision of the independence process. Latin American states joined the other developing country members in calling for maximum funding of technical assistance and economic development projects. They successfully created the Economic Commission for Latin America within the Economic and Social Council in 1948.

Latin Americans were less amenable to U.S. leadership in the 1960s and began to divide on cold war issues. Cuba joined the Soviet bloc after 1960; others increasingly adopted independent stances. They also began to divide on colonial issues, although they were virtually unanimous in condemning racism in South Africa. Most Latin Americans voted consistently to extend economic and technical programs and voted with considerable unity on humanitarian and social cooperation and administrative matters. They also tended to vote as a bloc in UN elections.

Latin America's regional self-perception has been enhanced by their membership in the UN System. They had formed a bloc at the San Francisco Conference in 1945, and thereafter they met as a regional caucusing group during annual General Assembly meetings, so as to ensure the representation of Latin American interests and maximum voting strength. The Latin American caucus is the oldest standing regional grouping in the UN. Although its decisions are not binding on members, it has succeeded in defining regional positions on issues before the UN, gained general agreement on tactics to be pursued, and negotiated the election of Latin Americans to fill offices in various UN bodies.

The caucuses were informal in nature until the Ninth General Assembly convened in 1953, when the procedures were formalized. Thereafter, the self-named Latin American Caucusing Group held regular biweekly meetings chaired by the Latin American delegate who had been elected a vice-president of the General Assembly. When the OAS imposed sanctions on Cuba in 1964, isolating it diplomatically, the Latin American group reverted to informal meetings to which Cuba was not invited (with one exception in March 1973). Cuba was readmitted in January 1975, and the formal caucus was reinstituted; in the meantime, the new Caribbean states were also invited to join.

UN Relationship to the Inter-American System

Some early proponents and founders of the United Nations argued that the global institution was incompatible with regional organizations.[6] More of them, including U.S. Secretary of State Cordell Hull, accepted the existence of regional organizations but insisted that they be superseded by the UN in authority. The members of the Inter-American System at the time were beginning the process of coordinating and extending the fifty-five-year-old American regional system on a permanent juridical basis; Latin Americans were concerned whether their regional system would preserve its freedom of action. Enough pressure was brought to bear at the organizing conference at San Francisco in 1945, particularly by the Latin American states acting as a bloc, to have the UN Charter sanction regional organization. Alberto Lleras Camargo of Colombia led the effort (he became the first secretary-general of the Organization of American States in 1948).

The charter specifies considerable UN direction of regional arrangements, but in fact the Inter-American System enjoyed significant autonomy for many years. Article 51 of the UN Charter recognized regional arrangements as being compatible with global organization and especially appropriate to the settlement of regional disputes. It gave the Security Council the right to intervene in those settlements and allowed individual states the right to appeal directly to the global body. In practice, however, the UN deferred to the Inter-American System. Although some regional disputes were taken directly to the UN, and some OAS decisions were appealed there, until the 1980s the Inter-American System for the most part was the primary forum for issues relating to American peace and security, with little UN action forthcoming.

A few examples suffice to illustrate the UN relationship with the Inter-American System. In June 1954 Guatemala appealed to the Security Council in accusing Honduras and Nicaragua of aggression. (Guatemala was not then a party to the Rio Treaty or the OAS Charter.) The Latin American members of the Security Council, supported by the United States, wanted to refer the matter to the OAS, but a resolution to that effect was vetoed by the Soviet Union. A French resolution calling for a cease-fire was then adopted. The Security Council considered a subsequent Guatemalan request for another review of the issue but declined to place the issue on its agenda.

The OAS decision to apply sanctions against the Trujillo regime in the Dominican Republic for its assassination attempt against the president of Venezuela was appealed to the UN in 1960. The Soviet Union tried in the Security Council to authorize the sanctions, which would have established the Security Council's authority over regional enforcement actions and provided a precedent for the Soviet Union to veto any future regional sanctions against Cuba. The Soviet proposal was voted down.

After the Bay of Pigs invasion in 1961, Cuba charged the United States and certain other Caribbean states with aggression and appealed to the Security Council for support. The council took no action. In settling the Cuban missile crisis in 1962, the United States and the Soviet Union agreed to have UN observers in Cuba monitor the removal of Soviet missiles; but Castro refused to receive a UN team, and it was never sent. In 1967 the Twelfth Meeting of Consultation of Ministers of Foreign Affairs expanded OAS sanctions against Cuba and reemphasized the practice of only reporting regional actions to the UN, as opposed to gaining UN approval. Also in 1967 the OAS established a permanent observer at the UN to act as liaison between the two organizations. In 1973 the attention of the Security Council was directed to disputes between the United States and Panama, and between Britain and Guatemala over Belize; no actions were taken.

The de facto independence of the Inter-American System in matters of peace and security eroded in the 1980s. By this time the system's collective security functions had significantly declined. Direct UN activities in hemispheric conflict occurred during the Anglo-Argentine War of 1982 and during the Central American conflict, and the UN provided the authority for the Haitian operation in 1994.

The UN Security Council, secretary-general, and General Assembly were all involved in the South Atlantic conflict. On April 3, 1982, the day after Argentina invaded and took control of the British Falkland Islands Colony, the Security Council adopted a resolution demanding immediate cessation of hostilities and the withdrawal of Argentine forces; it called on both parties to seek a diplomatic solution. The resolution became the foundation for British diplomacy throughout most of the crisis and the point of departure for other third-party efforts. UN Secretary-General Javier Pérez de Cuellar, a Peruvian diplomat, at first deferred to U.S. diplomacy; after its failure, however, the mediation efforts shifted to the secretary-general. The disputants could not agree on the critical issue of sovereignty, and the mediation effort collapsed. In the aftermath of the crisis (the fighting ended on June 14), nineteen other Latin American states joined Argentina in introducing, and having adopted, a resolution in the General Assembly calling for British-Argentine negotiations. The United States voted for the resolution, in a conciliatory gesture toward Argentina and the rest of Latin America.

In the 1980s and into the 1990s, elements of the UN system were closely involved in the efforts to accommodate Central American conflict. The inability of the Inter-American System to take authoritative action in Central America early in the conflict led to the first direct UN peacemaking and peacekeeping involvement in the Western Hemisphere. It was generally well received in Central America and by other

Latin Americans and opened the possibility of greater UN involvement in hemispheric security affairs and conflict resolution.

UN involvement was slow to develop, however. In 1983 and 1984 Nicaragua submitted resolutions to the Security Council to condemn the United States for aggression against Nicaragua; the United States vetoed them. The Security Council approved resolutions supporting the Contadora peace process in May 1983, and the General Assembly did the same in November 1983 and October 1984.

At this point the International Court of Justice (ICJ) asserted it authority over strenuous U.S. opposition.[7] On March 29, 1984, Nicaragua asked the UN Security Council to condemn the "escalation of acts of aggression" on the part of the United States with its recent mining of Nicaragua's harbors. The United States vetoed a resolution to that effect, and the Sandinista government presented its case to the ICJ. After arguing that Nicaragua's evidence was faulty, the United States challenged the court's jurisdiction and withdrew from further participation; the court agreed with Nicaragua that the case should proceed. Two years later, on June 17, 1986, the ICJ handed down its decision; it ruled that the United States had violated international law in mining Nicaraguan harbors and should make reparations. The key issues were decided by the same vote of 12–3; the dissenting judges were from the United States, Japan, and the United Kingdom. On July 31, 1986, the Security Council took up a Nicaraguan resolution for full U.S. compliance with the ICJ decision and for the cessation of U.S. support for the insurgent Contras. The United States vetoed the resolution, and neither the court nor the council had the capacity to enforce U.S. compliance.

Other UN organs then joined the OAS in accepting Central American requests to assist with the 1987 Central American agreement (Esquipulus II) for a comprehensive subregional peace plan. Over U.S. objections, UN Secretary-General Pérez de Cuéllar mediated negotiations that in 1989 resulted in the Security Council's approval of the organization and deployment of the military-civilian UN Observer Group in Central America (ONUCA). ONUCA engaged in extensive and effective peacekeeping and election monitoring operations in Central America. The UN and the Organization of American States worked out a division-of-labor arrangement for the use of available resources.

The United Nations responded to the 1991 military overthrow of Haitian President Jean-Bertrand Aristide; it joined with the OAS in an effort to restore Aristide to power. The process culminated with the formation of a multinational U.S.-led peacekeeping force authorized by the UN Security Council.

Developmental Organizations

With the establishment of the United Nations System, Latin American states immediately turned to various UN agencies as alternatives both to bilateral U.S. assistance and, increasingly, to OAS agencies, which they viewed as dominated by the United States. Their first major accomplishment was the creation in 1948 of the Economic

Commission for Latin America (ECLA) as a subagency of the UN Economic and Social Council (ECOSOC); it was headquartered in Santiago, Chile. In 1984 it was retitled the Economic Commission for Latin America and the Caribbean (ECLAC) to recognize the involvement of the newly independent Caribbean entities. Its general purpose was to formulate Latin American economic theory concerning development, trade, and regional integration and to coordinate policies designed to promote these enterprises. In 1962 ECLA founded the Latin American Institute for Economic and Social Planning (ILPES), also located in Santiago, to provide training, information, and advice to regional developmental agencies. The Latin American Demographic Center (CELADE), established in 1957 as a UN agency, was placed under ECLA's administration in 1975.

ECLA membership was initially open to American states that were UN members in the Americas and to states that had dependencies in the Americas. In mid-1998, ECLAC had forty full members: the thirty-three Latin American and Caribbean states, Canada, the United States, France, the Netherlands, and the United Kingdom; plus Portugal, Spain, and Italy, invited to adhere because of their special ties to the region. Five nonsovereign entities were admitted as associate members: Monserrat, the British Virgin Islands, the U.S. Virgin Islands, Puerto Rico, and the Netherlands Antilles. ECLAC meets approximately every two years; its sessions are attended by observers from the UN and certain of its specialized agencies and from other IGOs and some nongovernmental organizations. From 1948 to 1998, ECLAC held twenty-seven regular sessions.

ECLA initially served as a major advocate of unorthodox development theory and policy. It influenced Latin American economists and government officials to a considerable, but then declining, degree. The executive secretaries, all well-known Latin American economists, combined political economic theory with diplomatic activism to exert highly significant personal influence on institutional positions and activities.[8]

Gustavo Martínez Cabañas of Mexico was the first executive-director of ECLA, from 1949 to 1950. He was succeeded by Raúl Prebisch (1950–1963). Once the director of the Central Bank of Argentina, Prebisch was Latin America's best-known economist. ECLA became a proving ground for his structuralist theory (see Chapter 3), which held that underdevelopment was caused by a combination of domestic and international economic structural realities. He elaborated his thesis into a comprehensive Latin American economic development theory and then extended it to include the entire Third World. Prebisch left ECLA in 1963, but he had continuing influence as head of the United Nations Conference on Trade and Development (UNCTAD) until 1968, where he was a leading voice for developing countries at large. José Antonio Mayobre of Venezuela (1963–1967) and Carlos Quintana of Mexico (1967-1972) continued to follow the structuralist approach as successors to Prebisch at ECLA (1963–1972).

Uruguayan Enrique Iglesias was also one of Latin America's leading economists and diplomats. He headed ECLA for thirteen years (1972–1985) and incrementally shifted his own thinking and the organization's approach. He moved the institutional position from one that vigorously promoted state intervention for economic development and import-substitution industrialization to one that relied on developing a combination of internal and external markets and recognizing an important role for private enterprise in Latin American development. Iglesias resigned in 1985 to become foreign minister of Uruguay, as that country returned to elected civilian government; in 1987 he was appointed president of the Inter-American Development Bank. Norberto González of Argentina succeeded Iglesias for a brief period (1985–1987).

Gert Rosenthal, as executive-director of ECLAC since 1987, has presided over a difficult period of change. Structuralism was generally abandoned around Latin America, and neoliberalism ascended to the dominant position as regional economic doctrine. ECLAC statements acknowledge that the old ideas of structural dependency are no longer appropriate and embrace the tenets of neoliberalism. ECLAC has vigorously supported the revival of Latin American subregional economic integration, when accompanied by privatization of domestic enterprises and more openness to integration organization partners, as well as to the outside world—prominently the United States and Europe.

The United Nations Conference on Trade and Development (UNCTAD) was organized as an institution attuned to the interests of underdeveloped nations. Latin Americans had important influences in UNCTAD through their own concerted bloc action and by virtue of the fact that it was headed by Raúl Prebisch from 1963 to 1968. A series of global meetings has been held, convened about every four years: UNCTAD I (Geneva, 1964); UNCTAD II (New Delhi, 1968); UNCTAD III (Santiago, 1972); UNCTAD IV (Nairobi, 1976); UNCTAD V (Manila, 1979); UNCTAD VI (Belgrade, 1983); UNCTAD VII (Geneva, 1987); UNCTAD VIII (Cartagena, 1992); and UNCTAD IX (Johannesburg, South Africa, 1996). After the 1964 meeting UNCTAD became a permanent organ of the General Assembly.

Latin American states caucused as a regional bloc prior to each UNCTAD session, first in the Special Latin American Coordinating Committee (CECLA) before UNCTAD I, II, and III, and then in the Latin American Economic System (SELA). They adopted common regional developmental strategies that became dominant themes during the global meetings. The largely unproductive effort to improve terms of trade for developing nations was a great disappointment to them. It was apparently a source of frustration for Prebisch and perhaps led to his resignation as secretary-general of UNCTAD after the 1968 conference.

UNCTAD from the beginning was the centerpiece of the Third World effort to create a New International Economic Order (NIEO). This international regime, centered in UNCTAD but involving numerous other organizations and activities, is discussed below.

Financial Institutions

The Bretton Woods Conference in 1944 authorized the establishment of two companion financial organizations—the International Monetary Fund (IMF) and the

International Bank for Reconstruction and Development (IBRD), more commonly called the World Bank. The IMF was organized in 1945 and had the purpose of supporting international monetary stability. The World Bank commenced operations in 1946, initially helping reconstruct war-devastated Europe, and then assisting the economic development of its lesser-developed country members. Both institutions are highly active in Latin American and Caribbean. Both of them lend only to members; membership in the IMF is a prerequisite to membership in the World Bank. All states of the Americas are members except Cuba, which withdrew in 1960.

The World Bank had some activities in Latin America from the time it started operations in 1946. The UN Development Program (UNDP) instituted programs in Latin America after its inauguration in 1953. Two bank affiliates, the International Finance Corporation (IFC) and the International Development Association (IDA), were established—in 1956 and 1960, respectively—in response to the demands of developing nations for increased loans on more flexible terms than those being offered. Together the IBRD, IFC, and IDA make up the World Bank Group.

The World Bank was caught up in the Latin American debt crisis in the 1980s. Former U.S. congressman Barber B. Conable became bank president in March 1986, stating that he wanted it involved more deeply in the efforts dealing with the debt. An authority on economic policy, Conable strongly endorsed the role of the bank envisaged by U.S. Treasury Secretary James A. Baker in his initiative regarding the debt (see Chapter 13). As a congressman Conable had criticized the Reagan administration's initial suspicion of and hostility toward the World Bank. In 1991 Conable was succeeded by Lewis T. Preston as president of the bank; he resigned before the end of his term for reasons of health and was succeeded in March 1995 by James D. Wolfensohn. The World Bank's directors elect the president, but they have always accepted the recommendation of the U.S. president (the directorship of the International Monetary Fund by tradition is filled by a European).

The IMF was designed to encourage trade by contributing to the maintenance of stable currencies and rates of exchange. An autonomous agency, the IMF is not under the authority of the UN but is associated with it. It lends from funds contributed by member states to ease inflationary pressures and to cover trade deficits. Interest rates are nominal, but when negotiating "standby arrangements" for "drawing rights" with a potential recipient, the IMF usually insists on conditions for domestic economic reforms. Those reforms are based on orthodox monetarist policies.

After becoming IMF director in 1962, Pierre-Paul Schweitzer of France was able to improve the IMF reputation somewhat in Latin America. In 1972 U.S. efforts to have him replaced were strongly opposed by most Latin American governments. Schweitzer was more willing than his predecessors had been to recognize that some IMF conditions were politically unacceptable to Latin Americans, and he was more sympathetic to their needs. For example, he assisted them in negotiations with creditors when they fell behind in payments, including the instances of Chile, Argentina, and Brazil in the early 1970s. The next two IMF managing directors were also from France: Jacques de Larosiere, who served from 1978 to January 1987 (resigning about a year and a half before his second five-year term expired); and Michael Camdessus, formerly governor of the French central bank.

Tensions between the IMF and Latin American governments returned at high levels, however, with the onset of the Latin American debt crisis in 1981.[9] Faced with the mounting inability to make payments due in late 1982, Latin American governments sought agreements with the IMF and the principal creditors. The IMF, at the very center of the debt negotiations, remained committed to orthodox economics, stressing debtor austerity, lower imports, and increased exports as conditions ("conditionality") for loans—all measures aimed at reducing inflation and enhancing the ability to service debt and invest internally for sustained development. Creditor banks and governments generally required debtors to conclude agreements with the IMF as a prerequisite to renegotiating the lending arrangements. When austerity and credit targets were not met as agreed upon, the IMF did not hesitate to withhold portions of loans, nor did private creditors hesitate to interrupt loan disbursements. The IMF's monetarist policies were in opposition to the ECLA structuralist approach (until ECLAC changed its orientation in the 1980s), which created tension between the two agencies. Latin American governments allied with ECLA, whereas the United States supported the IMF. Latin Americans tended to view the IMF as an instrument of creditor states, especially the United States, and it became a frequent target of nationalist enmity.

The General Agreement on Tariffs and Trade (GATT) was concluded in Geneva in 1947, in the aftermath of the economic dislocations of World War II. The meeting, called by the UN Economic and Social Council, negotiated and signed the multilateral trade treaty (the GATT itself) as an interim agreement, and drafted a charter for a permanent international trade organization. The latter instrument was never ratified, however, so the GATT continued as the only basis for global negotiations to promote the development of an open world trade system; it created its own secretariat and grievance procedures. Its purpose has been to advance free trade through widespread multilateral negotiations to reduce tariff and other barriers to world trade.

GATT held eight "rounds" of talks, named for the city or country in which they were initiated. They began with the Geneva Round in 1947, with twenty-three states participating, and concluded with the Uruguay Round, which closed in 1993, with 108 state participants. The negotiators have applied the principle of incrementalism, seeking with each round to increase the number of negotiating states and to expand the sectors of goods, services, and investment covered. Of particular interest to Latin America and the Caribbean, in 1971 GATT approved the Generalized System of Preferences (GSP), allowing the more developed states to give preferential tariff treatment to the developing countries; the United States adopted the GSP in 1976.

With the new global and regional economic and political era emerging in the 1980s, given impetus by the end of the cold war, most Latin American and Caribbean states engaged in the Uruguay Round, which began in Punta del Este in 1986. An on-going European Community-U.S. dispute over agricultural subsidies effectively blocked agreement and the talks broke down; Latin Americans (and much of the rest of the developing world) were particularly interested in convincing the EC to change substantially its Common Agricultural Policy of subsidies to its farmers. By late 1991, however, the impasse seemed to have yielded to a new momentum.

The Bush administration's Enterprise of the Americas Initiative (EAI), proposed in June 1991, emphasized that a satisfactory conclusion of the Uruguay Round constituted one of the "basic stepping stones" to the realization of a western hemispheric free-trade system. Virtually all of the American states were basing their economic recovery or development on strategies of export-led growth and did not intend that regional groupings forego extraregional trade links. They generally acknowledged (1) that many important trade issues for the American states (such as agriculture and textiles) could not be satisfactorily settled only within inter-American contexts and required world-wide resolution; (2) that if GATT could deal successfully with the contentious issues on a global basis, they would vanish from the regional agenda; and (3) that the problems of Latin American and Caribbean economies would not be resolved simply by exporting to the United States, so that they must also look to European and Asian markets.[10] GATT was succeeded by the World Trade Organization (WTO) in 1995.

Environmental Provisions

Given the global nature of the environmental problems and issues, the Latin American and Caribbean states (and the Western Hemisphere international organizations in general) have followed the lead of the United Nations. The landmark United Nations World Environment Conference in Stockholm in 1972 established the environment-development connection and marked the emergence of environmental protection as a growing international issue. It challenged the established post–World War II view of economic or broader "national" development that was largely divorced from environmental considerations. The principal institutional outcome of the Stockholm conference was the UN Environmental Program (UNEP), which the General Assembly established in 1972.

In 1983 the General Assembly called for the organization of the World Economic Commission (Bruntland Commission). The commissions report in 1987 to the UN General Assembly focused on the new concept of "sustainable development."[11] The report reflected considerable change in the notion of development itself, from an earlier concentration on economic growth and industrialization to a greater emphasis on both development for social betterment and development sensitive to natural resource limitations. Further action followed the report. The World Bank increased its spending on environmental and human developmental projects; it had been criticized on those issues in the past. In 1989 the UN Economic Commission for Latin America and the Caribbean declared its support for environmental policy endeavors. In 1991 the United Nations Environment Facility, managed jointly by the UNDP, UNEP, and the World Bank, began its operations.

The second of the distinguishing environmental conferences, held in June 1992, was the United Nations Conference on Environment and Development (UNCED) in Rio de Janeiro, known as the Rio Summit, Earth Summit, and Eco 92. Delegates from 180 states adopted a series of agreements on principles and practices of sustainable development and global environmental preservation management. They included the Rio Declaration on Environment and Development, the Agenda 21 of guidelines for activities, and the Statement of Principles on the Management, Conservation, and Sustainable Development of all Types of Forests. Two conventions were signed—the Framework Convention on Climate Change and the Convention on Biological Diversity—which had been negotiated under the auspices of UNEP. A third instrument adopted through UNEP efforts was signed in Uruguay later in the year. In 1995 the UN opened its International Environmental and Technology Center in Japan and located one of six regional offices in Mexico, D.F.

In June 1997 the United Nations sponsored a five-day follow-up Earth Summit. Delegates from 180 states, including forty-four heads of state, met to assess progress since the 1992 Rio Summit and to establish guidelines for new agreements, including a treaty addressing deforestation and another on climate change and global warming (to be signed in Kyoto in December 1997). But disagreements between industrialized and developing countries over timetables for the reduction of global warming, and between the United States and other countries over targets for reducing air pollution, resulted in the lack of concrete commitments.

SOME GLOBAL REGIMES

Arms Control

Various Latin American states have adhered to a wide range of arms control agreements since the late 1950s. The regime governing arms control in Latin America is diffuse, including several treaties negotiated in different forums. The Antarctic Treaty of 1959 was the earliest of the post–World War II arms control treaties involving Latin American states. Because it goes beyond arms control as such and involves other issues it is discussed separately below.[12] The Latin American Nuclear-Free Zone is taken up in Chapter 7.

UN-Sponsored Treaties.   The Charter of the United Nations, unlike the Covenant of the League of Nations, gave disarmament and arms control no particular priority. Eventually, however, the UN Disarmament Commission was established in 1952. At first the preserve of the major world powers, the commission was broadened to allow membership of smaller states and was reconstituted in 1961 as the Eighteen Nation Disarmament Committee (ENDC). In 1969 membership was increased from eighteen to twenty-six, and the body was reorganized as the Committee on Disarmament (CCD). The ENDC included Brazil and Mexico; Argentina was added when the CCD was organized. Several multinational agreements to which Latin American states are a party emerged from these two committees.

A series of international arms control agreements were negotiated in the 1960s and 1970s under the auspices of the United Nations. The Limited (or Partial) Test Ban Treaty prohibits nuclear weapons tests as indicated in its formal title (Treaty Banning Nuclear Weapon Tests in the Atmosphere, in Outer Space, and Under Water, signed August 5, 1963, and entered into force October 10, 1963). Although it is of primary relevance to the nuclear powers, the treaty was open to all states, and eventually 103 states signed it. The Outer Space Treaty (Treaty on Principles Governing the Activities of States in the Exploration and Use of Outer Space, Including the Moon and Other Celestial Bodies, signed January 26, 1967, and entered into force October 10, 1967) is based on a concept embedded in the Antarctic Treaty: It seeks to prohibit military competition in outer space before it begins. The Seabed Arms Control Treaty (Treaty on the Prohibition of the Emplacement of Nuclear Weapons and Other Weapons of Mass Destruction on the Seabed and the Ocean Floor and in the Subsoil Thereof, signed February 11, 1971, and entered into force May 18, 1972) also sought to prevent the introduction of international conflict and nuclear weapons into locations that had been free of them. The Biological Weapons Convention (Convention on the Prohibition of the Development, Production, and Stockpiling of Bacteriological and Toxin Weapons and on Their Destruction, signed April 10, 1972, and entered into force in 1975) prohibits the development, production, stockpiling, or acquisition of biological agents or toxins "of types and in quantities that have no justification for the prophylactic, protective, or other peaceful use," as well as weapons and means of delivery.

Another antibiological warfare treaty, a product of the 1925 Geneva Conference for the Supervision of the International Traffic in Arms, was revived by the United Nations in 1969. The Geneva Protocol (Protocol for the Prohibition of the Use in War of Asphyxiating, Poisonous, or Other Gases, and of Bacteriological Methods of Warfare, signed June 17, 1925, and entered into force February 28, 1928) had been adhered to only by Chile, Mexico, and Venezuela among the Latin American states. The protocol restated certain provisions of the earlier peace treaties concluding World War I. It prohibited the use of gases and bacteriological weapons of war. Problems of treaty interpretation prevented the adherence of many states until 1969, when the CCD supported UN Secretary-General U Thant's plea that the 1925 protocol be widely adopted with the simple acknowledgment that it prohibited the use of all chemical and biological weapons of war. Numerous states, including nine in Latin America, then adopted the 1925 protocol.

The Nonproliferation Treaty.   The United States had a monopoly on nuclear weapons until 1949, when the Soviet Union achieved a nuclear capability. By 1964 the United Kingdom, France, and the People's Republic of China had joined the "nuclear club." The Partial Test Ban Treaty of 1963, written by the United States, the Soviet Union, and the United Kingdom, reflected a general concern about the spread of nuclear weapons and was intended to inhibit their proliferation. Virtually all states except France and China approved of the nonproliferation concept contained in the 1963 treaty. In 1967 a draft nonproliferation treaty was developed through the initiative of both nuclear and nonnuclear states. The following year, the Conference of Non-Nuclear Nations opened for signature the Treaty on the Non-Proliferation of Nuclear Weapons, usually referred to as the Non-Proliferation Treaty (NPT). It was signed July 1, 1968, and entered into force March 5, 1970.

The major thrust of the NPT is to prohibit those states possessing nuclear weapons from transferring them to nonnuclear states and to prohibit the latter from building or acquiring them. Negotiations of the draft treaty revealed deep suspicions on the part of many nonnuclear states. As a result, important modifications representing concessions by the nuclear powers were included in the final NPT. The nonnuclear states argued that, since they were giving up the choice of "going nuclear," the nuclear states should accept safeguards ensuring they were not violating treaty agreements. The NPT provides for safeguards to be administered by the IAEA, and for a Review Conference to be held every five years. The nuclear states also committed themselves to negotiations aimed at ending the strategic stalemate and seeking general and complete disarmament, as well as making peaceful nuclear technology available to the nonnuclear states on a nondiscriminatory basis.

The NPT was opened for signature in 1968, and in 1992 it was in force for 140 states (including the Holy See), a record number of adherents for an arms control agreement. Two nuclear powers—China and France—have not joined the NPT, and at least six states with significant nuclear activities (including Argentina and Brazil) remain outside the treaty. Twenty-seven of the thirty-three Latin American regional states are party to the NPT—all but Argentina, Brazil, Chile, Cuba, Guyana, and St. Kitts and Nevis. Brazil earlier had been a leader of the disarmament movement. By 1968, however, Brazil had been ruled for four years by an ambitious military government and was a potential nuclear power reluctant to adhere to the NPT. Argentina, also governed by a military regime, apparently felt it must have the same options as Brazil, its long-time rival. With rapprochement between the two states dating from 1979, and the return to constitutional civilian governments in both countries in the early 1980s, the possibility for their adherence was enhanced. In November 1990 and July 1991, respectively, the presidents of Argentina and Brazil signed two bilateral accords: one renouncing the manufacture of nuclear weapons and pledging to open negotiations with the IAEA to set up an inspection system, and another establishing a joint agency to monitor the safeguards agreement. In December 1992 they signed an agreement with the IAEA to carry out inspections in both countries. They have not indicated intent to join the NPT, even though their agreement with the IAEA provides safeguards as rigorous as the NPT regime.

On May 11, 1995, at the NPT Review and Extension Conference, the parties to the treaty decided unanimously to extend the treaty indefinitely. Many developing countries (particularly Venezuela and Mexico, though in the end they joined others in the unanimity) were frustrated with the permanent extension, considering it discriminatory, and expected the United States to make a deal, but it was uncompromising.

The Antarctic Treaty

The Antarctic Treaty of 1959 established a multinational collaborative regime for the region. It was signed in Washington on December 1, 1959, and entered into force on June 23, 1961, after ratification by the twelve signatory nations. Among them were the seven states who had claimed sovereignty over some part of the Antarctic continent (Argentina, Australia, Chile, France, New Zealand, Norway, and the United Kingdom; the claims made by Argentina, Chile, and the United Kingdom overlapped).[13] The other five signatories—Belgium, Japan, South Africa, the United States, and the Soviet Union—had explored the region but made no territorial claims. These twelve countries, as "consultative members," formed the Council of Claimant States, whose authority was restricted to making recommendations by unanimous vote. Four additional states later became consultative members—Poland in 1977, West Germany in 1981, and Brazil and India in 1983—raising the total number to sixteen. The treaty was also open to accession by other states, and twelve states became "acceding members." Uruguay became an acceding member in 1980, and in 1984 reaffirmed its possible rights over Antarctic territory. Other Southern Cone states have not participated—Peru has little interest in Antarctica, and Paraguay and Bolivia have ignored it.

The Antarctic Treaty made significant accomplishments after its inception. It succeeded in preventing conflict in the Antarctic, as it was designed to do. The signatory states agreed to set aside (but not renounce) their demands during the life of the treaty. The council also succeeded in its goals of internationalizing and demilitarizing Antarctica, prohibiting nuclear testing and radioactive waste disposal on the continent, and ensuring that the region was used for peaceful purposes (including, most prominently, cooperative exploration and scientific investigations). Signatory states were accorded free access to the entire region with mutual rights of inspection of all national installations. The treaty prohibits "any measures of a military nature, such as the establishment of military bases and fortifications, the carrying out of military maneuvers as well as the testing of any types of weapons." It allows military personnel and equipment to be used only for scientific and other peaceful purposes. No treaty violations have been reported.

Increasing pressures were exerted for changes in the Antarctic regime. At the first seven consultative meetings held under the treaty, the topic of resources was kept off the agenda (it had purposely not been addressed in the treaty), but in the 1970s concern was expressed about the future utility and continuing existence of the treaty if petroleum or natural gas should be discovered in the Antarctic or under the surrounding continental shelf. Consequently, in 1981, the consultative members agreed to establish principles for dealing with the issue of mineral resources. Events had caught up with Antarctic governance—especially the increased price of petroleum and improved technology for extracting resources in conditions of extreme cold. Marine resources, especially an abundant high-protein crustacean called krill, had also attracted attention. Japan, Poland, and the Soviet Union were the major harvesters, but other states indicated interest in having a share.

The status of the Antarctic Treaty was further complicated in the United Nations. Third World nations not a part of the Antarctic Treaty regime argued for globalization of the region's governance and distribution of its resources. On November 30, 1983, the United Nations General Assembly adopted a resolution calling for a thorough study of the issue. In response, the treaty nations tried to demonstrate the strength of the existing system. The Polar Research Board of the U.S. National Academy of Sciences held a workshop on the future of the Antarctic in January 1985 at Beardmore Station, a remote research camp near the South Pole. Twenty-five countries sent fifty-seven scientists, diplomats, international lawyers, environmentalists, and others to attend the workshop. The debate over whether Antarctica should be regulated by the Antarctic Treaty or by the United Nations became apparently a dead issue.

Law of the Sea

The Inter-American Dispute.   What began as a territorial sea issue between the United States and certain South American west coast states developed into a global concern in which all Latin American states became involved to some degree.[14] In 1947, presidential declarations emanating from Chile and Peru claimed sovereignty over the seas adjacent to their coasts extending to a distance of 200 nautical miles. In 1952 they were joined by Ecuador at the First Conference on the Exploitation and Conservation of the Maritime Resources of the South Pacific in Santiago. They signed a joint declaration establishing a 200-mile maritime zone, including both the sea and the underlying land area, over which they claimed "sole sovereignty and jurisdiction." Their rationale was that the offshore food and economic materials were essential national resources and that they had the right and duty to protect and regulate them against outside exploitation. They argued that the 200-mile boundary included the outer limits of the food-rich Humboldt Current, which formed a "natural" and specific maritime unit. The three states convened a second conference at Lima in December 1954, where they signed six supplementary agreements for joint defense in the event of outside violations of their sovereignty in the maritime zone. They created a standing committee, the South Pacific Commission, to hold annual consultative meetings.

Beginning in 1955, the United States sought, with no success, to negotiate its differences with the three South American states. The United States, along with other large maritime powers, adhered to the traditional three-mile limit in territorial seas and a contiguous twelve-mile zone reserved for exclusive fishing rights. The United States protested the South American claims as unilateral declarations at variance with the generally accepted limits of territorial waters. An attempt to negotiate the dispute was made at the Santiago Negotiations on Fishery Conservation Problems (September 14–October 5, 1955), attended by Chile, Peru, Ecuador, and the United States, but the fundamental disagreement remained. In February 1967 the United States proposed that the dispute be submitted to the International Court of Justice or that another conference be held. The South American states refused both proposals.

In September 1951 Ecuador seized and fined U.S.-owned tuna boats, accusing them of illegally fishing in Ecuadorian waters. Peru made its first such seizure in February 1955 and Chile in December 1957. The U.S. Congress had promulgated the Fishermen's Protective Act of 1954, which provided that in any case where a U.S. vessel was seized by a foreign country under territorial waters not recognized by the United States, the secretary of state should take action "to attend to the welfare of such vessel and its crew while it is held by such country and to secure the release of such vessel and crew" and to collect costs from the foreign country, and that the secretary of the treasury should reimburse the vessel's owners for any fines paid. A 1968 amendment broadened the scope of reimbursement and, more important, provided that if the foreign country did not reimburse the United States within 120 days of a claim, the secretary of state should withhold an amount equal to the claim from U.S. assistance funds programmed for the country. The Foreign Assistance Act of 1961 provided that, in determining a country's eligibility for assistance, consideration should be given to excluding those countries that had seized U.S. vessels. The Foreign Military Sales Act of 1963 provided that "no defense article or defense service shall be sold by the United States Government . . . to any country which . . . seizes or takes into custody or fines an American fishing vessel engaged in fishing more than twelve miles from the coast of that country."[15] By this time, the problem had evolved into a global issue.

The Global Concern. By the mid-1950s, a number of nations throughout the world, including many others in Latin America, began to assert claims to an extension of the territorial seas or contiguous areas. Several factors caused the increased pressures for a change in the international law of the sea, including a growth in the economic uses of the oceans, dramatic advances in the technology for exploiting ocean resources, an increased awareness of environmental problems, and a general desire of small states forming the global majority to have a voice in the shaping of international law. The scope of the issue was formidable. The oceans cover about 70 percent of the earth's surface, over which some 95 percent of world trade moves, and contain huge petroleum and other mineral reserves. Virtually all states had some interest in the rules governing the oceans. The United Nations first attempted to resolve some of the problems in 1958 at the First United Nations Conference on the Law of the Sea at Geneva. The conference partially codified the international law of the sea by adopting four conventions. The Second UN Law of the Sea Conference was held in 1960 to resolve more issues, but without success. In 1967 Malta placed its "Pardo Plan" on the UN General Assembly agenda. It addressed "the question of the reservation exclusively for peaceful purposes of the seabed and the ocean floor, and the subsoil thereof, underlying the high seas beyond the limits of national jurisdiction and the use of their resources in the interests of mankind." The General Assembly then created a thirty-two-nation Special Committee, which, after two years of study, produced a statement of principles but left many problems unresolved.

In December 1970 the General Assembly called for a Third UN Law of the Sea Conference to deal not only with the questions remaining from the previous two conferences but also with a number of new ones that had subsequently arisen. The Special Committee was enlarged to ninety-one nations and reconstituted as the UN Committee on the Peaceful Uses of the Seabed and the Ocean Floor Beyond the Limits of National Jurisdiction (Seabed Committee). It engaged in almost three years of preparatory work for a comprehensive conference. The Third United Nations Conference on the Law of the Sea (UNCLOS III) convened in December 1973. After nine years of intense negotiations among various nations of the world, it produced in 1982 a comprehensive treaty for a global law of the sea regime. Some 156 states participated, about 120 of which were coastal states.

Latin American Positions.   During the years of negotiations for a modern and comprehensive law of the sea, different approaches developed to several of the related issues. Some coastal states viewed the decision to extend their national jurisdiction seaward as a sovereign right, considering contiguous oceans as vital national resources subject to territorial state sovereignty. Chile, Peru, and Ecuador were joined by Brazil in claiming a 200-mile territorial sea.

Most Caribbean states held a different view, expressed in the Declaration of Santo Domingo, formulated at the Specialized Conference of Caribbean Countries Concerning the Problems of the Sea, attended by fifteen states in 1972. The declaration was signed by Colombia, Costa Rica, the Dominican Republic, Guatemala, Haiti, Honduras, Mexico, Nicaragua, Trinidad and Tobago, and Venezuela. Five delegations declined to sign: Barbados, El Salvador, Guyana, Jamaica, and Panama. The declaration favored state sovereignty extending only to a limit of twelve nautical miles seaward, with ships afforded innocent (nonbelligerent) passage through the territorial sea on a nondiscriminatory basis. The Santo Domingo Declaration also proposed the concept of the "patrimonial sea," an area, including the territorial sea, not to exceed 200 nautical miles, within which a state exercised rights over resources but not sovereignty. Thus a state could not regulate navigation through the area, but it could manage the living and nonliving resources of the ocean, seabed, and subsoil. The idea was used during UNCLOS III to bring about a compromise among positions regarding sovereignty and resource allocation.

The negotiations also proceeded in a North-South context. The Pardo Plan had first formulated the idea of the "common heritage of mankind"; it quickly became a Third World rallying point that was later applied to the future of the Antarctic Treaty. On April 30, 1982, the bulk of the Latin American states, like nearly all Third World states, voted in favor of the UN Convention on the Law of the Sea. The United States voted against it, and a number of developed states abstained. The vote was 130 states for the treaty, four opposed (United States, Israel, Turkey, and Venezuela), and seventeen abstentions (mostly the Soviet bloc, except for Romania, and the European states). The chief Third World negotiator was Alvaro de Soto of Peru.

The Law of the Sea Convention.   The Law of the Sea Convention was opened for signature in December 1982 and entered into force in November 1994 (after having received its sixtieth ratification as required). The United States was not among the signatories, although in 1994 President Clinton sent the treaty to the U.S. Senate for advice and consent. Most of the provisions had become the de facto source of the international law of the sea for both signatories and nonsignatories as soon as it was signed.

The treaty sets a twelve-mile territorial waters limit, establishes a 200-mile exclusive "economic zone" for coastal nations (with a definition of oil drilling rights), regulates shipping lanes and provides for rights of passage for civilian and military ships through narrow straits, guarantees free navigation for naval forces, regulates scientific exploration and fisheries, requires environmental protection and pollution controls, controls mining under the deep sea, and establishes a system of international courts to arbitrate disputes at sea.

From the start of the negotiations, provisions regulating the mining of the profuse mineral nodules that lie in the seabed were the focus of differences that finally could not be resolved. A compromise was struck with the establishment of a dual authority, one that would mine on behalf of the less-developed countries and another that would license private enterprise to have access to mining sites. But the Reagan administration, although acknowledging that the United States strongly desired almost all other treaty provisions, decided that Article 11 did not adequately protect the U.S. firms that were exploring and developing technology to mine the seabed.

THIRD WORLD ORGANIZATIONS

Latin America in the Third World

The membership of Latin American states in the Third World, transcending regional boundaries, constituted a loose global subsystem. Latin Americans sought alternatives to traditional power politics and the redistribution of political and economic power and rewards by aligning with other like-minded states in other parts of the globe. At the same time, Latin America's regional consciousness was reinforced, in that it behaved as a regional bloc within the Third World. Latin America was, at once, a regional unit with subregional distinctions and at least loosely part of the Third World, which in certain ways it led.

The term "Third World" entered the popular vocabulary after World War II. It came to refer to the countries of Asia, Africa, and Latin America, thus containing the majority of the world's populations, as distinguished from the First World (the United States and its partners) and the Second World (the Soviet Union and its Communist-state allies). The Third World was viewed as mostly nonaligned in international politics and composed of poor, developing countries economically dependent on the rich nations. Third World nations were said to have a sense of community based on their common conditions of poverty, colonial history, and economic dependency, and consequently to share the foreign policy orientations of nonalignment and developmentalism.

Some problems arose with this seemingly widely held view. The attempt to make precise definitions and identify common characteristics among Third World members revealed important exceptions that challenged the norms. Furthermore, Third World unity and sense of community was illusory. The Latin American region certainly defies easy or general categorization. Yet the concrete movements and organizations that evolved reflected real concerns and aspirations, and their complexities needed to be confronted. The Third World in the cold war era required a more discriminating definition, and the associated structures and processes more precise analysis, than those in the popular view.

The Third World evolved out of two separate but closely related associations, the Nonaligned Movement and the New International Economic Order. Thus, two parallel Third World conceptions of the international system emerged, one in reaction to the cold war and its aftermath and the other in response to the gap between rich and poor nations. The distinctions became blurred as each movement extended its agenda and grew in size. Both sought Third World unity through international conferences focusing on a wide range of economic, political, and security issues. Concerted action was difficult to achieve, however, given the large number of states involved, the diversity of interests, and the divisiveness of issues. Notions of nonalignment and development were variously interpreted by Third World governments. The divergences and regional and other issues generated tremendous strains in both movements.

The Latin American identification with the Third World, in the sense of both nonalignment and developmentalism, was a loose and often inexact one. By and large, the Latin American states identified first with their own regional developmental problems, perceiving a unique development tradition and tending to coalesce among themselves when confronting the international aspects of development. In fact, a clear Latin American bloc emerged within the Third World, in both the Nonaligned Movement and the NIEO, pressing regional positions on numerous issues.

The end of the cold war challenged the identity of both the Nonaligned Movement and the NIEO. Latin American interest in both movements consequently declined. The end of the cold war made irrelevant the always-too-simple perception of the international structure as one of the First, Second, and Third Worlds. Alignment became a non-issue. In fact, the Nonaligned Movement had already been increasingly concerned with the same developmental matters as the NIEO. But the demise of the Soviet Union reduced the leverage of the NIEO, since it no longer was able to exploit the rivalries of the two superpowers while remaining noncommittal itself.

The Nonaligned Movement

The Third World was first synonymous with the Nonaligned Movement, which traces its beginnings to the onset of the post–World War II cold war between East and West.[16] Certain states in Asia and Africa, most of them former European colonies that had recently gained their independence, were the first participants. They sought to avoid political and military entanglements in the cold war by forming a Third World in the bipolar structure between the First and Second Worlds dominated by the United States and the Soviet Union, respectively. Membership in the Nonaligned Movement was first indicated by attendance at a series of informal conferences beginning in 1947. The first major meeting was at Bandung, Indonesia, in April 1955, where leaders of twenty-nine Asian and African states, including the People's Republic of China, attended the landmark event and proclaimed themselves to be a third force in world affairs. They called for nonalignment in the cold war and condemned colonialism as an evil. No Latin American state attended.

The Belgrade Conference of 1961 was a significant gathering. It was the first nonaligned summit meeting (the twenty-five delegates were heads of state), and it expanded Third World membership beyond Africa and Asia with the presence of Yugoslavia and Cuba. Third World leaders had considered inviting several Latin American states to attend, but those who were approached were not interested because they had not been consulted about Cuba's invitation (although three states sent observers).

By agreement reached in Belgrade in 1961, summit Conferences of Nonaligned Nations (to be attended by heads of state) would be held approximately every three years. Nine additional nonaligned summits have convened: Cairo (1964), Lusaka (1970), Algiers (1973), Colombo (1976), Havana (1979), New Delhi (1983), Harare (1986), Belgrade (1989), Jakarta (1992). Membership expanded to include an increasing number of Latin American states after 1961. Eventually sixteen of them became full members of the movement, and an additional eight had attended nonaligned conferences as observers. The remaining nine regional states have not participated. Latin American regional organizations that sent observers were the Economic Commission for Latin America and the Caribbean, the Latin American Economic System, and the Latin American Energy Organization.

Cuba, under the revolutionary leadership of Fidel Castro, became Latin America's most active and prominent member. Castro was a leading figure at the Algiers summit in 1973, and he became president of the movement in 1979 for a four-year term. With Castro presiding at the sixth summit meeting in Havana in 1979, the members threatened to split over his proposal that the Soviet Union was the "natural ally" of the Nonaligned Movement in the struggle against imperialism and that the policies of nonaligned states should reflect the Soviet position. President Tito of Yugoslavia and other delegates to the conference strongly opposed Castro, maintaining that imperialism and colonialism in whatever form should be condemned. Little support for the Cuban view was forthcoming, and the opposition led by Tito won an overwhelming victory in expunging references to the natural allies thesis from the documents finally adopted. In addition, the annual Ministerial Meeting of the Coordinating Bureau (the executive committee of the movement) was abolished, depriving Castro of an important medium to express his views.

The Cuban chairmanship ran into further trouble in the immediate aftermath of the summit meeting. The annual meeting of nonaligned foreign ministers and delegation leaders in New York at the opening of the UN General Assembly session failed for the first time ever to produce any substantive statement or serious discussion of priorities for handling the UN debates. At the same session of the General Assembly, Cuba stood for election as a nonpermanent member of the Security Council. It should have been assured an easy victory, with a potential of eighty-eight votes from the nonaligned UN members, plus twelve from the Soviet bloc. However, Colombia was put up as a candidate against Cuba, and a total of 154 ballots produced a deadlock, with neither side obtaining the necessary two-thirds majority. The Soviet Union's invasion of Afghanistan further eroded Cuba's chances. Both candidates stood down in favor of Mexico, which was not a member of the Nonaligned Movement.

The Reagan administration after January 1981 made several policy changes on development issues, the law of the sea, the Middle East, Southern Africa, Central America, and military expenditures. Much of the Third World saw these changes as an unwelcome return to the cold war. The result within the Nonaligned Movement was a substantial shift in Cuba's favor against U.S. policy. With the end of the cold war a few years later, however, the old issues faded, and the Nonaligned Movement lost much of its reason for being. Fidel Castro did not attend the 1992 summit conference.

The New International Economic Order

Another Third World association came to be known as the New International Economic Order (NIEO).[17] Almost all Latin American states joined this association. The origins of the NIEO may be traced to the first United Nations Conference on Trade and Development (UNCTAD I) held in Geneva in 1961. UNCTAD began as an ad hoc body, but, guided by its first secretary-general, Raúl Prebisch of Argentina, the General Assembly converted it to a permanent organ in the United Nations System in December 1964. At UNCTAD I, Third World states had formed the Group of 77, a coalition to unify and articulate their objections to the global trade, aid, and development practices of the mid-1960s. It then expanded in number but kept its original name. The Group of 77, led by Algeria, used its numerical majority to convene the Sixth Special Session of the General Assembly in 1974 and to adopt a Declaration on the Establishment of a New International Economic Order. It also approved the Charter of Economic Rights and Duties of States sponsored by Mexican President Luís Echeverría. Thus, the formal establishment of the NIEO occurred in 1974, but it had grown out of earlier precedents and concerns. The NIEO created a north-south global confrontation between rich and poor nations on the idea that, by and large, the wealthy nations of the world were in the Northern Hemisphere and the poorer nations in the Southern Hemisphere. Consequently, the meaning of Third World was extended to be synonymous with the "south" in economic and developmental terms. The NIEO was pursued primarily through various United Nations organs. The Group of 77 met before sessions of the General Assembly and other gatherings to try to decide on a common course of action.

The Group of 77 had some success in its endeavors. It was instrumental in the creation of the Special United Nations Fund for Economic Development (SUNFED), the United Nations Capital Development Fund (UNCDF), and the International Development Association (IDA) as an affiliate of the World Bank. The Group of 77 organized a series of special UN conferences to address a wide range of other issues they considered crucial to their interests: on the environment, population, food, the law of the sea, disarmament, women, industrialization, desertification, technology transfer, rural development, and the role of science and technology in development. These conferences, however, rarely led to concrete results. The Group of 77 represented a majority of the UN membership and could pass any action that it chose in the General Assembly—if it maintained its cohesiveness. It was not, however, able to persuade or compel the North to adopt its tenets or prescriptions.

For most of Latin America most of the time, the Third World was synonymous with the developing world. The regional actors, including members of the Non-aligned Movement, seemed to have concluded that they shared special economic problems with other developing nations, particularly in their relations with the developed world. In fact, the Latin American region took the lead in addressing a wide range of issues beginning in the early 1960s. The important issues, from their points of view, involved development and the world economy, especially world trade, public assistance, and private investment. At the same time, Latin America approached the NIEO as a regional bloc, placing as much reliance on their own regional integration and caucusing organizations as on the NIEO.

With the end of the cold war and the NIEO's significantly reduced leverage, Latin Americans placed even less trust in the organization as a policy vehicle. The UNCTAD IX meeting in 1996 reflected the enormous changes in global politics. In the first place, it was held in South Africa, a state formerly anathema to the NIEO because of its racial policies but then presided over by Nelson Mandela, hero of the anti-apartheid movement. Developing countries had changed their perceptions and strategies, embracing free-market economies and competing with each other for private foreign investment and the presence of multinational corporations in their economies. UNCTAD IX itself adopted the new outlook, inasmuch as a report by the secretary-general, Rubens Ricupero, argued for the benefits of MNCs to economic development.

Commodity Agreements

Latin American states joined, and sometimes led, "commodity agreements," a process also referred to as "resources diplomacy."[18] States that produce primary materials, often having monocultural economies, were attracted to commodity agreements as a way to control markets for their export products. They sought to raise and then stabilize prices in world markets and assure export earnings over a long period of time. In general, commodity agreements represented further efforts on the part of Latin American (and other) states to gain economic strength in relation to the more industrialized and richer states.

The Organization of Petroleum Exporting Countries (OPEC) was one of the earliest and the most successful commodity agreements. Five relatively obscure underdeveloped states banded together in 1960 to form OPEC. It eventually comprised thirteen members, with its headquarters located in Vienna. Venezuela was a charter member, and Ecuador joined in 1973. A Venezuelan oil expert and government official, Juan Pablo Pérez Alfonso, played a prominent role in establishing OPEC. The stimulus occurred in 1959, when the major global oil companies acted in concert to reduce the price they paid for oil to the producing states. The original five OPEC members met in Baghdad the following year in order, according to their charter, "to create an organization for regular consultation and for the coordination of oil policies." OPEC came into prominence with the energy crises in the 1970s. By mid-1973, thirteen years after its modest beginnings, OPEC was powerful enough to quadruple the price of petroleum on world markets and bring about a major redistribution of international income in favor of its member states. But with the subsequent "oil glut" and chronic disagreements among the members states, OPEC lost much of its leverage and its prominence as an effective commodity agreement. In 1990 Ecuador withdrew from OPEC, and Venezuela became a reluctant participant.

A commodity agreement predating OPEC also enjoyed some success. An International Coffee Agreement signed in 1962 was the culmination of earlier efforts. Brazil had attempted from 1940 to 1945 to regulate production and achieve price stability in the global coffee market. The 1962 agreement, renewed for five years in 1968, was subscribed to by Brazil and Colombia (the world's largest coffee producers at the time), Ecuador, the Central American states, and a number of African producers. Consumer states also joined in agreeing to stabilize coffee prices. In 1962, when U.S. policy toward Latin America was cast in the context of the Alliance for Progress, any price increases resulting from the coffee agreement were viewed as a form of aid for development. Despite a great deal of internal dispute, especially between the Latin American and African groups, world coffee prices were brought under a modicum of control.

The coffee-producing states allowed the agreement to expire in 1973. They apparently felt that they no longer needed a formal agreement with the consumer states. Nevertheless, they were faced with the financial inability to limit coffee sales in order to keep prices at a desirable level. To this end, Venezuela in November 1974 announced that it would lend some of its profits from petroleum sales to Central America, so that Central America could withhold part of their coffee production from international markets. Brazil and Colombia said they would finance their own stockpiling.

OPEC's success catalyzed efforts to regulate other commodities through associations of producer nations. Other cartels with Latin American participants were created. An organization of copper producers, the Intergovernmental Council of Copper Exporting Countries (CIPIC), was established in 1967 and made up of Chile, Peru, Zambia, Zaire, and, later, Indonesia. The Organization of Iron Ore Exporting Countries (IOEC) was composed of Venezuela (a major leader), Chile, Peru, Brazil, Algeria, India, Australia, Canada, Sweden, Liberia, and Mauritania. Bolivia belonged to the International Tin Agreement (which collapsed in 1985). Jamaica is the chief producer and leader of the International Bauxite Association. Latin American banana producers organized the International Organization of Banana Exporters (IPEB).

Serious doubts exist about the viability of the cartels. A successful effort requires that producers are willing and able to withhold enough of their products to affect prices and that consumer demand remain relatively constant despite increased prices. These conditions are hard to satisfy, because producers often are unable to finance stockpiling or reduced production, and consumers often turn to substitutes or are willing to do without. Petroleum seemed to be the exception, because producers had the financial ability to control the volume of supply, and consumers had little choice other than to buy the crucial commodity at current world market prices. However, even OPEC ran into serious problems of supply, demand, and member-cohesion. Furthermore, high prices stimulated the major consumers to increase oil conservation efforts, seek alternative energy sources, and, for those able to do so, increase their own oil production.

NOTES

1. James Brown Scott, *The Hague Peace Conferences of 1899 and 1907*, 2 vols. (Baltimore: Johns Hopkins University Press, 1909); Carnegie Endowment for International Peace, *The Reports to the Hague Conferences of 1899 and 1907*, ed. James Brown Scott (Oxford: Clarendon Press, 1917).

2. J. Lloyd Mecham, *A Survey of United States-Latin American Relations*, (Boston: Houghton Mifflin, 1965), 99.

3. Augustín Edwards, *La América Latina y la Liga de las Naciones* (Santiago de Chile: Editorial Universitaria, 1937); and Warren H. Kelchner, *Latin American Relations with the League of Nations* (Boston: World Peace Foundation, 1929).

4. J. Fred Rippy, *Globe and Hemisphere* (Chicago: Henry Regnery, 1958), 519.

5. For good general works on the United Nations, see Evan Luard, *The United Nations: How It Works and What It Does*, 2d ed., rev. by Derek Heater (New York: St. Martin's, 1994); Karen A. Mingst and Margaret P. Karns, *The United Nations in the Post–Cold War Era* (Boulder, Colo.: Westview Press, 1995); and Thomas Weiss, David P. Forsythe, and Roger A. Coate, *The United Nations and Changing World Politics* (Boulder, Colo.: Westview Press, 1995).

6. See G. Pope Atkins, *Encyclopedia of the Inter-American System* (Westport, Conn.: Greenwood Press, 1997), 450–452.

7. The ICJ succeeded the Permanant Court of International Justice of the League of Nations in 1946. By informal agreement at the time, two of the fifteen judges were to be from Latin American states, rotating among themselves every two years; and in the 1970s the regional states agreed that one of those seats would be from a Commonwealth Caribbean Country. Larman C. Wilson and David W. Dent, *Historical Dictionary of Inter-American Organizations* (Lanham, Md.: Scarecrow, 1998), 107–109.

8. See Wilson and Dent, *Historical Dictionary of Inter-American Organizations,* 79.

9. See Manuel Pastor Jr., *The International Monetary Fund and Latin America: Economic Stabilization and Class Conflict* (Boulder, Colo.: Westview Press, 1987).

10. G. Pope Atkins, "Institutional Arrangements for Hemispheric Free Trade," *Annals of the American Academy of Political and Social Science* 526 (March 1993): 187. See Anne O. Krueger, ed., *The WTO As an International Organization* (Chicago: University of Chicago Press, 1998) and Asif H. Qureshi, *The World Trade Organization: Implementing International Trade Norms* (Manchester, U.K.: Manchester University Press, 1996).

11. World Commission on Environment and Development, *Our Common Future* (Oxford: Oxford University Press, 1987). See also Robert O. Keohane and Ilinor Ostrom, eds. *Local Commons and Global Interdependence* (London: Sage Publications, 1995); and Marian A.L. Miller, *The Third World in Global Environmental Politics* (Boulder: Lynne Rienner Publishers, 1995).

12. Background information in this section is based on U.S. Arms Control and Disarmament Agency, *Arms Control and Disarmament Agreements: Texts and History of Negotiations* (Washington, D.C.: 1975).

13. Jack Child, *Antarctica and South American Geopolitics: Frozen Lebensraum* (New York: Praeger, 1988); A. Jorgensen-Dahl and W. Ostreng, eds. *The Antarctic Treaty System in World Politics* (London: Macmillan, 1991); and Olav Schram Stokke and Davor Vidas, eds. *Governing the Antarctic: The Effectiveness and Legitimacy of the Antarctic Treaty System* (Cambridge, U.K.: Cambridge University Press, 1997).

14. See George V. Galdorisi and Kevin R. Vienna, *Beyond the Law of the Sea: New Directions for U.S. Oceans Policy* (Westport, Conn.: Praeger, 1997); David Larson, *Security Issues and the Law of the Sea* (Lanham, Md.: University Press of America, 1994; Francisco Orrego Vicuña, *Los Fondos Marinos y Oceánicos: Jurisdicción Nacional y Régimen Internacional* (Santiago de Chile: Editorial Andres Bello, 1976); Giulio Pontecorvo, ed., *The New Order of the Oceans* (New York: Columbia University Press, 1986); Bobbie B. Smetherman and Robert M. Smetherman, *Territorial Seas and Inter-American Relations* (New York: Praeger, 1974); and U.S. Arms Control and Disarmament Agency, *Arms Control and Disarmament Agreements*.

15. Virginia M. Hagen, *The Latin American-United States Fishing Rights Controversy with Specific Reference to Chile, Ecuador, and Peru* (Washington, D.C.: Library of Congress, 1969).

16. Robert A. Mortimer, *The Third World Coalition in International Politics* (Boulder, Colo.: Westview Press, 1984) is a chronological history.

17. Luciano Tomassini, ed., *El dialogo norte-sur: una perspectiva latinoamericana* (Buenos Aires: Editorial Belgrano, 1982); and Barry B. Levine, ed., *El desafío neoliberal: el fin del tercermundismo en América Latina* (Bogotá: Grupo Editorial Norma, 1992).

18. Amer Salih Araim, *Intergovernmental Commodity Organizations and the New International Economic Order* (New York: Praeger, 1990).

PART FOUR

■

Transnational Actors

Students of Latin America's international relations have long been aware of the significance of transnational phenomena. Over the past three decades it has been clear that nonstate actors are inescapable and integral elements of the international system. Although nation-states remain the most important units of the international system, they share influence with other entities capable of initiating interaction and determining international and transsocietal outcomes in the Latin American and Caribbean context. The most important of these transnational entities are identified and analyzed in this part of the book.

Among the many nonstate actors operating in the region, a number of them have emerged as the most significant and have captured the attention of analysts. They are divided into three categories. Chapter 10 deals with organizations that may claim to be autonomous actors—the Roman Catholic Church, Protestant churches, and international and multinational business enterprises. Chapter 11 addresses subnational actors that are part of transnational networks: international labor movements, transnational political parties, and guerrilla insurgency groups. Other transnational actors, better understood in the context of the phenomena of which they are a part, are taken up in Part V.

CHAPTER TEN

———————— ∎ ————————

Transnational Entities

This chapter deals with certain autonomous transnational actors and their special relationships with Latin America. The first, the Roman Catholic Church, is a unique actor with distinctive historical ties to Latin America. Organized around the sovereign state of the Holy See, the church forms a religious network continuously and intimately involved in the region from the time of European discovery of the New World to the present day. Protestant churches have become an important missionary challenge to Roman Catholicism, a surprising and relatively recent phenomenon that has had spectacular growth since the 1960s. Transnational private business enterprise has its roots in Latin America's nineteenth century international relations. Multinational corporations have been especially prominent regional actors since their accelerated growth after World War II; they have since played central international roles.

THE ROMAN CATHOLIC CHURCH

The Catholic Church as Global Political Actor

Church policy and influence in Latin America, emanating from the papacy in Rome, is a complex subject for several reasons. First, the Roman Catholic Church is a special kind of international actor; the Holy See around which it is centered is both a sovereign state presided over by the pope and headquarters for a worldwide religious organization. Second, the church is a transnational unit, but it is not as monolithic as its internal and global structures might imply. Nationalism, in Latin America and in other parts of the world, plays an important role in matters of religion and church politics, as in other social arenas. Finally, deep divisions within the church over many issues, a reality beginning in the Latin American colonial period, have complicated the policies of the Holy See and its relations with Latin American churches and states, as well as inter-Latin American church relations.

The Holy See and the Vatican State. The nature of the Roman Catholic Church as an actor in the modern international political system is unique. References to the papacy as a nonstate actor are technically inaccurate, since the Holy See and the Vatican in fact comprise a sovereign state, although the church predates the emergence of the modern nation-state by more than a millennium and has special characteristics. The Roman Catholic Church is the oldest important actor in the current international political system and is formally recognized by most of the nation-states. Its independent attributes and sovereign status date from the Peace of Westphalia of 1648, with the Lateran Pacts signed with Italy in 1929 (revised in 1984) further confirming its status.

The Holy See constitutes the central state of the Roman Catholic Church. Its sovereignty is vested in a sacerdotal monarchy (the papacy) that serves as the capital of the global Roman Catholic Church and has governmental jurisdiction and temporal and spiritual authority. The Holy See has legal personality in international law, which allows it to enter into treaties as a juridically equal state and to engage in formal diplomatic relations. The Holy See has exchanged diplomatic missions since the fourth century and today engages in a broad scope of diplomatic activity. It is formally recognized by about 120 nation-states and carries on diplomatic relations with them, including most of the Latin American states. Its participation in international organizations includes membership in a number of intergovernmental and nongovernmental organizations and permanent observer status in the United Nations System, the Organization of American States, and the Council of Europe. The Holy See is signatory to many treaties.

The State of the Vatican City is the territorial base of the Holy See, superseding the former Papal States; the pope is head of state. The Vatican City was created as a state in 1929 in a treaty agreement with the Italian state to administer the properties belonging to the Holy See. Although the Vatican does possess personality under international law and enters into international agreements (primarily in its relations with Italy), it does not exchange diplomatic representatives.[1]

Until the latter part of the nineteenth century, the pope not only led the universal church but also headed a relatively large European state. The Italian peninsula was divided into a number of separate entities, significant among them were the Papal States, with Rome as the capital city. During the revolutions and wars attendant to the unification of Italy under a monarch, the papacy lost control over much of its territory. By 1861 the Papal States had been conquered by military force and annexed to the Kingdom of Italy; in 1870 Italian troops occupied Rome, and the pope withdrew to the Vatican. Finally, the papacy and Italy signed the three Lateran treaties of 1929. Italy recognized the sovereignty of the Holy See and the creation of the State of the Vatican City; the pope dropped all claims to the former Papal States; and they both agreed on certain arrangements between church and state in Italy. Two additional pacts (concordats), signed by the Vatican and Italy in 1984 and put into effect the following year, revised parts of the Lateran treaties. These revisions changed certain aspects of the relationship between the Vatican and Italy, but had no real consequence for the international activities of the Holy See.

Decision-Making. Church divisiveness over social issues is instructive with regard to its policy-making procedures and reveals the decentralized nature of the church as a transnational actor. Some years ago Thomas Sanders pointed out the gap between the ideal church decision-making model and the way in which policy is really formulated, a reality that has fluctuated but persisted to the present day.[2] According to the ideal model, broad policies are made by the pope at the top of the church structure and then move downward through the hierarchy for implementation by bishops around the world, finally being applied by priests and laypeople. The emphasis throughout is on initiative and authority from above and obedience from below. In fact, according to Sanders, official church teachings have tended to lag behind social change, and the upper echelons of the hierarchy have been slow to absorb new social thought. The pope and most bishops have not been policy innovators; revision of papal policy has usually been in response to public pressures and to initiatives taken by lower-level church officials who eventually have been able to influence superior authorities.

Latin American Structures. A perception of Latin America as a distinct region has been revealed in church organizational structures. In 1858 the papacy established the Latin American Holy College (Colegio Pío Latinoamericano) in Rome, and in 1899 it sponsored the Latin American Plenary Council at the Vatican.[3] Much later, in 1953, Latin American bishops established a regional organization, the Conference of Latin American Bishops (Conferencia Episcopal Latinoamericana—CELAM). CELAM became an important inter-Latin American Catholic Church forum for debate and communication; the papacy has attempted to influence it in matters of papal policy. CELAM held its first conference in Rio de Janeiro in 1955, followed by assemblies in Bogotá (1968), Puebla (1979), and Santo Domingo (1992). CELAM searches for common positions among the bishops, takes into account papal teaching, issues policy statements, and offers guidance to national church officials. It has served the important function of regionally integrating the church in Latin America and eroding the old system of largely isolated national churches.

One Roman Catholic order that maintains extensive formal diplomatic relations with Latin America is the Sovereign Military Hospitaller Order of St. John of Jerusalem, of Rhodes, and of Malta (also known as the Knights of Malta, or the Knights of St. John, or the Knights Hospitallers). Founded in eleventh-century Jerusalem, this religious order later fought in the Crusades and eventually acquired great wealth and military power, including fortresses and fleets. Over the years it moved to Cyprus, to Rhodes, and to Malta, becoming in the process a powerful territorial state. French armed forces dislodged the order from Malta in 1798, after which its headquarters were located in Rome and dependent on the Holy See. Thus, by the time of Latin American independence, the Knights of Malta were no longer a military power and had lost their territorial base. Nevertheless, the order maintained its state status and supported diplomatic relations with the Holy See and with numerous nation-states around the world, today including nineteen states in Latin America. The order is, therefore, an actor in the Latin American subsystem. Although it still calls itself an order of chivalry of laypeople and priests with mixed religious and military purposes, its activities in Latin America and elsewhere are concerned almost exclusively with various kinds of welfare work.

Also of interest is the Missionaries of Charity, an international organization ministering to the destitute, founded in India in 1950 by an Albanian nun, Agnes Gonxha Bojaxhiu, who became universally known as Mother Teresa of Calcutta. (Mother Teresa was awarded the Nobel Peace Prize in 1979; she died in 1997.) The missionaries' first overseas mission was to Venezuela in 1965, followed, in Latin America and the Caribbean, by missions to Haiti, Peru, Panama, Paraguay, Brazil, Argentina, Bolivia, Chile, Colombia, Ecuador, Trinidad, Jamaica, Grenada, and Guyana. The sisters opened houses for the impoverished and terminally-ill, day care centers, and soup kitchens.[4]

Mention should be made of the important role played by foreign priests in the Latin American churches. After the nineteenth-century Latin American movements for independence, the church was subject to political attacks, often involving violence, by anticlerical liberal governments. As a result, the church was in a continuing state of crisis, unable to recruit sufficient clergy from local populations. Thus began the flow of clergy from Europe and subsequently from the United States. That movement continued after World War II, to the extent that today the percentage of foreign clergy is as high as 80 percent in some countries and is significant in almost all others. Most of them come from France, Spain, and the United States.

Papal Relations with Latin America

The papal role in Latin America has never been as great as might be expected, given the hierarchical church structure that stresses obedience to higher authority and the fact that a huge percentage of all Latin Americans are baptized in the Roman Catholic faith.[5] Since Latin American independence, four elements of international relations involving the papacy have stood out. They are, sequentially, (1) the transition from conflict to diplomatic linkages in the nineteenth century, a situation growing out of the long colonial era; (2) papal third-party conflict resolution in the twentieth century; (3) a series of papal visits to the region, beginning in 1969 and calculated as efforts to address human and theological issues and to ameliorate deep divisions over them within the church; and (4) deep concerns with the challenges of liberation theology and the spread of Pentecostal Protestantism.

Colonial Foundations.   Rome's presence was minimal during the Latin American colonial period, despite Catholic Spain's aim to conquer and rule its part of America in the name of God and the Gospel as well as for Gold and Glory. The Spanish crown jealously controlled religious as well as other affairs in the colonies, successfully resisting papal intrusion through the system of "royal patronage" (*patronato* *reál)*, in which the crown made ecclesiastical appointments, controlled finances, and made basic policy decisions. Portuguese officials followed the Spanish lead and also insisted on independence regarding church governance in Brazil. The Holy See generally accepted Spanish and Portuguese sovereign power over the church in America, taking little action to assert itself there.

During the Spanish American wars for independence, the pope supported the Spanish king. In 1816 the pope issued an encyclical calling for Spanish American Catholics to be faithful to the king.[6] The church in Spanish America was divided, however. Many of the lower clergy participated as patriots in the independence movements—the Mexican struggle, for example, was begun by two radical priests, although they were soon set aside by more conservative elites. The high clergy tended to be royalist until revolutionary success was evident, whereupon they generally supported the new states against Spain.

Nineteenth-Century Conflict and Accommodation. In the early national period, papal relations with the Latin American states were largely conflictual. Papal influence was mixed but, by and large, not great. The Holy See continued its close ties with Spain and the Holy Roman Empire, which, in turn, were often hostile toward Latin America. The Holy See's relations with Brazil were much better than those with other Latin American states. Rome was closely tied to Portugal, but the Brazilian independence movement had been nearly bloodless; independent Brazil was governed as a monarchy by the heirs to the Portuguese throne until 1889, so that Luso-Brazilian relations were relatively friendly. The Holy See and Brazil exchanged diplomatic representatives in 1830 and continuously maintained relations afterwards.

During this period, the Latin American churches were deeply divided over political issues and in sharp conflict with the temporal state. Church-state conflict existed virtually everywhere in the region to some degree; it was especially intense in Mexico and Colombia. The churches were caught up in political struggles, largely fought out between opposing upper class cliques organized into primitive political parties. Conservatives advocated traditionalism and authoritarianism, whereas liberals sought constitutional republicanism. One major issue stemmed from the nature of church-state relations inherited from the colonial period. During that time the church had enjoyed the legal status of an autonomous "estate," which included a number of special privileges, such as maintaining its own judicial system. Liberals wanted to end the church's special status as part of their overall attempt to create societies in which all individuals were subject to common constitutional provisions and legal systems. Liberal anticlericalism was also directed against church wealth in several states.

The church hierarchy in Latin America responded to the liberal challenge by allying with conservatives and some of the most reactionary elements of society, thus gaining a reputation for opposing social change and perpetuating economic injustice. The Holy See further alienated its detractors by systematic attacks on such liberal tenets as rationalism, public education, economic progress and materialism, and separation of church and state (as in the encyclical *Quanta Cura* in 1864); and by the doctrine of papal infallibility proclaimed in 1870, which made the pope's word final in matters of faith and doctrine.

The Latin American church-state conflict declined in the late nineteenth century, soon after the pope had suffered the loss of the Papal States in Italy and had become isolated in the Vatican. In this environment, the papacy pressed for expanded diplomatic relations, and by the beginning of the twentieth century it had established them with all Latin American states. These diplomatic channels were used to defend the church's property interests against liberal opposition. Anticlericalism remained strong among liberals, but an accommodation with the church was beginning to take place.

Third-Party Conflict Resolution. Two notable cases of successful papal mediation in serious Latin American conflicts—one involving Haiti and the Dominican Republic in the 1930s and the other Chile and Argentina in the 1970s and 1980s—illustrate papal activity in different parts of the region over time.

In October 1937, Dominican military forces attacked and killed large numbers of Haitian peasants near the border between the two countries. It was a bloody and tragic chapter in the long history of border disputes. A complex series of diplomatic maneuvering followed, and in time the dispute was taken up under two general inter-American treaties to which both countries were a signatory. The agreement reached was widely acclaimed as a successful utilization of the Inter-American System's structure for peaceful settlement. In fact, as the U.S. minister in the Dominican Republic observed at the time, the actual instrument of the settlement was the diplomacy of the papal nuncio who was accredited to both countries. The church offered a common meeting ground in an otherwise distrustful and hostile situation. The convention finally signed with the appearance of inter-American diplomacy was in fact the protocol originally drafted and urged on the two states by the papal nuncio.[7]

Argentina and Chile over the years contested the entire length of their mutual border. One issue involved a contentious and dangerous dispute over three islands in the Beagle Channel near Cape Horn. In 1971 they agreed to allow the British crown to arbitrate the dispute, and six years later an award was handed down that largely favored the Chilean claims. The Argentine military government rejected the decision, and in late 1978 the two countries were on the verge of war. The Holy See's observer to the Organization of American States urgently proposed papal mediation, which was readily accepted by both countries in January 1979. Almost two years later, in December 1980, the pope presented his peace proposal. Chile seemed ready to accept it, but Argentina stalled on responding. The effort was interrupted by the Anglo-Argentine war of 1982, but the papal role as third-party mediator was successfully revived. In January 1984, a month after the inauguration of civilian Argentine President Raúl Alfonsín, the two countries signed a declaration at public ceremonies in the Vatican, pledging to solve the "southern question" in the framework of papal mediation. In November 1984 the two countries signed a treaty, again at the Vatican.

Over the years, papal nuncios had attempted to mediate in internal as well as other international conflicts. They did so when dictators fell in the 1940s and 1950s in Colombia, Costa Rica, and Venezuela, for example, and they tried to avoid civil war in the Dominican Republic in 1965.

Papal Visits. When Pope Paul VI arrived in Bogotá on August 22, 1968, he became the first pontiff to visit Latin America. He attended the World Eucharistic Congress and, afterward, addressed the meeting of CELAM at Medellín. Pope John Paul II, after becoming pope in October 1978, made an extensive series of visits over the years to all parts of Latin America. Between 1979 and 1998 he traveled in the region on fourteen occasions: (1) in February 1979, to the Dominican Republic, Mexico, and the Bahamas; (2) in July 1980, to Brazil; (3) in 1983, to Central America; (4) in January and February 1985, to Venezuela, Ecuador, and Peru, with a stopover in (Anglican) Trinidad and Tobago; (5) in July 1986, to Colombia; (6) in April 1987, Chile and Argentina; (7) in May 1988, to Southern Cone states; (8) in 1990, to Mexico; (9) in October 1991, to Brazil; (10) in October 1992, to Santo Domingo (to commemorate Roman Catholicism's five hundred years in the Americas, and to attend the fourth assembly of CELAM); (11) in August 1993, to Jamaica and Mexico; (12) in February 1996, to El Salvador, Guatemala, Nicaragua, and Venezuela; (13) in October 1997, to Brazil; and (14) in January 1998, to Cuba. Almost one-fifth of Pope John Paul II's considerable overseas travel has been to Latin America.[8]

This extensive papal attention to Latin America is partly due to the fact that the region is on the verge of containing a majority of the entire world's Roman Catholics. Moreover, the Latin American church is severely divided over an array of fundamental social issues, creating some of the most controversial movements within Roman Catholicism. In addition, Protestant fundamentalist, evangelical, and Pentecostal groups since World War II have grown steadily in the region. These religious phenomena are largely a function of social factors.

The Church and Social Change

After World War I, new issues began to transcend those previously associated with church-state conflict. New social and economic concerns increasingly divided the church and complicated papal-Latin American relations. Important religious changes entered the Latin American political experience in the 1930s with the formation of Christian Democratic parties, Catholic Action groups, and Catholic labor unions. The upper clergy still tended to be conservative, but many local priests and laypeople became concerned with questions of the church's role in achieving social justice and economic development.

Beginning in the 1960s, social and economic change in Latin America accelerated dramatically. In response, church people occupied places across the entire spectrum: obedient conservatives, intransigent reactionaries, progressive reformers, and radical revolutionaries. In the 1960s the papacy finally addressed these questions directly, most notably in Pope John XXIII's encyclicals *Mater et Magistra* (1961) and *Pacem in Terris* (1963), and in Pope Paul VI's encyclical *Populorum Progreso* (1967). The worldwide ecclesiastical convention called Vatican II (1962–1965) dealt extensively with the social and economic issues. Papal positions were also articulated during the numerous visits to Latin America. In general, papal policy moved away from supporting the political and social status quo, opting for some measure of reform and opposing both reaction and revolution. Despite papal statements for change, however, the church was far from united. If anything, divisions intensified over social issues.

The lack of consensus within the church was clearly demonstrated during the visit of Pope Paul VI to Colombia in 1968 and during several trips of Pope John Paul II to the region after 1978. The debate from the beginning solidified opposing positions that continued over the years. Both popes reiterated their support for social progress but also maintained their theological conservatism and thus failed to appeal broadly to any faction. They chastised both the political Right and Left, arguing that the church must lead in the fight against poverty and injustice and oppose the concentration of wealth and power in the hands of the few, as well as the abuses of political authority. They rejected as un-Christian and impractical the idea that violence was necessary to counter these injustices; but they also alienated many progressives who would otherwise agree with notions of orderly peaceful reform by reemphasizing the ban on artificial contraception contained in the encyclical *Humanae Vitae*. Church progressives and numerous governments argued that without birth control and family planning programs, economic development would be impossible and, consequently, social injustice would persist.

Papal relations with the more radical movements within the Latin American church became increasingly important, and the related issues seemed to dominate the debate about the role of the church in social change. Some priests and laypeople argued for the relevance of Marxism to Christian social change. Some expressed admiration for slain revolutionary hero, Ernesto "Che" Guevara, and certain "Third World priests" joined guerrilla bands and engaged in violent acts. The young Colombian priest Camilo Torres Restrepo, for example, was killed by a Colombian army unit in 1966 while fighting as a member of a guerrilla group.[9] In fact, few priests joined guerrilla movements, and as military regimes disappeared and more democratic governments ascended, what came to be known as liberation theology, and related movements, became the much more important drive for change.

Liberation theology generated a great deal of controversy within the church, with considerable disagreement among Latin American bishops and conflict with the Holy See. Liberation theology is, in sum, a "theology of the poor," which argues that the church should play a central political role in the struggles for human rights and social and economic justice for the popular masses. A Peruvian priest, Gustavo Gutiérrez, is considered the first theologian to write about the various tenets that had been developing in theological terms since the late 1950s in Latin America. In time Gutiérrez was joined by a relatively small number of liberation theologians around the region, such as the Brazilian priest Leonardo Boff.[10] Much more numerous were priests and laypeople engaging in action. In particular, liberation theologians and their activist colleagues helped spawn "base communities" (*comunidades eclesiales de base*—CEBs). In practice, most CEBs were composed of groups of poor people who emphasized lay leadership and stressed experience and biblical traditions as the sources of valid religious values.

Critics and opponents sharply challenged liberation theology. They charged that it was Marxism in Christian disguise, that it was an inappropriate challenge to church authority and politicization of religion, and that it represented a "theology of violence." The detractors said that the gospel and atheistic materialism were inherently contradictory. Matters coalesced in September 1984 when Cardinal Joseph Ratzinger, prefect of the Vatican Congregation for the Doctrine of the Faith, issued "The Instruction on Certain Aspects of 'Liberation Theology.'"[11] The document pointed out the errors of the theology; in particular, it accused liberation theologians of using "concepts uncritically borrowed from Marxist ideology."

Those who did utilize Marxist concepts for analyzing society replied that they sought to recover the two-millennium Judeo-Christian tradition of biblical radicalism, and that Marxist analysis was merely an analytic tool for understanding modern class conflict and poverty. Peter Hebblethwaite argued that Pope John XXIII's encyclical, *Pacem en Terris*, justified such thinking, in that it held that "good and commendable elements" could be found in systems of thought that also contained "falsity."[12] Supporters also pointed out that the charge of politicization implied that Latin American religion in past ages was not political, which was clearly an insupportable proposition. What was new were the issues being addressed, not the church's political role. They argued that since the causes of poverty were part of social and economic structures, political action was necessary if those structures were to be changed. With regard to violence, some liberationists raised the question of whether it had ᵗheological significance but in fact did not dwell on this subject. According to Paul Sigmund, Gutiérrez proclaimed his adherence to Aquinas's Just War doctrine and expressed reservations concerning European "theologies of revolution" that appeared to "baptize" violence.[13]

Pope John Paul II remained unconvinced. He directly confronted liberation theology during his trips to Latin America. The papacy issued warnings to the Peruvian hierarchy about the dangers of liberation theology, silenced Leonardo Boff in 1985–1986 (Boff left the ministry in 1992), and censured the two priests—Miguel D'Escoto and Ernesto Cardenal—who served in the Nicaraguan revolutionary Sandinista government. The pope's actions were based partly on opposition to political action by the clergy, saying they should restrict themselves to traditional pastoral concerns, and partly on the principle of obedience to papal authority. In several messages during his visits, the pope objected to those who he said distorted the evangelical message and put it at the service of ideological and political strategies in search of "illusory earthly liberation." The gap between wealth and poverty was evil, he said, but the church's spiritual mission must never be relegated to a secondary place behind social concerns.

THE PROTESTANT CHALLENGE

From the colonial era until recent decades, Virginia Garrard-Burnett tells us, Spanish Americans widely thought of Protestantism as hostile to their faith and culture;

not until the early 1960s did Latin American perceptions change.[14] During the colo-nial period, Protestants in Spanish America were subject to persecution by the Inqui-sition; after independence their activities in the region were mostly confined to serv-ing alien European and North American residents. The first foreign missionaries in Latin America on a permanent basis arrived during the mid-nineteenth century and were mostly members of immigrant churches from Europe. From the 1860s into the 1880s, they were welcomed by certain liberal governments who saw Protestant activ-ities as supporting their anti-conservative reforms. They were followed by Protestant missionaries from the United States in the early twentieth century, who established a permanent presence for their denominations but converted few people. In the mean-time, fundamentalist Protestants had revolted against modernist biblical views, bro-ken away from the established "mainline" or "historical" churches, organized their own congregations, and undertaken activities in Latin America. In the 1940s some fundamentalists renamed themselves evangelicals, reflecting their desire to rise above sectarian disputes and to concentrate on evangelizing the world. Their activities also had minimal impact in Latin America.

Finally, in the early 1960s, Latin American conversion rates began to increase dra-matically, especially to Pentecostal evangelical churches. According to David Stoll, even though the majority of Protestant missionaries have come from non-Pente-costal backgrounds, between two-thirds and three-quarters of all Latin American Protestants belong to Pentecostal churches.[15] Their activities eventually eroded Ro-man Catholicism to some degree in virtually all Latin American countries, to the ex-tent that in the region at large they account for at least 12 percent of the population (a conservative estimate), with the number growing rapidly. They are above the re-gional average (up to 22 percent) in Argentina, Brazil, Chile, Colombia, Dominican Republic, Ecuador, Haiti, Paraguay, Venezuela, and most of Central America (ex-cepting Costa Rica and including Panama). In Guatemala, evangelicals account for one-third of the population, the vast majority of which are Pentecostals.

What accounts for this rapid Protestant, and particularly Pentecostal, success? One factor that has been suggested is the benefit for Protestantism in general of the changes in Roman Catholicism brought about by Vatican II, which stimulated many Latin Americans to leave the Catholic Church. Another is that, with the large bud-gets enjoyed by the Pentecostal churches, the Latin American Roman Catholic Church was increasingly constrained in the competition by its own restricted human and financial resources—as well as by the limits imposed by the Holy See.[16]

David Martin argues from a sociological viewpoint that in those parts of Latin America where faith remains but is "disarticulated" from Roman Catholicism, Protestantism can become "an empowering religion for the poor."[17] But why did Pentecostals have such appeal for the same sectors that seemed to support liberation theology? Why have the CEBs found themselves particularly vulnerable to competi-tion with Pentecostals in attracting the poor? Why would poor people, alienated from traditional Catholic social attitudes and seeking change through political ac-tivism, respond to the Pentecostal's detachment from the world? Stoll suggests that liberation theology did not express popular aspirations as effectively as it was presumed to; Garrard-Burnett adds that people seek out evangelical churches partly because they offer refuge from political involvement, including the danger posed by both church and state opponents of liberation theology. She also argues that observers overlook the complexity of Pentecostal detachment—as a pragmatic strategy for survival in this world as they await the next, adherents must build networks of emotional, economic, and even political support.[18]

The Holy See and the Roman Catholic Church in Latin America viewed Protestant expansion as a serious threat and responded with a sense of competition and conflict. Ken Serbin points out that Roman Catholic enmity does not extend to the presence of "mainline" Protestant denominations (Anglicans and Episcopalians, Methodists, Presbyterians, Lutherans, and others) who have established ecumenical relationships with Roman Catholics.[19] Considerable disagreement arose among Roman Catholics over how to respond to the threat. Some argued for a conservative approach that strengthened and preserved the existing church presence and activity. Others urged co-optation by way of a greater role for the laity. Pope John Paul in his later trips to Latin America called for a closing of Catholic ranks against the "invasion of sects" and for a "new evangelization" on the part of Roman Catholics. He used particularly strong language in 1991 in Brazil (the world's largest Roman Catholic country), accusing evangelical "sects" of offering "false mirages" and "distorted simplifications." He admonished Brazilian bishops to undertake Catholic evangelization to overcome the moral deterioration that had left Brazilians vulnerable to those overtures. The pope's concerns were echoed by sympathetic elements at the fourth CELAM assembly at Santo Domingo in 1992. In his visit to Mexico in 1993, the pope's condemnation of the condition of Indians seemed at least partially inspired by the numbers who had converted to Pentecostal evangelism.

BUSINESS ENTERPRISE AND
MULTINATIONAL CORPORATIONS

Corporations as System Actors

A multinational corporation (MNC) is a group entity with a legal personality. Although corporate control remains centered within some sovereign state, the corporation exhibits a great deal of independence as an actor in the international political system. The prefix "multi" indicates that MNCs have business activities in a number of states and have extensive resources. Other definitional distinctions have been offered to conceptualize the nature and roles of business organizations as actors in the international system. An "international" firm, with headquarters located in a specific state and ownership vested in that state's nationals, enters foreign markets by direct investment as an extension of the parent company in order to develop foreign sources of supply, primarily to serve its domestic (home) market. International corporations act across state boundaries but retain the nationality of their parent company, which makes the major policy decisions. A literally or purely "transnational" company, like the MNC, would allocate its resources apart from state boundary considerations, but unlike the MNC its ownership, management, and decisions would transcend national considerations. Most major global corporations today are MNCs, which dominate the world industrial order while remaining domiciled in industrial states. Although private business enterprise has long been a part of the international scene, the MNC is a relatively new actor in world politics.[20]

International companies originally were creations and subjects of the state. For example, in colonial America the Dutch West Indies Company was chartered by the sovereign monarch and, although funded by private capital, it was subject to royal control and entitled to state protection. Over the years, however, the nature of overseas business enterprises underwent dramatic changes, and, consequently, their roles as international actors changed. In the nineteenth century, business corporations began to develop in the capitalist economies in Great Britain, Europe, and the United States. They were not multinational in character, however, as their activities and power were restricted by the states granting corporate charters. International firms were generally limited to a specific economic activity, such as banking, mining, agriculture, or manufacturing, and their life spans and total assets were limited by law. By the time of World War I, however, according to Raymond Vernon "corporations could be formed by practically anyone for practically any purpose without limit of time or size." Even more important, he said, "corporations by this time had acquired the extraordinary right to own other corporations." Consequently, separate companies could be created to perform different aspects of a total business activity, but all of the activities would be subject to centralized control, coordination, and support.[21] Modern corporations acquired a distinct multinational character as they began to branch out into several different sovereign jurisdictions, with various enterprises linked together by a single corporate structure.

The growth of MNCs was especially significant after World War II, the size of their overseas assets dwarfing those of the past. U.S., European, and Japanese companies increased their foreign assets at rapid rates in virtually all parts of the world. Later, MNCs evolved in newly industrializing parts of the world, including Latin America. Well over 4,000 MNCs now exist, accounting for about one-third of the gross world production of goods and services. But a great proportion of the activity is controlled by a small number of large corporations in a few industrial sectors. In the petroleum industry, the "Seven Sisters"—Exxon (Standard Oil of New Jersey), Standard Oil of California, The Royal Dutch Shell Group, Texaco, Gulf, Mobil, and British Petroleum—dominate the world's oil production, control more than half of the oil tanker tonnage, and retail about half of the petroleum products on world markets. Nine automotive producers—General Motors, Ford, Chrysler, Volkswagen, Fiat, British Motors, Nissan, Toyota, and Honda—dominate global automotive markets. The electronics industry, the third largest industrial sector, is composed essentially of the major U.S., Japanese, and European firms. A half-dozen mining companies account for three-fourths of the international trade in metals and other ores, and a few companies control world chemical markets.

The main operational goal of both foreign and domestic corporate foreign policy is assumed to be the maximization of profits. Business enterprises, like states, act in their own interests, which, ultimately, are survival, security, and well-being. Once the fundamental concerns of assuring survival and securing resources are provided for, policy success is measured in terms of monetary profit and corporate growth. Thus, foreign operations are rationalized in economic terms, principally the beneficial employment of capital resources. Modern technology has increasingly stimulated the growth of large companies requiring access to global markets, and the world economy encourages direct overseas investment. But international and multinational business relations, involving as they do corporate relations with both foreign and home governments, are inseparable from politics. Companies have used many of the same strategies and tactics in external relations as states have, including cooperative ones such as negotiation and persuasion, as well as coercion and subversion. Consequently, MNCs have foreign departments or overseas divisions devoted to "foreign policy-making" and execution—these operations come complete with a foreign service and interact with sovereign states.

Corporate Actors in Latin America

International and multinational business enterprise in Latin America has been a controversial activity. Business entities have negotiated with sovereign states, but they have also engaged in espionage; they have pursued unsavory activities designed to influence foreign officials, such as bribery; and they have been involved in the subversion of governments. Spectacular examples of past business intervention include United Fruit Company activities in Central America from the early part of the twentieth century through the 1930s. Coercion through threats of violence to force small farmers to sell exclusively to United Fruit at company prices, bribery of public officials, and even the sponsoring of coups earned United Fruit the popular name of *el pulpo* (the octopus). Oil company ventures in Mexico and Peru also often involved corrupt practices. In a more recent example, oil companies whose interests had been expropriated in Cuba by the Castro regime exerted influential pressure on the U.S. government in favor of the Bay of Pigs. International Telephone and Telegraph (ITT) took measures in Chile to disrupt the Marxist government of Salvador Allende (1970–1973). Bribery of Latin American officials by U.S. companies, including United Brands in Honduras and Gulf Oil in Bolivia, was revealed in 1975.

Evidence also exists to support the view that U.S. companies cooperate with their Latin American hosts as good corporate citizens. For example, Stephen Rosenfield, writing in the *Washington Post* on January 28, 1972, reported on a series of discussions about relations between U.S. business firms and Latin American government officials, sponsored by the Council on Foreign Relations in 1971. He concluded that the proceedings revealed "not a calculated or malevolent or exploitation-minded conspiracy of the bureaucratic-investment complex"; rather, "there was evident an inclination to consider new forms of American economic participation on terms politically acceptable in the hemisphere, and a parallel inclination to avoid the kinds of political confrontation that would spoil the chances for future profit." In the latter 1980s and into the 1990s, the image of MNCs improved considerably, at least among those Latin American government officials and those in domestic sectors who embraced economic neoliberalism and sought increased foreign investment. Nevertheless, problems continued to arise in the post–cold war era, with allegations of wrongdoing and questionable business practices (such as bribery) being brought against corporations.

For many years a paramount issue was that of excessive foreign business profits from Latin American operations. Ascertaining the profits of foreign enterprises has been difficult to analyze, especially after the arrival of holding companies and large corporations with networks of branches and affiliates in several states, which often issued "no-par" common stock.[22] As John Hunter and James Foley have noted, no definition exists of what constitutes a "fair" or "excessive" rate of return.[23] Furthermore, the meaningfulness of available data is questionable. These authors, defining an annual rate of return as the ratio of total earnings to the total outstanding investment before the payment of corporate income taxes, pointed out that caution should be exercised in analyzing published figures, primarily because of the nature of accounting procedures. Rates of return depend on the value placed on assets, which is difficult to determine precisely. Capital is often invested in kind as well as money, and inflation makes further valuations problematical. In addition, in order to show a lower rate of return, foreign companies may purposely overvalue their assets or sell their locally produced products to their external parent at low prices.

Nevertheless, some conclusions have been made about past foreign business profits in Latin America. With regard to British investments in the nineteenth century into the twentieth, Van Alstyne concluded "that few British investors enjoyed anything better than a small return for their money, that the risks in many cases (particularly mining) were great and the losses considerable, and that salaried employees, manufacturers in Great Britain, exporters and shipping companies benefited more than did the direct investor."[24] Research by J. Fred Rippy focusing on U.S. investments during the first half of the twentieth century disclosed high yields for a few business organizations. Dividends paid by some small mining companies in Mexico were fantastic— one paid an annual average dividend of 945.8 percent from 1903 to 1927, and another an annual average of 124.5 percent from 1908 to 1926. Rippy calculated that the large mining and petroleum companies probably made large profits on their Latin American investments. He noted that Creole Petroleum Company in Venezuela paid an annual average dividend of 31.8 percent on its common stock from 1936 to 1951, and that International Petroleum Company in Peru and Colombia returned an average annual dividend of more than 40 percent from 1921 to 1950. However, Rippy said, many foreign business organizations in Latin America yielded only moderate profits or suffered heavy losses. Most agricultural enterprises had only a few profitable years, with the exceptions of the Cuban American Sugar Company and the United Fruit Company; those attempting to grow plantation rubber in Mexico and Central

America from 1890 to 1910 lost heavily. Finally, railways and public utilities were not among the business organizations enjoying high yields.

For the first ten years following World War II, the highest returns for U.S. investors in Latin America came from petroleum (24.4 percent) and agriculture (16.8 percent—mainly sugar). Returns came to 11.5 percent from mining, 14.4 percent from manufacturing, and 17.3 percent from trading companies. The lowest returns were from public utilities. The average return for the decade was 14.6 percent per year. During the period from 1960 to 1967, average rates of return for U.S. investments in manufacturing were generally lower in Latin America (10.3 percent) than in all other world regions except Canada.[25] In the 1980s, with the onset of the severe debt problem and spectacular Latin American inflation rates, the region became unattractive to foreign corporate investors because of the fear of large losses on investment. With increased political and economic stabilization by the end of the decade, however, investors again saw opportunities in the region and commenced to work out investment and profit remittance "rules of the game" in the context of bilateral arrangements and within economic integration organizations and other free agreements.

The Evolution of Business Activity in Latin America

British capital accounted for most of the foreign investment in Latin America from the early national period until the world depression of 1930. Toward the end of the nineteenth century, French, German, and U.S. capital became significant. By then, Latin America was receiving investments from virtually every nation in Europe and some from Japan. Most of the investment was portfolio in nature, financing projects through the purchase of Latin American government bonds and leaving operational administration to local management. However, important operations were also begun by foreign entrepreneurs through direct investment and management.

Toward the end of the nineteenth century, international business actors who were to enjoy many years of large-scale activity in Latin America began to appear. The most important sectors for foreign direct investments included extractive operations (petroleum production and tin, copper, and nitrate mining); forestry and agriculture (coffee, sugar, meats, and tropical fruits, including bananas); banking; and some specialized manufacturing areas. U.S. investors, unlike investors from other nations, were as interested in direct as in portfolio investments, and Latin American markets were seen to offer U.S. companies important opportunities. After 1930, portfolio investments greatly declined for a variety of reasons, and direct investments increased. U.S. capital came to assume a dominant position. In the 1930s and 1940s no less than 300 U.S. companies dominated foreign business operations in Latin America, and by 1950 U.S. investments were twice as large as all others combined. European and Japanese investments were sharply reduced, especially by the impact of two world wars.

A few examples suffice to illustrate the growth of business actors in the Latin American region. Richard Van Alstyne offered the case of George Drabble of Manchester, who in the late 1840s went to Buenos Aires and in time "played a part in the formation of every important enterprise in that country during the next two decades"—including the first railway line built in Argentina, the Bank of London and the River Plate, the Buenos Aires Tramway Company, the Buenos Aires and Rosario Railway, and the River Plate Fresh Meat Company.[26] Beginning in the late nineteenth century in Argentina, Armour and Company and Swift and Company competed with British concerns in meat processing and exporting. Both companies expanded to Uruguay and Paraguay, and through the 1960s those three countries were important suppliers for both companies' overall operations. In Chile and Peru, U.S. mining companies dominated copper and other mineral extraction from the late nineteenth century until the 1960s; the most important of these companies were Kennecott, Anaconda, and Cerro de Pasco. The Singer Company, founded in Boston in 1850, from the early days of its sewing machine business established foreign subsidiaries. By World War I, Singer was well established in all of Latin America. It remained so in the mid-1990s, with the Brazilian subsidiary one of its largest branches.

In Peru in the 1870s a U.S. adventurer and railroad builder, Henry Meiggs, built lines across the Andes and created a financial empire. In Peru at about the same time, a young Irish immigrant, William Russell Grace, began a small business of servicing ships that transported guano fertilizer. He parlayed this modest beginning into the large and highly diversified W. R. Grace and Company, a trading firm headquartered in New York and operating in all of Latin America. Known as Casa Grace in Latin America, its regional operations by the 1970s had dwindled to only a minority of its global business. During the latter part of the nineteenth century, Henry Meiggs's nephew, Minor Cooper Keith, established railways in Central America and then developed some banana plantations and shipping lines to U.S. ports. In 1899, after thirty years of intense rivalry with his competitors, Keith took over most of the other small banana companies and organized the United Fruit Company, thereafter a major political actor in Central America, with headquarters in New York. In 1970 the company acquired John Morrell and Company, adding meat packing to its Chiquita banana enterprise and changing its corporate name to United Brands. In 1984, Carl H. Lindner, a Cincinnati financier, gained controlling interest in United Brands. He broke up the United Brands conglomerate, selling off certain operations (but keeping the Morrell Co.). By 1990, when he renamed the company Chiquita Brands International, it was selling about one-third of the world's supply of bananas, most of which it grew in Central America. The company also applied the Chiquita name to other fruits and packaged goods.

The activities of oil companies have also been important in Latin America. The Standard Oil Company of New Jersey (created in 1873 by John D. Rockefeller as the Standard Oil Trust) and the binational Royal Dutch Shell Group (a merger in 1897 of the Royal Dutch Petroleum Company and the British-owned Shell Transport and Trading Company) established major operations in Mexico and Venezuela after the discovery of oil in both states in the 1890s. The largest single petroleum operation in Latin America for many years was run in Venezuela by the Creole Oil Company, a subsidiary of Standard Oil. Both Standard and Shell had difficulties with Mexico, beginning with the revolution in 1910, and were expropriated in 1938. In the 1930s Venezuela became the principal supplier for both companies, remaining so until their Middle East operations surpassed Venezuelan production in the 1960s. Venezuela nationalized the Standard and Shell operations in 1975. Gulf, Texaco, and other oil companies have also been active in a number of Latin American nations. They continued to operate in several countries, although they also were targets of Latin American nationalists and suffered expropriations, such as in Peru and Bolivia in the late 1960s.

European banks became well-established in the region during the nineteenth century and remained so to the present day. Among the most important was the Bank of London and South America (BOLSA), a joint Canadian-British chartered enterprise. It was acquired by Lloyds Bank of London in 1971. French and German banks also gained important positions in the banking sector. The U.S. Federal Reserve Act became effective in June 1914, allowing U.S. banks to establish overseas branches. They were led by the National City Bank of New York (later First National City Bank, and then Citibank), which in 1914 opened its first overseas branch in Buenos Aires; considerable and continuous activity throughout the region ensued. Other U.S. banks followed suit, with the Chase Manhattan Bank, the Bank of Boston, and the Bank of America prominent among them. After World War II, Canada's giant chartered banks, such as the Royal Bank of Canada and Bank of Nova Scotia, expanded into the British Caribbean colonial islands and territories. They dominated the banking systems of the independent Commonwealth Caribbean Countries and were active in the remainder of the circum-Caribbean.[27]

After World War II, U.S. and European companies placed a new emphasis on manufacturing, retailing, communications, and service industries in addition to the traditional concentration on extractive, agricultural, and trading concerns. International Telephone and Telegraph became a major and controversial actor in Latin America. Founded in 1920 by Virgin Islander Sosthenes Behn as a small telephone company in Puerto Rico, ITT became a worldwide telephone and cable communications firm operating extensively in Latin America. The Ford, Chrysler, General Motors, Volkswagen, Fiat, and Renault automotive companies placed assembly plants in Argentina, Brazil, and Mexico. Sears, Roebuck, and Company founded a chain of stores in several parts of the region, selling goods produced mostly by local industries. The hotel industry expanded far beyond the long-popular tourist areas in Mexico and the Caribbean. Much of the business initially belonged to the Intercontinental Hotel Corporation, a subsidiary of Pan American World Airways. In the 1960s the Sheraton and Hilton chains expanded significantly into Latin America; Sheraton was acquired by ITT. Japanese corporations did not engage in overseas production facilities to the same extent as U.S. and European companies; rather, they sold products through large trading companies serving industrial firms through overseas offices.

Important investment companies also appeared on the Latin American scene. Atlantic Community Development Group for Latin America (ADELA) was established in 1956 as a private multinational consortium sponsoring private foreign investment in Latin America. Capitalized by contributions from U.S. and European firms, it provided financial backing for new enterprises by Latin American business-people in a variety of fields. International Basic Economy Corporation (IBEC) was started by Nelson Rockefeller in 1947 to introduce new ventures to underdeveloped areas for both profit and local development. Significant Latin American ventures included the hybrid corn business in Brazil and the introduction of "supermarkets" to Venezuela, Peru, and Argentina.

Several multibusiness associations having a primary concern with Latin America have been organized. A nonprofit organization supported by member corporations, the United States Inter-American Council, was founded in New York in 1958. Its name was changed to Council for Latin America in 1965 and, in 1970, to Council of the Americas; it also opened a Washington office. The Council's stated purpose is "to further understanding and acceptance of the role of private enterprise as a positive force for the development of the Americas." The Inter-American Council for Commerce and Production (known by its Spanish acronym CICYP) was established in 1960 by U.S. and Latin American companies, individual businesspersons and economists, and developmental organizations. At its meetings in U.S. and Latin American cities, CICYP stressed the role of private enterprise in Latin American economic integration, active business participation in the making of public economic policy, and the need to stimulate foreign private investments through such vehicles as ADELA.

The 1970s into the 1980s was a period characterized by difficult MNC-Latin American relations, in contrast to the expansion of direct foreign investment in the 1950s and 1960s. Certain Latin American governments engaged in nationalizations, and many placed restrictions on the remittance of profits, discouraging MNC investments. Although commercial bank lending expanded significantly in the 1970s, the severe debt problems in the following decade further discouraged foreign private capital investment.[28] Existing ventures were scaled down or terminated, and new ones were generally not forthcoming.

After the mid-1980s and into the 1990s, investors again manifested interest in Latin America. Their increasing investment activity was sparked by developments in the region having to do with the end of the debt crisis and reduced inflation, and with newly adopted neoliberal government policies that lowered barriers to trade and put foreign firms on a non-discriminatory basis. After about 1987 U.S. companies significantly expanded their investments in Latin America, as markets there were increasingly opened. According to the UN Economic Commission on Latin America and the Caribbean, during the first three years of the 1990s U.S. direct investment in the region increased by $12.6 billion, or 16.6 percent, to $88.9 billion.[29] That amount represented 18.3 percent of total $486.7 billion U.S. investment abroad. In Latin America it continued to be concentrated in finance (with a share of 46 percent) and manufacturing (30 percent), followed by banking (9 percent), petroleum (5 percent), trade (4 percent), and all other categories (7 percent). Bermuda was the largest recipient of investment at $25.8 billion, an amount accounted for mostly by the financial sector and the repayments of loans by finance affiliates; Panama ranked third, at $11.5 billion, largely for the same reason. Other leading recipients, with more balanced investment sectors, were Brazil ($16.1 billion) and Mexico ($13.3 billion). MNC operations in Chile, Argentina, and Venezuela were also notable. The positive expectations of U.S. MNCs were also based on the possibilities for freer trade throughout the hemisphere held out by the Enterprise for the Americas Initiative, posed by the United States in June 1990. Most MNC executives looked favorably on the commencement of the North American Free Trade Agreement (NAFTA) in January 1994. In this regard, Canadian banks and companies have become major players, with Canada's generally increased interest in the region in the post–cold war era and, more specifically, as a partner in NAFTA.

NOTES

1. This definition draws on U.S. Department of State, "The Holy See," *Background Notes* (March 1987).
2. Thomas Sanders, "The Church in Latin America," *Foreign Affairs* 48 (January 1970): 285–299.
3. Víctor Alba, "Vatican Diplomacy in Latin America," in *Latin American Foreign Policies*, ed. Harold Eugene Davis and Larman C. Wilson (Baltimore: Johns Hopkins University Press, 1975).
4. Sister M. Noel Menezes, R.S.M., "Missionaries of Charity," in *Encyclopedia of Latin American History and Culture*, ed. Barbara A. Tennenbaum, vol. 4 (New York: Charles Scribner's Sons, 1996), 72.
5. A dated but useful history until the date of publication is Avro Manhattan, *Latin America and the Vatican* (London: Watts, 1946). General works that include transnational aspects are Edward L. Cleary and Hannah Stewart-Gambino, eds., *Conflict and Competition: The Latin American Church in a Changing Environment* (Boulder, Colo.: Lynne Rienner Publishers, 1992); Daniel H. Levine, *Religion and Political Conflict in Latin America* (Chapel Hill: University of North Carolina Press, 1986); and Edward A. Lynch, *Religion and Politics in Latin America* (New York: Praeger, 1991).
6. Alba, "Vatican Diplomacy in Latin America," 104.
7. G. Pope Atkins and Larman C. Wilson, *The Dominican Republic and the United States* (Athens: University of Georgia Press, 1998), 72–78.
8. Héctor Ferllini S., Miguel Díaz S., and Oscar Castillo, eds., *Un Viaje Histórico: El Papa en una Región de Conflicto* (San José: Urux Editores, 1983) includes pronouncements and speeches by Pope John Paul II during his 1983 visit to Central America and Haiti.
9. See Camilo Torres, *Revolutionary Priest: The Complete Writings and Messages of Camilo Torres*, ed. John Gerassi (New York: Random House, 1971); and Walter J. Broderick, *Camilo Torres: A Biography of the Priest-Guerrillero* (New York: Doubleday, 1975).
10. See Gustavo Gutiérrez, *Theology of Liberation: History, Politics, and Salvation* (Maryknoll, N.Y.: Orbis, 1973). Also of particular interest are Leonardo Boff, *Church Charisma and Power: Liberation Theology and the Institutional Church* (New York: Crossroad, 1985); and Ernesto Cardenal, *The Gospel in Solentiname*, 4 vols. (New York: Orbis 1976–1982). Philip Berryman, *Liberation Theology: Essential Facts About the Revolutionary Religious Movement in*

Latin America and Beyond (Philadelphia: Temple University Press, 1987) is an informative and sympathetic treatment of liberation theology by a U.S. priest; and Michael Novak, *Liberation Theology and the Liberal Society* (Washington, D.C.: AEI Press, 1987) is a negative critique by a U.S. conservative intellectual. See also Michael R. Candelaria, *Popular Liberation and Liberation: The Dilemma of Liberation Theology* (Albany: State University of New York Press, 1990); and Paul E. Sigmund, *Liberation Theology at the Crossroads: Democracy or Revolution?* (New York: Oxford University Press, 1990).

11. Sigmund, *Liberation Theology at the Crossroads*, chapter 9, notes that the Congregation for the Doctrine of the Faith was established in 1965 at the end of Vatican II as a more positively oriented theological body to replace the Holy Office. It had been created in 1908 to take over the functions of the Sacred Congregation of the Universal Inquisition, founded in 1542 to combat heresy.

12. Peter Hebblethwaite, *Pope John XXIII: Shepherd of the Modern World* (New York: Doubleday, 1985).

13. Sigmund, *Liberation Theology at the Crossroads*, 157.

14. This discussion depends on Virginia Garrard-Burnett, "Protestantism," in Tennenbaum, *Encyclopedia of Latin American History and Culture*, 475–477; and Virginia Garrard-Burnett and David Stoll, *Rethinking Protestantism in Latin America* (Philadelphia: Temple University Press, 1993). See also Edward L. Cleary and Hannah Stewart-Gambino, eds., *Power, Politics, and Pentecostals in Latin America* (Boulder, Colo.: Westview Press, 1997); Anne Motley Hallum, *Beyond Missionaries: Toward an Understanding of the Protestants in Central America* (Lanham, Md.: Rowman and Littlefield, 1966); David Martin, *Tongues of Fire: The Explosion of Protestantism in Latin America* (Oxford, U.K.: Basil Blackwell, 1990); Daniel R. Miller, *Coming of Age, Protestantism in Contemporary Latin America* (Lanham, Md.: University Press of America, 1994); and David Stoll, *Is Latin America Turning Protestant? The Politics of Evangelical Growth* (Berkeley: University of California Press, 1990).

15. It may be helpful to provide a modicum of definitional information. Fundamentalism is a movement in U.S. Protestantism that arose in the early twentieth century and that stresses scripture as the inerrant source of faith and doctrine and as literal historical record. Evangelical churches, based on the term "evangelize" (preaching the gospel and converting others to Christianity), emphasize the authority of New Testament scriptures over that of the church itself, as well as the personal nature of original sin and reconciliation of God through Christ. Pentecostal groups, a Protestant, evangelical subgroup, adopted their name with reference to the Christian belief in the descent of the Holy Ghost upon the apostles following the crucifixion and resurrection. David Stoll says Pentecostals "claim to receive special gifts from the Holy Spirit—speaking in tongues, faith healing, and prophecy—that non-Pentecostal fundamentalists and evangelicals eschew" (Garrard-Burnett and Stoll, *Rethinking Protestantism in Latin America*). A problem is posed by the fact that Latin American Protestants tend to call themselves *evangélicos* regardless of denomination.

16. Cleary and Stewart-Gambino, *Conflict and Competition*.

17. Martin, *Tongues of Fire*.

18. Garrard-Burnett and Stoll, *Rethinking Protestantism in Latin America*.

19. Ken Serbin, "Latin America's Catholic Church: Religious Rivalries and the North-South Divide." *North-South Issues* 2, no. 1 (1993).

20. Analytic treatments of MNCs reached their height in the mid-1970s and afterwards declined, as did external investment in the region. See Richard S. Barnet and Ronald E. Muller, *Global Reach: The Power of the Multinational Corporations* (New York: Simon and

Schuster, 1975); Jack N. Behrman, *The Role of International Companies in Latin America* (Lexington, Mass.: Lexington Books, 1972); Donald P. Irish, ed., *Multinational Corporations in Latin America* (Athens: Ohio University Press, 1978); Raymond Vernon, *Sovereignty at Bay: The Multinational Spread of U.S. Enterprises* (New York: Basic Books, 1971); Mira Wilkins, *The Emergence of Multinational Enterprise* (Cambridge: Harvard University Press, 1970); and Mira Wilkins, *The Maturing of Multinational Enterprise* (Cambridge: Harvard University Press, 1974). On more recent developments see Robert Grosse, *Multinationals in Latin America* (London: Routledge, 1989).

21. Vernon, *Sovereignty at Bay*, 1–2.

22. J. Fred Rippy, *Globe and Hemisphere* (Chicago: Henry Regnery, 1958), 47.

23. John M. Hunter and James W. Foley, *Economic Problems of Latin America* (Boston: Houghton Mifflin, 1975), 208–209.

24. Richard W. Van Alstyne, "Britain in Latin America after 1865," *Current History* 28 (March 1955): 153.

25. Rippy, *Globe and Hemisphere*, 47–52; Hunter and Foley, *Economic Problems of Latin America*, 208.

26. Van Alstyne, "Britain in Latin America after 1865."

27. John D. Hebron, "Turning Over a New Leaf in the Americas," *Hemisfile* 4 no. 1 (January/February 1993): 8–9.

28. Robert Grosse, *Multinationals in Latin America* (London: Routledge, 1989).

29. *CEPAL News*, vol. 13, no. 10, October 1993.

CHAPTER ELEVEN

■

Subnational Actors and Networks

Subnational actors (intrastate nongovernmental entities) are relatively autonomous parts of a state political system. They are transnational when they form relationships across state boundaries and become parts of transnational or transsocietal networks. The specific actors in this category in the Latin American and Caribbean context that are identified and analyzed in this chapter are political party associations, international labor movements, and guerrilla groups.

POLITICAL PARTY ASSOCIATIONS

Political Parties as Independent Actors

Political parties are groups that seek to obtain public office and political power by presenting candidates to the electorate. Transnational political parties transcend state boundaries and seek international acceptance in an organized way. The affiliates to a transnational party share a philosophy and common goals to some degree, coordinate their interests and ideas, and offer mutual support. The national identities of transnational parties may be primary, but their connections across national boundaries are discernible.

A number of transnational parties have been active in Latin America. The most important ones originated outside the region and later established Latin American counterparts, including the Communist parties organized in the Communist International (Comintern), the Social Democratic parties in the Socialist International, and the Christian Democratic parties in the Christian Democratic World Union. Political parties in the United States are only peripherally relevant to Latin America. The Democratic and Republican parties are essentially national parties and not internationalized. They have interests and sympathies abroad but have not established systematic transnational ties with kindred parties. Their Puerto Rican counterparts are active only in the context of U.S. national elections, in which Puerto Ricans vote.

The Comintern and the Socialist International both emerged from the nineteenth-century European socialist movement. The First International, originally called the Workers' International Association, was formed by Karl Marx in 1864 and dissolved in 1876. The Second International (the Labor International) held its first meeting in 1889 and continued until its collapse in 1914, with the outbreak of World War I. Neither the First nor Second International involved Latin America; except for small sections in the United States, both were European organizations.

Members of the internationals shared the goal of uniting the workers of the world and taking power from their class enemies, but tensions increased over the years between totalitarian and democratic strains of Marxism. They achieved separate identities after World War I and thereafter went their separate ideological and organizational ways as bitter rivals. The Third International, also called the Communist International and known as the Comintern, was founded by Lenin in 1919, following the successful Bolshevik Revolution of 1917 and the establishment of the Soviet Union. With the purpose of organizing revolutions through Communist parties in every country throughout the world, the Comintern developed extensive Latin American connections. It was dissolved in 1943.

Social Democrats, opposing Bolshevist totalitarianism, claimed to reconvene the Second International in 1920. In 1923 they called themselves the Socialist and Labor International and explicitly disassociated from the Comintern as a rival organization. The Socialist International remained an essentially European movement, with only a few, small American elements. It was interrupted by World War II, but in 1945 it reorganized as the International Socialist Conference with headquarters in London. It took the name Socialist International in 1951 at the pivotal Frankfurt Conference, which adopted the "Principles and Tasks of Democratic Socialism." In time the Socialist International expanded to include Social Democratic and Labor parties in many countries, including Latin America.

In the meantime, another competing party emerged with yet another distinct orientation. Christian Democratic parties appeared around Europe in the 1890s, espousing a sort of clerical Fabian socialism. More interest groups than political parties, they defended Roman Catholic interests on the grassroots level. The European organizations broadened their bases and became real political parties in the 1920s. They were still Roman Catholic in outlook, but they sought to appeal to the interests of broader segments of the electorate. They also shifted from socialism to traditional liberalism. This fundamental change was in opposition to events within the socialist movement—both the adoption of Bolshevism in the Communist International and the rise of trade union socialism in the Socialist International. The transnational Christian Democratic World Union was not formed until the late 1940s. By then its traditional liberal tenets (such as individualism, limited government roles, and laissez-faire economics) were identified with postwar conservatism. The transnational organization included Latin American counterparts.

Both the Social Democratic and Christian Democratic parties in Europe went through evolutionary stages of development that are relevant to understanding their Latin American connections. They gained governmental power in the 1920s and 1930s in Europe, but their general ineffectiveness convinced them of the need for broader electoral appeal. The religious base of the Christian Democrats precluded their appealing to anticlerical elements, whereas the trade unionist Social Democrats could make few inroads with propertied classes or industrial interests. After World War II, both parties reduced their ideological insistence in successful concerted efforts to broaden their political bases and consequently became the two major European parties. At the Frankfurt Conference in 1951, the Social Democrats acknowledged the utility of mixed private and public economic sectors, depending on individual national conditions, and in 1959 they formally disavowed Marxism and social revolution. Soon thereafter the Christian Democrats came to accept a degree of state intervention into economic and social affairs. Fundamental differences remained, however. In general, Christian Democrats may be characterized as moderate conservatives with a strong right wing, and the Social Democrats as moderate socialists with a strong left wing. Latin American counterparts did not necessarily follow the same process.

The Communist International and Latin America

In an earlier era international communism could have been called a major global transnational political movement.[1] After its founding in March 1919, the Comintern headquarters was in Moscow throughout its twenty-four year existence. The Comintern included members in almost all countries, and they sent delegates to Moscow to plan the promotion of Communist revolutions outside of the Soviet Union. The Soviet government denied that the Comintern was an instrument of the Soviet state, although in fact it viewed the organization as a tool of Soviet policy.

The founding of local Communist parties and the Latin American section of the Comintern created opportunities for extending revolutionary activities in the region. Under Comintern guidance, the Mexican Communist Party was more successful in fostering communism in Central America than in Mexico itself, as Mexicans preferred to make their own revolution without outside assistance. In South America the Argentine Communist Party was the first to join the Comintern. A South American Comintern secretariat was set up in Buenos Aires in 1930 and assigned the task of strengthening Communist influence and supervising the flow of agents in the Southern Cone.

Between the two world wars, Soviet policy was aimed at creating loyal and disciplined local Communist parties, with some success. In Chile, the organization of a strong Communist Party contributed to formation of a popular front coalition that brought the Radical Party to power in 1938. Thus, Chile became the third country, after France and Spain, to be ruled by popular fronts. Otherwise, the Soviet strategy was a failure.

Communism faced the continuing dilemma of reconciling Soviet foreign policy interests, the narrow Comintern sectarian approach, and the needs of local Communist parties. In Latin America in the late 1920s and throughout the 1930s, Comintern tactics made little progress toward revolution, but they did provoke a rupture of Soviet diplomatic relations with Mexico and Argentina in 1930, with Chile in

1932, and with Brazil and Uruguay in 1936. Dogmatic Comintern directives to local Communist parties and the Soviet preoccupation with domestic and proximate
international problems did not enhance revolutionary chances. Furthermore, radical
Latin American nationalists initially were more inclined to opt for Italian fascism
than for Soviet communism.

In 1943 Moscow announced that the Comintern had been dissolved. Throughout
the 1920s and 1930s, the Soviet Union had remained the world's only Communist
country; the Comintern purpose of sparking revolution elsewhere had obviously not
succeeded. Thereafter, Communist parties continued to work for the overthrow of
established governments without the Comintern; in Latin America they succeeded
nowhere. For a brief period during and immediately after World War II, from about
1941 to 1947, the Soviet Union and Latin American Communist parties did enjoy
influence in the region. The wartime alliance between the Soviet Union and the
Western powers facilitated the expansion of Soviet diplomatic contacts in the region,
and Latin American Communist parties achieved a certain level of prestige. Those
parties were directed by Moscow to support the Allied war effort and to use their influence to prevent strikes and the disruption of war production.

The onset of the cold war in 1947 reversed the trend. Soviet relations with Latin
America became increasingly strained, as Stalin bitterly criticized Latin American
governments for their close ties with the United States and demanded that the local
parties publicly declare their loyalty to the Soviet Union. Wartime goodwill toward
the Soviet Union dissipated, and the newly intransigent Communist parties were
outlawed. Better relations were not possible until after Stalin's death in 1953, but the
internecine strife among various revolutionary groups after the Castro revolution of
1959 severely detracted from the Communist parties' positions. The traditional
Latin American Communist parties remained loyal to the Communist Party of the
Soviet Union. Thus the disappearance of the Soviet-led international Communist
system with the ending of the cold war had drastic consequences not only for the organizational and financial status of the Communist parties of Latin America but for
their very ideological identity. Their ingrained dogmatism greatly limited their ability to find answers to these problems.

The Socialist International and Latin America

Social democracy has a long history in Latin America.[2] Some local parties, borrowing their social-democratic inspiration from Europe, date from the first decade of the
twentieth century. The importance to Latin America of the Socialist International
(SI), however, is a much more recent phenomenon. In fact, its real impact as an actor in Latin American international relations dates from about 1976, when it began
taking more interest in the Third World. After that date, the SI was more active in
Latin America than in any other region outside of Europe.

Despite the expressed desire at the Frankfurt Conference in 1951 to open to the
Third World and develop closer links with Latin American, Asian, and African par-

ties, the SI kept its essentially European character. In the 1970s some European leaders, notably Willy Brandt, Bruno Kreisky, and Olaf Palme, strongly advocated expanding membership into Third World regions. They argued that social democratic
solidarity and mutual support would have a positive influence in furthering the
struggle for social and economic equality on the part of popular movements. Willy
Brandt accepted the presidency of the SI at its Geneva Conference in November
1976, partly on the condition that the SI would actively seek institutional cooperation with like-minded Third World parties and movements. Political parties and organizations from forty-two countries were represented at the Geneva Conference. By
the mid-1980s, SI global membership had expanded to include sixty-four parties
and affiliated groups from fifty countries, fifty-two observer parties and liberation
fronts from thirty-seven countries, and ten international organizations as observers.
Those from Europe were in a distinct minority.

Latin American membership in the SI grew rapidly. Two of the three heads of
state present at the Geneva Conference in 1976 were from Latin America: President
Carlos Andrés Pérez of Venezuela, representing the Democratic Action Party, and
President Daniel Oduber of Costa Rica, representing the National Liberation Party.
The SI organized an ongoing Regional Conference on Latin America and the
Caribbean, which held periodic meetings in different Latin American capitals. By
1983 twenty Latin American parties and organizations were members of the SI.

The SI addressed a large number of issues concerning Latin America, both directly and indirectly. Among the first and continuing issues were the New International Economic Order (NIEO) and disarmament and arms control. The NIEO
continued as a major topic at subsequent meetings, reflecting Brandt's views on the
NIEO and the SI's new openness to the Third World. Calls were made for a new international financial and monetary system that would diminish the debts of the developing countries. Other resolutions emphasized disarmament, partly on the
grounds that it would release resources for development. The Latin American nuclear-free zone treaty was viewed with great favor.

A second set of major issues with particular relevance for Latin America dealt with
democracy, dictatorship, and human rights. Over the years a number of resolutions
were passed on general subjects, as well as on issues involving specifically named
countries. Resolutions were passed, for example, expressing regret over the proliferation of military dictatorships that institutionalized the use of terror and torture; supporting the peoples' struggles for a democratic system that respects human rights
and social development; calling for an end to arbitrary detention, tortures, and
killings; and demanding the restoration of political freedom and the right of political
parties and trade unions to work freely and openly. Other resolutions denounced
disappearances, arbitrary detention, and persecution in specific countries, while expressing solidarity with democratic elements against dictatorial regimes and welcom-
ing democratic elections held in several states. The Central American crisis beginning in the late 1970s occupied a great deal of SI attention, continuing into the late
1980s. Statements in the 1980s denounced U.S. policy toward Nicaragua (in fact,

deep divisions existed over attitudes toward the Sandinista government); supported the New Jewel Movement in Grenada; supported the Panamanian-U.S. treaties for the decolonization of the Panama Canal; declared solidarity with the Puerto Rican Independence Party; and demanded humane treatment of illegal immigrants.[3]

LABOR MOVEMENTS

Labor Unions as International Actors

A number of regionally organized labor organizations, comprising national Latin American members and usually affiliated with some larger world movement, have been significant twentieth-century actors in the Latin American subsystem.[4] International and multinational labor development has been slow and sporadic, however, and conflicts have often arisen between the different organizations. Latin American labor movements—stimulated by industrialization and the growth of the urban proletariat beginning in the late nineteenth century, but also including mine workers as an important labor sector—have tended to be organized along national rather than international lines. Labor eventually became politically strong, especially in Mexico, Chile, Argentina, Bolivia, Venezuela, Colombia, and Peru, and gained importance in Brazil, Uruguay, and Costa Rica. The first regional organizations were founded soon after World War I; but their development was slowed by disputes among national members about goals, and they were characterized by clashes between contending workers with opposing ideologies.

The Pan American Federation of Labor (PAFL) was organized in 1918, largely on the combined initiative of the American Federation of Labor (AFL) and the Regional Confederation of Mexican Labor (CROM), which was founded in the same year. PAFL was effective only until the late 1920s, although it was not formally disbanded until after World War II. Its most active members, in addition to U.S. and Mexican unions, were largely those from Central America and the Caribbean islands. PAFL engaged primarily in extending financial assistance to its poorer members and in public protests about U.S. imperialism in Mexico and the Caribbean.

About the time that PAFL ceased to be effective in the late 1920s, two new and more radical regional labor confederations appeared. Both were established in 1929 and reflected the split within Latin American labor movements between anarcho-syndicalists and Communists. Those unions associated with the former ideology founded the Continental Association of American Workers (Asociación Continental Americana de Trabajadores—ACAT). By 1929 anarcho-syndicalists had lost control of much of the Latin American labor movement to Communists, and ACAT never had much political impact, even though it continued to maintain a formal organization. Of more importance was its Communist-dominated rival, the Latin American Syndicalist Confederation (Confederación Sindical Latino Americana—CSLA), a product of the period of Communist history during which the Communist International instructed local Communist parties to establish separate labor union organizations under their control. Consequently, national affiliates of CSLA were established in those Latin American states where Communist parties existed. Some important national trade union organizations, insisting on autonomy of action, refused to join CSLA because it was directed from the Soviet Union. The most important example was the refusal of CROM of Mexico to join, even though it had declared itself both socialist and syndicalist. CSLA was dissolved in 1938 and superseded by a more broadly based labor organization.

When its founding congress met in Mexico City in 1938, the Confederation of Latin American Workers (Confederación de Trabajadores de América Latina—CTAL) represented the most ambitious and important effort to date to establish an all-inclusive regional trade union. CTAL involved collaboration among most communist, socialist, and liberal labor unions and paralleled popular front political party coalitions that were being formed at the same time. The guiding personality and long-term leader of CTAL was Vicente Lombardo Toledano, the radical Mexican intellectual, politician, and labor leader. Lombardo organized CTAL with the help of other Latin American trade union leaders, most prominently those from Cuba, Chile, and Colombia. Within a few years after its founding, CTAL's leadership became Communist-dominated and pro-Soviet. Lombardo's personal power declined after 1946, when his own union in Mexico, which he had founded in 1936, repudiated his leadership. Furthermore, with the onset of the cold war in 1947, collaboration ended between Communists and noncommunists in political parties and labor movements, and Communist labor influence declined drastically. CTAL lost the affiliation of several national unions that left in 1948 to found the Inter-American Federation of Labor. Until then CTAL had been the only labor confederation existing in Latin America. In 1950 it became the regional affiliate of the World Federation of Trade Unions (WFTU). Generally a Communist-dominated association with policy largely determined by the Soviet government, CTAL eventually was disbanded and replaced by the Single Central Association of Latin American Workers (Central Unica de Trabajadores de América Latina—CUTAL), but it lost a number of national member unions during the process of reorganization.

Most national Latin American trade unions belonged to the WFTU, a worldwide labor confederation, when it was founded in 1945. But in 1949 most of its noncommunist affiliates withdrew, and the WFTU became a leading organization for the Communist international front. In 1951 the WFTU was expelled from Paris, where it was founded, for "subversive activities." It moved its headquarters to Vienna but was ejected in 1956 for "endangering Austrian neutrality" and relocated in Prague, where it was lodged for almost 35 years. In 1991, with the end of the cold war, Czechoslovakia ordered the WFTU to leave, on the grounds that no Czech trade union was any longer a WFTU member. The collapse of communism in Central Europe and the Soviet Union, and the dissolution of the Soviet Union itself, greatly affected the WFTU and led numerous member unions to disaffiliate, although entities remained from about 150 states. Nevertheless, WFTU leadership acknowledged that the organization needed to reevaluate its orientation in the post–cold war world and perhaps even become a democratic organization.[5]

The Inter-American Federation of Labor (Confederación Interamericana de Trabajadores—CIT) was organized in 1948 by non-Communist ex-members of CTAL and other trade unions with the specific purpose of countering Communist influence in the Latin American labor movement. The efforts of the AFL of the United States and the APRA Party of Peru constituted the driving force behind the founding of CIT. CIT membership was inter-American in character, comprising twelve Latin American national labor confederations and the AFL of the United States and of Canada. CIT was superseded in 1951 with the founding in Mexico City of the Inter-American Regional Organization of Workers (Organización Regional Interamericana de Trabajadores—ORIT), which absorbed additional affiliates of CTAL at the time of its founding. ORIT was the American affiliate of the International Confederation of Free Trade Unions (ICFTU), founded in London in 1949 under U.S. and British labor leadership by those unions that withdrew from the Communist-controlled WFTU; its headquarters later moved to Brussels. ICFTU has worked closely with labor-oriented agencies in the United Nations system; it is especially interested in worker training and education. The American Federation of Labor and Congress of Industrial Organizations (AFL-CIO) of the United States has ties with ORIT and has given it financial and technical aid.

A potentially powerful rival to both CTAL and ORIT appeared in 1952 with the formation of the Unionized Latin American Workers' Group (Agrupación de Trabajadores Latino Americanos Sindicalizados—ATLAS) by Argentine president Juan Perón. ATLAS, under the direction of the General Confederation of Labor of Argentina, was intended as an instrument of Peronista foreign policy to help extend Argentine influence in Spanish America. As an international labor organization, it organized and affiliated as members a number of national labor confederations outside of Argentina. ATLAS was only of temporary importance, however; it disbanded after Perón fell from power in 1955. CTAL had offered an alliance to ATLAS in 1953, but it had been refused. After 1955 former ATLAS unions either joined ORIT or steered an independent course.

In 1954 an additional regional labor organization was founded, the Latin American Confederation of Christian Trade Unionists (Confederación Latino Americana de Sindicalistas Cristianos—CLASC). This organization is the Latin American regional affiliate of the International Federation of Christian Trade Unions founded in The Hague in 1920; its headquarters was later moved to Brussels. The parent world organization's program originally was based on the papal encyclical *Rerum Novarum* (1891), and later on *Quadragerimo Anno* (1931), although its affiliates included Protestant as well as Roman Catholic federations. CLASC also had links to international associations of Christian Democratic political parties and trade unions. Its own national affiliates in Latin America have included Christian trade unions and federations and a Catholic workers' association. CLASC, clearly leftist, was critical of the larger ORIT, which it considered to be dominated by the conservative U.S. labor movement. CLASC was also anticommunist, however, and thus opposed the moribund CUTAL.

U.S. Labor and Latin America

The U.S. labor movement has had periods of concern with and indifference to Latin American regional organizations. After its involvement with PAFL from 1918 until the late 1920s, the AFL had few contacts with the Latin American labor movement until after World War II, when it was instrumental in organizing CIT and the successor ORIT. In 1946 the AFL sent Serafino Romualdi as its "labor ambassador" to Latin America. Romualdi negotiated with noncommunist trade unions and federations both in and out of the Communist-led CTAL, and within two years the rival CIT had been established. Romualdi had served briefly with the Latin American department of the International Ladies Garment Workers Union before going to the region. Upon his return in 1948 he became head of the inter-American affairs section of the AFL and held a similar position with the AFL-CIO after the U.S. labor merger in 1955. Romualdi also served as assistant secretary of ORIT and labor adviser to the Alliance for Progress; he retired in 1964. Romualdi died three years later in Mexico while on a lecture trip to the Cuernavaca Labor College run by ORIT.[6]

In 1961 the AFL-CIO and a group of U.S. business corporations active in Latin America founded a U.S. Government-financed union-industry group called the American Institute for Free Labor Development (AIFLD). Romualdi was appointed its first director. The purpose of AIFLD in Latin America was to encourage the development of noncommunist trade unions, to the extent that a staff study by the U.S. Senate Foreign Relations Committee in 1968 criticized the AIFLD for being preoccupied with anticommunism in its Latin American operations. To the present day the AFL-CIO's foreign policies have continued to operate primarily through the AIFLD.

Changes in the foreign policies of U.S. labor in the late 1960s, extending into the 1990s, have had important implications for its Latin American relations—namely, a long period of reduced contacts. The AFL-CIO supported free trade as long as the balance of trade was favorable to the United States. The only qualifications were that agreements should be negotiated with states whose exports were harming specific U.S. industries and that the government should pay adjustment allowances for workers who were displaced because of foreign competition. But in the late 1960s, when the United States began to suffer large trade deficits, labor policy changed. The AFL-CIO began to champion protectionism in U.S. trade, favored a decrease rather than an increase in world economic interdependency, and drew back from its own commitments to international labor organizations.

In the early 1970s, U.S. labor leaders began to argue that protectionism was the only way for U.S. labor to guard against the effects of international competition. That position has continued into the mid-1990s. As trade balances turned against the United States, U.S. labor turned against free trade. Labor leaders complained that the tariff code and tax laws encouraged U.S.-based MNCs to manufacture in foreign settings at a lower cost and return finished products back to the United States. Consequently, they charged, U.S.-based MNCs were destroying jobs at home in their search for cheap labor abroad; in other words, by exporting jobs to their foreign subsidiaries and affiliates where lower labor costs prevailed, in order to produce goods that underpriced U.S.-made products, MNCs were quickly eliminating U.S. jobs. Arguing that labor was helpless in the changed international situation, U.S. labor leaders moved their trade policies away from supporting free-trade legislation.

In the post–cold war era, the U.S. and Latin American governments' neoliberal emphases on free-trade agreements caused U.S. labor to become even more vociferous in its opposition to arrangements for regional economic integration and free trade under the U.S. Enterprise for the Americas Initiative. It mounted serious but unsuccessful opposition to the approval by the U.S. Congress of the North American Free Trade Agreement, primarily out of fear that it would result in the migration of U.S. jobs to Mexico. Such concerns will likely constitute the most difficult issue for the AFL-CIO in any future debates over hemispheric free trade.

GUERRILLA INSURGENTS

Guerrilla groups have been a part of the Latin American scene since the early nineteenth century wars for independence, and of international significance since that time. They were most prominent, however, after the successful Cuban Revolution (1956–1959). The importance of guerrilla groups declined in the 1970s, as counterinsurgency operations by governments (including especially repressive military regimes) proved effective. In certain states, however, they remained or reappeared as important actors.

Insurgents Defined

The nature and scope of the meaning of guerrilla insurgency should be clarified. John Martz defined guerrilla warfare as "armed protest against nationally constituted authority by an organized force other than the regular military establishment pursuing a set of broadly explicit objectives which extend beyond a mere change of governmental personnel and denial of legitimacy to the existing regime."[7] In the same vein, Samuel Huntington noted that insurgency, which challenges political systems at a fundamental level and employs violence to bring about the collapse of an incumbent regime, should be distinguished from other forms of violence aimed at reaping rewards from the existing political system (such as power, money, or recognition).[8]

A further definitional problem is the indiscriminate way in which the terms "terrorist" and "terrorism" came to be used. These terms have emotional content that may disguise political preferences rather than reveal analytic precision. The result is a certain conceptual confusion surrounding the subject of entities that engage in violence against the existing order.

The essential problem in the case of Latin America is to distinguish between terrorist and guerrilla groups and terrorism and insurgency. For terrorists, terrorism is the principal component of ideology and the use of terror an exclusive instrument. They engage in random or planned violence through such methods as assassination, kidnapping, bombing, and hijackings, against the general public (noncombatants) or against government officials for political purposes. Their intent is to induce terror—an intense, overmastering fear—in the minds of their targets. This concept of "terrorist" is too narrow to define the organized insurgent guerrilla groups, which have been the more important actors in the Latin American context. Guerrillas do not necessarily employ the use of terror, and when they do, it is part of a larger set of instruments. Thus, guerrillas may avoid such use of violence and still be defined as guerrillas, whereas terrorists, by definition, engage essentially in terrorist acts. Although all guerrilla groups in Latin America have eventually used terror on some level (some more or less than others), few purely terrorist groups have existed. An important exception was the rise of urban guerrilla warfare in the late 1960s, which emphasized terrorism to such an extent that its difference from insurgency was blurred (calling such revolutionaries "guerrillas" was probably a misnomer). The revival of more familiar guerrilla warfare the during the 1970s seemed once again to emphasize the distinction. Many terrorists have come from the radical right, such as the death squads that operated in Argentina, Brazil, Guatemala, and El Salvador. They usually had government connections and were devoted to preserving, not destroying, the status quo.

Guerrillas and terrorists have other distinguishing characteristics. Terrorists tend to aim at the general public and individual government officials but recognize that they are not equipped to confront security forces effectively and try to avoid them. Guerrillas engage the security forces as primary targets. Terrorist groups tend to be small, organized around isolated cells in order to escape detection. Guerrillas have more complex organizations and utilize a visible hierarchical military command structure.

The Cuban Model

Contemporary guerrilla warfare in Latin America was introduced with Fidel Castro's successful movement in Cuba, which defeated dictator Fulgencio Batista and provided the dominant model for other guerrilla groups around the region.[9] In December 1956 Fidel Castro and his band of eighty-two guerrillas landed on the northeastern coast of Cuba in the old yacht *Granma*, initiating a two-year insurgency against dictator Fulgencio Batista. The small group of only a dozen survivors, known as the 26th of July Movement, made their way into the mountainous eastern portion of the island, called the Sierra Maestra. From there guerrilla activities increased, and the Batista regime was overthrown. On January 1, 1959, Castro assumed power as the leader of the Cuban state.

Fidelista movements became widespread around Latin America, seeking to emulate the Cuban success and looking to Havana for leadership. Similar conflicts emanated from the Caribbean and extended into South America and, to an extent, Mexico. After about a year of consolidating his power after January 1, 1959, Castro openly encouraged violent revolution in the rest of the hemisphere through active assistance by guerrilla movements, especially in Venezuela, Peru, and Guatemala. Guerrilla activities in Latin America intensified in 1963 and 1964, and Cuban support continued until about 1968. During that time, Cuba added Colombia to its list of targets, and Che Guevara led the insurgency in Bolivia. Not until twenty years later in Nicaragua, however, did a second movement succeed in destroying an existing political system and gaining control of the state. Although most Latin American guerrilla groups looked to Cuba for leadership, and although Castro exercised some influence over them, only a modicum of effort was made to organize these groups internationally. In December 1965 the Organization of Latin American Solidarity (OLAS) was organized under Cuban auspices as an agency to coordinate regional guerrilla activity. OLAS, a confederation of twenty-seven Latin American revolutionary movements, held its first conference in Havana in 1967.

Although Cuba urged and actively supported violent revolution in the rest of the region, the Soviet Union favored relations through "normal" diplomatic and economic channels. Soviet policy had continued to be generally unprovocative during World War II and through the 1950s; after the war its covert activities and its support for Latin American revolutionary groups vacillated. The Soviet Union urged caution in the early 1960s, following Castro's success in Cuba, and throughout the extended period of guerrilla warfare. Most orthodox (Moscow-oriented) Communist parties followed the Soviet lead and rejected armed insurgency in favor of more cautious tactics. China supported the militant Cuban posture for the violent overthrow of existing regimes, although it simultaneously attempted to increase its own diplomatic and trade contacts with Latin American states.

By late 1968 Castro had come to terms with the Soviet Union and tacitly accepted the Soviet doctrines of peaceful coexistence and evolutionary transition to socialism. Major guerrilla efforts had been liquidated in Peru and Bolivia and effectively controlled in Colombia, Venezuela, and Guatemala. Furthermore, economic problems forced Cuba to rely more on the Soviet Union. As the Cuban economy faltered, Soviet influence increased, and Cuban policy conformity may have been the price for continued Soviet assistance. Castro largely withdrew his support of insurgency movements, seeming to resign himself at least temporarily to the futility of exporting revolution. By 1970, after a year and a half of Cuban silence toward Latin American revolution, insurgent leaders began to criticize Castro for his withdrawal of support. The Soviet Union preferred cooperative state-to-state interaction after the mid-1960s, but it occasionally supported subversive activities that led to conflict with Latin American states—Colombia in 1967, Uruguay in 1968, Mexico and Ecuador in 1971, Bolivia in 1972, and Chile in 1973.

Considerable differences in ideology and tactical preferences were found among Fidelista revolutionaries, and between them and Soviet-supported Latin American Communist parties advocating orthodox Marxist-Leninist thought. Matters were even more complicated by China's positions on various issues and by its support for revolutionary activity in Latin America; by the survival of Maoism in Latin America after it had declined in the PRC itself; and by the influence of other ideologies, such as those of Trotsky, Bakunin, and certain Spanish theorists. In addition, an array of Latin American writers added their contributions to revolutionary literature. The most important Latin American theories, however, were the *foco* (rural cadre) concept of Fidelismo and ideas related to urban warfare.

The Castro experience served as the original principal source for guerrilla warfare doctrine. Ernesto "Che" Guevara's statements provide a starting point for an analysis of insurgency doctrine.[10] Guevara—who had been with Castro aboard the *Granma* and was a major figure in the subsequent insurgency movement and then in the revolutionary government, and who died in 1967 fighting in Bolivia (see below)—was a hero to revolutionaries and had great influence on their activities through his writings on guerrilla strategy. Guevara reflected to a degree the theories of Mao Tse-tung and Ho Chi Minh, in that he sought to establish a rural peasant base for revolution. He differed from Soviet (Leninist) theory by insisting that it was unnecessary to wait until all of the objective conditions for revolution were present, as he believed that an insurrectional cadre or core (*foco*) of thirty to fifty men could create the conditions to initiate the armed struggle. He also departed from Soviet doctrine by insisting that the guerrillas need not be tied to a political party. They were in "the vanguard," and after they gained power a revolutionary party could arise, as, he claimed, had been the course followed by the Cuban Revolution. The guerrilla *foco* would operate in the countryside (as in the Sierra Maestra) and create a peasant revolution. Unlike the theories of Mao and Ho, the *foco* would lead the revolution, not blend with the peasantry.

Regis Debray (1967) wrote a long pamphlet that also was viewed as a handbook on guerrilla warfare.[11] Debray was the radical intellectual scion of a wealthy, conservative, aristocratic French family. He taught at the University of Havana after Castro came to power and later was with Guevara in Bolivia. He used the Castro experience as the model for further Latin American revolution, dismissing all other strategies, and drew heavily on Guevara's and Castro's writings and speeches. Debray argued, in sum: (1) that guerrilla struggle was the only effective means of achieving political and social change in Latin America; (2) that revolutionary power resided not with political parties but in guerrilla cadres and their military leadership; (3) that, since Castro was correct in his dictum that "cities are the graveyards of revolutionaries," war must be fought in the countryside; and (4) that mobile guerrilla *focos* would make the revolution, eventually gaining mass support. Debray said that Castro's contribution to Marxism-Leninism was his insistence that guerrillas must assume both political and military leadership of the revolution and defer the creation of a party.

Some writers argued that Fidelismo was more a matter of tactics than of ideology. They pointed out that Castro's guerrilla warfare was not in fact set in the theoretical mold that he and others later claimed. He pragmatically used ideology as it suited his needs, coming to power through the confluence of several factors that did not conform to subsequent theoretical explanations. Castro won not with peasant militia (or the proletariat) but with middle-class revolutionaries, and his *foco* did not create a revolutionary situation where none had existed—victory was due to nonguerrilla factors. Guerrilla determination was important, but so were the mistakes and incompetence of the enemy. The turning point in the Cuban Revolution was when Batista responded to Castro by trying to control the major cities through repression, turning the urban middle class against him and losing his ability to rule. The regular armed forces were corrupt, undisciplined, and easily demoralized, and the Sierra Maestra provided a guerrilla sanctuary only because the army was unwilling to enter. Many significant revolutionary events occurred in the cities, initiated by urban guerrillas.

When Bolivian troops seized Guevara they found a 30,000-word personal handwritten diary that detailed the eleven-month guerrilla campaign.[12] Although Guevara repeated much of his earlier guerrilla doctrine in the diary, it also constituted a major source of evidence to argue the nonuniversality of the Cuban Revolution and its inapplicability to certain other situations. Guevara stressed the "continental magnitude of the task," writing that he wanted to create a series of "Vietnams," beginning in Bolivia and moving to neighboring nations. Yet his largely foreign band showed little understanding of Bolivian politics and culture; none of them spoke Quechua, the primary language of the Indians in their area of operations. Furthermore, the Bolivian government was able to capitalize on the popular perception that "foreigners" were attempting to capture the Bolivian nation, a situation that the guerrillas had not faced in Cuba. The regular Bolivian army units, unlike Batista's army in Cuba, were willing to encounter and able to defeat guerrillas in a mountainous environment. Most important, the diary bitterly described the Indian peasants' lack of support for the guerrillas and even their betrayal of the movement. The guerrillas were unable to replenish their personnel losses with a single peasant recruit.

Urban warfare theory rose to prominence following Guevara's defeat in Bolivia. A widely read booklet that advocated the initiation and development of guerrilla forces in urban areas was the forty-one-page *Minimanual of the Urban Guerrilla*, written in 1970 by Carlos Marighella, a Brazilian. It received Cuban support with its publication in the official organ *Tricontinental* and was circulated abroad. Marighella, a dissident former member of the Brazilian Communist Party and founder of an urban terrorist group in Brazil, was killed in a police ambush in São Paulo at the end of 1969. He had long opposed the rural guerrilla warfare thesis. Cuban support of his alternative strategy signified a fundamental change in Latin American insurgency thinking. Marighella summed up his strategy, in fact the fundamental statement about terrorism, in this manner: "It is necessary to turn political crisis into armed conflict by performing violent actions that will force those in power to transform the political situation of the country into a military situation. That will alienate the masses who, from then on, will revolt against the army and the police and thus blame them for this state of things."

This scenario for civil war—the strategy of militarization through urban terror that will invite repression and pave the way for popular revolt—proved to be utopian. Urban guerrillas discovered that the frequent popular response to indiscriminate terrorism was revulsion, and that if a government was sufficiently ruthless, effective repression was more likely to occur than popular uprising. And the paradoxical general result of experiences with brutal military regimes was a return to constitutionally elected presidents and the discrediting of both the extreme political Left and Right.

Latin American Guerrilla Movements

Significant guerrilla groups outside of Cuba first appeared in Peru.[13] In October 1959 a group of young radicals committed to Fidelismo broke away from the reformist Aprista Party, eventually organizing themselves as the Movement of the Revolutionary Left (MIR). After its leadership was killed in 1965 while fighting the Peruvian army, MIR was relatively inactive and finally dissolved. In 1962 some Peruvian Communist Party members broke away from MIR and formed the National Liberation Army (ELN); it, too, declined after 1965. A Trotskyite peasant movement, the Revolutionary Leftist Front (FIR), was very active from 1962 to 1964, but its leaders were imprisoned, and FIR dissolved.

In the meantime, the most effective Peruvian insurgency developed, and in the 1980s it posed a serious threat to Peruvian governments. Following the Sino-Soviet split in 1964, the Peruvian Communist Party divided into pro-Soviet and pro-Chinese groups; the Maoist factions further divided and realigned, out of which emerged in 1970 the Sendero Luminoso (Shining Path). Abimael Guzmán Reynoso (Comrade Gonzalo), a professor at the San Cristobal de Huamanga University in Ayacucho, led the group from the beginning. Its ideology has often been referred to as Maoist (the theory that revolution begins with rural peasant warfare that eventually encircles the cities), but it was rooted in the thinking of José Carlos Mariátegui (1895–1930), a prominent Peruvian intellectual who had advocated combined Marxist and nationalist solutions to his country's problems. Mariátegui was also founder of the party organization that had ultimately led through a long and circuitous route to the organization of the Sendero Luminoso. Indeed, the full original name of the movement was "The Revolutionary Student Front in the Shining Path of Mariátegui." Thus Maoism was blended with Mariátegui's concept of the Peruvian Indian's historical tradition of resistance, first to Spanish colonial rule and then to white and mestizo domination.

Guzmán built the Sendero Luminoso (SL) organization in the countryside, and in May 1980 it began to engage in acts of sabotage and terror. The SL also had an urban structure from the beginning. The first guerrilla operations included urban warfare in Lima, although action was concentrated in the mountainous Ayacucho Department. The SL thereafter proved to be a disciplined, effective, and particularly ruthless guerrilla movement. In 1986 it expanded its activities to other parts of the country, both rural and urban. Since the SL considered itself an indigenous non-aligned group and was openly contemptuous of other movements and their ideologies, it did not seek or receive outside assistance. The SL counted on support from *campesino* communities, which it recruited with a combination of rewards and severe punishment. In the mid-1980s, the SL forced a relationship with international drug traffickers in which the guerrillas attacked the army and the police in the prime coca growing regions in exchange for money and weapons.

Peruvian government ruthlessly pursued counterinsurgency in the 1980s with little success. Finally, in 1992, government forces captured Abimael Guzmán and other SL leaders in Lima. By this time some 20,000 Peruvians had been killed in the guerrilla struggle. Afterwards SL activity waned considerably.

In 1984 another terrorist group had emerged in Peru, the Castroite Movimiento Revolucionario Túpac Amaru (MRTA), in direct opposition to the SL. After the army captured the leader of the MRTA in 1992 that movement also began to disintegrate.

Among other early groups were those organized in Venezuela, a major target of Castro's own international activities. In 1960 a group split from the ruling reformist Democratic Action Party and formed the Movement of the Revolutionary Left (MIR). MIR engaged in joint operations with the guerrilla element of the Venezuelan Communist Party, organized in 1962 and called the Armed Forces of National Liberation (FALN). By 1966 the two organizations had withdrawn from armed revolutionary tactics, and three years later they accepted President Rafael Caldera's offer of amnesty and formed their own political parties. Some small guerrilla remnants remained and in early 1973 merged to form the Revolutionary Integration Organization (OIR), but it had little success. A political party of former insurgents sometimes held the balance of power in the Venezuelan Congress and, in 1989, it elected its candidate to a state governorship.[14]

One of the most effective groups operated in Uruguay. The National Liberation Front (FLN), popularly called the Tupamaros, was organized in 1963. Its operations increased in 1966, and it enjoyed considerable success for the next six years. In 1972, however, the Uruguayan army was given extraconstitutional powers and finally brought the Tupamaros under control.

Guerrilla activities in Colombia have been among the most persistent and longest lasting. The Fidelista National Liberation Army (ELNF) was formed in 1964. It was this group with whom the former Jesuit priest Camilo Torres was associated (see Chapter 10). After a number of its leaders were killed in 1972 and its commander defected in 1976, the ELNF adopted an essentially defensive posture. The Armed Forces of Colombia (FARC) was organized in 1966 and, supported by Cuba, became the most important guerrilla group in Colombia. The small Peking-oriented Popular Liberation Army (EPL) was formed in 1967, linked with the Revolutionary Workers Party (PRT), but it suffered severe losses in the late 1960s and early 1970s and became a minor factor. Unusual in its origins was the 19th of April Movement (M-19). Organized in 1974, it took its name from the presidential election of April 19, 1970, when the vaguely populist former dictator, General Gustavo Rojas Pinilla, was defeated. Also of note was the Indian-based group, Quintin Lame.

In 1984 Colombian President Belisario Betancur (1982–86) proposed a truce and an amnesty law, marking the beginning of negotiations with guerrilla groups aimed at national reconciliation. The process was continued during the presidency of Virgilio Barco (1986–90). In March 1990 the M-19 was finally persuaded to surrender its arms and join in electoral politics. Its presidential candidate in the May 1990 elections came in third, with 13 percent of the vote. Shortly thereafter, in late 1990 and 1991, the EPL, PRT, and Quintin Lame also abandoned the armed struggle in agreements with President César Gaviria Trujillo. The ELNF and FARC remained in the field, however, and posed a serious and effective challenge to Colombia's political processes. They soon controlled a majority of the state's territory and became involved in the drug traffic by levying lucrative "war taxes" on cocaine and heroin producers in return for physical protection. In October 1997 they sought to disrupt, with considerable effect, provincial and municipal elections through intimidation—setting off bombs, killing candidates, and threatening voters; the ELNF kidnapped two Organization of American States election monitors (who were later released). Right-wing, counter-revolutionary paramilitary groups are also involved in the areas where state control is lacking. In March 1998 the guerrillas, allied with drug producers, stepped up their attacks and threats of violence.

Insurgency in Brazil was fragmented, with competing groups organized along local rather than national lines. Two groups stood out among the many organizations that proliferated under frequently changing leadership—the National Liberation Action (ALN) and the Popular Revolutionary Vanguard (VPR). Both the ALN and the VPR were virtually eliminated by Brazilian forces in 1973, a date by which all Brazilian guerrilla forces had lost their effectiveness.

In Chile the most important of several guerrilla organizations was the Movement of the Revolutionary Left (MIR), formed in 1965 as a Fidelista group advocating armed struggle. It did not join Marxist President Allende's coalition government of 1970–1973 and, in fact, was highly critical of it. Most MIR leaders were arrested after the military coup in 1973. MIR continued to exist but disappeared in the late 1980s just prior to Chile's return to constitutional government.

Insurgency organizations in Argentina were among the most active. Some were formed in the early 1960s, but they did not become prominent until late in the decade. The three most important groups were the Montoneros (MPM), the Peronist Armed Forces (FAP), and Revolutionary Armed Forces (FAR). The three closely linked groups claimed to be both Fidelista and Peronista, although they were as much as ejected from the Peronist party in 1973 and 1974. Large numbers of terrorist political murders in the 1970s inspired like retaliation by right-wing groups. In 1976 the Peronist government began an intensive and bloody antiguerrilla campaign, which intensified after the military coup in 1977 into what the military regime justified as a necessary "dirty war." The guerrilla organizations were eliminated, but military actions went far beyond antiterrorism to deal brutally with many other people as well.

Insurgency in Bolivia was of special interest because of the direct connection with Cuban revolutionary leaders. Ernesto "Che" Guevara in Cuba made plans for guerrilla action in Bolivia, hoping to stimulate a South American continent-wide insurgency movement. He arrived in Bolivia in November 1966 and organized the National Liberation Army (ELN). It was initially composed of twenty Cubans (four of whom had been members of the Cuban Central Committee), twenty-nine Bolivians, and three Peruvians. After some initial successes in the Bolivian mountains, the ELN suffered increasing losses at the hands of the Bolivian army. In October 1967, Che and all but five guerrillas were killed by Bolivian military forces—an event that dealt a major blow to insurgency groups throughout Latin America. The ELN continued after Guevara's death, but in 1969 the new leadership was captured by government forces, and the ELN was disarmed. The Bolivian Movement of the Revolutionary Left (MIR), formed in 1971, suffered heavy losses the following year. Jaime Paz Zamora, who had led the MIR, became Bolivia's vice president in 1982 and was elected president in 1989 to succeed his uncle, Víctor Paz Estenssoro.

The first important guerrilla groups in Central America operated in Guatemala beginning in 1961. Three major ones were organized: the Revolutionary Armed Forces (FAR), the 13th of November Revolutionary Movement (MR-13), and the Organization of the Armed People. Guatemalan violence was extreme in the 1960s, as right-wing groups responded in kind to guerrilla terrorism. The Guatemalan army conducted a brutal counterinsurgency campaign in the early 1960s, along with large-scale Indian population resettlements. The guerrillas were weakened but managed to keep operating in remote areas; however, in 1980 they were routed by another ruthless army campaign. Two years later the three guerrilla groups formed the Guatemalan National Revolutionary Union, which was able to engage in skirmishes and attacks on infrastructure targets but not capable of engaging the army in sustained operations. On October 2, 1987, the Guatemalan government, represented by army generals, and the guerrilla alliance announced a cease-fire and began talks, seeking to end the twenty-six-year insurgency. The talks complied with the Central American peace agreement that had been signed by all Central American presidents in August 1987 (see Chapter 12 for more details on the Central American peace process and its relevance to ending insurgencies in most of the Central American states). The talks, in Madrid, Guatemala, and Mexico, took several years to complete, since they were sometimes deadlocked over human rights issues and interrupted by sporadic insurgent action (the guerrillas reorganized as the Guatemalan United Revolutionary Front—URNG). In mid-1993, after the army leaders forced the president to resign, the new president recommenced the peace negotiations.

In Nicaragua, a small Castroite organization was founded in 1961 called the Sandinist National Liberation Front (FSLN). It became inactive in 1970 but reactivated in 1972, as popular discontent with the ruling Somoza dictatorship increased. The Sandinistas and their allies finally overthrew General Somoza in 1979. As soon as the Sandinista guerrillas became governors they were opposed by counterrevolutionary guerrilla groups. Numerous organizations coalesced into three alliances. In time they were collectively known as the *Contras* and supported by the Reagan administration as a key element in its anti-Sandinista policies, but they were loosely connected and had continuous internal disputes. The National Democratic Front (FDN) coalition was formed in 1981 by former National Guard officers; they recruited widely within

Nicaragua, and in time their ranks included many teenagers. The FDN was based in Honduras and operated in northern Nicaragua, seeking to overthrow the Sandinistas. A coalition of Indian groups—the Sandinista Unity of Miskito, Sumas, and Ramas (MISURASATA), founded under another name in 1979 to oppose Somoza—was transformed in 1981 into an armed resistance against the Sandinista government. The government's resettlement of Indians as part of its counterinsurgency operations had led MISURASATA to join loosely with the FDN. In stark contrast to the FDN, the Democratic Revolutionary Alliance (ARDE) consisted of moderate political forces operating out of Costa Rica, which sought to return the Sandinista revolution to its original political pluralism. The two dominant forces were the Sandinista Revolutionary Front, led by a disillusioned Sandinista hero in the fight against Somoza, and the Democratic Movement, whose members included prominent civilians who had opposed Somoza, some who had been members of the Junta of Government after 1979, and some who had been Sandinista supporters. They put together their revolutionary front in early 1982 and made clear their distance from the FDN because of its *somocista* background and different political objectives.

The FDN had begun its operations with assistance from Argentine military intelligence officers and U.S. CIA agents. Most U.S. support went directly to the FDN, considered to be the best fighting force. In late 1984 legislation prohibited direct CIA help. In July 1985 the United States persuaded the feuding Contras to form the United Nicaraguan Opposition (UNO) to serve as an "umbrella" organization for the various rebel groups. Underlying the UNO effort was an attempt to enhance Contra acceptability with the reluctant U.S. Congress. The various elements formed the UNO Directorate but also acted independently.

In 1986 Congress authorized an overt assistance program, but with restrictions. The Iran-Contra affair in 1987, revealed in detail in congressional hearings, ended a covert operation that had been directed out of the National Security Council (NSC) staff organization, had relied on private funding and logistical support, and had been designed to overcome the post-1984 congressional prohibitions. In 1989 the badly split Contra leadership was reorganized under the Nicaraguan Resistance, a new "umbrella" unit with a five-member directorate. The power struggle continued, however, given impetus by two factors: On February 3, 1988, the U.S. Congress rejected any further public aid to the Contras, and on March 23 the Contra leadership and the Sandinista government signed a temporary cease-fire and began negotiations to make it permanent. The Contra alliance, which had been held together by a common enemy and U.S. support, was badly fractured.

The February 1990 elections—in which the United Nicaraguan Opposition (UNO), headed by presidential candidate Violeta Barrios de Chamorro, defeated the Sandinista Party and incumbent President Daniel Ortega—constituted a turning point in the Nicaraguan civil war. The Nicaraguan Resistance (Contras) did not transform itself into a political party for the elections, nor did it become a part of the UNO coalition. Rather, it shared a mutual animosity with the UNO toward the Sandinista government and was interested in voting it out of power.[15] On April 19,

1990, all parties (Contras, Miskito Indian rebels—then known as Yatama—Sandinistas, and the Chamorro government-elect), in concert with the UN Security Council and with U.S. backing, reached agreements to end the civil war. Nevertheless, political distrust and armed violence prevailed. Contra leaders were targets of assassinations, and they charged the Sandinistas with pursuing a systematic plan for their elimination. Hundreds of former Contras, known as recontras, returned to guerrilla warfare to protest the failure of the government to deliver on its promises. Ex-Sandinista army officers organized armed groups of former Sandinista soldiers in response, resulting in outbreaks of fighting. By early 1994, however, the government had managed to disarm both sides, despite the continuing political turmoil and sporadic terrorist acts.

In El Salvador, the Nicaraguan Revolution of July 1979 reinvigorated insurgent movements. The Farabundo Martí National Liberation Front (FMLN) had been formed in October 1980 to integrate five armed organizations. The Farabundo Martí Popular Forces of Liberation (FPL), founded in 1974, was the largest organization but suffered from violent internal disputes. A second FMLN guerrilla group was the Revolutionary Army of the People (ERP), and the Armed Forces of National Resistance (FARN) also joined. The Salvadoran Communist Party decided to join the armed conflict in 1979 in alliance with the FMLN. The small Central American Workers' Revolutionary Party (PRTC) adhered in late 1980.

The Democratic Revolutionary Front (FDR) was also established in 1980. It was a separate political wing attached to the FMLN that operated as a government-in-exile in Mexico, but it had no control over military decisions. The FDR was made up of democratic left organizations. Most important was the National Revolutionary Movement, a Social Democratic organization and member of the Socialist International. The Popular Socialist Christian Movement (MPSC), composed of former Christian Democrats who left the party in early 1980, was also part of the FDR. Much of the FDR membership had concluded that peaceful progress in El Salvador was no longer possible.

The FMLN initially followed a "total victory" strategy, which ended with the failure of the "final offensive" in January 1981 (just prior to the U.S. presidential inauguration). The insurgents then turned to sabotage of the country's infrastructure (the destruction of roads and bridges, communications facilities, electrical and water sources, and industrial plants). They refused government offers to participate in elections; they occasionally negotiated directly with the government, but the civil war continued unabated and stalemated.

In October 1987 intense negotiations occurred in compliance with the general Central American peace accord. Following the government's defeat in legislative elections in March 1988, however, the FMLN decided to press for a full-scale insurrection. While periodic UN-mediated negotiations occurred in 1990 and 1991 the war continued at a standoff. Finally, on January 16, 1992, the government and the insurgents signed a comprehensive peace agreement in Mexico, and a UN monitored cease-fire began on February 1. Under the pact, among other things, the

FMLN gave up the armed struggle, disarmed, and became a legally recognized political party; and the Salvadoran army was reduced in size by half, certain paramilitary units known for human rights abuses were disbanded, and a new integrated police force was created. On March 20, 1994, national elections were held as the culmination of the peace process that ended the civil war, followed by a presidential runoff vote on April 23. The presidency was won by Armando Calderon Sol of the conservative Republican Nationalist Alliance (ARENA). Nevertheless, the second-place showing by Rubén Zamora—formerly a central figure of the FDR and a presidential candidate of the Democratic Convergence leftist coalition (that included the FMLN)—and the election of FMLN candidates as mayors and members of the National Assembly established the former insurgents as a significant political presence in the new El Salvador.

NOTES

1. See Manuel Caballero, *Latin America and the Comintern, 1919–1943* (New York: Cambridge University Press, 1986). On Communist parties in Latin America, with reference to the Soviet role, see Donald L. Herman, ed., *The Communist Tide in Latin America* (Austin: University of Texas Press, 1973).

2. See Julius Braunthal, *History of the International*, 3 vols. (New York: Praeger; Boulder, Colo.: Westview Press, 1967–1980); Menno Vellinga, ed., *Social Democracy in Latin America: Prospects for Change* (Boulder, Colo.: Westview Press, 1993); and Felicity Williams, *La Internacional Socialista y América Latina: Una visión crítica* (México: Universidad Autónoma Metropolitano, 1984).

3. See Eusebio M. Mujal-Leon, *European Socialism and the Conflict in Central America* (New York: Praeger, 1989).

4. See Víctor Alba, *Politics and the Labor Movement in Latin America* (Stanford: Stanford University Press, 1968); Robert Alexander, *Organized Labor in Latin America* (New York: Free Press, 1965); Moises Poblete Troncoso and Ben G. Burnett, *The Rise of the Latin American Labor Movement* (New York: Bookman, 1960).

5. United Kingdom, Foreign and Commonwealth Office, "Twelfth World Trade Union Congress" *Background Brief* (October 1990) gives details about the WFTU.

6. See Serafino Romualdi, *Presidents and Peons: Recollections of a Labor Ambassador to Latin America* (New York: Funk and Wagnalls, 1967).

7. John D. Martz, "Guerrilla Warfare and Violence in Contemporary Latin America," *Annals of the Southeastern Conference on Latin American Studies* 1 (March 1970): 143.

8. Samuel P. Huntington, "Civil Violence and the Process of Development," in *Civil Violence and the Process of Development*, pt. 2 (London: International Institute for Strategic Studies, 1974), 3.

9. On the Cuban Revolution, see Ramon L. Bonachea and Marta San Martín, *The Cuban Insurrection, 1952–1959* (New Brunswick, N.J.: Transaction, 1974); Rolando E. Bonachea and Nelson P. Valdes, *Cuba in Revolution* (Garden City, N.Y.: Anchor, 1972); and K. S. Karol, *Guerrillas in Power: The Course of the Cuban Revolution* (New York: Hill and Wang, 1970).

10. See Ernesto "Che" Guevara, *Guerrilla Warfare* (New York: Monthly Review, 1961); Ernesto "Che" Guevara, *Obras Completas*, 5 vols. (Buenos Aires: Ed. Cepe, 1973–1974); John Gerassi, ed., *Venceremos! The Speeches and Writings of Che Guevara* (New York: Macmillan,

1968). See also Ernesto "Che" Guevara, *Guerrilla Warfare*, ed., with an introduction and case studies, Brian Loveman and Thomas M. Davies Jr. (Lincoln: University of Nebraska Press, 1985), in which the editors comment on Guevara's writings and add information on contemporary insurgencies. An excellent general analysis of the phenomenon of guerrilla warfare and its doctrines is Timothy P. Wickham-Crowley, *Exploring Revolution: Essays on Latin American Insurgency and Revolutionary Theory* (New York: M. E. Sharpe, 1991).

11. Regis Debray, *Revolution in the Revolution? Armed Struggle and Political Struggle in Latin America* (New York: Monthly Review, 1967).

12. Of the many editions of Guevara's Bolivian diary in several languages, the most useful in English are Robert Scheer, ed., *The Diary of Che Guevara—Bolivia: November 7, 1966–October 7, 1967* (New York: Bantam, 1968), which contains an introduction by Fidel Castro; and Daniel James, ed., *The Complete Bolivian Diaries of Che Guevara and Other Captured Documents* (New York: Stein and Day, 1968).

13. See Richard Gott, *Guerrilla Movements in Latin America* (London: Nelson, 1970); Robert Moss, *Urban Guerrillas* (London: Temple Smith, 1972), Timothy P. Wickham-Crowley, *Guerrillas and Revolution in Latin America: A Comparative Study of Insurgents and Regimes since 1956* (Princeton: Princeton University Press, 1992). Michael Radu and Vladimir Tismaneasu, *Latin American Revolutionaries: Groups, Goals, Methods* (Washington, D.C.: Pergamon-Brassey Publishers, 1990) is a thorough reference work. On the state of the Latin American Left, including continuing and former insurgents, see Jorge G. Castañeda, *Utopia Unarmed: The Latin American Left after the Cold War* (New York: Alfred A. Knopf, 1993).

14. Matthew Soberg Shugart, "Guerrillas and Elections: An Institutionalist Perspective of the Costs of Conflicts and Competition," *International Studies Quarterly* (June 1992), 129–130.

15. Shugart, "Guerrillas and Elections," 137–139, 142, 145.

PART FIVE

■

Interstate and
Transnational Relations

In this part of the book we acknowledge the distinction between interstate and transnational relations. But the analysis blends them in broad categories of interaction in order to reflect the realities of the international system and the Latin American and Caribbean subsystem. The four chapters are concerned with certain patterns of interaction and instruments of policy among state and nonstate actors and international institutions. In sequence, they have to do with (1) violence and its accommodation, in terms of interstate war, internal warfare, and approximations of war involving military intervention, espionage, subversion, and covert action; (2) interactions within the international economic system, such as commercial relations and foreign aid, not only in terms of the interests of states and transnational actors but in terms of societal development as well; (3) the relationship of different types of Latin American governing regimes (in democratic, authoritarian, and revolutionary categories) with outsiders, in terms of regime development or behavior; and (4) multifaceted intersocietal relations in which states have limited influence over (often highly diffused) transnational actors: movement of people, cultural interactions (such as formal cultural exchanges, communications phenomena, and entertainment and sports), and the illicit drug traffic.

CHAPTER TWELVE

■

Warfare and
Its Approximations

Certain realities and norms in the international relations of Latin America and the Caribbean have been coercive and violent in nature. This chapter examines those realities in the three categories. Warfare is classified in two ways: (1) interstate wars from the nineteenth century to the present, involving the threat or use of force in the regional subsystem; and (2) internal warfare since the 1950s, carried out by subnational guerrilla groups with transnational connections, to which the target states and external states have responded. Efforts at conflict resolution in both categories of warfare are part of the analysis. The idea of war is extrapolated to include the third category: the coercive diplomacy manifested in military intervention, espionage, subversion, and covert action. (Other kinds of coercive diplomacy are taken up in later chapters.) The three phenomena in fact overlap in content, a reflection of the hazy boundary between open warfare and coercive diplomacy.

THE SOURCES OF CONFLICT

Violence in the Latin American subsystem has arisen essentially from five sets of causes: (1) boundary and territorial disputes, (2) competition for resources, (3) imperial and other power disputes, (4) ideological competition, and (5) migration of people and goods. Specific cases of conflict often involve combinations of these sources.[1]

Boundary and territorial conflicts have loomed large as a special interest in the foreign policy of almost every Latin American state. Boundary or border disputes flow from disagreements over frontiers between contiguous sovereignties. They have been prevalent within the region to the extent that every Latin American state with a common land frontier with another has been in conflict; only Caribbean island-states with no contiguous neighbors have avoided such quarrels. Boundary or border disputes are related to territorial disputes, in that they may be part of larger controversies involving sovereign claims. Territorial conflicts are usually disputes over the possession of land terrain but may extend to oceanic rights. Border and territorial disputes had their roots in the Latin American colonial period, and several have persisted until recently. Undetermined national boundaries at independence and rival state ambitions gave rise to patterns of strife continuing to the present day. Many have been resolved or suspended, but some remain potential sources of serious conflict. Inter-American war, the most intense form of subsystem conflict, has been associated with boundary and territorial questions. The terrain in contention was in some instances of strategic or economic worth and in others of dubious value; they always had a highly nationalist content.

Resource conflicts have become increasingly important in furthering national development and economic well-being. Although the disputes involve land or ocean rights, the energy, strategic, or food resources are primarily at stake (such as petroleum, natural gas, minerals, hydroelectricity, and fish).

Both classic imperialism and simpler projections of state power are associated with balance-of-power systems and usually include questions of prestige or some other version of "national honor." They have been prominently pursued by the external great powers. A series of European military interventions and other forms of power politics occurred in all parts of Latin America throughout the nineteenth century. U.S. intervention in the circum-Caribbean has been a continuing twentieth century reality. Soviet attempts at subversion were prevalent between the two world wars, as have been U.S. covert activities since World War II. For those Latin American states with power ambitions, border, territorial, and oceanic disputes are related to the geopolitical-strategic thrust for territorial expansion and regional influence. Certain nonstate actors also are sources of conflict. Conspicuous examples are guerrilla warfare since the 1950s and the violent aspects of the drug traffic from the late 1970s; others include activities by international business enterprises and multinational corporations.

Often this competition for power has been intertwined with ideological conflict. The ideological category goes beyond simple power considerations, however, to deal with the struggle to impose or resist the imposition of political, economic, and social values. The principal rivalries have been between dictatorships and democracies, civilian and military regimes, and democratic capitalism and various forms of Marxism.

Conflicts arising from the migration of people and goods are also multifaceted. A majority of the nineteenth-century European interventions were responses to problems arising from commerce, investments, and immigrants. Foreign investors and resident aliens appealed to their governments for redress when Latin Americans defaulted on their debts or mistreated foreign persons and property. Those governments demanded indemnity from Latin American states and at times threatened or used military force to gain compliance. Other migration conflicts that have resulted from strains caused by strife involve the movement of people across frontiers for economic or political reasons. The flow of illicit drugs has lead to considerable violence on the part of traffickers and to contentious interstate relations.

NINETEENTH-CENTURY PATTERNS AND CASES

Mexico and International Conflict

In the nineteenth century, Mexico was especially vulnerable to external intrusions. These intrusions involved military intervention, occupation, and great loss of territory at the hands of the United States and Europeans. The last U.S. intervention in Mexico ended in 1914. Britain in 1808 was poised to send an invading force ashore but aborted the effort because of the necessities of the Napoleonic Wars. Spain sent an expedition to Mexico in 1829 in response to the expulsion of Spanish citizens, but it was repelled by disease and the Mexican army. In 1838–1839 France blockaded and bombarded Vera Cruz and forced payment of claims to its nationals; the action was dubbed the Pastry War because of the enormous claim submitted by a French pastry chef. But the most critical occurrences for Mexico were war with the United States and, later, occupation by France.

Mexico's relations with the United States were dominated by boundary and territorial questions in the nineteenth century. The frontier between the United States and Mexico had not been fixed when the latter won its independence; an 1819 treaty, reaffirmed in 1828, agreed to the Sabine River as a boundary. The United States, however, expanding westward across the continent to realize "manifest destiny," wanted to designate the Rio Grande (Rio Bravo) as the new boundary but could not gain Mexican agreement.[2]

The Mexican government generally ignored its sparsely inhabited northern territory and granted "Anglo" settlers the right to form a colony. U.S. citizens who began to settle there in the 1820s eventually clashed with the central Mexican government. In 1836 Texas declared its independence and defeated a Mexican army sent to put it down. Texans wanted to be annexed as a U.S. state, but statehood was denied, largely because of the slavery issue. They thereupon established the independent Republic of Texas, which the United States recognized in 1837. Despite the opposition of Britain and France, who wanted Texas to serve as a buffer between the United States and Mexico, the United States finally made Texas a state in 1845.

Continued disputes over the extent of the Texas territory after U.S. statehood resulted in the U.S.-Mexican war (1846–1848). Mexico said that Texas ended at the Nueces River; the United States claimed that Texas ended at the Rio Grande. Full-scale warfare ensued, ending with complete U.S. mastery. The war was settled by the Treaty of Guadalupe Hidalgo, signed on February 2, 1848. Under its terms, Mexico quit its claims to Texas, agreed on the Texas boundary fixed at the Rio Grande, and ceded the rest of its northern territory from Texas to the Pacific Ocean. The United States paid Mexico $15 million.[3] The vastness of the new acquisition—almost half of Mexico's territory—did not satisfy some U.S. expansionists. An "all-Mexico" movement demanded total annexation, but their ambitions were frustrated by the slavery issue. In 1853 the U.S. Minister to Mexico, James Gadsden, negotiated the purchase from Mexico of the Gila River valley in southern Arizona and New Mexico for $10 million.

Mexico was rocked by civil war beginning in 1857, and the government of Benito Juárez in 1861 declared bankruptcy and repudiated its foreign debts. France, Britain, and Spain collaborated to coerce Mexico to honor their nationals' heavy claims, some of which were fraudulent; their combined fleet landed troops at Vera Cruz. The following year, in 1862, Britain and Spain reached agreements with Mexico and withdrew. Napoleon III had much more in mind, however: He wanted to establish a French empire in Mexico in order to enhance French commerce, contain U.S. continental expansion, and curry favor with the church in France by punishing anticlerical Mexican liberals.

French troops occupied the capital, and France formed the Empire of Mexico, with prince Archduke Maximilian of Austria, a Roman Catholic, as the chief of state. In 1865, at the end of its own civil war, the United States, which had continued to recognize the Juárez government, demanded that French forces be withdrawn. Napoleon III removed French troops from Mexico, not only because of the U.S. position but also because of Mexican forces that continued their resistance outside the capital city, because of opposition in France, and because of a tenuous political position in Europe. With French military support gone, Juárez's army deposed Maximilian; he was convicted by court martial and executed.

The 1848 peace treaty between Mexico and the United States did not end their border friction. Numerous incidents continued to occur into the twentieth century. U.S. Marines landed in Mexico in 1913, as the Mexican revolution took an exceptionally violent turn. U.S. forces took Vera Cruz in 1914 and held it for almost seven months; General John J. Pershing led an expedition into northern Mexico in an unsuccessful attempt to capture General Francisco (Pancho) Villa. This was the last U.S. (or other foreign) military intervention in Mexico.

Southern Cone Conflicts

The nineteenth century witnessed a series of major South American wars or threats of war and power struggles. Involving in one way or another all of the subregional states, the wars were part of a larger expression of Southern Cone power politics and geopolitical thinking. The most intense leadership rivalry was among Argentina, Brazil, and Chile, the "ABC" states. Southern Cone conflicts left a legacy of territorial and boundary disputes, power struggles leading to war and threats of war, persistent claims of sovereignty, competition for resources, and enduring xenophobia toward neighbors.

The rivalry between Argentina and Brazil for control of the Rio de la Plata region centered on Uruguay in the early national period. Portugal and Spain had contested the region for two centuries in the colonial era as the major point of contact between their empires. Argentina unsuccessfully tried to maintain the viceroyalty of La Plata under its control during the wars for independence, and afterward it actively meddled in the other platine states. Brazil, after gaining independence in 1822, pursued an aggressive policy of "manifest destiny," clashing with Argentine ambitions.

Uruguayan patriots claimed independence from both Spain and Portugal and seceded from Buenos Aires. In 1822 Brazil annexed Uruguay as the Cisplatine
province of the Brazilian empire. In 1825 Uruguay declared its independence from
Brazil; Argentina entered the dispute on the side of the rebels; and an indecisive
three-year war ensued. Britain, its commercial interests in the area disrupted, intervened to force a settlement. It pressured Argentina and Brazil into signing the Treaty
of Montevideo (1828), in which both countries agreed to recognize Uruguayan independence so as to create a buffer state between them. But attempts to control
Uruguay continued throughout the nineteenth century, and intermittent Uruguayan
civil war invited Argentine and Brazilian intervention and claims for territory.

What Uruguayans called the Great War began in 1836. An alliance between Argentine dictator Juan Manuel de Rosas and an Uruguayan political faction, the Blan-
cos, conducted a siege of Montevideo from 1841 to 1851 against another faction,
the Colorados, allied with anti-Rosas Argentines. From 1845 to 1850 French and
British naval units blockaded Buenos Aires and thus supported the Montevideans.
After the withdrawal, Brazil joined the anti-Rosas alignment, partly because it was
assured of a favorable settlement of its Uruguayan boundary, and was soon victorious. In 1851 Brazil forced a treaty in which Uruguay gave up almost half its territory
along the northern frontier.

The Paraguayan War (1865–1870), known in Paraguay as the War of the Triple
Alliance, resulted from the alliance of the Uruguayan Colorados with Argentina and
Brazil to resist the expansionist moves of Paraguayan dictator Francisco Solano
López. A Blanco government, having poor relations with both Argentina and Brazil,
had responded to Paraguayan overtures for a common policy in 1862. López had in
mind a Paraguayan-led empire of central South American states, including Uruguay
and Bolivia. Paraguay invaded Argentina and Brazil near their Uruguayan borders,
and in May 1865 the triple alliance of those two states plus Uruguay was formed. A
five-year war resulted, ending in March 1970 with Paraguay's complete defeat. Most
of its male population was killed, and Argentina and Brazil took portions of its territory. Paraguay, no longer a power contender, was left as a buffer state between its
neighbors.[4]

Following the movements for independence, the entire boundary between Argentina and Chile from north to south was disputed. In 1881 a vague settlement
provided for the frontier to run along the "highest peaks" of the Andes, dividing the
watershed. This provision was interpreted differently by each state. War was narrowly averted over a portion of the northern frontier known as the Puna de Atacama.
After failing to reach agreement through direct diplomacy, Chile and Argentina
agreed to arbitration by the United States. In 1899 the U.S. arbiter divided the disputed territory, and the decision was accepted by both sides. Parts of the southern
boundary remained in dispute, however. The 1881 treaty had divided Tierra del
Fuego between the two states, giving Argentina sovereignty over Patagonia, and
Chile sovereignty over the Strait of Magellan (which Chile agreed to neutralize). Disagreements then arose over the precise demarcation, and in 1896 the disputants

turned to the British crown for arbitration. King Edward VII handed down his award in 1902.

Important conflicts on the west coast of South America that developed in the early independence period continued in some respects into the latter twentieth century. Chile, intent on dominating the Pacific coast, pursued aggressive policies toward Bolivia and Peru, who in 1836 formed an alliance. Chile, seeing a threat to its economic interests and strategic position, immediately went to war against the Peru-Bolivian Confederation. Argentina did the same in 1937, but, feeling less threatened than Chile, played a minor military role. Chile invaded Peru and defeated the combined Peru-Bolivian army in 1839, bringing an end to the Confederation.

The War of the Pacific (1879–1883) was a particularly serious conflict. In 1866 Chileans had discovered vast nitrate deposits in the barren Atacama Desert along the 800-mile Bolivian Pacific coastline, where few Bolivians had settled. In 1874 Bolivia ceded a portion of its Atacama territory to Chile. The Chileans mined and exported the nitrates under an agreement with Bolivia until 1878, when a dispute over taxes led to military confrontation. When Chile attacked the Bolivian desert regions in 1879, Peru entered the war on the side of Bolivia. Some major actions were fought at sea, where Chile had supremacy over Peru. The Chilean army invaded Peru and sacked and occupied Lima. U.S. and European governments unsuccessfully attempted to mediate a truce. Chile finally defeated the Peru-Bolivian alliance.

In the Ancón Treaty of October 20, 1883, Peru ceded its province of Tarapacá to Chile. Chile was to occupy the Peruvian provinces of Tacna and Arica for a ten-year period, after which a plebiscite was to determine their future status. Chile and Peru could not agree on the terms of the plebiscite, however, and its continuous postponement after 1893 embittered their relations for the next thirty-five years. A compromise was finally reached through U.S. good offices in the Washington Protocol of 1929. Chile annexed Arica and returned Tacna to Peru.

Chile and Bolivia signed a truce on April 4, 1884, which provided for an indefinite armistice and for Chilean occupation of Atacama. In 1888 Chile unilaterally made the Atacama territory its province of Antofagasta. A treaty formally ending the war was not signed until October 20, 1904. Under its provisions Bolivia gave up the territory, thereby confirming the loss of its coastline and access to the sea. In return, Chile indemnified Bolivia and agreed to build a railroad from La Paz to Arica for Bolivian use. Chile later allowed Bolivia to use Arica as a free port, but Bolivia never abandoned the idea of regaining its own Pacific port. In 1920 it appealed to the League of Nations for a seaport on the grounds that the 1904 treaty was null and void, but the League refused to intervene.[5]

The persistent Argentine-British Falklands/Malvinas dispute began with Argentina's independence. The Falkland Islands, known in Argentina as the Islas Malvinas and located some 300 miles east of southern Argentina, had an ambiguous early history that complicated later claims to its ownership. After discovery of the islands in 1592 France, Spain, and Britain made contending colonial claims. In 1820, Argentina (then the United Provinces of La Plata) took possession based on rights of succession to

Spanish territory. Britain later claimed ownership. At the same time, private U.S. sealing vessels were trespassing on the islands. The Argentine governor seized three of the vessels, which opened up a controversy between Argentina and the United States, during which the *USS Lexington* destroyed the Argentine colony on the Malvinas. Britain took advantage of the situation by occupying the islands with military force in 1833. A British naval unit drove off an Argentine settlement and established effective British control for the next century and a half. Argentina never accepted British rule, and it regularly protested and asserted its own sovereign claims.

TWENTIETH-CENTURY PATTERNS AND CASES THROUGH WORLD WAR II

U.S. Caribbean Imperialism

During the first third of the twentieth century, the United States pursued imperialism in the circum-Caribbean.[6] Its behavior was based especially on geopolitical-strategic calculations combined with economic motives and, sometimes, democratic purposes. The beginnings of U.S. imperialism in the region date from the U.S. victory in its ten-week war with Spain. In addition to colonizing Puerto Rico, the United States intervened on numerous occasions and in various ways in seven states between 1898 and 1934—Cuba, Panama, Haiti, Dominican Republic, Nicaragua, Honduras, and Guatemala. Intervention variously assumed the forms of troop landings and military occupations, the establishment of protectorates, electoral supervision, and the creation of customs receiverships. Most of the interventions were carried out with concern for the security of the Panama Canal, as it was being constructed and then went into operation. In the initial stages of imperialism, the United States asserted its new world power with little hesitation in order to attain canal rights and to secure the Caribbean approaches to the Central American isthmus. A secondary motive later developed—intervention in the name of democracy and antidictatorship. Some interventions occurred to protect the lives and property of U.S. citizens. For a time, the focus was on the protection of capital investments ("Dollar Diplomacy").

U.S. imperialism increased after the conclusion of the last European military intervention in a sovereign Latin America state—Venezuela in 1902–1903. Europeans residing in Venezuela had been heavily damaged in a civil war, but dictator Cipriano Castro excluded foreign claims. External states issued ultimatums and, when they were not met, Germany, Great Britain, and Italy blockaded Venezuela in concert. The United States had previously stressed that the Monroe Doctrine forbade territorial aggrandizement, but it did not protect any state against punishment for fiscal misconduct. After the blockade began, the United States successfully pressured the European states to accept arbitration of their grievances. In 1905 President Roosevelt issued his corollary to the Monroe Doctrine, and the United States thereafter engaged in its own Caribbean intervention, largely in order to preempt that of the Europeans.

U.S. troops were continuously based in Panama from 1902 to 1914 during the construction of the canal. They intervened there during local disturbances from 1918 to 1920 and in 1925. The United States exercised its rights of intervention in Cuba by establishing a provisional military government from 1906 to 1909; it also briefly sent in troops in 1912 and again in 1916 (with some troops remaining until 1922) and threatened to do so again on numerous other occasions. U.S. forces intervened in the Dominican Republic in 1905 to restore order; another troop intervention in 1916 was followed by the establishment of a U.S. military government that lasted until 1924. U.S. Marines occupied Nicaragua from 1912 to 1925 and from 1926 until 1933. Marines were sent to Haiti in 1914. After a brief withdrawal they returned in 1915 and remained until 1934. U.S. troops were in and out of Honduras between 1903 and 1925. A brief military intervention occurred in Guatemala in 1920 to protect U.S. diplomats and private interests during political disturbances.

The Taft administration (1909–1913) began the U.S. practice of "Dollar Diplomacy" in the Caribbean region. Secretary of State Philander C. Knox manipulated U.S. investments and loans by encouraging financial groups and consortia to extend them in the Dominican Republic, Haiti, and Nicaragua. This private capital involvement led to the landing of U.S. Marines to protect U.S. lives and property. The United States pursued arms control in Cuba and Nicaragua (and Mexico) through supervision of sales and embargoes. U.S. "fiscal intervention" took place under U.S.-administered customs receiverships in the Dominican Republic beginning in 1905, in Nicaragua from 1911, and in Haiti starting in 1916. The receiverships involved U.S. fiscal control of the economies and were designed to bring about responsible management and to arrange for a restructuring of international debts.

U.S. armed forces carried out "civic action" projects during their occupations of Cuba, Panama, Nicaragua, Haiti, and the Dominican Republic. Under the aegis of "civic action," internal order was restored, legal systems were reformed, highways were constructed, public education was improved, and sanitation and public health programs were instituted. Public schools were constructed, teachers were trained, and public administration programs were developed. Little political development took place, however.

President Woodrow Wilson added the element of pro-democracy and antidictatorship to U.S. interventions. It should be emphasized that military actions were not initially engaged in order to bring down dictatorships or promote constitutional-democratic practices, although the refusal to recognize new governments was so motivated. Once military occupation was begun, however, U.S. Marines trained, organized, and commanded the military and police forces in Nicaragua, Haiti, and the Dominican Republic, in the hope that they would be converted to apolitical forces and protect future constitutional governments upon the withdrawal of U.S. forces (a hope totally unrealized). The United States concurrently supervised elections prior to ending occupations. Such elections were held in Cuba, Panama, the Dominican Republic, Haiti, and Nicaragua. These Wilsonian practices were continued by Presidents Harding, Coolidge, and, for a time, Hoover.

The United States moved away from interventionist policies beginning in 1930. President Hoover reduced the number of troops in the Caribbean, and President Roosevelt largely based his Good Neighbor Policy on nonintervention. The last troop contingents left Nicaragua in 1933 and Haiti in 1934, leaving no U.S. troops in Latin America for the first time since 1919. No further direct military interventions occurred until 1965, when forces were sent to the Dominican Republic. President Roosevelt resisted State Department pressures for armed intervention against the repressive Machado dictatorship in Cuba in 1933, and the 1903 treaty with Cuba giving the United States interventionist rights was abrogated in 1934 (the United States retained the Guantanamo naval station). Likewise, the United States concluded a treaty with Panama in 1936, giving up rights to intervene in Panamanian affairs. The last customs receiverships, in Haiti and the Dominican Republic, were finally closed in 1941.

Soviet Subversion

After the Bolshevik Revolution of 1917, the Soviet Union attempted the contradictory policy of simultaneously creating loyal Communist parties in Latin America and establishing traditional diplomatic relations. After Uruguay recognized the Soviet Union in 1926, the Soviet embassy in Montevideo served as Latin American headquarters for the Comintern and the point of dissemination for revolutionary propaganda. Soviet efforts to stimulate armed insurrections through local Communist parties were attempted in Mexico (1929), Argentina (1930), Chile (1931), El Salvador (1932), Chile (1932), Cuba (1933), and Brazil (1935). The insurrections, all of which were suppressed, led to outlawing the Communist parties and rupturing relations with the Soviet Union—by 1939 all diplomatic relations between Latin American states and the Soviet Union had been severed. Soviet policy was much more cautious after 1935; Moscow instructed local Communist parties to participate in popular front coalitions.

Inter-Latin American Conflict

Haiti and the Dominican Republic, both located on the island of Hispaniola, viewed each other with suspicion.[7] After the Dominican Republic ejected Haitian occupation in 1844, border conflicts were frequent, aggravated by mutual racial enmities. In 1874 the two states agreed to a vague boundary, which was to be delineated by subsequent negotiations, but it remained undefined for the next six decades, and frequent border clashes occurred. In 1934 and 1935 the presidents of the two states exchanged visits and announced that all border difficulties had been resolved. As it turned out, the difficulties were more intense than ever. In October 1937 Dominican military forces killed at least 12,000, and perhaps as many as 25,000, Haitian peasants near the border. Little doubt exists that Dominican dictator Rafael Trujillo was responsible. A settlement was reached using the peacekeeping machinery of the Inter-American System, although the papal nuncio accredited to both states was in fact responsible for the settlement signed on January 31, 1938. The Dominican Republic agreed to pay $750,000 as indemnity to Haiti and to fix responsibility for the "incident."

The Chaco War between Bolivia and Paraguay from 1932 to 1935 was an especially violent and bloody conflict. The war originated in disputes over undetermined national frontiers.[8] The area of the Chaco Boreal, a triangle of territory bound by the Pilcomayo, Paraguay, and Parapeti rivers, was a void area until both Paraguay and Bolivia took increased interest in it. Paraguay desired to recover some of its lost national prestige after the War of the Triple Alliance; and Bolivia, after the War of the Pacific, looked for an outlet to the Atlantic through ports on the Paraguay River. Several frontier treaties were signed, but none went into effect. In 1906 Bolivia began building small forts in the disputed region, and Paraguay followed suit. Armed clashes in December 1928 led to full-scale war in 1932. Numerous attempts at mediation by elements of the League of Nations and of the Inter-American System, and certain American states acting individually and in concert, failed to settle the territorial issues or to bring the subsequent violence to a halt. By 1935 Paraguay was in control of most of the Chaco and, with both sides exhausted, a truce was agreed to.

A prolonged and difficult peace conference worked from 1935 until 1939 before it was able to arrive at a peace settlement. Argentina took the initiative to organize the process, and the meetings took place in Buenos Aires. The participants were the other Southern Cone countries (Argentina, Brazil, Chile, Peru, and Uruguay); the bitter belligerents, Bolivia and Paraguay; and the United States, which had been closely involved in prior peace efforts. The peace treaty adopted in 1938 gave Paraguay, as military victor, most of the disputed area; Bolivia gained port facilities and rights of passage through Paraguay. The financial and human costs for both sides were huge. Some 50,000 to 60,000 Bolivians and 35,000 to 40,000 Paraguayans had died in the war.

Peru and Ecuador had serious boundary disputes that dated from their earliest relations.[9] Upon independence they both claimed the sparsely inhabited Amazon provinces of Jaen and Maynas lying to the north of the Marañón River (which eventually flows into the Amazon River). Military movements by both sides occurred in the area between July 1941 and January 1942, but no major fighting took place. The United States, which entered World War II in December 1941, forced a settlement of the dispute and its destabilizing influences in South America. An agreement was reached in Rio de Janeiro on January 29, 1942, in which Ecuador (the weaker belligerent) accepted Peruvian sovereignty over the disputed territory, and the United States, Argentina, Chile, and Brazil were named guarantor states. A mixed Ecuadorian-Peruvian Boundary Commission was subsequently appointed to fix the boundary; but, after about 95 percent of the frontier had been marked, Ecuador protested that it did not conform to the agreement, and the commission's work was halted. The dispute remained unresolved, and violence was renewed on several occasions (see below); in each instance the guarantor states named in 1942 undertook their third-party role.

Colombia and Peru signed a treaty in 1922, fixing the boundary between them in the Amazon River Basin. In 1930 the demarcation was fixed by a bilateral commission. Under this plan, Colombia occupied a strip of territory called the "Leticia Trapezium," which included the Amazon River port town of Leticia. In September 1932, an irregular Peruvian band seized the town by force and ejected the Colombian officials. The Peruvian government at first repudiated the act, but later it supported the seizure, sent regular troops into the area, and declared the 1922 treaty invalid. Colombia then sent military forces to the Leticia territory, and in February 1933 the disputants severed diplomatic relations.

The Inter-American System and Brazil attempted to settle the matter but Peru adopted an uncompromising position. After a change of government in Peru, however, the disputants adopted a League of Nations proposal whereby they evacuated their troops from the area, and in June 1933, a League commission took over its administration. Peru and Colombia then continued their negotiations with Brazilian mediation, from October 1933 until May 1934, when an agreement was reached. A protocol was signed in which Peru expressed regret for the incidents causing the dispute, reestablished diplomatic relations, and confirmed the Lima Treaty of 1922. Colombia then reoccupied Leticia.

POST–WORLD WAR II PATTERNS AND CASES

U.S. Cold War Interventions

A new factor entered the Latin American subsystem after World War II with the creation of the U.S. Central Intelligence Agency (CIA).[10] During the cold war, CIA officials deliberately participated in the assassination of foreign leaders; trained private armies; bribed chiefs of state, labor union leaders, and other officials and political figures; and engaged in various activities to discredit or remove what were considered to be leftist Latin American governments. The CIA's covert interventions in Latin American politics became highly controversial in both Latin American and the United States.

In 1974 and 1975 the U.S. intelligence community was investigated by a presidential commission and select committees in both chambers of the U.S. Congress. Former directors of the CIA testified and stated their opposition to further assassinations as an instrument of U.S. foreign policy, a position reiterated by President Ford. The reform movement proved abortive, however, as Congress made do with the half-measure of "oversight," and the CIA interpreted its reporting requirements as narrowly as possible.[11] The Reagan administration gave free rein to the CIA. One result was the 1983–1984 mining of Nicaraguan harbors, which flouted the oversight prerogatives of the Senate Select Committee on Intelligence. As it turned out, questions about appropriate activities for an intelligence organization in a democratic nation and the legal basis for those activities still had not been resolved by the end of the cold war.[12]

The first important case of cold war conflict and U.S. covert intervention in Latin America occurred in Guatemala in 1954.[13] The situation was rooted in the 1944 overthrow of Dictator-General Jorge Ubico, after thirteen years in power. The following year, elected civilian president Juan Arévalo was inaugurated, and he promoted fundamental social reform. He was succeeded in 1951 by President Jacobo Arbenz Guzmán, who initiated a number of radical economic and social changes. His efforts eventually brought opposition from the United States, which accused him of bringing Communists into his government and allowing them too influence Guatemalan politics. Arbenz attempted to integrate the Indian majority into the national life through labor organization and agrarian reform, bringing strenuous opposition from the powerful landowning class. He employed Guatemalan and foreign leftists in his government (including the Argentine Ernesto "Che" Guevara) and broadened diplomatic contacts with Communist states. He expropriated United Fruit Company properties.

By early 1953 Guatemalan exiles were being trained in the neighboring states of Honduras and Nicaragua with CIA assistance and support. The resolution that Secretary of State John Foster Dulles pushed through the Tenth Inter-American Conference in 1954 was aimed at weakening Guatemala's position in the Inter-American System. In June 1954 ten member states, at the behest of the United States, invoked the Inter-American Treaty of Reciprocal Assistance (Rio Treaty), charging intervention by international communism in Guatemala and highlighting the danger posed to American peace and security. The OAS Council met provisionally as the Organ of Consultation and called for a foreign ministers' meeting. At the same time, a U.S.-sponsored exile force, led by Guatemalan Colonel Carlos Castillo Armas, invaded Guatemala from Honduras on June 18, 1954. Before an OAS fact-finding team could arrive in Guatemala, the coup had succeeded and Arbenz had been sent into exile; the foreign ministers meeting was canceled.

U.S. conflict with the Castro government in Cuba was the dominant focus of covert U.S. actions after 1959.[14] Castro's 26th of July Movement, which took power on January 1, 1959, originally seemed dedicated to liberal democracy. The United States recognized the Castro government on January 7, 1959. By the end of 1961, however, it was clear that Castro was running a dictatorship. On May 1, 1961, he formally announced that Cuba was "a socialist state," and the following December he stated that he would be a "Marxist-Leninist until the last day of my life." These developments were accompanied by Cuba's increasing orientation toward the Soviet Union. Castro defied the United States early in his regime. He confiscated U.S. and British oil refineries and other U.S. investments and property, abrogated the U.S.-Cuban mutual assistance pact, expelled U.S. military missions, and mounted a hostile propaganda campaign. The Eisenhower administration canceled all imports of Cuban sugar on July 6, 1960. Three days later Soviet Premier Nikita Khrushchev proclaimed Cuba a protectorate and threatened to defend it with missiles against the United States. Cuban-U.S. diplomatic relations were ruptured on January 3, 1961.

The United States led multilateral actions as well as took unilateral measures against Cuba. The principal early unilateral effort consisted of organizing and financing a Cuban exile invasion to overthrow Castro in April 1961. The 1,500-man force, which included a large number of disillusioned former Castro revolutionaries, landed at the Bay of Pigs on Cuba's southern coast in hopes of catalyzing a popular uprising. Planned under President Eisenhower and carried out under President Kennedy, it was an utter failure. The Cuban armed forces easily subdued and imprisoned the invaders.[15] Although the United States pledged to desist from any further invasions of Cuba as part of the settlement of the missile crisis with the Soviet Union in October 1962, it continued attempts to assassinate Castro. In 1975, Senate hearings revealed efforts made on Castro's life through various intermediaries from 1960 to 1965.

The United States employed clandestine operations in Chile to disrupt the elected Marxist government of President Salvador Allende from 1970 to 1973.[16] The Chilean election of 1970 was thrown to the congress when no candidate received a majority. ITT, the U.S. corporation, then offered a million dollars to the Nixon administration for a bribery scheme to seek Allende's defeat in the Chilean congressional runoff. The offer was made through John A. McCone, former director of the CIA and then an ITT board member. The U.S. government, which had financed Allende's opposition in the campaign, declined the offer on the grounds that it would be unworkable, but thereafter it made several efforts to "destabilize" the Allende government and discredit his experiment of "socialism in democracy."

U.S. officials, including military personnel, encouraged Chilean military dissidents to make a coup prior to Allende's inauguration. After Allende's inauguration, the United States encouraged and financed a wide spectrum of opposition groups, including other parties, certain trade and labor organizations, middle-class housewives, and right-wing terrorist groups; strikes and demonstrations were funded and coordinated through the CIA station in Santiago. In addition, the United States used its influence and voting power in the international lending agencies to put a "credit squeeze" on Chile. Finally, by mid-1973, Chile was in a desperate economic and social situation. The Chilean military overthrew Allende on September 11, 1973, in a brief but bloody coup in which Allende died.

The later disclosure that the CIA had financed the strikes that preceded the Chilean coup was confirmed by President Ford in a news conference in September 1974. Ford said that U.S. actions had been carried out in an attempt to help preserve opposition newspapers and parties in Chile. (In fact, the opposition press had continued to print during the Allende years, and opposition parties, including the most hostile, continued to function; only after the coup was the press suppressed and were political parties banned). Ford justified U.S. subversion in Chile as being "in the best interests of the Chilean people."

The United States sent troops to the Dominican Republic in 1965, in its first direct military intervention in Latin America since 1933.[17] The intervention took place in the aftermath of the thirty-one-year Trujillo dictatorship and in the context of U.S. experience with Castro's Cuba; it ended with Trujillo's assassination on May 30, 1961. Dominican individuals and groups with conflicting purposes struggled with each other after Trujillo's death, and none were satisfied with the results. On

April 24, 1965, a rebel army faction known as the "Constitutionalists" attempted a coup in support of civilian reformist politician Juan Bosch (who had been elected president and inaugurated in February 1963 but overthrown by a military coup seven months later). The opposing military "Loyalist" faction was supported by most military units and the national police. Military advantage fluctuated between the two sides during a civil war lasting more than four months and culminating with U.S. military intervention. The United States landed 405 marines in the capital city on April 28. The complement was increased thereafter, reaching a high of 23,000 troops (mostly from the U.S. Army) in the vicinity of Santo Domingo, with 10,000 more standing by offshore.

The United States justified the initial troop landing as protection for its nationals residing in the Dominican Republic. In an address to the nation on May 2, however, President Johnson asserted that Communists had joined the rebels and threatened to take control. Because "what began as a popular democratic revolution" had been "seized and placed into the hands of a band of Communist conspirators," said the president, the U.S. goal had changed "to help prevent another Communist state in this hemisphere." The United States then received OAS endorsement of its intervention, but only after a bitter debate, and the U.S. command was transformed into an international peacekeeping force. Except for the Brazilian contribution, the Latin American presence was a token one, and the peacekeeping mission in fact supported the Loyalist military faction. Finally, in late August, a settlement was signed by both sides. A year later, in September 1966, the peace force was withdrawn.

British Disputes

With Guyana.   Britain and Venezuela had disputed a large portion of British Guiana from the beginning of Venezuelan independence.[18] The problem continued after Britain granted the territory independence in 1966 as Guyana. The dispute had seemed settled in 1899 when the decision of an international court of arbitration was accepted by both parties. However, in 1962 Venezuela reasserted its claims, declaring the 1899 agreement void. Venezuela had hired U.S. attorneys to represent its case in 1899; in 1962 it discovered that the will of one of those attorneys had stated that a secret "deal" had been made between the British representatives and a Russian arbiter.

Venezuela wanted the boundary to be moved some 150 miles to the east to the Essequibo River, a change that would give Venezuela about 53,000 square miles of territory constituting approximately three-fifths of Guyana. Venezuela protested Guyanese independence, asserting that the boundary question should have first been settled. In 1966, Great Britain, Guyana, and Venezuela signed an agreement establishing a mixed border commission and providing that, if the commission failed to solve the problem by May 1970, the dispute would be referred to the World Court or the UN secretary-general. The mixed commission failed in its mission, but with direct negotiations the three states signed another agreement on June 18, 1970. The agreement suspended the 1966 protocol and provided for a twelve-year "cooling-off" period, to be extended automatically unless either Venezuela or Guyana decided otherwise. (The agreement was so extended in 1982). In the meantime, Guyana was free to develop the disputed area, and Venezuela was to press no further claims.

With Guatemala. A long history of conflict existed over the ownership of Belize, formerly the colony of British Honduras. Guatemala and Great Britain signed a treaty in 1850 in which Guatemala recognized British sovereignty over Belize in return for certain concessions, one of which was the construction of a road connecting Guatemala City with the Atlantic coast. Since Britain never built the road, Guatemala declared the treaty void in 1939 and reasserted its claims on the grounds of territory inherited from Spain. Britain replied that Spain never effectively controlled the area, that it was not a part of the colonial Guatemalan jurisdiction, and that, anyway, Spain had ceded the area to Britain in 1670. Britain maintained control.

Guatemala reasserted its claims in the 1950s, when Britain began to consider granting independence to Belize. Belize did not join the short-lived West Indies Federation formed in 1958 and refused a Guatemalan proposal in 1960 that it become an internally self-governing "free associated state" under Guatemalan sovereignty. Guatemala broke diplomatic relations with Britain in 1963, when the latter allowed Belize internal self-government. Guatemala and Belize both rejected a U.S. proposal in 1971 that Belize be granted immediate independence on condition it would "consult" with Guatemala on foreign and defense matters. Belize desired independence but feared a Guatemalan military invasion once British protection was gone; Britain was willing to grant independence but not to guarantee the defense of the new state. Finally, in 1991, Britain relented on the security issue and granted Belize independence, leaving a British force in Belize to guarantee its territorial integrity. Guatemala refused to recognized Belize as a new state.

Mexico laid claim to part of Belize based on succession rights to Spanish sovereignty, but only asserted its right to participate in any discussions on the status of the area. Mexico stated that it would not reactivate its claims if a solution was reached based on the wishes of the Belizen people.

On September 6, 1991, Guatemalan President Jorge Serrano recognized Belize as a sovereign state. Guatemala and Belize commenced diplomatic relations. Two years later, Guatemala and Belize pledged to refrain from using force against each other. In January 1994 Britain withdrew most of its garrison and handed over defense responsibilities to Belize.

With Argentina. In 1982 Britain's continuing dispute with Argentina over the Falkland or Malvinas Islands escalated into war.[19] In 1965 the United Nations General Assembly, at Argentina's behest, had approved a resolution urging the two states to negotiate a resolution of the sovereignty question. Britain acquiesced, and in 1971 agreements were reached on matters of commerce, communications, air service, educational and medical facilities, and cultural exchanges. In 1975, a British government study reporting the possibility of oil in the surrounding continental shelf complicated matters. Britain proposed a "lease-back" scheme, whereby Argentina would be granted formal sovereignty but Britain would continue administrative control in order to allow the Falkland inhabitants sufficient time to adjust to eventual Argentine governance. Settlers had migrated to the Falklands after the assertion of British control in 1833; in 1980 they numbered about 1,800. Most of the Falklanders strongly desired the status quo, wanting neither annexation to Argentina nor independence. The British Parliament defeated the lease-back formula in the face of opposition by the Falkland lobby.

Argentina then sought to recover the Malvinas by force. On April 2, 1982, Argentina invaded and took military control of the inhabited portions of the British Falkland Islands colony, saying it was enforcing its rightful sovereignty over the Islas Malvinas. The British government, led by Prime Minister Margaret Thatcher, dispatched a naval force to the South Atlantic, 7,000 miles from southern English ports, and appealed for support from the United Nations and the European Community (EC). The UN Security Council responded with Resolution 502, which condemned the Argentine action, demanded an immediate withdrawal of Argentine forces, and called on both governments to seek a diplomatic solution to their differences. The Soviet Union did not veto the resolution, apparently satisfied with the dilemma facing the United States. The EC also responded favorably to the British appeal, adopting a resolution on April 16 condemning the illegal Argentine aggression against a territory linked to the Community and urgently appealing to Argentina to implement UN Security Council Resolution 502. The EC also banned arms sales to and embargoed imports from Argentina.

The United States had quickly engaged in an intense mediation effort, hoping to commence negotiations and avoid open warfare. Secretary of State Alexander Haig pursued "shuttle diplomacy" from April 7–19, with visits to London and Buenos Aires. The Thatcher government argued that democracies should not appease dictators and must resist aggression, and insisted that Britain would not consider negotiations until Argentina unconditionally withdrew its troops in accordance with the Security Council resolution. A "paramount consideration" for the British was that the wishes of resident Falklanders be respected. The Argentine government, in turn, said it would not remove its troops nor begin negotiations until Britain recognized Argentine sovereignty over the islands and recalled its naval task force. The U.S. effort effectively ended in impasse on April 19.

Argentina turned to the Inter-American System for support. The initial response from other Latin American states was restrained. A meeting of the OAS Permanent Council from April 5–13 resulted only in a "resolution of concern" that offered its "friendly cooperation in the search for a peaceful settlement." Argentina invoked the Rio Treaty just as the U.S. mediation effort ended, and the Twentieth Meeting of Consultation of Ministers of Foreign Affairs was convened April 26–28. By this time British forces had penetrated the hemispheric security zone as defined in the Rio Treaty. The foreign ministers adopted a resolution supporting Argentine claims to sovereignty but refused to invoke any sanctions, as Argentina had requested, against Britain.

The United States ended its neutrality on April 30, in favor of Britain and in strong opposition to Argentina. Secretary Haig said that "in light of Argentina's failure to accept a compromise, we must take concrete steps to underscore that the United States cannot and will not condone the use of unlawful force to resolve disputes." Among other measures, the United States suspended all military exports and Export-Import Bank credits to Argentina. It promised material support for British forces on request, short of direct military involvement.

The EC, UN, and Inter-American System continued their efforts as military action escalated. EC support for the British position had faltered, especially with the heavy loss of life that followed the sinking of an Argentine cruiser on May 2. It was widely perceived that the British had violated their own rules of engagement and eroded its moral advantage as the victim of aggression. Following relentless British bargaining, however, the majority decided to extend the sanctions against Argentina indefinitely. In the UN Security Council, Secretary-General Javier Pérez de Cuellar reported that his efforts had brought no agreement. The inter-American foreign ministers meeting was reconvened May 27–29. The final resolution, adopted after a Latin American display of hostility toward the United States, condemned British counterforce but again refused sanctions.

After the military campaign came to an end on June 14, the EC lifted its sanctions. On July 12 President Reagan announced that U.S. economic sanctions were no longer necessary. (The ban on military transfers, predating the conflict and requiring a human rights certification to Congress, was not lifted until December 1983, when a new civilian government was inaugurated in Buenos Aires.) Britain continued its own sanctions and enforced a 200 nautical mile exclusion zone. It kept military power in the area ("Fortress Falklands"), despite the expense to the British treasury and the depletion of its NATO forces.

The disputants remained without diplomatic relations and technically at war, as Argentina had not formally declared an end to hostilities. Argentina continued to press its case for sovereignty in the United Nations. Communication did occur, however, with Argentina and Britain speaking through Brazil and Switzerland, respectively, as their intermediaries; direct secret talks, begun in December 1983, broke down in acrimony. Formal talks were finally commenced, and in February 1990, almost eight years after the South Atlantic war had ended, Britain and Argentina reestablished diplomatic relations. Subsequent agreements were signed regarding investment promotion, military movements in the South Atlantic, and air and sea links between Britain and Argentina. Argentina continued to claim sovereignty over the islands, and Britain continued to reject such claims.

Latin American Insurgency

Contemporary guerrilla warfare was introduced with Fidel Castro's successful exile invasion of Cuba and subsequent defeat of dictator Fulgencio Batista.[20] Similar conflicts emanated from the Caribbean but extended into South America and, to an extent, Mexico. After about a year of consolidating his power in the wake of the revolution 's success on January 1, 1959, Castro openly encouraged violent revolution in the rest of the hemisphere and gave direct assistance to guerrilla movements, especially in Venezuela, Peru, and Guatemala. Guerrilla activities in Latin America intensified in 1963 and 1964, and Cuban support continued until about 1968. During that time, Cuba added Colombia to its list of targets, and Che Guevara led the insurgency in Bolivia (see Chapter 11).

While Cuba urged and actively supported violent revolution in the rest of the region, the Soviet Union favored relations through "normal" diplomatic and economic channels. Soviet policy had continued to be generally unprovocative during World War II and through the 1950s, and after the war its covert activities and its support for Latin American revolutionary groups vacillated. The Soviet Union urged caution in the early 1960s, following Castro's success in Cuba, and throughout the extended period of guerrilla warfare. Most orthodox (Moscow-oriented) Communist parties followed the Soviet lead and rejected armed insurgency in favor of more cautious tactics. China supported the militant Cuban posture for the violent overthrow of existing regimes, although it simultaneously attempted to increase its own diplomatic and trade contacts with Latin American states.

By late 1968 Castro had come to terms with the Soviet Union and tacitly accepted the Soviet doctrines of peaceful coexistence and evolutionary transition to socialism. Major guerrilla efforts had been liquidated in Peru and Bolivia and effectively controlled in Colombia, Venezuela, and Guatemala. Furthermore, economic problems forced Cuba to rely more on the Soviet Union. As the Cuban economy faltered, Soviet influence increased, and Cuban policy conformity may have been the price for continued Soviet assistance. Castro largely withdrew his support of insurgency movements, seeming to resign himself at least temporarily to the futility of exporting revolution. By 1970, after a year and a half of Cuban silence toward Latin American revolution, insurgent leaders began to criticize Castro for his withdrawal of support. The Soviet Union preferred cooperative state-to-state interaction after the mid-1960s, but it occasionally supported subversive activities that led to conflict with Latin American states—Colombia in 1967, Uruguay in 1968, Mexico and Ecuador in 1971, Bolivia in 1972, and Chile in 1973.

Soviet-Cuban support of guerrilla warfare revived with the successful Sandinista-led Nicaraguan Revolution of 1979 and with increased insurgent activities in other Central American countries. In the new insurgent era, the Soviet Union and Cuba again disagreed over the appropriate approach. Their positions were reversed, however, with Cuba urging caution and the Soviets pressing an activist policy.

Inter-Latin American Disputes

Ecuador and Peru. Continuing conflict between Ecuador and Peru was an extension of the crisis of 1942.[21] In September 1955, Ecuador presented a complaint to the Council of the Organization of American States (OAS) that the presence of Peruvian army units on the border and nearby warships indicated an invasion of Ecuador. Ecuador had also submitted the matter directly to the guarantor states (Argentina, Brazil, Chile, and the United States) named in the Rio Protocol of 1942, requesting that they investigate the facts on site. The OAS Council deferred to that process. The guarantor states appointed a military investigating committee, which completed air and land reconnaissance over the area in question and observed nothing "abnormal." The matter, after some rhetorical flourishes by Ecuador and Peru in the OAS, was closed. However, in 1961 Ecuador declared the Rio Protocol null and void; yet Ecuador later in fact recognized the role of the guarantor states.

In January 1981 Peruvian aircraft attacked three Ecuadorian military outposts in the disputed area and evicted the troops. At Ecuador's request, the Nineteenth Meeting of Ministers of Foreign Affairs convened for a brief meeting in February and urged a cease-fire and the withdrawal of the military forces, to which both disputants agreed. The meeting then deferred to the actions of the four guarantor states, who sent a military commission to the area to monitor and assist the cease-fire and the troop withdrawals. Once again, the specific incident was thus settled but not the underlying dispute.

Ecuador and Peru engaged in a thirty-four-day undeclared war commencing on January 26, 1995 in the disputed border region. Ecuador again accepted the good offices of the guarantor states in order to end the hostilities and restore peace, seemingly accepting the Rio Protocol as the basis for negotiations. In February 1995 the disputants signed agreements providing for a cease-fire and for the separation of the armed forces, with outside observers verifying compliance. The cease-fire held, and the process of separating forces began on March 30; all troops were withdrawn by May 3. The guarantor and disputing states then met to agree on the creation of a demilitarized zone, prisoner exchange, the opening of the border, and the removal of mines in the area. The guarantor states continued to uphold the validity of the Río Protocol, but also seemed willing to consider its revision.

The Beagle Channel Dispute.   The dispute between Argentina and Chile over ownership of three islands in the Beagle Channel involved competing geopolitical and strategic calculations, access to possible petroleum and other resources, and the status of conflicting claims in the Antarctic. In 1971, Argentina and Chile agreed to submit their century-old dispute to binding arbitration as prescribed in existing bilateral treaties. Accordingly, the British crown appointed a five-judge international court of arbitration (all of the judges were members of the International Court of Justice). After six years of hearings and studies, the court rendered a decision in 1977, finding that the three islands (Picton, Lennox, and Nueva) were "unquestionably Chilean," thus giving Chile control of the resource-rich sea area. But in January 1978, in defiance of established international norms regarding peaceful settlement of disputes, the Argentine military government rejected the ruling. From its point of view, Chilean possession of the islands negated the fundamental Argentine bioceanic principle that Chile was by nature a Pacific coast power and that Argentina must have hegemony in the Atlantic zone; furthermore Chilean rights in the Atlantic Ocean would threaten Argentina's Antarctic claims.

When the disputants were on the verge of war in late 1978, the Holy See observer to the OAS proposed papal mediation. Both governments readily accepted this offer. The entire southern boundary zone, including the Beagle Channel and the contiguous oceanic triangle, was submitted for papal consideration. Two years later, on December 12, 1980, the pope presented his peace proposal. Chile was given sovereignty over the three islands plus a narrow fringe of territorial waters. Contiguous Atlantic waters were designated a condominium "sea of peace" reserved for common or concerted activities. Chile seemed ready to accept the papal decision, although it had resisted the sea-of-peace idea because the ocean resources were more important than the islands as such. Argentina did not reject the proposal, but it was clearly reluctant to accept a Chilean presence in the Atlantic. The process was interrupted by the Anglo-Argentine war of 1982.

After the war the negotiating climate for Argentina and Chile seemed unpropitious. Chile was convinced that Argentina had not negotiated in good faith since 1971 and had been too willing to consider the use of military force. Argentina strongly resented Chile's neutrality in the 1982 Anglo-Argentine war, which it saw as aiding Britain. The British crown had been removed from its traditional role as intermediary between Argentina and Chile, and the United States was in no position to take initiatives. The United Nations lacked precedents in regional American disputes, and the disputants were not inclined to submit to the Inter-American System. Holy See mediation remained open, but Argentina's stalling tactics seemed to devalue that option. Yet the new civilian government in Argentina was determined to overcame the difficulties. The papal mediating role was revived; on November 29, 1984, the foreign ministers of Argentina and Chile signed a treaty in the Vatican, which was ratified by both states and went into effect in 1985.

The treaty recognized Chilean possession of the three islands, with sovereignty extending south to Cape Horn, and gave Chile maritime jurisdiction over a surrounding twelve-mile-wide zone; Argentina had the right to exercise free navigation. Specific limitations on Chilean rights, however, removed the possibility of maritime projection or claims of sovereignty that would normally accompany territorial possession. That is, Chile had physical access to the Atlantic Ocean but did not hold rights to juridical claims. Argentina was given maritime jurisdiction over the area outside the twelve-mile zone. The sea-of-peace idea from the 1980 proposal had been discarded. The treaty specified that Argentine jurisdiction was not limited by requirements related either to sovereignty or joint economic exploitation. The bioceanic principle was recognized, with Cape Horn established as the base for maritime boundaries. The parties agreed to create a binational commission to facilitate the economic integration of the region, and to abstain from warfare in the area. The agreement was a clear compromise aimed at satisfying the fundamental concerns of each side. Chile got the islands and access to surrounding resources; Argentina retained control of the Atlantic area and jurisdiction over the eastern mouth of the Strait of Magellan to the north.

Caribbean Conflict.   After World War II a number of boundary and ideological clashes occurred in the Caribbean area.[22] External actors joined in urging, opposing, or resolving the conflicts in various patterns. The conflicts initially entailed disaffected exiles invading their own national homelands, and then extended to guerrilla warfare both in the Caribbean area and throughout much of the rest of Latin America.

Shortly after the war, exiles from a number of circum-Caribbean states gathered in other nearby states to plan revolutions. Considerable talk was heard about a Caribbean Legion, said to be sponsored by local reform governments in Cuba, Guatemala, and Costa Rica and composed of political exiles and adventurers dedicated to the overthrow of dictatorships in the Caribbean. Charles Ameringer concludes that the Caribbean Legion in fact never existed as a military organization with a permanent central command. Rather, he says, "the term was applied indiscriminately to a series of exile military operations and plots" with different leadership, sponsors, and objectives.[23] The dictators (especially Rafael Trujillo of the Dominican Republic and Anastazio Somoza of Nicaragua) in turn encouraged activities against their at least nominally democratic neighbors. Haiti, which was not so easily classifiable, was also involved.

To see the conflict simply as a confrontation between democracy and dictatorship distorts reality. In 1950 an OAS investigating committee issued a report noting that exiles fighting against their home governments tended to join with people of other nationalities who had similar purposes. It said that many of them were idealistic individuals who, deprived of democratic guarantees in their own states, sought to change political life. But others were "adventurers, professional revolutionaries, and mercenaries whose primary objective was the promotion of illegal traffic in arms and expeditions against countries with which they have no ties whatsoever." Whatever their motives, their activities involved the use of territory by states in violation of international obligations.[24]

El Salvador–Honduras War.   An interstate war occurred in 1967 between El Salvador and Honduras over boundary and migration issues.[25] For most of the twentieth century, Salvadorans had left their densely populated homeland and migrated, legally and illegally, to lightly populated Honduras across an ill-defined border. Their search for work and land provoked Honduran resentment, and military skirmishes frequently occurred. The worst fighting in sixty years occurred in a week-long undeclared war in July 1969. Honduras had instituted a land reform program affecting the Salvadoran land squatters just as an emotionally charged soccer championship series was being played by the two national teams. Following the rioting at the *futbol* match, Honduran mobs attacked Salvadoran aliens, diplomatic relations were suspended, and troops were placed on alert. The conflict was thus dubbed the "soccer war," but the conflict was hardly a trivial one. The armed forces launched full-scale attacks. The OAS arranged a truce, which went into effect on July 18, and maintained a peacekeeping team on the frontier. An estimated 3,000 persons were killed during the conflict and 7,000 injured, along with extensive property damage. The dispute was set aside with the onset of sustained Central American violence after 1979.

CENTRAL AMERICAN CONFLICT

The Nicaraguan Revolution

The 1979 Nicaraguan Revolution triggered complex, violent, and long-lasting strife in Central America.[26] The OAS became involved in the Nicaraguan civil war when the Seventeenth Meeting of Consultation of Ministers of Foreign Affairs convened in September 1978 to consider the worsening conflict. The Somoza dictatorship in Nicaragua favored the convocation so that it could "demonstrate to the world how foreign interventions are trying to implant Marxist-Leninist ideals" in Nicaragua—a reference to Cuban and Soviet support of the Sandinist National Liberation Front (FSLN). The Human Rights Commission visited Nicaragua, and its report in October 1978 was highly critical of human rights violations by the Somoza government. The OAS attempted to mediate the situation, but the government rejected as interventionist the call for an OAS-supervised referendum and for Somoza's resignation. In mid-October, the foreign ministers censured Nicaragua for its air attacks near the Costa Rican border, which injured Costa Rican civilians. In June 1979 the foreign ministers meeting issued its final resolution. It charged the Somoza regime with inhumane conduct and called for its immediate replacement by a pluralist representative government, the guarantee of respect for human rights for all Nicaraguans, and the holding of free elections.

After coming to office in 1977, President Carter had imposed sanctions related to human rights abuses against the Somoza regime, as well as the military junta in El Salvador and the Lucas García dictatorship in Guatemala. After the Sandinista-led revolution overthrew Somoza in 1979, President Carter accused the Soviet Union and Cuba of increased subversive activities in Central America. He was antagonistic toward the new Nicaraguan regime on the grounds that it was shipping Soviet-provided arms to leftist guerrillas in the emerging civil war in El Salvador. U.S. military transfers were resumed to the Salvadoran government despite the lack of substantive reforms.

Central American Complexities

Central American conflict exacerbated confrontations in the subregion's international relations, created new ones, and tapped into deep mutual suspicions among Central American neighbors.[27] Regional developments were further complicated by the involvement of external actors. For the United States, Central America became a primary foreign policy concern, and its policies were a source of sharp domestic and international debate. The United States continued to play the leading role in the area, but other states and groups were also prominent, as the U.S. Central American preserve became an internationalized arena. A striking new condition was the concerted assertiveness by Latin American states in opposition to U.S. actions. The principal initiatives for conflict resolution, which the United States greeted with a distinct lack of enthusiasm, were undertaken by local states in concert. The OAS and the UN, both of them at first on the periphery, eventually played critical roles.

The Reagan administration accused Nicaragua of transshipping Soviet-bloc arms to Salvadoran insurgents, and Cuba of providing arms and advisers to Central American guerrilla groups. The administration applied coercive and interventionist tactics, but added developmental measures in response to domestic and international criticism that recognized the complexities involved. But the thrust of policy was constant: the United States was unwilling to accept a Marxist government in Nicaragua and sought a military victory over leftist forces in El Salvador.

From 1981 to 1988, key U.S. policies included coercive pressures on Nicaragua, combined with aid and various overtures to other Central American states—with El Salvador the central concern. The United States armed, financed, and advised anti-Sandinista guerrillas (the Contras), conducted military maneuvers in and with Honduras and naval exercises near Nicaragua, applied an economic boycott against Nicaragua, and even mined its harbors. In the meantime, the U.S. invasion of Grenada in October 1983 (see below) led to speculation that it would be followed by military intervention in Nicaragua (in retrospect not a likely event after the end of 1981, primarily because of U.S. Army reluctance; U.S. officials never ruled it out, however). The Reagan administration in effect carried out an undeclared war with Nicaragua, while continuing formal diplomatic ties.

Military arms and advisers and economic aid to El Salvador increased dramatically. Assistance was increasingly sent to Honduras, which allowed training of Salvadoran forces on its territory, and where a significant portion of the Contra force operated. Guatemala, ruled by a brutally repressive regime, received only marginal U.S. aid. The United States also prevailed upon the military government in Argentina, which had no traditional interests in Central America, to send military advisers to Guatemala and El Salvador, to advise Honduras on intelligence matters, and to train the Contras along the Nicaraguan border. The Anglo-Argentine war in 1982, and the accompanying hostility toward the United States, brought the withdrawal of the Argentine military presence from Central America.

The United States also bargained with friendly governments. The Caribbean Basin Initiative (CBI), proposed in 1981 and implemented in 1984, provided for trade preferences and economic aid to friendly governments. It was framed in terms of the Soviet-Cuban threat, but it also recognized poverty as a source of instability. Increasingly strong pressure was asserted on the Salvadoran government to follow a centrist course, institute an effective agrarian reform program, curtail right-wing death squads, and hold free and fair elections. The United States also sought to legitimize governments in Honduras and Guatemala with elections and to improve their human rights records.

Cuba made no secret of its support for Nicaragua. Large numbers of Cuban teachers, medical and technical personnel, and military advisers were sent there, and Nicaraguans were trained in Cuba. Cuba provided training and equipment to guerrilla forces in El Salvador. The Soviets limited their direct involvement in the region, leaving much of the socialist bloc's activities in Nicaragua to East Germans, Czechs, and Bulgarians. Soviet military equipment was supplied, most notably tanks and he-

licopters, but not sophisticated aircraft. (See Chapter 5 for an analysis of Soviet behavior in Central America.)

Europeans exercised little influence on Central American events or on restraining
U.S. actions. They drew back from supporting Nicaragua as it increasingly mistreated the opposition and moved away from pluralism and nonalignment. Most of
all, the Grenada invasion in 1983 signaled that Central American conflict had entered a new and more serious phase. European governments wanted to avoid another
alliance problem with the United States, but made it clear that they opposed U.S.
military solutions in Central America. They also supported Latin American propositions for conflict resolution, directly challenging U.S. policies with formulas for negotiated settlements.

Conflict Resolution

Central American conflict differed from previous situations mainly by virtue of the
resistance of the local states to simple U.S.-enforced settlement. Despite the strong
and sustained assertion of U.S. power, it did not prevail. High U.S. officials from
time to time negotiated directly with Nicaraguans. Central American issues were
placed on the agenda of U.S.-Soviet negotiations. The several parties charged their
opponents with intransigence and insincerity, and little was accomplished toward
ending the conflict. The Inter-American System was involved in various aspects of
the early part of the conflict, but its effectiveness had declined and mutual security
provisions were not invoked. Its initial irrelevance largely explains why substitute
multilateral fora emerged.

Latin American states composing the Contadora Group (Colombia, Mexico,
Panama, and Venezuela) organized themselves at a summit meeting held on the
Panamanian island of Contadora in January 1983. The group proposed to serve as a
mediator in seeking peaceful negotiated outcomes in Central America. It drew up a
set of twenty-one principles designed to facilitate discussions between the United
States and Nicaragua and, in El Salvador, between the government and the insurgents.[28] The principles included, among other things, limiting arms flows, prohibiting all foreign bases, withdrawing external advisers (including Cuban, East European, and U.S.), and ending support for insurgents (both Salvadoran and
Nicaraguan). All five Central American states agreed to the list of principles.

On July 28, 1985, in order to provide new impetus to what was then recognized
as an stalled initiative, four South American states—Argentina, Brazil, Peru, and
Uruguay—joined in a Contadora Support Group. Ecuador had originally been a
participant but dropped out after a conflict with Nicaragua led to a rupture of relations. European governments and political groups generally applauded the Contadora initiative, saying it matched their own policy preferences. An extraordinary
meeting, held in September 1984 in Costa Rica, was attended by all EC foreign
ministers, representatives of the four Contadora countries and five Central American
countries, and observers from Spain and Portugal. European ambivalence was re-

flected in the EC reluctance to commit financial resources to the area, in spite of its formal endorsement of the Contadora proposal.

The Contadora initiative declined with time and events—and, its supporters argued, with U.S. intransigence. The Kissinger report claimed to favor a "comprehensive regional settlement" but refused to accept any regime (i.e., Nicaragua) that might serve as a "crucial stepping stone for Cuban and Soviet efforts to promote armed insurgency in Latin America." It bluntly said that "The United States cannot use the Contadora process as a substitute for its own policy."

In the wake of the Contadora impasse, President Oscar Arias of Costa Rica proposed a peace plan (for which he won the Nobel Peace Prize) that became the basis for a significant and continuing conflict resolution effort. On August 17, 1987, the five Central American presidents met in Guatemala City and formalized his proposal. They signed a document entitled "Procedure for the Establishment of a Firm and Lasting Peace in Central America," known informally as the "Esquipulus II Accords," after the town in Guatemala where the five presidents had earlier met (in June 1986) and discussed regional problems.

The plan had three interrelated purposes: the political reconciliation within each of the Central American states, the democratization of their domestic political processes, and the cessation of civil and international hostilities. In order to achieve national reconciliation, the plan called for the combination of a cease-fire in those countries where irregular or insurgent groups were active, amnesty policies to facilitate the cease-fire, and the beginning of dialogue between governments and all unarmed opposition groups as well as those who had accepted amnesty. In addition, the governments committed themselves to promoting pluralist and participatory democracy, including the restoration of individual freedoms and free and honest elections at an early date. Each state would create a representative National Commission of Reconciliation to verify compliance and to monitor the democratization process. Urgent measures would address the problems of refugees and displaced persons.

The cessation of hostilities also depended on international processes. Governments in and outside the region were urged to cease open and covert aid to any irregular forces or insurgent movements and to prevent the use of their territory in support of aggression against other states. The plan mandated creation of an International Commission for Verification and International Follow-up *(seguimiento)*, made up of the secretaries-general of the OAS and UN and the foreign ministers of Central America, the Contadora Group, and the Support Group. The commission undertook to ensure compliance with the various commitments. A timetable of deadlines was established; although they were seldom met, the process continued into the 1990s.

The UN and the OAS became increasingly involved in the Esquipulus II process. UN Secretary General Pérez de Cuéllar negotiated with Central American governments over the conditions and extent of possible UN diplomatic and military involvement in conflict resolution. In 1989 the Security Council approved the organization and deployment of the civilian-military UN Observer Group in Central America (ONUCA). ONUCA subsequently engaged in extensive peacekeeping and election monitoring operations in Central America. The OAS, which historically had dealt with Central American conflict but had been shunned in favor of the Contadora and Esquipulus processes, also played a significant role. It formed a partnership with the UN with a specified division of labor. The OAS was active in the peace verification process and assumed the delicate function of overseeing the resettlement of the Contras in 1990–91.[29]

The Central American peace process was persistently prosecuted into the mid-1990s, and fundamental goals envisioned in the Esquipulus II Accords were eventually realized. The process was particularly difficult in Nicaragua, El Salvador, and Guatemala. Internal social and political problems continued, but the civil wars and international conflicts ended.[30]

The Grenada Intervention

U.S. military intervention in 1983 in the Commonwealth Caribbean island-state of Grenada is understood as an adjunct of the Central American imbroglio; at the same time it was marked by particular dynamics.[31] When Britain granted independence to Grenada in 1974, Eric Gairy—a charismatic, popular, corrupt, long-established politician—was elected the first prime minister and sustained himself through repression and rigged elections. In March 1979, Maurice Bishop, leader of the opposition New Jewel Movement (NJM), led a coup d'état and established himself prime minister of the People's Revolutionary Government (PRG). The PRG suspended the constitution and parliament, detained political prisoners, closed the only independent newspaper, suspended habeas corpus, and refused to schedule elections. The Carter administration and some of the other Eastern Caribbean states were concerned that a coup against an at least technically democratic government might occur, and that Prime Minister Bishop and his colleagues were inclined to Marxism-Leninism. The Carter administration responded to Grenada's increasing ties with Cuba and the Soviet Union by refusing to exchange diplomats or to extend foreign assistance. It did not, however, treat Grenada as a major foreign policy problem.

The Reagan administration, emphasizing the NJM's Marxist-Leninism and Grenada's growing links to Cuba and the Soviet Union, intensified the antagonism with its own policy of diplomatic isolation and anticommunist rhetoric. It pointed to Cuba's shipments of arms and military advisors to Grenada and to its help in building an airport at Point Salines. The United States dismissed Grenada's claim that the airport was to facilitate tourism, pointing out that it could be used by Cuban and Soviet long-range military aircraft and claiming that it was part of the projection of Communist power in the circum-Caribbean. Secretary of Defense Caspar Weinberger called Grenada "a Cuban satellite."

Dissenters from the U.S. view pointed out that, in addition to Cuba's substantial help, British, European, and U.S. companies were involved in the airfield's construction, and the EC was co-financing it. They noted that other Caribbean states had built similar airports to support their tourist economies.

A power struggle within the NJM led to a coup d'état managed by Deputy Prime Minister Bernard Coard in league with the Commander of the People's Revolutionary Armed Forces, Hudson Austin. On October 13, 1983, they placed Bishop under house arrest. But during a pitched battle between thousands of Bishop loyalists and the Grenadian army, a zealous army officer ordered the execution of Bishop and seven of his colleagues (who had surrendered). General Austin formed a Revolutionary Council that imposed control.

The Reagan administration decided to intervene militarily into the Grenadian situation.[32] An immediate concern was the fate of some 1,000 U.S. nationals on the island, over half of them medical students, which presented a potential hostage crisis. Ignoring collective security provisions of the Rio Treaty and the OAS Charter, the United States persuaded the Organization of Eastern Caribbean States (OECS) to request its military assistance. The subsequent U.S. invasion of Grenada involved participation by certain OECS members, but other member states were bitterly opposed to the action.

The invasion force, which began to land on October 25, involved 5,000 U.S. personnel and a small number from OECS states. The British government raised a dissenting voice as the operation began, but Prime Minister Margaret Thatcher's personal appeal did not dissuade President Reagan. The invasion, code-named Operation Fury, was marred by errors in planning, intelligence lapses, and interservice rivalry. U.S. forces also encountered unexpectedly strong resistance from the Grenadian-Cuban forces. Nevertheless, the immediate objectives were realized: Governor General Sir Paul Scoon (who held a ceremonial post but reported to London) was released from de facto house arrest (although the helicopter that picked him up was hit by ground fire and nearly crashed); and the U.S. students and persons were picked up without injury and evacuated (although their rescue was more difficult and took much longer than anticipated). U.S. military elements nearly attacked the Venezuelan embassy by mistake. The hostilities ended on November 2, 1983; 19 Americans died and 115 were wounded; 25 Cubans were killed and 115 wounded; and 45 Grenadian civilians were killed and 358 wounded.

POST–COLD WAR EVENTS

The Panama Situation

Conflict between Panama and the United States, culminating in a unilateral U.S. military intervention, revolved around the actions of General Manuel Antonio Noriega, commander of the Panamanian Defense Force and de facto president of Panama.[33] Noriega had long had a close relationship with the CIA as a paid informant—about drug trafficking, among other things—despite U.S. knowledge that Noriega himself was involved in the drug trade, as well as in gun smuggling from the United States to Central America. The United States finally abandoned the relationship, and on February 4, 1988, federal grand juries in Florida indicted him for drug crimes. Noriega then forced the resignation of the Panamanian president; and in May 1989 he violently overturned the results of an election—which he had agreed to—when it was won by the opposition candidate, Guillermo Endara. Police brutality and grave human rights violations followed. The Bush administration backed Endara.

The Twenty-First Meeting of Consultation of Ministers of Foreign Affairs convened in May 1989 to consider the Panama situation. The foreign ministers held Noriega responsible for the crisis and condemned "the outrageous abuses perpetrated against the opposition candidates and citizenry." They sent a mediation commission, led by the OAS Secretary-General with three of the foreign ministers, to bring about a transfer of power through democratic means as soon as possible; the mandate was later amended to specify Noriega's resignation and a transfer of power by September 1, 1989 and the subsequent holding of free elections as soon as possible. Despite considerable effort, the OAS mission was unable to broker an agreement; Noriega refused to resign and continued the violence as the deadline for the transfer of power passed.

On December 20, 1989, President Bush ordered U.S. troops into Panama in what was called Operation Just Cause. In the ensuing days, the United States flew in 22,500 combatants to supplement the 13,000 troops permanently stationed in Panama as part of the U.S. Southern Command. President Bush, noting that Noriega had rejected the negotiations aimed at resolving the two-year crisis, said that U.S. goals were to safeguard the lives of Americans, to defend democracy in Panama, to combat drug trafficking, and to protect the integrity of the Panama Canal. Endara was installed as president under U.S. protection. After several days of military operations, U.S. forces defeated the Panamanian Defense Force and arrested Noriega. (He was taken to the United States, where he was tried, convicted, and imprisoned on drug trafficking charges.) The intervention was popular in the United States but widely criticized elsewhere. Despite the notable lack of sympathy for Noriega, the U.S. invasion and subsequent seizing of him reinforced Latin American misgivings about U.S. unilateralism.

The Meeting of Consultation reconvened and on December 22, 1989, adopted a resolution that deplored the U.S. invasion, declared the United States to be in violation of international law, called for the immediate cessation of hostilities, and demanded the withdrawal of U.S. forces. At the meeting's final session on January 9, 1990, the foreign ministers took up Nicaragua's charge that U.S. troops had violated its embassy in Panama City. They adopted a resolution condemning the presence of U.S. troops in the Nicaraguan embassy as a violation of certain international conventions.

The Haiti Situation

The overthrow in 1991 of Jean-Bertrand Aristide, Haiti's first democratically elected president, precipitated a long sequence of events that culminated with the military occupation of Haiti by a U.S.-led, UN-sanctioned peace force.[34] Lieutenant General Raoul Cédras, commander-in-chief of the army, led the coup and headed the subsequent military-civilian governing junta. Aristide, a prominent Roman Catholic priest championing Haiti's impoverished masses and advocating radical economic and social change, threatened the power of Haiti's political and social elite. Some of Aristide's followers committed violent acts that resulted in a number of deaths, which Aristide did not condemn. The elites had long used violence to maintain their privileged position.

The OAS responded to the coup, primarily through an ad hoc Meeting of Consultation of Ministers of Foreign Affairs. The ministers, seeking to restore the constitutional president and faced with a hostile and recalcitrant de facto junta in Haiti, urged member states to embargo most trade with Haiti and to freeze the assets of the Haitian state. The OAS secretary-general organized a civilian mission that went to Haiti to mediate negotiations for Aristide's return to power; on February 23, 1992, after months of difficult negotiations, the parties signed an agreement called the Protocol of Washington. But the Haitian de facto regime delayed ratifying it, and a large exodus of Haitian refugees left for the United States—a matter that was a major factor in U.S. policy-making throughout the course of the Haitian situation (see Chapter 14). In November 1992, with the failure of the embargo and the protocol, the OAS Permanent Council asked the UN secretary-general for support in applying sanctions and finding a solution to the crisis. The UN thereafter took the lead, while working in concert with the OAS.

In February 1993 the Haitian regime agreed to receive the UN-OAS International Civilian Mission in Haiti (MICIVIH). In June 1993, after continuous delays by the de facto government, the UN Security Council called for a worldwide embargo of Haiti on petroleum and arms and for a freeze of the regime's financial assets. Numerous states, including some in Latin America, did not apply the measures. Nevertheless, on July 3, 1993, Aristide and the regime signed an agreement, the Governors Island Accord, in New York. The pact called for the dismissal or resignation of Haiti's military leaders and for Aristide to return to Haiti on October 30, 1993 and resume his presidential authority, with a number of transitional measures to be taken by all parties. In September, the UN Security Council authorized establishment of a separate military-police operation, the United Nations Mission in Haiti (UNMIH), to assist in training the armed forces, reorganizing the police, and building the physical infrastructure. The first UNMIH contingent arrived at Port-au-Prince aboard the *USS Harlan County* on October 11, 1993, where a mob of armed civilian thugs and small boats blocked their landing and threatened U.S., UN, and OAS diplomats; the government made no moves to restore order. The Clinton administration ordered the ship to depart Haiti.

The UN Security Council immediately approved a resolution reimposing the global oil and arms embargo and the freeze on overseas financial assets; in a defiant violent act in Haiti, gunmen assassinated Aristide's minister of justice. The date for Aristide's return passed. For the next nine months, all efforts to find a diplomatic resolution were unsuccessful. During that time, the Security Council unanimously adopted a resolution to impose the trade embargo with an international naval blockade, and later authorized the United States to form a multinational force with the mandate "to use all necessary means to facilitate the departure of the military leadership [and] the prompt return of the legitimately elected President." President Clinton issued orders for the invasion of Haiti to begin on the early morning of September 19. He also accepted former President Jimmy Carter's proposal to undertake an urgent diplomatic effort to persuade the Haitian military leaders to depart peacefully. Carter immediately departed for Haiti, leading a delegation that also included Senator Sam Nunn (Democrat of Georgia) and former chairman of the Joint Chiefs, General Colin Powell. As the military force was preparing to land, the mission signed an agreement with General Cedras.

The agreement provided that "certain military officers of the Haitian armed forces" would accept "an early and honorable retirement," once the Haitian parliament had voted a general amnesty into law, or on October 15, 1994, whichever was earlier. Further, the economic embargo and economic sanctions would be "lifted without delay," and "forthcoming legislative elections will be held in a free and democratic manner." President Clinton said that the mission was designed to provide a secure environment for the restoration of President Aristide and democracy, to begin the professional retraining of the Haitian armed forces, and to facilitate a "quick handoff" to a UN peacekeeping force to maintain an orderly environment in which development aid could flow and free and fair elections could be held.

On September 19 the U.S.-led multilateral military force landed without opposition. By the end of the month some 20,000 troops were in Haiti, essentially a U.S. force backed by small contingents from other states. The National Assembly passed an amnesty bill allowing President Aristide to pardon military people accused of political offenses. The most prominent military personalities were dismissed, and Cedras resigned; all of them left the country. Aristide returned to Haiti on October 15 to resume power. Work began on disarming and retraining the police and the military; the Haitian armed forces were eventually disbanded. In March 1995 the U.S.-led military force was replaced by the United Nations Mission in Haiti (UNMIH), made up of some 6,000 personnel, about 2,400 of whom were from the United States. Haiti held legislative and municipal elections, with the UNMIH providing security and large numbers of electoral monitors present; these elections were followed by the presidential election in which Aristide's personal choice for his replacement, Rene García Preval, was elected president and inaugurated on February 7, 1996. With violence and crime a continuing problem, however, the UN Security Council authorized a reduced and reconstituted UN force to remain in Haiti.

NOTES

1. See the models of regional interstate conflict constructed by Jack Child, *Geopolitics and Conflict in South America: Quarrels Among Neighbors* (New York: Praeger, 1985); and Wolf Grabendorff, "Interstate Conflict Behavior and Regional Potential for Conflict in Latin America," *Journal of Inter-American Studies and World Affairs* 24 (August 1982): 267–294.

2. See Glen Price, *Origins of the War with Mexico* (Austin: University of Texas Press, 1967); and Otis A. Singletary, *The Mexican War* (Chicago: University of Chicago Press, 1960).

3. See K. Jack Bauer, *The Mexican War, 1846–1848* (Lincoln: University of Nebraska Press, 1992); and Richard Griswold del Castillo, *The Treaty of Guadalupe Hidalgo: A Legacy of Conflict* (Norman: University of Oklahoma Press, 1992).

4. See Charles J. Kolinski, *Independence or Death! The Story of the Paraguayan War* (Gainesville: University of Florida Press, 1965).

5. See Gonzalo Bulnes, *Guerra del Pacífico*, 2d ed., 3 vols. (Santiago de Chile: Editorial del Pacifico, 1955).

6. See William E. Kane, *Civil Strife in Latin America: A Legal History of U.S. Involvement* (Baltimore: Johns Hopkins University Press, 1972); Dana G. Munro, *Intervention and Dollar Diplomacy in the Caribbean, 1900–1921* (Princeton: Princeton University Press, 1964); Dana G. Munro, *The United States and the Caribbean Republics, 1921-1933* (Princeton: Princeton University Press, 1974); Ivan Musicant, *The Banana Wars: A History of United States Intervention in Latin America from the Spanish American War to the Invasion of Panama* (New York: Macmillan, 1990); Whitney T. Perkins, *Constraint of Empire: The United States and Caribbean Interventions* (Westport, Conn.: Greenwood Press, 1981); C. Neale Ronning, ed., *Intervention in Latin America* (New York: Knopf, l970); and Robert Freeman Smith, ed., *The Era of Caribbean Intervention, 1898–1930* (Malabar: Krieger Publishing, 1981).

7. See G. Pope Atkins and Larman C. Wilson, *The Dominican Republic and the United States* (Athens, University of George Press, 1998), 72–78.

8. See G. Pope Atkins, *Encyclopedia of the Inter-American System* (Westport, Conn.: Greenwood Press, 1997), 67–73; J. Lloyd Mecham, *The United States and Inter-American Security, 1889–1960* (Austin: University of Texas Press, 1961), 154–159; Leslie B. Rout, *Politics of the Chaco Peace Conference, 1935–39* (Austin: University of Texas Press, 1970); Bryce Wood, *The United States and Latin American Wars, 1932–1942* (New York: Columbia University Press, 1966), pt. 1; and David H. Zook, *The Conduct of the Chaco War* (New Haven: Bookman Associates, 1960).

9. See Atkins, *Encyclopedia of the Inter-American System*, 164–168. See also William Krieg, *Ecuadorian-Peruvian Rivalry in the Upper Amazon*, 2d ed. (Washington, D.C.: U.S. Department of State, 1986); J. Lloyd Mecham, *The United States and Inter-American Security, 1889–1960* (Austin: University of Texas Press, 1961), 166–170; Bryce Wood, *The United States and Latin American Wars, 1932–1942* (New York: Columbia University Press, 1966), 255–342; and David H. Zook, *Zarumilla-Marañon: The Ecuador-Peru Dispute* (New York: Bookman Associates, 1964).

10. See John Prados, *President's Secret Wars: CIA and Pentagon Covert Operations Since World War II* (New York: William Morrow, 1986).

11. U.S. Senate, Select Committee to Study Government Operations with Respect to Intelligence Activities, *Alleged Assassination Plots Involving Foreign Leaders, Interim Report and Final Report* (Washington, D.C.: Government Printing Office, 1975, 1976). At the same time, a book was published by former CIA operations officer, Philip Agee, *Inside the Company: CIA Diary* (Harmondsworth, U.K.: Penguin, 1975), an early account of clandestine activities in Latin America. Agee had spent much of his twelve-year CIA career from 1957 to 1969 in Ecuador, Uruguay, and Mexico. He portrayed himself as a "true believer" in the cold war against communism who, having become disillusioned with The Company (the CIA), determined not only to expose the agency but to urge its dismantlement. Agee, bitterly referred to by CIA officials as "our first defector," does not explain his conversion from zealous cold war

devotion to anticapitalist Marxism; but he offers a convincing account of covert CIA operations in Latin America. Those operations included the manipulation of foreign agents, news media, political parties, public officials, political leaders, and trade unions—and the use of bribery, blackmail, propaganda, wire-tapping, and other means of espionage. Agee discussed CIA interventions in elections and its role in assassination attempts and coups d'état, all aimed at weakening leftist forces. The foreign CIA agents and collaborators he listed by name included prominent figures from all walks of Latin American life.

12. Prados, *President's Secret Wars*.

13. Atkins, *Encyclopedia of the Inter-American System*, 201–202; Peiro Gleijeses, *Shattered Hope: The Guatemalan Revolution and the United States, 1944–1954* (Princeton: Princeton University Press, 1991); and Richard Immerman, *The CIA in Guatemala: The Foreign Policy of Intervention* (Austin: University of Texas Press, 1982).

14. Atkins, *Encyclopedia of the Inter-American System*, 112–116.

15. Trumbull Higgins, *The Perfect Failure: Kennedy, Eisenhower, and the CIA at the Bay of Pigs* (New York: Norton, 1987).

16. U.S. Senate, Select Committee to Study Government Operations with Respect to Intelligence Activities, *Covert Action in Chile, 1963–1973: Staff Report* (Washington, D.C.: Government Printing Office, 1975); and U.S. House of Representatives, Committee on Foreign Affairs, *The United States and Chile During the Allende Years: Hearings* (Washington, D.C.: Government Printing Office, 1975).

17. Atkins and Wilson, *The Dominican Republic and the United States*, 133–142; and Piero Gleijeses, *The Dominican Crisis: The 1965 Consitutionalist Revolt and American Intervention* (Baltimore: Johns Hopkins University Press, 1978).

18. Jacqueline Anne Braveboy-Wagner, *The Venezuelan-Guyana Border Dispute: Britain's Colonial Legacy in Latin America* (Boulder, Colo.: Westview Press, 1984).

19. This section is based on G. Pope Atkins, "Diplomacy in the South Atlantic Crisis," in *Latin America and Caribbean Contemporary Record*, vol. 2, ed. Jack W. Hopkins(New York: Holmes and Meier, 1984), 22–33. See also Peter Beck, *The Falklands as an International Problem* (London: Routledge, 1988); and G. M. Dillon, *The Falklands, Politics, and War* (New York: St. Martin's, 1989); Lawrence Freedman and Virginia Gamba-Stonehouse, *Signals of War: The Falklands Conflict of 1982* (Princeton: Princeton University Press, 1991); Lowell S. Gustafson, *The Sovereignty Dispute Over the Falkland (Malvinas) Islands* (New York: Oxford University Press, 1988); and Raphael Perl, *The Falkland Islands Dispute in International Law* (London: Oceana Publications, 1993).

20. The ideologies underpinning guerrilla warfare in Latin America and the characteristics of individual insurgency groups are analyzed at length in chapter 11; the subjects are revisited below in this chapter in the context of Central American conflict in the 1980s and 1990s. Here the matters are simply identified and generally acknowledged as a major form of warfare in the regional subsystem. For bibliographical information regarding the Cuban Revolution, guerrilla warfare, and the Latin American Left, see the notes to Chapter 11.

21. Based on Atkins, *Encyclopedia of the Inter-American System*, 164–168. See also Krieg, *Ecuadorian-Peruvian Rivalry in the Upper Amazon*; Mecham, *The United States and Inter-American Security*, 166–170; Wood, *The United States and Latin American Wars*, 255–342; and Zook, *Zarumilla-Marañon: The Ecuador-Peru Dispute*.

22. See Atkins, *Encyclopedia of the Inter-American System*, 50–55; Charles D. Ameringer, *The Caribbean Legion: Patriots, Politicians, and Soldiers of Fortune, 1946–1950* (University Park: Pennsylvania University Press, 1996) and *The Democratic Left in Exile: The Anti-Dictato-*

rial Struggle in the Caribbean, 1945–1959 (Coral Gables: University of Miami Press, 1974); and J. Lloyd Mecham, *The United States and Inter-American Security* (Austin: University of Texas Press, 1961), chapter 12.

23. Ameringer, *The Democratic Left in Exile*, chapter 2.

24. Investigating Committee of the Organ of Consultation, *Documents Submitted at the Meeting of March 13, 1950* (Washington, D.C.: Pan American Union, General Secretariat of the Organization of American States, 1950).

25. See Atkins, *Encyclopedia of the Inter-American System*, 169–172; and Thomas D. Anderson, *The War of the Dispossessed: Honduras and El Salvador, 1969* (Lincoln: University of Nebraska Press, 1981).

26. See Atkins, *Encyclopedia of the Inter-American System*, 356–358; and Robert A. Pastor, *Whirlpool: U.S. Foreign Policy toward Latin America and the Caribbean* (Princeton: Princeton University Press, 1992).

27. See Atkins, *Encyclopedia of the Inter-American System*, 58–67; Harold Blakemore, *Central American Crisis: Challenge to U.S. Diplomacy*, monograph supplement to *Conflict Studies* (London: 1984); Walter LaFeber, *Inevitable Revolutions: The United States in Central America*, 2d ed. (New York: W. W. Norton, 1993); Robert S. Leiken, *Central America: Anatomy of a Conflict* (New York: Pergamon Press, 1984); and Pastor, *Whirlpool*.

28. Bruce Michael Bagley, ed., *Contadora and the Diplomacy of Peace in Central America: The United States, Central America, and Contadora* (Boulder, Colo.: Westview Press, 1989); Bruce Michael Bagley, Roberto Alvarez, and Katherine P. Hagedorn, eds., *Contadora and the Central American Peace Process: Selected Documents* (Boulder, Colo.: Westview Press, 1985); and Jack Child, *The Central American Peace Process, 1983–1991* (Boulder, Colo.: Lynne Rienner Publishers, 1992).

29. Child, *The Central American Peace Process*.

30. For details of the processes in the various states, see Atkins, *Encyclopedia of the Inter-American System*, 172–176, 196–200, 352–356.

31. Robert J. Beck, *The Grenada Invasion: Politics, Law, and Foreign Policy Decisionmaking* (Boulder, Colo.: Westview Press, 1993); Jorge Heine, ed., *A Revolution Aborted: The Lessons of Grenada* (Pittsburgh: University of Pittsburgh Press, 1990); Kai P. Schoenhals and Richard A. Melanson, *Revolution and Intervention in Grenada: The New Jewel Movement, the United States, and the Caribbean* (Boulder, Colo.: Westview Press, 1985); and Paul Seabury and Walter A. McDougall, eds., *The Grenada Papers* (San Francisco: Institute for Contemporary Studies, 1984).

32. Beck, *The Grenada Invasion*, in a careful study not sympathetic to U.S. rationales, argues that without the unusual circumstances of the October 1983 situation the United States probably would not have taken the military action.

33. This discussion is based on Atkins, *Encyclopedia of the Inter-American System*, 404–407. See also Thomas Donnelly, Margaret Roth, and Caleb Baker, *Operation Just Cause: The Storming of Panama* (Lexington, Mass.: Lexington Books, 1992); and Bruce W. Watson and Peter G. Tsouras, eds., *Operation Just Cause: The U.S. Intervention in Panama* (Boulder, Colo.: Westview Press, 1990).

34. This treatment is based on Atkins, *Encyclopedia of the Inter-American System*, 206–215. See also Stephen Baranyi, "Peace Missions and Subsidiarity in the Americas: Conflict Management in the Western Hemisphere," *International Journal* 50, no. 2 (Toronto: Spring 1995): 358–364; and two reports by the Inter-American Commission on Human Rights, both titled *Report on the Situation of Human Rights in Haiti* (Washington, D.C.: Pan American Union, General Secretariat, Organization of American States, 1992 and 1994).

CHAPTER THIRTEEN

■

Economic Policies and Relations

The special nature of foreign economic policies and international economic relations—which also include political and social content and environmental concerns—compels a separate discussion. Their transnational nature must be stressed. A strong economy is a matter of national and international security, but, as Marian Irish and Elke Frank tell us, foreign economic policy is more complex than national security policy because there is "no single focus of economic power and no single focus for economic policy planning."[1] These phenomena involve a myriad of subnational interests with transnational ties, and they go far beyond state interests to include those of critically important nonstate transnational actors. The latter range from individuals in the general public to powerful multinational corporations, many of whom compete or cooperate with states in an autonomous manner. Furthermore, the notions of economic development underlying policies and relations have increasingly been tied to political, social, environmental, and other concerns, with continuing disagreements over what the connections should be. The chapter addresses these matters with reference to the Latin American and Caribbean subsystem.

SOME GENERAL CONSIDERATIONS

The economic policies and relations of the Latin American and Caribbean states, and the actions of outsiders with respect to them, are partly understood as a function of the nature of the regional states' economies and the particular problems they present. They are further understood in terms of the changing and competing conceptualizations of economic development.

Latin American and Caribbean Economies

The Latin American and Caribbean region contains economies ranging from the lowest category of development to highly industrialized systems.[2] With that caveat in mind, certain generalizations may be advanced.

A majority of the regional states remain characterized by economic monoculturism: national income depends on the export of a few, perhaps only one or two, agricultural, pastoral, or mineral items, which causes domestic economies to risk the vagaries of world markets. Without defensive measures, stagnation is averted as long as full export market demands exist, but economies deteriorate when products are sold in markets with declining prices.

Weaknesses in the industrial sector are characteristics of economic monoculturism. Latin America traditionally relied on external industrialized economies for manufactured goods as well as investment capital, for which it exchanged agricultural and mineral commodities. Industrialization has made some progress in most states and remarkable strides in a few, so that today industrial levels vary widely. Some economies are fairly well balanced industrially, including heavy industry. Brazil is especially notable, and Argentina, Chile, and Mexico have made advances in this regard. Others are in a moderate industrial development stage, such as Colombia, Peru, Venezuela, and Trinidad and Tobago. The remainder have the beginnings of industrialization or are as much as nonindustrial. Latin America in general has certain natural disadvantages that detract from its industrial potential. For example, coal resources are small and generally of low quality, and power sources are deficient. Hydroelectric potential is great, but the best sites are remote from urban centers. Platine states in the Southern Cone, led by Brazil and Argentina, have cooperated to their mutual benefit in dam building projects to realize hydroelectric potential.

A continuing myth, dating from the European discovery of the New World, pictures the Latin American region as possessing immense mineral resources that need only investment capital and managerial skills to be developed. The region is not generally so endowed, although a minority of states are especially rich in certain resources. Some of them rank high in world levels of reserves and production, such as Bolivia in tin; Chile in nitrates and copper; Mexico in silver, lead, and zinc; Peru in vanadium and bismuth; and Venezuela and Mexico in oil. Even though these minerals are crucial necessities for the external industrialized nations, the Latin American states only seldom have derived serious bargaining leverage, with the important exception of oil in the 1970s. In some states the heavy reliance on mineral resources continues, and the related problems of monoculturism persist. For this reason, many Latin American states have joined international commodity agreements (see Chapter 9).

With regard to the critical matter of oil resources, ten Latin American states produce oil, but it is significant as an export in only four of them—Venezuela, Mexico, Ecuador, and Colombia. Venezuela's petroleum industry began to grow especially in the 1920s, and thereafter it has consistently been among the world's major oil producers and exporters. Mexican reserves and production have also achieved a very high volume in world terms. With the energy crisis of the 1970s and dramatic increases in world market oil prices, Venezuela and Mexico profited enormously. Conversely, the decline of the price of oil in the 1980s and then the late 1990s was an key factor in their economic crises.

The high levels of external debt in relation to the size of Latin American economies was the most serious international economic problem throughout the 1980s. By the 1990s the debt continued as a vital consideration but had become subsumed under broader questions of international trade and investment. External debt is closely linked not only to trade balances but also to more general international relations and questions of internal stability. Latin American and Caribbean policy makers ask how dependent their states are on the international economic system and whether they are able to respond to outside pressures. During the debt crisis of the 1980s, they had to consider the effect of domestic austerity programs—negotiated with the International Monetary Fund in concert with external government and commercial bank creditors—on domestic developmental demands. They generally argued that too much austerity would bear too heavily on the poorest sectors of society, leading to social violence and ultimately to political chaos. Leaders of democratic polities, most of whom had succeeded military regimes that had presided over the increases in public debt, protested that their social stability and very democracies were at stake.

Concepts of Economic Development

After World War II, international economic policies having to do with the Latin American and Caribbean subsystem emerged in terms of changing and competing ideas of what constituted economic development. Latin American governments by and large came to emphasize economic growth, industrialization, and economic integration. The United States provided generally effective but relatively small technical assistance programs and loans to finance international trade, but it was unwilling to establish large economic development programs. It insisted on the private sector as the primary source of investment capital and on free trade as the vehicle for generating development funds. The United States considered these matters of secondary interest, especially after the advent of the cold war, when it primarily sought to organize the Latin American states into an inter-American anticommunist alliance. Latin Americans reluctantly acquiesced, but they made clear their strong desire for substantial multilateral economic development cooperation.

When Latin American pressures mounted in the late 1950s, and with the startling success of the Castro revolution in Cuba in 1959, U.S. and Latin American positions became (temporarily) complementary. The confluence of interests rested on different motivations, with Latin Americans seeking their own broad national development and the United States linking that development with political and social stability serving international security. As a result, at U.S. initiative, the Organization of American States (OAS) adopted the Alliance for Progress in 1961.

In the Alliance for Progress the American states agreed to work toward goals that emphasized broad elements of economic development, tied to political and social development. An underlying assumption was that economic development and social and political progress were inseparable and must occur simultaneously. So long as antiquated social structures, nondemocratic political systems, and politically-minded armed forces persisted, economic development was retarded; conversely, economic inequities impaired social and political progress. The United States feared that unstable and underdeveloped (broadly defined) Latin American states would be vulnerable to the spread of the Cuban Revolution.

The new developmentalism signaled fundamental changes in U.S. economic policies. The United States no longer insisted on the private sector as the primary source of investment capital. The provision of long-term loans repayable in soft currency for social purpose projects (such as low-cost housing, improved education, and land reform) revised the former U.S. policy of extending short-term hard currency loans to be spent primarily on U.S. products. A purpose of economic assistance had always been to support political stability; now social stability and democratic development were included in economic formulas, as well as providing a counter-ideology to communism.

After 1969 the United States in effect ended the Alliance for Progress, disappointed with its lack of results. It greatly reduced project funding for Latin American economic development and social change and reemphasized the importance of trade over aid and of foreign investment capital for economic development. The Latin American reaction was expressed in two parallel ideas: (1) collective economic security for development, saying that economic-social problems should be taken as seriously as the political-military conception of mutual security; and (2) cooperation for integral development, arguing that human aspects of the economic and social development of the people at large be emphasized. Economic security for development emphasized protection and guarantees against economic coercion by powerful industrial states and multinational corporations, which in turn would permit self-sustained integral development. For its part, integral development, which was considered indissolubly linked to security, emphasized societal progress over macroeconomic goals. Both ideas expressed a conviction to found political-economic relations on respect for "ideological pluralism"—presumably denying the requirement of embracing representative democracy or liberal economics as necessary developmental models. The United States objected to the idea of collective economic security on the grounds that it was too abstract and ill-defined, had little to do with economics, and did not confront the real causes of underdevelopment. Nothing came immediately of the Latin American efforts to change the bases for inter-American economic cooperation, but the ideas were kept alive.

In the 1980s, the Reagan administration's policies toward Central American conflict reluctantly revived developmentalism as a secondary element (see below). The assumptions behind those policies were reminiscent of Alliance for Progress precepts, although they aimed to serve even more closely anticommunist purposes in the restricted circum-Caribbean U.S. security zone.

In the 1980s inter-American economic policy attention centered on the severe Latin American and Caribbean external debt problem. By the end of the decade the matter of debt, considered worrisome but no longer in crisis, was subsumed under a new thrust for increased inter-American free trade and investment. At the same time, the Latin American ideas of collective economic security and integral development were revived but were framed in a tone that contrasted with the earlier aggressive hostility toward outsiders. The OAS Inter-American Economic and Social Council issued a report on the subject in 1982 that reiterated but moderated the former orientation.[3] The report continued to define integral development in human and socioeconomic terms, referring to the equitable distribution of developmental gains. Although not asserting the security argument, it emphasized the increasingly interdependent world in which Latin America and the Caribbean region suffered from the economic problems of the industrialized states, which created economic imbalances and social tensions to the point of a dependency relationship. The report favored continuation of Latin American and Caribbean strategies of export diversification and subregional economic integration, but acknowledged the necessity of co-operating closely with the United States and Canada (the former because of the sheer size of its economy).

Amendments to the OAS Charter went into effect in 1988 and officially adopted the purposes of integral development, indicating at least U.S. acquiescence. They added a chapter on the subject stating, among other things, that development "should constitute an integral and continuous process for the establishment of a more just economic and social order that will make possible and contribute to the fulfillment of the individual," to include economic, social, educational, cultural, scientific, and technological fields.

At about the same time, something of an international consensus on the notion of "sustainable development" became evident.[4] Sustainable development referred to the necessity of reconciling developmental and environmental policies with a dual awareness of necessary economic growth and natural resource limitations. In 1972 the United Nations World Environment Conference in Stockholm made the environment-development connection; until then development and the environment had been mostly separate considerations. The World Economic Commission (Bruntland Commission), organized in 1983 as a product of the Stockholm conference, gave continuing visibility to the idea. In the mid-1980s Latin Americans melded the idea of sustainable development with the existing concept of integral development, again with U.S. acquiescence if not enthusiasm.

By 1990 the political and economic transformations in Latin America, away from authoritarian governance and (with exceptions) state-dominated economies, had combined with the end of global East-West conflict to reopen the possibilities for complementary inter-American economic relations. The United States under the Bush administration had returned to a multilateral policy orientation toward the other Americas, which the Clinton presidency continued. A consensus reemerged among the American states (as had been established in the Alliance for Progress) about the essentiality of a combined economic-democratic subtext to the salient inter-American issues; at the same time, economic policies, now with strong U.S. support, continued to embrace the guiding concepts of integral and sustainable development. It should be noted, however, that important sectors in Latin America and the United States dissented from the newer approaches, with tensions between traditional notions of economic growth and industrialization and the new developmental paradigm.

PATTERNS OF COMMERCIAL RELATIONS

Nineteenth-Century Commercial Relations

Once Latin American barriers to investment and trade were dropped, along with their dependence on Spain and Portugal, in the early nineteenth century, Britain immediately dominated Latin American commerce and maintained an advantage over other industrial states. In the late nineteenth century British preeminence eroded, especially through the efforts of the United States and Germany. The Latin American states mainly had colonial plantation economies. The economically more powerful external states sought export markets for their manufactured goods, investment capital, technical skills, and surplus populations, and they cultivated Latin American sources of food and raw materials. The most efficient Latin American industries were often foreign owned and managed and produced for foreign rather than domestic markets.

Foreign capital was more attracted to portfolio than to direct investments.[5] Beginning with Argentina in 1824, most Latin American government bonds were sold in the London money market, with the remainder selling primarily in France and the United States. By 1827 every bond sale had been defaulted, a situation postponing further flotations for three to four decades (except for Brazil). British capital again financed large bond issues by fifteen Latin American governments in the 1860s and 1870s; by 1877 more than two-thirds of the total value was again in default. In the 1880s Latin American debt servicing improved. But French investors who purchased bonds in the 1860s and 1870s in Haiti, Mexico, Honduras, Peru, and Argentina suffered heavy losses when they were defaulted.[6]

Direct investment was important. Britain was especially well entrenched in Argentina, with holdings there representing between 40 and 50 percent of Britain's total Latin American investment. Britain also had substantial levels of investment in Brazil, Mexico, Venezuela, and Colombia. Some private U.S. capital migrated to Latin America before 1830; by 1870 virtually every Latin American state had received some such investments, with the preponderance in Mexico, Cuba, and Chile. U.S. capital flows increased dramatically after the Civil War. At the turn of the century about two-thirds of the U.S. investment in Latin America was concentrated in Mexico.[7] The main recipients of French capital were Brazil, Chile, and Mexico. By the turn of the century, foreigners owned all or most of Latin America's railroads, tramways, river shipping businesses, port facilities, and major mining companies; and a large number of ranches and farms, manufacturing and processing plants, forestry operations, commercial banks, and other enterprises; as well as all of the ocean shipping lines operating in the region.[8]

Commercial Relations Through World War II

As Latin American populations grew rapidly after 1900, demands for consumer goods increased. These goods were not available from domestic industries, however, and the region's international trade expanded dramatically. Total Latin American trade increased three-fold from 1885 to 1913, on the eve of World War I. Britain remained the principal trader and investor, but the United States registered the greatest increases and ranked second in both areas. German and French trade and investment also remained significant.

World War I cut off much of Europe's trade with Latin America. Trade recovered soon after the war but then contracted somewhat in the 1920s, standing at more than $5 billion at the end of the decade. During the postwar period up to 1930, U.S. investments more than tripled, with almost every Latin American state receiving some U.S. capital. British investments remained relatively stable until they began to decline after 1928, never to recover to their pre-1928 levels. German and French holdings declined in the 1920s. Regional trade and foreign investment shrank severely during the world depression, beginning in 1930; the lack of capital and purchasing power in markets around the globe were exacerbated by protectionist policies adopted by most trading partners. In addition to adopting economic controls, some Latin American states expropriated foreign enterprises, notably oil company subsidiaries in Mexico and Bolivia in 1938.

World War II stimulated Latin American international trade, especially with the Allies, who purchased the region's raw materials in large amounts for their war effort. However, new investment capital did not flow into the region until after the conflict was settled in 1945. During the postwar period, foreign corporations in Latin America still produced food and raw materials for export to industrial states, and the Latin American states continued to import capital machinery and manufactured goods. A number of them also imported significant amounts of agricultural products. Foreign exchange reserves that accumulated during the war were partly used to retire bonds at a rapid pace in order to reduce levels of portfolio investments. Some states repatriated a number of foreign enterprises. Argentina took over British railways and other transportation facilities, and several governments purchased public utilities from their foreign owners. However, total direct investments increased, with the United States the main source of capital. The levels of portfolio investment increased only slightly.

Post–World War II Relations

Trade and investment figures illustrate U.S. economic dominance during the postwar era.[9] For most Latin American states, at least one-third (often much more) of their total trade was with the United States. Through the 1960s U.S. investments accounted for about 40 percent of the total invested in Brazil, about half of that in Colombia and Peru, and almost 75 percent in Chile, with the largest single U.S. investment in Latin America in Venezuelan petroleum. Other nations were also active.

Germany and Japan were the strongest competitors to the dominant U.S. position. British investments and trade fell off sharply after World War II. France also had a low level of trade, except with Brazil. The United States and other investors suffered large losses with the nationalization and expropriation of foreign enterprise in Cuba after 1959, in Chile and Peru in the late 1960s and early 1970s, and especially in Venezuela in the mid-1970s. The Soviet Union and China mounted drives in the 1960s and 1970s to increase their trade with Latin America, but they held only a minor share, except for trade between the Soviet Union and Cuba.

The 1980s Debt Situation

Latin American international economic relations were dominated after the early 1980s by problems of external debt.[10] Although they were part of a global phenomenon, debt problems had special relevance for Latin America. The regional situation was distinguished from previous ones by its sheer magnitude. All Latin American states, as well as Caribbean ones, had accumulated high levels of debt in relation to the size of their economies and had encountered serious problems with servicing them. Almost two-thirds of all bank loans to developing countries beginning in the early 1970s went to Latin America. Activities related to the resolution of debt issues continued to dominate U.S., European, and Japanese economic relations with the regional states.

The problem began in the late 1960s when Latin American governments and private enterprises decided to accelerate domestic development by borrowing abroad from international lending institutions and private commercial banks. The arrangements included two types of creditors: private suppliers, such as commercial banks, which provided direct loans and markets for the flotation of bonds; and public sources, including bilateral government agencies and the multilateral (general and regional) financial institutions. Borrowers included Latin American governments, government agencies, and private sector entities. The doubling of oil prices in 1973 spurred further borrowing to pay for higher-priced oil imports, and a reduction in interest rates after 1976 accelerated borrowing even further.

Debt-service capacity remained satisfactory, except for occasional problems, until the end of the 1970s. Commercial banks competed vigorously to place loans in the profitable market. They operated on the theory that governments, by definition, were not vulnerable to bankruptcy, as were private corporations, and on the assumption that the IMF would rescue governments that encountered liquidity problems. Latin American governments, for their part, saw no need to adjust monetary or fiscal policies or engage in domestic austerity programs, and fiscal deficits increased. In a number of important cases, a significant portion of borrowed funds was diverted from developmental purposes to budgetary support, military expenditures, and capital flight. High-level corruption was sometimes a serious problem as well.

Not only did the size of public debt increase dramatically, but its structure also changed significantly. The greatest change was the increase in medium-term loans granted by private banks. Latin Americans gained unprecedented access to international bank syndicates and the Euromarket, and by 1980 the level of private-lender participation had grown from an insignificant proportion to more than two-thirds of the total.

A set of factors converged at the end of the 1970s to create the Latin American debt crisis. Another round of oil price increases worsened terms of trade. Renewed global recession sharply depressed prices for commodity exports, and interest rates increased. All of these problems, which added to debt-service burdens, were initially perceived as temporary phenomena that could be bridged through short-term borrowing. But the situation discouraged domestic savings and investment and encouraged massive capital flight, and Latin American economic growth rates declined for the first time in four decades. Borrowers had increasingly undertaken risky, short-term, variable-rate loans, further adding to the debt-servicing load. Banks began to refuse new loans, denying access to capital markets when debt servicing was the most difficult.

The debt problem became a crisis when Mexico, at the time the world's second largest debtor, announced on August 12, 1982, that it could no longer meet its external debt-service obligations. Thereafter other governments indicated illiquidity and inability to meet their foreign debts. With the advent of the debt predicament in 1982 and the accompanying decrease in borrowers' creditworthiness, Latin Americans increasingly requested debt rescheduling. Complex negotiations subsequently developed between the borrowing entities and private banks, multilateral financial institutions, and creditor governments.

At the time of the Mexican announcement in 1982, Latin American external debt totaled about $315 billion. The three largest economies (Brazil, Mexico, and Argentina) accounted for about two-thirds of the total. Brazil was the world's largest debtor, having reached a level of about $100 billion in 1982. Chile, Colombia, Peru, and Venezuela together held much of the remainder. All Latin American countries, however, had borrowed heavily in relation to the size of their economies. U.S. bank claims in Latin America totaled some $82.5 billion, about a quarter of their overseas lending. Two-thirds of that total was held by the nine largest U.S. banks. The exposure of European and Japanese banks was sizable but far smaller as a percentage of their total international claims. Many smaller banks participated in external credits through syndicates.

Two "clubs" represented creditor governments and private banks, respectively.[11] Neither club had a fixed membership or an institutional structure. The Paris Club was composed of sovereign representatives engaged in government-to-government loans. Originally established in 1956 to deal with the serious financial situation in Argentina, it operated again in the general financial crisis after 1982. The London Club of commercial banks was organized in the mid-1970s to systematize the proliferation of banking syndicates (themselves formed to raise the vast sums involved in the 1970s lending). It operated informally, meeting only when negotiations with a particular borrower were in progress. Although the Paris Club was concerned with the interests of commercial banks, it did not allow them to participate in its proceedings.

The Cartagena Group emerged to represent most of the Latin American debtor governments. When the presidents of Mexico and Brazil met soon after the onset of the crisis, they considered but rejected the repudiation of debts in favor of rescheduling them. The United Nations Commission for Latin America and the Caribbean (ECLAC) and the Latin American Economic System (SELA) subsequently issued a joint report and sponsored several meetings to discuss collective action. The most important of these meetings took place in Quito in January 1984, attended by representatives (including presidents and prime ministers) from twenty-six Latin American governments. The final report postulated a program of reduced debt payments and interest rates, a lengthening of maturities, and the elimination of trade barriers by developed countries. The indifferent response by creditors inspired eleven Latin American governments (Argentina, Bolivia, Brazil, Chile, Colombia, Dominican Republic, Ecuador, Mexico, Peru, Uruguay, and Venezuela) to meet at Cartagena, Colombia, in June 1984 to further consider a multilateral position. They issued a document establishing a formal consultative mechanism known as the Cartagena Group and agreed to meet regularly.

Two dissenting Latin American leaders offered their own widely publicized propositions. Peru's new President, Alan García (succeeding the Peruvian government that had been present at the formation of the Cartagena Group), stated at his inauguration in July 1985 that he intended to set aside no more than 10 percent of Peruvian export earnings for debt servicing. In April 1986 García further announced his intention of setting his own interest rate for servicing the debt. Cuban Premier Fidel Castro in July 1985 recommended direct creditor-debtor negotiations but said that if creditors were recalcitrant, then unilateral collective repudiation of debts should follow. Cuba was not a member of the Cartagena Group.

Almost all Latin American governments were involved in continuing negotiations with the International Monetary Fund (IMF), in which the United States played a major role, and with a consortium of private international banks led by New York-based Citibank. The IMF insisted that the governments adopt austerity programs aimed primarily at controlling inflation, reducing imports, and stimulating exports so as to generate foreign exchange for debt servicing and lessen the need to borrow from abroad in future years. The banks made refinancing of existing loans and negotiation of new ones contingent on such agreements. The IMF, in turn, made "bridging loans" to ease the shocks of austerity. The United States and the Bank for International Settlements (BIS) also provided some short-term bridging loans to help countries meet external liquidity requirements. When austerity and credit targets were not met, the IMF did not hesitate to withhold portions of loans, and private creditors did not hesitate to interrupt loan disbursements. Debtor countries were reluctant to adopt the austerity measures because of internal political opposition and fear of social disruption, a consideration particularly important for new, delicately balanced democratic governments and for those in the midst of moving toward democracy.

The U.S. government concurred in the positions taken by the IMF and commercial banks. In 1985, however, a modest change in emphasis evolved with what came to be called the "Baker Initiative." U.S. Treasury Secretary James Baker unveiled his ideas at a combined meeting of the IMF and the World Bank Group in Seoul, Korea, in October 1985. He proposed to build on the existing approach and seek growth in the debtor countries that would restore their creditworthiness. Baker called for a three-year term package of new commercial bank loans, netting $20 billion to fifteen principal debtor countries, ten of whom were from Latin America. Those countries would be required to undertake long-term structural reform policies and to open their economies to foreign trade and investment, as well as to accept a continued central role for the IMF and an expanded role for multilateral banking institutions. The initiative amended the original approach only marginally, not fundamentally.

Some three and a half years later, on March 14, 1989, U.S. Treasury Secretary Nicholas Brady announced another Third World debt relief proposal. The "Brady Plan" sought negotiations that encouraged debtor states to sell state-owned industries and reduce public spending; it also encouraged commercial banks to forgive part of the debt and accept lower interest payments—and even to cancel existing bank loans and related charges. The plan was aimed at reviving economic growth and decreasing political and social tensions resulting from economic dislocations. Whereas the Baker Initiative was based on new commercial bank loans, the Brady Plan called for debt relief and service cost reductions. Mexico was the initial and most important target of the Brady strategy, and after an eleven-month process of negotiating with the commercial banks, the IMF, and the World Bank an agreement was reached. Similar agreements were concluded with nine other Latin American states, among them Venezuela, Costa Rica, Argentina, Uruguay, and, in mid-1992, Brazil, the last of the major, targeted, sovereign Latin American borrowers to come to an agreement under the Brady Plan.

Before initiation of the Brady Plan, West Europeans had done little in order to ameliorate the debt crisis. They had looked to the United States for its resolution. The Brady Plan also failed to get the European's strong backing, since they were determined that commercial banks would not transfer their bad loans to the IMF and the World Bank. The banks themselves expected those international institutions and creditor states to provide them guarantees. Nevertheless, agreements between creditors and the major debtors for debt and servicing reductions were finally worked out. Japan was more positively active. In 1987 it instituted the Nakasone Plan, which recycled $65 billion of Japan's balance of payments surpluses over a five-year period to assist Third World debtor countries, the largest of which were in Latin America. In 1988 Japan followed with the Miyazawa Plan, which proposed a voluntary reduction of the bank debt through a conversion of the loans into guaranteed bonds—a year later the scheme was incorporated into the Brady Plan. Japan helped finance the debt reduction efforts of individual Latin American states, such as Mexico and Venezuela.[12] At the behest of the United States, Japan agreed to contribute $500 million to the IDB's Multilateral Investment Fund in support of Latin American private sector development. Canada, France, Portugal, and Spain also contributed in the combined amount of $257 million.

Debt, Trade, and Investment in the 1990s

By 1990 the debt problem was no longer considered to be in crisis. The situation remained serious and worrisome, however. Some obligations were not being serviced as agreed; any downturns in the global economy might revive the crisis; and poverty and social dislocations remained crucial domestic problems. But debt issues had become subsumed under larger considerations of international trade and investment. Official statements and studies issuing from the IDB, ECLAC, and SELA reflected the changed situation. They indicated that although the debt problem was a continuing reality, it had become more manageable, and most Latin American states had recovered their credibility with outside investors. Debt-reduction, lower interest rates, and varying degrees of economic recovery and opening had generally improved the financial outlook. The debt structure itself had improved, having been transformed into longer-term instruments (often into bond issues) that were traded on an active secondary market.[13] Foreign direct investment, which had sharply declined during the 1980s, grew rapidly at the end of the decade and into the 1990s, as new bank lending almost ceased. MNCs established new subsidiaries and expanded existing operations. Foreign investors purchased many of the formerly state-owned enterprises as they were privatized. Latin American governments also attracted a large return of flight capital that had earlier sought refuge in the United States and Europe.

U.S. ECONOMIC POLICIES AND AID PROGRAMS

The 1930s Through World War II

An early source of U.S. assistance to Latin America was the Export-Import Bank of Washington (EXIM, later EIB), established in 1934 to help promote the recovery of U.S. foreign trade after its sharp decline during the world depression. According to the EXIM report of December 31, 1941, a total of $48.5 million in loans had been disbursed to the twenty Latin American states as of that date. The most significant single project consisted of assisting in the export of U.S. equipment and services for the construction of a steel plant at Volta Redonda, Brazil. After the fall of France in 1940 and throughout World War II, EXIM loans to Latin America were aimed at developing sources of strategic raw materials and combating Axis economic penetration, as well as building the Pan American highway and other projects. The EXIM report of July 1, 1945, listed more than $4 billion in authorizations to Latin America from 1940 to 1945.

The first publicly funded U.S. technical assistance programs in Latin America were instituted in 1939. The programs were not intended for major capital investments or to promote large scale economic development, but to give limited assistance to specific projects jointly financed by the United States and the host government. In 1939 President Roosevelt established the Interdepartmental Committee on Scientific and Cultural Cooperation, which spent a total of $678,000 in Latin America through

1945. Most of the projects were in agriculture (notably a rubber development program), geology, civil aviation, child welfare, and statistical services. Another agency created in 1940, eventually called the Office of Inter-American Affairs, was devoted to U.S. technical assistance programs in Latin America; it was originally headed by Nelson A. Rockefeller. Viewed as a wartime agency only, it supervised a large number of cultural and commercial relations between the United States and Latin America. Technical assistance programs costing the United States $110 million through 1945 concentrated on the fields of health, agriculture, and education.

Post–World War II

The Truman administration from 1945 through 1952 attempted to explain to Latin America that problems in other parts of the world, first in Europe and then in Asia, were more pressing than those in Latin America.[14] Thus Latin Americans should depend primarily for funds on the newly created international lending agencies—the World Bank and the International Monetary Fund (IMF)—and private investment capital, rather than on direct U.S. economic assistance. Technical assistance programs, however, were continued. U.S. policy was geared to the cold war, and the prospect of both Soviet expansion into Latin America and internal Communist revolution seemed remote.

Beginning in 1945 EXIM was authorized to finance some foreign development projects on the assumption that they would increase markets for U.S. exports. EXIM was the main source of U.S. postwar economic assistance to Latin America, but it gave Europe priority, and the sums authorized for Latin America were relatively small. EXIM projects in 1951, in response to the military needs of the Korean conflict, were aimed at facilitating Latin American strategic raw material production. The Interdepartmental Committee on Scientific and Cultural Cooperation (ICSCC) and the Institute of Inter-American Affairs (IIAA)—a subagency of the Office of Inter-American Affairs that was transferred to the State Department when its parent was abolished—continued their technical assistance projects in the fields of agriculture, public health, elementary education, and vocational training. From 1946 through 1949 the ICSCC expended $10.4 million in Latin America, and the IIAA spent $21.6 million.

The United States inaugurated a worldwide technical assistance program in 1950 under the Act for International Development. The program was informally called "Point Four" because it was the fourth point of President Truman's economic policy announced in his inaugural address of 1949. Although the U.S. experience with technical assistance in Latin America largely provided the basis for global Point Four programs, the region itself received less assistance than did Europe and Asia. Public administration and the improvement of industrial productivity were added as new fields of endeavor in 1951.

The Mutual Security Act (MSA) of 1951 emphasized the relevance of economic and technical aid to security concerns in the context of the cold war. The Communist threat in Latin America was not considered great, however, and the area was of low priority in MSA programs. The Truman and Eisenhower administrations continued to stress the "trade not aid" concept in Latin America and opposed large-scale development spending. Nevertheless, Latin Americans benefited from several MSA programs, even if not to the extent they desired. In addition, the Agricultural Trade Development and Assistance Act of 1954 (PL480), an effort to reduce U.S. farm product surpluses in a constructive manner, provided for several programs, among them the overseas sale of surplus agricultural products followed by loans of "counterpart" funds that subsequently accumulated.

After Vice President Nixon's ill-fated Latin American trip in 1958, U.S. officials indicated a need to reexamine U.S. economic policy toward Latin America and showed a willingness to make changes. The Castro revolution in Cuba in 1959, and Cuba's association with the Soviet Union, further inspired U.S. attention to economic programs in the region. New developmental policies emerged toward the end of the Eisenhower administration. The Inter-American Development Bank was established in late 1959 with U.S. backing. In July 1960 the United States announced the $500 million Eisenhower Plan for Latin American economic development, aimed at halting "the further spread of communism in the Western Hemisphere." At U.S. urging, the "Act of Bogotá" was adopted at an inter-American meeting in September 1960 to give multilateral support to the Eisenhower Plan.

The new program represented some fundamental changes in U.S. economic policies toward Latin America. The provision of long-term loans, repayable in soft currency, for social purpose projects such as low-cost housing, improved education, and land reform revised the former policy of extending hard currency loans to be spent primarily on U.S. products. The United States continued to urge Latin Americans to provide an attractive climate for foreign investors in the economic development process, but it no longer insisted on private capital as the primary economic source.

The Alliance for Progress

Soon after his inauguration in 1961, President Kennedy proposed a ten-year Latin American economic, political, and social development program known as the Alliance for Progress.[15] The Alliance for Progress built on programs initiated by President Eisenhower. It had originally been inspired by Brazilian President Kubitschek's proposal in 1958 for an "Operation Pan America" to raise Latin American living standards dramatically. A few months after Kennedy's proposal, an inter-American agreement, the Charter of Punta del Este, was signed to make the Alliance a multilateral program. In general, the United States promised to give long-term development assistance to Latin America in a "decade of progress." The program, to be administered by the IDB, promised significant financial contributions as well as assistance in development planning and social reform. U.S. economic and social aid was closely linked to the fear that the Castro revolution would spread to other parts of the region.

The developmentalist policy of the Alliance for Progress continued through the Kennedy and Johnson administrations, but the Nixon administration quickly shifted to a "low profile" in economic as well as other affairs concerning Latin America. In his first presidential address on hemispheric policy on April 14, 1969, President Nixon referred to the Alliance as a "great concept" that had "done much good" in some countries. Although Nixon did not propose a formal end to the Alliance, he indicated that it would be downgraded on the grounds that it had not stimulated sufficient economic growth. He made no mention of its democratic or social purposes. Latin American economic aid expenditures declined after 1969, and policy rhetoric moved away from ideas and projects aimed at social change and economic development. The importance of trade over aid and of foreign investment capital for economic development was reemphasized. The Ford administration after 1974 made no basic changes in Nixon's economic policy toward Latin America. The Carter administration emphasized the human rights factor in its aid polices, which mainly affected military assistance programs, and economic assistance in general was not emphasized.

The Caribbean Basin Initiative

President Reagan announced the Caribbean Basin Initiative (CBI) at a meeting of the OAS in February 1982.[16] Congress subsequently passed the Caribbean Basin Economic Recovery Act, which went into effect on January 1, 1984, with the purpose of stimulating the trade and growth of selected circum-Caribbean beneficiary countries. It offered U.S. trade preferences by providing for duty free access to the U.S. market over a period of twelve years, restricting certain products from such entry. In 1990 Congress enacted legislation at President Bush's request making the CBI permanent. Eventually all circum-Caribbean states—with the exception of Cuba— and many of the dependencies were designated as beneficiaries. Cuba and Nicaragua had been excluded from the program from the beginning; Nicaragua was made eligible after its 1990 presidential elections ended authoritarian rule. Grenada had initially been proscribed but was declared eligible after the U.S. military intervention in 1983. Haiti had been a beneficiary until November 5, 1991, when the United States imposed an economic embargo in accordance with multilateral sanctions imposed by the OAS; after the U.S.-led, UN-sanctioned military mission entered the country in 1994, Haiti's eligibility was restored. The U.S. Virgin Islands and Puerto Rico, which are part of the U.S. state structure, are considered CBI beneficiaries for certain purposes.

The CBI as initially conceived closely fitted the Reagan administration's geopolitical views of the Caribbean Basin—sketched in terms of East-West conflict—and reflected changing views of the causes of Central American conflict. It blended opposition to Soviet expansionism with local developmentalism and the president's free-enterprise philosophy. Reagan's speech before the OAS and subsequent administration declarations all revealed this combination of concerns. He emphasized the strategic importance of the Caribbean to the United States, as well as U.S. economic interests and subregional economic problems, which he suggested threatened political and social stability and created conditions that could be exploited by the Soviet Union and Cuba. Economic problems also increased illegal immigration and facilitated the export of narcotics to the United States. In sum, a major border of the United States threatened to consist of hostile states, and the United States therefore had a vital interest in preventing economic collapse or the creation of Marxist-Leninist regimes in neighboring countries. By the time the 1990 measure was enacted, the cold war was over and the East-West aspects of the CBI were irrelevant.

The economic considerations of CBI programs were aimed at Caribbean export expansion and diversification and increased outside investment. The CBI "centerpiece" was the provision for duty-free access for most exports from designated Caribbean countries into U.S. markets. The exceptions included textiles and apparel, canned tuna, petroleum and petroleum products, most footwear, and certain leather and other goods. Sugar imports received limited duty-free treatment but were in effect subject to quota limits, in terms of the prior U.S. domestic sugar price support program. Sugar remained subject to the tariff-rate quota system announced on September 13, 1990. The 1986 law required ethanol imports to conform to special rules, allowed special access to the United States for apparel assembled in the Caribbean region from materials manufactured in the United States, and created a "safeguard mechanism" for U.S. industries injured by increased CBI imports. The CBI was supplemented by designated investment capital from Puerto Rico—low-cost funds derived from profits accumulated free of federal taxes by U.S. corporate subsidiaries in Puerto Rico under Section 936 of the U.S. tax code (thus called "936 funds"). Under this provision cooperative manufacturing ventures were promoted in which Caribbean countries supplied low-cost labor for the assembly of items manufactured in Puerto Rico and the United States.

The Andean Trade Initiative

On December 4, 1991, President Bush signed into law the Andean Trade Preference Act (ATPA). As the trade element of President Bush's "Andean Strategy" to deal with the narcotics traffic, the ATPA was a unilateral trade preference program aimed at promoting economic development through private sector initiative in the four Andean countries of Bolivia, Colombia, Ecuador, and Peru. It gave them duty-free entry into the U.S. market over a ten-year period (extending to December 4, 2001). Certain categories of products were excluded from duty-free entry, which were the same as under the CBI, except the ATPA also excludes rum. An official guidebook to the ATPA offered the following policy rationale: ATPA programs help Bolivia, Colombia, Ecuador, and Peru with economic development and diversification, as well as stimulate private sector initiative and offer new opportunities for U.S. entrepreneurs. If Andean coca growers and processors are to discontinue their activities, they must have viable alternatives to earn adequate income.[17]

Enterprise for the Americas Initiative

On June 27, 1990, President George Bush announced the Enterprise for the Americas Initiative (EAI), which contemplated a Western Hemisphere free-trade area. The centerpiece of the proposal, the North American Free Trade Agreement among Canada, Mexico, and the United States, went into effect on January 1, 1994, creating the world's largest free-trade zone. In the meantime, the United States signed "framework agreements" on trade and investment with all other countries in the Latin American region except for Cuba and Haiti (which was later included as a member of the Caribbean Community). (See Chapter 7 for details.) The EAI included a debt reduction element, which was in effect an extension of the Brady Plan. The United States proposed to ease some debt burden and to increase incentives for economic reform and environmental protection by agreeing, with conditions, to reduce bilateral government-to-government debt owed to the United States. A state's eligibility was determined by the degree of its movement toward an open investment regime. (As part of this approach, the United States would support natural resources management as an element of protecting the environment.) The program became operational on June 27, 1991, when the United States and Chile signed the first debt-reduction agreement. Subsequent arrangements were made with other Latin American borrowers. The EAI also contemplated the promotion of regional private investment with a Multilateral Investment Fund (MIF), which was established in the Inter-American Development Bank (IDB) on February 11, 1992, with initial capital of about $1.3 billion, including a U.S. pledge of $500 million.

TRADE AND AID POLICIES OF OTHER STATES

The United States stressed the multilateral nature of the CBI when it was conceived in 1982. Consultation with other governments did take place, and they supplemented the U.S. programs. But it was agreed that each state would develop its own approach, with only a modicum of coordination in order to avoid duplication. Much of the effort on the part of these and other actors—Canada, Europe, Japan, and international financial institutions—in fact predated the CBI itself and, presumably, would have continued without it.

The United Kingdom, France, and the Netherlands for many years tended to concentrate their aid in their current and former dependencies. This practice left few resources for assistance to the vast majority of the region. Europeans generally tied aid closely to their exports, looking to improve their own balance of trade more than to promote Latin American economic development. Assistance was designed to improve commercial positions, and credits and loans usually were granted only to finance Latin American purchases of European products. Germany was the exception. Like the United States, Germany perceived that its interests were best served by a stable and prosperous world and linked its aid to anticommunist ideology and the East-West conflict. Consequently, German economic aid to Latin America fit into its overall concern with the underdeveloped nations and centered on economic development programs initiated in the mid-1950s. Commercial goals were not lacking, and German aid credits were used to develop new export markets. However, in 1974 the German government reduced its development aid programs, stating, in effect, that easing its domestic tax burden took precedent over foreign assistance.

By the mid-1970s, members of the European Community (EC) had decided to direct their trade and aid policies toward Latin America through their own multilateral European institutions.[18] More than 80 percent of the trade between the EC and Latin America involved the seven largest Latin American economies (Argentina, Brazil, Chile, Colombia, Mexico, Peru, and Venezuela). The EC was Latin America's largest trading partner after the United States, although the level of trade tended to decline from the 1970s into the 1990s. The relationship with Latin America was of much less significance to Europe than to the United States. Nevertheless, Latin America received a proportionally higher level of exports from the EC than did other Less Developed Countries (LDCs), probably because it was the most economically advanced LDC region. Although Latin America represented a minor part of the EC's total trade, the area was a principal source of food and raw materials and an important market for manufactured surpluses.

In 1971 the EC introduced the Generalized System of Preference (GSP) as its principal concessionary policy toward LDCs. The GSP offered concessional terms of trade for certain Third World exports and later provided loans through the European Development Fund and the European Investment Bank, as well as other forms of export assistance. These measures were aimed at helping developing economies to be more competitive with the First World in gaining access to European markets. But Latin Americans were highly critical of EC practices. EC officials acknowledged the Latin American complaint that the system was too restrictive and that preferences were given on few of the products in the first rank of Latin American exports.

The EC also established special trade preferences for former colonies of its member states. After lengthy negotiations, the initial four-year Lomé Convention was signed in 1974 between the EC and forty-six states in Africa, the Caribbean, and the Pacific (the ACP countries). The third revision of the convention, which went into effect in 1990, is to expire in 2000. With each revision the number of eligible ACP countries expanded (in 1990 they numbered sixty-nine) and the benefits for them increased. Until 1990 the only Latin American regional beneficiaries were the twelve Commonwealth Caribbean Countries and Suriname, former colonies of the United Kingdom and the Netherlands, respectively. In that year the Dominican Republic, at Spain's urging, was allowed to adhere, and Haiti was brought in soon after. The Lomé system provides preferential markets for many products, special trade concessions (duty-free access to the EC market for most of their industrial and agricultural exports), a commodity export price stabilization agreement, cooperation in industrial and technical matters, increased aid disbursements and loans through the European Development Fund and the European Investment Bank, assistance in regional integration, and joint institutions.

The Latin American states not party to the convention expressed displeasure with the Lomé arrangements. They complained that Lomé meant they were faced with unfair terms of trade, not only in competition with the industrialized world but with much of the rest of the Third World as well. They reiterated pleas that the EC adopt a global policy toward LDCs and not favor the ACP partners to the detriment of others.

In the 1990s Europeans responded to Latin America's improved economic and political situation and to the shift from highly protected to more open market economies. But they were unwilling to accept more than modest financial costs in trade and investment relationships. A new temporary element was the European Community Special Andean Trade Program, designed to support efforts by Andean countries to combat drug production. The EC adopted a plan to assist Colombia, Peru, Bolivia, and Ecuador with trade concessions on a range of their export goods over a four-year period, expiring October 29, 1994. The program excluded certain agricultural products and live animals. The EC also established a special program of financial aid to Colombia, which had initiated the request for EC support, over the same four-year period.[19]

After President Bush presented his EAI proposal in 1990 for a hemispheric free-trade area, and the United States-Mexico-Canada NAFTA negotiations commenced, Europe reconsidered its position toward Latin America. Beginning in 1995, the European Union (the new designation as of 1992) undertook initiatives that, if realized, would establish highly significant transregional trading relations. In December 1995 the EU signed an Inter-Regional Framework Agreement with the Common Market of the South (MERCOSUR, including Brazil, Latin America's largest economy, and Argentina, the third largest), looking toward a free-trade agreement. The EU signed similar framework agreements in 1996 with Chile (which has a relatively small but open and stable economic system) and in 1997 with Mexico (the region's second largest economy and a NAFTA partner).

Japan adopted an increasingly global foreign policy as it became the world's second largest market economy. Most of Japan's aid to Latin America was in the form of export credits rather than economic development grants, similar to the U.S. practice through EXIM.[20] Japanese relations with Caribbean countries developed slowly, commensurate with its relatively limited interests in the region, but its engagement in the region expanded. Japan actively traded with Cuba, and it lent $10 million to Jamaica in 1981 for developmental purposes. In early 1986 Japan increased its trade credits and developmental assistance to the circum-Caribbean countries.

Latin America was not an important part of Canada's foreign assistance program until 1964. Thereafter, bilateral aid and some Canadian contributions to the IDB were restricted to purchases of Canadian goods. Canadian assistance to circum-Caribbean countries increased after the onset of Central American conflict in the late 1970s and the debt crisis of the early 1980s. Specifically, in early 1982 Canada announced an increase in developmental assistance to Central American countries, committing $105 million over a five-year period. In 1986 Canada announced a program to double its bilateral aid to the Commonwealth Caribbean—both the sovereign states and British dependencies—for the ensuing year, and simultaneously to implement a preferential free-trade arrangement for those countries along the lines of the CBI (called CARIBCAN). In March 1990, Canada announced that certain items were no longer excluded and that Canada would write off Can$182 million in CARIBCAN debts.

The Soviet Union's regional economic aid program outside of Cuba was small, but its trade concessions were generous in nature if not in amount.[21] Soviet economic aid to Cuba included balance-of-payments credits, technical assistance costs, project credits, and sugar subsidies. The Soviet Union normally did not provide aid in the form of either grants or outright loans. However, it gave trade transactions the character of economic assistance by allowing repayments in the form of commodities rather than currency.[22] This barter arrangement was automatically tied to Soviet products. Latin Americans complained about the inferior quality of Soviet goods and their overvaluation in account settlements. Except for Cuba, Latin American states enjoyed a trade surplus with the Soviet Union. Offers of economic aid and trade were often linked to the reestablishment of diplomatic relations with the Soviet Union.

Soviet foreign policy reorientations after 1985, and the subsequent dissolution of the Soviet Union, meant Moscow's at least temporary economic retirement from Latin America, with only a residual relationship with Cuba. With the decline of the Soviet economy, subsidies and assistance to Cuba were drastically reduced. Castro, with a huge stake in the status quo, vehemently protested the changing relationship. In 1990 the Soviets discontinued subsidizing petroleum deliveries to Cuba and Cuban sugar exports to the Soviet Union, which were especially heavy blows to the Cuban economy. In fact, the Soviets put all trade on a commercial basis at world market prices. In 1990–1991 the Soviet Union sharply cut its Cuban grant and technical aid programs, including the number of technicians and advisers in Cuba. In July 1993, Russia agreed to grant Cuba a $380 million credit, only a fraction of the assistance issuing from Moscow in previous years, to facilitate trade and to complete projects initiated by the former Soviet Union.[23]

The Holy See sponsored a development assistance program in support of papal pronouncements concerning social and economic justice for the poor. Pope Paul VI in 1969 established a Vatican Development Fund for Latin America to be funneled through the IDB. Interest-free, long-term loan projects were selected by the bank in consultation with the Vatican. According to a church communiqué, the fund would be used in "the fields of agrarian reform, over-all human well-being, workers' organizations and other areas of social and economic reform and general improvement in the developing countries which are members of the bank."

The stronger Latin American states sponsored assistance programs. Brazil, Mexico, Argentina, and Venezuela for a time provided economic aid and technical assistance to the poorer Latin American states. The most important programs were pursued by Venezuela, which used its oil wealth in the mid-1970s to enhance its emerging influence, especially in the circum-Caribbean, as well as to avoid the inflationary consequences of investing more money in the domestic economy than it could absorb. In 1974 Venezuela contributed more than $500 million for loans to be made through the IDB and the World Bank. In December of that year Venezuela compensated six Central American states for holding back part of their coffee harvests in order to raise prices. It provided subsidies to those particularly hurt by rising oil prices and gave direct aid to the most underdeveloped of them.

Latin American assistance activities were reduced with the debt crisis in the 1980s, but certain efforts nevertheless continued. In 1980 Mexico and Venezuela established a joint oil facility for the energy-deficient countries in the circum-Caribbean. The program financed almost a third of the petroleum requirements of nine countries (El Salvador, Guatemala, Honduras, Costa Rica, Nicaragua, Panama, Barbados, Jamaica, and the Dominican Republic), valued at a total of about $300 million annually. The facility continued despite the debt problems in both countries. In addition, Mexico granted trade preferences to El Salvador, Guatemala, Costa Rica, Panama, and members of CARICOM, and financed technical assistance programs around the area. Venezuela further assisted some of those economies in the 1980s by contributing direct Central Bank deposits (in Nicaragua, the Dominican Republic, Costa Rica, and Jamaica) and by granting developmental project loans to Central American countries. Colombia offered substantial trade credits and modest technical assistance programs to several countries in the circum-Caribbean.

NOTES

1. Marian Irish and Elke Frank, *U.S. Foreign Policy: Context, Conduct, and Content* (New York: Harcourt, Brace, Jovanovich, 1973), 243. See also the discussions elsewhere in this book on economic policies and relations, particularly those on development theories in Chapter 3, integration movements in Chapter 7, and international organization programs in Chapters 8 and 9 (which also address environmental matters).

2. See Victor Bulmer-Thomas, *The Economic History of Latin America Since Independence* (Cambridge, U.K.: Cambridge University Press, 1995); Colin Lewis, *Latin America in the World Economy* (Boulder, Colo.: Lynne Rienner Publishers, 1990); and Hilbourne A. Watson, ed., *The Caribbean in the Global Political Economy* (Boulder, Colo.: Lynne Rienner Publishers, 1994).

3. Inter-American Economic and Social Council, *Hemispheric Cooperation and Integral Development: Report for the Secretary General* (Washington, D.C.: General Secretariat of the Organization of American States, 1982). See also Antonio Jorge, ed., *Economic Development and Social Change: United States-Latin American Relations in the 1990s* (New Brunswick, N.J.: Transaction, 1992); and, by the president of the Inter-American Development Bank, Enrique V. Iglesias, *Reflections on Economic Development: Toward a New Latin American Consensus* (Baltimore: Johns Hopkins University Press, 1993).

4. See David Goodman and Michael Redclift, eds., *Environment and Development in Latin America: The Politics of Sustainability* (New York: St. Martins Press, 1991); Gordon J. MacDonald, Daniel L. Nielsen, and Marc A. Stern, eds., *Latin American Environmental Policy* (Boulder, Colo.: Westview Press, 1996); Heraldo Muñoz, ed., *Environment and Diplomacy in the Americas* (Boulder, Colo.: Lynne Rienner Publishers, 1992); Heraldo Muñoz and Robin L. Rosenberg, eds., *Difficult Liaison: Trade and Environment in the Americas* (Coral Gables: Uni-

versity of Miami, North-South Center, 1993; and Joseph S. Tulchin, ed., *Economic Development and Environmental Protection in Latin America* (Boulder, Colo.: Lynne Rienner Publishers, 1991).

5. See Carlos Marichal, *A Century of Debt Crisis in Latin America: From Independence to the Great Depression, 1820–1930* (Princeton: Princeton University Press, 1989). See also J. Fred Rippy, *British Investments in Latin America, 1822–1949* (Minneapolis: University of Minnesota Press, 1959); and D. C. M. Platt, *Latin America and British Trade, 1806–1914* (New York: Barnes and Noble, 1973).

6. J. Fred Rippy, *Globe and Hemisphere* (Chicago: Henry Regnery, 1958), 331–333.

7. Marvin Bernstein, ed., *Foreign Investment in Latin America* (New York: Knopf, 1966).

8. Rippy, *Globe and Hemisphere*, 334.

9. Some analyses of trade and investment that together provide a broad picture are: Donald Baerresen, Martin Carnoy, and Joseph Grunwald, *Latin American Trade Patterns* (Washington, D.C.: Brookings Institution, 1965); Bernstein, *Foreign Investment in Latin America*; Anthony T. Bryan, ed., *The Caribbean: New Dynamics in Trade and Political Economy* (New Brunswick, N.J.: Transaction, 1995); John M. Dyer, *United States-Latin American Trade and Financial Relations* (Coral Gables: University of Miami Press, 1961); Mark B. Rosenberg, ed., *The Changing Hemisphere Trade Environment: Opportunities and Obstacles* (Miami: Florida International University, 1991); Steven E. Sanderson, *The Politics of Trade in Latin American Development* (Stanford: Stanford University Press, 1992); and Dick Steward, *Trade and Hemisphere: The Good Neighbor Policy and Reciprocal Trade* (Columbia: University of Missouri Press, 1975).

10. Some broad treatments of the debt problem and its adjustment are William L. Canak, ed., *Lost Promises: Debt, Austerity, and Development in Latin America* (Boulder, Colo.: Westview Press, 1989); Robert Devlin, *Debt and Crisis in Latin America: The Supply Side of the Story* (Princeton: Princeton University Press, 1989); Jeffrey A. Frieden, *Debt, Development, and Democracy: Modern Political Economy and Latin America, 1965–1985* (Princeton: Princeton University Press, 1992); Robert Grosse, ed., *Government Responses to the Latin American Debt Problem* (Boulder, Colo.: Lynne Rienner, 1995); Antonio Jorge and Jorge Salazar-Carrillo, eds., *The Latin American Debt* (New York: St. Martin's Press, 1992); Robert A. Pastor, ed., *Latin America's Debt Crisis: Adjusting to the Past or Planning for the Future?* (Boulder, Colo.: Lynne Rienner Publishers, 1987); and Barbara Stallings and Robert Kaufman, *Debt and Democracy in Latin America* (Boulder, Colo.: Westview Press, 1989).

11. This discussion draws on F. Parkinson, "Some Legal and Institutional Aspects of the Debt Crisis," *Coexistence* 24 (Netherlands: 1987): 155–168.

12. Susan Kaufman Purcell and Robert M. Immerman, *Japan and Latin America in the New Global Order* (Boulder, Colo.: Lynne Rienner Publishers, 1992).

13. See Manuel R. Agosin, ed., *Direct Foreign Investment in Latin America* (Washington, D.C.: Inter-American Development Bank; Baltimore: Johns Hopkins University Press, 1995); August Blake Friscia and Charles J. L. T. Kovacs, *Beyond the Lost Decade: Debt and Development in Latin America* (Boulder, Colo.: Westview Press, 1993); and Robert Grosse, ed., *Private Sector Solutions to the Latin American Debt Problem* (New Brunswick, N.J.: Transaction, 1992).

14. See Philip M. Glick, *The Administration of Technical Assistance: Growth in the Americas* (Chicago: University of Chicago Press, 1957); Lincoln Gordon, *A New Deal for Latin America: The Alliance for Progress* (Cambridge: Harvard University Press, 1963); Roger D. Hansen, *U.S.-Latin American Economic Policy* (Washington, D.C.: Overseas Development Council, 1975); and John F. McCamant, *Development Assistance in Central America* (New York: Praeger, 1968).

15. See Jerome Levinson and Juan de Onís, *The Alliance That Lost Its Way: A Critical Report on the Alliance for Progress* (Chicago: Quadrangle Books, 1970); Herbert K. May, *Problems and Prospects of the Alliance for Progress* (New York: Praeger, 1968); and L. Ronald Scheman, ed., *The Alliance for Progress: A Retrospective* (New York: Praeger Publishers, 1988).

16. See U.S. House of Representatives, Committee on Foreign Affairs, *The Caribbean Basin Initiative, Hearings* (Washington, D.C.: Government Printing Office, 1981).

17. U.S. Department of Commerce and U.S. Agency for International Development, *Andean Trade Preference Act* (Washington, D.C.: Government Printing Office, July 1992).

18. See Alfred Glen Mower Jr., *The European Community and Latin America: A Case Study in Global Role Expansion* (Westport, Conn.: Greenwood Press, 1982). See also Susan Kaufman Purcell and Françoise Simon, eds., *Europe and Latin America in the World Economy* (Boulder, Colo.: Lynne Rienner Publishers, 1994).

19. U.S. Department of Commerce and U.S. Agency for International Development, *Andean Trade Preference Act*.

20. Purcell and Immerman, *Japan and Latin America in the New Global Order*.

21. See Robert K. Evanson, "Soviet Political Uses of Trade with Latin America," *Journal of Inter-American Studies and World Affairs* 27, no. 2 (1985): 99–127; and Comisión Económica para América Latina, *Relaciones Económicos de América Latina con los Países Miembros del Consejo de Asistencia Mutua Económica (CAME)* (Santiago: Naciones Unidas, 1982).

22. Herbert Goldhamer, *The Foreign Powers in Latin America* (Princeton: Princeton University Press, 1972), 184.

23. Cole Blasier, "Latin America Without the USSR," *North-South Issues* 2, no. 4 (1993).

CHAPTER FOURTEEN

—————— ■ ——————

Political Regimes and International Processes

The relationship of different Latin American governing regimes to international relations has been a significant foreign policy-making factor for both the regional and external actors. The related matters are both interstate and transnational in nature, dealing as they do with political-security considerations, transnational and intergovernmental actors and relations, and the impact on Latin American societal outcomes. In this chapter, after identifying the salient Latin American regime types so as to provide a frame of reference for subsequent analysis, two topics are analyzed: (1) the promotion of democracy and human rights as purposes of policy and relations, and the corollary of opposition to authoritarian and radical revolutionary regimes; and (2) military cooperation and its implications for Latin American political systems and the policies of outside states. The matter of social-revolutionary regimes is taken up in the context of the principal categories of dictatorship, military regimes, and democratic forms.

LATIN AMERICAN POLITICAL REGIMES

The political systems of Latin America have embraced several types of governance, with changes in regime types occurring in most of the states. Although each state has important individual political characteristics, as a general matter Latin Americans have long evidenced a tension between personalist dictatorships or military regimes and democratic forms, and revolutionary regimes have added to the mix.

When the Latin American states became independent in the early nineteenth century, almost all of them adopted the idea of republicanism with the presidential system. However, the widespread existence of the *caudillo* in Spanish America (referring to a local strongman, boss, or man on horseback), reflected a disposition for authoritarianism and personalism, with an emphasis on personalities rather than public issues. Brazil was unique, in that it was governed for the first six decades of independence by a relatively benign constitutional monarchy presided over by the heirs to the Portuguese throne, after which it also formally adopted the republican form. *Caudillismo,* typical of the nineteenth century, declined as a governmental form in the twentieth century. Nevertheless, some caudillos were still found in the 1960s; the last approximations disappeared only during the 1980s. In Brazil the counterpart, *coroneis,* was prevalent in regional politics during the monarchy and afterwards competed for national prominence (often in the form of state governors).

In the meantime, military regimes, in which the armed forces form the government, became more customary. In contrast to the traditional caudillos, who erected one-man dictatorships over the armed forces in order to consolidate personal power, the leaders of military regimes hold power as agents for the entire military organization and superimpose the military structure onto the government. Military regimes, although authoritarian, are by definition not personalist. Constitutional democracies, competing with personal dictators and military regimes, were established for various periods of time in several states (Chile traces its democratic beginnings to the 1830s), beginning in the late nineteenth and early twentieth centuries. It may be noted that Brazil was successfully governed by a constitutional monarch from 1822 to 1889, and Mexico and Haiti were less successfully governed by absolute monarchies for a time in the nineteenth century.

After World War II, an era of tentative democracy gave way to military regimes. From the 1960s into the 1980s, military rule was found in Latin America (albeit with important exceptions) to the extent that armed forces ruled a large majority of Latin Americans as never before. The military overthrew civilian governments not simply to reconstitute them, as had been the tradition, but for the purpose of long-term governance and the goal of solving national and international problems in terms of military standards. This was a phenomenon dubbed "bureaucratic authoritarianism," as well as "professional militarism" (in contrast to military professionalism).[1] By the end of the 1980s, discredited military regimes had given way to constitutional civilian governments or were finishing the process of doing so. The result was a new era of Latin American democracy, with certain deviations and its own characteristics.

The term "revolution" has, in the Latin American political vocabulary, been applied to four different types of political phenomena: (1) to describe the Latin American movements against colonial masters, which gained national independence but did little to change social structures; (2) to denote coups d'état *(golpes de estado),* in which chief executives are forcefully ejected or in which presidents extend the length of their tenures through extraconstitutional means *(continuismo)*; (3) to describe political and social change, in the sense of long-term evolutionary processes of reform, modernization, and development; and (4) to define violent movements that capture the state and fundamentally change the structure and processes of social and political systems. Our interest here is with the revolutionary regimes associated with the last category.

Social revolution refers to a movement—usually claiming an ideological inspiration—that takes political power and seeks to recast the political-economic system and social order. The most fundamental transformations tend to be the ways in which wealth is redistributed and new groups acquire dominant positions in matters of state.

In Latin America many such revolutions have been attempted, but only three success-ful ones have generally been recognized: the Mexican Revolution of 1910, the Cuban Revolution of 1959, and the Nicaraguan Revolution of 1979. One could say that a social revolution took place in Bolivia in 1954 but eventually disappeared; and that Guatemala was in the process of social revolution after 1944, but in 1954 it was cut short by counterrevolution. The government of Salvador Allende in Chile (1970–1973) also sought a social revolution, although through electoral-constitu-tional processes. Other candidates have been proposed. In the international sphere, social revolutions tend to pit themselves against external enemies to assist internal consolidation—the three Latin American revolutions emphasized above all occurred within the U.S. sphere of influence against the considerable displeasure and opposi-tion of the United States. Mexican revolutionaries did not make universal claims for their upheaval, whereas those in Cuba and Nicaragua saw themselves as models for the rest of Latin America and sought to export their movements by supporting like-minded insurgents elsewhere. The three revolutions have had different outcomes. Be-ginning in World War II, Mexican revolutionary purposes declined, although the mystique was rhetorically continued until the 1980s. The Cuban Revolution led by Fidel Castro survived constant U.S. opposition, but after 1989 the critical support of the Soviet Union disappeared, and Cuba compromised its revolutionary tenets. The Sandinista government in Nicaragua was also the target of U.S. hostility and only par-tially consolidated its political power; surprisingly, it held and lost elections in 1990 and then turned over government to the victorious opposition.[2]

DEMOCRACY, MILITARISM, AND DIPLOMACY

U.S. Policies

A fundamental issue for the United States has been whether to pursue republican forms of government (representative democracy) and the protection of human rights as goals of policy. It generally sympathized with democratic elements in Latin Amer-ica, but the actual promotion of representative democracy and respect for human rights received shifting emphasis and rationales over the years, often with ambiguity and vacillation. The concepts were rooted in American idealism and were not shared until recently by European states. Guided by realist tenets, Europeans saw the U.S. ef-forts as misguided and naive and saw no reason to make such considerations a part of their calculations. Until the latter twentieth century, only the United States among the major external states felt obliged to consider regime type as an element of diplo-matic recognition and other forms of pro-democratic, antiauthoritarian actions.

When the United States pursued policies of democratic development, they most often saw these policies as ways to promote Latin American stability and thus to contribute to security against outside threats. Determining the relationship between democratic development, political stability, and prevention of foreign control was a long-standing problem. On one side, analysts pointed out an inherent conflict between democratic development and political stability, as the latter concern caused the United States to tolerate and even support certain dictators and military regimes. Because they cooperated with the United States, these regimes were said to achieve stability. For the most part, the United States accommodated itself to such dictatorships and military regimes and regarded them as conducive at least to temporary stability. Another view maintained that ultimate stability could be achieved not by dictators and armed forces but only through open democratic societies and free elections in which all political groups shared equal opportunity. The reason for supporting Latin American democratic development in the image of U.S. values was the assumption that open societies and popular participation were the soundest paths to progress and political stability.

Especially after World War II, policy debates focused on whether instability was more the result of external subversion or of internal conditions. Related arguments concerned the relative merits of shoring up the status quo or encouraging reform (such arguments did not concern radical solutions, which were assumed by both sides to risk foreign orientation). The assumption that the departure of dictators created chaos, leading to opportunities for local Communists linked to the Soviet Union, had currency after the Cuban Revolution of 1959 and again with the Nicaraguan Revolution of 1979. By the mid-1980s, a consensus had been reached within U.S. policy circles that democratic forms in Latin America best served U.S. interests and should be promoted. The debate continued, however, over how to go about this enterprise.

A U.S. policy tradition on the question of relations with nondemocratic regimes was established at the very beginning of inter-American relations. The U.S. criteria for recognition throughout the nineteenth century and into the twentieth was established by President Thomas Jefferson during the Latin American movements for independence. When a new government came to power by whatever means, the United States normally recognized it, once its de facto rule was evidenced and its intention to honor its commitments indicated. Initial U.S. contacts with the new Latin America states in the early nineteenth century were slow to develop. The United States was sympathetic toward the Latin American revolutions, yet it remained neutral during the conflicts and did not begin to recognize the new nations until 1822. The War of 1812 had turned U.S. attention from Latin American affairs, and thereafter recognition would have jeopardized its negotiations with Spain for the U.S. acquisition of the Floridas. After a treaty on the matter was signed with Spain in 1821, the United States began to recognize Latin American sovereignties. The U.S. recognition policy that did not consider the political form of governments in power remained relatively constant thereafter for almost a century, during which time Latin American revolutions and dictatorial governments were frequent.

President Woodrow Wilson came to office in 1913, reoriented the traditional recognition policy, and revised U.S. democratic policies—with regard both to recognition policies and to the partial justification of the frequent U.S. interventions in the Caribbean. Wilson instituted the practice of refusing to recognize governments that came to power through *golpes de estado*, in an attempt to encourage democratic governments. This practice of "moral" recognition of "legitimate" governments was regarded by many Latin Americans as "diplomatic" or "indirect" intervention. President Wilson chose to depart from the Jeffersonian tradition on the grounds that recognizing unconstitutional (illegitimate) governments implied approval.

Wilson saw the lack of domestic stability in the Caribbean countries as a function of their lack of progress toward constitutional democracy. He assumed that democracy could be imposed by external guidance and that the United States had the responsibility for undertaking that role. Wilson's military actions were not primarily aimed at bringing down dictatorships or promoting constitutional-democratic practices; but once military occupation was begun, U.S. Marines attempted to transform local military and police forces into apolitical forces that would defend constitutional governments after the U.S. troops were gone. U.S. forces organized and supervised elections prior to departing. Presidents Harding, Coolidge, and Hoover (briefly) continued such actions. All such efforts to establish democracy were unsuccessful.

President Hoover, as part of his incremental shift to noninterventionist policies, reapplied de facto recognition to the many violent Latin American governmental changes occurring in 1930 and 1931. Conflict over recognition policy was minimal under the Franklin Roosevelt administration. Between 1931 and 1945, the United States responded to sixteen "unscheduled" changes of Latin American governments that it felt raised questions of recognition; ten cases resulted in prompt recognition, four in delayed recognition, and two in nonrecognition. Nonintervention came under some attack because it seemed to allow dictators to seize and maintain power unhindered by external constraints.

U.S.-Argentine conflict in 1945–1946 marked a temporary departure from the policy of nonintervention. Assistant Secretary of State Spruille Braden argued that since U.S. power in Latin America made some sort of intervention unavoidable—in that intervention occurred through inaction as well as action—the United States should use its formidable influence in a positive manner by assuming democratic leadership. Braden was especially antagonistic toward the military regime in Argentina and its major figure, Colonel Juan D. Perón. While U.S. Ambassador in Buenos Aires in 1945, Braden had openly campaigned against presidential candidate Perón; after assuming his position as Assistant Secretary of State, Braden supervised the issuance of the famous "Blue Book" in February1946, two weeks prior to the Argentine election, which described Perón's wartime collaboration with the Axis, his totalitarian practices, and his use of electoral intimidation. Perón made U.S. intervention a primary campaign issue and easily won the presidency. Several Latin American governments supported the United States, but most invoked the principle of noninterference in the internal affairs of others.

After the Argentine experience the United States returned to a policy of strict nonintervention. For example, in May 1950 Assistant Secretary of State Edward Miller stated that the maintenance of diplomatic relations with nondemocratic regimes was determined not by approval of the form of government but by whether a regime could maintain civil order and honor its international obligations—traditional principles again guided U.S. recognition policy. During the Truman administration, nineteen recognition cases arose; nine new governments were recognized, seven recognitions were delayed, and nonrecognition was decided in three instances.[3]

The Eisenhower administration continued to emphasize the principle of nonintervention, insistent that intervention to remove dictators would result in an aftermath of disorder and tension that would give Communists political opportunities. His administration made decisions regarding diplomatic relations in nineteen Latin American cases; they resulted in recognition on thirteen occasions, a single nonrecognition, three delayed recognitions, and the severance of relations in two instances.

Despite the Latin American consensus favoring the principle of nonintervention over any other, and the lack of significant support for nonrecognition as an instrument for the defense of democracy, many Latin Americans expressed discontent with U.S. policies. A dramatic manifestation was the violence that greeted Vice President Richard Nixon during a 1958 tour of South America; this violence in part reflected dissatisfaction with U.S. attitudes toward Latin American dictators. Nixon afterward recommended the half-measure that the United States extend a "cool handshake" to dictators and an *abrazo* to democracies.

The Alliance for Progress under President Kennedy asserted that Latin American economic and social development must occur within a democratic framework. This assumption was challenged by seven military coups overthrowing elected Latin American presidents between 1961 and 1963. The United States at first refused to recognize the military governments and suspended its foreign assistance; but by late 1963, policy had shifted to the accommodation of military coups and eventually to the recognition of the resulting governments and the restoration of most aid programs.

After the assassination of President Kennedy in November 1963 and the succession of Vice President Johnson, the United States did not oppose dictators or promote democracy through coercion. Of eight cases concerning diplomatic representation between 1963 and 1969, four resulted in recognition, three in delayed recognition, and one in the severance of relations. Assistant Secretary of State Thomas C. Mann expressed the U.S. position in a speech delivered in June 1964. Mann reaffirmed the American commitment to and preference for representative democracy and human rights. However, he noted the lack of support for proposals for collective action and rejected any form of unilateral intervention by the United States. In order to help democratic realization, Mann suggested continuous encouragement through diplomatic discussions and support for collective action in "those cases where repression, tyranny, and brutality outrage the conscience of mankind."

This policy position remained unchanged until the mid-1970s, since the Nixon-Ford administrations continued a pragmatic attitude toward military affairs. Both presidencies said that U.S. policy stressed continuity of relations with the new governments, which, they noted, was in accordance with the idea of a U.S. Senate Resolution in September 1969 stating that recognition did not imply the approval of a new government. The United States extended prompt recognition in all five cases of recognition that arose during the Nixon and Ford administrations. With regard to military aid, the 1969 Rockefeller Report stated: "In short, a new type of military man is coming to the fore and often becoming a major force for constructive change in the American republics. Motivated by increasing impatience with corruption, inefficiency and a stagnant political order, the new military man is prepared to adapt his authoritarian tradition to the goals of social and economic progress."[4]

President Jimmy Carter stated at Notre Dame University in May 1977 that "we are now free of that inordinate fear of communism which once led us to embrace any dictator who joined us in that fear." After discounting the Soviet threat, Carter rested his global policies on three commitments: (1) to consider human rights as a fundamental tenet of U.S. foreign policy; (2) to reduce the danger of nuclear proliferation and the spread of conventional weapons; and (3) to rely on all forms of military cooperation as exceptional rather than normal instruments of policy. In the Southern Cone the United States banned Argentina, Chile, Paraguay, and Uruguay from receiving further arms transfers and certain forms of economic aid; Brazil, offended by the State Department's 1977 report on its human rights situation, refused to accept any more U.S. military assistance. In Central America, the United States applied sanctions to El Salvador, Guatemala, and Nicaragua because of human rights abuses. After the overthrow of Anastasio Somoza in Nicaragua, however, and the accession of the Sandinista-dominated government, Carter feared that events in El Salvador would parallel those in Nicaragua. He lifted the ban on military assistance to El Salvador and resumed shipments to the military government despite the absence of any reforms. The Reagan administration made opposition to Communist expansion the basis for its regional policies. This approach necessitated the reduction of democratic and human rights concerns to a secondary position and worked to restore the military programs that had been considerably diminished in prior years.

With the end of the cold war, the United States and most of the Latin American and Caribbean states settled on democratic and economic reform and development as overarching foreign policy norms. Most of these policies were carried out within a multilateral orientation and are discussed below.[5]

Multilateral Diplomacy

The member states of the Inter-American System committed themselves to the promotion of representative democracy and the protection of human rights.[6] Although the system, beginning in 1901, adopted treaties on aspects of human rights, and in the latter 1930s and during World War II made representative democracy the goal of the "political defense" of the hemisphere, a more comprehensive approach was not developed until after the war. Despite the increased attention, however, actions were hesitant and qualified. For most Latin American members, nonintervention transcended democratic development. Furthermore, the largely successful U.S. effort to emphasize mutual security and convert the Inter-American System into an anticommunist alliance eroded commitments to democracy and human rights. In the late 1980s and continuing into the 1990s, when almost all Latin American states had constitutional governments and U.S. policies were no longer burdened with cold war calculations, an inter-American consensus emerged that democratic governance (in concert with economic reform) constituted the overarching hemispheric norm.

The 1948 Charter of the Organization of American States and other instruments strongly reaffirmed principles of democracy and human rights. The Ninth International Conference of American States in 1948, which adopted the OAS Charter, addressed the recognition of de facto governments following *golpes de estado*. The conference adopted a resolution declaring that continuity of diplomatic relations among the American states was desirable and that recognition did not indicate approval of a regime but only the acknowledgment of state authority. In the 1960s the OAS began to provide technical electoral assistance. The General Secretariat organized observer missions to presidential elections in the Dominican Republic (1961 and 1962), Nicaragua (1963), Costa Rica (1962), Honduras (1963), and, in 1966, Bolivia, Costa Rica, and the Dominican Republic. With Latin American sensitivities in mind, the First Symposium on Representative Democracy (December 1962) issued a report arguing that OAS assistance in elections did not constitute "interference or intervention in the internal affairs" of a requesting state.

The Inter-American Commission on Human Rights was established in 1960 as an OAS advisory group; its pursuit of cases of human rights violations was limited to the use of moral suasion and required that it work in concert with accused governments. In 1965 the commission was given an expanded mandate, and it made investigations in the Dominican Republic, Honduras, El Salvador, and Haiti; its findings led to no further action. The 1967 amendments to the OAS Charter, which went into effect in 1970, raised the commission to the status of an organ under the cognizance of the General Assembly. In 1974 the commission presented detailed reports of grave human rights violations by the Brazilian and Chilean governments, but the OAS General Assembly declined to act on either case. In 1976 the commission's annual report found flagrant human rights violations by sixteen member states, with emphasis on Chile; and its 1977 report detailed violations in Argentina, Bolivia, El Salvador, Guatemala, and Nicaragua. On both occasions the assembly again declined to take any action. In 1978 the American Convention on Human Rights, which had been signed in 1969, finally went into effect for the ratifying states. The convention expanded the commission's authority and established the Inter-American Court of Human Rights, with jurisdiction limited to cases voluntarily brought by states subscribing to the convention. At the 1981 General Assembly meeting, the commission submitted reports on violations in Argentina, Bolivia, El Salvador, Guatemala, and Nicaragua; the assembly simply acknowledged their receipt.

Following the political transformations in Latin America and the end of East-West conflict, the terms of the inter-American debate about democracy and human rights had changed, no longer shaped by cold war calculations and decreasingly so by a preoccupation with nonintervention. Beginning in 1989, the technique of OAS electoral observation missions was revived. Since then, about half the Latin American states and Suriname have allowed OAS electoral observation missions to monitor and sometimes to assist in their elections. In 1991, the OAS issued the Santiago Commitment to Democracy and the Renewal of the International System, declaring the members' "firm political commitment to the promotion and protection of human rights and representative democracy as indispensable conditions for the stability, peace, and development of the regions." It mandated "adoption of efficacious, timely, and expeditious procedures to ensure the promotion and defense of democracy." OAS members acted in terms of the Santiago Declaration when constitutional rule was abrogated in Haiti in 1991, in Peru in 1992, in Guatemala in 1993, and in Suriname in 1994—with certain multilateral responses, without the approval of the respective governments, in all cases. In 1997 an OAS Charter amendment went into effect providing for the temporary suspension of member states in which the democratic process had been illegally interrupted.

The Summit of the Americas in December 1994 pursued matters of democratic development as one of its basic themes. The meeting issued a Plan of Action, stating, among other things, that "the strengthening, effective exercise and consolidation of democracy constitute the central political priority of the Americas," and that "the Organization of American States is the principal hemispheric body for the defense of democratic values and institutions."

Although the OAS endorsed extensive joint action related to democracy and human rights, past experience and current events confirmed the difficulties confronted by external actors. Various statements during the debates and in related documents acknowledged that democracy would emerge according to the conditions within each society; that outsiders had a limited role to play, in the sense that they could help or hurt a situation but not determine or enforce democratic success; and that democratic development depended essentially on leadership and developments within the individual states themselves. Nevertheless, the actions described above indicated that most member states agreed on the value of an assertive response to the overthrow of democratic governments. By their acceptance of the notion that multilateral action was necessary and proper to help consolidate democracy and prevent reversals, they seemed to have moderated their views of nonintervention, sovereignty, and self-determination. That acceptance was qualified, however, particularly with regard to the sensitive issue of the use of force; most Latin American governments continued to be strongly opposed to unilateral undertakings and unwilling to accept collective military action for the defense of democratic rule.

MILITARY COOPERATION

In a purely military sense, the rationale for maintaining armed forces is either to perform protective functions for the state—defending against both external and internal threats—or to act offensively against the state's antagonists—compelling them to accede to its demands. In addition to the roles of war, defense, and internal security, military establishments traditionally have played some part in national development ("civic action"). Defensive and aggressive use of force has been important in Latin America, and the idea of nation-building dates from the early nineteenth century; but the domestic political roles of the Latin American armed forces and their intervention into politics have been their most significant activities. Their historic importance has been in the domestic realm: Armed forces have served as supports for dictatorships, constituted their own governments, and operated as key actors in domestic politics when not directly in power. Thus, interstate military relations and their impact on Latin American politics and political systems is viewed primarily (but not exclusively) in a transnational context.

An important problem to consider is that of the military influence of large, external states on weaker, regional ones. Specifically, we need to (1) evaluate the Latin American aspirations and needs that have led them to seek out or accept foreign military assistance; (2) analyze the military means employed by external and regional states to achieve their foreign policy ends and identify the subsequent patterns of military interaction that emerged; and (3) consider the consequences of the foreign military influences for Latin American military establishments, civil-military relations, and foreign policy.

The military element of international relations encompasses a wide variety of policy choices and of interactions through which states attempt to influence each other. Military influences are transmitted by several diplomatic instruments; those techniques short of war, and cooperative rather than conflictual in nature, include sending missions to other states (military, naval, air, and police), providing training and education facilities for foreign personnel, engaging in the arms trade, exchanging armed service attachés through embassy structures, making visits, and awarding honors.

Latin American Military Modernization

Given the Latin American desire for military modernization, cooperative military interaction involving the Latin American subsystem has been the result of international rivalry among external states for influence in the region. Toward the end of the nineteenth century, Latin American states began to develop their military establishments—most of which had been born during the earlier wars for independence—as a concomitant to the general thrust for national modernization. Thereafter, Latin American governments generally conceded that their continuous attempts to modernize and professionalize their military establishments required substantial foreign assistance. The Latin American armed forces underwent extensive development with active assistance from Europe and the United States, both in terms of professional training and in the acquisition of arms and equipment. As a result, levels of military modernization and foreign military influences in the region varied widely, and complex patterns of international military competition emerged.

The motives of the extraregional states in giving military assistance were several. In general terms military assistance was used as a way to gain political and economic as well as military influence in Latin America. Cooperative military instruments included sending military missions and instructors to other states, providing training and educational facilities for foreign personnel, pursuing diplomatic activities (such as exchanging armed service attachés, making visits, and awarding honors), and engaging in the arms trade.

Patterns of Relations to World War I

From the late nineteenth century until World War I, Latin American plans for military and naval reorganization and development led to sharp competition among the external states who vied to be entrusted with the task. Some foreign influence existed in the regional armies and navies dating from the wars for independence, but it was not until the Latin American states decided to develop their military establishments systematically that foreign training became an important part of Latin American international politics.

In the pre-World War I period, Germany and France were the most important military competitors, and Great Britain and the United States, both renowned commercial shipbuilders, retained the most influence in naval affairs. The German and French armies enjoyed high prestige and the support of their home governments in overseas activities. Their competition for military influence in Latin America and elsewhere was an extension of Franco-German antagonism in Europe. Germany was predominant in Chile's and Argentina's military affairs, whereas France prevailed in Peru, Uruguay, and Brazil. The two states competed with rough equality in Bolivia, Paraguay, and Guatemala. The United States exerted direct military influence on armies in those states in the Caribbean where it practiced post-1898 intervention. Influence was mixed in Ecuador, Venezuela, and Colombia, and was not significant in the other regional states.

External military assistance usually involved sending armed forces missions and instructors to Latin America and offering the Latin American state the use of military facilities in the external state. German and French missions and instructors were invited to perform a variety of tasks in the major South American states. Chile, the first to begin military modernization, received its first German adviser in 1885. Thereafter the number of German officers increased, and they achieved positions far in excess of foreign officers elsewhere in Latin America. They reorganized the Chilean army, organized a general staff, established general conscription, reformed military education, and assumed direct command and training of troops. The German role became important in Argentina in 1899, when a military mission was engaged to organize and staff the new Army War College. It was later involved in other training schools and in writing Argentina's obligatory conscription law. Peru was the first Latin American state to establish close military collaboration with France and became a center of French military influence in Latin America. A French military mission arrived in 1896 and reorganized the Peruvian army along French lines. France also held a leading military position in Brazil. A French mission was engaged by the state of São Paulo in 1906 to train public forces and to establish a cadet school. Latin American military personnel were assigned overseas for professional training and education, regimental service, and observation at maneuvers. A few were sent to the United States, but most went to Europe, primarily to those states that sent missions to Latin America.

Latin American states also entered into armaments contracts with European munitions firms and U.S. and European shipbuilders, committing most regional armies and navies almost completely to foreign manufactures. Armaments orders were largely by-products of foreign service mission employment. The Latin American states, as a rule, were not weapons manufacturers and imported almost all of their armaments and equipment. The competition in military affairs affected the general competition in the export trade, as military orders could increase a country's volume of export trade considerably. In the industrial sphere, bitter rivalry developed among Krupp of Germany, Schneider-Creusot of France, and other arms manufacturers. Leading European armament firms made advances to Latin American governments until improved Latin American financial situations enabled them to make immediate payment. The French government, in granting general-purpose loans to Latin American governments, insisted on linking them to purchases from Schneider-Creusot. In spite of the French efforts, the German firms of Krupp and Mauser held the largest share of the Latin American military market prior to World War I. These relations were disrupted by the demands of World War I.

The Interbellum Period

After World War I Latin American military leaders complained that their lack of war experience seriously handicapped service training. By then the last wars in which they had participated were more than a generation removed, and only a few Latin American officers had observed the recent war in Europe firsthand. They had been left behind by the revolutionary developments in military technology and tactics. Latin American military men thus felt that it was essential for them to learn from those who had recent experience and knowledge in modern war.

Outside of those small Caribbean states where the United States was directly intervening, at first it seemed that France would be free of military competition in Latin America. Not only was the military reputation of France, as the leading European power, at its zenith, but the Versailles Treaty prohibited Germany from sending military missions and instructors abroad and abolished all German military educational institutions that might receive foreign officers. The treaty bound thirteen Latin American states and prohibited Germany from aiding the military forces of any other state in any way. French military circles confidently expected to inherit the prewar German position in South America in a period marked by severe legal restrictions on Germany. As it turned out, however, the Versailles Treaty proved to be ineffective, and Germany soon returned to a position of influence.

The first years after the war witnessed a surge in French influence in Latin American armies, but the region soon received training missions not only from France, and eventually Germany, but also from Italy, Great Britain, the United States, and even Switzerland and Spain. The number of missions contracted by Latin American governments increased substantially in the 1920s and 1930s. Air and police missions were added to the traditional army and naval missions. Especially notable was the accelerated employment of air force training missions consequent to the rapid development of military aviation during the war. Italy entered the South American military scene in the 1920s and eventually gained influence in Latin American military aviation. Britain and the United States initially followed their tradition of viewing military relations in essentially commercial terms, but in the 1930s they began to aim at counter-influencing the presence of Germany and other Axis states for political reasons. Japan attempted to compete in the arms market but was relatively unimportant. A small number of Russian officers of the old Tsarist army, several of high rank and reputation, came to Latin America for military employment after the Bolshevik Revolution of 1917, and some of them participated in the Chaco War between Bolivia and Paraguay in the 1930s.

As in the prewar period, the South American states were the most important arenas of competition during the years between the world wars. Chile reengaged German military instructors in 1924, over vigorous French protests based on the Versailles Treaty. German officers returned to Argentina in the 1920s and remained until 1940. Germany had a military monopoly in Bolivia between the wars until 1935 (the end of the Chaco War), after which an Italian military mission was engaged. Military relations remained intimate between France and Peru, with French officers assuming important army positions. France also sent air and naval missions to Peru, although the United States later sent a naval mission and replaced the French position in the Peruvian navy. France also resumed its work in Brazil in the 1920s in the state of São Paulo. It added missions to the Brazilian federal army and air force, including direction of the general staff school. A large and influential U.S. naval mission went to Brazil in 1922. Paraguay, Ecuador, Colombia, Venezuela, and Guatemala continued their eclectic ways, turning to more than one external military source. Chile and Peru played surrogate roles for Germany and France, respectively. They sent training missions and instructors to other Latin American states and received other Latin American personnel in their military institutions, thus further transmitting their mentors' systems.

The external states continued to perceive the economic advantages inherent in dominant military influence, since the Latin American states required foreign armaments to continue their military modernization. They hoped that the partisan efforts of their officers would lead to extensive arms contracts. Furthermore, Latin American military establishments were expected to urge the adoption and imitation of foreign production practices and techniques within their own newly established armaments industries, which would lead to foreign industrial involvement in the region.

The persuasive counsel of foreign military advisers gave the initial impetus for this development. Thus, the arms trade continued to be closely linked to military diplomatic activities. Foreign military officers were instrumental in establishing and promoting the new armaments industries because they were interested in seeing the Latin American units armed with implements with which the instructors were familiar. Military and diplomatic personnel cooperated closely with the representatives of their home commercial arms firms. Often the commercial representatives in Latin America were either retired or reserve officers. Thus, military instructors and missions stimulated the international arms trade.

World War II

During the period surrounding World War II, the United States sought to displace European military influence in all of Latin America beyond most of the Caribbean area, where it was already predominant. As a result, military cooperation was established between the United States and almost all of Latin America, and the phase of European military influence in Latin America ended. With the rise of fascism and threat of war in Europe, and the consequent dangers perceived for the Americas, the United States urged the establishment of multilateral inter-American arrangements for hemispheric defense. During the war, an additional set of bilateral military relationships were established, which set precedents for postwar interaction. By the time war broke out in Europe in September 1939, the United States and other American governments had issued neutrality proclamations. However, most Latin American states were unable to patrol their own coastal waters effectively, so the United States secured permission for military bases and certain other rights and facilities from them. After the fall of France in 1940, U.S. negotiations with most Latin American states led to further base rights agreements, whereby U.S. requests were granted for airfields to be used as aircraft ferry relay points. The United States constructed or refurbished some Latin American naval bases, and agreements were signed permitting the United States to use Latin American airports, to fly over their territories, and to station maintenance personnel in the area.

In the late 1930s the United States began to substitute its military missions and instructors for those of the European states, continuing its efforts during the war and immediately after. The Lend-Lease Act of March 11, 1941, ended legal restrictions on the supplying of arms to Latin America, allowing bilateral military assistance to be extended to certain Latin American states. Although Lend-Lease was designed to assist U.S. allies most directly involved in the European war, the president was empowered to transfer military articles to any state whose defense was deemed vital to the security of the United States. All Latin American states were declared eligible for aid except Argentina and Panama—Argentina had refused to cooperate with hemispheric defense plans, whereas Panama had other special military arrangements with the United States. Brazil received by far the largest portion of Lend-Lease arms furnished to Latin America, most of which were used to equip its expeditionary infantry force that saw action in Italy. Mexico (which sent an aircraft squadron to the Philippines), Chile, and Peru received most of the remainder.

Post–World War II

After World War II the United States became Latin America's main source of military assistance, providing both standardized military equipment and training. By 1946 the United States was the only external state maintaining missions in Latin America, with seventeen of them in thirteen states. In the first part of the postwar period the United States continued to rationalize military assistance in terms of the need for cooperative efforts toward a common hemispheric defense. The wartime principles of hemispheric defense were reaffirmed on a continuing basis in the Inter-American Treaty of Reciprocal Assistance (Rio Treaty) of 1947. Thereafter, U.S. officials claimed that the Rio Treaty was the "cornerstone" of U.S. military commitments to the region, and the framework for regional and bilateral military programs.

From the end of World War II until 1952 the United States had no well-organized program of military assistance in Latin America. President Truman asked the U.S. Congress on two occasions, in 1946 and 1947, for authority to institute a program of inter-American military cooperation, but Congress refused the requests. The United States continued to supply some military equipment under the Lend-Lease Act, but only that which had previously been committed for delivery as of the end of the war. Under the Surplus Property Act of 1944, which authorized direct sales of U.S. military surpluses at reduced prices, Latin Americans purchased small arms, light naval vessels, and artillery pieces. The Mutual Defense Act of 1949 enabled Latin Americans, as signatories of the Rio Treaty, to purchase arms from the United States. However, no grant aid was available, and requests for material far exceeded the amount available.

The most important basis for U.S.-Latin American military relations during most of the 1950s and until 1961 was the Mutual Security Act of 1951, passed in response to the Korean War. Portions of the legislation dealing with Latin America made military assistance contingent on the recipients' participation in "missions important to the defense of the Western Hemisphere." The act made it clear that it would be desirable to standardize the equipment, organization, and methods of the Latin American armed forces, and to orient them toward the United States and mutual security, in order to prevent Latin American arms purchases elsewhere, which might invite non-hemispheric military missions and advisers to the region. The United States also wanted to ensure the accessibility of strategic raw materials. Most of all, U.S. policy pronouncements claimed that the United States was not anxious to assume major responsibilities in Latin America in case of war. It desired to help the Latin American countries achieve a capability to protect their own territory, thus sparing the United States the necessity of assigning large numbers of troops to the region.

The assertion that the primary purpose of military aid was to strengthen Latin America's own capability to contribute to hemispheric defense cannot be accepted as the basis for U.S. policy. U.S. military planners seemed to recognize that an all-out Soviet attack on Latin America was a remote possibility, and that even if such an attack occurred the United States obviously would have to assume the burden of defense and retaliation. The military resources of Latin America in relation to the Soviet Union were so limited that massive aid would have been required to enable them to withstand a major attack. Even with such aid, the contribution they could make to self-defense against military aggression would inevitably be small. The United States at the time considered Latin America to be far behind the front lines of the cold war. The fact that military equipment assigned to Latin America was small in quantity and obsolete in quality indicated an assumption that U.S. armed forces would have been necessary to resist certain kinds of external attack. The conclusion to be made is that military aid was extended to preempt Latin American relations with other external actors and to promote internal stability in the Latin American states.

Under the provisions of the Mutual Security Act, Latin American states were able to make cash purchases of weapons and equipment. In addition, the act authorized direct grants of military equipment for selected states under bilateral agreements, called Mutual Defense Assistance pacts. A total of sixteen such agreements were signed in the 1950s. Two kinds of U.S. military missions were authorized under the Mutual Security Act: (1) Military Assistance Advisory Groups (MAAG) to administer military transfers under the Mutual Defense Assistance agreements; and (2) Service Training Missions to help train Latin American armed forces in an advisory capacity. Every Latin American state received at least one kind of mission and sometimes both. In addition, Latin American personnel were trained at U.S. military centers in the United States and Panama.

With the Alliance for Progress and an emphasis on economic and social development in Latin America, U.S. policy openly shifted from an emphasis on hemispheric defense to the combating internal subversion. The shift began near the end of the Eisenhower administration and was consummated in 1961 at the beginning of the Kennedy presidency. Economic and social development were assumed to occur best in a stable political environment. Military aid aimed at countering internal Communist subversion and insurgency was said to help promote that stability. A modicum of resources, such as small amounts for antisubmarine warfare, continued to be put into hemispheric defense, but internal stability clearly was the overriding goal.

Military assistance programs continued to consist of furnishing technical advisers, supplying grant material, and sponsoring formal training, as well as selling equipment for cash. The content of these programs, however, was changed to support Latin American counterinsurgency capabilities. Throughout the 1960s, U.S. officials, stressing the low probability of attack on Latin America from outside the hemisphere, attempted to discourage Latin American states from building up large conventional military forces and particularly discouraged arms purchases involving sophisticated aircraft and expensive naval vessels. Such expenditures were considered unwarranted diversions of resources from economic and social development projects; military replacement items should be of a kind and cost that would increase internal capabilities and enhance national development. In 1963 the International Police Academy was established in Washington, D.C., operated by the Agency for International Development. It was charged with assisting Latin American police forces in maintaining civil security—specifically, in combating urban guerrilla activities.

Under the Alliance for Progress, Latin American armed forces placed a new emphasis on civic action, substantively supported by U.S. funds, equipment, and advisers. A number of enterprises fell under this rubric. The by-products of military training that were transferred to civilian life ranged from the literacy training of recruits to the teaching of technical skills that enhanced civilian occupations. Other functions were directly aimed at assisting economic and social development, such as exploring remote areas and opening new land, building schools and highways, improving sanitation and health facilities—and other projects useful to civilians, especially in rural areas.

A wide variety of objectives were pursued and variously stressed as functions of civic action. Emphasis was placed on economic and social development through nation-building and on strengthening the economy by modernizing basic facilities and improving the infrastructure. A related idea was that the armed forces should justify their expensive public maintenance by helping to develop their nations. Another goal was improving the image of the military and the central government in the eyes of a skeptical public. Special stress was placed on the relationship of civic action to counterinsurgency (the two doctrines were developed simultaneously in the 1960s). Here the intent was to rectify those conditions believed to inspire insurgency, such as poverty and unfulfilled expectations for a better life.[7]

The United States sharply diminished its military presence in Latin America beginning in the late 1960s. Officials declared that not only was the hemispheric defense concept outdated but internal insurgency threats also were at a low level. Furthermore, Latin American counterinsurgency capabilities had improved. Consequently, personnel assigned to military groups were reduced, and grant assistance funds were cut. A reduced training program and grant assistance fund were maintained.

An important debate in the U.S. Congress in 1967 revolved around the concern that scarce Latin American resources were being unduly devoted to military expenditures to the detriment of social and economic development. The Foreign Military Sales Act of that year imposed a limit of $75 million on direct arms sales to Latin America. Latin American states simply turned to other suppliers, especially European ones. In 1971 President Nixon exercised his discretionary authority and raised the ceiling to $150 million, a figure then agreed to by Congress in the legislation for fiscal year 1972. The rationale for the increased limit was that Latin Americans had a legitimate need to update their military equipment and that experience had shown that they would simply acquire what they wanted elsewhere at an increased cost, if the United States was unresponsive to their requests. Latin Americans would also view the U.S. position as indifferent and paternalistic. U.S. balance-of-payments problems gave further impetus to increased arms exports, and the sales ceiling was eliminated altogether in 1974.

Competitors in the Arms Trade

The United States was Latin America's chief, but not exclusive, source of military assistance for the first two decades after World War II. After the war, France, Britain, Italy, Spain, West Germany, and Belgium again received small numbers of Latin American officers in their educational and training institutions. However, other states had a primary concern with trade and lacked security interests in the region. With the exception of Soviet relations with Cuba after 1960, with Peru after 1968, and with Chile from 1970 to 1973, sales of military equipment by other states than the United States were essentially of economic significance, related to the balance of payments rather than to the balance of power. Great Britain and France pursued a policy of virtually unrestricted arms sales in the profitable Latin American market. Germany, beginning in the late 1960s, adopted a similar policy after lifting prior restrictions on arms transfers to developing nations.

When the United States de-emphasized counterinsurgency and restricted arms sales to Latin America, the regional states turned to Europe as their chief suppliers. At the same time, the larger South American states competed vigorously to modernize their armed forces. Consequently, the volume and sophistication of arms transfers to Latin America increased dramatically. According to a study by the U.S. Department of State in 1973, surveying arms sales to Latin America (excluding Cuba), from 1966 to 1973, Latin American states placed a total of $1.7 billion in orders, 75 percent of them in Western Europe (mainly Britain, France, and West Germany).[8] The United States received 13 percent of those orders, Canada 10 percent, and Australia 2 percent. Six South American states (Argentina, Brazil, Chile, Colombia, Peru, and Venezuela) placed 97 percent of the orders. Naval and air forces accounted for about 90 percent of arms expenditures by the six states, and ground forces accounted for the remaining 10 percent.

The Soviet-Peruvian military relationship that began in 1973 continued through the latter 1980s. Peru was the only South American nation receiving military transfers from the Soviet Union, primarily sales of helicopters and tanks. Soviet military advisers and technicians were resident in Peru, and Peruvian military personnel were trained in the Soviet Union. The Soviet fishing fleet that operated off the South American Pacific coast was granted access to Peruvian ports for support and maintenance.

The Human Rights Factor

Dramatic reductions in U.S. military assistance to Latin America began with a 1976 congressional action and were extended by President Carter after 1977. The International Security Assistance and Arms Export Control Act of 1976 virtually eliminated several key elements of the aid program. It directed the elimination of U.S. military advisory groups around the world, unless specifically authorized by Congress. Those in Latin America were reduced to three military personnel, with some specifically authorized exceptions.

President Carter introduced far-ranging executive restrictions on U.S. arms transfers. He stated that henceforth U.S. arms transfers would be viewed as exceptional rather than normal foreign policy instruments, that the United States as the world's largest arms exporter would take the initiative in reducing arms sales, and that human rights considerations in recipient countries would be an important factor in military assistance decisions. Congress approved the new presidential orientation. In 1976 Congress had required that reports be issued on those countries for which security was proposed and had mandated an associated review process; the extent of the "report cards" and the review process was expanded during the Carter administration. As a result, the United States ended its military assistance and prohibited arms transfers to Argentina, Chile (beginning in 1976), El Salvador, Guatemala, Nicaragua, Paraguay, and Uruguay. Sales to Brazil were not so prohibited, but Brazil refused to accept further military aid in reaction to the publication of negative reports on the status of human rights there. All states claimed unwarranted interference in their internal affairs.

Because U.S. policies in the Southern Cone had revolved around questions of human rights and military assistance during the Carter administration, President Reagan had to observe legislative controls and prohibition of arms transfers because of human rights violations in Argentina, Chile, Paraguay, and Uruguay. Among several actions taken to reverse human rights policies toward the Southern Cone, the Reagan administration introduced legislation to repeal the ban on U.S. arms sales to Argentina and Chile. Congress agreed but required a presidential certification that both countries had made significant progress on human rights problems. These efforts came to an abrupt end, however, with the outbreak of the Anglo-Argentine military conflict in March 1982. After the return to democracy in Argentina in December 1983, the administration certified to Congress that Argentina had improved its human rights record and was eligible for military transfers that had been prohibited since 1977. With the return to democracy in other Southern Cone states (Uruguay, Brazil, and Bolivia joined Argentina; Peru had followed constitutional procedures since 1978), General Augusto Pinochet in Chile and Alfredo Stroessner in Paraguay stood alone as military heads of government. Prior U.S. prohibitions on arms transfers remained in effect for Chile and Paraguay; they were lifted elsewhere. Bolivia and Peru were central to U.S. efforts to control the international narcotics traffic, but bilateral programs designed to cut off the drug flow at its sources enjoyed little success.

Arms Transfers Revived

The Reagan administration revived transfers of weapons and equipment to Latin America, as a logical part of its policies that were based on opposition to Soviet-Cuban expansionism. Reagan's approach differed from Carter's in three main ways: (1) Arms transfers would have a central role in U.S. diplomacy for hemispheric security; (2) human rights concerns would be subordinate to security interests in decisions about military relations; and (3) commercial sales would be encouraged and would include making sophisticated weapons available to Latin American armed forces. U.S. officials said that the policy was designed (1) to counter Soviet arms transfers that destabilized regions of strategic importance to the United States, (2) to establish the United States as a reliable supplier and thereby strengthen ties with allies. They said the Carter policy had been proven ineffective because the Soviet Union and other major arms suppliers had not slackened their activities. Officials denied charges that commercial considerations were the main driving force behind the new policy, which in practice amounted to a license for U.S. industry to sell anything anywhere.

While the Reagan administration sought to reelevate military assistance as an instrument of policy, legislative prohibitions and congressional controls in terms of human rights continued. Earlier decisions prohibiting arms transfers to Argentina, Chile, Paraguay, Uruguay, and Guatemala remained in effect, and questions were raised about human rights conditions in El Salvador. The administration itself chose to chastise Nicaragua, with whom it had hostile relations, about its human rights record. Reagan's effort to create an inter-American front against Communist penetration in the Southern Cone involved improving relations with military regimes in Argentina, Chile, Uruguay, and Paraguay. Cultivating their cooperation required, as a first step, reversing extant sanctions.

In April 1981, the administration introduced legislation to repeal the ban on arms sales to Argentina, followed by a similar request with respect to Chile. After considerable resistance, Congress agreed to lift sanctions on both countries, but only after the president had certified to Congress that they had made significant progress on human rights problems. The State Department decided to consider the Argentine and Chilean cases simultaneously because of their dispute over islands in the Beagle Channel, not wanting to appear to take sides. The case for Chile was difficult because Chile would not cooperate in resolving the murder case of Orlando Letelier (a former Chilean ambassador to the United States) and an associate who had been assassinated in Washington. The Anglo-Argentine war of 1982 suspended certification considerations for a year and a half.

Prime Minister Thatcher also expressed concern that the United States had dropped its prohibition of arms sales to Argentina and that any resumption of such transfers would enhance Argentina's ability to attack the islands. Supporters of the U.S. action pointed out that no statutory reasons remained to justify continuation of the previously well-founded discrimination, that in any case those arms could be obtained from numerous sources other than the United States, and that Alfonsín had pledged both not to use force in the dispute and to reduce Argentina's arms purchases. It was also noted that the United Kingdom was selling weapons to Chile that could be used to attack Argentina. On December 10, 1983, inauguration day of the newly elected Argentine civilian President Raúl Alfonsín, President Reagan certified to Congress that Argentina had improved its human rights record and was eligible for the resumption of military transfers. A similar move was taken toward Uruguay in 1984, with the end of the military regime and the return to democracy there. By then, General Augusto Pinochet of Chile and Alfredo Stroessner in Paraguay stood alone as military heads of state, and U.S. prohibitions on arms transfers remained in effect for both governments.

Human rights concerns in Central America posed special considerations. In Guatemala, General Roméo Lucas García presided over probably the most violently repressive regime in Latin America. The Reagan administration indicated its willingness to resume military aid to help combat Guatemala's insurgency problem, but the scale of state terrorism was so high that the administration could not convince Congress to resume military ties. Congress relented in the case of El Salvador but by law required the executive to certify that El Salvador was making a "concerted and significant effort to comply with internationally recognized human rights," was "achieving substantial control over all elements of its armed forces," and was "committed to the holding of free elections at an early date." Certification was made in February 1981. With the subsequent holding of elections in El Salvador, the end of the Lucas García dictatorship in Guatemala and the holding of elections there, the resumption of the electoral process in Honduras, and the improved but still problematical human rights situations in all three countries, U.S. military transfers were unfettered. Arms transfers were again conducted, this time in the larger context of Central American conflict (see below).

The administration was free to act independently when arms transfers did not involve questions of human rights. As a candidate, Reagan had pledged to promote weapons sales abroad and did so once in office. The State Department instructed U.S. diplomats, including armed services attachés, to assist U.S. manufacturers in marketing arms abroad. It canceled President Carter's order prohibiting such cooperation. Reagan approved sales of advanced aircraft to Third World states. Venezuela was a principal recipient, as the Reagan administration acceded to its request to purchase eighteen F-16s on a cash basis. Concerns were expressed that the sale presaged unrestrained transfers of highly advanced weaponry in Latin America. As it turned out, other countries did not have the economic resources to buy extensive military arms.

Post–Cold War Development

From the late 1980s, the United States shifted its priorities regarding military relations with Latin America away from counterinsurgency operations and dedicated even fewer resources to programs involving the Latin American armed forces. Activities emphasized supporting the armed forces for actions against the drug traffic and, to a lesser extent, against other transnational criminal activities; training them for participation in international UN-sponsored peacekeeping operations; and offering technical assistance and some funding for the specific problem of removing the huge number of anti-personnel mines in Central America (a consequence of internal wars in the 1980s). Direct military assistance was at a very low level, and most sales of military equipment (until 1997) were intended for anti-drug operations—and most of those transfers were to Colombia.[9]

A continuing and accelerated controversy involved the training courses provided at the U.S. School of the Americas at Fort Benning, Georgia (where it had been moved after many years of operation in Panama). Critics of the school had long argued for closing the school, pointing to its graduates, who included those who had overthrown civilian governments and numerous others who had been charged with human rights violations. They were particularly outraged in 1996 by the revelations that a counterinsurgency training manual in the 1980s had recommended such measures as torture and murder. School officials disavowed the tactics and in their courses significantly increased the human rights content.[10] The school's supporters denied any connection between the training and the contrary behavior of some of its graduates and asserted the necessity for the United States to remain engaged with armed forces in the new era of Latin American democratization.

Further controversy arose in 1997 when the Clinton administration lifted the continuing restrictions on U.S. sales of advanced weapons systems—including combat jet aircraft and other "sophisticated" military equipment—to Latin America. The ensuing debate over the wisdom of this development was a familiar one. Many armed forces officials in the region welcomed the decision, saying that after several years of severely reduced military spending they needed to upgrade their eroded resources. Detractors—among them Latin American government officials and U.S. and Latin American military analysts and human rights organizations—were concerned that such sales would set off a dangerous regional arms race in sophisticated weaponry, a race Latin American states could financially ill-afford. Such weapons, they said, were unrelated to current security threats. Critics also noted the U.S. commercial interest underlying the decision and the lobbying power of U.S. defense contractors, who sought to increase foreign arms sales in the wake of the significant decrease of U.S. Defense Department arms procurement with the end of the cold war.

Some Consequences of Military Cooperation

International military cooperation forms a special area of consideration for development theory and policies, particularly in the Latin American context. All Latin American states and their military establishments have depended at some time and to some extent on foreign powers for their military modernization. External states gain influence when Latin American states rely on them for arms acquisitions, military organizations, and tactics based on the external models. But such matters as military philosophy and ideology and civil-military relations, are difficult to measure and to assign causality.

A major debate among decision makers in seller states (especially the United States) and an important domestic issue among certain political groups in Latin America is the question of the allocation of resources for military expenditures that could be better spent for economic development or applied to a reduction of national expenditures. A related assumption voiced by critics of the arms trade, at least throughout the twentieth century, is that it has stimulated arms races among the regional states. The result may be that domestic political conflict in Latin American politics will intensify and that efforts to reduce those expenditures by external pressures will be futile. That arms purchases are directly related to arms races and the possibilities of armed international conflict has also been debated. A state's purported fear of an external military threat may be an excuse to buy arms for purposes of national military prestige and for the maintenance of a military establishment by professional military men acting in their own self-interest.

The political-developmental effects of both military and economic programs have been subject to much criticism. Beginning in the late 1950s an analytical point of departure concerning foreign military influences in Latin America was the "traditionalist" versus "revisionist" debate. These positions may be equated with "idealism" and "realism," respectively, in the debate over developmentalism and military cooperation. Although most of that debate referred to U.S. influences, similar positions may be assumed regarding the European states in Latin America prior to World War II, particularly those of Germany and France.[11] The debate itself faded in the 1980s, as the Latin American military regimes disappeared, but the basic opposing tenets have continued to arise whenever external military aid is discussed.

The traditional/idealist view linked international military relations to the frequent role of the Latin American armed forces as the direct arbiters of domestic politics. It maintained that Latin American military establishments were essentially defenders of the status quo and thwarted political, social, and economic development. Furthermore, a number of traditionalist critics of U.S. military assistance programs saw a causal relationship between military aid and conservative or reactionary Latin American militarism that impeded national development. As a result, these critics claimed a positive correlation between military assistance and the increase in or maintenance of Latin American militarism, holding the United States responsible.

The revisionist/realist school held, contrarily, that the fact of political involvement by Latin American military establishments was an expression, rather than a cause, of underdevelopment, and that the armed forces could be mobilized to perform useful nation-building functions. This school claimed that the military in Latin America was peculiarly suited to strike a balance between stability and change, since it embodied a combination of authority and reform-mindedness (this argument is rarely heard in the new democratic era). A few military regimes themselves claimed to have abandoned their role as defenders of the status quo and as allies of the upper class against civilian governments who sought reform. Revisionists tended to deny causal relationships between military assistance and militarism, stressing internal rather than foreign factors.

Revisionists correctly insisted that military regimes be viewed as part of the total structure and function of society. Their stress on military regimes as effective instruments of modernization, however, is at least open to question and, in view of the Latin American experience with military regimes over the past two decades, essentially discredited. The "revisionist" U.S. policy adopted in 1963, essentially unchanged until 1976, and revived in Central American policy in the 1980s tended especially to a simplistic faith in the modernizing possibilities of the Latin American military. This undifferentiated view ignored that individual officers or groups acted in a predatory manner. The recent experience of a number of military governments challenges the assumption that even reform-minded military rule can be an effective instrument for progress. The record so far shows some achievements but mostly only partial success or outright failure. Furthermore, the blatantly repressive nature of certain military regimes flies in the face of developmentalist tenets and supports the traditionalist-idealist view. Especially in Southern Cone politics, concepts of "security" have justified military rationales for domestic intervention and repression.

A shortcoming of both theoretical perspectives, and of state policies based on them, is that they assumed the institutional nature of all Latin American armed forces. They saw them as organized into a cohesive military establishment and acting as a disciplined corporate entity, either for good or evil. Theories of Latin American civil-military relations must allow for the reality of "noninstitutionality" as a continuing rather than transitory state in certain cases. In these instances, theory must also take into account the consequences of personalities and interpersonal relationships—that is, theorists must consider relations revolving around personal interactions among a chief executive, important military officers, and their key associates, rather than processes involving a bureaucratically well-organized "presidency" and "military establishment."

Dependency theory also addressed the consequences of international military cooperation. The arms trade did not necessarily involve a political function if it was viewed by the actors strictly as a commercial transaction. If Latin American industries were unable to produce equipment, arms, and munitions in sufficient quantity or to provide updated models and spare parts, the Latin American armed services may have become dependent on foreign manufacturers. The relative independence in military affairs on the part of major states, and even some smaller ones, indicated that dependency might be broken by local policy efforts despite the wishes of outside suppliers.

The impact of one military establishment on the institutions of another was not necessarily the most important consequence of military interaction. The professional level achieved by the regional armed forces varied widely, as they first copied European military establishments, especially French and German ones, and later those of the United States. The various external styles were reflected in Latin American military organization, training and educational methods, strategy and tactics, and arms acquisitions. This observation is superficial, however, if the impact was not of political consequence. It is not enough to observe, for example, that one or another Latin American army adopted French, German, or U.S. training methods or organizational schemes and then conclude that an influential linkage exists. Imitation may have been manifested only in appearances, with actual military behavior taking place that was alien to the external model. For example, the Prussian General Staff system was emulated by most Latin American states between 1890 and World War II. Yet it was also almost universally adopted around the globe by Germany's friends and enemies alike, and even by its major rivals for influence in Latin America (France and the United States). Logically, the adoption of the German staff system did not necessarily indicate direct German political influence. Likewise, after World War II, most Latin American states imitated the U.S. Department of Defense and armed forces organization; but differing relations existed with the United States, and there were varying patterns of civil-military relations within Latin America as well. The analyst must attempt to ascertain how far the imitation of external military systems led with regard to the substantive attitudes of Latin American military men toward their civil-military relations.

Trends in external military aid and Latin American militarism—the decade-and-a-half rise from the mid-1960s to the late 1970s in the military dominance of Latin America, despite a sharp decrease in U.S. assistance—present an incongruity for dependency theory and the traditionalist critique. Irving Louis Horowitz concluded that if theories of dependency explained Latin American militarism, we might have anticipated a reduction rather than a pronounced increase in militarization. He argued that Latin American militarism was not so much a function of either dependency or developmentalism as it was a response to the military dynamics and specific domestic conditions. Although neither dependency nor developmental perspectives were entirely removed from the realities of hemispheric conditions, it was clear that Latin American militarism should not be perceived as a mechanical response to foreign pressures, especially when such pressures move counter to observable trends.[12]

The new international security concerns in the post–cold war period have brought on new concerns about civil-military relations in Latin America. Some people fear that the armed forces may use expanded national security roles as a rationale for reestablishing repressive military regimes (as they did in the past)—or that they may at least risk increased militarization of Latin American societies and undermine democratic institutions. Many Latin American armed forces officers worry that the new security roles—especially in UN peacekeeping and internal counter-narcotics operations—detract from their traditional missions and increase factional divisions within their own institutions. Others argue that the revised national security priorities should strengthen the democratic nature of civil-military relations. In any event, Latin Americans have been faced with deciding on the role of their armed forces in the context of their new domestic and international political environments.[13]

NOTES

1. Frederick M. Nunn, *The Time of the Generals: Latin American Professional Militarism in World Perspective* (Lincoln: University of Nebraska Press, 1992).

2. Social-revolutionary regimes have been considered elsewhere in this book: with references to the policies of Mexico and Cuba; in terms of early Soviet policies and the later connection with Cuba and Nicaragua; and, especially, regarding U.S. efforts during the cold war to unilaterally intervene against what it saw as Communist or potentially Communist regimes, and to transform the multilateral Inter-American System into an anticommunist al-

liance. Of particular interest is Cole Blasier, *The Hovering Giant: U.S. Responses to Revolutionary Change in Latin America*, rev. ed. (Pittsburgh: University of Pittsburgh Press, 1985), a thorough treatment of the subject highly critical of U.S. attitudes.

3. U.S. Department of State, *U.S. Policy Toward Latin America: Recognition and Non-Recognition of Governments and Interruption in Diplomatic Relations, 1933–1974* (Washington, D.C.: 1975). Other similar statements below are taken from this source.

4. *The Rockefeller Report on the Americas*, New York Times edition (Chicago: Quadrangle, 1969), 32–33.

5. Of interest is Michael J. Kryzanek, *Leaders, Leadership, and U.S. Policy in Latin America* (Boulder, Colo.: Westview Press, 1992), an innovative treatment of U.S. policy actions in terms of their ability to deal with various categories of Latin American political regimes and their leaders, with reference to issues of drugs, debt, development, and intervention. See also Lars Schoultz, *Human Rights and United States Policy Toward Latin America* (Princeton: Princeton University Press, 1981), an excellent scholarly treatment of the subject.

6. The following discussion is based on G. Pope Atkins, *Encyclopedia of the Inter-American System* (Westport, Conn.: Greenwood Press, 1997), 122–133. See also Thomas Buergenthal, Robert Norris, and Dinah Shelton, *Protecting Human Rights in the Americas: Selected Problems*, 3d. ed. (Kehl, Germany: N. P. Engel, 1990); Tom Farer, ed., *Beyond Sovereignty: Collectively Defending Democracy in the Americas* (Baltimore: Johns Hopkins University Press, 1996); Cecilia Medina Quiroga, *The Battle of Human Rights: Gross, Systematic Violations and the Inter-American System* (Dordrecht; Boston: M. Nijhoff, 1988); and Lars Schoultz, William C. Smith, and Augusto C. Varas, eds., *Security, Democracy, and Development in the Western Hemisphere* (New Brunswick, N.J.: Transaction, 1994).

7. Willard F. Barber and C. Neale Ronning, *Internal Security and Military Power: Counterinsurgency and Civic Action in Latin America* (Columbus: Ohio State University Press, 1966) remains an insightful work, highly skeptical about the utility of counterinsurgency, civic action, and U.S. assistance.

8. U.S. Department of State, *Arms Sales in Latin America* (Washington, D.C.: 1973).

9. For a good summary analysis of these matters, see Richard L. Millett, "The United States and Latin America's Armed Forces," *Journal of Interamerican Studies and World Affairs* 39, no. 1 (Spring 1997), 121–136.

10. Millett, "The United States and Latin America's Armed Forces," 126–127.

11. The analytic concepts regarding the roles of Latin American armed forces have been periodically reviewed. See G. Pope Atkins, "The Armed Forces in Latin American Politics," in *Civil-Military Relations*, ed. Charles Cochran (New York: Free Press, 1974); Richard C. Rankin, "The Expanding Institutional Concerns of the Latin American Military Establishments," *Latin American Research Review* 9 (Spring 1974): 81–108; Riordan Roett and James F. Tierney, eds., "The Military in Latin America," *International Journal of Politics* 1 (Summer-Fall 1971): entire issue; they have been updated by Paul Zagorsky, *Democracy vs. National Security: Civil-Military Relations in Latin America* (Boulder, Colo.: Lynne Rienner Publishers, 1992).

12. Irving Louis Horowitz, "From Dependency to Determinism: The New Structure of Latin American Militarism," *Journal of Political and Military Sociology* 5 (Fall 1977): 217–238.

13. G. Pope Atkins, "Redefining Security in Inter-American Relations: Implications for Democracy and Civil-Military Relations," in *To Sheathe the Sword: Civil-Military Relations in the Quest for Democracy*, ed. John P. Lovell and David Albright (Westport, Conn.: Greenwood Press, 1997), 173–174.

CHAPTER FIFTEEN

■

Intersocietal Relations

Four highly multifaceted, transnational, intersocietal phenomena are examined in this chapter: the movement of people, the illicit drug traffic, public and private cultural exchanges, the cultural diffusion among societies. The movement of people is not, as Doris Meissner points out, a discrete social phenomenon unrelated to larger matters; it is also a function of politics, economics, law, demographics, human rights, and security concerns.[1] The long-standing illegal drug traffic—originating in and flowing through and out of the region—emerged in the 1980s as a widely recognized source of criminality, violence, economic and political power, social problems, and governmental dilemmas. Transnational cultural relations involve the public and private transmittal of societal values (to include related government propaganda efforts). Cultural diffusion has multiple sources. It is partly a consequence of the above phenomena: Human migrations, cultural exchanges, and the drug traffic each have their transnational societal consequences; they are joined by the informal transnational proliferation of the news and entertainment media, educational connections, sports, popular culture, and other transnational associations.

THE MOVEMENT OF PEOPLE

Basic Concepts

The movement of people involves migrants and refugees and related state policies and actions. International migrants (people who move from one country to settle in another) are both emigrants (from the country they leave) and immigrants (to the one they enter); émigrés are those who migrate especially for political reasons. Refugees are those who flee a country and enter another for reasons of personal safety. Asylum is either temporary refuge provided to political transgressors within a state by the embassy or military facilities of another, or protection offered by a state to exiled dissidents from another state. The specific meanings of these generic terms and the formal and informal rules governing the movements themselves have changed with altered conditions, as will be indicated below.

399

The problem of refugees and asylees as matters of policy and law requires further commentary. Not until well into the twentieth century were international norms and legal standards adopted that affected the Western Hemisphere. The Inter-American System issued four formal instruments between 1928 and 1954 that addressed matters of refugees and asylum.[2] The United States was not a party to them because it did not recognize the doctrine of asylum as part of international law. The Sixth International Conference of American States in 1928 adopted the Convention on Asylum, which sixteen Latin American states subsequently ratified. It excluded from the right of asylum common criminals and deserters from the armed forces, and provided for specific rules to be followed by all parties in the cases of asylum granted to political offenders. Two conventions, signed in 1933 and 1954, respectively, amended the 1928 instrument in certain particulars. The Tenth Inter-American Conference in 1954 adopted the Convention on Territorial Asylum, providing that every state had the sovereign right "to admit into its territory such persons as it deems advisable, without . . . giving rise to complaint by any other State," and laying out specific rules for the granting of asylum.

Today's international law regarding refugees, essentially the legacy of World War II, is provided by the 1967 United Nations Protocol Relating to the Status of Refugees. It defines refugees as people who have suffered persecution or likely to face it "for reasons of race, religion, nationality, membership of particular social groups or political opinion" and are therefore unwilling to return to their country of former residence. Refugees have the right not to be forcibly returned.[3] In addition to this legally-defined group of individuals, the victims of war and repression are also generally considered refugees.[4] In both the legal and general senses the Latin American region has yielded serious refugee predicaments.

Increasingly since the 1960s, asylum has come to be an important process for the inter-American protection of human rights. Recent refugee problems—as in Central America, Cuba, and Haiti—and more interest in human rights issues have broadened the concept of asylum. Adolfo Aguillar points out two trends as of the mid-1990s: (1) refugees do not necessarily ask for individual protection but may seek refuge on the basis of group persecution; and (2) refuge is increasingly a multilateral matter, as international organizations have become more active—the United Nations Human Rights Commission is the lead agency— superseding bilateral interstate processes and challenging state sovereignty on such matters.[5]

Movements into Latin America and the Caribbean

Migrations of people created all of the human groups that make up the Americas. As a result of their complexities, Latin American country populations are dissimilar in many respects. They have, inter alia, combined aboriginal, Iberian, African, and other cultural heritages to the extent that no typical Latin American individual or nation-state exists. A similar general statement can be made about the newer Caribbean nation-states.

Migrants from Asia, who moved by land beginning possibly 40,000, and at least 12,000, years ago, were the first people to inhabit what came to be known as the Americas. By the time of European expansion into the Western Hemisphere after 1492, groupings of Indians (misnamed by Christopher Columbus) ranged from primitive nomadic tribes to the advanced civilizations of the Aztec and Inca empires (more complex than some of those in Europe at the time). The Spanish and Portuguese came first as conquerors and then as settlers, with a total of approximately one million colonists each from Spain and Portugal. Most of the Indians in the Caribbean islands were killed off, mainly through Spanish maltreatment and disease; Spaniards then placed those on the continental mainland in servile status.[6]

Spain and Portugal introduced some twelve million Black Africans, shipped across the Atlantic Ocean (the horrific Middle Passage) in the three-century slave trade (which corresponded to the Iberian colonial period); they composed the largest population group in colonial Latin America.[7] African slave labor flowed to the Caribbean and the rest of Spanish America and to Portuguese Brazil, as well as to British America (even to non-plantation regions) and to French Canada. In Latin America and the Caribbean most slaves were placed in less populated areas—where Indians had been destroyed or had not settled—as laborers on sugar and cacao plantations or in gold, silver, and diamond mines. The British, French, and Dutch also brought African slaves to their Caribbean possessions. The British brought in East Indians (from South Asia) as indentured immigrant labor from the 1830s until World War II. Chinese "coolies" were transported as "contract labor" to various parts of the region.

Immigrants from most parts of the globe migrated to the New World, mostly after the Latin American states became independent (only a small number went to the colonies), adding to the racial and cultural mix. Large-scale immigration occurred in the last two decades of the nineteenth century and continued until World War I, which interrupted the flow. Migration slowly recovered in the 1920s, but it was subsequently impeded by global depression and disrupted by World War II. In the postwar period, another wave of substantial migration commenced but then tapered off.

A number of factors encouraged the movement of people in the latter part of the nineteenth century from Europe to Latin America—they were essentially the same ones that lie behind the contemporary migrations to the United States. In Europe, populations increased as industrialization accelerated, a transformation that was accompanied by increased life expectancy; people also moved from farms to factories, reducing agricultural output while the demand for food was increasing. For most of Europe the changes resulted in social dislocations, excess population, a surplus of investment capital for export, and the need to import food and raw materials. Latin American circumstances—especially in southern South America—complemented the European situation. The region was lightly populated and had a potential for significant production of food and of raw materials; the countries there desired to develop their economies and societies but needed people, capital, and technical assistance to produce commodities for export.[8] Latin Americans were concerned with underpopulation throughout the nineteenth century into the twentieth. In 1810 the entire regional population was about 20 million; by 1900 that amount was little more than 60 million.

The major Latin American recipients of immigrants were Argentina, Uruguay, and Brazil, followed by Chile, Mexico, and Venezuela; every Latin American country received some immigrants. Most of them were Spanish, Portuguese, and Italian, with substantial numbers of French, German, British, and other nationalities; most Japanese immigration occurred in the 1930s, especially to Brazil, with many emigrants also going to Peru and Bolivia.

Numerous émigrés and refugees migrated to Latin America and were added to the mix of migrants.[9] At mid-century, refugees arrived in Latin America, escaping the consequences of the failed 1848 European Liberal Revolutions. A substantial number of Italian emigrants before 1880 were political exiles, mostly republicans and socialists, who left because of the failure of the *risorgimiento* (the movement to unify Italy under a single secular state). After that date the majority of Italian emigrants were from the poorest socioeconomic strata, escaping conditions in the south.[10] European political upheavals in the 1920s and 1930s stimulated migration to Latin America. After Benito Mussolini became premier of Italy in 1922, antifascist republicans and socialists went to the Americas. During the Spanish Civil War (1936–1939) and after General Francisco Franco's victory, refugees (including many intellectuals) went to Mexico and, in fewer numbers, to Argentina as favored destinations.[11] Germans, including many Jews, fled after Adolph Hitler's rise to the chancellorship in 1933; Mussolini's onerous racial laws of 1938 caused many Italian Jews to depart.[12]

Migration had economic and political consequences for the sending countries.[13] The departure of migrants from their homelands frequently alleviated economic stresses and the attendant political tensions. Migration reduced, but did not resolve, unemployment and overcrowding in Italy, Spain, Portugal, and Japan. Overseas migrants sometimes facilitated trade relations when they formed trading companies that introduced new forms of commerce. Emigrants sending remittances back to their families, an important consideration especially to the economically-motivated waves of European migration to the Americas, provided direct economic benefits to the old country. Emigration was not without cost to the homelands, however, especially if the migrants were skilled workers.

The hopes of certain states that immigrant communities would further their political influence in Latin America were not generally realized. Emigrants were not automatically sympathetic to the homeland even when loyal to their original nationality in a cultural sense. Politically motivated refugees were usually antagonistic to the governments they had left behind, and economic emigrants were averse to the socioeconomic structure they had abandoned. Intellectuals and professional and white collar émigrés often carried bitter ideological, political, and racial enmities and could in fact be damaging critics of the regimes they had fled. Later generations tended to behave as local citizens rather than as "foreigners."

After World War II the image remained of Latin America as underpopulated and with huge open spaces available to mass migration from a crowded world. Although the region did have much unoccupied territory, and several states could in theory have provided more people with living space, economic conditions in particular mitigated against supporting larger populations. Economic growth was insufficient to decrease poverty levels in countries with high population growth rates; the problem was not the lack of people but of capital and technology. Consequently, Latin American states no longer recruited new settlers, as they had in the last century. At the same time migrant labor from Europe and Asia looked elsewhere, and the initial wave of postwar migration subsided. Furthermore, Latin America's economic and political problems created its own significant emigration.

U.S. Immigration and Refugee Policies

The Open Hemispheric Door. Until 1968 the United States had few restrictions on migration from the other Americas. U.S. officials generally did not view the matter as a foreign policy priority until well into the cold war—first with specific regard to the aftermath of the Castro revolution of 1959, and then in more general terms in the 1980s. Thus U.S. policy makers traditionally treated immigration and refugee matters as a low priority to be dealt with by law enforcement agencies, state and local authorities, and nongovernmental organizations and churches that dealt with human requirements.14

During the nineteenth century the United States had no comprehensive immigration legislation. Although a series of specific laws excluded certain groups, particularly Chinese, none of them mentioned Latin Americans. The Immigration Act of 1924 introduced national origins quotas but specifically exempted migrants coming from the independent states of the Western Hemisphere. All immigrants, however, had to meet employment and self-support requirements in order to qualify for visas. The Immigration and Nationality Act of 1952 revised the 1924 quota system but, like the earlier law, placed no restrictions on Latin American states. (The 1952 act prohibited Communists from entering the United States.) The 1965 Immigration and Nationality Act, which went into effect in 1968, put a ceiling on Western Hemisphere immigration for the first time. It restricted the region to an annual maximum of 120,000 immigrants but without the "per-country" restrictions imposed elsewhere. The act of 1976 applied the country limits to the Americas.15

The special treatment of Latin America prior to the 1965 law derived from the role of Mexico and the Caribbean countries as sources of cheap labor and from the U.S. view of their strategic location, which dictated the desirability of a stable region. Mexican migration had particular implications: The U.S.-Mexico border marked a huge contrast between the standards of living of neighboring states with distinct cultures. For many years Mexicans had moved across the porous border in search of jobs and safety; particularly numerous were the permanent and seasonal workers whom U.S. employers actively recruited. After passage of the 1924 Act, many Mexicans, unable to qualify for immigration visas, had simply entered illegally across the Rio Grande.[16]

During World War II, with the large movement of U.S. labor into war-related industries, the United States and Mexico formalized the de facto enlistment of Mexicans in a temporary *bracero* (labor) program for crop harvesting and railway maintenance, with U.S. government subsidies for transportation, housing, health, and certain other costs. The two governments signed the first of a series of agreements in August 1942. A revised temporary postwar agreement gave way to special U.S. legislation, enacted after negotiations with Mexico (further worker shortages had resulted from the Korean war). The Migrant Labor Agreement of 1951 provided for the recruitment of Mexican farmworkers to assist in the harvest of agricultural crops. The act was amended and extended on five occasions, at the instance of certain farming interests, until it was finally terminated in 1964.[17] The following year, the Immigration and Nationality Act provided for the entry of agricultural labor in general. Mexico remained the leading origin of immigrants from all countries.[18]

Other Latin American migrants established communities in the United States, especially those coming from the circum-Caribbean. The flow increased after World War II, although it was relatively modest until the 1980s. Many Central Americans migrated to the United States in search of employment; others were displaced by social problems and violent political events. Cuba, the Dominican Republic, and Haiti were also sources of migrants, escaping brutal dictatorships as well as poor economic conditions. In all instances, established communities in the United States facilitated rapid expansion of movement in response to later economic pressures and violence.[19]

The Cuban Revolution of 1959, which precipitated an outflow of people fleeing the new regime, presented an important special case of refugee flows and U.S. policy. According to Christopher Mitchell, the Cuban Revolution of 1959 marked a major turning point for the United States with regard to the linkage between foreign policy and immigration, not only because for the first time "high politics" were prominent considerations in the making of refugee policy but also because refugee policy itself played a key role in the formation of the flow of people.[20]

After coming to power, Fidel Castro encouraged the exodus of the Cuban middle classes, whom he saw as potential political opponents. The United States welcomed them; no legal obstacles to their entry existed, and they were deemed to symbolize the Cuban regime's lack of legitimacy and stability. Aristide Zolberg points out that the Cubans were initially expected to be temporary exiles who would return home after the Castro regime was overthrown—but the unsuccessful invasion at the Bay of Pigs by a U.S.-sponsored Cuban exile force in April 1962 brought an end to that expectation.[21] During the October 1963 missile crisis and the U.S. blockade, Castro disallowed further emigration; when he reopened the border in 1965, President Lyndon Johnson responded with the comment that "those who seek refuge here will find it." An airlift of "freedom flights" was begun and operated until 1973. In 1976, Cuba and the United States agreed to allow exiles in the United States to visit Cuba and some political prisoners in Cuba to go to the United States.

New Priorities. Since about 1980, the United States has made global immigration (legal and illegal) and refugee issues high foreign policy priorities. The decade of the 1980s was a historic high period for the United States, with the number of immigrants outnumbered only by those in the first decade of the twentieth century.[22] The migration from Latin America and the Caribbean had a prominent place in U.S. decisions. Largely the consequence of deteriorating political and economic conditions exacerbated by U.S. policies, the augmented movements followed the established flows from Mexico, Central America, Cuba, and Haiti. U.S. laws and policies—which, along with public opinion, underwent changes during this last decade of the cold war—were marked by inconsistency and controversy.

After 1979 U.S. actions reflected cold war calculations that outward migration (in particular refugees) weakened Communist adversaries and revealed their illegitimacy. The United States thus welcomed most refugees from Cuba; it also pressed Nicaragua to permit freedom of exit but urged those who left to seek haven in neighboring countries. Other circum-Caribbean migrants were not accorded the same special treatment, despite the repression, violence, and economic dislocations in several of their home countries.

The Refugee Act of 1980 was intended to provide systematic procedures for dealing with refugees but, because of cold war exigencies, was not fully implemented until 1991 (see below). In the interim, refugee settlement and asylum adjudication continued to operate according to the prior rules in force. Two crises early in the 1980s, regarding Cuban and Haitian refugees, respectively, marked another turning point for U.S. policies concerning the foreign policy-migration linkage and initiated the continuing public debate in the United States.

The "Mariel Crisis" in Cuba began in April 1980, when some 10,000 Cubans invaded the Peruvian embassy in Havana and demanded political asylum. In response, the Castro government opened Mariel harbor for anyone to leave; the Cuban exile community in Florida launched a massive boat lift, and the Carter administration reluctantly allowed entry of the refugees. Within five months about 130,000 Cubans had arrived in the southern United States, including about 8,000 criminals and others released from prisons and mental institutions (they were in effect pushed out of Cuba). In July 1981 the Reagan administration announced it would henceforth interdict boats across the Florida straits and turn their passengers back to Cuba. In December 1984 Cuba and the United States reached an agreement, whereby Cuba would take back 2,476 "excludables" (mostly common criminals) and the United States would accept former political prisoners as refugees and resume issuance of immigration visas to other qualified Cubans. Cuba suspended the agreement in May 1985 when the United States launched Radio Marti; by then a small number of excludables remained in U.S. prisons. The Mariel episode attracted considerable attention in the United States and challenged the cold war policy whereby any refugees from Communist countries were welcome.[23]

Simultaneous with the Mariel crisis in 1980, and in contrast to policies toward Cuba, the United States denied asylum requests to the vast majority of Haitians who made boat landings on the Florida coast. In 1981 the Reagan administration began seizing and detaining Haitians who arrived in the United States, and, with Haitian dictator Duvalier's formal agreement, ordered the U.S. Coast Guard to interdict Haitian vessels, perform a summary review of the migrants' claims for asylum, and return to Haiti those deemed to have no case. With successful challenges in U.S. courts by human rights groups, however, most of the arrested Haitians were released, and many of them were granted amnesty. But the interdiction of "boat people" continued until 1991. Over the ten-year period of that policy, the Coast Guard intercepted some 24,600 Haitians, only twenty-eight of whom were permitted to enter the United States to apply for asylum.[24]

Also notable were the increased numbers of people from the Dominican Republic, which shared with Haiti the island of Hispaniola, who went to the United States during the 1980s. Primarily seeking economic opportunity, they were facilitated by the long-established Dominican communities in the United States (New York City was a favored destination). Many of them entered under the "family reunion" priorities of U.S. immigration law. As of 1986 remittances from Dominicans in the United States almost equaled the annual Dominican government budget and a quarter of its foreign exchange earnings.[25]

Large numbers of Central Americans left their homes after 1979 because of civil and international wars and degraded economies. The close U.S. involvement in Central American conflict was one of the significant factors in sustaining the outflow of people. The United States created the Contra insurgents to fight the Sandinista regime in Nicaragua and imposed economic sanctions against the country. The United States also supported and guided other Central American counterinsurgency and related operations that disrupted economies and displaced people (see Chapter 12).[26]

About two million Central Americans were displaced. Large numbers of them sought refuge in neighboring countries and the United States, including between 300,000 and 500,000 Nicaraguans and more than a million Salvadorans. Many of the latter went to Mexico and even more to the United States, where they became by far the largest Central American community. Refugees from Guatemala went mostly to neighboring Mexico, with significant numbers also seeking refuge in the United States. The United States allowed few admissions of displaced Central Americans under the 1980 refugee law, on the grounds that safe havens were available in neighboring countries; U.S. officials categorically saw them as illegal aliens and treated them accordingly, even though they qualified either as refugees under international law or as economic migrants. From 1984 to 1990, fully 64 percent of all asylum cases adjudicated in the United States on a worldwide basis originated in El Salvador, Guatemala, and Nicaragua. Most of the appeals were rejected, but those from Nicaragua were most likely to be approved (26 percent, compared to 2.6 percent for El Salvadorans and 1.8 percent for Guatemalans).[27]

The U.S. Immigration Reform and Control Act (IRCA) of 1986, more than fifteen years in the making, was finally adopted after numerous compromises among numerous U.S. interest groups. The primary concern was illegal immigration, much of which came from Mexico. The matter was dealt with in three principal ways: (1)

the legalization of undocumented immigrants; (2) the enforcement of employer sanctions, making it illegal to hire workers who did not have appropriate work-eligibility documents (nondiscrimination provisions were also included); and (3) improved border controls. Under IRCA, the United States legalized almost 3 million undocumented aliens, the largest number of whom came from Mexico; but it had little success enforcing employer sanctions or improving border controls. With regard to Mexico, IRCA sought to regularize the status of Mexican undocumented migrants so as to contribute to the country's social and economic stability.

U.S. public opinion toward immigrants and refugees became generally more ambivalent during the 1980s, with deep divisions reflected in a contentious public debate. The ambivalence and divisiveness were carried over into the 1990s post–cold war period. Officials had to deal with the different preferences of human rights organizations, employers of migrant labor, ethnic groups, and state and local governments, as well as hostile public opinion. Large sectors of the U.S. public challenged both the traditional view of immigrants and refugees as deserving of personal opportunity and safe haven; a growing number of people saw migrants (legal and illegal) posing economic, social, and cultural threats, unfairly competing for jobs, and placing unacceptable costs on public educational, health, and welfare systems; some asserted the problem of alien criminals, drug traffickers, and terrorists (although little evidence indicates significant links to migration).[28] Another broad section of the public remained committed to the American humanitarian tradition regarding immigrants and refugees and opposed to the inconsistencies of cold war-based decisions about who should enter, although many people from this sector agreed that tighter regulation of illegal entrants was required.

Post–Cold War Changes.   The Bush administration in 1990 sought to make immigration, refugee, and asylum procedures more even handed. By 1991 it had fully implemented the languishing Refugee Act of 1980 and cooperated with Congress to adopt the Immigration Act of 1990. The Refugee Act, an amendment of the 1952 law, mandated the first permanent procedures for admitting and resettling refugees in the United States. It defined refugees to conform with the 1967 United Nations Protocol Relating to the Status of Refugees, and stated the intent to protect them without regard to ideological orientation. It provided that refugees and asylees were eligible for permanent resident status after a year of continuous presence in the United States. The Immigration Act, dealing with legal flows of immigrants, increased the number of annual admissions and created categories that did not count against the ceiling. The preference system was reformulated by identifying immigrants as either "family-based" (relatives of U.S. citizens) or "independent" (a new classification designed to attract more highly skilled people). The act also provided "temporary protected status" for people escaping armed conflict, natural disasters, or other extraordinary and temporary conditions.[29] Specific country policies were slow to change, however, despite the Bush administrations efforts in the new post–cold war environment.

Erratic outflows of people seeking to enter the United States from Cuba and Haiti put them at the front of U.S. concerns. Economic conditions in Cuba deteriorated after the retirement and then desolation of the Soviet Union, conditions that were exacerbated in 1992 by increased U.S. sanctions. Consequently, more Cubans sought to migrate, and loose Cuban controls made relatively easy their departure by boat and rafts (a perilous undertaking). The United States feared a repetition of the Mariel boat lift and dissuaded Cubans in Florida from staging one. Nevertheless, the numbers became so great that in August 1994 the Clinton administration ordered the Coast Guard to interdict or rescue the small vessels but not to allow them to enter the United States. The migrants were given safe haven at U.S. bases at Guantanamo Bay and in Panama. Cuba and the United States reached an agreement whereby Cuba would stop the flow "using mainly persuasive methods," and the United States would accept at least 20,000 Cuban immigrants a year (at the time the number was about 3,000 per year).[30]

The negotiations were anathema to politically active, conservative Cuban-Americans, who wanted no relief of potential threats to the Castro regime. Kathleen Newland notes that until the 1994 events, U.S. refugee actions toward Cuba had been "an outpost of cold war policy in a post–cold war world."[31] Since the 1960s the overwhelming number of Cubans who had left their homeland had been admitted to the United States as asylees, even those whose clear intent was economic immigration; the 1994 occurrence signaled the end of that long-standing policy (the Mariel crisis of 1980 notwithstanding).

In Haiti, the large numbers of people seeking asylum in the United States continued until the elected, popular, reformist president, Jean-Bertrand Aristide, was inaugurated in 1991. During Aristide's short tenure, the number of migrants dropped sharply; but his overthrow and replacement in September 1991 by a brutal de facto military government led to a huge upsurge in the numbers of Haitians leaving for the United States. As before, they were interdicted at sea; but with the Coast Guard cutters overwhelmed by the numbers, President Bush ordered that Haitians be taken to Guantanamo Bay for safe haven and for screening as to their eligibility for asylum. Almost a third of them were deemed to have a well-founded fear of persecution and proceeded to the United States for further processing. In May 1992—with the process being challenged in the courts, and heavily criticized by human rights advocates and the UN High Commissioner for Refugees as contrary to international law—President Bush ordered the repatriation of all Haitians intercepted at sea without the amnesty screening. The Bush administration opened processing centers in Haiti where people could apply for refugee status. President Clinton, who as a candidate had severely criticized the Bush policy of forcible return, continued the Bush approach when he was faced with the imminence of a huge influx of Haitians. Clinton pledged to solve the problem by restoring Aristide to the presidency, but with the slowness of the restoration process the boat exodus was resumed and the processing facilities were swamped. The Haitian refugee policy remained in flux for more than two and a half years. In September 1994 a U.S.-led, United Nations-sponsored military force entered Haiti and restored Aristide; the mass exodus ended.[32]

THE DRUG TRAFFIC

In the early 1980s, the problem of the illicit drug traffic entered inter-American relations as a compelling, acrimonious, and intractable high priority issue. Although it had existed for many years, its expansion after the late 1970s made it an enormous business enterprise with social, economic, and political implications that created major policy dilemmas for all governments involved.[33]

International Drug Control Efforts

Governments did not consider drug abuse an international problem until the twentieth century. Even with increasing illicit drug flows and international interdependence and cooperation in the nineteenth century, the concept of "free trade" included narcotics. When the drug problem finally emerged as an international issue, the concern focused on the human consequences of drug use as a matter of public health; the concern then expanded "as the scope and impact of illicit drug trafficking took on more ominous dimensions."[34]

The first formal international agreement for the control of illicit drugs, proposed by the United States, was The Hague International Opium Convention of 1912.[35] Most Latin American states signed the instrument and several ratified it, but none actually put it into practice. After World War I the League of Nations instituted two regulatory agencies—the Permanent Central Opium Board and the Drug Supervisory Board. The League also sponsored the adoption of three instruments (in 1925, 1931, and 1936), but the United States signed only one of them, and Latin Americans (other than Mexico and Uruguay) were generally not concerned with drug regulation.

At the end of World War II, the United Nations succeeded the League of Nations as the center of international efforts to counter drug trafficking. It took over the multilateral agencies and established the United Nations Commission on Narcotic Drugs as the central body. The UN sponsored the drafting of three conventions that provided a worldwide juridical framework under UN administration. The Single Convention on Narcotic Drugs of 1961, amended by a 1972 protocol, terminated, replaced, unified, and expanded the earlier six conventions and two amending protocols, going back to 1912, that were still in force (the latest of which was a 1953 protocol). The single convention established the International Narcotics Control Board (INCB) to oversee treaty compliance. Two additional instruments followed: the 1971 Convention on Psychotropic Substances and the 1988 Convention Against Illicit Traffic in Narcotic Drugs and Psychotropic Substances. In 1971 the UN established the Fund for Drug Abuse Control to provide technical and financial assistance for action programs. In December 1990 the Seventeenth Special Session of the General Assembly, devoted entirely to drug abuse control, approved creation of a United Nations International Drug Control Program. It also merged operational agencies into a single entity, the United Nations International Narcotics Control Program (UNDCP). Furthermore, the UN initiated a succession of regional instruments and programs, which, because of related inter-American undertakings, were minor compared to other world regions. Until the mid-1980s, however, Latin Americans had little enthusiasm for the UN endeavors. The producer nations especially were not prone to implement international agreements.

The Inter-American Situation

The United States has provided the primary market of users and distributors of illicit drugs, whereas people from most Latin America and Caribbean countries are part of the chain of its production, transportation, financing, marketing, and distribution (including in the United States). These linkages created their own transnational culture.

Market demand stemmed primarily from drug consumption in the United States, which provided the world's largest market for illicit drugs. In the latter 1980s, U.S. consumers spent about $110 billion annually on illegal drugs, a figure corresponding to almost 3 percent of GNP. Those consumers numbered some 25 to 30 million marijuana smokers, 5 to 6 million cocaine users, and more than a half-million heroin takers. With the growth of drug-related crime and violence, narcotics financing of organized crime, and the negative social consequences of increasing numbers of youth involved with drugs, the drug traffic became a major public issue in the United States.

As the U.S. market became saturated, traffickers looked for new markets to absorb the increasing supply. By the end of 1986, Europe had begun to import significant amounts of illicit drugs, and by mid-1987 it was evident that even Latin American societies were subject to increasing cocaine use.

Suppliers in other countries, especially in Latin America, responded to the U.S. demand. Latin America was the source of all the cocaine, four-fifths of the marijuana, and two-fifths of the heroin consumed in the United States. Mexico, Colombia, Peru, and Bolivia were the key regional sources of drug production and shipping. Almost all of the other Latin American and Caribbean countries were involved to some extent in those enterprises and in "money laundering" and transshipment along alternate trafficking routes. The Colombian Medellín Cartel became the largest cocaine cartel in the world and accumulated vast wealth and power; it was later replaced by the rival Colombian Cali Cartel. The immense wealth of drug traffickers enabled them to corrupt civil, police, and armed forces officials to varying degrees; they were willing to assassinate those who refused to cooperate. In those states most involved in the drug enterprise, corruption undermined the legitimacy of governments, and violence intimidated them. Drugs became a major source of income for many Latin American farmers; they financed a large underground economy outside of state authority. In some countries the traffickers arranged with insurgency groups to exchange money for protection.

Inter-American Cooperation

Eventually inter-American counter-narcotics measures were undertaken. Despite considerable bilateral and multilateral efforts sustained by significant resources, and certain operational successes, governments and societies have been frustrated in the attempts to control the drug traffic.

Cooperative international drug eradication and interdiction programs, led by the United States, were undertaken. In 1982 President Ronald Reagan declared a "war on drugs." U.S. policy makers had determined that they could not quickly modify domestic consumer behavior very much and so decided to emphasize the attack on the source and flow of drugs, beginning with bilateral actions. Interagency field efforts were taken on with Mexico. Colombia agreed to extradite its citizens to the United States for trial. The United States entered into agreements with Peru in 1982 and Bolivia in 1983 designed to eradicate the supply of drugs and induce small farmers to switch to other crops. In 1986 the United States and Bolivia cooperated in an exercise called Operation Blast Furnace. U.S. Army helicopters airlifted Bolivian National Police on a series of raids aimed at destroying the laboratories that processed the coca leaf and the coca fields themselves. In 1988 Operation Snowcap—headed by the U.S. Drug Enforcement Agency (DEA) and assisted by U.S. Special Forces, the U.S. Border Patrol, and police in several Latin American countries—conducted anti-cocaine activities.

The U.S. Anti-Drug Abuse Act of 1986 was designed to strengthen the U.S. antinarcotics efforts at home and abroad. It sought to lower domestic demand with tougher law enforcement, educational programs, drug testing, treatment and rehabilitation programs, and increased penalties for traffickers. It increased resources for the interdiction of the drug traffic and for eradication, crop substitution, and enforcement programs abroad. The law mandated the annual International Narcotics Control Strategy Report to assess the situation in the drug producing and trafficking nations around the world, nineteen of which were in Latin America. The president was required to certify whether those countries were cooperating fully with the United States in narcotics control before they could receive foreign aid; trade and economic sanctions were also provided for. Sanctions were imposed on Bolivia in 1986 and 1987 for not acting seriously to eradicate its coca crop. In 1988 Panama was "decertified" because of the activities of General Manuel Noriega. While cooperating with the CIA and DEA, Noriega had created a large narcotics-trafficking and money-laundering center. A U.S. federal court convicted him in absentia on drug-related charges.

The Reagan administration and bipartisan majorities in the Congress stayed the course on the "supply-side" approach to international drug control. They continued the focus on the eradication of drug cultivation and processing in supplier countries and crop substitution programs for the growers, as well as on interdiction of narcotics shipments, increased U.S. military roles in the efforts, and better law enforcement by police and courts in source states. On the domestic "demand-side," policy emphasized law enforcement over prevention and treatment. In late 1988, the Congress, disappointed with the results so far, enacted a second Anti-Drug Abuse Act. In effect the law mandated a shift in emphasis rather than a fundamental change in strategy. More resources were put into demand-side efforts, particularly in law enforcement, and supply-side efforts were continued.[36]

Certain multilateral efforts were pursued on subregional levels. The first initiative, undertaken in 1976 by ten South American states, was the South American Agreement on Narcotic Drugs and Psychotropic Substances. Among other things, the agreement set up seven training centers (in Buenos Aires, Caracas, Lima, Brasília, and Santiago) for treatment and rehabilitation, preventive education, suppression of illegal trafficking, documentation, customs, canine training, and the regulation of licit drugs. The Caribbean Community (CARICOM) from the mid-1980s initiated programs in the fields of law enforcement, epidemiology, preventive education, and treatment. The five Central American states in December 1990 established the Permanent Central American Commission for the Eradication of the Production, Traffic, Consumption and Use of Narcotic Drugs and Psychotropic Substances, and Related Offenses to coordinate activities and promote cooperative efforts.[37]

Until the mid-1980s, the Inter-American System was at an impasse over the drug issue. The United States blamed Latin America as the supplier, and Latin Americans condemned the United States for creating the drug consumption market.[38] Eventually, the American states understood that the transnational problem required multilateral resolution, and important measures were undertaken within the Organization of American States (OAS).[39] In April 1986 in Rio de Janeiro the OAS adopted a major program for regional anti-narcotics cooperation, and the following November the Inter-American Drug Abuse Control Commission (CICAD) was created to implement the program. In 1990 the Meeting of Ministers Alliance of the Americas against Drug Trafficking met in Ixtapa, Mexico. The ministers evaluated the course of the Program of Rio and made recommendations for revisions in its priorities and operations. CICAD adopted five priority lines of action to implement the Programs of Rio and Ixtapa: legal development, education for prevention, community mobilization, a uniform inter-American statistical system, and an inter-American drug information system. CICAD and UN agencies have coordinated their undertakings in order to avoid duplication of efforts and to preserve their scarce resources.

The Bush administration, which took office in January 1989, also pursued a supply-side strategy in the continuing war on drugs. It increased funding for demand control with an emphasis on law enforcement. In particular, it attempted further to "militarize" the international war on drugs.[40] In late 1989, the administration expanded the role of the U.S. armed forces in counter-production and interdiction actions, despite opposition from military leaders. On December 20, 1989, the U.S. armed forces unilaterally intervened in Panama, removed General Noriega from power, and sent him to the United States for trial on drug-trafficking and money-laundering charges (he was subsequently convicted and imprisoned). Shortly after the intervention, on February 15, 1990, President Bush participated at the Andean Drug Summit in Cartagena with the presidents of Colombia, Peru, and Bolivia. It produced several bilateral agreements between the United States and the other states, one pledging more consultation and collaboration in the war on drugs and others regarding intelligence gathering and sharing, extradition, the problem of money laundering, the illegal small arms trade, and public awareness.[41]

Soon after the Cartagena meeting the Bush administration announced its "Andean Strategy," which contained a number of elements. A $2.2 billion development aid package for Bolivia, Colombia, and Peru was conditioned on their acceptance of military aid. The Andean Trade Preference Act was enacted into law as the trade element of the Andean Strategy, offering a unilateral U.S. trade preference program for Bolivia, Colombia, Ecuador, and Peru (see Chapter 13). Thus both aid and trade aimed to help the Andean states move away from coca cultivation and trafficking to other crops and forms of livelihood. Military aid was designed to convince the Andean states to deploy their public forces into zones of narcotics production and transport. The U.S. Army drew up a plan envisioning coordinated attacks by the armed forces of Bolivia, Colombia, and Peru on drug cartel targets, to the dismay of many high-ranking U.S. military officials and government leaders in the three Andean states.

A second summit was held from February 26–27, 1992, in San Antonio, Texas, attended by the presidents of Bolivia, Colombia, Ecuador, Mexico, Peru, and the United States and the foreign minister of Venezuela. U.S. proposals contained no shifts in premises or priorities, and the Latin Americans continued to insist on less U.S. unilateralism and more economic aid. The participants signed an agreement pledging more cooperation in their anti-narcotics actions, including the creation of regional police training centers, mutual legislation to control money laundering and chemical shipments, and improved means of sharing intelligence and evidence. Neither development aid nor coordinated Andean military action were mentioned.[42]

The Clinton administration, which took office in January 1993, shifted the operational focus of anti-drug efforts. Experts in the field generally agreed that the drug traffic had not been significantly reduced, despite years of expensive and intense efforts to restrict it. A National Security Council review concluded that U.S. military interdiction efforts had little effect in reducing the flow of cocaine into the United States. By the end of 1993 a revised U.S. approach had been decided upon. Congress reduced overall aid to the Andean states for drug control and cut military and police aid in particular. The administration decreased funding for the U.S. armed forces counter-narcotics programs, reducing their roles in drug interdiction, but increased resources for cocaine eradication in the Andean states and law enforcement on the U.S.-Mexican border. On the demand-side, the administration shifted the emphasis to treatment and prevention programs over law enforcement. On January 11, 1994 a State Department official said that rather than focus on interdiction (which had proved a failure in the past) the United States alternatively would concentrate on drug-crop eradication and local police training, crop substitution, and programs to reduce the demand for drugs in the United States. Officials did not indicate why they expected these policies, which had been tried in the past—and found wanting—to succeed. The OAS-sponsored Summit of the Americas in December 1994 discussed the drug problem extensively and made important specific recommendations for CICAD to set in motion.

CULTURAL RELATIONS

Transnational cultural relations refer to how the sum total of the ways of living (shared attitudes and values) associated with a society are transmitted beyond its own boundaries and how recipient societies respond to this transmission. The process of transmission may be formal or informal and promoted under either public or private auspices. Formal governmental cultural exchanges and programs and the activities of private cultural exchange organizations have been important, but of considerably more significance has been the transnational mix of governmental and (often more important) nongovernmental intersocietal transactions.

States commonly seem to assume that cultural exchange facilitates the realization of political goals. Although cultural exchange may be unnecessary when interests are complementary, or, conversely, may be unable to overcome wide divergences of interest, cultural relations may assist cooperation or mitigate conflict. Some states have emphasized the economic value of cultural exchange. French officials, for example, have said that foreign students trained in French culture were the best promoters of French products, commercial methods, and technology.[43] Cultural relations have also been pursued in essentially ideological terms, such as the French "civilizing mission," the U.S. "democratizing mission," and the Spanish pursuit of "racial solidarity."

Although cultural relations in a broad sense existed throughout Latin American history, systematic governmental or nongovernmental activity is a twentieth century phenomenon. However, during the nineteenth century and well into the twentieth, important informal relationships were established. For example, educated Latin Americans (especially South Americans) were attracted to French culture throughout the nineteenth century. They adopted French philosophies, traveled to France, and sent their children to be educated there. French governments were unwilling to enter into cultural exchange with Latin America even during the height of the country's cultural influence at the turn of the century and up to World War I.

Spanish cultural policies toward Latin America have been of special interest. A small precursor Pan-Hispanic cultural movement began in the mid-nineteenth century, but the idea received little attention until the 1890s. This movement—known as *hispanismo* or, sometimes, *hispanoamericanismo*—was advocated by a group of Spanish luminaries that included Rafael Altamira, José Ortega y Gassett, José F. Gómez, Adolfo Gonzáles Posada, Miguel de Unamuno, and others. They attempted to persuade Spanish governments to establish official programs based on their ideas. The movement was later fostered by institutes for Spanish-American studies in Spanish universities, several journals on the subject, student and professorial exchanges, and Pan-Hispanic political and commercial organizations.

Early advocates of *hispanismo* championed not only a cultural community among Spanish-speaking peoples, stressing kindred race and cultural solidarity, but also political rapprochement and increased economic interaction for the mutual benefit of Spain and America. Some writers called for some sort of confederation or league among Hispanic peoples, but this idea remained vague. Hostility toward the Pan-

American movement sponsored by the United States was a constant theme, and *hispanoamericanistas* viewed Yankee imperialism and materialism as a major threat to Hispanic values in Latin America. Antiyankeeism was stimulated by the war of 1898 and given further impetus by the long period of U.S. intervention in the Caribbean that followed. A Hispano-American cultural and economic congress was held in Madrid in 1900 with Spanish American attendance, signaling the official beginning of *hispanismo*. Further congresses assembled in different Spanish cities in 1908, 1910, 1912, and 1914. The Spanish government modestly supported the movement, sending representatives to Spanish American centenary celebrations (beginning with Argentina in 1910) and subsidizing several Pan-Hispanic political and commercial organizations. It sponsored scholarships and fellowships for student and professor exchange.[44] Latin American hostility toward Spain lessened somewhat, and trade slightly increased.

Most students of the movement have viewed *hispanismo* basically as a cultural, partially economic, nonaggressive liberal movement stressing race, culture, and commerce, designed to promote Hispanic civilization and solidarity and to defend the culture against U.S. incursions. An important work by Frederick Pike confirms these features but also emphasizes that the Spanish adherents of the movement held antirevolutionary sentiments and represented the status quo. Pike believes that Spanish liberal and conservative supporters of *hispanismo* alike wished to prevent social revolution on both sides of the Atlantic. This sharing of social conservatism, in effect, left as the main difference between them the conservatives' rigid Roman Catholicism and the liberals' strong anticlericalism.[45]

In the late 1930s, after falangist dictator General Francisco Franco came to power, *hispanismo* was converted to *hispanidad*, a concept fundamentally different from its predecessor. *Hispanidad* was widely popularized by Ramiro de Maeztu, an ex-anarchist turned falangist, in his book *Defensa de la Hispanidad*, first published in 1934.[46] He described the concept in mystical and reactionary terms, seeking revindication of Spanish world power. For inspiration, he turned to the sixteenth century, when Spanish imperial power had reached its zenith. According to the falangists, the bases for Spanish greatness had been devotion to the church, military and naval strength, and a hierarchical social order. That greatness had declined, and Spain had suffered three centuries of humiliation, the theory continued, because of the pagan Renaissance, the Protestant Reformation, and the consequent eroding effects of relativism in religion, egalitarian political ideals, and economic materialism. Falangists admired and felt a spiritual kinship with Italian fascism and German Nazism. But they insisted that falangism was distinctly Spanish, rooted in the values of the Middle Ages when, it was claimed, Spain was already fascist. To promote Spanish regeneration in the 1930s, falangists called for reinstitution of religious intolerance and the Inquisition, the recovery of military strength and military values, and the resumption of empire in America (including large portions of the United States). England continued to be the eternal enemy, and France was vilified, but the United States and Pan Americanism received the most vociferous hostility. Falangism was also anti-Masonic, anti-Semitic, antidemocratic, antisocialist, and anticommunist. The reestablishment of the American empire was absurd as a practical policy goal. Franco probably sought at most some degree of Spanish American sympathy for his regime.

Immediately after the Spanish Civil War and during World War II, organizations associated with the falangists engaged in a propaganda campaign in Latin America, sometimes in concert with German Nazi and Italian fascist groups, even though Spain remained neutral throughout the war. Brazilian dictator Getulio Vargas initially sympathized with falangism and allowed Rio de Janeiro to serve as the Latin American center for Spanish propaganda activities, but Brazil nevertheless eventually sided with the Allies in World War II. (Actually, Vargas first sympathized with the Salazar brand of fascism in Portugal, which was older than the Franco regime.) Spain also cultivated relations with authoritarian governments in Argentina and Peru. It was active in Chile but eventually broke relations with that government. Spain financed the travel of sympathetic Latin American politicians, intellectuals, and students to Spain and established an Institute of Hispanic Studies in Madrid to give a scholarly veneer to *hispanidad*. Pan Hispanism was received enthusiastically in Latin America by right-wing elements. Its appeal was essentially restricted to those elements by the end of World War II and the defeat of the Axis powers.

During World War I and the following interbellum period, the leading external competitors disseminated propaganda in Latin America. During the war the regional states were courted by both sides of the conflict—by France, Great Britain, and then Italy and the United States on the one hand, and by Germany, supported by neutral Spain, on the other. Notable at the time was the work of the American Committee on Public Information (the Creel Committee), the first U.S. experiment in government-supported cultural exchange in Latin America. Created by President Wilson in 1917 and headed by journalist George Creel, the agency established a network of contacts around Latin America. These contacts, usually resident U.S. newspaper correspondents but sometimes government officials and Latin American nationals, distributed various kinds of communications media and advised on the content best received in their areas.[47]

During the 1920s and especially the 1930s, as international frictions increased, external propagandizing in Latin America continued apace. Italy, Germany, and Spain actively sought to take advantage of their national communities in the region, but with mixed success. Those communities often were deeply divided among themselves over loyalty to European governments, even though they generally had affection for the former national homeland. After the United States announced its Good Neighbor Policy in 1933, European propaganda lost much of its appeal because it had a high antiyankee content.

Until the mid-1930s, virtually all United States and inter-American cultural activities were voluntary and nongovernmental, sponsored by individuals, universities, foundations, and other private organizations. The Inter-American System first introduced cultural cooperation in December 1936 with a series multilateral conventions that emphasized student and teacher exchanges and scientific cooperation. In 1938 the Eighth International Conference of American States passed resolutions approving more social, educational, and cultural cooperation, and in that year the Department of State established its first agencies to administer official activities and to assist private agencies in their cultural programs (they had a strong Latin American focus). These measures were in response to the ideological content of the German, Italian, and Spanish dictators' cultural activities in Latin America.[48]

Regularized cultural exchange programs were prevalent after World War II. The most important ones were maintained by France, the United States, West Germany, Great Britain, Spain, and the Soviet Union, although the People's Republic of China, East Germany, Italy, Iran, Korea, and the United Arab Republic (UAR) also undertook some modest activities in the region. In addition, Argentina, Brazil, Mexico, Chile, and Cuba developed intraregional communications and educational exchange programs.

Several external states maintained publicly funded cultural centers around the region. Most of them were private organizations receiving financial support from their home governments, including France's Alliance Francaise, Germany's Goethe Institute, the United Kingdom's British Council, Spain's Instituto de Cultura Hispanica, and the United States Information Agency. All of them engaged in a wide range of activities. They gave high priority to language classes (except for the Spanish-run centers), the operation of libraries, and various cultural programs. They provided scholarships for Latin Americans to study abroad, offered travel programs for the exchange of artists, intellectuals, and athletes, and distributed films, books, magazines, and newspapers. Most of the major external states sent government-supported teachers to staff schools originally intended to serve the children of their own nationals, but enrollments in these schools include large numbers of Latin American children as well. All major government broadcast services were aired to Latin America.[49]

The Inter-American System substantially increased its cultural cooperation, but such activities never reached high priority levels on its agenda of activities. The 1948 Charter of the Organization of American States established the Inter-American Cultural Council and its permanent commission, the Inter-American Committee for Cultural Action, to promote educational, cultural, and scientific relations. The 1967 charter amendments established the new Inter-American Council for Education, Science, and Culture as the expanded and upgraded successor to the cultural council, which was made the Permanent Executive Committee of the new entity. Subsequent charter amendments continued the same arrangement and purposes of promoting inter-American educational, scientific, and cultural cooperation and exchange.

At the 1994 Summit of the Americas, the leaders of the American states determined to strengthen cultural exchange and information flows, partly as a way to introduce a human element into free-trade processes. The Department of Cultural Affairs in the General Secretariat of the OAS was to have primary responsibility for reinforcing cultural cooperation.[50]

CULTURAL DIFFUSION

Momentous, rapidly increasing, and interrelated transnational phenomena have had major sociocultural implications for Latin American and Caribbean societies and their linkages with the outside world. They include the cultural impacts of migration, drug trafficking, proliferation of news and entertainment media, popular culture, sports, educational connections, and other transnational associations—as well as the economic relationships discussed in Chapter 13. Cultural diffusion has increased, particularly since World War II; it received great impetus in the 1980s for a variety of reasons; and with the end of the cold war it has continued unabated. The rapid development of communications and information technology has enormously facilitated these developments. The cultural spread and dispersion is also part of the decreasing importance of state and societal boundaries, given the difficulty of monitoring such extensive cross-border flows of people, data, capital, services, and criminal activity.[51] The following discussion briefly explores in a general and speculative way some of the sociocultural processes and consequences associated with the phenomena identified above.

Migrant communities are a special case in point, especially the millions of Latin Americans resident in the United States, with many of them moving back and forth to their homelands. Doris Meissner notes that migrants tend to go where connections have already been made and that "migration streams become sustained by factors that are independent of the original reasons that led migrants to leave." Attracted by the opportunities (economic and political) for a better life in the United States, they often join relatives and friends who had previously moved there. Consequently, once begun, migration is likely to continue.[52] Furthermore, as Patricia Pessar observes, unlike earlier immigrants from Europe who sought to settle permanently and assimilate into the dominant culture, recent Latin American immigrants are "constructing transnationalized lives."[53]

This situation has created ambivalence about national self-identity and country loyalty. Put another way, the developing transnational identity transcends both the original home country and the newly adopted one. As people circulate between the two, they adopt dual social identities that reach across national borders. Many transnational communities in the United States create their own social, economic, and political networks in the community's distinct interests. Although U.S. life may be difficult because of competition for jobs and discrimination against those who are mestizo, black, or mulatto, migrants earn more money than would be possible in the homeland and have the benefits of the U.S. public education system, medical care, and welfare system. Yet migrants also tend to remain ethnically, socially, and economically tied to their countries of origin. Many of them intend to work in the United States in order to save sufficient money to return home and start a business or retire (although this is often an unrealized hope). Some maintain a household in each country to assure legal status in the former country of residence. Remittances are an important economic-social-familial way that loyalties are linked.

Educational connections are an important source of transnationalization. Over the decades many thousands of Latin American and Caribbean students have participated in high school exchanges and earned undergraduate, graduate, and professional degrees in the United States. At the same time, the U.S. government and private foundations have provided funds to institutes and programs in the region. A result has been that U.S. educational models have been accepted as ways to improve educational institutions in the region. A larger societal and political consequence has been the establishment of intellectual, professional, and policy linkages between U.S. and Latin American educators and public and private leaders. As a general matter, a network of academics and policy makers who exchange information and advice seems to have developed. On this elite level, a few examples of prominent Latin Americans illustrate the point. César Gaviria Trujillo, former president of Colombia and appointed secretary-general of the Organization of American States in 1994, attended high school for a year in California; Sixto Durán Ballén, former president of Ecuador, graduated from Columbia University; Alberto Fujimori, president of Peru, studied at the University of Michigan; Ernesto Zedillo, president of Mexico, earned a Ph.D. from Yale; Ernesto Pérez, former president of Panama, graduated from Harvard. An exceptionally large number of cabinet ministers, especially in finance and economics positions, and other high level policy officials have been educated and trained at U.S. institutions (a general commitment to democratic development and free markets, perhaps at least partially connected to the educational experience and resulting personal connections, seems to link the contemporary leadership class). The influence extends to the growing Latin American and Caribbean middle class who have also studied in the United States. English is the common language of the evolving Latin American and Caribbean commercial and technocratic elites. Special mention is made of the role of Howard University in connecting African-Americans in the United States with black Third World leaders, in terms of both alumni and visitor programs; special connections have developed in the Caribbean (for example, Eric Williams, former prime minister of Trinidad and Tobago, was a graduate of Howard).

Popular culture—reflected and transmitted in various forms of visual and performance entertainment, as well as in commercial consumerism and information and opinion representations (by way of cinema, theater, radio, television, electronic and press news media, commercials, music, and sports)—has been a primary avenue of cultural diffusion. The role of motion pictures and television in the North Americanization process deserves further commentary. From its earliest days, the U.S. motion picture industry has exported its products. TV relied on U.S. commercials promoting U.S. products, and TV and the movies (which were also transmitted over television) portrayed the lifestyles, values, and material goods of the highly developed, prosperous, and secularized U.S. society. As Latin Americans have adopted neoliberal economics, they have further opened themselves to U.S. consumerism. It should also be noted that Caribbean music has been an expanding influence in the cultural linkages, with many musicians from the region achieving considerable success in the United States (and in Europe).

On a smaller but important scale, baseball has evolved as a notable transnational cultural matter in the circum-Caribbean. Baseball has long been the national sport of Cuba, the Dominican Republic, Nicaragua, Venezuela, and Panama, where players become popular heroes—today probably even more than in the United States, where football and basketball pose strong competition. In those countries, star baseball players are national heroes; and local teams are sources of national pride, as teams from the region have competed well with the United States and, literally, beat U.S. teams at their own game (which was something of a symbol of resistance to U.S. power).[54] Since the 1970s, that pride had also stemmed from the fact that more and more Latin players have been recruited to play in the U.S. major leagues, where they have excelled. In the 1890s U.S. seamen introduced baseball to Cubans; Cuban sugar workers in turn took it to nearby countries, where local teams were organized. During the U.S. Caribbean military interventions and occupations, U.S. military personnel reinforced the sport by playing baseball as members of and against the local teams. In the 1930s the U.S. Negro Leagues played exhibitions with the local teams throughout the Caribbean, where they were very popular; they recruited the best players. Beginning in the 1950s, after Jackie Robinson (in 1947) and then other U.S. black baseball players had broken the color line, the U.S. major leagues recruited a long line of Latin American players. The phenomenon took off in the 1970s and has dramatically increased ever since—between 1977 and 1997 the number of Caribbean players on major league teams doubled. At the beginning of the 1997 season, of the 200 foreign-born players on the thirty U.S. major league team rosters, 184 of them were from the circum-Caribbean and Mexico (about 16 percent of the total number). The Dominican Republic (where the local organization of baseball and U.S. major league interest is the most intense) had the most, with fifty-seven players (Venezuela was second with twenty of them).[55]

The "North Americanization" of Latin American culture is a long-standing issue. Indicated elsewhere in the book are elements and forms of Latin American nationalism based on cultural factors that resist cultural intrusions as dangers to native values. The issue of cultural imperialism and U.S. threats to Latin American cultural identities was revived in the 1960s and 1970s as part of the more general erosion of inter-American cooperation. Since the 1980s, with increasingly transnationalized relations, cultural questions have become even more complex.

North Americanization alludes to the spread of U.S. cultural values by way of commerce, migration, educational exchange, sports, and popular culture—all facilitated by modern telecommunications, transportation systems, the news media, radio and television, and motion pictures. It also refers to the influence of U.S. culture on Latin Americans and Caribbeans in the United States, as immigrants, exiles, students, and travelers. U.S. actors in particular have had an enormous influence on the region—in matters of migration, economic affairs, the drug traffic, and the concomitant social and cultural consequences. At the same time, Latin Americans, particularly from the Caribbean area, have had a significant impact on the United States in the same areas. In the 1950s the expression "North Americanization of the

Caribbean" arose with reference to the consequences of U.S. economic and cultural influences on Caribbean societies; it continues to have currency. In the 1960s the reciprocal impact was recognized with the phrase "Caribbeanization of the United States," which gained broader recognition in the 1980s and 1990s.

The process of North Americanization has been met with divided Latin American and Caribbean views about the United States. On the one hand, a strong reaction against North Americanization has displayed resentment of U.S. cultural influence. Although the current phenomena are not a consequence of overt U.S. government policies, so that in the traditional sense of power politics cultural imperialism is not the issue, some of the elements of transnationalism sprang from what were originally ingredients of the imperial relationship, dating primarily from the beginning of the twentieth century. Latin Americans who resent or fear these U.S. (or other foreign) influences continue to see them as continuing cultural imperialism (as do some IR analysts), in the sense that such imperialism is essentially an extension of the past into the new transnational context.

At the same time, a large number of Latin Americans, many of whom have adopted English as a second language, welcome or accept U.S. ideas, values, products, and lifestyles (those who are members of the transnational migrant societies are prime, but far from exclusive, examples). Many Latin Americans developed a preference for U.S. consumer goods and other products and for the materialist, secular lifestyle; in certain countries it also included the passion for baseball and, in many parts of the region, the borrowing of the U.S. educational model. (A serious problem is that economic revival has not particularly benefited the large poor sectors of society.) With reference to the Commonwealth Caribbean, Aggrey Brown says that the "present conceptions of cultural imperialism are misconceived and the very concept of cultural imperialism itself is a misdiagnosis—the people of the region are willing consumers and cultural ennui is the price we pay for passive consumption."[56] Others equate North Americanization with modernization, seeing it as an inevitable consequence of societal proximity, migration, commerce, and cultural contact.

U.S. citizens have also reacted to transnationalization and the reciprocal Latin American influence. Caribbeanization has changed the political, social, and popular cultural scenes in several cities (notably, for example, in New York and Miami) and affected public policies in several states. As indicated above, it has fueled the continuing debate about immigration policy.

Certain paradoxes are also evident. For example, the influence of the higher educational models has both advanced and reduced the North Americanization of Latin American and Caribbean institutions: University reforms emulating foreign models have made those institutions more self-sufficient. On another plane, the U.S. invention of baseball provides a source of national pride in the circum-Caribbean, as people there have made a U.S. export their own sport. On the other side of the equation, it should be noted that portions of the U.S. public have their own doubts about the export of U.S. popular culture, citing those elements that celebrate crassness and violence and fearing that it presents an exaggerated and negative view of the

United States to the world. Some analysts point out that in the case of cinema, "Hollywood" or the "American" motion picture industry is itself transnational—in terms of its major stars and investors and owners of production studios—and that perhaps the industry is part of a developing global mass culture. Other aspects of transnationalism are worrisome to all parties: With more open borders crime has become a transcontinental problem, as criminal organizations manage the flow of drugs and a vast illegal trade in automobiles, weapons, and migrants.

NOTES

1. Doris Meissner, "Immigration and Refugee Policy," in *The United States and Latin America: Redefining U.S. Purposes in the Post-Cold War Era*, ed. G. Pope Atkins (Austin: Lyndon B. Johnson School of Public Affairs, University of Texas at Austin, 1992), 63.

2. For details, see G. Pope Atkins, *Encyclopedia of the Inter-American System* (Westport, Conn.: Greenwood Press, 1997), 29–31. See also C. Neale Ronning, *Diplomatic Asylum: Legal Norms and Political Reality in Latin American Relations* (The Hague: Nijhoff, 1957); and Keith W. Yundt, *Latin American and Political Refugees* (New York: Praeger, 1988).

3. Carl Kaysen, "Refugees: Concepts, Norms, Realities, and What the United States Can and Should Do," in *Threatened Peoples, Threatened Borders: World Migration and U.S. Policy*, ed. Michael S. Teitelbaum and Myron Weiner (New York: W. W. Norton and Co., 1995), 244–245.

4. Meissner, "Immigration and Refugee Policy," 64.

5. Adolfo Aguilar Zinser, "Asylum," in *Encyclopedia of Latin American History and Culture*, ed. Barbara A Tennenbaum, vol. 1 (New York: Charles Scribner's Sons, 1996), 229.

6. See John E. Kicza, ed., *The Indian in Latin American History: Resistance, Resilience, and Acculturation* (Wilmington, Del.: Scholarly Resources, 1993).

7. For recent informative and provocative treatments providing a variety of analytic view points, see Robin Blackburn, *The Making of New World Slavery: From the Baroque to the Modern, 1492–1800* (New York: Verso, 1997); Madeleine Burnside, *Spirits of the Passage: The Transatlantic Trade in the Seventeenth Century* (New York: Simon and Schuster, 1997); Darién J. Davis, ed., *Slavery and Beyond: The African Impact on Latin American and the Caribbean* (Wilmington, Del.: Scholarly Resources, 1995); Hugh Thomas, *The Slave Trade: The Story of the Atlantic Slave Trade: 1440–1870* (New York: Simon and Schuster, 1997); John Thornton, *Africa and the Africans in the Making of the Atlantic World, 1400–1680* (Cambridge: Cambridge University Press, 1992).

8. Magnus Morner, with the collaboration of Harold Sims, *Adventurers and Proletarians: The Story of Migrants in Latin America* (University of Pittsburgh Press, 1985).

9. The following discussion incorporates information from Herbert Goldhamer, *The Foreign Powers in Latin America* (Princeton: Princeton University Press, 1972), chapter 5.

10. Fabio Luca Cavazza, *Italy and Latin America* (Santa Monica, Calif.: Rand, 1967).

11. See Patricia W. Fagen, *Exiles and Citizens: Spanish Republicans in Mexico* (Austin: University of Texas Press, 1973).

12. The special situation of the Jewish presence in Latin America as both religious and cultural communities is analyzed by Martin A. Cohen, ed., *The Jewish Experience in Latin America*, 2 vols. (New York: American Jewish Historical Society, 1971); Judith Laikin Elkin, *Jews of the Latin American Republics* (Chapel Hill: University of North Carolina Press, 1980); Judith

Laikin Elkin and Gilbert W. Merkx, eds., *The Jewish Presence in Latin America* (Boulder, Colo.: Westview Press, 1988); and Saúl Sosnowski, "Jews," in *Encyclopedia of Latin American History and Culture*, ed. Barbara A. Tennenbaum, vol. 3 (New York: Charles Scribner's Sons, 1996), 320–322.

13. The following two paragraphs rely on Goldhamer, *The Foreign Powers in Latin America*, 90–103.

14. Meissner, "Immigration and Refugee Policy," 63.

15. Sergio Díaz-Briquets, "Relationship Between U.S. Foreign Policies and U.S. Immigration Policies," in Teitelbaum and Weiner, *Threatened Peoples, Threatened Borders*.

16. See Mark Reisler, *By the Sweat of Their Brow: Mexican Immigrant Labor in the United States, 1900–1940* (Westport, Conn.: Greenwood Press, 1976).

17. J. Lloyd Mecham, *A Survey of United States–Latin American Relations* (Boston: Houghton Mifflin, 1965), 374, 376–377. See Barbara A. Driscoll, *The Tracks North: The Railroad Bracero Program of World War II* (Austin: University of Texas Press, 1997).

18. Díaz-Briquets, "Relationship Between U.S. Foreign Policies and U.S. Immigration Policies." See also Wayne A. Cornelius and Jorge A. Bustamante, eds., *Mexican Migration to the United States: Origins, Consequences, and Policy Options* (San Diego: Center for U.S.-Mexican Studies, University of California at San Diego, 1989).

19. See Aristide R. Zolberg, "From Invitation to Interdiction: U.S. Foreign Policy and Immigration since 1945," in Teitelbaum and Weiner, *Threatened Peoples, Threatened Borders*, 144–152.

20. Christopher Mitchell, "Introduction," in *Western Hemisphere Immigration and United States Foreign Policy*, ed. Christopher Mitchell (University Park: Pennsylvania State University Press, 1992). See also Felix Roberto Masud-Piloto, *From Welcomed Exiles to Illegal Immigrants: Cuban Migration to the U.S., 1959–1995* (Lanham, Md.: University Press of America, 1996).

21. Zolberg, "From Invitation to Interdiction," 126–129.

22. Meissner, "Immigration and Refugee Policies," 64.

23. See David W. Engstrom, *Presidential Decision Making Adrift: The Carter Administration and the Mariel Boatlift* (Lanham, Md.: Rowman and Littlefield, 1997); and Mario A. Rivera, *Decision and Structure: U.S. Refugee Policy and the Mariel Crisis* (Lanham, Md.: University Press of America, 1991).

24. Kathleen Newland, "The Impact of U.S. Refugee Policies on U.S. Foreign Policy: A Case of the Tail Wagging the Dog?" in Teitelbaum and Weiner, *Threatened Peoples, Threatened Borders*, 198–202. See also Robert S. Kahn, *Other People's Blood: U.S. Immigration Prisons in the Reagan Decade* (Boulder, Colo.: Westview Press, 1996).

25. Zolberg, "From Invitation to Interdiction," 152–154. See also G. Pope Atkins and Larman C. Wilson, *The Dominican Republic and the United States* (Athens: University of Georgia Press, 1998), 78–79, 160–164, 197.

26. On this point, see Meissner, "Immigration and Refugee Policies," 64; Kaysen, "Refugees," 250; and Sharon Stanton Russell, "Migration Patterns of U.S. Foreign Policy Interest," in Teitelbaum and Weiner, *Threatened Peoples, Threatened Borders*, 74–75. See also Elizabeth G. Ferris, *The Central American Refugees* (New York: Praeger, 1987).

27. Russell "Migration Patterns of U.S. Foreign Policy Interest." Russell notes that despite the Reagan administration's assertion that a Communist takeover of El Salvador would precipitate a mass exodus to the United States, a much larger migration of Salvadorans than of Nicaraguans from Sandinista-governed Nicaragua in fact went to the United States.

28. Warren Zimmerman, "Migrants and Refugees: A Threat to Security?" in Teitelbaum and Weiner, *Threatened Peoples, Threatened Borders*, 89–94.

29. Yundt, *Latin American States and Political Refugees*; and Russell, "Migration Patterns of U.S. Foreign Policy Interest," 48–56.

30. Zolberg, "From Invitation to Interdiction," 126–29.

31. Newland, "The Impact of U.S. Refugee Policies on U.S. Foreign Policy," 196–198.

32. Newland, "The Impact of U.S. Refugee Policies on U.S. Foreign Policy," 198–202.

33. William O. Walker, *Drug Control in the Americas*, rev. ed. (Albuquerque: University of New Mexico Press, 1989) is a good historical review of inter-American drug control efforts. See Bruce M. Bagley and William O. Walker III, eds., *Drug Trafficking in the Americas* (New Brunswick, N.J.: Transaction, 1995); Patrick Clausen and Rensselaer Lee III, *The Andean Cocaine Industry*, 2d ed. (New York: St. Martin's Press, 1998); Elizabeth Joyce and Carlos Malamud, eds., *Latin America and the International Drug Trade* (New York: St. Martin's Press, 1997); Scott B. MacDonald, *Dancing on a Volcano: The Latin American Drug Trade* (New York: Praeger, 1988); Donald J. Mabry, ed., *The Latin American Narcotics Trade and U.S. National Security* (Westport, Conn.: Greenwood Press, 1989); Raphael F. Perl, ed., *Drugs and Foreign Policy: A Critical Review* (Boulder, Colo.: Westview Press, 1994); Peter Dale Scott and Jonathan Marshall, *Cocaine Politics: Drugs, Armies, and the CIA in Central America*, updated ed. (Berkeley: University of California Press, 1998); Peter H. Smith, ed., *Drug Policy in the Americas* (Boulder, Colo.: Westview Press, 1992); William O. Walker III, ed., *Drugs in the Western Hemisphere: An Odyssey of Cultures in Conflict* (Wilmington, Del.: Scholarly Resources, 1996). A thorough reference source is Bruce M. Bagley, ed., *Drug Trafficking in the Americas: An Annotated Bibliography* (Boulder, Colo.: Lynne Rienner Publishers, 1996).

34. Irving Tragen, "World-Wide and Regional Anti-Drug Programs," in Perl, *Drugs and Foreign Policy*.

35. For details of these earlier efforts, see Atkins, *Encyclopedia of the Inter-American System*, 148–149.

36. Bruce M. Bagley, "Narcotics Traffic" in Atkins, *The United States and Latin America*.

37. The above information is supplied by Tragen, "World-Wide and Regional Anti-Drug Programs," 172–173.

38. Irving G. Tragen, *Overview of the Drug Problem in the Americas* (Washington, D.C.: General Secretariat, Organization of American States, July 1989), 1.

39. For details, see Atkins, *Encyclopedia of the Inter-American System*, 151–152.

40. Bagley, "Narcotics Traffic."

41. Bruce M. Bagley, "After San Antonio," *Journal of Interamerican Studies and World Affairs* 34, no. 3 (Fall 1992): 1–12.

42. Bagley, "After San Antonio."

43. Goldhamer, *The Foreign Powers in Latin America*, 131–132.

44. J. Fred Rippy, *Globe and Hemisphere* (Chicago: Henry Regnery, 1958), 205–209, 512–515.

45. Frederick B. Pike, *Hispanismo, 1898–1936: Spanish Conservatives and Liberals and Their Relations with Spanish America* (Notre Dame: University of Notre Dame Press, 1971).

46. Ramiro de Maeztu, *Defensa de la Hispanidad*, 4th ed. (Madrid: Cultura Española, 1941).

47. James R. Mock, "The Creel Committee in Latin America," *Hispanic American Historical Review* 22 (May 1942): 262–279.

48. Atkins, *Encyclopedia of the Inter-American System*, 158; and Mecham, *A Survey of United States-Latin American Relations*, 128–130. See Samuel Shapiro, ed., *Cultural Factors in Inter-American Relations* (Notre Dame: University of Notre Dame Press, 1968).

49. Goldhamer, *The Foreign Powers in Latin America*, chapter 9.

50. Atkins, *Encyclopedia of the Inter-American System*, 159, 163.

51. In the introduction to Hopeton S. Dunn, ed., *Globalization, Communications and Caribbean Identity* (New York: St. Martin's, 1995), Dunn gives a good synopsis of the global and regional forces at work. See also Yosef Lapid and Friedrich Kratochwil, eds., *The Return of Culture and Identity to IR Theory* (Boulder, Colo.: Lynne Rienner Publishers, 1996).

52. Meissner, "Immigration and Refugee Policies," *passim*; see also Ransford W. Palmer, ed., *U.S.-Caribbean Relations: Their Impact on Peoples and Culture* (Westport, Conn.: Praeger, 1998).

53. Patricia Pessar, "Emigration," in *Encyclopedia of Latin American History and Culture*, ed. Barbara A. Tennenbaum, vol. 4 (New York: Charles Scribner's Sons, 1996), 488–489. See also Sergio Díaz-Briquets and Sidney Weintrab, *The Effects of Receiving Country Policies on Migration Flows* (Boulder, Colo.: Westview Press, 1991).

54. Alan Klein, *Sugarball: The American Game, the Dominican Dream* (New Haven: Yale University Press, 1991); See also Joseph L. Arbena, ed., *Sport and Society in Latin America: Diffusion, Dependency, and the Rise of Mass Culture* (Westport, Conn.: Greenwood Press, 1988); and Michael M. Olesak and Mary Adams Olesak, *Béisbol: Latin Americans and the Grand Old Game* (Grand Rapids, Mich.: Master's Press, 1991).

55. See Mark Maske, "Baseball Is Fast Becoming the International Pastime," *Washington Post,* 20 January 1998; and Murray Chass, "A New Baseball Strategy: Latin American Bargains," *New York Times,* 22 March 1998.

56. Aggrey Brown, "Caribbean Cultures and Mass Communication Technology: Re-Examining the Cultural Dependency Thesis," chapter 3 in Dunn, *Globalization, Communications and Caribbean Identity*.

INDEX